About the Cover Image

Fire Brigade

Taken just after the Civil War, this image captures five members of a private fire brigade. Before the arrival of government-run fire departments, private fire brigades raced through the streets to see who could be first to arrive at fires because insurance companies paid individual brigades to save buildings. The pride of the men engaged in this dangerous work shines through. Library of Congress, Prints & Photographs Division, Reproduction number LC-DIG-ppmsca-11010 (digital file from original item, front) LC-DIG-ppmsca-11011 (digital file from original item, back).

The American Promise

A HISTORY OF THE UNITED STATES

VOLUME I: TO 1877

EIGHTH EDITION

James L. Roark
Emory University

Michael P. Johnson
Johns Hopkins University

François Furstenberg
Johns Hopkins University

Patricia Cline Cohen
University of California, Santa Barbara

Sarah Stage
Arizona State University

Susan M. Hartmann
The Ohio State University

Sarah E. Igo
Vanderbilt University

bedford/st.martin's
Macmillan Learning
Boston | New York

For Bedford/St. Martin's

Vice President, Editorial, Macmillan Learning Humanities: Leasa Burton
Senior Program Director for History: Michael Rosenberg
Senior Program Manager for History: William J. Lombardo
History Marketing Manager: Melissa Rodriguez
Director of Content Development, Humanities: Jane Knetzger
Senior Developmental Editor: Leah R. Strauss
Senior Content Project Manager: Kendra LeFleur
Senior Workflow Project Supervisor: Susan Wein
Production Supervisor: Lawrence Guerra
Executive Media Project Manager: Michelle Camisa
Media Editor: Mary Starowicz
Editorial Assistant: Julia Bell
Editorial Services: Lumina Datamatics, Inc.
Composition: Lumina Datamatics, Inc.
Cartographer: Mapping Specialists, Ltd.
Text Permissions Manager: Kalina Ingham
Senior Photo Permissions Editor: Cecilia Varas
Photo Researcher: Naomi Kornhauser
Director of Design, Content Management: Diana Blume
Text Design: SPi Global
Cover Design: William Boardman
Cover Image: Library of Congress, Prints & Photographs Division, Reproduction number
  LC-DIG-ppmsca-11010 (digital file from original item, front)
  LC-DIG-ppmsca-11011 (digital file from original item, back).
Printing and Binding: LSC Communications

Manufactured in the United States of America.

For information, write: Bedford/St. Martin's, 75 Arlington Street, Boston, MA 02116

ISBN 978-1-319-17765-2   (Combined Edition)
ISBN 978-1-319-20889-9   (Volume 1)
ISBN 978-1-319-20890-5   (Volume 2)

Acknowledgments

PREFACE: Why This Book This Way?

We are delighted to present the eighth edition of *The American Promise*. Our book has always been shaped by firsthand knowledge that the survey course is one of the most difficult to teach and, for many, also the most difficult to take. From the outset we have sought to meet this challenge by providing a story students enjoy for its **readability, clear chronology, and lively voices of ordinary Americans**. *The American Promise* delivers a narrative with political backbone, documents and features for analysis and discussion, and overall support for teaching. We remain committed to making the book the most teachable and readable introductory American history text available.

New Authors for the Eighth Edition

With the eighth edition, we are delighted to welcome two new coauthors to the book. François Furstenberg is Professor of History at Johns Hopkins University, and Sarah Igo is the Andrew Jackson Professor of American History and Director of American Studies at Vanderbilt University. Both are universally recognized as outstanding scholars, and equally important, they are excellent teachers, able to engage and stimulate their students. Their deep knowledge of eighteenth- and nineteenth-century America (François) and of recent America (Sarah) and their outstanding skills in the classroom mean that they are ideal additions to our author team.

What Makes *The American Promise* Special

The American Promise grew out of many conversations among ourselves and with others about the teaching and learning of history. We know that instructors want a U.S. history text that introduces students to overarching trends and developments and, at the same time, gives voice to the diverse people who have made American history. We know that students of history often come away overwhelmed and confused about what information is most important to know. Because many students have difficulty understanding the most important concepts when they read a traditional U.S. survey text, we seek to provide a text that does not overwhelm them with detail, offers clear signposts about the key questions to focus on, and introduces them to historical thinking skills.

The approach of our narrative is reflected in our title, *The American Promise*. We **emphasize human agency** and demonstrate our conviction that the essence of America has been its promise. For millions, the nation has held out the promise of a better life, unfettered worship, equality before the law, representative government, democratic politics, and other freedoms seldom found elsewhere. But none of these promises has come with any guarantees. Throughout our history, the promise has been marred by disappointments, compromises, and denials, but it lives on. Throughout the narrative, we demonstrate how much of American history is a continuing struggle over the definition and realization of the nation's promise.

We offer **a clear chronology and a framework that braids political and social history,** as we have found that students need both the structure a political narrative provides *and* the insights gained from examining social and cultural experience. To write a comprehensive, balanced account of American history, we focus on the public arena—the place where politics intersects social and cultural developments—to show how Americans confronted the major issues of their day and created far-reaching historical change.

New to This Edition

An Inquiry-Based Model

With the eighth edition, we present the narrative within a unique pedagogical design orchestrated to aid students' understanding of the most important developments while also fostering students' ability to think historically. The pedagogical format will be familiar to instructors who have previously assigned the version of the book called *Understanding the American Promise.* We continue to employ innovative pedagogy to help students understand the book's major arguments and also begin to grasp the **question-driven methodology** that is at the heart of the historian's craft.

▶ New Pedagogical Design. Our pedagogical design reinforces the truth that history is a discipline rooted in debate and inquiry. Each chapter begins with an **opening question** that drives students toward the overarching themes of the chapter, followed by a **brief chapter introduction** that identifies in simple, straightforward terms the most important events and people to be discussed. The chapter then turns to a story of one individual that emphasizes human agency and invites students to evaluate to what extent individuals make history. Individuals profiled in **An American Story** include Deborah Sampson (chapter 7). Alexander Hamilton (chapter 9), Robert Smalls (chapter 15), Frances Willard (chapter 20), and Lieutenant Frederick Downs Jr. (chapter 29).

▶ Helping Students Understand the Narrative. Too often textbook authors write with other historians in mind. In this eighth edition, we tried particularly hard to keep our focus on students. To make American history more easily understood, we have reexamined our language to make sure our telling of the story is clear, direct, and accessible. Where possible, we have streamlined the story to keep from overwhelming students with details and to help them understand what is important. We've rethought our chapter-opening questions to make them precise and aimed at the heart of the chapter. For example, chapter 7 asks, "How did the United States gain its independence in the Revolution?," chapter 14 asks, "How did the issue of slavery drive the United States toward civil war in the mid-nineteenth century?," and chapter 25 asks, "How and why did the United States fight World War II?"

Section-opening headings expressed as questions and **section-ending quick review questions** model the kinds of questions historians ask and help students engage in inquiry-based reading and understanding. **Section-based chronologies** of historical developments help students keep events in context as they read. Because students often have difficulty seeing the forest for the trees, **chapter locators** at the foot of the page remind students of where they are in the chapter's larger progression of events and concepts. **Skills-based marginal questions** that address each chapter's major ideas appear throughout each chapter. **Key terms** highlighted in the text and also defined in the margins further remind students of what's most important to know.

To engage students in this American story and to portray fully the diversity of the American experience, we stitch into our narrative **the voices of hundreds of contemporaries**. The book is rich with many viewpoints from people from all walks of life. Now we highlight two **evocative quotes** per chapter, highlighting voices of both ordinary Americans and notable figures.

One of *The American Promise*'s unique pedagogical features is the **Chapter Study Guide** that provides a structured five-step process to help students build deep understanding of the chapter material. In **Step One**, students identify the chapter's key terms and explain why each term matters. In **Step Two**, they begin to apply their understanding of the chapter material through activities that ask them to consider comparison, change over time, or cause and effect. **Step Three** helps students put it all together with analytical, synthetic questions. In **Step Four**, students consider the connection between two events or circumstances to think about the relation between major events and developments. Finally, **Step Five** invites students to make connections between the past and present day.

We animate the story **with a vivid map and art program.** In total, there are more than 165 maps in *The American Promise*. A **map activity** in each chapter engages students in reading maps and making connections and thus enhances geographical literacy. The book contains more than 250 images, many of which are historical artifacts that underscore the importance of material culture. Two **visual activities** in each chapter reinforce the role of images as historical evidence and help students sharpen their skills for interpreting visual images. Throughout each chapter, a wide variety of visual material reinforces important historical concepts. Some narrative material has been moved into figures and tables to clarify and underscore certain developments and provide an alternative mode of learning.

Updates to the Narrative

The eighth edition has been significantly updated to reflect current scholarship. Two sections of the book in particular have been substantially revised. The coverage of early American history from the Seven Years' War through the early Republic has been updated by François Furstenberg (chapters 6–11), and the last chapters in the book have been revised and restructured by Sarah Igo to provide a better chronological balance in coverage of the post-1960s period (chapters 26–31).

▶ **Updated and Expanded Coverage of Early American History.** A major area of revision focused on inserting Native American history more fully into the narrative of early American history. Chapters 6–11 now focus much more on Native Americans' struggles in the west to maintain their autonomy and territorial sovereignty, struggles which had a decisive effect on many of the great events of early American history, from the Seven Years' War to the American Revolution, the drafting of the Constitution, and beyond. We hope students will have a better understanding of the complex interplay of forces at work in early American history, forces in which Europeans were not the only main actors. This emphasis extends to the maps (such as Map 6.1, European Areas of Influence and the Seven Years' War, 1756–1763), where we have made changes to better locate and emphasize Native American peoples.

The second major area of revision focused on incorporating transnational forces more fully into the narrative. Thus, the discussions of the Seven Years' War, the Revolution, and the political conflicts of the 1790s and beyond all emphasize the importance of European imperial objectives and of wars in Europe and the Caribbean. It's important to remember, for example, that battles in North America were only part of the war we know as the "American Revolution." Fighting also took place in the Caribbean, in Europe, and even in India.

▶ **Updated and Revised Organization of U.S. History since 1945.** The last six chapters of the book (chapters 26–31) have been thoroughly updated to include new scholarship on global political developments, social movements, technological innovations, and environmental challenges. These chapters have also been restructured to provide a better chronological balance in coverage of the post-1960s period. Chapters 26 and 27 employ longer timeframes, allowing students to grasp (in chapter 26) how Cold War foreign policy and ongoing militarization shaped geopolitics, the federal state, and domestic affairs from 1945 all the way to 1960. Chapter 27 considers domestic policy and culture during the same years, highlighting postwar continuities and departures from the New Deal era. Chapter 28 emphasizes the complex roots and tactics of the "rights revolution," emphasizing the dynamic between grassroots protest and national policy-making. Chapter 29 revolves less around the Vietnam War itself than the interrelated geopolitical and social challenges of the later 1960s and 1970s, including military defeat, racial tensions, the oil crisis, and stagflation. Chapter 30 begins with Reagan's election and closes at the turn of the twenty-first century, allowing the events of the 1980s and 1990s—for example, the end of the Cold War, the outbreak of new global conflicts, and the "culture wars"— to be considered in the same frame. Chapter 31 now opens with the 9/11 attacks and offers a full analysis of the Obama years as well as Trump's election and the first two years of his administration. It includes new material on immigration debates, natural disasters, surveillance technologies, and the twenty-first-century economy.

▶ **Enriched Coverage of Science and Technology.** In response to reviewers who noted students' interest in technology, we have included more coverage of issues related to science and technology. From railroads and airplanes to telephones and the evolution of the Internet, technological change has been one of the drivers of American history and, of course, remains so today. The theme extends to coverage of related environmental issues. Some highlights of this coverage include a new section on the latest DNA evidence of the first human migrants to the New World (chapter 1); a new map activity that asks students to connect environmental/geographical considerations to politics (chapter 6); a consideration of the centrality of steam power and railroads in early industrialization (chapter 12); a discussion of Custer that employs recent developments in disaster archaeology, as well as a reconsideration of the role of hydraulic mining in western development (chapter 17); a feature on the technology of electricity with up-to-date inclusion on Tesla's role (chapter 18); new material on conservation and Hetch Hetchy Valley (chapter 21); new coverage of radar technology (chapter 25); and a discussion of the personal computer revolution and the federal government's subsidizing of the high-tech sector in the 1980s, as well as a fuller description of the information economy and tech boom in the 1990s (chapter 30).

Evaluating of Primary Sources

Primary sources form the heart of historical study, and we are pleased to offer the **Analyzing Historical Evidence** feature. This feature, which appears in every chapter, juxtaposes two to four primary documents to dramatize the human dimension of major events and show varying perspectives on those events. Each feature also provides students with an opportunity to build and practice their skills of historical interpretation. Because students are so attuned to visuals and instructors deeply value their usefulness as primary sources, we have included both text and visual sources in this new feature. Images including photographs of artifacts of daily life in Chaco Canyon, depictions of Native American battles, early examples of photojournalism, political cartoons, and more show students how to mine visual documents for evidence about the past.

Each feature includes three **Questions for Analysis** to help students understand the significance of the featured topic, its context, and how it might be viewed from different angles. Each of the questions fits in one of the following Historical Skill categories: Summarize the Argument, Analyze the Evidence, Consider the Context, Recognize Viewpoints, and Ask Historical Questions. Topics include "Enslavement by Marriage," "The Nation's First Formal Declaration of War," "The Meaning of Freedom," "The Final Push for Woman Suffrage," and "Protecting Gay and Lesbian Rights." These features are available both in print and online and are easily assigned in LaunchPad, along with multiple-choice quizzes that measure student comprehension.

Highlighting the Stories of Individuals

In addition to the Analyzing Historical Evidence feature, each chapter also contains a **Spotlight** feature. Some of the essays focus on how historians make and support historical arguments, such as "Why Did Cortés Win?" (chapter 2) and "How Could a Vice President Get Away with Murder?" (chapter 10). Other essays illuminate the stories of individuals or groups who sought their own versions of the promise of America, such as "A Slave Sues for Her Freedom" (chapter 8) and "How Did Textile Workers Try to Improve Their Wages and Working Conditions?" (chapter 24). Finally, some essays offer a global perspective by connecting U.S. history to developments around the world, such as "Did France and Spain Accomplish Their Objectives in the American Revolution?" (chapter 7) and "1968: A Year of Global Unrest" (chapter 29). Each feature includes three **Questions for Analysis**. Each of the questions fits in one of the following Historical Skill categories; Summarize the Argument, Analyze the Evidence, Consider the Context, Recognize Viewpoints, and Ask Historical Questions.

Helping Instructors Teach with Digital Resources for the Classroom

The eighth edition of *The American Promise* offers flexibility in formats, including easy-to-use digital resources that can make an immediate impact in classrooms. *The American Promise* is offered in Macmillan's premier learning platform, **LaunchPad**, an intuitive interactive e-book and course space. Ready to assign as is, with key assessment resources built into each chapter, instructors can also edit and customize **LaunchPad** as their imaginations and innovations dictate. Free when packaged with the print text, **LaunchPad** grants students and teachers access to a wealth of online tools and resources built specifically for our text to enhance reading comprehension and promote in-depth study.

Developed with extensive feedback from history instructors and students, **LaunchPad** for *the American Past* includes the complete narrative of the print book, the companion reader *Reading the American Past* with accompanying auto-graded exercises, guided reading exercises, primary source quizzes, video sources, map activities, flashcards, and **LearningCurve**, an adaptive learning tool that is designed to get students to read before they come to class. With **source-based questions in the test bank and in LearningCurve** and the ability to **sort test bank questions by chapter learning objectives**, instructors now have more ways to test students on their understanding of sources and narrative in the book.

Available for the first time with this edition, **Achieve Read & Practice** puts the most affordable and easy-to-use e-book with built-in assessment into the hands of students wherever they go. **Achieve Read & Practice**'s interactive e-book, adaptive quizzing, and gradebook is built with an intuitive interface that can be read on mobile devices and is fully accessible and available at a discounted price so anyone can use it. It comes preloaded with **LearningCurve adaptive quizzing**, which, when assigned, ensures students come to class prepared. Instructors can set due dates for reading assignments and **LearningCurve** quizzes in just a few clicks, making it an effective option for a simple and affordable way to engage students with the narrative.

To learn more about digital product offerings, see the "Versions and Supplements" section on page xi.

Acknowledgments

We gratefully acknowledge all of the helpful suggestions from those who have read and taught from previous editions of *The American Promise* and cared enough to take the time to advise us. We hope that our many classroom collaborators will be pleased to see their influence in the eighth edition. In particular, we wish to thank the talented scholars and teachers who gave generously of their time and knowledge to review the previous edition in preparation for its revision: Ann Ackerman, *Nashua County College*; Ian Aebel, *Harris-Stowe State University*; Joseph Bagley, *Georgia State University*; Timothy Buckner, *Troy University*; Kara Carroll, *Central New Mexico Community College*; Leilah Davidson, *Northern Arizona University*; Wayne Drews, *Kennesaw State University*; Donna Dunakey, *Florida Southwestern State College— Thomas Edison*; Robert Genter, *Nassau Community College*; Jessica Gerard, *Ozarks Technical Community College*; Diane Gill, *North Lake College*; Patricia Herb, *North Central State College*; Peter Hoffer, *University of Georgia*; Andrew Hollinger, *Tarrant County College NE*; Robin Krawitz, *Delaware State University*; Alan Lehmann, *Blinn College—Brenham*; Alexander Marriott, *Alvin College*; Michael McCormick, *Houston Community College*; Stacy Reikowsky, *North Dakota State University*; Gary Ritter, *Central Piedmont Community College*; Carey Roberts, *Liberty University*; Scott Seagle, *University of Tennessee at Chattanooga*; Edward Simmons, *Georgia Gwinnett College*; John Smith, *Texas A&M—Commerce*; David Toye, *Northeast State Community College NE*; James Tuten, *Juniata College*; Leah Vallely, *Calhoun Community College*; Stephanie Vincent, *Kent State University—Main*.

A project as complex as this requires the talents of many individuals. First, we would like to acknowledge our families for their support, forbearance, and toleration of our textbook responsibilities. We would also like to thank the many people at Bedford/St. Martin's and Macmillan Learning who have been crucial to this project. Thanks are due to Leah R. Strauss, senior developmental editor, who shepherded the project from start to finish, always with good humor; William J. Lombardo, senior program manager for history; Michael Rosenberg, senior program director for history; and Leasa Burton, vice president, for their support and guidance. Thanks are also due to Mary Starowicz, media editor; Mollie Chandler, associate editor; and Julia Bell, editorial assistant. We thank history marketing manager Melissa Rodriguez and marketing assistant Morgan Ratner. We thank senior content project manager Kendra LeFleur, who pulled together the many pieces related to copyediting, design, and composition. Thanks are also due to Naomi Kornhauser for her diligent visual source research; workflow manager Susan Wein; designer Jerilyn Bockorick; copy editor Jeannine Thibodeau; proofreaders Arthur Johnson and Kim Kosmatka; indexer Sonya Dintaman; cover designer William Boardman; and executive media project manager Michelle Camisa who oversaw the production of digital components of *The American Promise*.

VERSIONS AND SUPPLEMENTS

Adopters of *The American Promise* and their students have access to abundant print and digital resources and tools, the acclaimed Bedford Series in History and Culture volumes, and much more. The LaunchPad course space for *The American Promise* provides access to the narrative and a wealth of primary sources and other features, along with assignment and assessment opportunities. Achieve Read & Practice supplies adaptive quizzing and our mobile, accessible Value Edition e-book in one easy-to-use, affordable product. See below for more information, visit the book's catalog site at **macmillanlearning.com**, or contact your local Bedford/St. Martin's sales representative.

Get the Right Version for Your Class

To accommodate different course lengths and course budgets, *The American Promise* is available in several different versions and formats to best suit your course needs. The comprehensive *The American Promise* includes a full-color art program, a robust set of features, and a chapter study guide. *The American Promise*, Concise Edition, provides the unabridged narrative in full color, with a streamlined art and feature program, at a lower price. *The American Promise*, Value Edition, offers a trade-sized two-color option with the unabridged narrative and selected art and maps at a steep discount. The Value Edition is also offered at the lowest price point in loose-leaf format, and all of these versions are available as e-books. For the best value of all, package a new print book with LaunchPad or Achieve Read & Practice at no additional charge to get the best each format offers. LaunchPad users get a print version for easy portability with an interactive e-book for the full-feature text and course space, along with LearningCurve and loads of additional assignment and assessment options. Achieve Read & Practice users get a print version with a mobile, interactive Value Edition e-book plus LearningCurve adaptive quizzing in one exceptionally affordable, easy-to-use product.

Combined Volume (Chapters 1–31): available in a comprehensive edition, Concise Edition, Value Edition, loose-leaf, and e-book formats and in LaunchPad and Achieve Read & Practice

Volume 1, To 1877 (Chapters 1–16): available in a comprehensive edition, Concise Edition, Value Edition, loose-leaf, and e-book formats and in LaunchPad and Achieve Read & Practice

Volume 2, From 1865 (Chapters 16–31): available in a comprehensive edition, Concise Edition, Value Edition, loose-leaf, and e-book formats and in LaunchPad and Achieve Read & Practice

As noted below, any of these volumes can be packaged with additional titles for a discount. To get ISBNs for discount packages, visit **macmillanlearning.com** or contact your Bedford/St. Martin's representative.

Assign LaunchPad—an Assessment-Ready Interactive e-Book with Sources and Course Space

Available for discount purchase on its own or for packaging with new books at no additional charge, LaunchPad is a breakthrough solution for history courses. Intuitive and easy-to-use for students and instructors alike, Launch-Pad is ready to use as is; it can be edited, customized with your own material, and assigned quickly. LaunchPad for *The American Promise* includes Bedford/St. Martin's high-quality content all in one place, including the full interactive e-book and the companion reader *Reading the American Past*, plus Learning-Curve adaptive quizzing, guided reading activities designed to help students read actively for key concepts, auto-graded quizzes for each primary source, and chapter summative quizzes. Through a wealth of formative and summative assessments, including the adaptive learning program of LearningCurve (see the full description ahead), students gain confidence and get into their reading *before* class. These features, plus additional primary source documents, video sources and tools for making video assignments, map activities, flashcards, and customizable test banks, make LaunchPad an invaluable asset for any instructor.

LaunchPad easily integrates with course management systems, and with fast ways to build assignments, rearrange chapters, and add new pages, sections, or links, it lets teachers build the courses they want to teach and hold students accountable. For more information, visit **launchpadworks.com**, or to arrange a demo, contact us at **historymktg@macmillan.com**.

Assign LearningCurve So Your Students Come to Class Prepared

Students using **LaunchPad** or **Achieve Read & Practice** receive access to **LearningCurve** for *The American Promise*. Assigning **LearningCurve** in place of reading quizzes is easy for instructors, and the reporting features help instructors track overall class trends and spot topics that are giving students trouble so instructors can adjust their lectures and class activities. This online learning tool is popular with students because it was designed to help them comprehend content at their own pace in a nonthreatening, game-like environment. The feedback for wrong answers provides instructional coaching and sends students back to the book for review. Students answer as many questions as necessary to reach a target score, with repeated chances to revisit material they haven't mastered. When **LearningCurve** is assigned, students come to class better prepared.

Assign Achieve Read & Practice So Your Students Can Read and Study Wherever They Go

Available for discount purchase on its own or for packaging with new books at no additional charge, **Achieve Read & Practice** is Bedford/St. Martin's most affordable digital solution for history courses. Intuitive and easy to use for students and instructors alike, **Achieve Read & Practice** is ready to use as is and can be assigned quickly. **Achieve Read & Practice** for *The American Promise* includes the Value Edition interactive e-book, **LearningCurve** adaptive quizzing, assignment tools, and a gradebook. All this is built with an intuitive interface that can be read on mobile devices and is fully accessible, easily integrates with course management systems, and is available at a discounted price so anyone can use it. Instructors can set due dates for reading assignments and **LearningCurve** quizzes in just a few clicks, making it a simple and affordable way to engage students with the narrative and hold students accountable for course reading so they will come to class better prepared. For more information, visit **macmillanlearning.com/ReadandPractice**, or to arrange a demo, contact us at **historymktg@macmillan.com**.

Tailor Your Text to Match Your Course with Bedford Select for History

Create the ideal textbook for your course with only the chapters you need. Starting from the Value Edition history text, you can rearrange chapters, delete unnecessary chapters, select chapters of primary sources from the companion reader, add primary source document projects from the Bedford Document Collections, or choose to improve your students' historical thinking skills with the Bedford Tutorials for History. In addition, you can add your own original content to create just the book you're looking for. With Bedford Select, students pay only for material that will be assigned in the course, and nothing more. Order your textbook every semester, or modify from one term to the next. It is easy to build your customized textbook without compromising the quality and affordability you've come to expect from Bedford/St. Martin's. For more information, talk to your Bedford/St. Martin's representative or visit **macmillanlearning.com/bedfordselect**.

▷ iClicker

iClicker, Active Learning Simplified

iClicker offers simple, flexible tools to help you give students a voice and facilitate active learning in the classroom. Students can participate with the devices they already bring to class using our **iClicker** Reef mobile apps (which work with smartphones, tablets, or laptops) or **iClicker** remotes. We've now integrated **iClicker** with Macmillan's **LaunchPad** to make it easier than ever to synchronize grades and promote engagement—both in and out of class. **iClicker** Reef access cards can also be packaged with **LaunchPad** or your textbook at a significant savings for your students. To learn more, talk to your Macmillan Learning (Bedford/St. Martin's) representative or visit **www.iclicker.com**.

Take Advantage of Instructor Resources

Bedford/St. Martin's has developed a rich array of teaching resources for this book and for this course. They range from lecture and presentation materials and assessment tools to course management options. Most can be found in **LaunchPad** or can be downloaded or ordered from the Instructor Resources tab of the book's catalog site at **macmillanlearning.com**.

▶ **Bedford Coursepack for Blackboard, Canvas, Brightspace by D2L, or Moodle.** We can help you integrate our rich content into your course management system. Registered instructors can download coursepacks that include our popular free resources and book-specific content for *The American Promise*. To find your version or download your coursepack, visit **macmillanlearning.com**.

▶ **Instructor's Resource Manual.** The instructor's manual offers both experienced and first-time instructors tools for presenting textbook material in engaging ways. It includes content learning objectives, annotated chapter outlines, and strategies for teaching with the textbook, plus suggestions on how to get the most out of **LearningCurve** and a survival guide for first-time teaching assistants.

▶ **Guide to Changing Editions.** Designed to facilitate an instructor's transition from the previous edition or version of *The American Promise* to this new edition, this guide presents an overview of major changes and of changes within each chapter.

▶ **Online Test Bank.** The test bank includes a mix of fresh, carefully crafted multiple-choice, matching, short-answer, and essay questions for each chapter. Many of the multiple-choice questions feature a map, an image, or a primary source excerpt as the prompt. All questions appear in Microsoft Word format and in easy-to-use test bank software that allows instructors to add, edit, re-sequence, filter (by question type or learning objective), and print questions and answers. Instructors can also export questions into a variety of course management systems.

▶ *The Bedford Lecture Kit:* **Lecture Outlines, Maps, and Images.** Look good and save time with *The Bedford Lecture Kit*. These presentation materials include fully customizable multimedia presentations built around chapter outlines that are embedded with maps, figures, and images from the textbook, and they are supplemented by more detailed instructor notes on key points and concepts. These materials are downloadable from the Instructor Resources tab at **macmillanlearning.com**.

Print, Digital, and Custom Options for More Choice and Value

For information on free packages and discounts up to 50 percent, contact your local Bedford/St. Martin's representative or visit **macmillanlearning.com**.

▶ *Reading the American Past,* **Eighth Edition.** Edited by Michael P. Johnson, one of the authors of *The American Promise*, and designed to complement the textbook, *Reading the American Past* provides a broad selection of more than 150 primary source documents, as well as editorial apparatus to help students understand the sources. Available free when packaged with the print text and included in the LaunchPad e-book with auto-graded quizzes for each source. Also available on its own as a downloadable e-book.

▶ **Bedford Select for History.** Create the ideal textbook for your course with only the chapters you need. Starting from a Value Edition history text, you can rearrange chapters, delete unnecessary chapters, select chapters of primary sources from the companion reader and add primary source document projects from the Bedford Document Collections, or choose to improve your students' historical thinking skills with the Bedford Tutorials for History. In addition, you can add your own original content to create just the book you're looking for. With Bedford Select, students pay only for material that will be assigned in the course, and nothing more. Order your textbook every semester, or modify from one term to the next. It is easy to build your customized textbook without compromising the quality and affordability you've come to expect from Bedford/St. Martin's.

▶ **Bedford Tutorials for History.** Designed to customize textbooks with resources relevant to individual courses, this collection of brief units, each sixteen pages long and loaded with examples, guides students through basic skills such as using historical evidence effectively, working with primary sources, taking effective notes, avoiding plagiarism and citing sources, and more. Up to two tutorials can be added to a Bedford/St. Martin's history survey title at no additional charge, freeing you to spend your class time focusing on content and interpretation. For more information, visit **macmillanlearning.com/historytutorials**.

▶ **Bedford Document Collections for U.S. History.** These affordable, brief document projects provide five to seven primary sources, an introduction, historical background and other pedagogical features. Each curated project—designed for use in a single class period and written by a historian about a favorite topic— poses a historical question and guides students through analysis of the sources. Examples include Witch Accusations in Seventeenth-Century New England; The Legend of John Henry: Folklore and the Lives of African Americans in the Postwar South; and The Texas Rangers: Vanguard of Anglo Settlement in the Lone Star State. For more information, visit **macmillanlearning.com/bdc/ushistory/catalog**. You can also select up to two document projects from the collection to add in print for free to customize your Bedford/St. Martin's textbook. Additional document projects can be added for a reasonable cost. For more information, visit **macmillanlearning.com/custombdc/ushistory** or contact your Bedford/ St. Martin's representative.

▶ **The Bedford Series in History and Culture.** The more than one hundred titles in this highly praised series combine first-rate scholarship, historical narrative, and important primary documents for undergraduate courses. Each book is brief, inexpensive, and focused on a specific topic or period. Recently published titles include *The Chinese Exclusion Act and Angel Island: A Brief History with Documents,* by Judy Yung; *American Working Women in World War II: A Brief History with Documents,* by Lynn Dumenil; *Brown v. Board of Education: A Brief History with Documents,* Second Edition, by Waldo E. Martin Jr.; and *Defending Slavery: Proslavery Thought in the Old South,* by Paul Finkelman. For a complete list of titles, visit **macmillanlearning.com**. Package discounts are available.

▶ *Rand McNally Atlas of American History.* This collection of more than eighty full-color maps illustrates key events and eras from early exploration, settlement, expansion, and immigration to U.S. involvement in wars abroad and on U.S. soil. Introductory pages for each section include a brief overview, timelines, graphs, and photos to quickly establish a historical context. Free when packaged.

▶ *The Bedford Glossary for U.S. History.* This handy supplement for the survey course gives students historically contextualized definitions for hundreds of terms—from *abolitionism* to *zoot suit*—that they will encounter in lectures, reading, and exams. Free when packaged.

▶ Trade Books. Titles published by sister companies Hill and Wang; Farrar, Straus and Giroux; Henry Holt and Company; St. Martin's Press; Picador; and Palgrave Macmillan are available at a 50 percent discount when packaged with Bedford/St. Martin's textbooks. For more information, visit **macmillanlearning .com/tradeup**.

▶ *A Pocket Guide to Writing in History.* Updated to reflect changes made in the 2017 *Chicago Manual of Style* revision, this portable and affordable reference tool by Mary Lynn Rampolla provides reading, writing, and research advice useful to students in all history courses. Concise yet comprehensive advice on approaching typical history assignments, developing critical reading skills, writing effective history papers, conducting research, using and documenting sources, and avoiding plagiarism—enhanced with practical tips and examples throughout—have made this slim reference a best seller. Package discounts are available.

▶ *A Student's Guide to History.* This complete guide to success in any history course provides the practical help students need to be successful. In addition to introducing students to the nature of the discipline, author Jules Benjamin teaches a wide range of skills, from preparing for exams to approaching common writing assignments, and explains the research and documentation process with plentiful examples. Package discounts are available.

▶ *Going to the Source: The Bedford Reader in American History.* Developed by Victoria Bissell Brown and Timothy J. Shannon, this reader combines a rich diversity of primary and secondary sources with in-depth instructions for how to use each type of source. Mirroring the chronology of the U.S. history survey, each of the main chapters familiarizes students with a single type of source—from personal letters to political cartoons—while focusing on an intriguing historical episode such as the Cherokee Removal or the 1894 Pullman strike. The reader's wide variety of chapter topics and sources provokes students' interest as it teaches them the skills they need to successfully interrogate historical sources. Package discounts are available.

▶ *America Firsthand.* With its distinctive focus on first-person accounts from ordinary people, this primary documents reader by Anthony Marcus, John M. Giggie, and David Burner offers a remarkable range of perspectives on America's history from those who lived it. Popular Points of View sections expose students to different perspectives on a specific event or topic. Package discounts are available.

BRIEF CONTENTS

CONTENTS

1
ANCIENT AMERICA

2
EUROPEANS ENCOUNTER THE NEW WORLD

Photo: Everett Collection Historical/Alamy.

Photo: Courtesy of Toronto Public Library.

Photo: Library of Congress, 3a03340.

12
THE NORTH AND WEST
1840–1860 *326*

13
THE SLAVE SOUTH
1820–1860 *358*

14
THE HOUSE DIVIDED
1846–1861 *390*

Photo: Library of Congress, 3g02439.

Photo: Library of Congress, 3a33960.

Photo: Library of Congress, 3a06152.

15
THE CRUCIBLE OF WAR
1861–1865 *420*

16
RECONSTRUCTION
1863–1877 *456*

Photo: Library of Congress, 3c17998.

Photo: Alabama Department of Archives and History, Montgomery, Alabama.

APPENDICES

I. Documents

II. Government and Demographics

MAPS, FIGURES, AND TABLES

Map Activities are listed in blue

Maps

Figures and Tables

SPECIAL FEATURES

Area ceded by
Great Britain,
1818

Area ceded by
the United States
to Great Britain,
1818

OREGON COUNTRY
Agreement with Britain,
1846

(OREGON TERRITORY)

**LOUISIANA
PURCHASE**
from France, 1803

Missouri R.

N. Platte R.

Platte R.

S. Platte R.

(UTAH TERRITORY)

**MEXICAN CESSION,
1848**

CALIFORNIA
(1850)

(Claim waived by
Texas, 1850)

Red R.

TEXAS
Annexed, 1845

(NEW MEXICO TERRITORY)

**PACIFIC
OCEAN**

TEXAS
(1845)

GADSDEN PURCHASE
from Mexico, 1853

Rio Grande

Areas ceded by Britain, 1842
(Webster-Ashburton Treaty)

St. Lawrence R.

MAINE
(1820)

Lake Superior

VERMONT
(1791)

N.H.
(1788)

(MINNESOTA
TERRITORY)

WISCONSIN
(1848)

Lake Huron

Lake Michigan

NEW YORK
(1788)

MASS.
(1788)

Lake Ontario

MICHIGAN
(1837)

RHODE
ISLAND
(1790)

Lake Erie

PENN.
(1787)

Connecticut R.

Hudson R.

CONNECTICUT
(1788)

IOWA
(1846)

OHIO
(1803)

Delaware R.

NEW JERSEY
(1787)

ILLINOIS
(1818)

INDIANA
(1816)

Missouri R.

Potomac R.

DELAWARE
(1787)

MARYLAND
(1788)

Ohio R.

KENTUCKY
(1792)

James R.

*Chesapeake
Bay*

MISSOURI
(1821)

Gained by treaty
with Britain, 1783

VIRGINIA
(1788)

Cumberland R.

Tennessee R.

NORTH
CAROLINA
(1789)

Cape Fear R.

ARKANSAS
(1836)

TENNESSEE
(1796)

SOUTH
CAROLINA
(1788)

THE ORIGINAL THIRTEEN COLONIES

Proclamation Line of 1763

(INDIAN
TERRITORY)

Mississippi R.

ATLANTIC
OCEAN

Savannah R.

MISSISSIPPI
(1817)

ALABAMA
(1819)

GEORGIA
(1788)

LOUISIANA
(1812)

THE UNITED STATES
IN 1853

0   150   300 miles

0   150   300 kilometers

Areas taken from Spain
in 1810, 1813

FLORIDA
(1845)

FLORIDA
Treaty with Spain,
1819

Gulf of Mexico

(1789) Date of statehood

The American Promise

A HISTORY OF THE UNITED STATES

ANCIENT AMERICA

BEFORE 1492

How did ancient Americans shape North America before 1492? This chapter surveys the history of ancient Americans before Europeans arrived in 1492. It explores the major ancient American cultures that evolved for thousands of years after the first humans arrived in the New World.

This chapter will explore the following questions:

- Why do historians rely on the work of archaeologists?

- When and how did humans migrate into North America?

- When and why did Archaic hunter-gatherers inhabit ancient America?

- How did agriculture influence ancient American cultures?

- What ancient American cultures inhabited North America in the 1490s?

- How did the Mexican empire amass power and riches?

- Conclusion: How did ancient Americans shape their world and ours?

AN AMERICAN STORY

Nobody today knows his name. Almost a thousand years ago, ancient Americans buried a man with elaborate rituals at Cahokia, the largest residential and ceremonial site in what is now the United States. Located in southwestern Illinois near the Mississippi River, Cahokia had a population of more than 20,000. Cahokians' burial rituals suggest that the man was a very powerful person who represented spiritual and political authority.

Archaeologists—scientists who study the objects left behind by ancient peoples—discovered what we know about the Cahokians and this leader whom they buried. Cahokia attracted the attention of archaeologists because ancient Americans built hundreds of earthen mounds in the region. Atop Monks Mound, a huge pyramid that is the single biggest structure ever built by ancient North Americans, Cahokia's political and religious leaders performed ceremonies watched by thousands who crowded a nearby plaza roughly the size of fifty football fields. These ceremonies were probably intended to demonstrate that the leaders had access to supernatural forces. At the far edge of the plaza, Cahokians buried the man in a mound about 6 feet high and 250 feet long.

Before Cahokians lowered their leader into his grave sometime around AD 1050, they first placed the body of another man facedown in the dirt. On top of that man, Cahokians draped a large cape made of 20,000 shell beads crafted into the likeness of a bird. They then laid the leader faceup on the beaded cape with his head pointing southeast, aligned with the passage of the sun across the sky during the summer solstice. Experts speculate that Cahokians sought to pay homage not only to this man of importance but also to the awe-inspiring forces that governed their lives: darkness and light, earth and sun.

To accompany their leader, Cahokians also buried hundreds of beautifully crafted arrowheads and other artifacts along with the bodies of seven adults who probably were the leader's relatives or servants. Not far away, archaeologists discovered several amazing mass graves. One contained fifty-three young women who had been killed by poison, strangulation, or having their throats slit. Other graves contained forty-three more sacrificed women and forty-three additional men and women who had been executed at the burial site. In all, more than 270 people were buried in the mound with the leader.

Nobody knows exactly who the powerful man was or why Cahokians buried him as they did. Most likely he was a supreme leader of some sort. To date, archaeologists have found no similar burial site in all of ancient North America. Most likely, the man's burial and the human sacrifices that accompanied it were major public rituals that displayed the fearsome power he wielded, the respect he commanded, and the supernatural authority his survivors intended to honor. Much remains unknown and unknowable about him and his fellow Cahokians, just as it does with other ancient Americans. The history of ancient Americans is therefore necessarily incomplete and controversial. Still, archaeologists have learned a great deal about ancient peoples who shaped the history of America before 1492.

▼ **Cahokia Mother and Child** This ceramic effigy of a mother nursing her baby illustrates the skill of Cahokia's pottery makers as well as the human face of the tens of thousands of people who inhabited Cahokia and surrounding settlements when the site's massive mounds were used for burials and other rituals. National Geographic Image Collection/Alamy Stock Photo

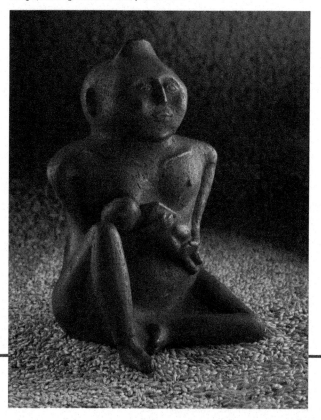

Why do historians rely on the work of archaeologists?

rchaeologists and historians seek to learn about people who lived in the past, but they usually employ different methods to obtain information. Both archaeologists and historians study artifacts as clues to the activities and ideas of the humans who created them. They concentrate, however, on different kinds of artifacts. Archaeologists tend to focus on physical objects, such as bones, spear points, pots, baskets, jewelry, clothing, and buildings. Historians direct their attention mostly to writings, such as letters, diaries, laws, speeches, newspapers, and court cases. The concentration of historians on writings and of archaeologists on other physical objects denotes a rough cultural and chronological boundary between the human beings studied by the two groups of scholars, a boundary marked by the use of writing.

Writing is defined as a system of symbols that record spoken language. Writing originated among ancient peoples in China, Egypt, and Central America about eight thousand years ago, within the most recent 2 percent of the 350,000 years that modern human beings have existed. While people who inhabited North America in 1492 expressed themselves with many kinds of symbols (for example, in their pottery, textiles, and tools), they did not use writing. Ancient Americans invented hundreds of spoken languages; they learned to survive in almost every natural environment; they chose and honored leaders; they traded, warred, and worshipped; and above all, they learned from and taught one another. Still, much of what we would like to know about their experiences remains unknown because they did not write about it.

Archaeologists specialize in learning about people who did not document their history in writing. They study the millions of artifacts ancient peoples created. They also examine geological strata, pollen, and other environmental features to reconstruct as much as possible about the world inhabited by ancient peoples. This chapter relies on such archaeological studies to sketch a brief overview of ancient America, the long first phase of the history of what became the United States. Although ancient Americans and their descendants resided in North America for thousands of years before Europeans arrived, their history cannot be reconstructed with the detail and certainty made possible by writing.

COMPARE AND CONTRAST

How do archaeologists' methods of studying people in the past differ from those of historians?

ANALYZE EVIDENCE

What sources do historians use to learn about ancient American societies?

QUICK REVIEW

Why do historians rely on archaeologists to understand the history of ancient Americans?

When and how did humans migrate into North America?

he first human beings to arrive in the Western Hemisphere emigrated from Siberia. They brought with them hunting skills, weapon- and tool-making techniques, and other forms of human knowledge developed millennia earlier in Africa, Europe, and Asia. These first Americans hunted large mammals, such as the mammoths they had learned in Europe and Asia to kill, butcher, and process for food, clothing, and building materials. Most likely, small groups of these first Americans wandered into the Western Hemisphere more or less accidentally in pursuit of prey.

African and Asian Origins

Human beings lived elsewhere in the world for hundreds of thousands of years before they reached the Western Hemisphere. Millions of years before humans existed anywhere on the globe, North and South America became detached from the gigantic common landmass scientists now call Pangaea. About 240 million years ago, powerful forces deep within the earth fractured Pangaea and slowly pushed continents apart to their present positions (**Map 1.1**). This process of continental drift encircled the land of the Western Hemisphere with large oceans that isolated it from the other continents long before the earliest human beings first appeared in Africa about five million years ago.

Millions of years later, about 320,000 BP, modern humans evolved in Africa. (The abbreviation *BP*, which stands for "years before the present," indicates dates earlier than two thousand years ago; for more recent dates, the common and familiar notation *AD* is used, as in AD 1492.) All human beings throughout the world today ultimately came from descendants of these ancient Africans. Slowly, over many thousands of years, some descendants walked out of Africa and scattered into Europe and Asia. Land that connected Africa to Europe and Asia made possible their migration. But for about 97 percent of the time, *modern humans* have inhabited the earth, none of them managed to cross the oceans that isolated North and South America from Africa and Eurasia.

Two major developments made it possible for ancient humans to migrate to the Western Hemisphere. First, people successfully adapted to the frigid environment near the Arctic Circle. By about 25,000 BP, humans had become permanent residents of extremely cold regions such as northeastern Siberia. Siberian women used bone needles to sew animal skins into warm clothing to protect their families from the frigid climate.

Second, changes in the earth's climate reconnected North America to Asia. During the last global cold spell—which endured from about 25,000 BP to 15,000 BP—snow piled up in glaciers and sea levels dropped, exposing a wide land bridge that connected Asian Siberia to American Alaska. Experts call this land bridge **Beringia**. Since the

CHRONOLOGY

ca. 25,000–15,000 BP
– Glaciation exposes Beringia land bridge.

ca. 20,000 BP
– Ancient people inhabit Alaska.

ca. 16,000 BP
– Some ancient people move south along Pacific coast.

ca. 14,600–14,200 BP
– Coastal migrants occupy sites in Oregon and Chile.

ca. 13,000 BP
– Southern overland migrants, the first Americans arrive in United States and spread throughout hemisphere.
– Paleo-Indians use Clovis points.

Beringia
The land bridge between Siberia and Alaska that allowed people to migrate into the Western Hemisphere.

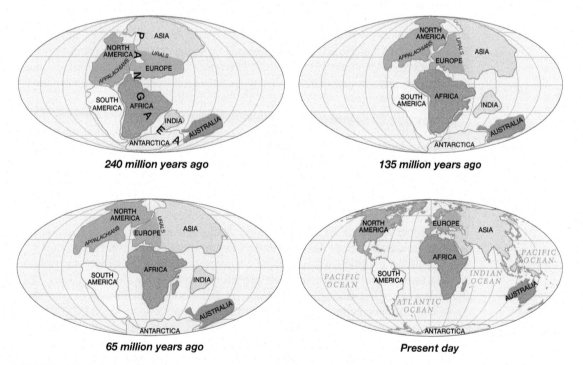

240 million years ago

135 million years ago

65 million years ago

Present day

MAP 1.1 ▲ Continental Drift

Massive geological forces separated North and South America from other continents eons before human beings evolved in Africa five million years ago.

When and why did Archaic hunter-gatherers inhabit ancient America?	How did agriculture influence ancient American cultures?	What ancient American cultures inhabited North America in the 1490s?	How did the Mexican empire amass power and riches?	Conclusion: How did ancient Americans shape their world and ours?

> "As these hunters slowly ventured east, they eventually became pioneers of human life in the Western Hemisphere. Although they did not know it, they revolutionized the history of humanity."

global climate is much warmer now, Beringia lies submerged beneath the ocean that separates Siberia from Alaska. While Beringia was above sea level, glaciers a half-mile thick covered what is now western Canada and reached to the Pacific coast, blocking human access to the rest of the hemisphere. Still, Siberian hunters roamed Beringia for thousands of years in search of mammoths, bison, and smaller animals. As these hunters slowly ventured east, they eventually became pioneers of human life in the Western Hemisphere. Although they did not know it, they revolutionized the history of humanity.

DNA extracted from rare fragments of ancient human bones and teeth confirms that several groups of people migrated through Beringia and into North America as the glaciers slowly melted over thousands of years. Scientists can extrapolate the approximate dates of their arrival by analyzing DNA. Archaeological evidence that documents the exact pathways and cultures of the earliest migrants has not been found, and much remains unknown. Still, experts have shown that ancient people inhabited what is now Alaska before 20,000 BP. They remained there and in the northern reaches of what is now Canada for thousands of years until they eventually died out for unknown reasons.

Around 20,000 BP, another group of ancient people with a distinctive DNA profile took advantage of the gradual shrinking of glaciers to begin to move south into Canada and eventually into what is now the United States. Some of these southern migrants traveled along the narrow strip of coastal land exposed by the melting glaciers until they reached ice-free land along the West Coast. We know little about these coastal migrants because their campsites and burials are now submerged under the Pacific Ocean. Within a thousand years or so after 16,000 BP, these coastal migrants spread all the way to South America. Although their remains are very rare, excavations at Paisley Caves in Oregon and more than 6,000 miles south at Monte Verde in Chile prove that these first hunters descended from ancient Siberians and inhabited these sites between 14,600 and 14,200 BP.

Another group of southern migrants tracked their animal prey over and around the melting glaciers as the climate gradually warmed during roughly the next 6,000 years. Some of them had reached what is now Montana by about 13,000 BP, as proven by recently analyzed DNA from a child's burial. Later generations of almost all Native Americans up to the present day share the distinctive DNA profile of these southern overland migrants. Although these people were not the first humans to arrive in America, they deserve to be called the first Americans since they were the ancestors of almost all the ancient Americans who populated the hemisphere after 13,000 BP. A third, much later pulse of migrants from Siberia arrived about 5,000 BP. Some of them migrated south as far as Arizona and became the ancestors of the Navajo and Apache people.

Beringia

CONSIDER CAUSE AND EFFECT

What developments allowed ancient humans to migrate to the Western Hemisphere?

Paleo-Indian Hunters

Archaeologists refer to these southern overland migrants and their descendants for the next few thousand years as Paleo-Indians. They speculate that when Paleo-Indians made it south of the glaciers they entered a hunters' paradise teeming with wildlife that had never before confronted human predators armed with razor-sharp spears. The abundance of game presumably made hunting relatively easy. Ample food permitted the Paleo-Indian population to grow. Within a thousand years or so after 13,000 BP, Paleo-Indians inhabited almost all of the Western Hemisphere.

The first Americans used a distinctively shaped spearhead known as a Clovis point, named for the place in New Mexico where it was first excavated. Archaeologists' discovery of abundant Clovis points throughout North and Central America in sites occupied about 13,000 BP provides evidence that these nomadic hunters shared not

Paleo-Indians
Archaeologists' term for the first migrants into North America and their descendants who spread across the Americas between about 15,000 BP and 13,500 BP.

Clovis point
Distinctively shaped spearhead used by Paleo-Indians and named for the place in New Mexico where it was first excavated.

| Why do historians rely on the work of archaeologists? | **When and how did humans migrate into North America?** |

▶ **Clovis Spear Points** These spear points, discovered in north-central Colorado in 1977, were crafted by Clovis people around 11,000 BP. They illustrate a feature common to Clovis points throughout the hemisphere, namely the design the maker used to skillfully chip away small fragments of stone and create the point used for killing animals. The stone for these points came from sites hundreds of miles away in Texas and Nebraska, documenting long-distance trade among Clovis people. Drake Clovis Cache. Smithsonian Institution, National Museum of Natural History, Department of Anthropology. Image by Marcia Bakry

just DNA but also a common way of life. Typically, all Paleo-Indians hunted large game such as mammoths and bison, but they probably also killed smaller animals. Concentration on large animals, when possible, made sense because just one mammoth supplied meat for months. Some Paleo-Indians even refrigerated mammoths they killed by filling the body cavities with stones and submerging the carcasses in icy lakes for later use. In addition to food, mammoths provided Paleo-Indians with hides and bones for clothing, shelter, tools, and much more.

About 11,000 BP, Paleo-Indians confronted a major crisis. The mammoths and other large mammals they hunted became extinct. The extinction occurred gradually, stretching over several hundred years. Scientists are not completely certain why it happened, although environmental change probably contributed to it. About this time, the earth's climate warmed, glaciers melted, and sea levels rose. Mammoths and other large mammals may have had difficulty adapting to the warmer climate. Many archaeologists also believe, however, that Paleo-Indians contributed to the extinctions in the Western Hemisphere by killing large animals more rapidly than the animals could reproduce. Some experts dispute this overkill interpretation, but warming environmental changes had occurred for millions of years before the arrival of Paleo-Indians without triggering the extinction of large animals. The presence of skilled Paleo-Indian hunters seems to have made a decisive difference. Whatever the causes, after the extinction of large mammals, Paleo-Indians literally inhabited a new world.

Paleo-Indians adapted to the extinction of their large-animal prey by making two important changes in their way of life. First, hunters began to prey more intensively on smaller animals. Second, Paleo-Indians devoted more energy to foraging—that is, to collecting wild plant foods such as roots, seeds, nuts, berries, and fruits. When Paleo-Indians made these changes, they replaced the apparent uniformity of the big-game-oriented Clovis culture with great cultural diversity adapted to the many natural environments throughout the hemisphere.

These post-Clovis adaptations to local environments resulted in an astounding variety of Native American cultures that existed when Europeans arrived in AD 1492. By then,

ANALYZE EVIDENCE
What did Paleo-Indians living throughout the Western hemisphere have in common?

CONSIDER CAUSE AND EFFECT
What caused the diversity of Paleo-Indian cultures after about 11,000 BP?

▶ **Folsom Discovery** The discovery of this spear point stuck between the ribs of an ancient bison near Folsom, New Mexico, revolutionized our understanding of ancient Americans. Since the bison was known to have been extinct for about 10,000 years, ancient Americans must have been hunting them at least 10,000 years ago. This discovery prompted the search for more human artifacts that proved humans resided in America for thousands of years before the extinction of the ancient bison. Courtesy of the Center for the Study of the First Americans, Texas A&M University.

| When and why did Archaic hunter-gatherers inhabit ancient America? | How did agriculture influence ancient American cultures? | What ancient American cultures inhabited North America in the 1490s? | How did the Mexican empire amass power and riches? | Conclusion: How did ancient Americans shape their world and ours? |

hunter-gatherer
A way of life that involved hunting game and gathering food from naturally occurring sources.

Archaic Indians
Hunting and gathering peoples who descended from Paleo-Indians and dominated the Americas from 10,000 BP to between 4000 and 3000 BP.

hundreds of tribes inhabited North America alone. Hundreds more lived in Central and South America. Still more hundreds of ancient American cultures had disappeared or been transformed as their people constantly adapted to environmental and other challenges.

QUICK REVIEW

How did Paleo-Indians adapt to environmental changes?

When and why did Archaic hunter-gatherers inhabit ancient America?

Archaeologists use the term *Archaic* in two ways: first, to describe the many different hunting and gathering cultures that descended from Paleo-Indians; and second, to refer to the long period of time when those cultures dominated ancient America—roughly from 10,000 BP to somewhere between 4000 BP and 3000 BP. The Archaic era in the history of ancient America followed the Paleo-Indian big-game hunters and came before the development of agriculture. However, even after ancient Americans began to engage in agriculture, the **hunter-gatherer** way of life persisted for millennia.

Like their Paleo-Indian ancestors, **Archaic Indians** hunted with spears, but they also took smaller game with traps, nets, and hooks. Unlike their Paleo-Indian predecessors, many Archaic peoples became excellent basket makers in order to collect and store seeds, roots, nuts, and berries they gathered from wild plants. They prepared food from these plants by using a variety of stone tools. A characteristic Archaic artifact is a grinding stone used to pulverize seeds into edible form. Most Archaic Indians migrated from place to place to gather plant food and hunt animals. They usually did not establish permanent villages, although they often returned to the same river valley or fertile meadow year after year. In regions with especially rich resources—such as present-day California and the Pacific Northwest—they developed permanent settlements. Archaic peoples followed these common practices in distinctive ways in the different environmental regions of North America (**Map 1.2**).

Great Plains Bison Hunters

After the extinction of the largest game animals, some hunters began to concentrate on bison in the massive herds that grazed the grassy plains that stretched hundreds of miles east of the Rocky Mountains. For almost a thousand years after the big-game extinctions, Archaic Indians hunted bison with Folsom points, named after a site near Folsom, New Mexico, discovered in 1908 by an African American cowboy named George McJunkin. Until this discovery, experts had believed that ancient Americans arrived in the New World fairly recently, about three thousand years ago. McJunkin's discovery revealed a Folsom point stuck between two ribs of a giant bison, where a Stone Age hunter had plunged it more than ten thousand years earlier. McJunkin's discovery proved for the first time that ancient Americans had inhabited the New World for more than ten thousand years.

Like their nomadic ancestors, Folsom and other Archaic hunters moved constantly to maintain contact with their prey. And like Paleo-Indians, these hunters had to get close enough to spear their prey. To make it easier to hunt with spears, Great Plains

Why do historians rely on the work of archaeologists?	When and how did humans migrate into North America?

hunters often stampeded bison herds over cliffs and then slaughtered the injured animals that plunged to the bottom.

Bows and arrows did not reach Great Plains hunters until about AD 500. They largely replaced spears, which had been hunters' weapons of choice since the migration across Beringia thousands of years earlier. Bows permitted hunters to wound animals from farther away. Arrows made it possible to shoot repeatedly. Arrowheads were easier to make and therefore less costly to lose than the larger, heavier spear points. These new weapons did not otherwise change age-old ways of hunting. Although we often imagine bison hunters on horseback, in reality ancient Great Plains people hunted on foot. Horses did not arrive on the Great Plains until Europeans imported them decades after 1492. Only then did Great Plains bison hunters obtain horses and become expert riders.

Great Basin Cultures

Archaic peoples in the Great Basin between the Rocky Mountains and the Sierra Nevada inhabited a region of great environmental diversity defined largely by the amount of rain. While some lived on the shores of lakes and marshes fed by the rain and ate fish, others hunted deer, antelope, bison, and smaller game. To protect against shortages in fish and game caused by the fickle rainfall, Great Basin Indians relied on plants as their most important food. Unlike meat and fish, plant food could be collected and stored for long periods. Many Great Basin peoples gathered piñon nuts as a dietary staple. Great Basin peoples adapted to the severe environmental challenges of the region and maintained their Archaic hunter-gatherer way of life for centuries after Europeans arrived in AD 1492.

COMPARE AND CONTRAST
How did Archaic peoples' ways of life differ from Paleo-Indians'?

Pacific Coast Cultures

The richness of the natural environment made present-day California the most densely settled area in all of ancient North America. The land and ocean offered such ample food that California peoples remained hunters and gatherers for hundreds of years after AD 1492. The diversity of California's environment produced variety among native peoples. The mosaic of Archaic settlements in California included about five hundred separate tribes speaking some ninety languages, each with local dialects. No other region of comparable size in ancient North America exhibited such cultural variety.

The Chumash, one of the many California cultures, inhabited the region surrounding what is now Santa Barbara about 5000 BP. Comparatively plentiful food resources—especially acorns—permitted Chumash people to establish relatively permanent villages. Conflict, probably caused by competition for valuable acorn-gathering territory, often broke out among the villages, as documented by Chumash skeletons that display clear signs of violence. Although few other California cultures achieved the population density and village settlements of the Chumash, all shared the hunter-gatherer way of life and reliance on acorns as a major food source.

Another rich natural environment lay along the Pacific Northwest coast. Like the Chumash, Northwest peoples built more or less permanent villages. After about 5500 BP, they concentrated on catching whales and large quantities of salmon, halibut, and other fish, which they dried to last throughout the year. They also traded with people who lived hundreds of miles from the coast. Fishing freed Northwest peoples to develop sophisticated woodworking skills. They fashioned elaborate wood carvings that denoted wealth and status, as well as huge canoes for fishing, hunting, and conducting warfare against neighboring tribes. Archaic northwesterners often fought with one another over access to prime fishing sites.

Ancient California Peoples

When and why did **Archaic hunter-gatherers inhabit ancient America?**

How did agriculture influence ancient American cultures?

What ancient American cultures inhabited North America in the 1490s?

How did the Mexican empire amass power and riches?

Conclusion: How did ancient Americans shape their world and ours?

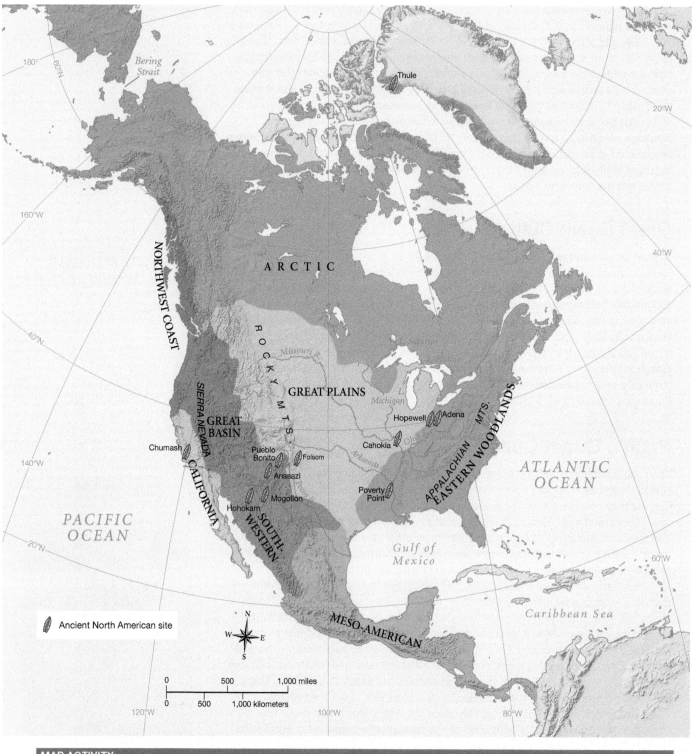

MAP ACTIVITY

MAP 1.2 ▲ Native North American Cultures Environmental conditions defined the boundaries of the broad zones of cultural similarity among ancient North Americans.

READING THE MAP: What crucial environmental features set the boundaries of each cultural region? (The topography indicated on Map 1.3, "Native North Americans about 1500," may be helpful.)

CONNECTIONS: How did the natural environment affect the development of different groups of Native American cultures?

Why do historians rely on the work of archaeologists?	When and how did humans migrate into North America?

◄ **Ozette Whale Effigy** This carving of a whale fin decorated with hundreds of sea otter teeth was discovered along with thousands of other artifacts of daily life at Ozette, an ancient village on the tip of the Olympic Peninsula in present-day Washington. The village was inundated by a catastrophic mudslide about five hundred years ago. The whale fin illustrates the importance of whale hunting to the residents of Ozette. Richard Alexander Cooke III.

Eastern Woodland Cultures

East of the Mississippi River, Archaic peoples adapted to a forest environment that included the major river valleys of the Mississippi, Ohio, Tennessee, and Cumberland; the Great Lakes region; and the Atlantic coast (see **Map 1.2**). Throughout these diverse locales, Archaic peoples pursued similar survival strategies.

Woodland hunters stalked deer as their most important prey. Deer supplied Woodland peoples with food as well as hides and bones that they crafted into clothing, weapons, and many other tools. Like Archaic peoples elsewhere, Woodland natives gathered edible plants, seeds, and nuts. About 6000 BP, some Woodland groups created more or less permanent settlements of 25 to 150 people, usually near a river or lake that offered a wide variety of plant and animal resources. Woodland burial sites suggest that life expectancy was about eighteen years, a short time to learn the skills necessary to survive, reproduce, and adapt to change.

Around 4000 BP, Woodland cultures added two important features to their basic hunter-gatherer lifestyle: agriculture and pottery. Trade and migration from Mexico brought gourds and pumpkins to Woodland peoples, who also began to cultivate sunflowers and small quantities of tobacco. Corn, which had been grown in Mexico and South America since about 7000 BP, also traveled north and became a significant food crop among Eastern Woodland peoples around 2500 BP. Most likely, women learned how to plant, grow, and harvest these crops as an outgrowth of their work gathering edible wild plants. Cultivated crops did not end Woodland peoples' dependence on gathering wild plants, seeds, and nuts.

Like agriculture, pottery probably originated in Mexico. Pots were more durable than baskets for cooking and storing food and water, but they were also much heavier, causing nomadic peoples to shun them. The permanent settlements of Woodland peoples made the heavy weight of pots much less important than their advantages compared to leaky and fragile baskets. While pottery and agriculture introduced changes in Woodland cultures, these ancient Americans retained the other basic features of their Archaic hunter-gatherer lifestyle until 1492 and beyond.

QUICK REVIEW

Why did Archaic Americans shift away from big-game hunting to foraging and preying on smaller animals?

When and why did Archaic hunter-gatherers inhabit ancient America?	How did agriculture influence ancient American cultures?	What ancient American cultures inhabited North America in the 1490s?	How did the Mexican empire amass power and riches?	Conclusion: How did ancient Americans shape their world and ours?

How did agriculture influence ancient American cultures?

CHRONOLOGY

ca. AD 500–1400
- Hohokam culture develops in Arizona.

ca. AD 800–1500
- Mississippian culture flourishes in Southeast.

ca. AD 1000–1200
- Anasazi peoples build cliff dwellings and pueblos.

pueblos
Multiunit dwellings, storage spaces, and ceremonial centers—often termed *kivas*—built by ancient Americans in the Southwest for centuries around AD 1000.

CONSIDER CAUSE AND EFFECT

Why did southwestern people adopt agriculture?

CONSIDER CAUSE AND EFFECT

How did the Pacific coast environment shape the ways of life of the groups who lived there?

Among Eastern Woodland peoples and most other Archaic cultures, agriculture supplemented but did not replace hunter-gatherers' food sources. Reliance on wild animals and plants required most Archaic groups to remain small and mobile. But beginning about 4000 BP, distinctive southwestern cultures began to *depend* on agriculture and to build permanent settlements. Later, around 2500 BP, Woodland peoples in the vast Mississippi valley began to construct burial mounds and other earthworks that suggest the existence of social and political hierarchies that archaeologists term *chiefdoms*. Although the hunter-gatherer lifestyle never entirely disappeared, agricultural settlements and chiefdoms were important innovations in the Archaic way of life.

Southwestern Cultures

Ancient Americans in present-day Arizona, New Mexico, and southern portions of Utah and Colorado developed cultures characterized by agricultural settlements and multiunit dwellings called **pueblos**. All southwestern peoples confronted the challenge of a dry climate and unpredictable fluctuations in rainfall that made the supply of wild plant food very unreliable. They probably adopted agriculture in response to this basic environmental uncertainty.

About 3500 BP, southwestern hunters and gatherers began to cultivate corn, their signature food crop. **(See "Spotlight: How Did Ancient Americans' Corn Spread throughout the World?" on page 14.)** The demands of corn cultivation required hunter-gatherers to restrict their migratory habits and settle in one place in order to tend the crop. Since they had to water their fields, southwestern people became irrigation experts, conserving water from streams, springs, and rainfall and distributing it to thirsty crops.

About AD 200, small farming settlements began to appear throughout southern New Mexico, marking the emergence of the Mogollon culture. Typically, a Mogollon settlement included a dozen pit houses, each made by digging a pit about fifteen feet in diameter and a foot or two deep and then erecting poles to support a roof of branches or dirt. Larger villages usually had one or two bigger pit houses that may have been the predecessors of the circular kivas, the ceremonial rooms that became a characteristic of nearly all southwestern settlements. About AD 900, Mogollon culture began to decline, for reasons that remain obscure.

Around AD 500, while the Mogollon culture prevailed in New Mexico, other ancient people migrated from Mexico to southern Arizona and established the distinctive Hohokam culture. Hohokam settlements used sophisticated grids of irrigation canals to plant and harvest crops twice a year. Hohokam settlements reflected Mexican cultural practices that northbound migrants brought with them, including the building of sizable platform mounds and ball courts. About AD 1400, Hohokam culture declined partly because centuries of irrigation probably made the soil become salty, which reduced crop yields and led to food shortages.

North of the Hohokam and Mogollon cultures, in a region that encompassed southern Utah and Colorado and northern Arizona and New Mexico, the Anasazi culture began to flourish about AD 100. The early Anasazi built pit houses on mesa tops and used irrigation much as did their neighbors to the south. Beginning around AD 1000, some Anasazi began to move to large, multistory cliff dwellings whose spectacular ruins

Why do historians rely on the work of archaeologists?	When and how did humans migrate into North America?

◀ **Ancient Agriculture** Dropping seeds into holes punched in cleared ground by a pointed stick known as a "dibble," this ancient American farmer sows a new crop. Previously planted seeds—including the corn and beans immediately opposite him—bear fruit for harvest. Created by a sixteenth-century European artist, the drawing misrepresents who did the agricultural work in many ancient American cultures— namely, women. The Morgan Library & Museum / Art Resource, NY.

READING THE IMAGE: In what ways has this ancient farmer modified the natural environment?
CONNECTIONS: What were the advantages and disadvantages of agriculture compared to hunting and gathering?

still exist at Mesa Verde, Colorado, and elsewhere. Other Anasazi communities—like the one known as **Pueblo Bonito**, whose impressive ruins can be visited at Chaco Canyon, New Mexico—erected huge stone-walled pueblos with enough rooms to house everyone in the settlement. **(See "Analyzing Historical Evidence: Artifacts of Daily Life in Chaco Canyon" on page 16.)** Anasazi pueblos and cliff dwellings typically included one or more kivas used for secret ceremonies, restricted to men, that sought to communicate with the supernatural world. The alignment of Chaco buildings with movements of the sun and moon shows that Anasazi studied the sky carefully, probably because they believed supernatural powers in the heavens governed their lives in every way. Pueblo Bonito stood at the center of thousands of smaller Chaco pueblos that supplied food and other goods to support Bonito's spiritual and political elites. Exactly how Pueblo Bonito elites exercised power over the network of smaller pueblos is not known, but it probably involved a combination of violence and spiritual ceremonies performed in the kivas. A disastrous drought plagued the region for about fifty years after AD 1130, triggering the disappearance of the Anasazi culture. The prolonged drought probably intensified conflict among the pueblos and made it impossible to depend on the tried-and-true techniques of irrigated agriculture that had been successful for centuries. By AD 1200, the large Anasazi pueblos had been abandoned. Some Anasazi migrated toward regions with more reliable rainfall and settled in Hopi, Zuñi, and Acoma pueblos that their descendants in Arizona and New Mexico have occupied ever since.

Pueblo Bonito
The largest residential and ceremonial site, containing more than six hundred rooms and thirty-five kivas, in the major Anasazi cultural center of Chaco Canyon in present-day New Mexico.

Woodland Burial Mounds and Chiefdoms

No other ancient Americans created dwellings similar to southwestern pueblos, but around 2500 BP, Woodland peoples throughout the Mississippi River watershed began to build **burial mounds**. The size of the mounds, the labor and organization required

burial mounds
Earthen mounds constructed by ancient American peoples, especially throughout the gigantic drainage of the Ohio and Mississippi rivers, after about 2500 BP.

| When and why did Archaic hunter-gatherers inhabit ancient America? | **How did agriculture influence ancient American cultures?** | What ancient American cultures inhabited North America in the 1490s? | How did the Mexican empire amass power and riches? | Conclusion: How did ancient Americans shape their world and ours? |

How Did Ancient Americans' Corn Spread throughout the World?

Corn on the cob slathered with butter, salted popcorn, corn chips—Americans produce and consume more corn than any other nation on earth. Today, each American eats an average of fifty-two quarts of popped corn a year. Popcorn grown in the United States is also munched in Mexico City, Tokyo, Seoul, Beijing, and London, and corn on the cob is sold at Moscow's famed Gorky Park. Yet popcorn and corn on the cob account for a tiny fraction of the gigantic mountain of thirty-four billion bushels of corn produced across the globe each year, one-third of it in the United States. All of that corn is descended from a plant domesticated and cultivated by ancient Americans beginning about ten thousand years ago.

The ancient ancestor of what we know today as corn is a grass called *teosinte*. Ancient people in central Mexico, probably women, selected desirable seeds from *teosinte* and over many generations managed to transform the small grass seeds into rows of corn kernels arrayed around a central cob. Slowly, during thousands of years, ancient agriculturalists developed many varieties of corn adapted to different growing conditions, with different nutritional qualities and varying productivity (the number of kernels grown from one corn seed). The remarkable adaptability of the corn plant and the high food value of the corn kernels caused the crop to spread among ancient Americans throughout the Western Hemisphere.

▶ This sixteenth-century watercolor of a Native American woman in Florida shows her extending a gift of hospitality with ears of corn in one hand and a basket of corn mush in the other. The watercolor captures the gift of corn ancient Americans bestowed on people throughout the world today. The Trustees of the British Museum/ Art Resource, NY.

chiefdom
Hierarchical social organization headed by a chief. Archaeologists believe Woodland chiefdoms commanded the labor required to construct burial mounds.

to erect them, and differences in the artifacts buried with certain individuals suggest the existence of a social and political hierarchy that archaeologists term a chiefdom. Experts do not know the name of a single chief, nor do they understand how chiefs exercised their power. But the only way archaeologists can account for the complex and labor-intensive burial mounds is to assume that a person—whom scholars term a *chief*—commanded the labor and obedience of very large numbers of other people, who made up the chief's chiefdom.

Between 2500 BP and 2100 BP, Adena people built hundreds of burial mounds radiating from central Ohio. In the mounds, the Adena usually included grave goods

Why do historians rely on the work of archaeologists?	When and how did humans migrate into North America?

Entirely unknown to Europeans when they arrived in the New World in 1492, corn acquired the name by which it is known in most of the world today: *maize*, which is derived from *mahiz* ("life-giver"), the word for corn Christopher Columbus learned from the Taino. It is no wonder ancient Americans worshipped maize gods, given how important corn was to their survival. Columbus and other Spaniards carried corn back to Europe in 1493, and within a generation, corn seeds had sprouted for the first time not only in Europe but also in the Middle East, Africa, India, and China.

At first, people outside the Americas did not find corn an appetizing food. An English botanist in the seventeenth century spoke for many others when he declared corn a food of the "barbarous Indians which know no better." He pronounced corn "a more convenient food for swine than for man." But Europeans in the New World, following Native American foodways, soon learned to eat corn ground into meal, often mixed with vegetables or meat, moistened, and served as a kind of mush they called samp or hominy or grits. Or they made a cornmeal dough that they baked in the coals of a fire or on an iron griddle to produce corn bread, which they also called hoecake, johnnycake, or corn pone—all of them adaptations of ancient American tortillas. Corn helped sustain Euro-Americans in the New World for centuries after 1492, just as it had ancient Americans for thousands of years before Europeans arrived.

Today corn is grown throughout the world and is a major commodity in global trade. The United States grows more than half of global corn exports, while Argentina, Brazil, and Ukraine account for another third. This exported corn goes to countries all around the world. Japan takes about a fifth of the global corn imports, and another third of corn imports goes to South Korea, Mexico, Egypt, and Taiwan.

Corn connects the United States to the rest of the world in many more ways than the export of millions of bushels of corn kernels. Only about a fifth of the U.S. corn crop is exported annually. The rest is used in dozens of products that Americans consume themselves as well as export to countries around the globe. The seventeenth-century English botanist was correct that corn is an excellent food for animals. Today, about half of the American corn crop is fed to livestock. Chances are that the beef, chicken, pork, and dairy products in American supermarkets came from animals that ate corn. And the United States exports billions of dollars' worth of corn-fed meat and dairy products to the rest of the world every year. Exports also include corn sugar used to sweeten hundreds of processed foods and corn byproducts used in products as varied as skateboards, toothpaste, tires, batteries, and lipstick. Even pulling into a gas station for a fill-up often means pumping gasoline mixed with ethanol made from corn—about a fourth of the American corn crop is used to make ethanol fuel, a product that reduces American dependence on foreign sources of oil.

Questions for Analysis

ASK HISTORICAL QUESTIONS: How did ancient Americans contribute to the evolution of corn? Why does the United States produce so much corn today?

CONSIDER THE CONTEXT: How did corn contribute to changes in ancient American cultures and societies? Why did corn spread so rapidly throughout the world?

ANALYZE THE EVIDENCE: In what ways is corn used today? How do these compare to how ancient Americans used corn?

such as spear points and stone pipes as well as thin sheets of mica (a glasslike mineral) crafted into animal or human shapes. Sometimes burial mounds were constructed all at once, but often they were built up slowly over many years.

About 2100 BP, Adena culture evolved into the more elaborate Hopewell culture, which lasted about five hundred years. Centered in Ohio, Hopewell culture extended throughout the enormous drainage of the Ohio and Mississippi rivers. Hopewell people built larger mounds than their Adena predecessors and filled them with magnificent grave goods that Hopewell groups reserved for their most important leaders. Most people were cremated, not buried. Hopewell burial rituals

| When and why did Archaic hunter-gatherers inhabit ancient America? | **How did agriculture influence ancient American cultures?** | What ancient American cultures inhabited North America in the 1490s? | How did the Mexican empire amass power and riches? | Conclusion: How did ancient Americans shape their world and ours? |

15

Artifacts of Daily Life in Chaco Canyon

Like archaeologists, historians study artifacts—physical objects—to investigate the past. Since ancient Americans did not use writing, their artifacts serve as documents of a sort. Pictured here are artifacts made and used more than a thousand years ago by residents of Pueblo Bonito in Chaco Canyon, located in the arid region at the intersection of present-day Utah, Colorado, Arizona, and New Mexico.

The largest of many buildings in Chaco Canyon, Pueblo Bonito originally stood four or five stories tall and included more than six hundred rooms, including thirty-five kivas, the circular structures visible around the perimeter of the large plazas. Chaco residents covered each kiva with a roof, creating a darkened underground space for ceremonial rituals. The ceremonies remain unknown, but less mysterious are the routines of daily life that sustained Chacoan people for centuries at Pueblo Bonito.

Among the thousands of artifacts excavated at Pueblo Bonito are these objects Chaco residents used routinely in their daily lives. Imagine a woman at Pueblo Bonito setting out on a spring day to plant corn, her family's most important food. She might strap on sandals, like the one shown on the facing page woven from fibers of the yucca plant. To dig a hole for planting corn seeds, the woman might use a digging stick like the one shown on the facing page, tipped by the horn of a mountain sheep and tightly bound with sinew to a cottonwood branch and covered with animal hide to protect the binding.

Once harvested and dried, corn needed to be ground in order to be cooked and eaten. Our imagined woman used the small flat stone (the *mano*) and the larger stone slab (the *metate*)

▲ **Pueblo Bonito, Chaco Canyon, New Mexico** Manfred Gottschalk/Alamy Stock Photo.

to grind the corn. Some rooms at Pueblo Bonito contained numerous grinding stones.

To cook the cornmeal, the woman mixed it with water, perhaps using a ceramic ladle—like the one shown on the facing page crafted by a Chaco pottery maker—to dip water from a storage pot. To kindle a fire, she might use the Chacoan fire starter kit shown here. After heating the cornmeal gruel in a ceramic pot, she might use the ladle again to transfer servings into small bowls for eating.

Examine these objects and think carefully about them. Each object required a great deal of learning and experience to create it and use it effectively. Consider in detail, step by step, what activities went into the making and use of each artifact.

brought many people together to honor the dead person and to help build the mound. Hopewell mounds often reached one hundred feet high and thirty feet in diameter. Grave goods at Hopewell sites testify to the high quality of Hopewell crafts and to a thriving trade network that ranged west to Wyoming and south and east to Florida.

Hopewell culture declined about AD 400 for reasons that are unknown. Archaeologists speculate that bows and arrows, along with increasing reliance on agriculture, made small settlements more self-sufficient and therefore less dependent on the central authority of the Hopewell chiefs who were responsible for the burial mounds.

Why do historians rely on the work of archaeologists?	When and how did humans migrate into North America?

▲ Sandal

▲ Digging Stick

► Ladle

► Mano and Metate

▼ Fire Starter Kit

Questions for Analysis

ANALYZE THE EVIDENCE: What kinds of material, knowledge, skill, and activity were required to make and use each of these artifacts?

CONSIDER THE CONTEXT: What do these artifacts suggest about food production and consumption in Chaco Canyon? What do these artifacts reveal about the society and culture of Chacoan people?

ASK HISTORICAL QUESTIONS: How did Chacoan culture, as revealed by these artifacts, compare to the lifestyles of ancient Americans in other regions at about the same time? How do these artifacts differ from artifacts of Paleo-Indians and Archaic hunters and gatherers described in the chapter? What changes might account for the differences?

Source: All images courtesy National Park Service, Chaco Culture National Historic Park.

Four hundred years later, another mound-building culture flourished. The Mississippian culture emerged in the floodplains of the major southeastern river systems about AD 800 and lasted until about AD 1500. Major Mississippian sites, such as the one at **Cahokia**, included huge mounds with platforms on top for ceremonies and for the residences of great chiefs. Most likely, the ceremonial mounds and ritual practices were influenced by Mexican cultural expressions brought north by traders and migrants. At Cahokia, skilled farmers supported the large population with ample crops of corn. In addition to mounds, Cahokians erected what archaeologists call woodhenges (after the famous Stonehenge in England)—long wooden poles set

Cahokia
The largest ceremonial site in ancient North America, located near the Mississippi River across from present-day St. Louis, where thousands of inhabitants built hundreds of earthen mounds between about AD 800 and AD 1500.

| When and why did Archaic hunter-gatherers inhabit ancient America? | **How did agriculture influence ancient American cultures?** | What ancient American cultures inhabited North America in the 1490s? | How did the Mexican empire amass power and riches? | Conclusion: How did ancient Americans shape their world and ours? |

◀ **Mexican Ball Court** The Mexica and other Mesoamerican peoples commonly built special courts (or playing fields) for their intensely competitive ball games. This rare model of a ball court, made in Mexico sometime between 2200 BP and AD 250, shows a game in progress, complete with players and spectators. Players wore padded belts and used their hips to hit the hard rubber ball through the goal. Spectators bet on the games, and losing players were often killed. A few ball courts have been excavated in North America, providing compelling evidence of one of the many connections between ancient Mesoamericans and North Americans. Yale University Art Gallery.

upright in the ground and carefully arranged in huge circles. Experts believe that Cahokians probably built woodhenges partly for ceremonies linked to celestial observations.

The large plazas at Cahokia were used for religious and political ceremonies as well as for playing the Cahokians' signature game of chunkey, which involved rolling a concave stone disk and trying to throw a spear that landed as close as possible to where the stone stopped. The game of chunkey spread throughout Mississippian cultures. Chunkey stones are commonly found in Mississippian graves, evidence of the importance Cahokians attached to chunkey, even in the hereafter.

Cahokia and other Mississippian cultures dwindled by AD 1500. When Europeans arrived, most of the descendants of Mississippian cultures, like those of the Hopewell culture, lived in small, dispersed agricultural villages supported by hunting and gathering. Clearly, the conditions that caused large chiefdoms to emerge—whatever they were—had changed, and chiefs no longer commanded the sweeping powers they had once enjoyed.

QUICK REVIEW

How and why did southwestern cultures differ from Woodland cultures?

What ancient American cultures inhabited North America in the 1490s?

On the eve of European colonization in the 1490s, Native Americans lived throughout North and South America, but their total population is uncertain. Some experts claim that Native Americans who inhabited what are now the United States and Canada numbered eighteen million to twenty million. Other experts place the population at no more than one million. A prudent estimate is about four million, or about the same as the number of people living on the small island nation of England at that time. The vastness of North America meant that the overall density of the ancient American population in North America was low, just 60 people per 100 square miles, compared to more than 8,000 in England. The survival strategies of hunting, gathering, and agriculture spread ancient Americans across the continent, but some regions supported more people than others (**Figure 1.1**).

| Why do historians rely on the work of archaeologists? | When and how did humans migrate into North America? |

Density

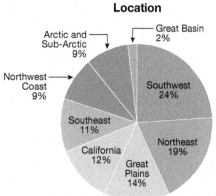

Location

FIGURE 1.1 ▲ Native American Population in North America about 1492 (Estimated)

Just before Europeans arrived, Native American population density varied widely, depending largely on the availability of natural resources. The Pacific coast, with its rich marine resources, had the highest concentration of people. Overall, the population density of North America was less than 1 percent that of England, which helps explain why Europeans viewed North America as a relatively empty wilderness.

Eastern Woodland and Great Plains Peoples

About one-third of native North Americans inhabited the enormous Woodland region east of the Mississippi River. Their population density was about average for North America as a whole. Eastern Woodland peoples clustered into three broad linguistic and cultural groups: Algonquian, Iroquoian, and Muskogean.

Algonquian tribes inhabited the Atlantic seaboard, the Great Lakes region, and much of the upper Midwest (**Map 1.3**). The relatively mild climate along the Atlantic permitted the coastal Algonquians to grow corn and other crops as well as to hunt and fish. Around the Great Lakes and in northern New England, however, cool summers and severe winters made agriculture impractical. Instead, the Abenaki, Penobscot, Chippewa, and other tribes concentrated on hunting and fishing, using canoes both for transportation and for gathering wild rice.

Inland from the Algonquian region, Iroquoian tribes occupied territories centered in Pennsylvania and upstate New York, as well as in the hilly upland regions of the Carolinas and Georgia. Iroquoian tribes differed from their neighbors in three important ways. First, their success in cultivating corn and other crops allowed them to build permanent settlements, usually consisting of several longhouses housing five to ten families. Second, Iroquoian women headed family clans and even selected the chiefs (normally men) who governed the tribes. Property of all sorts belonged to women. Third, for purposes of war and diplomacy, Iroquoian tribes—including the Seneca, Onondaga, Mohawk, Oneida, and Cayuga—allied in the League of Five Nations, which remained powerful well into the eighteenth century.

Muskogean peoples spread throughout the woodlands of the Southeast, south of the Ohio River and east of the Mississippi. Including the Creek, Choctaw, Chickasaw, and Natchez tribes, Muskogeans inhabited a bountiful natural environment that provided abundant food from hunting, gathering, and agriculture. Remnants of the earlier Mississippian culture still existed in Muskogean religion. The Natchez, for example,

| When and why did Archaic hunter-gatherers inhabit ancient America? | How did agriculture influence ancient American cultures? | **What ancient American cultures inhabited North America in the 1490s?** | How did the Mexican empire amass power and riches? | Conclusion: How did ancient Americans shape their world and ours? |

19

MAP 1.3 ▲ Native North Americans about 1500

Distinctive Native American peoples resided throughout the area that, centuries later, became the United States. This map shows the approximate location of some of the larger tribes about 1500. Lack of space on the map requires many other peoples who inhabited North America at the time to be omitted.

worshipped the sun and built temple mounds modeled after those of their Mississippian ancestors, including Cahokia.

Great Plains peoples accounted for about one out of seven native North Americans. Inhabiting the huge region between the Rocky Mountains and the Mississippi River, many tribes had migrated to the Great Plains within the century or two before the 1490s, forced westward by Iroquoian and Algonquian tribes. Some Great Plains tribes—especially the Mandan and Pawnee—farmed successfully, growing both corn and sunflowers. But the Teton Sioux, Blackfeet, Comanche, Cheyenne, and Crow on the northern plains, and the Apache and other nomadic tribes on the southern plains, depended on bison for subsistence.

Southwestern and Western Peoples

Southwestern cultures included about a quarter of all native North Americans. These descendants of the Mogollon, Hohokam, and Anasazi cultures lived in settled agricultural communities, many of them pueblos. They continued to grow corn, beans, and squash, using methods they had refined for centuries.

Why do historians rely on the work of archaeologists?

When and how did humans migrate into North America?

However, their communities came under attack by a large number of warlike Athapascans who invaded the Southwest beginning around AD 1300. The Athapascans—principally Apache and Navajo—were skillful warriors who preyed on the sedentary Pueblo Indians, reaping the fruits of agriculture without the work of farming.

About a fifth of all native North Americans resided along the Pacific coast. In California, abundant acorns and nutritious marine life continued to support high population densities, but this abundance retarded the development of agriculture. Similar dependence on hunting and gathering persisted along the Northwest coast, where fishing reigned supreme. Salmon were so plentiful at The Dalles, a prime fishing site on the Columbia River on the border of present-day Oregon and Washington, that Northwest peoples caught enough to trade dried fish as far away as California and the Great Plains. It is likely that The Dalles was the largest Native American trading center in ancient North America, although other ancient trading centers, such as Pueblo Bonito and Cahokia, also existed.

Cultural Similarities

While trading was common, all native North Americans in the 1490s still depended on hunting and gathering for a major portion of their food. Most of them also practiced agriculture. Some used agriculture to supplement hunting and gathering; for others,

▲ **Ancient American Weaving** This workbasket of a master weaver illustrates the technology of ancient American textile production. Found in a woman's grave in the Andes dating from one thousand years ago, the workbasket contains tools and thread for every stage of textile production. Weaving—like cooking, hunting, and worship—depended on human knowledge that survived only when passed from an experienced person to a novice. Museum of Fine Arts, Boston, Massachusetts, USA/Gift of Charles H. White/Bridgeman Images.

READING THE IMAGE: What human activities produced the tools in the workbasket?
CONNECTIONS: How did young people learn such survival skills as hunting, food gathering, cooking, weaving, and cooperation from their elders?

When and why did Archaic hunter-gatherers inhabit ancient America?	How did agriculture influence ancient American cultures?	**What ancient American cultures inhabited North America in the 1490s?**	How did the Mexican empire amass power and riches?	Conclusion: How did ancient Americans shape their world and ours?

the balance was reversed. People throughout North America used bows, arrows, and other weapons for hunting and warfare. To express themselves, they drew on stones, wood, and animal skins; wove baskets and textiles; crafted pottery, beads, and carvings; and created songs, dances, and rituals.

North American life did not include features common in Europe during the 1490s. Native North Americans did not use writing, wheels, or sailing ships. They had no large domesticated animals such as horses or cows. Their only metal was copper. However, the absence of these European conveniences mattered less than Native Americans' adaptations to local natural environments and to the social environment among neighboring peoples, adaptations that all native North Americans held in common.

It would be a mistake, however, to conclude that native North Americans lived in blissful harmony. Archaeological sites provide ample evidence of violent conflict. Warfare was common, making violence and fear typical features of ancient American life. Warfare not only killed people and destroyed their settlements, but victors usually took captives, especially women and children, and often treated them as slaves. Skeletons, like those at Cahokia, not only bear marks of wounds but also exhibit clear signs of ritualistic human sacrifice. Religious, ethnic, economic, and familial conflicts must have occurred, but they remain in obscurity, because they left few archaeological traces. In general, anxiety and instability must have been at least as common among ancient North Americans as feelings of peace and security.

Native North Americans not only adapted to the natural environment but also changed it in many ways. They built thousands of structures, from small dwellings to massive pueblos and enormous mounds, permanently altering the landscape. Their food-gathering techniques selected productive and nutritious varieties of plants, thereby shifting the balance of local plants toward useful varieties. The first stages of North American agriculture, for example, probably involved ancient Americans gathering wild seeds and then sowing them in a meadow for later harvest. To clear land for planting seeds, native North Americans set fires that burned off thousands of acres of forest.

Ancient North Americans also used fires for hunting. Hunters often started fires to frighten and force together deer, bison, and other animals, making them easier to kill. Indians also started fires along the edges of woods to burn off shrubby undergrowth. The fires allowed tender young plants to sprout and attract deer and other game, who then came within convenient range of hunters' weapons. The burns also encouraged the growth of sun-loving food plants that Indians relished, such as blackberries, strawberries, and raspberries.

Because the fires set by native North Americans usually burned until they ran out of fuel or were extinguished by rain or wind, enormous regions of North America were burned. In the long run, fires created and maintained a diverse and productive natural environment. Fires, like other activities of native North Americans, shaped the landscape of North America long before Europeans arrived in 1492.

ANALYZE EVIDENCE

What evidence shows that native North Americans engaged in conflict and warfare?

CONSIDER CAUSE AND EFFECT

In what ways did ancient Americans shape the landscape and environment of North America before 1492?

QUICK REVIEW

What traits did native North American cultures share?

Why do historians rely on the work of archaeologists?

When and how did humans migrate into North America?

How did the Mexican empire amass power and riches?

The vast majority of ancient Americans who lived in the Western Hemisphere in the 1490s inhabited Mesoamerica and South America, where the population approximately equaled that of Europe. Like their counterparts north of the Rio Grande, these people lived in a natural environment of tremendous diversity. Among all these cultures, the Mexica stood out. Their empire stretched from coast to coast across central Mexico, encompassing approximately six million people. Their significance in the history of the New World after 1492 dictates a brief survey of their culture and society.

The Mexica began their rise to prominence about 1325, when small bands settled on a marshy island in Lake Texcoco, the site of the future city of Tenochtitlán, the capital of the Mexican empire. Resourceful, courageous, and cold-blooded warriors, the Mexica often hired out as mercenaries for richer, more settled tribes.

By 1430, the Mexica succeeded in asserting their dominance and leading their own military campaigns in an ever-widening arc of empire building. Despite pockets of resistance, by the 1490s the Mexica ruled an empire that contained about as many people as lived in Spain. The empire exemplified the central values of Mexican society. The Mexica worshipped the war god Huitzilopochtli. Warriors held the most exalted positions in the social hierarchy, even above the priests who performed the sacred ceremonies that won Huitzilopochtli's favor. In almost constant battles to defend and extend the empire, young Mexican men exhibited the courage and daring that would allow them to rise in the carefully graduated ranks of warriors. The Mexica believed capturing prisoners was the ultimate act of bravery. Warriors usually turned over the captives to Mexican priests, who sacrificed many of them to Huitzilopochtli by cutting out their hearts. The Mexica believed that human sacrifice fed the sun's craving for blood, which kept the sun aflame and prevented the coming of everlasting darkness and chaos.

CHRONOLOGY

ca. AD 1325
– Small bands of Mexica settle on a marshy island in Lake Texcoco.

ca. AD 1490
– Mexican empire stretches from coast to coast in central Mexico and encompasses six million people.

AD 1492
– Christopher Columbus arrives in New World, beginning European colonization.

Mexica
The Mexica commanded an empire that stretched from coast to coast across central Mexico and encompassed as many as six million people.

◀ **Mexican Human Sacrifice** This late-sixteenth-century painting depicts human sacrifice at the temple of Tenochtitlán, a common Mexican ritual before Spanish conquest. Mexicans believed that cutting the heart from a sacrifice victim fed the sun with human blood and assured that the sun would continue to warm and nourish the world. Spaniards considered these rituals barbaric and banned them. DEA/G. Dagli Orti/De Agostini/Getty Images.

| When and why did Archaic hunter-gatherers inhabit ancient America? | How did agriculture influence ancient American cultures? | What ancient American cultures inhabited North America in the 1490s? | **How did the Mexican empire amass power and riches?** | Conclusion: How did ancient Americans shape their world and ours? |

The empire contributed far more to Mexican society than victims for sacrifice. At the most basic level, the empire functioned as a military and political system that collected **tribute** from subject peoples. The Mexica forced conquered tribes to pay tribute in goods, not money. Tribute redistributed to the Mexica was as much as one-third of the goods produced by conquered tribes. It included everything from candidates for human sacrifice to textiles and basic food products, as well as exotic luxury items such as gold, turquoise, and rare bird feathers.

Tribute reflected the fundamental relations of power and wealth that pervaded the Mexican empire. The relatively small nobility of Mexican warriors, supported by a still smaller group of priests, possessed the military and religious power to command the obedience of hundreds of thousands of non-noble Mexicans and of millions of non-Mexicans in subjugated colonies. Mexican elites exercised their power to obtain tribute and thereby to redistribute wealth from the conquered to the conquerors, from the commoners to the nobility, from the poor to the rich. This redistribution of wealth made possible the achievements of Mexican society that amazed the Spaniards after AD 1492: the huge cities, teeming markets, productive gardens, and storehouses stuffed with gold and other treasures.

On the whole, the Mexica did not interfere much with the internal government of conquered regions. Instead, they usually permitted the traditional ruling elites to stay in power—so long as they paid tribute. Subjugated communities felt exploited by the constant payment of tribute to the Mexica. The high level of discontent among subject peoples was the soft, vulnerable underbelly of the Mexican empire, a fact that Spanish intruders exploited after 1492 to conquer the Mexica.

UNDERSTAND POINTS OF VIEW

How did people conquered by Mexicans view the Mexican empire?

QUICK REVIEW

How did the Mexican empire display the central values of Mexican society?

Conclusion: How did ancient Americans shape their world and ours?

Ancient Americans shaped the history of human beings in the New World for more than thirteen thousand years. They established continuous human habitation in the Western Hemisphere from the time the first big-game hunters crossed Beringia until 1492 and beyond. Much of their history remains lost because they relied on oral rather than written communication. But much can be pieced together from artifacts they left behind at camps, kill sites, and ceremonial and residential centers such as Cahokia and Pueblo Bonito. Ancient Americans achieved their success through resourceful adaptation to the hemisphere's many and changing natural environments. They also adapted to social and cultural changes caused by human beings—such as marriages and deaths as well as political struggles and warfare among chiefdoms. Their creativity and artistry are unmistakably documented in their

Why do historians rely on the work of archaeologists?

When and how did humans migrate into North America?

numerous artifacts. Those material objects sketch the only likenesses of ancient Americans we will ever have—blurred, shadowy images that are unmistakably human but forever silent.

When European intruders began arriving in the Western Hemisphere after 1492, their ideas about the promise of the New World were strongly influenced by the diverse peoples they encountered. Europeans coveted Native Americans' wealth, labor, and land. Christian missionaries sought to save Native Americans' souls. For their part, Native Americans marveled at European technological novelties such as sailing ships, steel weapons, gunpowder, and horses, while often reserving judgment about or rejecting Europeans' Christian religion.

In the centuries following 1492, as the trickle of European strangers became a flood of newcomers from both Europe and Africa, Native Americans and colonial settlers continued to encounter one another. Peaceful negotiations as well as violent conflicts over both land and trading rights resulted in chronic fear and mistrust. While the era of European colonization marked the beginning of the end of ancient America, the ideas, subsistence strategies, and cultural beliefs of native North Americans remained powerful among their descendants for generations, and they persist today.

When and why did Archaic hunter-gatherers inhabit ancient America?

How did agriculture influence ancient American cultures?

What ancient American cultures inhabited North America in the 1490s?

How did the Mexican empire amass power and riches?

Conclusion: How did ancient Americans shape their world and ours?

STEP 1

EXPLAIN WHY IT MATTERS

Put your reading into practice. Identify each term below, and then explain why it matters in U.S. history.

TERM	WHO OR WHAT & WHEN	WHY IT MATTERS
Beringia (p. 5)		
Paleo-Indians (p. 6)		
Clovis point (p. 6)		
hunter-gatherer (p. 8)		
Archaic Indians (p. 8)		
pueblos (p. 12)		
Pueblo Bonito (p. 13)		
burial mounds (p. 13)		
chiefdom (p. 14)		
Cahokia (p. 17)		
Mexica (p. 23)		
tribute (p. 24)		

STEP 2

MOVE BEYOND THE BASICS

To demonstrate a more advanced understanding, describe the cultural differences of Native American peoples in 1492.

Native Americans in 1492	Geography and Climate	Economy and Lifestyle (sources of food and material goods, economic organization, trade)	Social/Political Organization (religion, family structures, social hierarchy)
Southwestern Cultures			
Eastern Woodland Cultures			
Pacific Coast Cultures			
Great Basin Cultures			
Great Plains Cultures			

STEP 3 **PUT IT ALL TOGETHER** Now, try to explain the big picture. Remember to use specific examples from the chapter in your answers.

THE FIRST AMERICANS

- When and how did humans first arrive in the Americas?

- How did Paleo-Indians adapt to the extinction of large mammals around 11,000 BP?

AGRICULTURE AND ADAPTATION

- How did Archaic Americans differ from their Paleo-Indian ancestors?

- How did the advent of agriculture change the cultures of ancient Americans?

NATIVE AMERICAN CULTURES IN 1490

- What accounts for the different regional Native American populations about 1490?

- How did the Mexica differ from the ancient Americans in North America?

LOOKING BACKWARD, LOOKING AHEAD

- What accounts for the diversity of Indian peoples on the eve of European contact?

STEP 4 **CONNECT THESE EVENTS** How did the environmental changes experienced by the Paleo-Indians give way to new forms of agriculture for Archaic Indians?

STEP 5 **CONNECT TO THE PRESENT** How do ancient American cultures persist in the United States and the world today?

2

EUROPEANS ENCOUNTER THE NEW WORLD

1492–1600

How did the first century of contact between Europeans and the New World change both?

This chapter explains how, when, and why Europeans came to the New World, where Spaniards eventually established a colonial empire. Europeans' encounters with Native Americans during the sixteenth century changed both the New and Old Worlds.

This chapter will explore the following questions:

- Why did Europeans launch explorations in the fifteenth century?

- What did Spaniards discover in the western Atlantic?

- How did Spaniards conquer and colonize New Spain?

- How did New Spain influence Europe?

- Conclusion: What did the New World promise Europeans?

AN AMERICAN STORY

Two babies were born in southern Europe in 1451, one in a castle and the other in a cottage. The baby girl, Isabella, was born the daughter of the king of Castile, who ruled the large central region of present-day Spain. The baby boy, Christopher, was the son of a weaver near Genoa in what is now Italy. Forty-one years later, the lives and aspirations of these two people intersected in southern Spain and permanently changed the history of the world.

Isabella received an excellent education and became a strong, resolute woman. In 1469, she married Ferdinand, the king of Aragon, a region of northeastern Spain. Five years later, Isabella ascended to the throne of Castile. Queen Isabella and King Ferdinand battled to unite the monarchies of Spain, to complete the long campaign known as the Reconquest to eliminate Muslim strongholds on the Iberian Peninsula, and to purify Christianity. They sought to rally support for their efforts to defend Christianity, persecute Jews, and defeat Muslims by traveling throughout their realms with a large entourage, including a choir, impressing everybody with their regal splendor.

Tagging along in the royal cavalcade of advisers, servants, and hangers-on who moved around Spain with the monarchs was Christopher Columbus, an experienced sailor and deeply religious man. Columbus was obsessed with a scheme to sail west across the Atlantic Ocean to reach the riches of China and Japan. In 1486, Columbus finally won a chance to pitch his plan to Isabella and Ferdinand. They rejected his proposal. The earth was too big, the ocean between Europe and China was too wide, and no sailors or ships could possibly withstand such a long voyage. Columbus did not give up. Year after year, he tried to get Isabella to support his risky scheme. Finally in mid-April 1492, she agreed to sponsor and partially fund his plan, which she hoped would expand the wealth and influence of her monarchy.

Columbus hurriedly organized his expedition. Just before sunrise on August 3, 1492, the three ships under his command caught the tide out of a harbor in southern Spain and sailed west. Barely two months later, in the predawn moonlight of October 12, 1492, Columbus glimpsed an island on the western horizon. At daybreak, he rowed ashore and claimed possession of the land for Isabella and Ferdinand, while curious islanders crowded around.

Columbus's encounters with Isabella and those islanders in 1492 transformed the history of the world. They unexpectedly made Spain the most important European power in the Western Hemisphere for more than a century. Long before 1492, other Europeans had expanded the limits of the world known to them. Their efforts helped make Columbus's voyage possible. But without Isabella's sponsorship, Columbus almost certainly would never have made his voyage. With her support and his own perseverance, Columbus blazed a watery trail to a world that neither he nor anyone else in Europe knew existed. Isabella, Ferdinand, and subsequent Spanish monarchs sought to reap the rewards of what they considered their empire across the Atlantic. The many Spaniards who came after Columbus created a distinctively Spanish colonial society in the New World during the sixteenth century. They conquered, enslaved, and killed Native Americans, built new institutions, and extracted great wealth that enriched the Spanish monarchy and made Spain the envy of other Europeans.

▼ **Spanish Tapestry** This detail from a lavish sixteenth-century tapestry depicts Columbus (kneeling) receiving a box of jewels from Queen Isabella (whose husband, King Ferdinand, stands slightly behind her) in appreciation for his voyages to the New World. Julio Donoso/Sygma via Getty Images.

Why did Europeans launch explorations in the fifteenth century?

CHRONOLOGY

Mid-Fourteenth Century
- Black Death kills approximately one-third of Europe's population.

1415–1460
- The Portuguese, led by Prince Henry the Navigator, use new navigational tools and techniques to aid maritime exploration.

1480
- Portuguese ships reach Congo.

1488
- Bartolomeu Dias rounds Cape of Good Hope.

1498
- Vasco da Gama sails to India.

Black Death
A disease in the mid-fourteenth century that killed about a third of the European population.

Historically, the East—not the West—attracted Europeans. Europeans first ventured across the North Atlantic about AD 1000, when Norsemen built a small fishing village at L'Anse aux Meadows on the tip of Newfoundland that lasted for about ten years. When the world's climate cooled, ice choked the North Atlantic and the Norse left. Other Europeans remained completely unaware of a landmass in the western Atlantic. Instead of looking to the West, wealthy Europeans wanted luxury goods from Asia and Africa. European merchants competed to satisfy those desires by trading with the East. This long-distance trade gave Europeans new information about the world they inhabited. A few people—sailors, merchants, and aristocrats—took the risks of exploring beyond the limits of the world known to Europeans. Those risks could be deadly. But sometimes they paid off with new information, new experiences, and new opportunities. Eventually, risk-takers discovered a world entirely new to Europeans.

Mediterranean Trade and European Expansion

From the twelfth through the fifteenth centuries, Mediterranean trade routes funneled spices, silk, carpets, ivory, and gold into continental Europe from Persia, Asia Minor, India, and Africa (**Map 2.1**). The Italian cities of Venice, Genoa, and Pisa dominated this lucrative trade. Italian merchants and bankers became rich and fiercely defended their near monopoly of the trade in Eastern luxuries. The satisfying profits of the Mediterranean trade offered merchants few incentives to look for alternatives. They had no desire to seek new routes to the East or to discover new lands.

Changes in European societies encouraged some people to undertake unusual risks. In the mid-fourteenth century, an epidemic of bubonic plague (the **Black Death**, as it was called) killed at least a third of the European population. This catastrophe had major long-term consequences. It drastically reduced the population, making Europe's limited food supply more plentiful for survivors. Many survivors also inherited property from plague victims, giving them new chances for a better life.

Understandably, most Europeans saw the world as a place of alarming risks. The delicate balance of health, harvests, and peace could quickly be tipped toward disaster by epidemics, famine, and violence. Most people protected themselves from the constant threat of calamity by living amid kinfolk and friends, by maintaining good relations with the rich and powerful, and by worshipping the supernatural. But the insecurities and uncertainties of fifteenth-century European life also encouraged a few to take greater risks, such as embarking on dangerous sea voyages through uncharted waters to points unknown.

In European societies, exploration voyages promised fame and fortune to those who succeeded, whether they were kings or commoners. Monarchs such as Isabella sponsored exploration to enlarge their realms and enrich their dynasties. More territory meant more subjects who could pay more taxes, provide more soldiers, and participate in more commerce, magnifying the monarch's power and prestige. Voyages of exploration also could stabilize the monarch's rule by diverting ambitious and disruptive noblemen toward distant lands. Some explorers, like Columbus, were commoners who hoped for elevation to the aristocracy as a reward for their daring exploits.

Scientific and technological advances also helped set the stage for exploration. The invention of movable type by Johannes Gutenberg around 1450 in Germany made printing

MAP 2.1 ▲ European Trade Routes and Portuguese Exploration in the Fifteenth Century

The trade of Italian cities with Asia was slowly undermined during the fifteenth century by Portuguese explorers who hopscotched along the coast of Africa and eventually found a sea route that opened the rich trade of the East to Portuguese merchants.

easier and cheaper. Print enormously expanded the diffusion of all kinds of information among literate Europeans such as Isabella and Columbus. By 1400, crucial navigational aids employed by maritime explorers like Columbus were already available: compasses; hourglasses; and the astrolabe and quadrant, which helped determine latitude (the distance north or south of the equator). Many people throughout fifteenth-century Europe knew about such technological advances. But the Portuguese were the first to use them in a campaign to sail beyond the limits of the world known to Europeans.

A Century of Portuguese Exploration

With only 2 percent of the population of Christian Europe, Portugal devoted far more energy and wealth to the geographic exploration of the world between 1415 and 1460 than all other European countries combined. As a Christian kingdom, Portugal cooperated with Isabella and Ferdinand in the Reconquest, the centuries-long drive to expel the Muslims from the Iberian Peninsula. The religious zeal that propelled the Reconquest also justified expansion into what the Portuguese considered heathen lands. A key victory came in 1415, when Portuguese forces conquered Ceuta, the Muslim bastion at the mouth of the Strait of Gibraltar, which gave Portugal access to the Atlantic coast of Africa.

Reconquest
The centuries-long drive by the Christian kingdoms of Spain and Portugal to expel Muslims from the Iberian Peninsula.

| What did Spaniards discover in the western Atlantic? | How did Spaniards conquer and colonize New Spain? | How did New Spain influence Europe? | Conclusion: What did the New World promise Europeans? |

◀ **Ivory Saltcellar** This exquisitely carved sixteenth-century ivory saltcellar for Portuguese tables combines African materials, craftsmanship, and imagery. Designed to hold table salt in the central globe, the saltcellar dramatized African trade and quietly suggested the beneficial influence of Portuguese in Africa. akg-images.

Prince Henry the Navigator, son of the Portuguese king, was the most influential advocate of Portuguese exploration. From 1415 until his death in 1460, Henry collected the latest information about sailing techniques and geography, supported new crusades against the Muslims, sought fresh sources of trade to fatten Portuguese pocketbooks, and pushed explorers to go even farther. Expeditions to Africa promised to capture wheat fields from their Moroccan owners and to obtain gold, which had become scarce because of expanding commerce within Europe and because of the Mediterranean trade's exchange of European gold for Eastern luxuries.

Neither the Portuguese nor anybody else in Europe knew the immensity of Africa, whose Atlantic coastline stretched for more than seven thousand miles. At first, Portuguese explorers cautiously hugged the Atlantic coast of Africa, seldom venturing beyond sight of land. By 1434, they reached the northern edge of the Sahara Desert, where they learned to ride strong westerly currents that carried them far out to sea until they caught favorable easterly winds that turned them back toward land and allowed them to reach Cape Verde by 1444.

The Portuguese developed the caravel to stow the supplies necessary for long sea voyages and to withstand the battering of waves in the open ocean. Fast, sturdy caravels became explorers' preferred ships. In caravels, Portuguese mariners sailed into and around the Gulf of Guinea and as far south as the Congo by 1480.

Fierce African resistance confined the Portuguese to coastal trading posts, where they bartered successfully for gold, slaves, and ivory. Powerful African kingdoms welcomed Portuguese trading ships loaded with iron goods, weapons, textiles, and ornamental shells. Portuguese merchants learned that building relatively peaceful trading posts on the coast offered them more profit and safety than attempting to conquer and colonize inland regions. In the 1460s, the Portuguese used African slaves to develop sugar plantations on the Cape Verde Islands, starting a system that would be transplanted to the New World in the centuries to come.

About 1480, Portuguese explorers, eager to bypass Mediterranean traders, began a conscious search for a sea route to Asia. In 1488, Bartolomeu Dias sailed around the Cape of Good Hope at the southern tip of Africa and hurried back to Lisbon with the exciting news that it appeared to be possible to sail on to India and China. In 1498, after ten years of careful preparation, Vasco da Gama commanded the first Portuguese fleet to sail to India. Portugal quickly capitalized on the commercial potential of da Gama's new sea route around Africa to the East. By the early sixteenth century, the Portuguese controlled a far-flung commercial empire in India, Indonesia, and China (collectively referred to as the East Indies). The new sea route to the East eliminated the lengthy overland travel of the Mediterranean trade and allowed Portuguese merchants to charge much lower prices for the Eastern goods they imported.

Portugal's African explorations during the fifteenth century broke the monopoly of the old Mediterranean trade with the East, dramatically expanded the world known to Europeans, established a network of Portuguese outposts in Africa and Asia, and developed methods of sailing the high seas that Columbus used on his historic voyage west.

CONSIDER CAUSE AND EFFECT

Why did Portugal sponsor a campaign of geographic exploration?

UNDERSTAND POINTS OF VIEW

Why did the Portuguese seek to undermine the Mediterranean trade with the East?

QUICK REVIEW

Why did European exploration increase during the fifteenth century?

Why did Europeans launch explorations in the fifteenth century?

CAPITAESQVEVIERÃOANODE
S33·

◀ **Portuguese Merchant Fleet** This 1533 drawing of the Portuguese merchant fleet on the way to trade in the East Indies illustrates the kinds of ships able to withstand the long ocean voyage as well as the large scale of Portugal's investment in the trade. The drawing suggests the pride in the trade felt by the Portuguese monarchy as well as by the merchants and sailors aboard the vessels, each of which is carefully named. akg-images.

What did Spaniards discover in the western Atlantic?

The Portuguese and other experts believed that sailing west across the Atlantic to Asia was literally impossible. The European discovery of America required someone bold enough to believe that the experts were wrong. That person was Christopher Columbus. His explorations inaugurated a geographic revolution that forever changed Europeans' understanding of the world and its peoples, including themselves. Columbus's landfall in the Caribbean initiated a thriving exchange between the people, ideas, cultures, and institutions of the Old and New Worlds that continues to this day.

The Explorations of Columbus

Columbus went to sea when he was about fourteen and eventually made his way to Lisbon, where he married Felipa Moniz, whose father had been raised in the household of Prince Henry the Navigator. Through Felipa, Columbus gained access to Portuguese explorers' maps and other information about sailing the tricky Atlantic winds and currents. Like other educated Europeans, Columbus believed that the earth was a sphere. Theoretically it was possible to reach the East Indies by sailing west. With flawed calculations, Columbus estimated that Asia was only about 2,500 miles away, a shorter distance than Portuguese ships routinely sailed between Lisbon and the Congo. In fact, the shortest distance to Japan from Europe's jumping-off point was nearly 11,000 miles. Convinced by his faulty calculations, Columbus became determined to prove the experts were wrong and he was right.

In 1492, after years of unsuccessful lobbying in Portugal, Spain, England, and France, Columbus finally won financing for his journey from the Spanish monarchs, Isabella and Ferdinand. They saw the venture as an inexpensive gamble: Their

CHRONOLOGY

1492
– Christopher Columbus lands in Caribbean and encounters Tainos.
– Columbian exchange begins.

1493
– Columbus makes second voyage to New World.

1494
– Portugal and Spain sign Treaty of Tordesillas.

1497
– John Cabot searches for Northwest Passage.

1513
– Vasco Núñez de Balboa crosses Isthmus of Panama.

1519
– Ferdinand Magellan sets out to sail around world.

| What did Spaniards discover in the western Atlantic? | How did Spaniards conquer and colonize New Spain? | How did New Spain influence Europe? | Conclusion: What did the New World promise Europeans? |

Columbus's First Voyage to the New World, 1492–1493

Tainos
Indians who inhabited San Salvador and were the first people Columbus encountered in the New World.

PLACE EVENTS IN CONTEXT

How did European ideas shape Columbus's perceptions of the Tainos he encountered in 1492?

Treaty of Tordesillas
The 1494 treaty drew an imaginary line west of the Canary Islands; land discovered west of the line belonged to Spain, and land to the east belonged to Portugal.

potential loss was small, but their potential gain was huge. They gave Columbus a letter of introduction to China's Grand Khan, the ruler they hoped he would meet on the other side of the Atlantic.

After frantic preparation, Columbus and his small fleet—the *Niña* and *Pinta*, both caravels, and the *Santa María*, a larger merchant vessel—headed west. Six weeks after leaving the Canary Islands, Columbus landed on a tiny Caribbean island about three hundred miles north of the eastern tip of Cuba.

Columbus claimed possession of the island for Spain and named it San Salvador, in honor of the Savior, Jesus Christ. He called the islanders "Indians," since he assumed that they inhabited the East Indies somewhere near Japan or China. The islanders called themselves Tainos, which in their language meant "good" or "noble." As agricultural people, Tainos grew cassava, corn, cotton, tobacco, and other crops. Instead of dressing in the finery Columbus had expected to find in the East Indies, Tainos "all . . . go around as naked as their mothers bore them," Columbus wrote. Although Columbus concluded that Tainos "had no religion," in reality they worshipped gods they called *zemis*, ancestral spirits who inhabited natural objects such as trees and stones. Tainos had no riches. "It seemed to me that they were a people very poor in everything," Columbus wrote.

What Tainos thought about Columbus and his sailors we can only surmise since they left no written documents. At first, Columbus got the impression that Tainos believed Spaniards came from heaven. But after six weeks of encounters, Columbus decided that "the people of these lands do not understand me nor do I, nor anyone else that I have with me, [understand] them." The confused communication between Spaniards and Tainos suggests how strange each group seemed to the other. Columbus's perceptions of Tainos were shaped by European attitudes, ideas, and expectations, just as Tainos' perceptions of the Europeans were no doubt colored by their own culture.

Columbus and his men understood perfectly that they had made a momentous discovery. In 1493, when Queen Isabella and King Ferdinand learned Columbus's news, they were overjoyed. With a voyage that had lasted barely eight months, Columbus catapulted Spain into a serious challenger to Portugal, whose explorers had not yet sailed to India or China. The Spanish monarchs elevated Columbus to the nobility with the title "Admiral of the Ocean Sea." The seven Tainos he brought to Spain were baptized as Christians. King Ferdinand served as their godfather.

The Spanish monarchs rushed to obtain the pope's support for their claim to the new lands in the West. When the pope, a Spaniard, agreed, the Portuguese feared that their own claims to recently discovered territories were in jeopardy. To protect their claims, the Portuguese and Spanish monarchs negotiated the Treaty of Tordesillas in 1494. The treaty drew an imaginary line eleven hundred miles west of the Canary Islands (**Map 2.2**). Land discovered west of the line (namely, the islands that Columbus discovered and any additional land that might be found) belonged to Spain. Portugal claimed land to the east (namely, its African and East Indian trading empire). The people who inhabited the lands on both sides of the line were not consulted about the treaty.

Isabella and Ferdinand moved quickly to realize the promise of their new claims. In the fall of 1493, they sent Columbus west once again, this time with a fleet of seventeen ships and more than a thousand men who planned to locate the Asian mainland, find gold, and get rich. Before Columbus died in 1506, he returned to the New World two more times (in 1498 and 1502) without giving up his belief that the East Indies were there, somewhere. Other explorers continued to search for a passage to the East or some other source of profit. Before long, however, prospects of beating the Portuguese to Asia began to dim along with the hope of finding piles of gold.

Still, Columbus's discoveries forced sixteenth-century Europeans to think about the world in new ways. He proved it was possible to sail from Europe to the western rim of the Atlantic and return to Europe. Most important, Columbus's voyages demonstrated that lands and peoples entirely unknown to Europeans existed across the Atlantic.

Why did Europeans launch explorations in the fifteenth century?

MAP 2.2 ▲ European Exploration in Sixteenth-Century America

This map illustrates the approximate routes of early European explorations of the New World.

The Geographic Revolution and the Columbian Exchange

Within thirty years of Columbus's initial discovery, Europeans' understanding of world geography underwent a revolution. An elite of perhaps twenty thousand people with

What did Spaniards discover in the western Atlantic?	How did Spaniards conquer and colonize New Spain?	How did New Spain influence Europe?	Conclusion: What did the New World promise Europeans?

▲ **Inca Goddess** This sixteenth-century Inca effigy depicts a goddess of agriculture clothed in ears of corn and varieties of squash. Over millennia, these foods became staples of the diets of ancient peoples throughout the hemisphere, and then, after the arrival of Europeans, throughout the globe. Such ancient American plants were important components of the Columbian exchange between the New and Old Worlds. Private Collection/Bridgeman Images.

Columbian exchange
The transatlantic exchange of goods, people, and ideas that began when Columbus arrived in the Caribbean, ending the age-old separation of the hemispheres by the Atlantic Ocean.

CONSIDER CAUSE AND EFFECT

How did the Columbian exchange affect Native Americans and Europeans?

access to Europe's royal courts and trading centers learned the exciting news about global geography. It took another generation of additional exploration before they could comprehend the larger contours of Columbus's discoveries.

European monarchs hurried to stake their claims to the newly discovered lands. In 1497, King Henry VII of England sent John Cabot to look for a Northwest Passage to the East Indies across the North Atlantic (see Map 2.2). Cabot reached the tip of Newfoundland, which he believed was part of Asia, and hurried back to England, where he assembled a small fleet and sailed west in 1498. But he was never heard from again.

Three thousand miles to the south, a Spanish expedition landed on the northern coast of South America in 1499 accompanied by Amerigo Vespucci, an Italian businessman. In 1500, Pedro Álvars Cabral commanded a Portuguese fleet that looped westward into the Atlantic bound for the Indian Ocean, but accidentally made landfall on the east coast of Brazil.

By 1500, European experts knew that several large chunks of land cluttered the western Atlantic. A few cartographers speculated that these chunks linked to one another in a landmass that was not Asia. In 1507, Martin Waldseemüller, a German cartographer, published the first map that showed the New World separate from Asia. He named the land America, in honor of Amerigo Vespucci.

Two additional discoveries confirmed Waldseemüller's speculation. In 1513, Vasco Núñez de Balboa crossed the Isthmus of Panama and reached the Pacific Ocean. Clearly, more water lay between the New World and Asia. Ferdinand Magellan discovered just how much water when he led an expedition to sail around the globe in 1519. Sponsored by Spain, Magellan's voyage took him first to the New World, around the southern tip of South America, and into the Pacific. Crossing the Pacific took almost four months, decimating his crew with hunger and thirst. Philippine tribesmen killed Magellan. A remnant of his expedition continued on to the Indian Ocean and managed to transport a cargo of spices back to Spain in 1522.

In most ways, Magellan's voyage was a disaster. One ship and eighteen men crawled back from an expedition that began with five ships and more than 250 men. But the geographic information Magellan provided left no doubt that America was a continent separated from Asia by the enormous Pacific Ocean. Magellan's voyage made clear that it was possible to sail west to reach the East Indies, but that was a terrible way to go. After Magellan, most Europeans who sailed west set their sights on the New World, not on Asia.

Columbus's arrival in the Caribbean anchored the western end of what might be imagined as a sea bridge that spanned the Atlantic, connecting the Western Hemisphere to Europe. Somewhat like the Beringian land bridge traversed by the first Americans thousands of years earlier (see chapter 1), the new sea bridge established a connection between the Eastern and Western Hemispheres. The Atlantic Ocean, which had isolated America from Europe, became an aquatic highway, thanks to sailing technology, intrepid seamen, and their European sponsors. This new sea bridge launched the **Columbian exchange**, a transatlantic trade of goods, people, and ideas that has continued ever since.

Spaniards brought novelties to the New World that were commonplace in Europe, including Christianity, iron technology, sailing ships, firearms, wheeled vehicles, and horses. Unknowingly, they also carried many Old World viruses and bacteria that caused devastating epidemics of smallpox, measles, and other diseases that killed the vast majority of Indians during the sixteenth century and later. European diseases made the Columbian exchange catastrophic for Native Americans. In the long term, these diseases helped transform the dominant peoples of the New World from Native Americans, who had inhabited the hemisphere for more than fourteen thousand years, to descendants of Europeans and Africans, who had arrived only recently.

Ancient American people, goods, and ideas made the return trip across the Atlantic. In 1495, Columbus himself sent more than five hundred enslaved Indians to be sold in European markets, the first of thousands more. He also introduced Europeans to New

Why did Europeans launch explorations in the fifteenth century?

◄ **Smallpox Victims** This sixteenth-century picture shows four Mexican smallpox victims lying on woven mats while a Mexican healer treats a fifth victim. In reality, there were no known remedies for smallpox, which Spaniards brought to Mexico. Millions died from smallpox, and those who survived were often horribly disfigured and demoralized. Sarin Images/Granger.

World foods such as corn and potatoes that became important staples in Old World diets, especially for poor people. Columbus's sailors became infected with syphilis in sexual encounters with New World women and unwittingly carried the deadly disease back to Europe. New World tobacco created a European fashion for smoking that ignited quickly and has yet to be extinguished. But for almost a generation after 1492, this Columbian exchange did not reward Spaniards with the riches they yearned to find.

QUICK REVIEW

How did New World discoveries revolutionize Europeans' understanding of global geography?

How did Spaniards conquer and colonize New Spain?

During the sixteenth century, the New World helped Spain become the most powerful monarchy in both Europe and the Americas. Initially, Spaniards enslaved Caribbean Indians and put them to work growing crops and mining gold. As Columbus declared, "the Indians [of New Spain] . . . were and are *the greatest wealth* . . . because they are the ones who dig, and harvest, and collect the bread and other supplies, and gather the gold from the mines, and do all the work of men and beast alike." But the profits from these early ventures barely covered the monarchs' costs of maintaining Spanish settlers. After almost thirty years of exploration, the promise of Columbus's discovery began to fade.

| What did Spaniards discover in the western Atlantic? | **How did Spaniards conquer and colonize New Spain?** | How did New Spain influence Europe? | Conclusion: What did the New World promise Europeans? |

CHRONOLOGY

1519
– Hernán Cortés searches for wealth in Mexico.

1520
– Mexicans in Tenochtitlán revolt against Spaniards.

1521
– Cortés conquers Mexicans.

1532
– Francisco Pizarro begins conquest of Peru.

1539
– Hernando de Soto explores southeastern North America.

1540
– Francisco Vásquez de Coronado explores Southwest and Great Plains.

1542
– Juan Rodríguez Cabrillo explores California coast.

1549
– Repartimiento reforms replace encomienda.

1565
– St. Augustine, Florida, is settled.

1598
– Juan de Oñate explores New Mexico.

1599
– Acoma pueblo revolts against Oñate.

In 1519, however, that promise was realized in Hernán Cortés's march into Mexico. Within the next thirty years, Spanish conquests extended from northern Mexico to southern Chile, and New World riches filled Spanish treasure chests. Cortés's expedition served as the model for Spaniards' and other Europeans' expectations that the New World could yield profits for its conquerors. Those profits came at the expense of native peoples victimized by forced labor, violent conquest, and deadly epidemics.

The Conquest of Mexico

Hernán Cortés, an obscure nineteen-year-old Spaniard, arrived in the New World in 1504. Throughout his twenties, Cortés fought in the conquest of Cuba and elsewhere in the Caribbean. In 1519, the governor of Cuba authorized him to organize an expedition of about six hundred men and eleven ships to investigate rumors of a fabulously wealthy kingdom somewhere in the interior of the mainland.

A charismatic and confident man, Cortés could not speak any Native American languages. He landed first on the Yucatán peninsula with his ragtag army and had the good fortune to receive the gift of a young girl named Malinali from a local Tobascan chief. She spoke several native languages, including Nahuatl, the language of the Mexica, the most powerful people in what is now Mexico and Central America (see chapter 1). Malinali, whom Spaniards called Marina, had acquired her linguistic skills painfully. Born into a family of Mexican nobility, she learned Nahuatl as a child. After her father died and her mother remarried, her stepfather sold her as a slave to Mayan-speaking Indians, who subsequently gave her to the Tobascans, who in turn presented her to Cortés. Malinali soon learned Spanish and became Cortés's interpreter, one of his several mistresses, and the mother of his son. Malinali was the Spaniards' lifeline of communication with the Indians. "Without her help," wrote one Spaniard who accompanied Cortés, "we would not have understood the language of New Spain and Mexico." By the time Malinali died at age twenty-four, the people she had grown up among—who had taught her languages, enslaved her, and given her to Cortés—had been conquered by Spaniards with her help.

In Tenochtitlán, the capital of the Mexican empire, the emperor Montezuma heard about strange creatures sighted along the coast. The emperor sent representatives to bring the strangers large quantities of food. Before the Mexican messengers served food to the Spaniards, the Mexicans sacrificed several hostages and soaked the food in their blood. This ritual disgusted the Spaniards and might have been enough to turn them back to Cuba. But along with the food, the Mexicans brought the Spaniards another gift, a "disk in the shape of a sun, as big as a cartwheel and made of very fine gold," as a Mexican recalled. Here was conclusive evidence that the rumors of fabulous riches heard by Cortés must be true. In August 1519, Cortés marched inland to find Montezuma. Leading about three hundred fifty men, Cortés had to live off the land, establishing peaceful relations with local tribes when he could and killing them when he thought it necessary. On November 8, 1519, Cortés reached Tenochtitlán, where Montezuma welcomed him and showered the Spaniards with lavish hospitality. Quickly, Cortés took Montezuma hostage and held him under house arrest, hoping to make him a puppet through whom

"Columbus declared 'the Indians [of New Spain] . . . were and are *the greatest wealth* . . . because they are the ones who dig, and harvest, and collect the bread and other supplies, and gather the gold from the mines, and do all the work of men and beast alike.'"

Why did Europeans launch explorations in the fifteenth century?

◀ **Cortés Arrives in Tenochtitlán** In this portrayal of Cortés and his army arriving in the Mexican capital, Malinali stands at the front of the procession, serving as the Spaniards' translator and intermediary with Montezuma (not pictured). Painted by a Mexican artist after the conquest, the work displays the choices the Mexica faced: accept the peaceful overtures of Cortés (doffing his hat) or face his battle-ready soldiers. Bibliothèque Nationale, Paris, France/De Agostini Picture Library/Bridgeman Images.

READING THE IMAGE: How did each of the different kinds of people illustrated in the portrait contribute to the Spanish conquest of Tenochtitlán?

CONNECTIONS: How did Cortés's conquest of Tenochtitlán compare to Mexicans' conquest of the numerous people in their empire?

the Spaniards could rule the Mexican empire. This uneasy peace existed for several months until one of Cortés's men led a brutal massacre of many Mexican nobles, causing the people of Tenochtitlán to revolt. Montezuma was killed, and Mexicans mounted a ferocious assault on the Spaniards. On June 30, 1520, Cortés and about one hundred other Spaniards fought their way out of Tenochtitlán, losing much of the gold they had confiscated, since it proved too heavy to carry away quickly. Cortés and his men retreated about a hundred miles to Tlaxcala, a stronghold of bitter enemies of the Mexicans. Tlaxcalans allowed Cortés to regroup, obtain reinforcements, and plan a strategy to conquer Tenochtitlán.

In the spring of 1521, Cortés and thousands of Indian allies laid siege to the Mexican capital. With a relentless, scorched-earth strategy, Cortés finally defeated the last Mexican defenders on August 13, 1521. The great capital of the Mexican empire "looked as if it had been ploughed up," one of Cortés's soldiers remembered. **(See "Spotlight: Why Did Cortés Win?" on page 40.)**

Cortés's Invasion of Tenochtitlán, 1519–1521

The Search for Other Mexicos

Lured by their hunger for gold, Spanish **conquistadors** (soldiers who fought in conquests) quickly fanned out from Tenochtitlán in search of other sources of treasure. The most spectacular prize fell to Francisco Pizarro, who conquered the **Incan empire** in Peru. The Incas controlled a vast, complex region that stretched along the western coast of South America for more than two thousand miles and contained more than nine million people. In 1532, Pizarro and his army of fewer than two hundred men captured the Incan emperor Atahualpa and held him hostage. As ransom, the Incas gave Pizarro the largest treasure yet produced by the conquests: gold and silver equivalent to half a century's worth of precious metal production in Europe. With the ransom safely in their hands, the Spaniards murdered Atahualpa. The spectacular Incan treasure proved that at least one other Mexico did indeed exist, and it spurred Spaniards' search for others.

conquistadors
Spanish explorers and soldiers who conquered Native Americans in the New World.

Incan empire
A region under the control of the Incas and their emperor, Atahualpa, that stretched along the western coast of South America.

| What did Spaniards discover in the western Atlantic? | **How did Spaniards conquer and colonize New Spain?** | How did New Spain influence Europe? | Conclusion: What did the New World promise Europeans? |

Why Did Cortés Win?

By conquering Mexico, Hernán Cortés demonstrated that the New World could enrich the Old. But how did a few hundred Spaniards so far away from home defeat millions of Indians fighting on their home turf?

First, several military factors favored the Spaniards. They possessed superior military technology, which partially offset the Mexicans' superior numbers. They fought with weapons of iron and steel against the Mexicans' stone, wood, and copper. They charged on horseback against Mexican warriors on foot. They ignited gunpowder to fire cannon and muskets toward attacking Mexicans, whose only source of power was human muscle.

However, the Spaniards' weaponry alone was not enough to overpower the Mexicans' immense numerical superiority. The Spanish forces also had superior military organization, although they were far from a highly disciplined, professional fighting force. Cortés's army was composed of soldiers of fortune, young men who hoped to fight for God and king and get rich. The unsteady discipline among the Spaniards is suggested by Cortés's decision to beach and dismantle the ships that had brought his small army to the Mexican mainland, thereby stranding his men with no choice but to go forward. Still, the Spaniards formed a well-oiled military machine compared to the Mexicans. Spanish tactics concentrated soldiers to magnify the effect of their firepower and to maintain communication during the thick of battle. In contrast, Mexicans tended to attack from ambush or in waves of frontal assaults, showing great courage but little organization or discipline. In the siege of Tenochtitlán, for example, when Mexicans had Spaniards on the run, they often paused

▲ This sixteenth-century painting illustrates the war clubs, spears, and feather shields Mexican warriors deployed against the steel swords and armor of attacking Spaniards. Album/Oronoz/SuperStock.

to sacrifice Spanish soldiers they had captured, taking time to skin "their faces," one Spaniard recalled, "which they afterward prepared like leather gloves, with their beards on."

But perhaps the Spaniards' most fundamental military advantage was their concept of war. The Mexican concept was shaped by the nature of their empire. The Mexicans fought to impose their tribute system on others and to take captives for sacrifices. They believed that war would make their adversaries realize the high cost of continuing to fight and would give them incentive to surrender and pay tribute. To the Spaniards, war meant destroying the enemy's ability to fight. In short, the Spaniards sought total victory; the Mexicans sought surrender. All these military factors

Juan Ponce de León sailed to Florida in 1521 to find riches, only to be killed in battle with Calusa Indians. A few years later, Lucas Vázquez de Ayllón explored the Atlantic coast north of Florida to present-day South Carolina. In 1526, he established a small settlement on the Georgia coast that he named San Miguel de Gualdape, the first Spanish attempt to establish a foothold in what is now the United States. Sickness and hostile Indians soon swept away this settlement. In 1528, Pánfilo de Narváez surveyed the Gulf coast from Florida to Texas, but his expedition ended disastrously with a shipwreck near present-day Galveston, Texas.

Why did Europeans launch explorations in the fifteenth century?

weakened the Mexicans' resistance but are still insufficient to explain Cortés's victory.

European viruses proved to be at least as significant as military technology. When the Mexicans confronted Cortés and his men, smallpox and measles viruses that the Spaniards had brought with them to Mexico weakened the Mexicans. A smallpox epidemic struck the Caribbean in 1519 and lasted through 1522, killing thousands of Indians and leaving many others too sick to fight. As one Mexican explained to a Spaniard shortly after the conquest, the plague lasted for months, "striking everywhere in the city and killing a vast number of our people." While Mexicans were decimated by their first exposure to smallpox and measles, Spaniards were for all practical purposes immune, having previously been exposed to the diseases.

Christianity was as much a part of the conquistadors' armory as swords and gunpowder. Spaniards' Christianity was a confident and militant faith that commanded its followers to destroy idolatry, root out heresy, slay infidels, and subjugate nonbelievers. Mexicans' religious doctrine caused them to be hesitant and uncertain in confronting Spaniards when they were most vulnerable. At first, Mexicans worried that Spaniards were immortal, an illusion Cortés tried to maintain by hiding the bodies of Spaniards who died.

Mexican military commanders often turned to their priests for military guidance. Spaniards routinely celebrated mass and prayed before battles, but Cortés and his subordinates—tough, wily, practical men—made the military and diplomatic decisions. When Spaniards suffered defeats, they did not worry that God had abandoned them. In contrast, when Mexicans lost battles advised by their priests, they confronted the distressing fear that their gods no longer seemed to listen to them. The deadly sickness sweeping through the countryside also seemed to show that their gods had abandoned them. "Cut us loose," one Mexican pleaded, "because the gods have died."

Finally, politics proved decisive in the Mexicans' defeat. Cortés shrewdly exploited the tensions between Mexicans and the people in their empire. Cortés reinforced his small army with thousands of Indian allies who were eager to seek revenge against their Mexican conquerors. With skillful diplomacy, Cortés obtained cooperation from thousands of Indian porters and food suppliers. Besides fighting alongside Cortés, Spaniards' Indian allies provided the invaders with a fairly secure base from which to maneuver against Mexicans' stronghold. Hundreds of thousands of other Indians helped Cortés by failing to come to Mexicans' defense. These passive allies of the Spaniards prevented Mexicans from fully capitalizing on their overwhelming numerical superiority. In the end, the political tensions created by the Mexican empire proved to be its crippling weakness.

Questions for Analysis

SUMMARIZE THE ARGUMENT: What factors were most significant in allowing Cortés and the Spaniards to overwhelm the much more numerous Mexican forces?

ANALYZE THE EVIDENCE: What military technologies aided the Spaniards? How did disease influence conquest? To what extent did ideas contribute to the Mexicans' defeat?

CONSIDER THE CONTEXT: To what extent was this conquest a clash of cultures? How did conquest change Spaniards' thinking about their New World empire? How did conquest shape New Spain?

In 1539, Hernando de Soto, a seasoned conquistador, set out with more than six hundred men to find another Peru in North America. Landing in Florida, de Soto slashed his way through much of southeastern North America for three years. De Soto typified the viewpoint of other conquistadors when he told an Indian leader in Georgia that he "was the child of the Sun, coming from its abode, and that he was going about the country seeking the greatest prince there and the richest region." After the brutal slaughter of many Native Americans and much hardship, de Soto died in 1542. His men buried him in the Mississippi River and turned back to Mexico, disappointed.

| What did Spaniards discover in the western Atlantic? | **How did Spaniards conquer and colonize New Spain?** | How did New Spain influence Europe? | Conclusion: What did the New World promise Europeans? |

▶ **Zuñi Defend Their Pueblo against Coronado** This sixteenth-century drawing by a Mexican artist shows Zuñi bowmen fighting back against Coronado's men and the entreaties of Christian missionaries. The drawing depicts a Zuñi defender aiming his arrow at a Mexican missionary armed with a crucifix, a rosary, and the Bible. Ms Hunter 242 f.317r The Spanish Conquest, from "Historia de Tlaxcala" by Diego Munoz Camargo (pen & ink on paper)/Mexican School, (16th century)/UNIVERSITY OF GLASGOW LIBRARY/© Glasgow University Library, Scotland/Bridgeman Images.

READING THE IMAGE: How did this picture convey Spaniards' point of view about Zuñi opposition to Coronado and his men? CONNECTIONS: Why did missionaries seek to convert Native Americans to Christianity, and why did many Native Americans resist the missionaries' efforts?

Tales of the fabulous wealth of the mythical Seven Cities of Cíbola also lured Francisco Vásquez de Coronado to search the Southwest and Great Plains of North America. In 1540, Coronado left northern Mexico with more than three hundred Spaniards, a thousand Indians, and a priest who claimed to know the way to what he called "the greatest and best of the discoveries." Cíbola turned out to be a small Zuñi pueblo of about a hundred families. When the Zuñi shot arrows at the Spaniards, Coronado attacked the pueblo and routed the defenders after a hard battle. Convinced that the rich cities must lie somewhere over the horizon, Coronado kept moving all the way to central Kansas, before deciding in 1542 that the rumors he had pursued were just that.

The same year Coronado abandoned his search for Cíbola, Juan Rodríguez Cabrillo's maritime expedition sought to find wealth along the coast of California. Cabrillo died on Santa Catalina Island, offshore from present-day Los Angeles, but his men sailed on to Oregon, where a ferocious storm forced them to turn back toward Mexico.

These probes into North America by de Soto, Coronado, and Cabrillo persuaded other Spaniards that enormous territories stretched northward from Mexico but their inhabitants had little to loot or exploit. After a generation of vigorous exploration, Spaniards concluded that there was only one Mexico and one Peru.

Spanish Outposts in Florida and New Mexico

Disappointed by the explorers' failure to discover riches in North America, the Spanish monarchy insisted that a few settlements be established in Florida and New Mexico to give a token of reality to Spain's territorial claims. Settlements in Florida would have the additional benefit of protecting Spanish ships from pirates and privateers who lurked along the southeastern coast, waiting for the Spanish treasure fleet when it sailed toward Spain.

Why did Europeans launch explorations in the fifteenth century?

In 1565, the Spanish king sent Pedro Menéndez de Avilés to found St. Augustine in Florida, the first permanent European settlement within what became the United States. By 1600, St. Augustine had a population of about five hundred, the only remaining Spanish beachhead on North America's vast Atlantic shoreline.

More than sixteen hundred miles west of St. Augustine, Spaniards founded another outpost in 1598. Juan de Oñate led an expedition of about five hundred people to settle northern Mexico, now called New Mexico, and claim the booty rumored to exist there. Oñate had impeccable credentials for both conquest and mining. His father helped to discover the bonanza silver mines of Zacatecas in central Mexico, and his wife, Isabel Tolsa Cortés Montezuma, was the granddaughter of Cortés and the great-granddaughter of Montezuma. When Oñate and his companions reached pueblos near present-day Albuquerque and Santa Fe, he sent out scouting parties to find the legendary treasures of the region and to locate the ocean, which he believed must be nearby. Meanwhile, many of his soldiers planned to mutiny, and relations with the Indians deteriorated. When Native Americans in the Acoma pueblo revolted against the Spaniards, Oñate ruthlessly suppressed the uprising, killing eight hundred men, women, and children. Oñate's response to the **Acoma pueblo revolt** reconfirmed Spaniards' military superiority, but it did not bring peace or stability to the region. After another pueblo revolt occurred in 1599, many of Oñate's settlers returned to Mexico, leaving New Mexico a small, dusty assertion of Spanish claims to the North American Southwest.

Acoma pueblo revolt
Revolt against the Spanish by Indians living at the Acoma pueblo in 1599.

New Spain in the Sixteenth Century

For all practical purposes, Spain was the dominant European power in the Western Hemisphere during the sixteenth century (**Map 2.3**). Portugal claimed the giant territory of Brazil under the Tordesillas Treaty, but was far more concerned with exploiting its hard-won trade with the East Indies than with colonizing the New World. England and France were absorbed by European matters and largely lost interest in America until late in the century. In the decades after 1519, Spaniards created the distinctive colonial society of **New Spain**, which showed other Europeans how the New World could be made to serve the purposes of the Old.

The Spanish monarchy gave the conquistadors permission to explore and plunder what they found. **(See "Analyzing Historical Evidence: Justifying Conquest" on page 46.)** The crown took one-fifth of any loot confiscated, called the "royal fifth," and allowed

New Spain
Spanish colony in the New World that governed for the benefit of Spain.

◀ **Potosí Silver Mine** In 1545, colonists discovered the massive silver deposits at Potosí in what is now Bolivia. Employing Indians more or less as slave laborers to mine and process the ore, as shown in this painting from about 1585, Potosí produced more than half the world's silver during the last half of the sixteenth century. Potosí made a huge contribution to the wealth that flowed from New Spain to the Spanish monarchy as well as to the oppression of Native Americans who worked in and around the mine. Granger, NYC–All Rights Reserved.

| What did Spaniards discover in the western Atlantic? | **How did Spaniards conquer and colonize New Spain?** | How did New Spain influence Europe? | Conclusion: What did the New World promise Europeans? |

MAP ACTIVITY

MAP 2.3 ▲ Sixteenth-Century European Colonies in the New World Spanish control spread throughout Central and South America during the sixteenth century, with the important exception of Portuguese Brazil. North America, though claimed by Spain under the Treaty of Tordesillas, remained on the margins of Spain's New World empire.

READING THE MAP: Track Spain's efforts at colonization by date. How did political holdings, the physical layout of the land, and natural resources influence where Spaniards directed their energies?
CONNECTIONS: What was the purpose of the Treaty of Tordesillas? How did the location of silver and gold mines affect the geographical limits of New Spain?

the conquerors to divide the rest. In the end, most conquistadors received very little after the plunder was divided among leaders such as Cortés and his favorite officers. To compensate his disappointed, battle-hardened soldiers, Cortés gave them Indian towns Spaniards had subdued.

Why did Europeans launch explorations in the fifteenth century?

The distribution of conquered towns institutionalized the system of *encomienda*, which empowered the conquistadors to rule the Indians and the lands in and around their towns. The concept of encomienda was familiar to Spaniards, who had used it to govern regions captured from Muslims during the Reconquest. In New Spain, encomienda transferred to the Spanish *encomendero* (the man who "owned" the town) the tribute that the town had previously paid to the Mexican empire. In theory, the encomendero was supposed to guarantee order and justice, be responsible for the Indians' material welfare, and encourage them to become Christians.

encomienda
A system that allowed the Spanish *encomendero,* or "owner" of a town, to collect tribute from the town in return for providing law and order and encouraging "his" Indians to convert to Christianity.

Catholic missionaries worked hard to convert Indians. They fervently believed that God expected them to save Indians' souls by convincing them to abandon their old sinful beliefs and to embrace the one true Christian faith. But after baptizing tens of thousands of Indians, the missionaries learned that many Indians continued to worship their own gods. Most priests came to believe that Indians were lesser beings inherently incapable of fully understanding Christianity.

In practice, encomenderos were far more interested in what Indians could do for them than in what they or the missionaries could do for Indians. Encomenderos subjected Indians to chronic overwork and brutal abuse. According to one Spaniard, encomenderos forced "all males to the harshest and most iniquitous and brutal slavery that man has ever devised for oppressing his fellow-men, treating them . . . worse than animals." Spaniards enslaved tens of thousands of Indians, many of whom, one priest reported, "were brought into Mexico City in great flocks, like sheep, so they could be branded easily." Economically, encomienda recognized a fundamental reality of New Spain: The most important treasure Spaniards could plunder from the New World was not gold but uncompensated Indian labor.

UNDERSTAND POINTS OF VIEW
Why did Spaniards come to New Spain in the sixteenth century?

The practice of coerced labor in New Spain grew directly out of Spaniards' assumption that they were superior to Indians. As one missionary put it, Indians "are more stupid than asses and refuse to improve in anything." Therefore, most Spaniards assumed, Indians' labor should be organized by and for their conquerors. Spaniards seldom hesitated to use violence to punish and intimidate recalcitrant Indians.

Encomienda engendered two groups of influential critics. A few missionaries were horrified at the brutal mistreatment of Indians. "What will [Indians] think about the God of the Christians," Friar Bartolomé de Las Casas asked, when they see their friends "with their heads split, their hands amputated, their intestines torn open? . . . Would they want to come to Christ's sheepfold after their homes had been destroyed, their children

> "'What will [Indians] think about the God of the Christians,' Friar Bartolemé de Las Casas asked."

imprisoned, their wives raped, their cities devastated, their maidens deflowered, and their provinces laid waste?" Unlike most Spaniards, Las Casas believed that Indians "are by nature of very subtle, lively, clear, and most capable understanding." While he and other outspoken missionaries softened few hearts among the encomenderos, they won some sympathy for Indians from the Spanish monarchy and royal bureaucracy. The Spanish monarchy moved to abolish encomienda in an effort to replace swashbuckling old conquistadors with royal bureaucrats as the rulers of New Spain.

In 1549, a reform called the *repartimiento* began to replace encomienda. It limited the labor an encomendero could command from his Indians to forty-five days per year from each adult male. The repartimiento, however, did not challenge the principle of forced labor, nor did it prevent encomenderos from continuing to cheat, mistreat, and overwork their Indians, many of whom were put to work in silver mines. Mining was grueling and dangerous work. One Spaniard claimed that ten Indians died for every peso earned in the mines, which was an exaggeration. But the mines were deadly for Indians and fabulously profitable for Spaniards. During the entire sixteenth century, precious-metal exports from New Spain to Spain were

| What did Spaniards discover in the western Atlantic? | **How did Spaniards conquer and colonize New Spain?** | How did New Spain influence Europe? | Conclusion: What did the New World promise Europeans? |

45

Justifying Conquest

The immense riches Spain reaped from its New World empire came largely at the expense of Native Americans. A few individual Spaniards raised their voices against the brutal exploitation of Indians. Their criticisms prompted the Spanish monarchy to formulate an official justification of conquest that, in effect, blamed Indians for resisting Spanish dominion.

DOCUMENT 1

Montecino's 1511 Sermon

In 1511, a Dominican friar named Antón Montecino delivered a blistering sermon that astonished the Spaniards gathered in the church in Santo Domingo, headquarters of the Spanish Caribbean.

Your greed for gold is blind. Your pride, your lust, your anger, your envy, your sloth, all blind. . . . You are in mortal sin. And you are heading for damnation. . . . For you are destroying an innocent people. For they are God's people, these innocents, whom you destroyed. By what right do you make them die? Mining gold for you in your mines or working for you in your fields, by what right do you unleash enslaving wars upon them? They have lived in peace in this land before you came, in peace in their own homes. They did nothing to harm you to cause you to slaughter them wholesale. . . .

Are you not under God's command to love them as you love yourselves?

Are you out of your souls, out of your minds? Yes. And that will bring you to damnation.

Source: Zvi Dor-Ner, *Columbus and the Age of Discovery* (New York: William Morrow, 1991), 220–21.

DOCUMENT 2

The Requerimiento

In 1512 and 1513, King Ferdinand met with philosophers and theologians and concluded that their holy duty to spread Christianity justified conquest. To buttress this claim, the king had his advisers prepare the requerimiento.

According to the requerimiento, Indians who failed to welcome Spanish conquest and all its blessings deserved to die. Conquistadors were commanded to read the requerimiento to the Indians before any act of conquest.

On the part of the King . . . [and] queen of [Spain], subduers of the barbarous nations, we their servants notify and make known to you, as best we can, that the Lord our God, living and eternal, created the heaven and the earth, and one man and one woman, of whom you and we, and all the men of the world, were and are descendants. . . .

God our lord gave charge to one man called St. Peter, that he should be lord and superior to all the men in the world, that all should obey him, and that he should be the head of the whole human race, wherever men should live . . . and he gave him the world for his kingdom and jurisdiction. . . .

[The Pope] who succeeded that St. Peter as lord of the world . . . made donation of these islands and mainland to the . . . king and queen [of Spain]. . . .

So their highnesses are kings and lords of these islands and mainland by virtue of this donation; and . . . almost all those to whom this has been notified, have received and served their highnesses, as lords and kings, in the way that subjects ought to do, with good will, without any resistance, immediately, without delay, when they were informed of the aforesaid facts. And also they received and obeyed the priests whom their highnesses sent to preach to them and to teach them our holy faith; and all these, of their own free will, without any reward or condition have become Christians, and are so, and their highnesses have joyfully and graciously received them, and they have also commanded them to be treated as their subjects and vassals; and you too are held

worth twenty-five times more than the next most important export, leather hides (**Figure 2.1**).

For Spaniards, life in New Spain after the conquests was relatively easy. As one colonist wrote to his brother in Spain, "Don't hesitate [to come]. . . . This land [New Spain] is as good as ours [in Spain], for God has given us more here than there, and we shall be better off." During the century after 1492, about 225,000 Spaniards settled in the colonies. Virtually all of them were poor young men of common (non-noble) lineage who came directly from Spain. Laborers and artisans made up the largest proportion, but soldiers and sailors were also numerous. Men vastly outnumbered women.

The gender and number of Spanish settlers shaped two fundamental features of the society of New Spain. First, Europeans never made up more than 1 or 2 percent of the total

Why did Europeans launch explorations in the fifteenth century?

and obliged to do the same. Wherefore, as best we can, we ask and require that you consider what we have said to you, and that you take the time that shall be necessary to understand and deliberate upon it, and that you acknowledge the Church as the ruler and superior of the whole world, and the high priest called Pope, and in his name the king and queen [of Spain] our lords, in his place, as superiors and lords and kings of these islands and this mainland . . . and that you consent and permit that these religious fathers declare and preach to you. . . .

If you do so . . . we . . . shall receive you in all love and charity, and shall leave you your wives and your children and your lands free without servitude, that you may do with them and with yourselves freely what you like and think best, and they shall not compel you to turn to Christians unless you yourselves, when informed of the truth, should wish to be converted to our holy Catholic faith. . . . And besides this, their highnesses award you many privileges and exemptions and will grant you many benefits.

But if you do not do this or if you maliciously delay in doing it, I certify to you that with the help of God we shall forcefully enter into your country and shall make war against you in all ways and manners that we can, and shall subject you to the yoke and obedience of the Church and of their highnesses; we shall take you and your wives and your children and shall make slaves of them, and as such shall sell and dispose of them as their highnesses may command; and we shall take away your goods and shall do to you all the harm and damage that we can, as to vassals who do not obey and refuse to receive their lord and resist and contradict him; and we protest that the deaths and losses which shall accrue from this are your fault, and not that of their highnesses, or ours, or of these soldiers who come with us.

Indians who heard the requerimiento could not understand Spanish, of course. No native documents survive to record the Indians' thoughts when they heard the Spaniards' official justification for conquest, even when it was translated into a language they recognized. But one conquistador reported that when the requerimiento was translated for two chiefs in Colombia, they responded that if the pope gave the king so much territory that belonged to other people, "the Pope must have been drunk."

Source: Adapted from A. Helps and M. Oppenheim, eds., *The Spanish Conquest in America and Its Relation to the History of Slavery and to the Government of the Colonies,* 4 vols. (London, 1900–1904), 1:264–67.

Questions for Analysis

ASK HISTORICAL QUESTIONS: To what degree did Spaniards believe their New World conquests were moral and just? How did Christianity influence Spaniards' ideas about conquest?

ANALYZE THE EVIDENCE: How did the requerimiento address the criticisms of Montecino? According to the requerimiento, what choices did Native Americans and Spaniards have?

CONSIDER THE CONTEXT: Since few Native Americans could understand the requerimiento when it was read to them, what purpose did the requerimiento serve? Who were its intended audiences?

RECOGNIZE VIEWPOINTS: According to the requerimiento, why were Native Americans responsible for Spanish cruelty? What arguments might Native American leaders have made against the requerimiento?

population. Although Spaniards ruled New Spain, the population was almost wholly Indian. Second, the shortage of Spanish women meant that Spanish men frequently married Indian women or used them as concubines. As a Spanish merchant in Mexico City wrote to a relative in Castile, "though there in Spain it might shock you that I have married an Indian woman, here one loses nothing of his honor." The relatively few women from Spain usually married Spanish men, contributing to a tiny elite defined by European origins.

The small number of Spaniards, the masses of Indians, and the frequency of intermarriage created a steep social hierarchy defined by perceptions of national origin and race. Natives of Spain—*peninsulares* (people born on the Iberian Peninsula)—enjoyed the highest social status in New Spain. Below them but still within the white elite were *creoles,* the children born in the New World to Spanish

creoles
Children born to Spanish parents in the New World who, with the *peninsulares*, made up the tiny portion of the population at the top of the colonial social hierarchy.

What did Spaniards discover in the western Atlantic?	**How did Spaniards conquer and colonize New Spain?**	How did New Spain influence Europe?	Conclusion: What did the New World promise Europeans?

FIGURE 2.1 ▶ New World Gold and Silver Imported into Spain during the Sixteenth Century, in Pesos

Spain imported more gold than silver during the first three decades of the sixteenth century, but the total value of this treasure was quickly eclipsed during the 1530s and 1540s, when rich silver mines were developed. Silver accounted for most of the enormous growth in Spain's precious-metal imports from the New World.

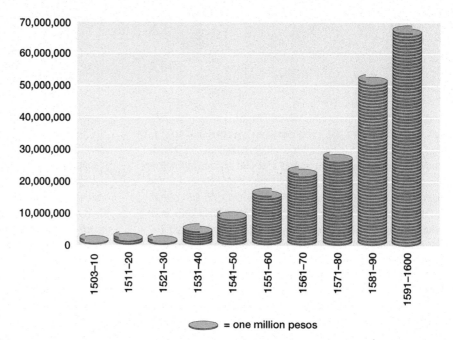

= one million pesos

men and women. Together, peninsulares and creoles made up barely 1 or 2 percent of the population. Below them on the social pyramid was a larger group of *mestizos*, the offspring of Spanish men and Indian women, who accounted for 4 or 5 percent of the population. Some mestizos worked as artisans and labor overseers and lived well, and a few rose into the ranks of the elite, especially if their Indian ancestry was not obvious from their skin color. Most mestizos, however, were lumped with Indians, the enormous bottom slab of the social pyramid.

The society of New Spain established a pattern that would shape other European colonies in the New World: a steep social pyramid stratified by social origin and race. All Europeans of whatever social origin considered themselves superior to all Native Americans. In New Spain, they were a dominant minority in both power and status.

ANALYZE EVIDENCE

How did New Spain's society reflect Spaniards' attitudes about race?

The Toll of Spanish Conquest and Colonization

By 1560, the major centers of Indian civilization had been conquered, their leaders overthrown, their religion held in contempt, and their people forced to work for the Spaniards. Profound demoralization pervaded Indian society. A Mexican poet wrote:

Nothing but flowers and songs of sorrow are left in Mexico . . .
Where once we saw warriors and wise men . . .
We are crushed to the ground; we lie in ruins.
There is nothing but grief and suffering in Mexico.

Adding to the culture shock of conquest and colonization was the deadly toll of European diseases. As conquest spread, Indians succumbed to epidemics of measles, smallpox, and respiratory illnesses. They had no immunity to these diseases because they had not been exposed to them before the arrival of Europeans. By 1570, the Indian population of New Spain had fallen about 90 percent from what it was when Columbus arrived, a catastrophe unequaled in human history. A Mayan Indian recalled that

Why did Europeans launch explorations in the fifteenth century?

when sickness struck his village, "The dogs and vultures devoured the bodies. The mortality was terrible. . . . So it was that we became orphans. . . . We were born to die." For most Indians, New Spain was a graveyard.

For Spaniards, Indian deaths meant that the most valuable resource of New Spain—Indian labor—dwindled rapidly. By the last quarter of the sixteenth century, Spanish colonists began to import African slaves. Some Africans had come to Mexico with the conquistadors. One Mexican recalled that among Cortés's men were "some black-skinned one[s] with kink[y] hair." In the years before 1550, while Indian labor was still adequate, only 15,000 slaves were imported from Africa. The relatively high cost of African slaves kept imports low, totaling approximately 36,000 from 1550 to the end of the century. During the sixteenth century, New Spain continued to rely primarily on the coerced labor of a shrinking number of Indians.

▲ **Racial and Cultural Blending in New Spain** In 1599 the Native American artist Adrián Sanchez Galque painted Don Francisco de Arobe (center) and his two sons, Don Domingo and Don Pedro. The painting was commissioned to convey their loyalty to the king of Spain. The painting depicts the racial and cultural amalgamation underway among the people of New Spain. Arobe and his sons had Spanish names, appear to be a mixture of African and Spanish or Native American ancestry, wore Spanish-style clothing, and adorned themselves with Native American–style jewelry. Album/Alamy Stock Photo.

QUICK REVIEW

What shaped New Spain's distinctive economy and society?

How did New Spain influence Europe?

The riches of New Spain helped make the sixteenth century the Golden Age of Spain. After Queen Isabella and King Ferdinand died, their sixteen-year-old grandson became King Charles I of Spain in 1516. Three years later, just as Cortés ventured into Mexico, King Charles became Holy Roman Emperor Charles V. His empire encompassed more territory than that of any other European monarch. He used the wealth of New Spain to promote his interests in sixteenth-century Europe. He also sought to defend orthodox Christianity from the insurgent heresy of the Protestant Reformation. The power of the Spanish monarchy spread the message throughout sixteenth-century Europe that a New World empire could bankroll Old World ambitions.

The Protestant Reformation and the Spanish Response

In 1517, Martin Luther, an obscure Catholic priest in Germany, initiated the Protestant Reformation by publicizing his criticisms of the Catholic Church. Luther's ideas won the sympathy of many Catholics, but they were considered extremely dangerous by church officials and by monarchs such as Charles V, who believed that just as the church spoke for God, they ruled for God.

Luther preached a doctrine known as "justification by faith." Individual Christians could obtain salvation and life everlasting only by having faith that God would save them. Giving monetary offerings to the church, following the orders of priests, or participating in church rituals would not bring believers closer to heaven. The only true source of information about God's will was the Bible, not the church. By reading the

Protestant Reformation
A religious rupture that began in 1517 with Martin Luther's critiques of the Roman Catholic Church, and precipitated the enduring division between Protestants and Catholics.

| What did Spaniards discover in the western Atlantic? | How did Spaniards conquer and colonize New Spain? | **How did New Spain influence Europe?** | Conclusion: What did the New World promise Europeans? |

49

COMPARE AND CONTRAST

How did Martin Luther's ideas about Christianity differ from Charles V's?

TRACE CHANGE OVER TIME

Why did Spain's economy decline during the sixteenth century, despite its riches from New Spain?

Bible, any Christian could learn as much about God's commandments as any priest. Indeed, Luther called for a "priesthood of all believers."

In effect, Luther charged that the Catholic Church was in many respects fraudulent. Luther declared that the church had neglected its true purpose of helping individual Christians understand the spiritual realm revealed in the Bible and had wasted its resources in worldly conflicts of politics and wars. Luther hoped his ideas would reform the Catholic Church, but instead they ruptured forever the unity of Christianity in western Europe.

Charles V pledged to exterminate Luther's Protestant heresies. The wealth pouring into Spain from the New World fueled his efforts to defend orthodox Catholic faith against Protestants, as well as against any other challenge to Spain's supremacy. As the most powerful monarch in Europe, Charles V, followed by his son and successor Philip II, assumed responsibility for upholding the existing order of sixteenth-century Europe.

American wealth, particularly Mexican silver, fueled Spanish ambitions, but Charles V's and Philip II's expenses for constant warfare far surpassed the revenues arriving from New Spain. To help meet military expenditures, both kings raised taxes in Spain more than fivefold during the sixteenth century. Since the wealthy nobility were exempted from taxation, the tax burden fell mostly on poor peasants. The monarchy's ambitions impoverished the vast majority of Spain's population and brought the nation to the brink of bankruptcy. When taxes failed to produce enough revenue to fight its wars, the monarchy borrowed heavily from European bankers. By the end of the sixteenth century, interest payments on royal debts swallowed two-thirds of the crown's annual revenues. In retrospect, the riches from New Spain proved a short-term blessing but a long-term curse.

Most Spaniards, however, looked upon New Spain as a glorious national achievement that displayed Spain's superiority over Native Americans and other Europeans. They had added enormously to their own knowledge and wealth. They had built mines, cities, Catholic churches, and even universities on the other side of the Atlantic. These military, religious, and economic achievements gave them great pride and confidence.

Europe and the Spanish Example

The lessons of sixteenth-century Spain were not lost on Spain's European rivals. Spain proudly displayed the fruits of its New World conquests. In 1520, for example, the German artist Albrecht Dürer wrote in his diary that he "marveled over the subtle ingenuity of the men in these distant lands [of New Spain]" who created such things as "a sun entirely of gold, a whole fathom [six feet] broad." But the most exciting news about "the men in these distant lands" was that they could serve the interests of Europeans, as Spain had shown. With a few notable exceptions, Europeans saw the New World as a place for the expansion of European influence, a place where, as one Spaniard wrote, Europeans could "give to those strange lands the form of our own."

France and England tried to follow Spain's example. Both nations warred with Spain in Europe, preyed on Spanish treasure fleets, and ventured to the New World, where they too hoped to find an undiscovered passageway to the East Indies or another Mexico or Peru.

In 1524, France sent Giovanni da Verrazano to scout the Atlantic coast of North America from North Carolina to Canada, looking for a Northwest Passage to the East Indies (see Map 2.2). Eleven years later, France probed farther north with Jacques Cartier's voyage up the St. Lawrence River. Encouraged, Cartier returned to the region with a group of settlers in 1541, but the colony they established—like the search for a Northwest Passage—came to nothing. English attempts to follow Spain's lead were slower but equally ill fated. Not until 1576, almost eighty years after John Cabot's voyages, did the English try again to find a Northwest Passage. This time Martin Frobisher sailed into the frigid waters of northern Canada (see Map 2.2). Like many other explorers mesmerized by the Spanish example, Frobisher believed he had found gold. But the tons of "ore" he hauled back to England proved worthless, and English interests shifted southward to the giant region on the northern margins of New Spain.

Why did Europeans launch explorations in the fifteenth century?

English explorers' attempts to establish North American settlements were no more fruitful than their search for a northern route to China. Sir Humphrey Gilbert led expeditions in 1578 and 1583 that made feeble efforts to found colonies in Newfoundland until Gilbert vanished at sea. Sir Walter Raleigh organized an expedition in 1585 to settle Roanoke Island off the coast of present-day North Carolina. The first group of explorers left no colonists on the island, but in 1587 Raleigh sent a contingent of more than one hundred settlers to Roanoke under John White's leadership. White went back to England for supplies, and when he returned to Roanoke in 1590, the colonists had disappeared. Roanoke colonists most likely died from a combination of natural causes and unfriendly Indians. Neither mines nor a route to Asia turned up, and the colony was abandoned. By the end of the century, England had failed to secure a New World beachhead.

Roanoke Settlement, 1585–1590

QUICK REVIEW

How did New Spain influence Europe?

Conclusion: What did the New World promise Europeans?

The sixteenth century in the New World belonged to the Spaniards who employed Columbus and to the Indians who greeted him as he stepped ashore. The Portuguese, whose voyages to Africa and Asia set the stage for Columbus's voyages, won the important consolation prize of Brazil, but Spain hit the jackpot. Isabella of Spain helped initiate the Columbian exchange between the New World and the Old, which massively benefited first Spain and later other European countries and which continues to this day. The exchange also subjected Native Americans to the ravages of European diseases and Spanish conquest. Spanish explorers, conquistadors, and colonists forced Indians to serve the interests of Spanish settlers and the Spanish monarchy. The exchange illustrated one of the most important lessons of the sixteenth century: After millions of years, the Atlantic no longer was an impermeable barrier separating the Eastern and Western Hemispheres. After the voyages of Columbus, European sailing ships regularly bridged the Atlantic carrying people, products, diseases, and ideas from one shore to the other.

No European monarch could forget the seductive lesson taught by Spain's example: The New World could vastly enrich the Old. Spain remained a New World power for almost four centuries, and its language, religion, culture, and institutions left a permanent imprint. By the end of the sixteenth century, however, other European monarchies had begun to contest Spain's dominion in Europe and to make forays into the northern fringes of Spain's New World preserve. To reap the benefits Spaniards enjoyed from their New World domain, other monarchs had to learn a difficult lesson: how to deviate from Spain's example. That discovery lay ahead.

While England's rulers eyed the huge North American hinterland of New Spain, they realized that it lacked the two main attractions of Mexico and Peru: incredible material wealth and large populations of Indians to use as workers. In the absence of gold and silver booty and plentiful native labor in North America, England would need to find some way to attract colonizers to a region that—compared to New Spain—did not appear very promising. During the next century, England's leaders overcame these dilemmas by developing a distinctive colonial model, one that encouraged land-hungry settlers from England and Europe to engage in agriculture with other sources of unfree labor: indentured servants from Europe and slaves from Africa.

| What did Spaniards discover in the western Atlantic? | How did Spaniards conquer and colonize New Spain? | How did New Spain influence Europe? | **Conclusion: What did the New World promise Europeans?** |

STEP 1

EXPLAIN WHY IT MATTERS

Put your reading into practice. Identify each term below, and then explain why it matters in U.S. history.

TERM	WHO OR WHAT & WHEN	WHY IT MATTERS
Black Death (p. 30)		
Reconquest (p. 31)		
Tainos (p. 34)		
Treaty of Tordesillas (p. 34)		
Columbian exchange (p. 36)		
conquistadors (p. 39)		
Incan empire (p. 39)		
Acoma pueblo revolt (p. 43)		
New Spain (p. 43)		
encomienda (p. 45)		
creoles (p. 47)		
Protestant Reformation (p. 49)		

STEP 2

MOVE BEYOND THE BASICS

The exercise below represents a more advanced understanding of the chapter material. In this exercise, you will consider the similarities and differences in the exploration and conquest of two Spanish explorers—Columbus and Cortés. What were the motivations behind each man's expeditions? How did these expeditions affect the peoples each encountered? And what were the benefits of each for the kingdom of Spain?

Explorer	Motivations	Impact on New World Peoples	Benefits for Spain
Columbus			
Cortés			

STEP 3

PUT IT ALL TOGETHER

Now, try to explain the big picture. Remember to use specific examples from the chapter in your answers.

EXPANSION AND EXPLORATION

- Why did the Portuguese explore the west coast of Africa?

- What was the Columbian exchange? Why was it important?

CONQUEST AND COLONIZATION

- How did New Spain reflect the values, beliefs, and goals of the Spanish conquerors?

- How did Spanish conquest and colonization affect the peoples of the Americas?

THE IMPACT OF DISCOVERY IN EUROPE

- How did New World wealth influence the clash between Protestants and Catholics in sixteenth-century Europe?

- What lessons did other European powers learn from Spain's experience in the New World?

LOOKING BACKWARD, LOOKING AHEAD

- How did the isolation of the people of the Americas before 1492 affect the course and consequences of European expansion in the New World?

STEP 4

CONNECT THESE EVENTS

In what ways did the start of the Columbian exchange begin a period of decline for Native Americans in the New World?

STEP 5

CONNECT TO THE PRESENT

How does the cultural encounter between the Old and New Worlds in the sixteenth century compare to encounters between very different cultures today?

3

THE SOUTHERN COLONIES IN THE SEVENTEENTH CENTURY

1601–1700

What shaped England's southern colonies during the seventeenth century? This chapter examines the founding of Virginia, the development of tobacco agriculture in the Chesapeake region, the shift from indentured servitude to enslaved labor, and the early years of South Carolina.

This chapter will explore the following questions:

- How did settlers' encounters with Native Americans shape the colony of Virginia?
- How did tobacco influence Chesapeake society?
- Why did Chesapeake society change by the 1670s?
- Why did a slave labor system develop in England's southern colonies?
- Conclusion: How did export crops contribute to the growth of the southern colonies?

AN AMERICAN STORY

In September 1662, shortly after her twenty-third birthday, Anne Orthwood sailed out of her native Bristol, England, toward the English colony of Virginia. Born to an unwed mother, Anne grew up with the stigma of being a bastard. Since Bristol was a thriving seaport, Anne probably heard that jobs in Virginia were plentiful and workers were few. Hundreds of people sailed from Bristol to Virginia every year, most of them poor young men who agreed to become indentured servants. Anne probably also heard about the shortage of women in Virginia. The promise of both work and marriage proved irresistible. In August 1662, Anne signed an indenture to a ship's surgeon who agreed to pay her way to Virginia in exchange for her agreement to work for four years as a servant.

Anne's fate mirrored that of thousands of other indentured servants, the largest group of immigrants to England's southern colonies in the seventeenth century. When Anne arrived in Virginia, the surgeon sold her indenture—and thus her—to William Kendall, a wealthy planter and prominent official on Virginia's Eastern Shore. Kendall himself had come to Virginia as a servant in 1650, but unlike Anne, he was from a respectable family and had received a valuable education. When he became free in 1654, he amassed more than 25,000 acres of land, thanks to his two marriages to wealthy widows. When Anne joined Kendall's household, residing among seven or eight other servants, two slaves, a free black man, and numerous relatives was Kendall's nephew, John.

Like Anne, John was young, unmarried, and recently arrived from England. William Kendall refused to allow his nephew to get mixed up with a lowly servant woman, and a bastard at that. Kendall decided to separate Anne and John by selling her indenture—and thus her—to a tenant farmer who lived several miles away.

As young people will, Anne and John found a way to get together. At a tavern in November 1663, Anne and John Kendall met. She became pregnant. Later, when pressed during childbirth as to who was the father, Anne admitted that it was John: "Three tymes She thought hee had to doe with her, but twice She was Certaine." After the birth of twin boys, Anne died, as did one of her babies. Her other son, Jasper, was indentured while still a baby to a Virginia planter; after twenty-two years of servitude, he became a free man. John Kendall never acknowledged Jasper as his son, but he did follow his uncle William's advice and married a wealthy widow.

Like so many other Virginia colonists, Anne gambled her freedom for the promise of a better life in Virginia, and she lost. Other former servants gambled and won, grandly like William and John Kendall, or modestly like Anne's son Jasper.

During the seventeenth century, English colonists learned how to grow enormous quantities of tobacco and export most of it to England. Tobacco production required hard labor and people who were willing—or could be forced—to do it. While New Spain took advantage of Native American labor, the Native Americans in British North America mostly refused to be conscripted into the English colonists' fields. Instead, the settlers depended on the labor of family members, indentured servants, and by the last third of the seventeenth century, African slaves. By the end of the century, the southern colonies had become sharply different from both New Spain and seventeenth-century England. In ways unimaginable to the earliest settlers, the colonists paid homage to the international market and the English monarch by working hard to make a good living growing crops for export to England.

▼ **Indentured Servant** This eighteenth-century portrait of an English servant by William Hogarth perhaps somewhat resembled indentured servant Anne Orthwood, who had immigrated to Virginia nearly a century earlier. No likeness of her exists. Unlike Orthwood, most servants who came to the Chesapeake during the seventeenth century were young boys. *Heads of Six of Hogarth's Servants*, detail, by William Hogarth. © Tate, London / Art Resource, NY.

How did settlers' encounters with Native Americans shape the colony of Virginia?

Virginia Company
A joint-stock company organized by London investors in 1606 that received a land grant from King James I in order to establish English colonies in North America.

Algonquian Indians
People who inhabited the coastal plain of present-day Virginia, near the Chesapeake Bay, when English colonists first settled the region.

Jamestown
The first permanent English settlement in North America, established in 1607 by colonists sponsored by the Virginia Company.

In 1606, England's King James I granted the Virginia Company more than six million acres in North America. He hoped to create the English equivalent of Spain's New World empire. Enthusiastic reports from the Roanoke voyages twenty years earlier (see chapter 2) claimed that in Virginia "the earth bringeth foorth all things in aboundance . . . without toile or labour." Virginia Company investors hoped to profit by finding a valuable crop for colonists to export, discovering deposits of gold or silver, or raiding Spanish treasure ships. Such hopes failed to appreciate the difficulty of adapting English expectations to New World realities. The Jamestown settlement, named for the king, struggled to survive for nearly two decades until the royal government replaced the private Virginia Company, which never earned a profit.

The Fragile Jamestown Settlement

King James believed that England could encroach on the outskirts of Spain's New World empire. An influential advocate of colonization claimed that "God hath reserved" the lands "lying north of Florida" to be brought "unto Christian civility by the English nation." The king acted upon this sentiment by granting the Virginia Company a royal license to poach on both Spanish claims and the chiefdom of Powhatan, who ruled about fifteen thousand Algonquian Indians near the coast of the Chesapeake Bay.

English merchants pooled their capital and shared risks by investing in joint-stock companies like the Virginia Company. The London investors in the Virginia Company hoped not just to trade but also to found an empire that would strengthen England. A proponent of colonization claimed that colonies would provide work for swarms of poor "valiant youths [in England who were] rusting and hurtfull by lack of employment." As colonists, these poor English youth could work, earn wages, and buy English goods while sending back resources to England that otherwise had to be imported from elsewhere.

In pursuit of this plan, the ships *Susan Constant*, *Discovery*, and *Godspeed* carried 144 English colonists toward Virginia in December 1606. A few weeks after they arrived at the mouth of Chesapeake Bay in April 1607, they went ashore on a small peninsula of the territory ruled by Powhatan, where they quickly built a fort, the first building in Jamestown. The fort showed the colonists' awareness that they needed to protect themselves from Indians and Spaniards. Spain planned to wipe out Jamestown, but never did. Powhatan's people, however, defended Virginia as their own. For weeks, the new settlers and Powhatan's warriors skirmished. English firearms repelled Indian attacks, but the Indians' superior numbers and knowledge of the wilderness made it risky for settlers to venture far beyond the fort.

The settlers soon confronted invisible dangers: disease and starvation. Saltwater and freshwater mixed in the swampy marshland surrounding Jamestown, creating an ecological zone where diseases thrived, especially since the colonists neglected careful sanitary habits. During the summer, many of the Englishmen lay "night and day groaning in every corner of the Fort most pittiful to heare," wrote one of the settlers. The colonists increased their misery by bickering among

◀ **Secotan Village** This engraving was copied from an original drawing John White made in 1585 when he visited the village of Secotan on the coast of North Carolina. The drawing shows daily life in the village, which may have resembled one of Powhatan's settlements. This drawing conveys the message that Secotan was orderly, settled, religious, harmonious, and peaceful, and very different from English villages. Service Historique de la Marine, Vincennes, France/Bridgeman Images.

READING THE IMAGE: What does this image say about Indian life in Secotan?

CONNECTIONS: How did Indian society differ from the English tobacco society that emerged later?

themselves, leaving crops unplanted and food supplies shrinking. "For the most part [the colonists] died of meere famine," a settler wrote; "there were never Englishmen left in a forreigne Countrey in such miserie as wee were in this new discovered Virginia."

Powhatan's people came to the rescue of the weakened and demoralized Englishmen. Early in September 1607, they began to bring corn to the colony for barter. Accustomed to eating food derived from wheat, English people considered corn the food "of the barbarous Indians which know no better . . . a more convenient food for swine than for man." The hungry colonists soon overcame their prejudice against corn. Jamestown leader Captain John Smith recalled that the settlers "would have sould their soules" for half a basket of Powhatan's corn. Indians' corn acquired by both trade and plunder managed to keep thirty-eight of the original settlers alive until a fresh supply of food and 120 more colonists arrived from England in January 1608. One colonist moaned that "this place [is] a meere plantacion of sorrowes and Cropp of trobles, having been plentifull in nothing but want and wanting nothing but plenty." The Virginia Company sent hundreds of new settlers to Jamestown each year, each of them eager to find the promised paradise. But most settlers went instead to early graves.

| How did tobacco influence Chesapeake society? | Why did Chesapeake society change by the 1670s? | Why did a slave labor system develop in England's southern colonies? | Conclusion: How did export crops contribute to the growth of the southern colonies? |

◄ Pocahontas in England Pocahontas, one of Powhatan's daughters, married colonist John Rolfe and traveled to England in 1616, where she posed for this portrait dressed in English clothing, the only likeness of her that survives. The portrait captures the novelty of England for Pocahontas and of Pocahontas for the English. The portrait uses her Algonquian name, "Matoaks," as well as her adopted English name, "Rebecka." She died in England soon after the portrait was made. Private Collection / Peter Newark American Pictures / Bridgeman Images.

Cooperation and Conflict between Natives and Newcomers

Powhatan's people stayed in contact with English settlers but maintained their distance. For one thing, the colonists smelled bad since they rarely bathed, unlike the Indians. The Virginia Company boasted that the settlers bought from the Indians "the pearles of earth [corn] and [gave] to them the pearles of heaven [Christianity]." In fact, few Indians became Christians, and the English devoted little effort to converting them. Marriage between Indian women and English men was rare, despite the tiny number of English women in Virginia during the early years. Few settlers bothered to learn the Indians' languages.

Powhatan's people regarded the English with suspicion for good reason. Although the settlers often made friendly overtures to the Indians, they did not hesitate to use their guns and swords to enforce English notions of proper Indian behavior. When Indians refused to trade their corn to the settlers, the English pillaged their villages and confiscated their corn.

The Indians retaliated against English violence, but for fifteen years they did not organize an all-out assault on the European intruders, probably for several reasons. Although Christianity held few attractions for the Indians, the power of the settlers' God impressed them. One chief told a colonist that "he did believe that our [English] God as much exceeded theirs as our guns did their bows and arrows." Powhatan probably concluded that these powerful strangers would make better allies than enemies. As allies, the English strengthened Powhatan's rule over the tribes in the region.

The colonists also traded with Powhatan's people, usually exchanging European goods for corn. Native Virginians eagerly traded corn to obtain the intruders' iron and steel knives, axes, and pots.

But why were the settlers unable to feed themselves for more than a decade? First, as the high death rate suggests, many settlers were too sick to be productive. Second, very few farmers came to Virginia in the early years. Instead, most of the newcomers were gentlemen and their servants who, in the words of one colonist, "never did know what a day's work was." The proportion of gentlemen in Virginia in the early years was six times greater than in England, a reflection of the Virginia Company's urgent need for investors and settlers. John Smith declared repeatedly that in Virginia "there is no country to pillage [as in New Spain]. . . . All you can expect from [Virginia] must be by labor." For years, however, colonists clung to ideas that made more sense in labor-rich England than in labor-poor Virginia.

CONSIDER CAUSE AND EFFECT

Why was the early Virginia colony so fragile? How did the colonists overcome that fragility?

How did settlers' encounters with Native Americans shape the colony of Virginia?

The Virginia colony created difficulties for Powhatan's chiefdom. Steady contact between natives and newcomers spread European diseases among the Indians, who suffered deadly epidemics. To produce enough corn for trade with the English, Indian women had to spend more time growing and harvesting crops. But from the Indians' viewpoint, the most important fact about the always-hungry colonists was that they were not going away.

Powhatan died in 1618, and his brother Opechancanough replaced him as supreme chief. In 1622, Opechancanough organized an all-out assault on the English settlers. As an English colonist observed, "When the day appointed for the massacre arrived [March 22], a number of savages visited many of our people in their dwellings, and while partaking with them of their meal[,] the savages, at a given signal, drew their weapons and fell upon us murdering and killing everybody they could reach[,] sparing neither women nor children." In all, the Indians killed 347 colonists, nearly a third of the English population. But the attack failed to dislodge the colonists. Instead, in the years to come the settlers unleashed a murderous campaign of Indian extermination that pushed the Indians beyond the frontiers of white settlement. After 1622, most colonists considered Indians their perpetual enemies. As an Englishman declared, the "murdered carcasses" of the colonists "speak, proclaim, and cry, *This our earth is truly English, and therefore this Land [of Virginia] is justly yours O English.*"

From Private Company to Royal Government

In the immediate aftermath of the 1622 uprising, the survivors became demoralized because, as one explained, the "massacre killed all our Countrie . . . [and] burst the heart of all the rest." The disaster prompted a royal investigation of affairs in Virginia. The investigators discovered that the high death rate among the colonists was caused more by disease and mismanagement than by Indian raids. In 1624, King James canceled the charter of the Virginia Company and made Virginia a **royal colony**. Now, the king, rather than the private investors of the Virginia Company, ruled the colony, an arrangement that lasted until 1776.

The king appointed the governor of Virginia and his council, but other features of local government established under the Virginia Company remained intact. In 1619, for example, the company inaugurated the **House of Burgesses**, an assembly of representatives (called burgesses) elected by the colony's inhabitants. Under the new royal government, laws passed by the burgesses had to be approved by the king's bureaucrats in England, rather than by the Virginia Company. Otherwise, the House of Burgesses continued as before, making it the oldest representative lawmaking assembly in the English colonies. Under the new royal government, all free adult men in Virginia could vote for the House of Burgesses, which was far more democratic than the English House of Commons.

The failure of the Virginia Company marked the end of the first phase of colonization of the Chesapeake region. From the first 105 adventurers in 1607, the population had grown to about twelve hundred by 1624. Despite death rates higher than the worst epidemics in London, new settlers still came. Their arrival and King James's willingness to take over the struggling colony reflected a fundamental change in Virginia. After years of experimentation, it was finally becoming clear that English settlers could make a fortune in Virginia by growing tobacco.

royal colony
A colony ruled by a king or queen and governed by officials appointed to serve the monarchy and represent its interests.

House of Burgesses
Virginia's assembly of representatives elected by inhabitants that was established by the Virginia Company and continued after the settlement became a royal colony.

COMPARE AND CONTRAST
How did Virginia's government change when it became a royal colony?

QUICK REVIEW

What explains Powhatan's responses to English colonists?

| How did tobacco influence Chesapeake society? | Why did Chesapeake society change by the 1670s? | Why did a slave labor system develop in England's southern colonies? | Conclusion: How did export crops contribute to the growth of the southern colonies? |

How did tobacco influence Chesapeake society?

Tobacco grew wild in the New World, and Native Americans used it for thousands of years before Europeans arrived. Many sixteenth-century European explorers noticed the Indians' habit of "drinking smoke." Sailors returning from the New World "suck in as much smoke as they can," one Spaniard observed, "[and] in this way they say that their hunger and thirst are allayed, their strength is restored and their spirits are refreshed; [and] . . . their brains are lulled by a joyous intoxication." That joyous intoxication—"a bewitching quality," England's King James called it—made tobacco irresistible to most Europeans.

At the beginning of the seventeenth century, tobacco was scarce and therefore expensive. In 1603, for example, England imported only about 25,000 pounds of tobacco, all from New Spain. By 1700, England imported more than 35 million pounds of tobacco, almost all from the Chesapeake colonies. The huge increase in the tobacco supply caused prices to plummet. A quantity of tobacco that sold for a dollar in 1600 cost less than two and a half cents by 1700. The low prices made possible by bumper crops harvested by planters in the Chesapeake transformed tobacco consumption in England and elsewhere in Europe. Annual per capita tobacco use in England grew more than 200-fold during the seventeenth century. As the English king observed, the Chesapeake colonies were "wholly built upon smoke."

By 1700, nearly 100,000 colonists lived in the Chesapeake region, including present-day Virginia, Maryland, and northern North Carolina (**Map 3.1**). Although the colonists differed in wealth, landholding, access to labor, and religion, they shared a dedication to growing tobacco. In 1700, they exported more than thirty-five million pounds of tobacco, five times more per capita than in 1620. Chesapeake colonists clearly mastered the demands of tobacco agriculture. The "Stinkinge Weede" (a common seventeenth-century term for tobacco) also mastered the colonists. Settlers lived by the rhythms of tobacco agriculture. Their endless need for labor attracted droves of English indentured servants to grueling work in tobacco fields with the promise of eventual freedom.

Tobacco Agriculture

Initially, the Virginia Company had no plans to grow tobacco. "As for tobacco," one colonist recalled, "we never then dreamt of it." Colonist John Rolfe planted West Indian tobacco seeds in 1612 and learned that they flourished in Virginia. By 1617, the colonists had grown enough tobacco to send the first commercial shipment to England, where it sold for a high price. After that, Virginia pivoted from a colony of rather aimless adventurers to a society of dedicated tobacco planters. A demanding crop, tobacco required close attention and a great deal of hand labor year-round. Like the Indians, the colonists "cleared" fields by cutting a ring of bark around each tree

◀ **Tobacco Cutter** Planters in the southern colonies of British North America shipped tobacco to England, where tobacconists used machines like the one shown here to chop the leaves into small pieces for smoking. Tobacco merchants often flavored the chopped leaves with oils, herbs, and spices. The illustration on the side of the cutter refers to the Native American origins of tobacco. Historisch Museum Haarlem.

How did settlers' encounters with Native Americans shape the colony of Virginia?

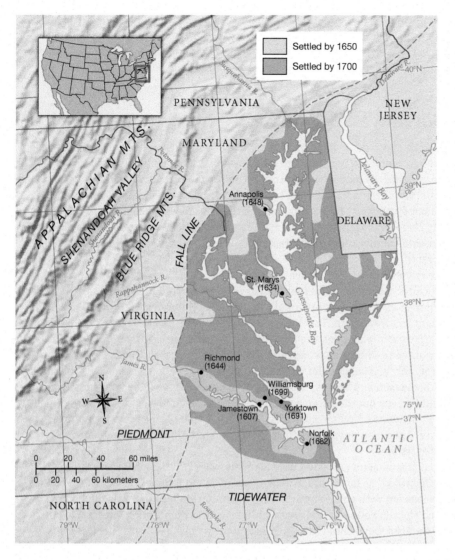

MAP 3.1 ▲ Chesapeake Colonies in the Seventeenth Century

This map illustrates the close association between land and water in the settlement of the Chesapeake in the seventeenth century. The fall line indicates the limit of navigable water, where rapids and falls prevented travel farther upstream.

(a procedure known as "girdling"), which killed the tree. Girdling brought sunlight to clearings but left fields studded with tree stumps that made plowing nearly impossible. Instead, colonists tilled their tobacco fields with heavy hoes. To plant, a visitor observed, farmers "just make holes [with a stick] into which they drop the seeds," much as the Indians did. Colonists young and old enjoyed the fruits of their labor. "Everyone smokes while working or idling," a traveler reported, including "men, women, girls, and boys, from the age of seven years." English settlers worked hard because their labor promised greater rewards in the Chesapeake region than in England. One colonist proclaimed that "the dirt of this Province affords as great a profit to the general Inhabitant, as the Gold of Peru doth to . . . the Spaniard." Although he exaggerated, a hired man could in fact expect to earn two or three times more in Virginia's tobacco fields than in England. Better still, in Virginia land was so abundant that it was extremely cheap compared with land in England.

| **How did tobacco influence Chesapeake society?** | Why did Chesapeake society change by the 1670s? | Why did a slave labor system develop in England's southern colonies? | Conclusion: How did export crops contribute to the growth of the southern colonies? |

By the mid-seventeenth century, common laborers could buy a hundred acres of land for less than their annual wages—which was impossible in England. To encourage settlement, the royal government even gave new settlers who paid their own transportation to the Chesapeake a grant of fifty acres of free land, called a "headright."

A Servant Labor System

Headrights, cheap land, and high wages gave poor English folk like Anne Orthwood powerful incentives to immigrate to the New World. Yet many poor people could not scrape together the money to pay for a trip across the Atlantic. Their poverty and the colonists' crying need for labor led to the creation of a servant labor system.

About 80 percent of the immigrants to the Chesapeake during the seventeenth century came as indentured servants. Instead of a society based on slave labor, the seventeenth-century Chesapeake region was mainly a society of white servants and ex-servants.

Relatively few African slaves were brought to the Chesapeake in the half-century after settlement. The first known Africans arrived in Virginia in 1619 aboard the *White Lion*, an English privateer that seized them from a Portuguese slave ship bound for South America. The "20. And odd Negroes," as one colonist called them, had been captured and enslaved in Angola in west-central Africa. A few more slaves trickled into the Chesapeake region during the next several decades. Until the 1670s, however, only a small number of enslaved people labored in Chesapeake tobacco fields. Some men and women of African descent occasionally became indentured servants, served out their terms of servitude, and became free. A few slaves escaped bondage by purchasing their freedom. These people were exceptions, however. Almost all people of African descent in the Chesapeake region were enslaved for life.

The great majority of indentured servants were white people from England, like Anne Orthwood. To buy passage aboard a ship bound for the Chesapeake, a person had to come up with about a year's wages. Earning wages at all was difficult in England since job opportunities were shrinking. Many landowners needed fewer farmhands because they shifted from growing crops to raising sheep in newly enclosed fields. Unemployed people drifted into English seaports such as Bristol, Liverpool, and London, where they learned about the plentiful jobs in North America. Unable to pay for their trip across the Atlantic, poor immigrants agreed to a contract called an indenture, which functioned as a form of credit. By signing an indenture, an immigrant borrowed the cost of transportation to the Chesapeake from a merchant or ship captain in England. To repay this loan, the indentured person agreed to work in the colonies as a servant for four to seven years.

Once the indentured person arrived in the colonies, the merchant or ship captain sold his contract for the immigrant's labor to a local tobacco planter. The planter paid about twice the cost of transportation and agreed to provide the servant with food and shelter. When the indenture expired, the planter owed the former servant "freedom dues," usually a few barrels of corn and a suit of clothes.

Ideally, indentures allowed poor immigrants like Anne Orthwood to trade their most valuable assets—their freedom and their ability to work—for a trip to the New World and a period of servitude followed by freedom in a land of opportunity. "What's a four years Servitude," a Maryland servant asked, "to advantage a man all the remainder of his dayes?" Planters reaped more immediate benefits. Servants meant more hands to

indentured servants
Poor immigrants who signed contracts known as indentures, in which they agreed to four to seven years of labor in North America in exchange for transportation from England, as well as food and shelter during their period of servitude.

"'What's a four years Servitude,' a Maryland servant asked, 'to advantage a man all the remainder of his dayes?'"

How did settlers' encounters with Native Americans shape the colony of Virginia?

grow more tobacco. A planter expected a servant to grow enough tobacco in one year to cover the price the planter paid for the indenture. Servants' labor during the remaining three to six years of the indenture promised a handsome profit for the planter. No wonder one Virginian declared, "Our principall wealth . . . consisteth in servants." Although many servants died before their indentures expired, like Orthwood did, planters still profited because they received a **headright** of fifty acres of land from the colonial government for every newly purchased servant.

About three out of four servants were young men between the ages of fifteen and twenty-five when they arrived in the Chesapeake. Typically, they shared the desperation of sixteen-year-old Francis Haires, who indentured himself for seven years because, according to his contract, "his father and mother and All friends [are] dead and he [is] a miserable wandering boy." Like Francis, most servants had no special training or skills, although the majority had some experience with agricultural work. "Hunger and fear of prisons bring to us onely such servants as have been brought up to no Art of Trade," one Virginia planter complained. A skilled craftsman could obtain a shorter indenture, but few risked coming to the colonies since their prospects were better in England.

Women were almost as rare as skilled craftsmen in the Chesapeake and much more desired. In the early days of the tobacco boom, the Virginia Company shipped young single women servants to the colony as prospective wives for male settlers willing to pay "120 weight [pounds] of the best leaf tobacco for each of them." The company reasoned that, as one official wrote in 1622, "the plantation can never flourish till families be planted, and the respect of wives and children fix the people on the soil." Even so, women remained a small minority of the Chesapeake population until the late seventeenth century.

The servant labor system reinforced the gender imbalance. Although female servants cost about the same as men and generally served for the same length of time, planters preferred male servants because, as one explained, they were "the mor[e] excellent and yousefull Cretuers" for field work. Servant women hoed and harvested tobacco fields and did household chores, such as cooking, washing, cleaning, gardening, and milking.

headright
Fifty acres of free land granted by the Virginia Company to planters for each indentured servant they purchased.

PLACE EVENTS IN CONTEXT
How did economic conditions in England influence immigration to the Chesapeake?

The Rigors of Servitude

Servants—whether men or women, whites or blacks, English or African—tended to work together and socialize together. In general, common day-to-day experiences caused servants—regardless of their race or gender—to consider themselves somewhat separate from free people, whose ranks they longed to join eventually.

Servant life was harsh by the standards of seventeenth-century England and even by the frontier standards of the Chesapeake. Unlike servants in England, Chesapeake servants like Anne Orthwood had no control over who purchased their labor and them—for the duration of their indenture. They were "sold here upp and downe like horses," one observer reported. But tobacco planters' need for labor silenced complaints about treating servants as property.

"The Servants of this Province," one boasted, "live more like Freemen than the most Mechanick Apprentices in London, wanting for nothing that is convenient and necessary, and . . . are extraordinary well used and respected." Some servants became free and prospered, as Anne Orthwood's master William Kendall did. Many other servants did not feel well used and respected when confronted by the rigors of labor in tobacco fields. Severe laws aimed to keep servants in their proper places. James Revel, an eighteen-year-old indentured to a Virginia tobacco planter, declared he was a "slave" sent to hoe "tobacco plants all day" from dawn to dusk. Punishments for servants' petty crimes stretched servitude far beyond the original terms of indenture.

■ Farm or plantation

Hog Island
Jamestown
James River

Settlement Patterns along the James River

How did tobacco influence Chesapeake society?	Why did Chesapeake society change by the 1670s?	Why did a slave labor system develop in England's southern colonies?	Conclusion: How did export crops contribute to the growth of the southern colonies?

Enslavement by Marriage

A white indentured servant woman named Eleanor Butler—Irish Nell—immigrated to Maryland and married a slave named Charles in 1681. More than eighty years later, descendants of Irish Nell and Charles named Mary and William Butler petitioned a Maryland court to free them from "a state of perpetual Slavery" in which they were held by a planter named Richard Boarman. Since seventeenth-century documents that could prove the race and status of Irish Nell and Charles did not exist, the court collected testimony in 1767 from white witnesses who knew the couple or had heard about them. The court eventually refused to grant freedom to Mary and William Butler, but the testimony the court gathered about Irish Nell and Charles, excerpted here, reveals assumptions about race, status, and gender that were common in the seventeenth-century Chesapeake region.

Samuel Abell, Junior, 49: said "that . . . Mr Richard Boarman the Defendant . . . told him . . . that Lord Baltimore a good many years ago, came into this Country to live and brought with him a woman named Butler . . . to wash and Iron and boarded with his Grand Father, and that sometime after they had been there, the said woman called Butler fell in Love with one of his Grand Father's Negroes and wanted to marry him, and upon my Lord, being informed that she wanted to marry the negro, my Lord sent for her in, and chid [chided] her, and told her that if she married the negro she would by that means enslave herself, and her posterity, upon which the woman told him that she had rather marry the negro under them circumstances, than to marry his Lordship with all his Country, upon which he told her she might go and marry him, and be dammed, accordingly she went and was married to the negro. . . . [Abell] asked . . . [Boarman] if there were not a good many of that Family; he said there was about one hundred and twenty of them, but the negroes by their Count made near three hundred of them, for that they had taken even some Salt water [African-born] negroes, into their count, and upon asking . . . [Boarman] how they came to be slaves as they came of a white woman; he said he claimed them by a Law of this province whereby white women marrying of slaves should become slaves to the house of her Husband's master, and he took out of his pocket a paper which he said was a copy of the act, and it appeared to be a copy of an act."

Thomas Bowling, 63: said "that . . . Irish Nell told [his mother] the day she expected to be married, she was early up intending to clear the house out, and a Gentleman . . . asked her if she was the Girl that was to be married that day to the negro? She said Yes, he then chid her, and told her, she would put a mark by that upon her Children and bring them into Slavery, that if she would marry a white man her Children might be of Credit in the world, otherwise they wou'd be in Slavery, upon which she fell a crying, and said it was to her Choice, she wou'd rather have Charles than have your Lordship."

Edward Edelen, 50: said "that . . . his Father . . . heard Lord Baltimore ask for Eleanor Butler a servant woman of Major Boarmans, when she came to him he said, I understand you are going to be married today to Negro Charles, he said to her what a pitty so likely a young Girl as you are should fling herself away so as to marry a negro, and he said not only that, but you'l make slaves of your Children and their posterity."

Benjamin Jameson, 48: said "that . . . [he] heard old Mrs Ruthom . . . say, that she was at Major Boarmans when the

---

Richard Higby, for example, received six extra years of servitude for killing three hogs. After midcentury, the Virginia legislature added three or more years to the indentures of most servants by requiring them to serve until they were twenty-four years old.

Women servants like Anne Orthwood were subject to special restrictions. They could not marry until their servitude expired. A servant woman, the law assumed, could not serve two masters at the same time: one who owned her indentured labor and another who was her husband. Since men greatly outnumbered women, servant women were pressured to engage in sexual relations regardless of marriage. As a rule, if a woman servant gave birth to a child, she had to serve two extra years and pay a fine, because lawmakers believed caring for her child would rob her indenture owner of part of her labor. If she died, as Anne Orthwood did, her child would become a servant until the child turned twenty-one, as Anne's son Jasper did.

How did settlers' encounters with Native Americans shape the colony of Virginia?

same Nell and Charles . . . was married . . . that she heard several people wish them much Joy, and that she behaved as a Bride, and that he has heard his mother say that . . . my Lord asked . . . [Nell] how she would like to go to bed to a Negro? She answered him that she rather go to bed to Charles than his Lordship."

Mary Crossen, 74: said "that she knew Eleanor Butler a white woman commonly called Irish Nell . . . that she does not know that Nell was a free woman but appeared to her, to do as she pleased, that she was a hard labouring body, and made Good Crops."

William Simpson, 49: said . . . "that he remembers Nell Butler and Negro Charles, and they passed as man and wife and called themselves so, and that Charles he believes was a salt water negro, and always understood was a slave of Major William Boarmans."

Joseph Jameson, 52: said "that he knew Irish Nell very well, that she lived . . . within a [mile?] of his Fathers, that she had a Daughter living with her, who died as a slave of Mr Boarman, and being asked how he knew she was a slave? Says she worked among the other slaves and lived as they did, she there died . . . that all the Descendants of the said Nell that he knew lived and died slaves they working and living as such except the said Kate who he had heard from the neighbour-hood . . . has purchased her freedom."

William McPherson, 60: said "that he knew Eleanor Butler, commonly called Irish Nell about fifty years ago . . . that he has seen Nell and Charles together and the Negro Charles called the said Nell his old woman, and she called him her old man, that he never knew of the said Nell being held as a slave, that when Charles went to [John] Saunders's quarter Nell went there also and acted as a Cook . . . that [when] John Saunders hired Negro Charles . . . that Eleanor Butler either came with him or followed him there and acted as a free woman and took in spinning and acted as a midwife . . . that . . . he has heard, that the Children of Nell . . . were held as slaves."

Source: Depositions from *Butler v. Boarman*, 1H. & McH. 371 (1770), Provincial Court, Judgment Record, Liber DD 17, Folio 236–243, Maryland State Archives.

Questions for Analysis

ASK HISTORICAL QUESTIONS: Why were Irish Nell and her descendants enslaved? What assumptions about race, gender, and social order contributed to their enslavement?

ANALYZE THE EVIDENCE: According to the witnesses, why did Irish Nell marry Charles? Why did Charles marry Irish Nell? What did it mean to the witnesses that Irish Nell was a white woman? To what extent are the testimonies reliable evidence?

CONSIDER THE CONTEXT: How did the witnesses learn about Irish Nell and Charles? What do the testimonies suggest about the neighborhood where Irish Nell and Charles resided? What do they suggest about the relationship between servants and slaves?

RECOGNIZE VIEWPOINTS: Why did Lord Baltimore warn Irish Nell about marrying Charles? How did Nell's viewpoint differ from that of Lord Baltimore and other white Marylanders?

Such harsh punishments reflected four fundamental realities of the servant labor system. First, planters' need for labor caused them to demand as much labor as they could get from their servants. Second, servants hoped to survive their servitude and use their freedom to obtain land and start a family. Third, since servants saw them-selves as free people temporarily in servitude, they often made grudging, halfhearted workers. Finally, planters put up with this arrangement because the alternatives were less desirable.

Planters could not easily hire free men and women because land was readily avail-able and free people preferred to work for themselves on their own land. Nor could planters depend on much labor from family members because families were few, were started late, and thus produced few children. And until the 1680s and 1690s, enslaved Africans were expensive and hard to come by. Before then, masters who wanted to

UNDERSTAND POINTS OF VIEW

How did the expectations of indentured servants differ from those of tobacco planters?

How did tobacco influence Chesapeake society?	Why did Chesapeake society change by the 1670s?	Why did a slave labor system develop in England's southern colonies?	Conclusion: How did export crops contribute to the growth of the southern colonies?

Bristol Docks This painting of the docks in Bristol, England, portrays a scene common at ports throughout the seventeenth-century Atlantic world. Tobacco flooded into Bristol in the seventeenth century while Bristol merchants also became active in the African slave trade, trading British goods on the West African coast for slaves, who were then taken to the New World to be sold to eager sugar and tobacco planters. Bristol Museum and Art Gallery, UK/Bridgeman Images.

grow more tobacco had few alternatives to buying indentured servants. **(See "Analyzing Historical Evidence: Enslavement by Marriage" on page 64.)**

Cultivating Land and Faith

Villages and small towns dotted the rural land-scape of seventeenth-century England, but in the Chesapeake, towns were few and far between. Instead, tobacco farms occupied small clearings surrounded by hundreds of acres of wilderness. Since tobacco was a labor-intensive crop that quickly exhausted the fertility of the soil, each farmer cultivated only 5 or 10 percent of his land at any one time. Tobacco planters sought land with access to a navigable river in order to minimize the work of transporting the heavy barrels of tobacco onto ships. A settled region of the Chesapeake was therefore a network of tobacco farms located near waterways.

Most Chesapeake colonists were Protestants rather than Catholics. All English colonists were required to attend worship services on Sunday and to conform to the rituals and beliefs of the Church of England. Few ministers migrated to the Chesapeake, however, and many of them did not uphold high standards of piety and devotion. Certainly, some colonists took their religion seriously. Church courts punished sinners and served notice on parishioners who spent Sundays "goeing a fishing." But on the whole, religion did not awaken the zeal of Chesapeake settlers, certainly not as it did for New England settlers in these same years (as discussed in chapter 4). The religion of the Chesapeake colonists was Anglican in word and form, but their faith lay in the turbulent, competitive, high-stakes gamble of survival as tobacco planters.

Like Virginia, the Catholic colony of Maryland worshipped at the altar of tobacco. In 1632, England's King Charles I granted his Catholic friend Lord Baltimore about six and a half million acres in the northern Chesapeake region. Lord Baltimore intended to create a refuge for Catholics, who suffered severe discrimination in England. He fitted out two ships, the *Ark* and the *Dove*; gathered about 150 settlers; and sent them to the new colony, where they arrived in March 1634. Maryland, however, failed to live up to Baltimore's hopes. The colony's population grew very slowly for twenty years, and most settlers were Protestants rather than Catholics. The religious turmoil of the Puritan Revolution in England (see chapter 4) spilled across the Atlantic, creating conflict between Maryland's few Catholics—most of them wealthy and prominent—and the Protestant majority, most of them neither wealthy nor prominent. Maryland's leaders hoped to attract decent people as servants, unlike those in Virginia, described by one Marylander as "the scumme of the people, . . . vagrants and runnewayes from their m[aste]rs, deabauched, idle, lazie squanderers, [and] jaylbirds." During the 1660s, however, Maryland began to attract settlers very much like Virginia's, and most

How did settlers' encounters with Native Americans shape the colony of Virginia?

of them were Protestants. Although Catholics continued to exert influence in Maryland, the colony's society, economy, politics, and culture became nearly indistinguishable from Virginia's. Both colonies shared a devotion to tobacco, the true faith of the Chesapeake.

QUICK REVIEW

Why did most immigrants to the Chesapeake come as indentured servants?

Why did Chesapeake society change by the 1670s?

The servant labor system increased inequality in Chesapeake society and led to Bacon's Rebellion in 1676. The rebellion prompted reforms that stabilized relations between elite planters and their lesser neighbors. The reforms paved the way for a social hierarchy that emphasized racial differences and diverted attention from inequality in landholding and wealth. Amid this social and political evolution, Chesapeake colonists' dedication to growing tobacco did not change.

Social and Economic Polarization

The first half of the seventeenth century in the Chesapeake was the era of the yeoman—a free farmer who owned a small plot of land sufficient to support a family and worked largely by servants and a few family members. A small number of elite planters had larger estates and commanded ten or more servants. But for the first several decades, few men lived long enough to accumulate fortunes that set them much apart from their neighbors.

Until midcentury, the principal division in Chesapeake society was less between rich and poor planters than between free farmers and servants. Although these two groups contrasted sharply in their legal and economic status, their daily lives had many similarities. Servants looked forward to the time when their indentures would expire and they, too, would become free and eventually own land.

Three major developments splintered this rough frontier equality during the third quarter of the century. First, as planters grew more and more tobacco, the ample supply depressed tobacco prices in European markets. Cheap tobacco reduced planters' profits and made saving enough to become landowners more difficult for freed servants. Second, because the death rate in the Chesapeake colonies declined, more and more servants survived their indentures, causing landless freemen to become more numerous and discontented. Third, declining death rates also encouraged the formation of a planter elite. By living longer, successful planters became even more successful. The wealthiest planters also began to buy slaves as well as to set themselves up as merchants.

By the 1670s, the society of the Chesapeake had become polarized. Landowners—the planter elite and the more numerous yeoman planters—clustered around one pole. Landless colonists, mainly free former servants, surrounded the other pole. Each group eyed the other with suspicion and mistrust. For the most part, planters saw landless freemen as a dangerous rabble rather than as fellow colonists with legitimate grievances. Virginia's governor William Berkeley feared the political threat to the ruling elite posed by "six parts in seven [of Virginia colonists who] . . . are poor, indebted, discontented, and armed."

CHRONOLOGY

ca. 1600–1650
– Yeoman farmers predominate in Chesapeake region.

1644
– Opechancanough leads second uprising.

1650–1660
– Navigation Acts require colonial products be shipped through English ports on English ships.

1661–1676
– No elections called in House of Burgesses.

1670
– House of Burgesses outlaws voting by poor men.

1676
– Bacon's Rebellion erupts.

| How did tobacco influence Chesapeake society? | **Why did Chesapeake society change by the 1670s?** | Why did a slave labor system develop in England's southern colonies? | Conclusion: How did export crops contribute to the growth of the southern colonies? |

Government Policies and Political Conflict

In general, government enforced the difference between servants and masters with an iron fist. Poor men complained that "nether the Governor nor Counsell could or would doe any poore men right, but that they would shew favor to great men and wronge the poore." Most Chesapeake colonists, like most Europeans, assumed that "great men" should bear the responsibilities of government. Until 1670, all freemen could vote, and they routinely elected prosperous planters to the legislature. No former servant served in either the governor's council or the House of Burgesses after 1640. Yet poor Virginians believed that the "great men" used government offices to promote their selfish personal interests rather than governing impartially.

As discontent grew among poor colonists during the 1660s and 1670s, colonial officials tried to keep political power in safe hands. Beginning in 1661, for example, Governor William Berkeley did not call an election for the House of Burgesses for fifteen years. In 1670, the House of Burgesses outlawed voting by poor men, allowing only men who were both landowners and heads of households to vote.

The king also began to tighten the royal government's control of trade in order to strengthen the monarchy and to collect more revenue from the Chesapeake colonies. A series of English laws funneled colonial trade exclusively into the hands of English merchants and shippers. The **Navigation Acts** of 1650 and 1651 specified that colonial goods had to be transported in English ships with predominantly English crews. A 1660 act required colonial products to be sent only to English ports. A 1663 law provided that all goods sent to the colonies must pass through English ports and be carried on English ships manned by English sailors. Taken together, these navigation acts reflected the English government's belief in mercantilism, namely that what was good for England (channeling all trade through English hands) should determine colonial policy.

Mercantilism underlay the import duty on tobacco imposed by the Navigation Act of 1660. The law placed an import tax of two pence on every pound of colonial tobacco brought into England, which was about as much as a Chesapeake farmer received for growing tobacco. The import tax gave the king a major financial interest in the size of the tobacco crop, which yielded about a quarter of all English import taxes during the 1660s.

CONSIDER CAUSE AND EFFECT

How did Virginia's declining death rate during the seventeenth century affect the colony's society?

Navigation Acts

English laws passed in the 1650s and 1660s requiring that English colonial goods be shipped through English ports on English ships in order to benefit English merchants, shippers, and seamen.

ANALYZE EVIDENCE

What evidence indicates that Virginia's social and economic divisions grew in the 1660s and 1670s?

Bacon's Rebellion

Colonists, like residents of European monarchies, accepted class divisions and inequality as long as they believed that government officials ruled for the general good. When rulers violated that expectation, ordinary people believed rebellion was justified. In 1676, **Bacon's Rebellion** began as a dispute over Virginia's Indian policy. Before it ended, the rebellion caused upheaval throughout Chesapeake politics and society, leaving in its wake death, destruction, and hostility between the great planters and their poorer neighbors.

Opechancanough, the Algonquian chief who had led the Indian uprising of 1622 in Virginia, organized another surprise attack in 1644, killing about five hundred Virginia colonists in two days. During the next two years of bitter fighting, the colonists eventually gained the upper hand and murdered the old chief. After the war, the Indians gave up all claims to land already settled by the English. In return, the Indians received a guarantee that wilderness land beyond the fringe of English settlement belonged exclusively to the Indians. The colonial government hoped this arrangement would reduce contact between settlers and Indians and maintain peace.

The policy might have worked if the Chesapeake population had not grown. But the number of land-hungry colonists multiplied. In their quest for land, they encroached steadily on Indian land. During the 1660s and 1670s, violence between colonists and

Bacon's Rebellion

A rebellion in 1676 led by frontier settler Nathaniel Bacon, who sought to attack both Indians and wealthy planters favored by the Virginia government.

How did settlers' encounters with Native Americans shape the colony of Virginia?

▶ **Governor William Berkeley** This portrait illustrates the distance that separated Governor Berkeley and the other Chesapeake grandees from poor planters, landless freemen, servants, and slaves. Berkeley's clothing suited the genteel homes of Jamestown, not the rustic dwellings of lesser Virginians. His haughty, satisfied demeanor suggests his lack of sympathy for poor Virginians, who, he was certain, deserved their lot. National Gallery of Art, Washington, D.C./ SuperStock.

Indians repeatedly flared along the frontier. The government, located in the tidewater region near the coast, far from the danger of Indian raids, tried to calm the conflict and reestablish peace.

Frontier settlers thirsted for revenge against what their leader, Nathaniel Bacon, termed "the protected and Darling Indians." Bacon proclaimed his "Design not only to ruine and extirpate all Indians in Generall but all Manner of Trade and Commerce with them." Bacon also urged the colonists to "see what spounges have suckt up the Publique Treasure." He charged that grandees, or elite planters, operated the government for their private gain, a charge that made sense to many colonists. In fact, officeholders had profited enough to buy slaves to replace their servants.

By the 1660s, government officials owned about 70 percent of all the colony's slaves. Bacon voiced the grievances of the small planters and poor farmers against both the Indians and the colonial rulers in Jamestown. **(See "Spotlight: Why Did English Colonists Consider Themselves Superior to Indians and Africans?" on page 70.)**

Hoping to maintain the fragile peace on the frontier in 1676, Governor Berkeley pronounced Bacon a rebel, threatened to punish him for treason, and called for new elections of burgesses who Berkeley believed would support his get-tough policy. To Berkeley's surprise, the elections backfired. Almost all the old burgesses were voted out of office. Replacing them were local leaders, including Bacon, who criticized the rule of the elite planters.

In June 1676, the new legislature passed reform measures known as Bacon's Laws. Among other changes, the laws gave local settlers a voice in setting tax rates, forbade officeholders from demanding bribes or extra fees for carrying out their duties, placed limits on holding more than one office at a time, and restored the vote to all freemen. The reforms motivated elite planters to convince Governor Berkeley that Bacon and his men were a greater threat than Indians.

When Bacon learned that Berkeley had once again branded him a traitor, he declared war against Berkeley and the other grandees. For three months, Bacon's forces fought Indians, destroyed grandees' plantations, and attacked Jamestown. Berkeley's loyalists retaliated by plundering the homes of Bacon's supporters. The fighting continued until Bacon unexpectedly died, most likely from dysentery, and several English ships arrived to increase Berkeley's strength. With the rebellion crushed, Berkeley hanged several of Bacon's allies and destroyed farms that belonged to Bacon's supporters.

The rebellion did nothing to remove the grandees from their positions of power. If anything, it strengthened them. When the king learned of the turmoil in the Chesapeake and its devastating effect on tobacco exports and customs duties, he ordered an investigation. Royal officials replaced Berkeley with a governor more attentive to the king's interests, nullified Bacon's Laws, and imposed an export tax on tobacco as a way to pay the expenses of the colony's government without getting the consent of the tightfisted House of Burgesses.

| How did tobacco influence Chesapeake society? | **Why did Chesapeake society change by the 1670s?** | Why did a slave labor system develop in England's southern colonies? | Conclusion: How did export crops contribute to the growth of the southern colonies? |

Why Did English Colonists Consider Themselves Superior to Indians and Africans?

Were seeds of the racial prejudice that is such a powerful force in American history planted in the seventeenth-century Chesapeake? To answer that question, historians have paid close attention to the language colonists used to describe Indians, Africans, and themselves.

In the mid–1500s, the English adopted the words *Indian* and *Negro* from Spanish, where they had come to mean, respectively, an aboriginal inhabitant of the New World and a black person of African ancestry. Both terms were generic, homogenizing an enormous variety of tribal affiliations, languages, and cultures. Neither term originated with the people to whom it referred. The New England minister Roger Williams, who published a book on Indian languages in 1643, reported, "They have often asked mee, why we call them Indians," a poignant question that reveals the European origins of the term, dating back to Columbus.

After *Indians,* the word the settlers used most frequently to describe Native Americans was *savages.* The Indians were savages in the colonists' eyes because they lacked the traits of English civilization. As one Englishman put it in 1625, the natives of Virginia were "so bad a people, having little of humanitie but shape, ignorant of Civilitie, of Arts, of Religion; more brutish than the beasts they hunt, more wild and unmanly than that unmanned wild countrey, which they range rather than inhabite; captivated also to Satans tyranny in foolish pieties, mad impieties, wicked idlenesse, busie and bloudy wickednesse." Some English colonists counterbalanced this harsh indictment with admiration for certain features of Indian behavior. They praised Indians' calm dignity and poise, their tender love and care for family members, and their simple, independent way of life in apparent harmony with nature.

Color was not emphasized as a feature of the Indians' savagery. During the seventeenth century, colonists never referred to Indians as "red." Instead, they saw Indians' skin color as tawny or tanned, the "Sun's livery," as one settler

▲ This lavish portrait of two seventeenth-century aristocratic ladies illustrates common European attitudes toward Africans. Both ladies appear completely at ease with the black servant boy. They gaze confidently at the viewer while the boy stares at the black lapdog, whose color and protruding eyes he shares, along with an ornamental collar. The portrait suggests that the ladies consider the African boy an inferior pet akin to the dog. RMN–Grand Palais/Art Resource, NY.

In the aftermath of Bacon's Rebellion, tensions between great planters and small farmers moderated. Bacon's Rebellion showed, a governor of Virginia said, that it was necessary "to steer between . . . either an Indian or a civil war." The ruling elite concluded that it was safer for the colonists to fight the Indians than to fight each other, and the government made little effort to restrict settlers' encroachment on Indian land. The export duty on tobacco allowed the colonial government to reduce

How did settlers' encounters with Native Americans shape the colony of Virginia?

wrote. To the English, tanned skin denoted a member of the working class who spent his or her days toiling under the sun. Pale skin was fashionable and signified high status. Many settlers held the view that Indians were innately white, like the English, but in other ways woefully un-English.

Despite their savagery in English eyes, Indians controlled two things colonists desperately wanted: land and peace. Early in the seventeenth century, when English settlements were small and weak, peace with the Indians was a higher priority than land. In this period, English comments on Indian savagery noted the obvious differences between settlers and Indians, but the colonists' need for peace kept them focused on ways to coexist with the Indians. By the middle of the seventeenth century, violent conflict with Indians erupted repeatedly as colonial settlements grew and their desire for land increased. The violence convinced settlers that the only way to achieve both land and peace was to eliminate the Indians, by either killing them or pushing them far away from colonial settlements. English assumptions of their superiority to Indians provided justification and a gloss of respectability to the colonists' violent and relentless grab of Indian land.

The colonists identified Africans quite differently. Their most common term for Africans was *Negroes*, but the other was neither *savage* nor *heathen*. It was *black*. What struck English colonists most forcefully about Africans was not their un-English ways but their un-English skin color.

Black was not a neutral color to the colonists. According to the *Oxford English Dictionary* (which catalogs the changing meaning of words), *black* meant to the English people who settled the Chesapeake "deeply stained with dirt; soiled, dirty, foul . . . having dark or deadly purposes, malignant; pertaining to or involving death, deadly; baneful, disastrous, sinister . . . foul, iniquitous, atrocious, horrible, wicked." *Black* was the opposite of *white*, which signified purity, beauty, and goodness—qualities the colonists identified with themselves. By the middle of the seventeenth century, colonists referred

to themselves not only as English but also as free, hinting that they believed that people who were not English were not free. After about 1680, colonists often referred to themselves as white, acknowledging the color of free people. By the end of the seventeenth century, blacks were triply cursed in English eyes: un-English, un-white, and un-free.

Virginians did not legally define slavery as permanent, lifelong, inherited bondage until 1660. The sparse surviving evidence demonstrates, however, that colonists practiced slavery on a small scale from the start. The debasements of slavery, especially as it became more common, strengthened the colonists' prejudice toward blacks, while racial prejudices buttressed slavery.

Colonists' attitudes toward Indians and Africans exaggerated and hardened English notions about social hierarchy, about superiority and inferiority. Colonists' convictions of their own superiority to Indians and Africans justified, they believed, their exploitation of Indians' land and Africans' labor. Those justifications planted the seeds of pernicious racial prejudices that flourished in America for centuries.

Questions for Analysis

SUMMARIZE THE ARGUMENT: How did colonists' views of Indians and Africans indicate their views about themselves? What were the consequences of English colonists' belief in their own superiority?

ANALYZE THE EVIDENCE: How did the words colonists used to describe Indians and Africans indicate their beliefs? How did colonists' views of Indians differ from their views of Africans?

CONSIDER THE CONTEXT: What basic contexts of ideas, identities, and desires shaped the colonists' views of Indians and Africans?

taxes on all free Virginians by 75 percent between 1660 and 1700, a very popular policy. In the long run, however, the most important contribution to political stability was the declining importance of the servant labor system. During the 1680s and 1690s, fewer servants arrived in the Chesapeake, partly because of improving economic conditions in England. Fewer immigrants meant that the number of poor, newly freed servants also declined. In 1700, about one-third of freed colonists still

TRACE CHANGE OVER TIME

How did the servant labor system influence Virginia's Indian policy?

| How did tobacco influence Chesapeake society? | **Why did Chesapeake society change by the 1670s?** | Why did a slave labor system develop in England's southern colonies? | Conclusion: How did export crops contribute to the growth of the southern colonies? |

worked as tenants on land owned by others, but the Chesapeake was in the midst of transitioning to a slave labor system that de-emphasized the differences between poor farmers and rich planters and magnified the differences between whites and blacks.

QUICK REVIEW

How did Bacon's Rebellion influence social and political conflict in the Chesapeake?

Why did a slave labor system develop in England's southern colonies?

slavery
Lifelong bondage and coerced labor imposed on captured Africans and usually inherited by their New World descendants.

Unlike the Spaniards in New Spain, English colonists did not succeed in forcing Indians to become laborers. They turned instead to another source of workers used by the Spaniards and Portuguese: enslaved Africans. European colonizers eventually built African slavery into the most important form of coerced labor in the New World.

During the seventeenth century, English colonies in the West Indies followed the Spanish and Portuguese examples and developed sugar plantations with slave labor. In the English North American colonies, however, a slave labor system did not emerge until the last quarter of the seventeenth century. During the 1670s, settlers from Barbados brought slavery to the new English mainland colony of Carolina, where the imprint of the West Indies remained strong for decades. In Chesapeake tobacco fields at about the same time, slave labor began to replace servant labor, the crucial step in the transition to a society of freedom for whites and slavery for Africans.

Indians Revolt in New Mexico and Florida

While English colonies in the Chesapeake grew and prospered with the tobacco trade, the northern outposts of the Spanish empire in New Mexico and Florida stagnated. Only about fifteen hundred Spaniards lived in Florida, and roughly twice as many inhabited New Mexico, yet both colonies required costly deliveries of supplies. One royal governor complained that "no [Spaniard] comes . . . to plow and sow [crops], but only to eat and loaf."

Instead of attracting settlers and growing crops for export, New Mexico and Florida housed soldiers and Spanish missionaries who tried to convert Indians to Christianity. In both colonies, Indians outnumbered Spaniards ten or twenty to one. Royal officials hoped that the missionaries would pacify the Indians and be a relatively cheap way to preserve Spain's footholds in North America. The missionaries baptized thousands of Indians in New Mexico and Florida during the seventeenth century, but they also planted the seeds of Indian uprisings against Spanish rule.

Dozens of missionaries came to Florida and New Mexico, as one announced, to free the Indians "from the miserable slavery of the demon and from the obscure darkness of their idolatry." The missionaries followed royal instructions that Indians should be taught "to live in a civilized manner, clothed and wearing shoes . . . [and] given the use of . . .

How did settlers' encounters with Native Americans shape the colony of Virginia?

bread, linen, horses, cattle, tools, and weapons, and all the rest that Spain has had." In effect, the missionaries sought to convert the Indians not just to Christianity but also to ways of life that Spaniards considered civilized.

The missionaries sponsored scores of Catholic churches across Florida and New Mexico. Adopting common practices in New Spain, they forced Indians to construct these churches and to pay tribute in the form of food, blankets, and other goods. Although the missionaries congratulated themselves on the many Indians they converted, their coercive methods undermined their goals. A missionary reported that an Indian in New Mexico asked him, "If we [missionaries] who are Christians caused so much harm and violence [to Indians], why should they become Christians?"

The Indians retaliated repeatedly against Spanish exploitation, but the Spaniards suppressed the violent uprisings by taking advantage of the disunity among the Indians, much as Cortés did in the conquest of Mexico (see chapter 2). In 1680, however, the native leader Popé organized the **Pueblo Revolt**, ordering his followers, as one recounted, to "break up and burn the images of the holy Christ, the Virgin Mary, and the other saints, the crosses, and everything pertaining to Christianity." During the revolt, Indians attacked churches, killed two-thirds of the Spanish missionaries, and drove Spaniards out of New Mexico to present-day El Paso, Texas. The Spaniards managed to return to New Mexico by the end of the seventeenth century, but only by limiting the missionaries and reducing labor exploitation. Florida Indians never mounted a unified attack on Spanish rule, but they too organized sporadic uprisings and resisted conversion, causing a Spanish official to report by the end of the seventeenth century that "the law of God and the preaching of the Holy Gospel have now ceased."

> "'If we [missionaries] who are Christians caused so much harm and violence [to Indians], why should they become Christians?'"

Pueblo Revolt
The revolt of Pueblo Indians in 1680 against the Spanish in New Mexico, under the leadership of Popé.

▲ **Spanish Missionary in Florida** This sixteenth-century picture illustrates the methods Spanish missionaries used to teach Christianity to Native Americans. The picture shows the importance of reading and the punishment given students who did not measure up to the missionaries' expectations. The Granger Collection, New York.

READING THE IMAGE: Aside from the doctrines of Christianity, what are the Native American students being taught by these methods of instruction?

CONNECTIONS: How did missionary activity among the English colonists in the seventeenth-century southern colonies differ from that in New Spain?

| How did tobacco influence Chesapeake society? | Why did Chesapeake society change by the 1670s? | Why did a slave labor system develop in England's southern colonies? | Conclusion: How did export crops contribute to the growth of the southern colonies? |

The West Indies: Sugar and Slavery

Barbados
Island in the English West Indies that produced sugar during the seventeenth century and provided a major source of wealth for England.

The most profitable part of England's New World empire during the seventeenth century lay in the Caribbean (**Map 3.2**). The tiny island of Barbados, colonized in the 1630s, was the jewel of the English West Indies. During the 1640s, a colonial official proclaimed Barbados "the most flourishing Island in all those American parts, and I verily believe in all the world for the production of sugar." Sugar commanded high prices in England, and planters rushed to grow as much as they could. By midcentury, annual sugar exports from the English Caribbean totaled about 150,000 pounds; by 1700, exports multiplied to 50 million pounds.

Sugar transformed Barbados and other West Indian islands. Poor farmers could not afford the expensive machinery needed to refine sugarcane juice into sugar, but planters with enough capital could get rich. By 1680, the wealthiest Barbadian sugar planters were four times richer than tobacco grandees in the Chesapeake. The sugar grandees differed from their Chesapeake counterparts in another crucial way: The average sugar baron in Barbados owned 115 slaves in 1680.

African slaves planted, cultivated, and harvested the sugarcane that made West Indian planters wealthy. Beginning in the 1640s, Barbadian planters purchased thousands of enslaved Africans to work their plantations, causing the African population on the island to mushroom. During the 1650s, when people of African descent made up only 3 percent of the Chesapeake population, they had already become the majority in Barbados. By 1700, slaves accounted for more than three-fourths of the island's population (**Figure 3.1**).

For slaves, work on a sugar plantation was a life sentence to brutal, unending labor. Slaves suffered high death rates. Since enslaved men outnumbered women two to one, few slaves could form families and have children. These grim realities meant that in Barbados and elsewhere in the West Indies, the slave population grew very slowly by natural means. Instead, the slave population increased because planters continually purchased more enslaved Africans. Although sugar plantations did not gain a foothold in North America in the seventeenth century, the West Indies still exerted a powerful influence on the development of slavery in the mainland colonies.

COMPARE AND CONTRAST
How did the English colonies in the West Indies differ from Virginia?

Carolina: A West Indian Frontier

The early settlers of what became South Carolina were immigrants from Barbados. In 1663, a Barbadian planter named John Colleton and a group of seven other men obtained a charter from England's King Charles II to establish a colony north of the Spanish territories in Florida. The men, known as "proprietors," hoped to siphon settlers from Barbados and other colonies and encourage them to develop a profitable export crop comparable to West Indian sugar or Chesapeake tobacco. The proprietors enlisted the English philosopher John Locke to help draft the *Fundamental Constitutions of Carolina*, which provided for religious liberty and political rights for small property holders while envisioning a landed aristocracy supported by bound laborers and slaves. Following the Chesapeake example, the proprietors also offered headrights of up to 150 acres of land for each settler, a policy that eventually undermined the *Constitutions*'s goal of a titled aristocracy by spreading landownership broadly among the settlers. In 1670, the proprietors established the colony's first permanent English settlement, Charles Towne, later called Charleston (see Map 3.2).

As the proprietors had planned, most of the early settlers were from Barbados, and they brought their slaves with them. More than a fourth of the early settlers were slaves, and by 1700, slaves made up about half the Carolina population. The new

How did settlers' encounters with Native Americans shape the colony of Virginia?

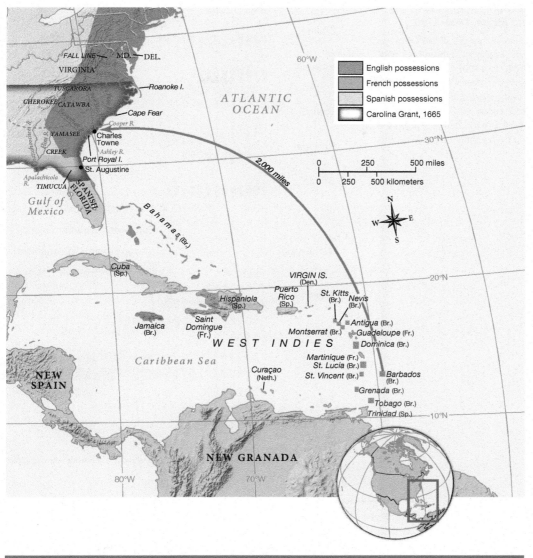

MAP 3.2 ▲ The West Indies and Carolina in the Seventeenth Century Although Carolina was geographically close to the Chesapeake colonies, it was culturally closer to the West Indies in the seventeenth century because its early settlers—both blacks and whites—came from Barbados. South Carolina maintained strong ties to the West Indies for more than a century.

READING THE MAP: Locate English colonies in America and English holdings in the Caribbean. Which European country controlled most of the mainland bordering the Caribbean? Where was the closest mainland English territory?

CONNECTIONS: Why were colonists in Carolina so interested in Barbados? What goods did they export? Describe the relationship between Carolina and Barbados in 1700.

colony's association with Barbados was so close that English officials routinely referred to "Carolina in ye West Indies."

The Carolinians tried to match their semitropical climate with profitable export crops of tobacco, cotton, indigo, and olives. Mostly, their experiments proved disappointing. In the mid-1690s, however, colonists identified a hardy strain of rice

How did tobacco influence Chesapeake society?	Why did Chesapeake society change by the 1670s?	**Why did a slave labor system develop in England's southern colonies?**	Conclusion: How did export crops contribute to the growth of the southern colonies?

Before 1640, Spain and Portugal sent four out of five European migrants to the New World, virtually all of them bound for New Spain or Brazil. But from 1640 to 1700, nearly as many migrants came from England as from all other European nations combined, a measure of the growing significance of England's colonies. From 1492 to 1700, more enslaved Africans than Europeans arrived in the New World. What explains the shifts in the destinations of enslaved Africans? Were there comparable shifts among European immigrants?

Before 1580*

Spain

Portugal

1580–1640

Spain

Portugal

Britain

France

Netherlands

= 10,000 people

Europeans = darker colors

African slaves = lighter colors

1640–1700

Spain

Portugal

Britain

France

Netherlands

*Note: Before 1580, migration from Britain, France, and the Netherlands was negligible.

and took advantage of the knowledge of rice cultivation among their many African slaves to build rice plantations. Settlers also sold livestock and timber to the West Indies, as well as another "natural resource." They captured and enslaved several thousand local Indians and sold them to Caribbean planters. Both economically and socially, seventeenth-century Carolina was a frontier outpost of the West Indian sugar economy.

Slave Labor Emerges in the Chesapeake

By 1700, more than eight out of ten people in the southern colonies of English North America lived in the Chesapeake. Until the 1670s, almost all Chesapeake colonists were white people from England. By 1700, however, one out of eight people in the region was a person of African descent. A few black people had lived in the Chesapeake since the 1620s, but the black population grew fivefold between 1670 and 1700, as hundreds of tobacco planters made the transition from servant to slave labor.

Planters saw several advantages to buying slaves. Although slaves cost three to five times more than servants, slaves never became free. Because the death rate had declined by the 1680s, planters could reasonably expect a slave to live longer than

How did settlers' encounters with Native Americans shape the colony of Virginia?

▲ **Sugar Plantation** This portrait of a Brazilian sugar plantation shows cartloads of sugarcane being hauled to the mill, which is powered by a waterwheel (far right), where the cane is squeezed between rollers to extract the sugary juice. The juice is then distilled over a fire tended by the slaves until it has the desired consistency and purity. Courtesy of the John Carter Brown Library at Brown University.

a servant's period of indenture. Slaves also promised to be a perpetual labor force since children of slave mothers inherited the status of slavery. And unlike servants, slaves could be controlled politically. A slave labor system promised to avoid the political problems caused by the servant labor system, such as Bacon's Rebellion. Slavery kept discontented laborers in permanent servitude, and their skin color was a badge of their bondage. (For more about slavery, see chapter 5.)

The slave labor system polarized Chesapeake society along lines of race and status. All slaves were black, and nearly all blacks were slaves. Almost all free people were white, and all whites were free or only temporarily bound in indentured servitude. Unlike Barbados, however, the Chesapeake retained a white majority. Among white people, huge differences of wealth and status still existed. By 1700, more than three-quarters of white families had neither servants nor slaves. But poor white farmers enjoyed the privileges of free status. They could own property, get married, have families, and pass on their property and their freedom to their descendants. They could move when and where they wanted and associate freely with other people. They could serve on juries, vote, and hold political office. They could work, loaf, and sleep as they chose. These privileges of freedom—none of them possessed by slaves—made poor white folks feel they had a genuine stake in the existence of slavery, even if they did not own a single slave. By emphasizing the privileges of freedom shared by all white people, the slave labor system reduced the tensions between poor folk and grandees that plagued the Chesapeake region in the 1670s.

In contrast to slaves on sugar plantations in Barbados, most enslaved people in the seventeenth-century Chesapeake colonies had frequent and close contact with white people. Slaves and white servants performed the same tasks on tobacco plantations, often working side by side in the fields. Slaves took advantage of every opportunity to slip away from white supervision and seek out the company of other slaves. Planters often feared that slaves would use such seemingly innocent social pleasures for political ends, either to run away or to conspire to strike against their masters. Slaves often did run away, but they were usually captured or returned after a brief absence. Despite planters' nightmares, slave uprisings did not occur.

| How did tobacco influence Chesapeake society? | Why did Chesapeake society change by the 1670s? | **Why did a slave labor system develop in England's southern colonies?** | Conclusion: How did export crops contribute to the growth of the southern colonies? |

▶ **Portrait of an African** During the first half of the seventeenth century, while the earliest enslaved Africans were being imported into the North American colonies, Peter Paul Rubens, an artist in Antwerp, Belgium, painted this sensitive, humane portrait of an African man in Europe. Whether the man was enslaved is not known. Still, the painting highlights the obvious humanity of this African man at the very time tens of thousands of other Africans—for whom no contemporary images exist—were victimized by the inhumane degradations and oppressions of enslavement in the New World. Album / Alamy Stock Photo.

CONSIDER CAUSE AND EFFECT

How did the development of the slave labor system in Virginia reshape the colony?

Although slavery resolved the political unrest caused by the servant labor system, it created new political problems. By 1700, the bedrock political issue in the southern colonies was keeping slaves in their place—at the end of a hoe. The slave labor system in the southern colonies stood roughly midway between the sugar plantations and black majority of Barbados to the south and the small farms and homogeneous villages that developed in seventeenth-century New England to the north (see chapter 4).

QUICK REVIEW

Why did slave labor largely replace the Chesapeake servant labor system by 1700?

Conclusion: How did export crops contribute to the growth of the southern colonies?

By 1700, the colonies of Virginia, Maryland, and Carolina were firmly established. The crops they grew for export provided a livelihood for many, a fortune for a few, and valuable income for shippers, merchants, and the English monarchy. The colonial societies differed from English society in most respects, yet the colonists considered themselves English people who happened to live in North America. They claimed the same rights and privileges as English men and women,

How did settlers' encounters with Native Americans shape the colony of Virginia?

while they denied those rights and privileges to Native Americans and enslaved Africans.

The English colonies also differed from the example of New Spain. Settlers and servants flocked to English colonies, in contrast to Spaniards, who trickled into New Spain. Few English missionaries sought to convert Indians to Protestant Christianity, unlike the numerous Catholic missionaries in the Spanish settlements in New Mexico and Florida. Large quantities of gold and silver never materialized in English North America. English colonists never adopted the system of encomienda (see chapter 2). Yet important forms of coerced labor and racial distinctions that developed in New Spain had North American counterparts. English colonists employed servants, like Anne Orthwood, and enslaved Africans while defining themselves as superior to both Indians and Africans.

By 1700, the remnants of Powhatan's people still survived. As English settlement pushed north, west, and south of Chesapeake Bay, the Indians faced the new colonial world that Powhatan had encountered when the first colonists arrived at Jamestown. By 1700, the descendants of Powhatan and other Native Americans understood that the English had come to stay.

Economically, the southern colonies developed from the struggling Jamestown settlement that could not feed itself into a major source of profits for England. The European fashion for tobacco provided livelihoods for numerous white families and riches for elite planters. After 1700, growing numbers of enslaved Africans were forced to grow tobacco in the Chesapeake and rice in Carolina. The slave society that dominated the eighteenth-century southern colonies was firmly rooted in the developments of the seventeenth century.

A desire for land, a hope for profit, and a dream for security motivated southern white colonists. Realizing these aspirations involved great risks, considerable suffering, and frequent disappointment as well as seizing Indian lands and coercing labor from servants and slaves. By 1700, despite huge differences in individual colonists' success in achieving their goals, tens of thousands of white colonists who were English immigrants or descendants of immigrants considered the southern colonies their home, shaping the history of the region and of the nation as a whole for centuries to come.

| How did tobacco influence Chesapeake society? | Why did Chesapeake society change by the 1670s? | Why did a slave labor system develop in England's southern colonies? | **Conclusion: How did export crops contribute to the growth of the southern colonies?** |

CHAPTER 3 STUDY GUIDE

STEP 1

EXPLAIN WHY IT MATTERS

Put your reading into practice. Identify each term below, and then explain why it matters in U.S. history.

TERM	WHO OR WHAT & WHEN	WHY IT MATTERS
Virginia Company (p. 56)		
Algonquian Indians (p. 56)		
Jamestown (p. 56)		
royal colony (p. 59)		
House of Burgesses (p. 59)		
indentured servants (p. 62)		
headright (p. 63)		
Navigation Acts (p. 68)		
Bacon's Rebellion (p. 68)		
slavery (p. 72)		
Pueblo Revolt (p. 73)		
Barbados (p. 74)		

STEP 2

MOVE BEYOND THE BASICS

Chart the key features of the southern colonies, including their population, major economic activities, and social and political tensions.

Date	Population	Economy	Social and Political Tensions
1607			
1620			
1650			
1700			

STEP 3 — PUT IT ALL TOGETHER

Now, try to explain the big picture. Remember to use specific examples from the chapter in your answers.

JAMESTOWN AND THE CHESAPEAKE

- How did interactions with Native Americans shape Jamestown's early history?

- How did tobacco transform the Chesapeake?

SLAVERY

- How did sugar contribute to the development of African slavery in the New World?

- How did the introduction of African slaves affect Chesapeake society?

INDENTURED SERVITUDE AND BACON'S REBELLION

- How did indentured servants influence the development of Chesapeake society?

- What caused Bacon's Rebellion? What were its consequences?

LOOKING BACKWARD, LOOKING AHEAD

- How did the English southern colonies in the seventeenth century differ from their counterparts in sixteenth-century New Spain?

- How did the introduction of African slaves contribute to the emergence of a distinct southern colonial society?

STEP 4 — CONNECT THESE EVENTS

How did Bacon's Rebellion contribute to the emergence of slave labor in England's southern colonies?

STEP 5 — CONNECT TO THE PRESENT

To what extent do ideas about inequality and race common in the seventeenth-century southern colonies continue to be important today?

4

THE NORTHERN COLONIES IN THE SEVENTEENTH CENTURY

1601–1700

How did the New England and middle colonies develop during the seventeenth century? This chapter explores the influence of religion in the evolution of England's northern colonies as well as the social and economic changes caused by growing population and increasing commerce.

This chapter will explore the following questions:

- Why did Puritans emigrate to North America?
- How did New England society change during the seventeenth century?
- How did the middle colonies differ from New England and the southern colonies?
- How did the English empire influence the colonies?
- Conclusion: Was there an English model of colonization in North America?

AN AMERICAN STORY

Roger Williams and his wife, Mary, arrived in Massachusetts in February 1631. Fresh from a fine education at Cambridge University, the twenty-eight-year-old Williams was "a godly [Puritan] minister," wrote Governor John Winthrop, whose Boston church asked Williams to become its preacher. But New England's premier Puritan church was not pure enough for Roger Williams.

Williams refused the invitation and moved to Plymouth colony, where he sought to learn the language, religion, and culture of the Narragansett Indians. Williams believed that "Nature knows no difference between Europeans and [Native] Americans in blood, birth, [or] bodies . . . God having made of one blood all mankind." He insisted that the colonists respect the Indians since all human beings— Christians and non-Christians alike—should live according to their consciences as revealed to them by God.

Williams condemned English colonists for what he called their "sin of unjust usurpation" of Indian land. He believed that English claims to Indian lands were legally, morally, and spiritually invalid. In contrast, Massachusetts officials defended colonists' settlement on Indian land. Governor Winthrop declared, "if we leave [the Indians] sufficient [land] for their use, we may lawfully take the rest, there being more than enough for them and us." Winthrop's arguments prevailed, but Williams refused to knuckle under. "God Land," he said, "[is] as great a God with us English as God Gold was with the Spaniards." Although New Englanders claimed to worship the one true God in heaven, Williams declared, "the truth is the great Gods of this world are God-belly, God-peace, God-wealth, God-honour, [and] God-pleasure."

Williams believed that the Bible obscured the Word of God in "mist and fog." He denounced as impure, ungodly, and tyrannical the claim that New England government enforced God's commandments in the Bible. He argued that forcing people to attend church was "False Worshipping" that promoted "spiritual drunkenness and whoredom." The only way to become a true Christian was by God's gift of faith revealed to a person's conscience. He believed that laws regulating religious behavior amounted to "spiritual rape." Governments should tolerate all religious beliefs because only God knows the Truth.

New England's leaders rejected Williams's arguments and banished him for his "extreme and dangerous" opinions. In January 1636, he fled south to Narragansett Bay, where he and his followers established the colony of Rhode Island, and enshrined "Liberty of Conscience" as a fundamental ideal.

Although New England's leaders expelled Williams from their holy commonwealth, his dissenting ideas in fact arose from orthodox Puritan doctrines, which inspired believers to read the Bible and draw their own conclusions with the guidance of educated ministers. During the seventeenth century, however, New England's Puritan zeal cooled, and the promise of a holy New England faded.

Late in the century, the new middle colonies of New York, New Jersey, and Pennsylvania were founded, featuring greater religious and ethnic diversity than New England. Religion remained important throughout all the colonies, but it competed with the growing faith that a better life required less focus on salvation and more attention to worldly concerns of family, work, and trade.

Throughout the colonies, settlements encroached on Indian land, causing violent conflict to flare up repeatedly. Political conflict also arose among colonists, particularly in response to major political upheavals in England. By the end of the seventeenth century, the English monarchy exerted greater control over North America and the rest of its Atlantic empire, but the products, people, and ideas that pulsed between England and the colonies energized both.

▼ **Bay Psalm Book** This first book printed in America contains psalms that Puritans sang as routine parts of their religious services. Although 1,700 copies of the Bay Psalm book were printed in 1640—enough for wide distribution among the early settlers—heavy use (indicated by the handwriting on the left-hand page) and the ravages of time have left only eleven surviving copies. This rare book recently sold for more than $14 million. Polaris/Newscom.

Why did Puritans emigrate to North America?

CHRONOLOGY

1534
– English Reformation begins.

1558–1603
– Elizabeth I reigns in England.

1603–1625
– James I reigns in England.

1620
– Plymouth colony founded by Pilgrims.

1629
– Massachusetts Bay Company receives royal charter.

1630
– John Winthrop leads Puritan settlers to Massachusetts Bay.

English Reformation
Abolished the Catholic Church in England and declared King Henry VIII head of the new Church of England.

Puritans
Dissenters from the Church of England who wanted a genuine Protestant Reformation rather than the partial Reformation sought by Henry VIII.

Puritans who emigrated to North America sought to escape the turmoil and persecution they suffered in England, long-term consequences of the English Reformation. They also wanted to build a new, orderly, Puritan version of England. They established a small settlement at Plymouth in 1620, followed a few years later by larger settlements sponsored by the Massachusetts Bay Company. Allowed to govern themselves through royal charter, these Puritans could organize the new colonies according to their religious faith. Although many immigrants to New England were not Puritans, Puritanism remained a paramount influence in New England's religion, politics, and community life during the seventeenth century.

Puritan Origins: The English Reformation

The religious roots of the Puritans who founded New England reached back to the Protestant Reformation, which began in Germany in 1517 (see chapter 2). The English church initially remained within the Catholic fold. Henry VIII, who reigned from 1509 to 1547, realized that the Reformation offered him an opportunity to break with Rome and take control of the Catholic Church in England. In 1534, Henry formally initiated the **English Reformation**. He insisted that Parliament outlaw the Catholic Church and proclaim him "the only supreme head on earth of the Church of England." Henry seized the vast properties of the Catholic Church in England. For example, twenty-one Catholic bishops in England owned over 175 palaces and houses, which now belonged to the king, along with many thousand acres of land. Henry also claimed the privilege of appointing all leaders in the church hierarchy.

In the short run, the English Reformation allowed Henry VIII to achieve his political goal of controlling the church. In the long run, however, the Reformation brought to England the political and religious turmoil that Henry had hoped to avoid. Henry himself sought no more than a halfway Reformation. Protestant doctrines held no attraction for him. In almost all matters of religious belief and practice, he remained an orthodox Catholic. Many English Catholics wanted to revoke the English Reformation. They hoped to return the Church of England to the pope and to restore Catholic doctrines and ceremonies. But many other English people insisted on a genuine, thoroughgoing Reformation. These people came to be called **Puritans**.

During the sixteenth century, Puritanism was less an organized movement than a set of ideas and religious principles that appealed strongly to many dissenting members of the Church of England. They sought to eliminate what they considered the offensive features of Catholicism that remained in the religious doctrines and practices of the Church of England. For example, they wanted to do away with the rituals of Catholic worship and instead emphasize that Christians needed to follow God's commandments as revealed in the Bible. At the outset of the English Reformation, few Bibles were available to ordinary Christians and they were written in Latin, which only priests and well educated laypeople could read. The new technology of printing and English translations of the Bible made it available for the first time to literate believers in England. All Puritans shared a desire to read the Bible and make the English church thoroughly Protestant.

The fate of Protestantism waxed and waned under the monarchs who succeeded Henry VIII. In 1558, Elizabeth I, the daughter of Henry and his second wife, Anne Boleyn, became queen. During her long reign, Elizabeth reaffirmed the English Reformation and tried to position the English church between the extremes of Catholicism and Puritanism. Like her father, she desired a church that would strengthen the monarchy and the nation. By the time Elizabeth died in 1603, many people in England looked on Protestantism as a defining feature of national identity.

Why did Puritans emigrate to North America?

◄ **Queen Elizabeth** This sixteenth-century portrait of Queen Elizabeth celebrates English victory over the Spanish Armada in 1588 that eventually allowed England's empire to spread to North America. Ann Ronan Pictures/Print Collector/Getty Images.

When Elizabeth's successor, James I, became king, English Puritans petitioned for further reform of the Church of England. James authorized a new translation of the Bible, known ever since as the King James Version. However, neither James I nor his son Charles I, who became king in 1625, was receptive to the ideas of Puritan reformers. James and Charles moved the Church of England away from Puritanism. They enforced conformity to the Church of England and punished dissenters. In 1629, Charles I dissolved Parliament—where Puritans were well represented—and initiated aggressive anti-Puritan policies. Many Puritans despaired about continuing to defend their faith in England and made plans to emigrate to Europe, the West Indies, or America.

The Pilgrims and Plymouth Colony

One of the first Protestant groups to emigrate, later known as Pilgrims, professed an unorthodox view known as separatism. These **Separatists** sought to withdraw from the Church of England, which they considered utterly corrupt. In 1608, they moved to Holland. By 1620, they realized that they could not live and worship there as they had hoped. William Bradford, a Separatist leader, recalled that "many of their children, by . . . the great licentiousness of youth [in Holland], and the manifold temptations of the place, were drawn away by evil examples." Bradford and other Separatists believed that America promised to better protect and preserve their children and their community. Separatists obtained permission to settle in the extensive territory granted to the Virginia Company (see chapter 3). In August 1620, Pilgrim families boarded the *Mayflower*, and after eleven weeks at sea all but one of the 102 immigrants arrived at the outermost tip of Cape Cod in present-day Massachusetts.

The Pilgrims realized immediately that they had landed far north of the Virginia grants and had no legal authority to settle in the area. To provide order, security, and a claim to legitimacy, they drew up the Mayflower Compact on the day they arrived. They pledged to "covenant and combine ourselves together into a civil Body Politick, for our better Ordering and Preservation." The signers (all men) agreed to enact and obey necessary and just laws. The Pilgrims settled at Plymouth and elected William Bradford their governor. That

Separatists
Puritans who sought to withdraw or separate from the Church of England.

| How did New England society change during the seventeenth century? | How did the middle colonies differ from New England and the southern colonies? | How did the English empire influence the colonies? | Conclusion: Was there an English model of colonization in North America? |

85

first winter, which they spent aboard their ship, "was most sad and lamentable," Bradford wrote later. "In two or three months' time half of [our] company died . . . being the depth of winter, and wanting houses . . . [and] being infected with scurvy and other diseases."

In the spring, Indians rescued the floundering Plymouth settlement. First Samoset and then Squanto befriended the settlers. Samoset had learned English from previous contacts with sailors and fishermen who had visited the coast to dry fish before the Plymouth settlers arrived. Squanto had been kidnapped by an English trader in 1614 and taken as a slave to Spain, where he escaped to London and learned English before finally making his way back home. Samoset arranged for the Pilgrims to meet and establish good relations with Massasoit, the chief of the Wampanoag Indians, whose territory included Plymouth. Squanto, Bradford wrote, "was a special instrument sent of God for their [the Pilgrims'] good. . . . He directed them how to set their corn, where to take fish, and to procure other commodities." With the Indians' guidance, the Pilgrims managed to harvest enough food to guarantee their survival through the coming winter, an occasion they celebrated in the fall of 1621 with a feast of thanksgiving attended by Massasoit and other Wampanoags.

Plymouth colony remained precarious for years, but the Pilgrims persisted, living simply and coexisting in relative peace with the Indians. One settler contrasted the group's improved circumstances with their former homes in England by noting, "We are all free-holders [here], the [landlords'] rent-day doth not trouble us." By 1630, Plymouth had become a small permanent settlement, but it failed to attract many other English Puritans.

The Founding of Massachusetts Bay Colony

In 1629, shortly before Charles I dissolved Parliament, a group of Puritans obtained a royal charter for the Massachusetts Bay Company. The charter provided the usual privileges granted to joint-stock companies, including land for colonization that spanned present-day Massachusetts, New Hampshire, Vermont, Maine, and upstate New York. A unique provision of the charter allowed the government of the Massachusetts Bay Company to be located in the colony rather than in England. With this permission, Puritan emigrants exchanged their status as a harassed minority in England for self-government as an empowered majority in Massachusetts.

John Winthrop, a prosperous lawyer and landowner, led the emigrants and became governor of the new colony. In March 1630, eleven ships crammed with seven hundred passengers sailed for Massachusetts. Six more ships and another five hundred emigrants followed a few months later. Unlike the Separatists, Winthrop's Puritans aspired to reform the corrupt Church of England (rather than separate from it) by setting an example of godliness in the New World. "For England's sake they are going from England to pray without ceasing for England," wrote one Puritan emigrant.

Winthrop proclaimed the cosmic significance of their journey in a sermon aboard the ship *Arbella* while still at sea—one of the most famous sermons in American history. The Puritans had "entered into a covenant" with God to "work out our salvation under the power and purity of his holy ordinances," Winthrop declared. This agreement with

◀ **John Winthrop** This portrait of John Winthrop was painted in England shortly before Winthrop departed for New England. The portrait displays the alert, intense, sober gaze characteristic of Puritan leaders. Winthrop's lace collar (or ruff), however, was an English fashion that New England Puritans detested. If the portrait had been made in New England, Winthrop would not have been wearing the ruff and lace-trimmed sleeves. American Antiquarian Society, Worcester, Massachusetts, USA / Bequest of William Winthrop / Bridgeman Images.

Why did Puritans emigrate to North America?

God meant that the Puritans had to make "extraordinary" efforts to "bring into familiar and constant practice" religious principles that most people in England ignored. To achieve their pious goals, the Puritans had to subordinate their individual interests to the common good. "We must be knit together in this work as one man," Winthrop preached. "We must delight in each other, make others' conditions our own, rejoice together, mourn together, labor and suffer together." The stakes could not be higher, Winthrop told his listeners: "We must consider that we shall be as a city upon a hill. The eyes of all people are upon us."

> "Winthrop told his listeners: 'We must consider that we shall be as a city upon a hill. The eyes of all people are upon us.'"

That belief shaped seventeenth-century New England as profoundly as tobacco shaped the Chesapeake. Winthrop's vision of a city on a hill fired the Puritans' fierce determination to keep their covenant and live according to God's laws, unlike the backsliders and compromisers who accommodated to the Church of England. Their resolve to adhere strictly to God's plan charged nearly every feature of life in seventeenth-century New England with a distinctive, high-voltage piety.

Winthrop chose to settle on the peninsula that became Boston, and other settlers clustered at promising locations nearby (**Map 4.1**). The new colonists had "all things to do, as in the beginning of the world," Winthrop's son wrote later. Unlike the early Chesapeake settlers, the first Massachusetts Bay colonists encountered few Indians because the local population had been almost entirely exterminated by an epidemic. Still, many of the colonists succumbed to diseases. During the first year, more than two hundred settlers died, including one of Winthrop's sons and eleven of his servants. Winthrop himself remained confident and optimistic. He wrote to his wife that "I like so well to be heer as I do not repent my comminge. . . . I would not have altered my course, though I had forseene all these Afflictions." And each year from 1630 to 1640, ship after ship followed in the wake of Winthrop's fleet, bringing more than twenty thousand new settlers.

Often, when the Church of England cracked down on a Puritan minister in England, he and many of his followers moved together to New England. Smaller groups of English Puritans moved to the Chesapeake and elsewhere in the colonies, including New Amsterdam (present-day New York). By 1640, New England had one of the highest ratios of

COMPARE AND CONTRAST
What did the Puritans and Pilgrims have in common and how did they differ?

MAP ACTIVITY

MAP 4.1 ◀ New England Colonies in the Seventeenth Century New Englanders spread across the landscape town by town during the seventeenth century. (For the sake of legibility, only a few of the more important towns are shown on the map.)

READING THE MAP: Using the dates on the map, create a chronology of the establishment of New England towns. What physical features correspond to the earliest habitation by English settlers?
CONNECTIONS: Why were towns so much more a feature of seventeenth-century New England than of the Chesapeake (see chapter 3)? How did Puritan dissent influence the settlement of New England colonies?

How did New England society change during the seventeenth century?	How did the middle colonies differ from New England and the southern colonies?	How did the English empire influence the colonies?	Conclusion: Was there an English model of colonization in North America?

preachers to population in all of Christendom. Several ministers sought to bring Christianity to the Indians in order to replace what a missionary termed the Indians' "unfixed, confused, and ungoverned . . . life, uncivilized and unsubdued to labor and order." The missionaries established "praying towns" to encourage Indians to adopt English ways. But the colonists focused far less on saving Indians' souls than on saving their own.

The occupations of New England immigrants reflected the social origins of English Puritans. On the whole, the immigrants came from the middle ranks of English society. The vast majority were either farmers or tradesmen. Indentured servants, whose numbers dominated the Chesapeake settlers, accounted for about a fifth of those headed for New England. Most New England immigrants paid their way to Massachusetts. They were encouraged by the promise of bounty in New England. As Winthrop wrote to his son, "Here can be no want of anything to those who bring means to raise [it] out of the earth and sea." **(See "Spotlight: How did Seventeenth-Century Colonists View Nature?" on page 90.)**

In contrast to Chesapeake newcomers, New England immigrants usually arrived as families. In fact, more Puritans came with family members than did any other group of immigrants in all of American history. Unlike immigrants to the Chesapeake, women and children made up a solid majority in New England.

As Winthrop reminded the first settlers in his *Arbella* sermon, each family was a "little commonwealth" that mirrored the hierarchy among all God's creatures. Just as humankind was subordinate to God, so young people were subordinate to their elders, children to their parents, and wives to their husbands. The immigrants' family ties reinforced their religious beliefs with the interlocking institutions of family, church, and community.

COMPARE AND CONTRAST

How did the seventeenth-century New England colonies compare to the Chesapeake colonies?

QUICK REVIEW

Why was the concept of a "little commonwealth" important in the New England colonies?

How did New England society change during the seventeenth century?

Calvinism
Doctrines of John Calvin emphasizing predestination, namely the idea that God had determined which souls would receive eternal salvation.

predestination
Doctrine stating that God determined whether individuals were destined for salvation or damnation before their birth.

visible saints
Puritans who had passed the tests of conversion and church membership and therefore appeared to be among God's elect.

The New England colonists, unlike their counterparts in the Chesapeake, settled in small towns, usually located on the coast or by a river (see Map 4.1). Massachusetts Bay colonists founded 133 towns during the seventeenth century, each with one or more churches. Church members' fervent piety, supported by the institutions of local government, enforced remarkable conformity in the small New England settlements. During the century, tensions within the Puritan faith and changes in New England communities splintered religious orthodoxy and weakened Puritan zeal. By 1700, however, Puritanism retained a distinctive influence in New England.

Church, Covenant, and Conformity

Puritans believed that a church consisted of men and women who had entered a solemn covenant with one another and with God. Winthrop and others who signed the covenant of the first Boston church in 1630 agreed to "Promisse, and bind our selves, to walke in all our wayes according to the Rule of the Gospell, and in all sincere Conformity to His holy Ordinaunces." Each person who wanted to join the church had to persuade existing members that she or he had fully experienced conversion and could abide by the covenant.

Why did Puritans emigrate to North America?

Puritans embraced a distinctive version of Protestantism derived from **Calvinism**. John Calvin, a leader of Reformation Protestantism, insisted that Christians strictly discipline their behavior to conform to God's commandments in the Bible. Like Calvin, Puritans believed in **predestination**—namely, that before the creation of the world God decided which few human souls would receive eternal life. Only God knew the identity of these fortunate predestined individuals—called the "elect" or "saints." Nothing a person did in his or her lifetime could influence God's choice or reveal whether the person was among the elect and predestined for everlasting life in heaven or was damned to eternal hell with the doomed multitude.

Despite the impossibility of knowing whether one was among the elect, Puritans believed that if a person lived a rigorously godly life—constantly winning the daily battle against sin—his or her behavior was likely to be a hint, a visible sign, that he or she was one of God's chosen few. Puritans thought that "sainthood" would become visible in individuals' behavior, especially if they were privileged to know God's Word as revealed in the Bible.

The connection between sainthood and saintly behavior, however, was far from certain. Some members of the elect, Puritans believed, had not heard God's Word. One reason Puritans required all town residents to attend church services (despite Roger Williams' criticisms) was to enlighten anyone who was ignorant of God's Truth. The slippery relationship between saintly behavior and God's predestined election caused Puritans to worry constantly that individuals who acted like saints were fooling themselves and others. Nevertheless, Puritans thought that **visible saints**—persons who passed Puritans' demanding tests of conversion and church membership—probably were among God's elect.

Since members of Puritan churches fervently hoped that God had chosen them to receive eternal life, they tried hard to demonstrate saintly behavior. To live up to their covenant, they had to help one another and discipline the entire community to behave according to saintly standards. Church members kept an eye on the behavior of everybody in town. By overseeing every aspect of life, the visible saints enforced a remarkable degree of conformity in Puritan communities. Total conformity, however, was never achieved. Ardent Puritans differed among themselves, as Roger Williams demonstrated. Non-Puritans shirked the saints' rules, such as the Massachusetts servant who declared that "if hell were ten times hotter, [I] would rather be there than [I] would serve [my] master."

CHRONOLOGY

1636
- Rhode Island colony established.
- Connecticut colony founded.

1636–1637
- Pequot War fought between colonists and Pequot Indians.

1638
- Anne Hutchinson excommunicated.

1642
- Puritan Revolution inflames England.

1649
- English Puritans win civil war.

1656
- Quakers arrive in Massachusetts and are persecuted.

1662
- Many Puritan congregations adopt Halfway Covenant.

1692
- Salem witch trials held.

THE
World turn'd upside down:
OR,
A briefe defcription of the ridiculous Fafhions of thefe diftracted Times.

By T.J. a well-willer to King, Parliament and Kingdom.

VISUAL ACTIVITY

◀ **The Puritan Challenge to the Status Quo** The World Turn'd Upside Down, a pamphlet printed in London in 1647, satirizes the Puritan notion that the contemporary world was deeply flawed. The pamphlet refers to the "distracted Times" of the Puritan Revolution in England. The drawing on the title page ridicules criticisms of English society that also were common among New England Puritans. British Library, London, UK / © British Library Board. All Rights Reserved / Bridgeman Images.

READING THE IMAGE: The drawing shows at least a dozen examples of the conventional world of seventeenth-century England turned upside down. Can you identify them?

CONNECTIONS: Puritans would claim that the artist was wrong—that the conventional world turned God's order upside down. How might the drawing have been different if a devout Puritan had drawn it?

How did New England society change during the seventeenth century?	How did the middle colonies differ from New England and the southern colonies?	How did the English empire influence the colonies?	Conclusion: Was there an English model of colonization in North America?

How Did Seventeenth-Century Colonists View Nature?

A cascade of novelty swept across Europe during the sixteenth and seventeenth centuries. New continents, new peoples, new plants and animals, new religions, and new ideas caused some thinkers to reconsider the basic character of the world and the place of human beings within it. Building on discoveries made in the sixteenth century by Copernicus and other astronomers, Galileo insisted, for example, that the earth did not rest at the center of the universe, but instead moved around the sun, demoting the globe and its inhabitants from the hub to an outer orbit. Isaac Newton, to take another example, invented the mathematics of bodies in motion—calculus, familiar to students for hundreds of years afterward—and worked out the theory of the invisible force that governs all matter—gravity. These and other scientific advances seemed to some people to contradict Christian ideas about God's sovereignty and much else. Was gravity just another name for God? Or was gravity the way God chose to order creation? Newton and most other seventeenth-century scientists believed that God created gravity and the rest of the natural order much like a watchmaker built a complex mechanical clock. Setting the clock in motion, God then stepped back and allowed the universe to operate by natural laws like gravity that did not need his constant supervision or intervention.

Settlers in seventeenth-century British colonies in North America lived thousands of miles and a mental world away from centers of advanced scientific thinking in London, Paris, Berlin, and elsewhere in Europe. Seventeenth-century colonists typically believed they and the earth stood at the center of God's vision. God constantly intervened in the world to express his pleasure or displeasure with humans' behavior, they thought. Violent thunderstorms, destructive winds, hail, floods, droughts, disease epidemics, and much else that we might consider acts of nature seventeenth-century colonists interpreted instead as signs of God's anger that people were not living up to his expectations. New Englanders in particular worried that God was punishing them for falling short of his biblical commandments.

God also sometimes rewarded colonists for obeying his divine laws. A Connecticut man, for example, reported that "we have had of late, great stormes of rain & wind, & sometimes of thunder and lightning, whereby some execution hath been done by the Lord's holy Hand, though with sparing mercy to mankind." The storms killed nine oxen, seven hogs, and a dog, but a nearby family of children left alone by their parents suffered "no hurt to any of them, more than amazing fear."

We might believe these children were lucky, having avoided harm by accident or coincidence. But colonists saw the children's safety as a "remarkable providence," an instance of God's gracious protection of his precious loved ones. Puritans welcomed remarkable providences as reassuring evidence of God's satisfaction that they were fulfilling the obligations of their holy covenant, at least temporarily.

Despite the importance of religion, churches played no direct role in the civil government of New England communities. Puritans did not want to mirror the Church of England, which they considered a puppet of the king rather than an independent body that served the Lord. They were determined to insulate New England churches from the contaminating influence of the civil government and its merely human laws. Ministers were prohibited from holding government office.

Puritans had no qualms, however, about their religious beliefs influencing New England governments. As much as possible, the Puritans tried to bring public life into conformity with their view of God's law. For example, fines were issued for Sabbath-breaking activities such as working, traveling, ice-skating, playing a flute, smoking a pipe, and visiting neighbors.

Puritans practiced other purifications of English practices that they considered corrupt. They refused to celebrate Christmas or Easter because the Bible did not mention either one. They outlawed religious wedding ceremonies. A magistrate married couples in a civil ceremony. They banned cards, dice, shuffleboard, and other games of chance, as well as music and dancing. "Mixt or Promiscuous Dancing. . . of Men and Women,"

Why did Puritans emigrate to North America?

When a bolt of lightning stunned another colonist, God's divine intervention shielded him and he survived unhurt, as did the Bible he was carrying under his arm, which was "left untouched" by the lightning except for the "whole book of Revelation [which] was carried away."

Colonists stayed alert to any unusual happening: a strange cloud formation; an unusual noise in the night; an ominous comet streaking across the sky; the "monstrous" birth of a calf with two heads or, worse, of a deformed human fetus. Colonists referred to such events as "wonders" that signaled God's awareness of every detail of their lives. Wonders seemed to be omens of God's judgment, but it was often difficult to decipher whether an omen meant God was angry or pleased. Overall, signs of an angry, vengeful God seemed to predominate, worrisome evidence to many colonists that they were failing—individually and collectively—to win God's favor. But another interpretation of wonders worried colonists even more. Maybe that two-headed calf or fiery comet was the work of Satan, whose powers for evil always warred against colonists' desires to live in godly ways.

Wonders and remarkable providences revealed seventeenth-century colonists' view of nature as ordered or disordered by mysterious, supernatural power. To them, nature was not a Newtonian clock set in motion by a distant God, but an enchanted environment that God and Satan battled over constantly, storm by storm, comet by comet. Colonists could

try to align themselves with God and reject Satan, but they could scarcely comprehend, much less change, the mysterious forces that governed nature and themselves. The orderly, harmonious, and law-abiding nature assumed by a Newtonian "watchmaker God" made no sense to seventeenth-century colonists. Instead, God watched and cared about every second of the lives of every creature on earth. They mattered to him, and, if they knew what was good for them, he better matter to them lest their chance for salvation slip away for all eternity.

Questions for Analysis

SUMMARIZE THE ARGUMENT: According to this essay, how did seventeenth-century colonists' views of nature differ from those of leading European scientists?

ANALYZE THE EVIDENCE: What does the colonial reaction to "wonders and remarkable providences" discussed in this essay reveal about colonists' view of nature? How might leading European scientists of the era have interpreted these events?

CONSIDER THE CONTEXT: How might life in the seventeenth-century colonies have influenced colonists' views about nature and themselves? Why might colonists and European scientists have had such contrasting views of God and nature?

could not be tolerated, according to one minister, since "the unchaste Touches and Gesticulations used by Dancers have a palpable tendency to that which is evil."

Government by Puritans for Puritanism

It is only a slight exaggeration to say that Puritans governed seventeenth-century New England for Puritanism. The charter of the Massachusetts Bay Company empowered the company's stockholders, known as freemen, to meet as the General Court and make the laws needed to govern the company's affairs. The colonists transformed this arrangement for running a joint-stock company into a structure for governing the colony. Hoping to ensure that godly men would decide government policies, the General Court expanded the number of freemen in 1631 to include all male church members. Only freemen had the right to vote for governor and other officials. When the size of the General Court grew too large to meet conveniently, the freemen agreed in 1634 that each town would send two deputies to the General Court to act as the colony's

PLACE EVENTS IN CONTEXT

Why did Puritans insist that colonial government should have no power over churches?

| **How did New England society change during the seventeenth century?** | How did the middle colonies differ from New England and the southern colonies? | How did the English empire influence the colonies? | Conclusion: Was there an English model of colonization in North America? |

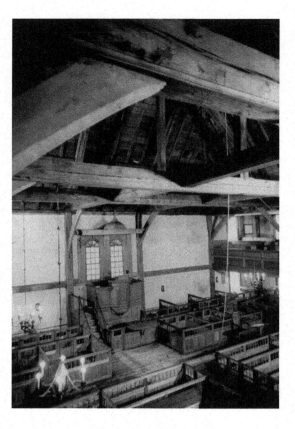

▶ **Puritan MeetingHouse** This photograph of a seventeenth-century Puritan meetinghouse exhibits the plain, unadorned style of worship in New England's churches. Puritans rejected stained glass windows common in English churches, which they considered idolatrous. The only music Puritans permitted in churches came from the voices of the congregation, rather than from an organ or other musical instrument. As the architecture of this meetinghouse suggests, the congregation was expected to focus not on eye-catching religious decorations, but instead on the Bible, on the words of the preacher, and on each person's relationship to the Almighty. Eliot Elisofon/Getty Images.

legislative assembly. All other men were classified as "inhabitants," who had the right to vote, hold office, and participate fully in town government.

A "town meeting" was composed of a town's inhabitants and freemen who chose the selectmen who administered local affairs. New England town meetings routinely practiced a level of democratic participation that had no equal elsewhere in the world. Almost every adult man could speak out and vote in town meetings, but all women— even church members—were prohibited from voting. This widespread political participation tended to reinforce conformity to Puritan ideals.

The General Court granted land for town sites to pious petitioners, once the Indians agreed to give up their claim to the land, usually in exchange for manu-factured goods. William Pynchon, for example, purchased the site of Springfield, Massachusetts, from the Agawam Indians for "eighteen fathams [arm's lengths] of Wampum [strings of shell-beads used in trade], eighteen coates, 18 hatchets, 18 hoes, [and] 18 knives." Town founders then apportioned land among themselves and any newcomers they approved. Most family plots were fifty to one hundred acres, causing land in New England to be much more equally distributed than in the Chesapeake.

The physical layout of New England towns encouraged settlers to look inward toward their neighbors, multiplying the opportunities for godly vigilance. Most people considered the forest that lay just beyond every settler's house an alien environment. Footpaths con-necting one town to another were so poorly marked that even John Winthrop once got lost and spent a sleepless night in the forest only a half mile from his house.

The Splintering of Puritanism

Almost from the beginning, John Winthrop and other leaders had difficulty enforcing their views of Puritan orthodoxy. In England, persecution as a dissenting minority uni-fied Puritan voices in opposition to the Church of England. In New England, however,

Why did Puritans emigrate to North America?

the promise of a godly society and the Puritans' emphasis on individual Bible study led toward different visions of godliness. New England's leaders believed that dissenters like Roger Williams who disagreed with their religious and political order were wrong. Dissent must be caused either by mistaken beliefs or by the evil power of Satan, they believed. As one Puritan minister proclaimed, "The Scripture saith . . . there is no Truth but one." Accordingly, dissent was intolerable.

A few years after arriving in Massachusetts, Winthrop confronted dissenter Anne Hutchinson, a devout Puritan woman steeped in Scripture and absorbed by religious questions. The mother of fourteen children, Hutchinson assisted neighboring women during childbirth. In 1634, she began to give weekly lectures about recent sermons delivered by local ministers. The women who gathered at Hutchinson's home listened to her preach about the "covenant of grace"—the idea that the only way individuals could be saved was by God's grace in choosing them to be members of the elect. Hutchinson contrasted this familiar Puritan doctrine with the covenant of works, the belief that a person's behavior—one's works—could win God's favor and ultimately earn a person salvation, a view Puritans believed was wrong and sinful.

The meetings at Hutchinson's house alarmed her nearest neighbor, Governor Winthrop, who believed that she was undermining the good order of the colony. In 1637, Winthrop had formal charges brought against Hutchinson and denounced her lectures as "not tolerable nor comely in the sight of God nor fitting for your sex." A leading minister told her, "You have stept out of your place, you have rather bine a Husband than a Wife and a preacher than a Hearer; and a Magistrate than a Subject."

Winthrop and other Puritan elders referred to Hutchinson and her followers as **antinomians**, people who believed that Christians could be saved by faith alone and did not need to act in accordance with God's law as set forth in the Bible and as interpreted by the colony's leaders. Hutchinson nimbly defended herself against the accusation of antinomianism. Yes, she acknowledged, she believed that men and women were saved by faith alone; but no, she did not deny the need to obey God's law. "The Lord hath let me see which was the clear ministry and which the wrong," she said. How could she tell which ministry was which, Winthrop asked. "By an immediate revelation," she replied, "by the voice of [God's] own spirit to my soul." Winthrop seized this statement as the heresy of prophecy, the view that God revealed his will directly to a believer instead of exclusively through the Bible, as every right-minded Puritan knew.

In 1638, the Boston church formally excommunicated Hutchinson. The minister decreed, "I doe cast you out and . . . deliver you up to Satan." Banished, Hutchinson and her family moved first to Roger Williams's Rhode Island and then to present-day New York, where she and most of her family were killed by Indians.

The strains within Puritanism exemplified by dissenters like Anne Hutchinson and Roger Williams caused communities to splinter repeatedly during the seventeenth century. Thomas Hooker, a prominent minister, clashed with Winthrop and other leaders over the composition of the church. Hooker argued that men and women who lived godly lives should be admitted to church membership even if they had not experienced conversion. In 1636, Hooker led an exodus of more than eight hundred colonists from Massachusetts to the Connecticut River valley, where they founded Hartford and neighboring towns. In 1639, the towns adopted the Fundamental Orders of Connecticut, a quasi-constitution that could be changed only by the vote of freemen, who did not have to be church members, although nearly all of them were.

Other Puritan churches divided and subdivided throughout the seventeenth century as acrimony developed over doctrine and church government. Sometimes churches split over the appointment of a controversial minister. These divisions arose from uncertainties and tensions within Puritan belief. As the colonies matured, other tensions surfaced.

antinomians
Individuals who believed that Christians could be saved by faith alone and did not need to act in accordance with God's law as set forth in the Bible.

How did New England society change during the seventeenth century?	How did the middle colonies differ from New England and the southern colonies?	How did the English empire influence the colonies?	Conclusion: Was there an English model of colonization in North America?

Religious Controversies and Economic Changes

A revolutionary change in the fortunes of Puritans in England had major consequences in New England. Disputes between King Charles I and Parliament, which was dominated by Puritans, escalated in 1642 to civil war in England, a conflict known as the **Puritan Revolution**. Parliamentary forces led by the staunch Puritan Oliver Cromwell were victorious. They beheaded Charles I in 1649 and proclaimed England a Puritan republic. From 1649 to 1660, England's rulers were Puritans and their supporters.

When the Puritan Revolution began, the stream of immigrants to New England dwindled, creating hard times for the colonists. They could no longer consider themselves a city on a hill that set a godly example for humankind. Puritans in England, not New England, were reforming English society. Also, when immigrant ships seldom came, the colonists faced sky-high prices for scarce English goods and few customers for their own colonial products. When they searched to find new products and markets, they established the enduring patterns of New England's economy.

New England's rocky soil and short growing season ruled out cultivating the southern colonies' crops of tobacco and rice that found ready markets in Atlantic ports. Exports that New Englanders could not get from the soil they took instead from the forest and the sea. By the 1640s, fur-bearing animals had become scarce unless fur trappers and traders went far beyond the frontiers of English settlement. Trees from the seemingly limitless forests of New England proved a longer-lasting resource. Masts for ships and staves for barrels of Spanish wine and West Indian sugar were crafted from New England timber.

Fish were the most important New England export. Dried, salted codfish from the rich North Atlantic fishing grounds found markets in southern Europe and the West Indies. The fish trade also stimulated colonial shipbuilding and trained generations of fishermen, sailors, and merchants. But the lives of most New England colonists revolved less around fish, fur, and timber than around their farms, churches, and families.

Although immigration came to a standstill in the 1640s, the colonial population continued to boom, doubling every twenty years. In New England, almost everyone got married, and women often had eight or nine children. Long, cold winters reduced warm-weather diseases such as malaria and yellow fever, making the death rate lower than in the South. By the end of the seventeenth century, the total New England population of about 100,000 roughly equaled that in the southern colonies.

During the second half of the seventeenth century, under the pressures of steady population growth (**Figure 4.1**) and participation in the Atlantic economy, the red-hot piety of the Puritan founding generation cooled. After 1640, the population grew faster than church membership. Boston's churches in 1650 could house only about a third of the city's residents. By the 1680s, women made up the majority of church members throughout New England. In some towns, only 15 percent of the adult men belonged to churches. A growing fraction of New Englanders, especially men, practiced what one historian has called "horse-shed Christianity." They attended sermons but afterward loitered outside near the horse shed, gossiping about the weather, fishing, their crops, or the scandalous behavior of neighbors. This slackening of piety led the Puritan minister Michael Wigglesworth to ask, in verse:

> How is it that
> I find In stead of holiness Carnality;
> In stead of heavenly frames an Earthly mind,
> For burning zeal, luke-warm Indifferency,
> For flaming love, key-cold Dead-heartedness. . . .
> Whence cometh it, that Pride, and Luxurie
> Debate, Deceit, Contention and Strife,
> False-dealing, Covetousness, Hypocrisie
> . . . amongst them are so rife,
> . . . that an honest man can hardly
> Trust his Brother?

Puritan Revolution
English civil war which began in 1642 and ended with the execution of Charles I in 1649, resulting in Puritan rule in England until 1660.

CONSIDER CAUSE AND EFFECT

Why did piety decline in New England during the seventeenth century?

Why did Puritans emigrate to North America?

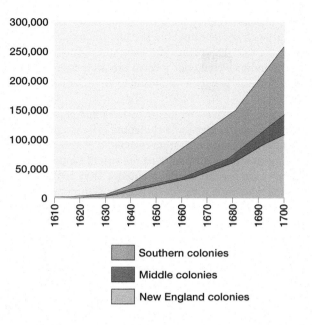

300,000

250,000

200,000

150,000

100,000

50,000

0

1610 1620 1630 1640 1650 1660 1670 1680 1690 1700

Southern colonies

Middle colonies

New England colonies

FIGURE 4.1 ◀ Population of the English North American Colonies in the Seventeenth Century

The colonial population grew at a steadily accelerating rate during the seventeenth century. New England and the southern colonies each accounted for about half the total colonial population until after 1680, when growth in Pennsylvania and New York contributed to a surge in the population of the middle colonies.

Most alarming to Puritan leaders was that many of the children of the visible saints of Winthrop's generation failed to experience conversion and become full church members. Puritans tended to assume that sainthood was inherited—that there was a good chance the children of visible saints were also among the elect. As these children grew up during the 1640s and 1650s, however, they seldom experienced the inward transformation of being born again that signaled conversion and qualification for church membership. The problem of declining church membership and the

◀ New England Mother and Child This seventeenth-century painting of Elizabeth Freake and her baby Mary illustrates the evolution of New England society away from the Puritan austerity of the founders and toward worldly elegance and display. Both mother and daughter appear prosperous, healthy, and somewhat proud. Worcester Art Museum, Massachusetts, USA/Bridgeman Images.

READING THE IMAGE: What does the clothing of Elizabeth and Mary suggest about their religion?

CONNECTIONS: Why did New England's Puritan zeal diminish in the latter third of the seventeenth century?

| How did New England society change during the seventeenth century? | How did the middle colonies differ from New England and the southern colonies? | How did the English empire influence the colonies? | Conclusion: Was there an English model of colonization in North America? |

watering-down of Puritan orthodoxy became urgent during the 1650s when the children of saints, who had grown to adulthood in New England but had not experienced conversion, began to have their own children. Their sons and daughters—the grandchildren of Winthrop's generation of founders—could not receive the protection that baptism afforded against the terrors of death, because according to church rules, their parents had not experienced conversion.

Puritan churches debated what to do. To allow anyone, even the child of a saint, to become a church member without conversion was an unthinkable retreat from fundamental Puritan doctrine. In 1662, Massachusetts ministers reached a compromise known as the **Halfway Covenant**. Unconverted children of saints would be permitted to become "halfway" church members. Like regular church members, they could baptize their infants. But unlike full church members, they could not take communion or have voting privileges in the church. The Halfway Covenant generated a controversy that sputtered through Puritan churches for the remainder of the century. With the Halfway Covenant, Puritan churches came to terms with the lukewarm piety that had replaced the founders' burning zeal.

Nonetheless, New England communities continued to enforce piety with holy rigor. Beginning in 1656, small bands of **Quakers**—members of the Society of Friends, as they called themselves—began to arrive in Massachusetts. Quakers believed that God spoke directly to each individual through an "inner light" and that individuals did not need either a preacher or the Bible to discover God's Word. Maintaining that all human beings were equal in God's eyes, Quakers refused to conform to mere human creations such as laws and governments, unless God demanded. Women often took a leading role in Quaker meetings, in contrast to Puritan congregations, where women remained subordinate although they greatly outnumbered men.

New England communities treated Quakers with ruthless severity. Some Quakers were branded on the face "with a red-hot iron with [an] H. for heresie." When Quakers refused to leave Massachusetts, Boston officials hanged four of them between 1659 and 1661.

New Englanders' partial success in realizing the promise of a godly society ultimately undermined the intense appeal of Puritanism. In the pious Puritan communities of New England, leaders tried to eliminate sin. In the process, they diminished the sense of complete human depravity that was the wellspring of Puritanism. As minister Cotton Mather bemoaned, "*Religion* brought forth *Prosperity*, and the *Daughter* destroy'd the *Mother*."

Witch trials held in Salem, Massachusetts, signaled the erosion of religious confidence. From the beginning of English settlement in the New World, more than 95 percent of all legal accusations of witchcraft occurred in New England, a hint of the Puritans' preoccupation with sin and evil. In Salem in 1692, witnesses accused more than one hundred people of witchcraft, a capital crime. **(See "Analyzing Historical Evidence: Hunting Witches in Salem, Massachusetts" on page 98.)** Bewitched young girls shrieked in pain, their limbs twisted into strange contortions, as they pointed out the witches who tortured them. According to the trial court record, the bewitched girls declared that "the shape of [one accused witch] did oftentimes very grievously pinch them, choke them, bite them, and afflict them; urging them to write their names in a book"—the devil's book. Most of the accused witches were older women, and nearly all of them were well known to their accusers. The Salem court hanged nineteen accused witches and pressed one to death under heavy stones. The Salem witchcraft trials displayed New England colonists' enduring belief in the supernatural origins of evil and their gnawing doubts about the strength of their faith. Why else, after all, had so many New Englanders given in to what their accusers and the judges believed were the temptations of Satan?

Halfway Covenant
A compromise that allowed the unconverted children of visible saints to become "halfway" members of the church and baptize their own children, even though they were not full church members.

Quakers
Members of the Society of Friends who believed that God spoke directly to each individual through an "inner light."

Why did Puritans emigrate to North America?

◄ Witches Show Their Love for Satan
Witches debased themselves by standing in line to kiss Satan's buttocks—or so it was popularly believed. This seventeenth-century print portrays Satan with clawlike hands and feet, the tail of a rodent, the wings of a bat, and the head of a lustful ram attached to the torso of a man. Notice that women predominate among the witches eager to express their devotion to Satan. The Granger Collection, New York.

QUICK REVIEW

Why did New England churches adopt the Halfway Covenant?

How did the middle colonies differ from New England and the southern colonies?

South of New England and north of the Chesapeake, a group of middle colonies were founded in the last third of the seventeenth century. Before the 1670s, few Europeans settled in the region. For the first two-thirds of the seventeenth century, the most important European outpost in the area was the relatively small Dutch colony of New Netherland. By 1700, however, the English monarchy had seized New Netherland, renamed it New York, and encouraged the creation of a Quaker colony in Pennsylvania led by William Penn. Unlike the New England colonies, the middle colonies of New York, New Jersey, and Pennsylvania originated as land grants by the English monarch to one or more proprietors, who then possessed both the land and the extensive, almost monarchical, powers of government (**Map 4.2**). These middle colonies attracted settlers of more varied European origins and religious faiths than were found in New England.

From New Netherland to New York

In 1609, the Dutch East India Company sent Henry Hudson to search for a Northwest Passage to the Orient. Hudson sailed up the large river that now bears his name until it dwindled to a stream that obviously did not lead to China. A decade later, the

CHRONOLOGY

1609
– Henry Hudson searches for Northwest Passage.

1626
– Manhattan Island purchased; New Amsterdam founded.

1664
– English seize Dutch colony; rename it New York.
– Colony of New Jersey created.

1681
– Colony of Pennsylvania founded.

| How did New England society change during the seventeenth century? | **How did the middle colonies differ from New England and the southern colonies?** | How did the English empire influence the colonies? | Conclusion: Was there an English model of colonization in North America? |

Hunting Witches in Salem, Massachusetts

I n the summer of 1692, many people in and around Salem, Massachusetts, accused dozens of their neighbors and kinfolk of being witches. Officials convened a special court to hear the testimony of the accusers and to examine the accused. In the end, nineteen convicted witches were hanged, and more than 150 accused witches crammed the jails before the trials were finally called off.

DOCUMENT 1

Witnesses against Accused Witch Susanna Martin, 1692

Neighbors lined up to give testimony that, in their minds, proved that the accused were witches. Like many other accused people, Susanna Martin pleaded not guilty to witchcraft. The court, persuaded by the testimony of witnesses, sentenced her to death, and she was executed on July 19, 1692.

Bernard Peache testify'd, That being in Bed on a Lords-day Night, he heard a scrabbling at the Window, whereat he then saw, *Susanna Martin* come in, and jump down upon the Floor. She took hold of this Deponents Feet, and drawing his Body up into an Heap, she lay upon him, near Two Hours; in all which time he could neither speak nor stirr. At length, when he could begin to move, he laid hold on her Hand, and pulling it up to his mouth, he bit three of her Fingers, as he judged, unto the Bone. Whereupon she went from the Chamber, down the Stairs, out at the Door. . . .

John Kembal . . . Being desirous to furnish himself with a Dog, he applied himself to buy one of this Martin. . . . But she not letting him have his Choice [Kembal went to another neighbor to get a puppy]. Within a few days after, [when] this *Kembal* . . . came below the Meeting-House, there appeared unto him, a little thing like a *Puppy*, of a Darkish Colour; and it shot Backwards and forwards between his Leggs. He had the Courage to use all possible Endeavors of Cutting it, with his Axe; but he could not Hit it. . . . Going a little further, there appeared unto him a Black Puppy, somewhat bigger than the first; but Black as Cole. Its motions were quicker than those of his Ax; it Flew at his Belly and away; then at his Throat, also over his Shoulder. . . . His heart now began to fail him, and he thought the Dog would have Tore his Throat out. But he recovered himself, and called upon God in his Distress; and Naming the Name of JESUS CHRIST, it Vanished away at once. . . . [The next day, Susanna Martin told other people that he had been frightened by puppies, although] Kembal [said he] had mentioned the Matter to no Creature Living.

Joseph Ring . . . has been strangely carried about by *Demons*, from one *Witch-Meeting* to another, for near two years together. . . . Afterwards . . . this poor man would be visited with unknown shapes . . . which would force him away with them, unto unknown Places, where he saw meetings, Feastings, Dancings. . . . When he was brought into these Hellish meetings, one of the First things they still did unto him, was to give him a knock on the Back, whereupon he was . . . as if Bound with chains, uncapable of Stirring out of the place, till they should Release him. . . . There often came to him a man, who presented him a Book, whereto he would have him set his Hand; promising to him, that he should then have even what he would; and presenting him with all the delectable Things, persons, and places that he could imagine. But he refusing to subscribe, the business would end with dreadful Shapes,

---

Dutch government granted the West India Company—a group of Dutch merchants and shippers—exclusive rights to trade with the Western Hemisphere. In 1626, Peter Minuit, the resident director of the company, purchased Manhattan Island from the Manhate Indians for trade goods worth the equivalent of a dozen beaver pelts. New Amsterdam, the small settlement established at the southern tip of Manhattan Island, became the principal trading center in **New Netherland** and the colony's headquarters.

Unlike the English colonies, New Netherland did not attract many European immigrants. Like New England and the Chesapeake colonies, New Netherland never realized its sponsors' dreams of great profits. The company tried to stimulate immigration by granting patroonships—allotments of eighteen miles of land along the Hudson River—to wealthy stockholders, who would bring fifty families to the colony and settle them as serf-like tenants on their huge domains. Only one patroonship succeeded; the others failed to attract settlers, and the company eventually reclaimed much of the land.

New Netherland
Dutch colony on Manhattan Island.

Why did Puritans emigrate to North America?

Noises and Screechings, which almost scared him out of his witts. . . . He saw the Prisoner [Susanna Martin], at several of those Hellish Randezvouzes. Note, This Woman was one of the most Impudent, Scurrilous, wicked creatures in the world & she did now throughout her whole Trial, discover herself to be such an one. Yet when she was asked what she had to say for her self, her Cheef Plea was, *That she had Led a most virtuous and Holy Life.*

Source: Cotton Mather, *The Wonders of the Invisible World* (Boston, 1692), 115–26.

DOCUMENT 2

Robert Calef, *More Wonders of the Invisible World*, 1700

A few New Englanders spoke out against the witch-hunt as the persecution of innocent people. Robert Calef, a Boston merchant, wrote a scathing criticism of the witch trials and their supporters.

And now to sum up all in a few words, we have seen a biggotted zeal, stirring up a blind, and most bloody rage, not against enemies, or irreligious, profligate persons—but . . . against as virtuous and religious as any they have left behind them in this country . . . and this by the testimony of vile varlets, as not only were known before, but have been further apparent since, by their manifest lives, whoredoms, incest &c. The accusations of these, from their spectral sight, being the chief evidence against those that suffered; in which accusations they were upheld by both magistrates and ministers, so long as they apprehended themselves in no danger. And then, tho' they could defend neither the doctrine nor the practice, yet none of them have in such a publick manner as the case requires, testified against either;

tho', at the same time they could not but be sensible what a stain and lasting infamy they have brought upon the whole country, to the indangering of the future welfare not only of this but of other places, induced by their example . . . occasioning the great dishonour and blasphemy of the name of God . . . and as a natural effect thereof, to the great increase of Atheism.

Source: Robert Calef, *More Wonders of the Invisible World* (London, 1700), unpaginated "Epistle to the Reader."

Questions for Analysis

ASK HISTORICAL QUESTIONS: Why were witnesses, the Salem court, and many people in the region so obsessed with witches that they seemed to suspect their malevolent influence in the ordinary events of daily life?

ANALYZE THE EVIDENCE: What evidence did accusers offer as proof that Susanna Martin was a witch? What did Calef think about such evidence? If the evidence was not the work of the devil or witches, what did it indicate?

CONSIDER THE CONTEXT: How did the 1692 witchcraft trials reflect changes in New England society since the time of John Winthrop and the founding generation? What do the testimonies of the accusers and the criticisms of Calef suggest about the strength and confidence of Puritans' belief in their covenant with God?

RECOGNIZE VIEWPOINTS: Why did Calef denounce the witchcraft trials? How would the witnesses respond to Martin's claim that she had led a most virtuous and holy life?

Though few in number, New Netherlanders were remarkably diverse, especially compared with the mostly English settlers to the north and south. Religious dissenters and immigrants from Holland, Sweden, France, Germany, and elsewhere made their way to the colony. A minister of the Dutch Reformed Church complained to his superiors in Holland that several groups of Jews had recently arrived, adding to the religious mixture of "Papists, Mennonites and Lutherans among the Dutch [and] many Puritans . . . and many other atheists . . . who conceal themselves under the name of Christians."

The West India Company struggled to govern the ethnically and religiously diverse colonists. Peter Stuyvesant, governor from 1647 to 1664, pointed out to company officials in Holland that "the *English* and *French* colonies are continued and populated by their own nation and countrymen and consequently [are] bound together more firmly and united," while the "colonies in *New-Netherland* are only gradually and slowly peopled by the scrapings of all sorts of nationalities (few excepted), who consequently have the

How did New England society change during the seventeenth century? | **How did the middle colonies differ from New England and the southern colonies?** | How did the English empire influence the colonies? | Conclusion: Was there an English model of colonization in North America?

MAP 4.2 ▶ Middle Colonies in the Seventeenth Century For the most part, settlers in the middle colonies in the seventeenth century clustered along the Hudson and Delaware rivers. The geographic extent of the colonies shown in this map reflects land grants authorized in England. Native Americans rather than colonists inhabited most of this area.

least interest in the welfare and maintenance of the commonwealth." Stuyvesant tried to enforce conformity to the Dutch Reformed Church, but the company—eager for more immigrants—declared that "the consciences of men should be free and unshackled," making a virtue of New Netherland necessity. The company never permitted the colony's settlers to form a representative government. Instead, the company appointed government officials who established policies, including taxes, which many colonists deeply resented.

In 1664, New Netherland became New York. Charles II, who became king of England in 1660 when Parliament restored the monarchy, gave his brother James, the Duke of York, an enormous grant of land that included New Netherland. The duke quickly organized a small fleet of warships, which appeared off Manhattan Island in late summer 1664, and demanded that Stuyvesant surrender. With little choice, he did.

As the new proprietor of the colony, the Duke of York exercised almost the same unlimited authority over the colony as had the West India Company, although the duke never set foot in the colony. Like the Dutch, the duke permitted "all persons of what Religion soever, quietly to inhabit . . . provided they give no disturbance to the publique peace, nor doe molest or disquiet others in the free exercise of their religion." This policy of religious toleration was less an affirmation of liberty of conscience than a recognition of the reality of the most ethnically and religiously diverse colony in seventeenth-century North America.

New Jersey and Pennsylvania

The creation of New York led indirectly to the founding of two other middle colonies, New Jersey and Pennsylvania. In 1664, the Duke of York subdivided his grant and gave the portion between the Hudson and Delaware rivers to two of his friends. The proprietors of this new colony, New Jersey, quarreled and called in a prominent English Quaker, William Penn, to settle their dispute. Penn eventually worked out an agreement that continued New Jersey's proprietary government. In the process, Penn himself became intensely interested in what he termed a "holy experiment" of establishing a genuinely Quaker colony in America.

Unlike most Quakers, William Penn came from an eminent family. His father had served both Cromwell and Charles II and had been knighted. Born in 1644, the younger Penn trained for a military career, but the ideas of dissenters from the reestablished Church of England appealed to him, and he became a devout Quaker. By 1680, Penn

CONSIDER CAUSE AND EFFECT

What accounts for the ethnic and religious diversity of New Netherland and New York?

Why did Puritans emigrate to North America?

◀ **New Amsterdam** The settlement on Manhattan Island appears in the background of this 1673 Dutch portrait of New Amsterdam. In the foreground, the Dutch artist placed native inhabitants of the mainland, drawing them to resemble Africans rather than Lenni Lenape (Delaware) Indians. The portrait contrasts orderly, efficient, businesslike New Amsterdam with the exotic natural environment of America. © Collection of the New-York Historical Society, USA/ Bridgeman Images.

had published fifty books and had spoken at countless public meetings, but he had failed to win official toleration for Quakers in England.

The Quakers' concept of an open, generous God who made his love equally available to all people continually brought them into conflict with the English government. Quaker leaders were ordinary men and women, not specially trained preachers. Quakers allowed women to assume positions of religious leadership. "In souls there is no sex," they said. Since all people were equal in the spiritual realm, Quakers considered social hierarchy false and evil. They called everyone "friend" and shook hands instead of curtsying or removing their hats—even when meeting the king. These customs enraged many non-Quakers and provoked innumerable beatings and worse. Penn was jailed four times for such offenses.

Despite his many run-ins with the government, Penn remained on good terms with Charles II. Partly to rid England of the troublesome Quakers, Charles made Penn the proprietor of a new colony of some 45,000 square miles called Pennsylvania in 1681.

Toleration and Diversity in Pennsylvania

Quakers flocked to Pennsylvania in numbers exceeded only by the great Puritan migration to New England fifty years earlier. Between 1682 and 1685, nearly eight thousand immigrants arrived. Penn wrote in 1685 that the settlers were "a collection of divers nations in Europe: as, French, Dutch, Germans, Swedes, Danes, Finns, Scotch-Irish, and English; and of the last equal to all the rest." The settlers represented a cross section of the artisans, farmers, and laborers who predominated among English Quakers.

Quaker missionaries also encouraged immigrants from the European continent, and many came, giving Pennsylvania greater ethnic diversity than any other English colony except New York. The Quaker colony prospered, and the capital city, Philadelphia, soon rivaled New York as a center of commerce. By 1700, the city's five thousand inhabitants participated in a thriving trade exporting flour and other food products to the West Indies and importing English textiles and manufactured goods.

Penn wanted to live in peace with the Indians who inhabited the region. His Indian policy expressed his Quaker ideals and contrasted sharply with the hostile policies of the other English colonies. As he explained to the chief of the Lenni Lenape (Delaware) Indians, "God has written his law in our hearts, by which we are taught and commanded to love and help and do good to one another . . . [and] I desire to enjoy [Pennsylvania lands] with your love and consent." Penn instructed his agents to obtain the Indians' consent by purchasing their land, respecting their claims, and dealing with them fairly.

How did New England society change during the seventeenth century?

How did the middle colonies differ from New England and the southern colonies?

How did the English empire influence the colonies?

Conclusion: Was there an English model of colonization in North America?

▶ **Quaker Couple** This seventeenth-century picture of a Quaker couple illustrates their plain clothing and modest habits. The woman and man do not appear poor; their clothing fits them and is well made, but the colors in their clothing are somber and muted, unlike the richly ornamented and brightly colored clothes worn by prosperous non-Quakers. Private Collection / The Stapleton Collection / Bridgeman Images.

Penn declared that the first principle of government was that every settler would "enjoy the free possession of his or her faith and exercise of worship towards God." Accordingly, Pennsylvania tolerated Protestant believers of all kinds as well as Roman Catholics. All voters and officeholders had to be Christians, however. Penn's government did not compel settlers to attend religious services, as in Massachusetts, or to pay taxes to maintain a state-supported church, as in Virginia.

Despite these policies of toleration, Pennsylvania was as much a Quaker colony as New England was a stronghold of Puritanism. "Government seems to me a part of religion itself," Penn wrote, "for there is no power but of God. The powers that be, are ordained of God: whosoever therefore resists the power [of government] resists the ordinance of God." Penn believed that government had two basic purposes: "to terrify evil-doers . . . [and] to cherish those that do well." Penn had no hesitation about using civil government to enforce religious morality. One of the colony's first laws provided severe punishment for "all such offenses against God, as swearing, cursing, lying, profane talking, [and] drunkenness . . . which excite the people to rudeness, cruelty, looseness, and irreligion."

As proprietor, Penn had extensive powers subject only to review by the king. He appointed a governor, who maintained the proprietor's power to veto any laws passed by the colonial council, which was elected by property owners who possessed at least one hundred acres of land or who paid taxes. The council had the power to originate laws and administer all the affairs of government. A popularly elected assembly served as a check on the council; its members had the authority to reject or approve laws supported by the council.

Penn stressed that the exact form of government mattered less than the men who served in it. In Penn's eyes, "good men" staffed Pennsylvania's government because Quakers dominated elective and appointive offices. Quakers, of course, differed among themselves. Members of the assembly struggled to win the right to debate and amend laws, especially tax laws. They finally won the battle in 1701, when a new Charter of Privileges gave the proprietor the power to appoint the council, and in turn stripped the council of all its former powers and gave them to the assembly, which became the only one-house legislature in all the English colonies.

COMPARE AND CONTRAST

How did Pennsylvania compare with the New England and southern colonies?

Why did Puritans emigrate to North America?

How did the English empire influence the colonies?

Proprietary grants to faraway lands were a cheap way for the king to reward friends. As the colonies grew, however, the grants became more valuable.

After 1660, the king took initiatives to funnel colonial trade through English hands and to consolidate royal authority over colonial governments. Influenced by economic and political considerations and triggered by King Philip's War between colonists and

CHRONOLOGY

1675–1676
– King Philip's War fought between colonists and Indians.

1686
– Dominion of New England created.

1688
– England's Glorious Revolution restores Protestant monarchy.

1689–1697
– King William's War pits Britain against France in North America.

MAP 4.3 ▲ American Colonies at the End of the Seventeenth Century

By the end of the seventeenth century, settlers inhabited a narrow band of land that stretched from Boston to Norfolk, with pockets of settlement farther south. Native Americans, France, and Spain contested the colonies' claims to enormous tracts of land to the west.

| How did New England society change during the seventeenth century? | How did the middle colonies differ from New England and the southern colonies? | **How did the English empire influence the colonies?** | Conclusion: Was there an English model of colonization in North America? |

Native Americans, the royal initiatives defined the basic relationship between the colonies and England that lasted until the American Revolution (**Map 4.3**).

Royal Regulation of Colonial Trade

English economic policies toward the colonies were designed to yield customs fees for the monarchy and profitable business for English merchants and shippers. Also, the policies were intended to divert the colonies' trade from England's enemies, especially the Dutch and French.

The Navigation Acts of 1650, 1651, 1660, and 1663 (see chapter 3) set forth two fundamental rules governing colonial trade. First, goods shipped to and from the colonies had to be transported in English ships using primarily English crews. Second, the Navigation Acts listed colonial products that could be shipped only to England or to other English colonies. These regulations prevented Chesapeake planters from shipping their tobacco directly to the European continent. But they interfered less with the commerce of New England and the middle colonies, whose principal exports of fish, lumber, and flour could legally be sent directly to their most important markets in the West Indies.

TRACE CHANGE OVER TIME

How did the colonies' economic relationship with England change during the seventeenth century?

By the end of the seventeenth century, colonial commerce was defined by English regulations that subjected merchants and shippers to royal supervision and gave them access to markets throughout the English empire. In addition, colonial shipping received protection from the English navy. By 1700, colonial goods (including those from the West Indies) accounted for one-fifth of all English imports and for two-thirds of all goods re-exported from England to the European continent. In turn, the colonies absorbed more than one-tenth of English exports. The commercial regulations of the empire gave economic value to England's proprietorship of the American colonies.

King Philip's War and the Consolidation of Royal Authority

The monarchy also took steps to exercise greater control over colonial governments. Virginia had been a royal colony since 1624; Maryland, South Carolina, and the middle colonies were proprietary colonies with close ties to the crown. The New England colonies possessed royal charters, but they had developed their own distinctively Puritan governments. Charles II, whose father, Charles I, had been beheaded by Puritans in England, took an interest in harnessing the New England colonies more firmly to the English empire. The occasion was a royal investigation following **King Philip's War**.

King Philip's War
War begun by Metacomet (King Philip) in 1675, in which the colonists finally prevailed after much bloodshed.

A series of skirmishes in the Connecticut River valley between 1636 and 1637 culminated in the Pequot War when colonists massacred hundreds of Pequot Indians. In the decades that followed, New Englanders established relatively peaceful relations with the more potent Wampanoags, while they steadily encroached on Indian land. In 1642, a native leader urged warring tribes to band together against the English. "We [must] be one as they [the English] are," he said; "otherwise we shall be gone shortly, for . . . these English having gotten our land, they with scythes cut down the grass, and with axes fell the trees, and their cows and horses eat the grass, and their hogs spoil our clam banks, and we shall all be starved."

Such grievances accumulated until 1675, when the Wampanoags, led by

"In 1642, a native leader urged warring tribes to band together against the English. 'We [must] be one as they [the English] are,' he said; 'otherwise we shall be gone shortly...'"

Why did Puritans emigrate to North America?

their chief Metacomet, whom the colonists called King Philip, attacked English settlements in western Massachusetts. Militias from Massachusetts and other New England colonies counterattacked against the Wampanoags, Nipmucks, and Narragansetts in a deadly sequence of battles that killed more than a thousand colonists and thousands more Indians. The Indians destroyed thirteen English settlements and partially burned another half dozen. Mary Rowlandson, a Massachusetts minister's wife who was captured during an Indian attack, recalled later that it was a "solemn sight to see so many Christians lying in their blood . . . like a company of sheep torn by wolves. All of them stripped naked by a company of hell-hounds, roaring, singing, ranting and insulting, as if they would have torn our very hearts out."

By the spring of 1676, Indian warriors ranged freely within seventeen miles of Boston. The colonists finally defeated the Indians, mainly with a scorched-earth policy of burning their food supplies. King Philip's War left the New England colonists with a large war debt, a devastated frontier, and an enduring hatred of Indians. A colonial officer justified destroying the Indians by likening them to vermin: "Yea Rats and Mice, or Swarms of Lice a Nation may destroy."

In 1676, an agent of the king arrived to investigate whether New England was abiding by English laws. Not surprisingly, the king's agent found many deviations from English rules, and the monarchy decided to govern New England more directly. In 1684, an English court revoked the old Massachusetts charter, the foundation of the Puritan colony's government. Two years later, royal officials incorporated Massachusetts and the other colonies north of Maryland into the Dominion of New England. To govern the Dominion, the English sent Sir Edmund Andros to Boston. Some New England merchants cooperated with Andros, but most colonists were offended by his flagrant disregard for such Puritan traditions as keeping the Sabbath. A visiting Englishman claimed that Bostonians were "great Censors of

King Philip's War, 1675

◀ **Metacomet** This eighteenth-century engraving illustrates the artist's image of Metacomet, the native leader of what colonists recalled as King Philip's War. The engraving depicts Metacomet's Indian style of dress, a sharp contrast to colonists' clothing. Yet the clothing is made of textiles obtained in trade with colonists, indicating the partial adoption of colonial goods. His musket and powder horns emphasize the danger Metacomet and other Indians posed to the colonists by making effective use of the colonists' own weaponry. Library of Congress, 3b42346.

| How did New England society change during the seventeenth century? | How did the middle colonies differ from New England and the southern colonies? | **How did the English empire influence the colonies?** | Conclusion: Was there an English model of colonization in North America? |

105

CONSIDER CAUSE AND EFFECT

Why did the English monarchy establish the Dominion of New England?

other Men's Manners, but extremely careless of their own." Worst of all, the Dominion of New England invalidated all land titles, confronting landowners in New England with the horrifying prospect of losing their land.

Events in England, however, permitted Massachusetts colonists to overthrow Andros and retain title to their property. When Charles II died in 1685, his brother James II, a zealous Catholic, succeeded him. James's aggressive campaign to appoint Catholics to government posts created such unrest that in 1688 a group of Protestant noblemen in Parliament invited the Dutch ruler William III of Orange to claim the English throne.

When William III landed in England at the head of a large army, James fled to France, and William III and his wife, Mary II (James's daughter), became corulers in the relatively bloodless "Glorious Revolution." William and Mary restored Protestant influence in England and its empire. Rumors of the Glorious Revolution raced across the Atlantic and emboldened colonial uprisings against royal authority in Massachusetts, New York, and Maryland.

In Boston in 1689, rebels tossed Andros and other English officials in jail, destroyed the Dominion of New England, and reestablished the former charter government. New Yorkers followed the Massachusetts example. Under the leadership of Jacob Leisler, rebels seized the royal governor in 1689 and ruled the colony for more than a year. That same year in Maryland, the Protestant Association, led by John Coode, overthrew the colony's pro-Catholic government, fearing it would not recognize the new Protestant king.

But these rebel governments did not last. When King William III's governor of New York arrived in 1691, he executed Leisler for treason. Coode's men ruled Maryland until the new royal governor arrived in 1692 and ended both Coode's rebellion and Lord Baltimore's proprietary government. In Massachusetts, John Winthrop's city on a hill became another royal colony in 1691. The new charter said that the governor of Massachusetts would be appointed by the king rather than elected by the colonists' representatives. But perhaps the most unsettling change was the new qualification for voting. Possession of property replaced church membership as a requirement for voting in colony-wide elections. Wealth replaced God's grace as the defining characteristic of Massachusetts citizenship.

QUICK REVIEW

Why did the Glorious Revolution in England lead to uprisings in the American colonies?

Conclusion: Was there an English model of colonization in North America?

By 1700, the northern English colonies had developed along lines quite different from the example set by their southern counterparts. Emigrants came with their families and created settlements unlike the scattered plantations and largely male environment of early Virginia. Puritans in New England built towns and governments around their churches and placed worship of God, not tobacco, at the center of their society. They depended chiefly on the labor of family members rather than on indentured servants and slaves.

Why did Puritans emigrate to North America?

The convictions of Puritanism that motivated John Winthrop and others to reinvent England in the colonies dimmed as New England matured and dissenters such as Roger Williams multiplied. Catholics, Quakers, Anglicans (members of the Church of England), Jews, and others settled in the Middle and southern colonies, enjoying the rare toleration of religious differences, especially in Pennsylvania and New York. At the same time, northern colonists, like their southern counterparts, developed an ever-increasing demand for land that inevitably led to bloody conflict with the Indians, who were killed or pushed away. By the closing years of the seventeenth century, the royal government in England intervened to try to moderate those conflicts and to govern the colonies more directly for the benefit of the monarchy. Assertions of royal control triggered colonial resistance that was ultimately suppressed, resulting in Massachusetts losing its special charter and becoming instead a royal colony much like the other English colonies in North America.

During the next century, the English colonial world would undergo surprising new developments built on the achievements of the seventeenth century. Immigrants from Scotland, Ireland, and Germany streamed into North America, and unprecedented numbers of African slaves were imported into the southern colonies. On average, white colonists attained a relatively comfortable standard of living, especially compared with most people in England and continental Europe. While religion remained important, the intensity of religious concern that characterized the seventeenth century declined during the eighteenth century. Colonists worried more about prosperity than about providence, and their societies grew increasingly secular, worldly, and diverse.

| How did New England society change during the seventeenth century? | How did the middle colonies differ from New England and the southern colonies? | How did the English empire influence the colonies? | **Conclusion: Was there an English model of colonization in North America?** |

107

CHAPTER 4 STUDY GUIDE

STEP 1

EXPLAIN WHY IT MATTERS

Put your reading into practice. Identify each term below, and then explain why it matters in U.S. history.

TERM	WHO OR WHAT & WHEN	WHY IT MATTERS
English Reformation (p. 84)		
Puritans (p. 84)		
Separatists (p. 85)		
Calvinism (p. 88)		
predestination (p. 88)		
visible saints (p. 88)		
antinomians (p. 93)		
Puritan Revolution (p. 94)		
Halfway Covenant (p. 96)		
Quakers (p. 96)		
New Netherland (p. 98)		
King Philip's War (p. 104)		

STEP 2

MOVE BEYOND THE BASICS

To demonstrate a more advanced understanding, compare and contrast the northern colonies—why they were settled, their social and political structures, and their economies.

Colony	Reasons for Settlement	Social/Political Structures (religion, family, legal system)	Economic (land use and distribution, industry, income, labor)
Plymouth			
Massachusetts Bay			
Rhode Island			
New Netherland/New York			
Pennsylvania			

STEP 3

PUT IT ALL TOGETHER

Now, try to explain the big picture. Remember to use specific examples from the chapter in your answers.

NEW ENGLAND

- What kind of society did the early settlers of New England hope to create?

- What challenged Puritan domination of New England?

THE MIDDLE COLONIES

- How did the settlement of the middle colonies differ from that of New England and the southern colonies?

- What explains tolerance for religious and ethnic diversity in the middle colonies?

THE EMPIRE

- How did the English empire seek to regulate colonial trade?

- How did colonists respond to the English empire's efforts to consolidate its political authority?

LOOKING BACKWARD, LOOKING AHEAD

- How did European colonization of the Americas in the seventeenth century differ from Spanish colonization in the previous century?

- How did growth and development of English colonies in the seventeenth century set the stage for conflict between England and its colonies in the eighteenth century?

STEP 4

CONNECT THESE EVENTS

How did the excommunication of Anne Hutchinson and the establishment of the Halfway Covenant demonstrate a declining importance of religion and Puritan zeal in the colonies during the seventeenth century?

STEP 5

CONNECT TO THE PRESENT

To what extent have the religious ideas of seventeenth-century colonists shaped features of American life today?

5

COLONIAL AMERICA IN THE EIGHTEENTH CENTURY

1701–1770

What were the most important changes in colonial America between 1701 and 1770? This chapter explores the evolution of different colonial societies in New England, the middle colonies, and the southern colonies. Despite regional differences, common experiences and ideas created a growing sense of unity among the colonists.

This chapter will explore the following questions:

- How did the British North American colonies change during the eighteenth century?
- What changed in New England life and culture?
- Why did the middle colonies grow rapidly?
- Why did slavery come to define the southern colonies?
- What unified colonists in British North America during the eighteenth century?
- Conclusion: Why did British North American colonists develop a dual identity?

AN AMERICAN STORY

The brothers Ancona and Little Ephraim Robin John lived in Old Calabar in West Africa. The brothers were part of a slave-trading dynasty headed by their relative Grandy King George, one of the most powerful leaders of the Efik people. Grandy King George owned hundreds of slaves whom he employed to capture still more slaves in the African interior. He sold these captives to captains of European slave ships for transport to sugar, tobacco, and rice fields in the New World.

British slave ship captains and African rivals conspired in 1767 to destroy Grandy King George's control of the slave trade. In a bloody battle, Little Ephraim and Ancona Robin John were themselves enslaved and transported across the Atlantic to the West Indies.

Unlike most slaves, the Robin John brothers spoke and wrote English, a skill they had learned as slave traders in Old Calabar. The Robin Johns escaped from the man who bought them in the West Indies and boarded a ship "determined to get home," Little Ephraim wrote. But the ship captain took them to Virginia instead and sold them as slaves. Their new master "would tie me up & whip me many times for nothing at all," Ancona testified, adding that he "was exceeding badly man ever I saw." After their Virginia master died in 1772, the Robin Johns heard that a slave ship from Old Calabar had recently arrived, and the captain promised to take them back to Africa if they would run away. They did, but the captain betrayed the Robin Johns and took them to Bristol, England, where he sought to sell them as slaves yet again.

While imprisoned in Bristol harbor, the Robin Johns smuggled letters to a Bristol slave trader they had known in Old Calabar. With his help, the Robin Johns appealed to the chief justice of England for their freedom on the grounds that they were unjustly enslaved because they "were free people . . . [who] had not done anything to forfeit our liberty." After complex negotiations, they won their freedom.

The Robin Johns converted to Christianity in Bristol, but they longed to return to Africa. In 1774, they left Bristol as free men on a slave ship bound for Old Calabar, where they resumed their careers as slave traders.

The Robin Johns' quest to escape enslavement and reclaim their freedom was shared but not realized by millions of Africans, who were victims of slave traders such as Grandy King George and numberless merchants, ship captains, and colonists. In contrast, tens of thousands of Europeans voluntarily crossed the Atlantic to seek opportunities in the North American colonies — often by agreeing to several years of servitude. Both groups often experienced the violence and deceit beneath the surface of the eighteenth-century Atlantic commerce that linked Britain, Africa, the West Indies, and colonial America. Many people, like the Robin Johns, turned to religious faith as a source of meaning and hope in an often cruel and unforgiving society.

The flood of free and unfree newcomers crossing the Atlantic contributed to unprecedented population growth in eighteenth-century British North America. In contrast, Spanish and French colonies in North America remained thinly populated outposts of European empires interested principally in maintaining a toehold in the vast continent. While the New England, middle, and southern colonies retained regional differences, commercial, cultural, and political developments built unifying experiences and attitudes among the colonists.

▼ **Captured into Slavery** African men, women, and children kidnapped or sold into the transatlantic slave trade were typically captured in the interior by other Africans who tied them up and marched them in a so-called coffle, as shown here, to prison-like holding pens on the African coast. African traders sold the enslaved people to European traders, who carried them to colonies in the New World. Hunger, disease, and violence killed roughly as many as slaves as did the brutal conditions of the transatlantic Middle Passage. Florilegius/SSPL/Getty Images.

How did the British North American colonies change during the eighteenth century?

The most important fact about eighteenth-century British America is phenomenal population growth: from about 250,000 in 1700 to more than two million by 1770. This eightfold growth of the colonial population signaled the maturation of a distinctive colonial society. In 1700, there were nineteen people in England for every American colonist. By 1770, there were only three. Colonists of different ethnic groups, races, and religions lived in varied environments under thirteen different colonial governments, all of them part of the British empire.

In general, the growth and diversity of the eighteenth-century colonial population derived from two sources: immigration and **natural increase** (growth through reproduction). Natural increase contributed about three-fourths of the population growth, immigration about one-fourth. Immigration shifted the ethnic and racial balance among the colonists, making them by 1770 less English and less white than ever before. Fewer than 10 percent of eighteenth-century immigrants came from England; about 36 percent were Scots-Irish, mostly from northern Ireland; 33 percent were brought from Africa, almost all of them slaves; nearly 15 percent had left the many German-language principalities (the nation of Germany did not exist until 1871); and almost 10 percent came from Scotland. In 1670, more than 9 out of 10 colonists were of English ancestry, and only 1 out of 25 was of African ancestry. By 1770, only about half of the colonists were of English descent, while more than 20 percent descended from Africans. Overall, by 1770, the people of the colonies had a distinctive colonial—rather than English—profile (**Map 5.1**).

The booming population of the colonies points toward a second major feature of eighteenth-century colonial society: an expanding economy. The nearly limitless wilderness stretching westward made land relatively cheap compared with its price in the Old World. The abundance of land made labor precious, and the colonists always needed more. The bottomless demand for labor was the fundamental economic environment that sustained the mushrooming population. Economic historians estimate that free colonists (those who were not indentured servants or slaves) had a higher standard of living than the majority of people elsewhere in the Atlantic world.

natural increase
Growth of population through reproduction, as opposed to immigration.

CONSIDER CAUSE AND EFFECT

What made the colonists in 1770 different from those in 1700 and from English society?

UNDERSTAND POINTS OF VIEW

What made the North American colonies attractive to voluntary immigrants during the eighteenth century?

QUICK REVIEW

How did the North American colonies achieve the remarkable population growth of the eighteenth century?

What changed in New England life and culture?

The New England population grew sixfold during the eighteenth century but lagged behind the growth in the other colonies. Most immigrants chose other destinations because New England's land was relatively densely settled and because Puritan orthodoxy discouraged newcomers of other faiths. As the population grew, many settlers in search of farmland left towns, causing Puritan communities to lose

MAP 5.1 ◀ Europeans and Africans in the Eighteenth Century

This map illustrates regions where Africans and certain immigrant groups clustered. It is important to avoid misreading the map. Predominantly English and German regions, for example, also contained colonists from other places. Likewise, regions where African slaves resided in large numbers also included many whites, slave masters among them. The map illustrates the diversity of eighteenth-century colonial society.

much of their cohesion. Still, networks of economic exchange tied New Englanders to their neighbors, to Boston merchants, and to the broad currents of Atlantic commerce. In many ways, trade became a faith that competed strongly with the traditions of Puritanism.

Natural Increase and Land Distribution

The New England population grew mostly by natural increase, much as it had during the seventeenth century. The perils of childbirth gave wives a shorter life expectancy than husbands, but wives often lived to have six, seven, or eight babies. Anne Franklin and her husband Josiah, a soap and candlemaker in Boston, had seven children before Anne died. Josiah quickly married his second wife, Abiah, and the couple had ten more children, including their son Benjamin, who became one of the most prominent colonial leaders of the eighteenth century. Like many other New Englanders, Benjamin Franklin felt hemmed in by family pressures and lack of opportunity. He ran away from Boston when he was seventeen to "assert my freedom," as he put it, landing first in New York and then in Philadelphia.

The growing New England population pressed against a limited amount of land (see Map 5.1). As the northernmost British colonies, New England had frontiers inhabited by powerful Native Americans, especially the Iroquois and Mahicans, who

What changed in New England life and culture?	Why did the middle colonies grow rapidly?	Why did slavery come to define the southern colonies?	What unified colonists in British North America during the eighteenth century?	Conclusion: Why did British North American colonists develop a dual identity?

▲ **New York Harbor** This portrait of New York harbor in about 1756 illustrates the importance of Atlantic commerce to the prosperous city in the background. The painting emphasizes a variety of oceangoing ships in the foreground. During its busiest seasons, the harbor commonly had ten times as many ships at anchor, which was nearly impossible for the artist to depict. © Collection of the New-York Historical Society, USA/Bridgeman Images.

READING THE IMAGE: How does the painting reflect New York's participation in Atlantic commerce?

CONNECTIONS: Why were port cities the largest and most prosperous cities in eighteenth-century America?

jealously defended their territory. Disputes with the French and Catholic colony of New France also menaced the British and mostly Protestant New England colonies.

During the seventeenth century, New England towns parceled out land to individual families. In most cases, the original settlers practiced partible inheritance—that is, they subdivided land more or less equally among sons. By the eighteenth century, the original portions of land allotments had to be further subdivided. Many plots of land became too small to support a family. Sons who could not hope to inherit enough land moved away from the town where they were born.

During the eighteenth century, colonial governments in New England abandoned the seventeenth-century policy of granting land to towns. Needing money, the governments of both Connecticut and Massachusetts sold land directly to individuals, including speculators. Now money, rather than membership in a community bound together by a church covenant, determined whether a person could obtain land. The new land policy eroded the seventeenth-century pattern of settlement. As colonists spread north and west, they tended to settle on individual farms rather than in the towns and villages as in the seventeenth century. Far more than in the seventeenth century, eighteenth-century New Englanders regulated their behavior by their own individual choices.

partible inheritance
System of inheritance in which land was divided equally among sons.

Farms, Fish, and Atlantic Trade

A New England farm was a place to get by, not to get rich. New England farmers grew food for their families, but their fields did not produce large surpluses that could be sold. Instead of one big crop, farmers grew many small ones. If farmers had extra, they sold to or bartered with neighbors. Poor roads made travel difficult, time-consuming, and expensive, especially with bulky and heavy agricultural goods. The one major agricultural product the New England colonies exported—livestock—walked to market on its own legs. By 1770, New Englanders had only one-fourth as much wealth per capita as free colonists in the southern colonies.

How did the British North American colonies change during the eighteenth century?

MAP 5.2 ▲ Atlantic Trade in the Eighteenth Century

This map illustrates the economic outlook of the colonies in the eighteenth century—east toward the Atlantic world rather than west toward the interior of North America. The long distances involved in the Atlantic trade and the uncertainties of ocean travel made it difficult for Britain to govern the colonies and regulate colonial commerce.

As consumers, New England farmers participated in a diversified commercial economy that linked remote farms to markets throughout the Atlantic world. Merchants large and small stocked imported goods—British textiles, ceramics, and metal goods; Chinese tea; West Indian sugar and rum; and Chesapeake tobacco. Farmers' needs supported local shoemakers, tailors, wheelwrights, and carpenters. Larger towns, especially Boston, housed skilled tradesmen such as cabinetmakers, silversmiths, and printers. Shipbuilders, sailors, and fishermen were among the many New Englanders who made their fortunes at sea. Fish accounted for more than a third of New England's eighteenth-century exports. Livestock and timber made up another third. The West Indies absorbed two-thirds of all New England's exports. Slaves on Caribbean sugar plantations ate dried, salted codfish caught by New England fishermen, filled barrels crafted from New England timber with molasses and refined sugar, and loaded those barrels aboard ships bound ultimately for Europeans with a taste for rum (made from molasses) and sweets. The rest of New England's exports went to Britain and continental Europe (**Map 5.2**). This Atlantic

PLACE EVENTS IN CONTEXT

How did slavery in the British colonies shape New England's economy?

| What changed in New England life and culture? | Why did the middle colonies grow rapidly? | Why did slavery come to define the southern colonies? | What unified colonists in British North America during the eighteenth century? | Conclusion: Why did British North American colonists develop a dual identity? |

commerce benefited the entire New England economy, providing jobs for laborers and tradesmen as well as for ship captains, clerks, merchants, and sailors.

Merchants dominated Atlantic commerce. The largest and most successful New England merchants lived in Boston at the hub of trade between local folk and the international market. The magnificence of a wealthy Boston merchant's home stunned John Adams, who termed it a house that seemed fit "for a noble Man, a Prince." Such luxurious Boston homes contrasted with the modest dwellings of Adams and other New Englanders, one measure of the unequal distribution of wealth that developed in Boston and other seaports during the eighteenth century.

By 1770, the richest 5 percent of Bostonians owned about half the city's wealth. The poorest two-thirds of the population owned less than one-tenth of the city's wealth. Still, the incidence of genuine poverty did not change much. About 5 percent of New Englanders qualified for poor relief throughout the eighteenth century. Overall, colonists were better off than most people in England.

New England was more English in origin than any other colonial region. People of African ancestry (almost all of them slaves) numbered more than fifteen thousand by 1770. But white people made up 97 percent of the population. Most New Englanders had little use for slaves on their family farms. Instead, the few slaves lived in towns, especially Boston, where most of them worked as domestic servants and laborers.

By 1770, the population, wealth, and commercial activity of New England differed from what they had been in 1700. Ministers still enjoyed high status, but Yankee traders had replaced Puritan saints as the symbolic New Englanders. Atlantic commerce competed with religious convictions in ordering New Englanders' daily lives.

CONSIDER CAUSE AND EFFECT

Why were slaves scarce in the New England colonies?

QUICK REVIEW

Why did settlement patterns in New England change during the eighteenth century?

Why did the middle colonies grow rapidly?

CHRONOLOGY

1700–1770
- Population of Pennsylvania, New York, New Jersey, and Delaware increases tenfold, largely as result of immigration.
- Germans make up largest percentage of migrants from European continent.

1720–1770
- Middle colonies' per capita consumption of imported goods from Britain more than doubles.

1733
- Benjamin Franklin publishes *Poor Richard's Almanack*.

In 1700, the middle colonies of Pennsylvania, New York, New Jersey, and Delaware had only half the population of New England. But by 1770, the population of the middle colonies had multiplied tenfold and nearly equaled the population of New England. Immigrants—mainly German, Irish, Scottish—made the middle colonies a uniquely diverse society. By the late eighteenth century, barely one-third of Pennsylvanians and less than half the total population of the middle colonies traced their ancestry to England. New white settlers, both free and in servitude, poured into the middle colonies because they perceived unmatched opportunities.

German and Scots-Irish Immigrants

Germans made up the largest contingent of migrants from the European continent to the middle colonies. By 1770, about 85,000 Germans had arrived in the colonies. Their fellow colonists often referred to them as **Pennsylvania Dutch**, an English corruption of *Deutsch*, the word the immigrants used to describe themselves.

Most German immigrants came from what is now southwestern Germany, where, one observer noted, peasants were "not as well off as cattle elsewhere." German immigrants included artisans and merchants, but the great majority were farmers

How did the British North American colonies change during the eighteenth century?

and laborers. Economically, they represented "middling folk," neither the poorest (who could not afford the trip) nor the better-off (who did not want to leave).

By the 1720s, Germans who had established themselves in the colonies wrote back to their friends and relatives, as one reported, "of the civil and religious liberties [and] privileges, and of all the goodness I have heard and seen." Such letters convinced still more Germans to pull up stakes and embark for the middle colonies.

Similar motives propelled the Scots-Irish, who considerably outnumbered German immigrants. The "Scots-Irish" actually hailed from northern Ireland, Scotland, and northern England. Like the Germans, the Scots-Irish were Protestants, but with a difference. Most German immigrants worshipped in Lutheran or German Reformed churches. Many others belonged to dissenting sects such as the Mennonites, Moravians, and Amish, who sought relief from persecution for their refusal to bear arms and to swear oaths, practices they shared with the Quakers. In contrast, the Scots-Irish tended to be militant Presbyterians, who seldom hesitated to bear arms or swear oaths. Like German settlers, Scots-Irish immigrants were clannish, residing when they could among relatives or neighbors from the old country.

In the eighteenth century, wave after wave of Scots-Irish immigrants arrived, culminating in a flood of immigration in the years just before the American Revolution. Deteriorating economic conditions in northern Ireland, Scotland, and England pushed many toward America. One Ulster Scot remarked that "oppression has brought us" to the "deplorable state . . . [that] the very marrow is screwed out of our bones." Most of the immigrants were farm laborers or tenant farmers fleeing droughts, crop failures, high food prices, or rising rents. They came, they told British officials, because of "poverty," the "tyranny of landlords," and their desire to "do better in America."

Both Scots-Irish and Germans probably heard the common saying "Pennsylvania is heaven for farmers [and] paradise for artisans," but they almost certainly did not fully understand the risks of their decision to leave their native lands. Ship captains, aware of the hunger for labor in the colonies, eagerly signed up the penniless German emigrants as redemptioners, a variant of indentured servants. A captain would agree to provide transportation to Philadelphia, where redemptioners would obtain the money to pay for their passage by borrowing it from a friend or relative who was already in the colonies, or as most did, by selling themselves as servants. Many redemptioners traveled in family groups, unlike impoverished Scots-Irish emigrants, who usually traveled alone and paid for their passage by contracting as indentured servants before they sailed to the colonies.

Redemptioners and indentured servants were packed aboard ships "as closely as herring," one migrant observed. Seasickness, exhaustion, poverty, poor food, bad water, inadequate sanitation, and tight quarters encouraged the spread of disease. When one ship finally approached land, a passenger wrote, "everyone crawls from below to the deck . . . and people cry for joy, pray, and sing praises and thanks to God." Unfortunately, their troubles were far from over. Unlike indentured servants, redemptioners negotiated independently with their purchasers about their period of servitude. Typically, a healthy adult redemptioner agreed to four years of labor. Indentured servants commonly served five, six, or seven years.

"God Gives All Things to Industry": Urban and Rural Labor

An indentured servant wrote in 1743 that Pennsylvania was "the best poor Man's Country in the World." Although the servant reported that "the Condition of bought Servants is very hard" and that masters often failed to live up to their promise to provide decent food and clothing, opportunity was abundant in the middle colonies because there was more work to do than workers to do it.

Pennsylvania Dutch
Name given by other colonists to German immigrants to the middle colonies.

Scots-Irish
Protestant immigrants from northern Ireland, Scotland, and northern England.

redemptioners
A kind of indentured servant.

COMPARE AND CONTRAST
How did the experiences of German and Scots-Irish immigrants to the middle colonies compare?

| What changed in New England life and culture? | **Why did the middle colonies grow rapidly?** | Why did slavery come to define the southern colonies? | What unified colonists in British North America during the eighteenth century? | Conclusion: Why did British North American colonists develop a dual identity? |

Most servants toiled in Philadelphia, New York City, or one of the smaller towns and villages. Artisans, small manufacturers, and shopkeepers prized the labor of male servants. Female servants usually worked in households, where nearly all of them cleaned, washed, cooked, or minded children. From the masters' viewpoint, servants were a bargain. A master could purchase five or six years of a servant's labor for approximately the wages a common laborer would earn in four months.

Since a slave cost about three times more than a servant, only prosperous colonists could afford the long-term investment in slave labor. Most farmers in the middle colonies used family labor, not slaves. Wheat, the most widely grown crop, did not require more labor than farmers could typically muster from relatives, neighbors, and a hired hand or two. Consequently, although people of African ancestry (almost all slaves) increased to more than thirty thousand in the middle colonies by 1770, they accounted for only about 7 percent of the total population and much less outside the cities.

Most slaves came to the middle colonies and New England after a stopover in the West Indies. Very few came directly from Africa. Slaves—unlike servants—could not charge masters with violating the terms of their contracts. Colonial laws punished slaves much more severely than servants for the same offense. Officials worried, for example, about "tippling" houses where "Negro Slaves and divers other person of Idle and suspected character . . . [were] drinking and behaving disorderly to the Great Disturbance of the Inhabitants . . . [by] offending against the peace of our . . . Lord the King his Crown and Dignity." Small numbers of slaves managed to obtain their freedom, but no African Americans escaped whites' firm convictions about black inferiority.

Whites' racism and blacks' low social status made African Americans scapegoats for Euro-Americans' suspicions and anxieties. In 1741, when arson and several unexplained thefts plagued New York City, officials suspected a murderous slave conspiracy and executed thirty-one slaves. On the basis of little evidence other than the slaves' "insolence" (refusal to conform fully to whites' expectations of servile behavior), city authorities burned thirteen slaves at the stake and hanged eighteen others. Although slaves were certainly impoverished, they were not among the poor for whom the middle colonies were reputed to be the best country in the world.

Immigrants swarmed to the middle colonies because of the availability of land. The Penn family (see chapter 4) encouraged immigration to bring in potential buyers for their enormous tracts of land in Pennsylvania. From the beginning, Pennsylvania followed a policy of negotiating with Indian tribes to purchase additional land. This policy reduced the violent frontier clashes more common elsewhere in the colonies. Few colonists drifted beyond the northern boundaries of Pennsylvania. Owners of the huge estates in New York's Hudson valley preferred to rent rather than sell their land, and therefore they attracted fewer immigrants. The Iroquois Indians dominated the lucrative fur trade of the St. Lawrence valley and eastern Great Lakes. They vigorously defended their territory from colonial encroachment, causing most settlers to prefer the comparatively safe lands of Pennsylvania.

Since the cheapest land always lay at the margin of settlement, would-be farmers tended to migrate to promising areas just beyond already improved farms. By midcentury, settlement had reached the eastern slopes of the Appalachian Mountains, and newcomers spilled south down the fertile valley of the Shenandoah River into western Virginia and the Carolinas. Thousands of settlers migrated from the middle colonies through this back door to the South. Abraham Lincoln's great-grandfather, John Lincoln—whose own grandfather, Mordecai, had migrated from England to Massachusetts in the 1630s—moved his family in the 1760s from Pennsylvania down the Shenandoah Valley into Virginia, where the future president's grandfather, also named Abraham, raised his family, including the future president's father, Thomas Lincoln.

Patterns of Settlement, 1700–1770

How did the British North American colonies change during the eighteenth century?

▲ **Bethlehem, Pennsylvania** This view of Bethlehem, Pennsylvania, in 1757 dramatizes the profound transformation of the natural landscape humans wrought in the eighteenth century. In less than twenty years, precisely laid-out orchards and fields replaced forests and glades. By carefully penning their livestock (lower center right) and fencing their fields (lower left), farmers safeguarded their livelihoods from the risks and disorders of untamed nature. Individual farmsteads (lower center) and brick town buildings (upper center) integrated the bounty of the land with community life. Few eighteenth-century communities were as orderly as Bethlehem, but many affected a comparable transformation of the environment. The New York Public Library/Art Resource, NY.

READING THE IMAGE: What does this painting indicate about the colonists' priorities?
CONNECTIONS: Why might Pennsylvanians have been so concerned about maintaining order?

Farmers like the Lincolns made the middle colonies the breadbasket of North America. They planted a wide variety of crops to feed their families, but they grew wheat in abundance. Flour milling was the number one industry and flour the number one export, accounting for about three-fourths of all exports from the middle colonies. Farmers profited from the grain market in the Atlantic world. By 1770, a bushel of wheat was worth twice as much (adjusted for inflation) as it had been in 1720. The steady rise of grain prices after 1720 helped make the standard of living in rural Pennsylvania higher than in any other agricultural region of the eighteenth-century world.

The comparatively widespread prosperity of all the middle colonies permitted residents to indulge in a half-century shopping spree for British imports. Commerce was so popular that a prominent New Yorker asked a friend in London to send him a few goods to "please a little boy & Girl who want to be merchants as soon as they can speak like their play fellows the Dutch Children here." The middle colonies' per capita consumption of imported goods from Britain more than doubled between 1720 and 1770, far outstripping the per capita consumption of British goods in both New England and the southern colonies.

Philadelphia stood at the crossroads of trade in wheat exports and British imports. Merchants occupied the top stratum of Philadelphia society. In a city where only 2 percent of the residents owned enough property to qualify to vote, merchants built grand homes and dominated local government. Many of Philadelphia's wealthiest merchants were Quakers. Quaker traits of industry, thrift, honesty, and sobriety

| What changed in New England life and culture? | **Why did the middle colonies grow rapidly?** | Why did slavery come to define the southern colonies? | What unified colonists in British North America during the eighteenth century? | Conclusion: Why did British North American colonists develop a dual identity? |

encouraged the accumulation of wealth. One colonist complained that a Quaker "prays for his neighbors on First Days [Sabbaths] and then preys on him the other six."

The lower ranks of merchants included aspiring tradesmen, such as Benjamin Franklin. In 1728, Franklin opened a small shop, run mostly by his wife, Deborah, that sold a little of everything: cheese, codfish, coffee, goose feathers, soap, and occasionally a slave. In 1733, Franklin began to publish *Poor Richard's Almanack*, which preached the likelihood of long-term rewards for tireless labor. The *Almanack* quickly became Franklin's most profitable product. Poor Richard's advice that "God gives all Things to Industry" might be considered the motto for the middle colonies. The promise of a worldly payoff made work a secular faith. Many Pennsylvanians thought less about the pearly gates of heaven than about their pocketbooks. Poor Richard advised, "Work as if you were to live 100 years, Pray as if you were to die Tomorrow." Although Quakers remained influential in Pennsylvania, Franklin spoke for most colonists with his down-to-earth advice about work, discipline, and thrift that celebrated the spark of ambition and the promise of worldly gain.

QUICK REVIEW

Why did immigrants flood into Pennsylvania during the eighteenth century?

Why did slavery come to define the southern colonies?

CHRONOLOGY

1711
– North Carolina founded.

1732
– Georgia founded.

1739
– Stono Rebellion takes place in South Carolina.

1770
– Southern colonies supply 90 percent of all North American exports to Britain.

Between 1700 and 1770, the population of the southern colonies of Virginia, Maryland, North Carolina, South Carolina, and Georgia grew almost ninefold. By 1770, about twice as many people lived in the South as in either the middle colonies or New England. As elsewhere, natural increase and immigration accounted for the rapid population growth. Many Scots-Irish and German immigrants funneled from the middle colonies into the southern backcountry. Other immigrants were indentured servants (mostly English and Scots-Irish). But slaves made the most striking contribution to the booming southern colonies, transforming the racial composition of the population. Slavery came to define the southern colonies during the eighteenth century, shaping the region's economy, society, and politics.

The Atlantic Slave Trade and the Growth of Slavery

The number of southerners of African ancestry (nearly all of them slaves) rocketed from just over twenty thousand in 1700 to well over four hundred thousand in 1770. The black population increased nearly three times faster than the South's briskly growing white population. Consequently, the proportion of southerners of African ancestry grew from 20 percent in 1700 to 40 percent in 1770.

Southern colonists clustered in two geographic and agricultural zones. The colonies in the Upper South, surrounding Chesapeake Bay, specialized in growing tobacco, as they had since the early seventeenth century. Throughout the eighteenth century, nine out of ten southern whites and eight out of ten southern blacks lived in the Chesapeake region. The Upper South retained a white majority during the eighteenth century.

MAP 5.3 ▲ **The Atlantic Slave Trade** Although the Atlantic slave trade lasted from about 1450 to 1870, it peaked during the eighteenth century, when more than six million African slaves were imported to the New World. Only a small fraction of these slaves were taken to British North America. Most went to sugar plantations in Brazil and the Caribbean.

READING THE MAP: Where in Africa did most slaves originate?

CONNECTIONS: Why were so many more African slaves sent to the West Indies and Brazil than to British North America?

In the Lower South, a much smaller cluster of colonists inhabited the coastal region and specialized in the production of rice and indigo (a plant used to make blue dye). Lower South colonists made up only 5 percent of the total population of the southern colonies in 1700, but inched upward to 15 percent by 1770. South Carolina was the sole British colony along the southern Atlantic coast until 1732. (North Carolina, founded in 1711, was largely an extension of the Chesapeake region.) Georgia was founded in 1732 as a refuge for poor people from England. Georgia's leaders banned slaves from 1735 to 1750. But few settlers arrived until Georgia lifted the prohibition on slavery after 1750 and slaves were imported in large numbers. In South Carolina, in contrast to Georgia and every other British mainland colony, slaves outnumbered whites almost two to one. In rice-growing regions along the South Carolina coast, the ratio of blacks to whites was greater than ten to one.

The enormous growth in the South's slave population occurred through natural increase and the flourishing Atlantic slave trade (**Table 5.1** and **Map 5.3**). Slave ships brought almost 300,000 Africans to British North America between 1619

TABLE 5.1 Slave Imports, 1451–1870

Estimated Slave Imports to the Western Hemisphere	
1451–1600	275,000
1601–1700	1,341,000
1701–1810	6,100,000
1811–1870	1,900,000

What changed in New England life and culture?	Why did the middle colonies grow rapidly?	**Why did slavery come to define the southern colonies?**	What unified colonists in British North America during the eighteenth century?	Conclusion: Why did British North American colonists develop a dual identity?

and 1780. Of these Africans, 95 percent arrived in the South and 96 percent arrived during the eighteenth century. Unlike indentured servants and redemptioners, these Africans did not choose to come to the colonies. Most of them had been born into free families located within a few hundred miles of the West African coast. Although they shared African origins, they came from many different African cultures, such as Akan, Angolan, Asante, Bambara, Gambian, Igbo, and Mandinga, among others. They spoke different languages, worshipped different deities, observed different rules of kinship, grew different crops, and recognized different rulers. The most important experience they had in common was enslavement.

Captured in war, kidnapped, or sold into slavery by other Africans, they were brought to the coast, sold to African traders who assembled slaves for resale, and sold again to European or colonial ship captains, who packed two hundred to three hundred or more aboard ships that carried them on the **Middle Passage** across the Atlantic, and then sold them yet again to colonial slave merchants or southern planters.

Middle Passage
The Atlantic crossing by slave ships traveling from West Africa to the Americas.

Olaudah Equiano published an account of his enslavement that reveals the common experiences of millions of other Africans swept up in the slave trade. In 1756, when he was eleven years old, Africans kidnapped Equiano in what is now Nigeria. They sold him to other Africans, who in turn eventually sold him to a slave ship on the coast. Equiano wrote that he "had never heard of white men or Europeans, nor of the sea," and he feared that he was "going to be killed" and "eaten by those white men with horrible looks, red faces, and loose hair." Once the ship set sail, many of the slaves, crowded together in suffocating heat fouled by filth of all descriptions, died from sickness. "The shrieks of the women and the groans of the dying rendered the whole a scene of horror almost inconceivable," Equiano recalled. Most of the slaves on the ship were sold in Barbados, but Equiano and other leftovers were shipped off to Virginia, where he "saw few or none of our native Africans and not one soul who could talk to me." Equiano felt isolated and "exceedingly miserable" because he "had no person to speak to that I could understand." Finally, the captain of a tobacco ship bound for England purchased Equiano, and he traveled as an enslaved sailor between North America, England, and the West Indies for ten years until he succeeded in buying his freedom in 1766.

"Equiano wrote that he 'had never heard of white men or Europeans, nor of the sea,' and he feared that he was 'going to be killed.'"

Only about 15 percent of the slaves brought into the southern colonies came aboard ships from the West Indies, as Equiano did. All the other slaves brought into the southern colonies came directly from Africa. And almost all the ships that brought them (roughly 90 percent) belonged to British merchants. Most of the slaves on board were young adults, with men usually outnumbering women two to one. Children under the age of fourteen, like Equiano, typically accounted for no more than 10 to 15 percent of a cargo.

The death rate during the Middle Passage varied greatly from ship to ship. On average, about 15 percent of the slaves died, but sometimes half or more perished. The average death rate among the white crew of slave ships was often nearly as bad. In general, the longer the voyage lasted, the more people died. Slaves and crew succumbed not only to epidemic diseases, such as smallpox and dysentery, but also to acute dehydration caused by fluid loss from perspiration, vomiting, and diarrhea, combined with a severe shortage of drinking water.

◄ **Olaudah Equiano** Painted after he had bought his freedom, this portrait evokes Equiano's successful acculturation to eighteenth-century English customs. In his *Interesting Narrative*, Equiano wrote that he "looked upon [the English] . . . as men superior to us [Africans], and therefore I had the stronger desire to resemble them, to imbibe their spirit and imitate their manners." Library of Congress, 3b01988.

How did the British North American colonies change during the eighteenth century?

Normally, at any one time an individual planter bought a relatively small number of newly arrived Africans, or new Negroes, as they were called. **(See "Spotlight: Why Did Few Colonists Oppose the African Slave Trade?" on page 124.)** New Negroes were often deeply depressed, demoralized, and disoriented. Planters expected their other slaves—either those born into slavery in the colonies (often called country-born or creole slaves) or Africans who had arrived earlier—to help new Negroes become accustomed to their strange new surroundings. Planters' preferences for slaves from specific regions of Africa aided slaves' acculturation (or seasoning, as it was then called) to the routine of bondage in the southern colonies. Chesapeake planters preferred slaves from Senegambia, the Gold Coast, or—like Equiano—the Bight of Biafra, which together accounted for about 40 percent of Africans imported to the Chesapeake. South Carolina planters favored slaves from the central African Congo and Angola regions, the origins of about 40 percent of the slaves they imported. Although slaves spoke many different languages, enough linguistic and cultural similarities existed that they could usually communicate with other Africans from the same region.

New Africans had to adjust to the physical as well as the cultural environment of the southern colonies. Slaves who had just endured the Middle Passage were poorly nourished, weak, and sick. In this vulnerable state, they encountered the alien diseases of North America without having developed a biological arsenal of acquired immunities. As many as 10 to 15 percent of newly arrived Africans died during their first year in the southern colonies. Still, the large number of newly enslaved Africans made the influence of African culture in the South stronger in the eighteenth century than ever before—or since.

While newly enslaved Africans poured into the southern colonies, slave mothers bore children, which caused the slave population in the South to grow rapidly. Slave owners encouraged these births. Thomas Jefferson explained, "I consider the labor of a breeding [slave] woman as no object, that a [slave] child raised every 2 years is of more profit than the crop of the best laboring [slave] man." Although slave mothers loved and nurtured their children, the death rate among slave children was high. The ever-present risk of being separated by sale also brought grief to many slave families. Nonetheless, the growing number of slave babies set the southern colonies apart from other New World slave societies, where death rates were so high that deaths were greater than births. The high birthrate in the southern colonies meant that by the 1740s, despite the arrival of newly enslaved Africans, the majority of southern slaves were born in the colonies.

new Negroes
Term given to newly arrived African slaves in the colonies.

CONSIDER CAUSE AND EFFECT
Why did the population of the southern colonies increase more than that of the middle colonies and New England?

Slave Labor and African American Culture

Southern planters expected slaves to work from sunup to sundown and beyond. George Washington wrote that his slaves should "be at their work as soon as it is light, work til it is dark, and be diligent while they are at it." The conflict between the masters' desire for maximum labor and the slaves' reluctance to do more than necessary made the threat of physical punishment a constant for eighteenth-century slaves. Masters preferred black slaves to white indentured servants because slaves served for life and because colonial laws did not limit the force masters could use against slaves. Enslaved people often resisted their masters' demands, one traveler noted, because of their "greatness of soul"—their stubborn unwillingness to conform to their masters' definition of them as merely slaves.

Some slaves escalated their acts of resistance to direct physical confrontation with the master, the mistress, or an overseer. But a hoe raised in anger, a punch in the face, or a desperate swipe with a knife led to swift and predictable retaliation by whites. Throughout the southern colonies, the balance of physical power rested securely in the hands of whites.

| What changed in New England life and culture? | Why did the middle colonies grow rapidly? | **Why did slavery come to define the southern colonies?** | What unified colonists in British North America during the eighteenth century? | Conclusion: Why did British North American colonists develop a dual identity? |

123

Why Did Few Colonists Oppose the African Slave Trade?

During the eighteenth century, the African slave trade carried more enslaved Africans across the Atlantic than ever before or since. From today's perspective, we might expect many people to have spoken out against the booming trade. But before the American Revolution, critics of the African slave trade were few, far between, and not influential. Why?

Enslaved Africans opposed becoming commodities in the transatlantic slave trade, but they had little power to resist. For centuries, in Europe, Africa, Asia, and the Middle East, enslavement had been considered a legitimate fate for people captured during a war. Kidnapping for the purpose of enslavement was widely thought to be illegitimate, but in practice the boundary between legitimate and illegitimate enslavement was murky and almost impossible to enforce. Africans captured other Africans, whether legitimately or illegitimately, and ultimately sold the captives to European slave traders. Slaves aboard as many as one-tenth of all ships in the African trade tried to escape their bondage by revolting. But nearly all revolts occurred while slaves and ships were in sight of the African coast, strong evidence that hopes of escape evaporated as Africa slipped out of sight on the eastern horizon.

The horrors of the slave trade were no secret, but most people in the colonies as well as in Britain and on the European continent considered pain and suffering a regrettable but inescapable part of life. The brutality inflicted on enslaved Africans seemed to many colonists an extreme form of the harsh conditions of life everyone confronted and took for granted. Occasionally colonists acknowledged the miseries of enslavement by referring to slaves as "poor Negroes" or "poor Africans," terminology that showed a measure of sympathy and a sense

▲ Benjamin Lay, pictured here in 1750, was an uncompromising opponent of slavery at a time when most people, including his fellow Quakers, did not consider slavery a problem. Born in England, Lay spent more than a decade in Barbados, where the brutality inflicted on slaves persuaded him to speak out. He immigrated to Pennsylvania in 1731 and campaigned vigorously against the evils of slavery, prisons, capital punishment, meat-eating, and other common practices until he died in 1759. History and Art Collection / Alamy Stock Photo.

that slaves were unlucky victims of circumstance. But this sympathy was tempered by deeply held racial prejudices that justified vicious mistreatment of blacks, whom Euro-Americans considered inferior.

PLACE EVENTS IN CONTEXT

Why did slave revolts rarely occur in the colonies during the eighteenth century?

Stono Rebellion
Slave uprising in Stono, South Carolina, in 1739.

Rebellion occurred, however, at Stono, South Carolina, in 1739. A group of about twenty slaves attacked a country store, killed the two storekeepers, and took the store's guns, ammunition, and powder. The rebels plundered and burned several plantations and killed more than twenty white men, women, and children. A mounted force of whites quickly put down the rebellion. They placed the rebels' heads atop mileposts along the main road, grim reminders of the consequences of rebellion. The South Carolina legislature enacted a harsh slave code in 1740 to punish with the utmost severity enslaved "negroes from the coast of Africa who are generally of a barbarous and savage disposition." The Stono Rebellion illustrated that eighteenth-century slaves had

How did the British North American colonies change during the eighteenth century?

Leading merchants who bought and sold enslaved Africans in ports such as Charleston, Philadelphia, Providence, New York, and Boston profited from the trade and did all they could to keep it going. They wanted enslaved Africans to be healthy and robust because then they could be sold for higher prices. Slave traders believed that brutality was necessary to prevent revolts by enslaved Africans, who greatly outnumbered the crewmen aboard slave ships. Far from condemning or stigmatizing slave traders, other colonists respected them, bought slaves from them, borrowed money from them, and did not object to their daughters marrying them. Some colonists saw the slave trade as a prime example of the great freedom colonists enjoyed as members of the British empire. Even most Christians who sought to live up to the biblical commandment to "do unto others as you would have them do unto you" felt few pangs of conscience about the African slave trade.

A few renegade Quakers became outspoken antislavery activists during the first half of the eighteenth century. Although Quakers were a tiny minority of colonists, they often prospered and bought slaves. A small number of Quakers, however, denounced slavery and the trade in slaves because they promoted worldliness and luxury rather than the Quakers' simple life of faith and suffering. In 1738, Pennsylvania Quaker Benjamin Lay went so far as to kidnap a white child belonging to a Quaker slaveholder in order to demonstrate the violence of the slave trade. Lay believed that owning slaves corrupted all Quakers' faith. He dramatized the violence of the trade at the 1738 Philadelphia Yearly Meeting of Quakers by plunging a sword into a Bible hollowed out to hold a container of pokeberry juice, splattering the blood-red juice on his fellow believers. Beginning in the 1740s, New Jersey Quaker John Woolman visited individual Quaker slaveholders and quietly talked to them

about his belief that God expected people "to exercise goodness toward every living creature," especially slaves, who were suffering. Woolman, like Lay, worked to persuade slaveholders to liberate their slaves and in that way purge slaveholding from the Quaker faith in order to purify their church and fulfill their divine obligation to be kind to all creatures. Anthony Benezet, another Philadelphia Quaker, proclaimed that "nothing can be more inconsistent with the Doctrines and Practice of our meek Lord and Master, nor stained with a deeper Dye of Injustice, Cruelty and Oppression . . . [than] the SLAVE TRADE." The efforts of Lay, Woolman, Benezet, and others led the Philadelphia Quaker meeting in 1758 to encourage Quakers to free their slaves and to ban slaveholders from participating in the affairs of the church. But for the most part, these pioneering antislavery initiatives were confined to a small number of Quakers and ignored by the vast majority of colonists, for whom the African slave trade remained business as usual.

Questions for Analysis

SUMMARIZE THE ARGUMENT: Why did the African slave trade create so little opposition among colonists? Why did a few Quakers oppose the trade?

ANALYZE THE EVIDENCE: How did supporters of the African slave trade justify its cruelty and violence? What arguments did Quakers use to denounce slavery and the slave trade?

CONSIDER THE CONTEXT: How did colonists' attitudes toward the slave trade reflect their thinking about markets, freedom, inequality, and race?

no chance of overturning slavery and very little chance of defending themselves in any bold strike for freedom. No other similar uprisings occurred during the colonial period.

Slaves maneuvered constantly to protect themselves and to gain a measure of autonomy within the boundaries of slavery. In Chesapeake tobacco fields, most slaves were subject to close supervision by whites. In the Lower South, the **task system** gave slaves some control over the pace of their work and some choice in the use of the rest of their time. A "task" was typically defined as a certain area of ground to be cultivated or a specific job to be completed. A slave who completed the assigned task might use the remainder of the day, if any, to work in a garden, fish, hunt, spin, weave,

task system
A system of labor that assigned slaves a daily task and allowed them to do as they wished if their task was completed.

| What changed in New England life and culture? | Why did the middle colonies grow rapidly? | **Why did slavery come to define the southern colonies?** | What unified colonists in British North America during the eighteenth century? | Conclusion: Why did British North American colonists develop a dual identity? |

◀ **Colonial Slave Drum** An African in Virginia made this drum sometime around the beginning of the eighteenth century. The drum combines deerskin and cedarwood from North America with African workmanship and designs. During rare moments of respite from their work, slaves played drums to accompany dances learned in Africa. They also drummed out messages from plantation to plantation. © The Trustees of the British Museum/Art Resource, NY.

sew, or cook. When masters sought to boost productivity by increasing tasks, slaves did what they could to defend their customary assignments.

Eighteenth-century slaves also planted the roots of African American lineages that branch out to the present. Slaves valued family ties, and as in West African societies, kinship structured slaves' relations with one another. Slave parents often gave a child the name of a grandparent, aunt, or uncle. In West Africa, kinship identified a person's place among living relatives and linked the person backward to ancestors in the past and forward to descendants in the future. Newly imported African slaves usually arrived alone, like Equiano, without kin. Often slaves who had traversed the Middle Passage on the same ship adopted one another as "brothers" and "sisters." Likewise, as new Negroes were seasoned and incorporated into existing slave communities, established families often adopted them as fictive kin.

When possible, slaves expressed many other features of their West African origins in their lives on New World plantations. They gave their children African names such as Cudjo, Quash, Minda, or Fuladi. They grew food crops they had known in Africa, such as yams and okra. They constructed huts with mud walls and thatched roofs similar to African residences. They fashioned banjos, drums, and other musical instruments, held dances, and observed funeral rites that echoed African practices. In these and many other ways, slaves drew upon their African heritages as much as the oppressive circumstances of slavery permitted.

Tobacco, Rice, and Prosperity

Slaves' labor bestowed prosperity on their masters, British merchants, and the monarchy. Slavery was so important and valuable that one minister claimed in 1757 that "to live in Virginia without slaves is morally impossible." The southern colonies supplied 90 percent of all North American exports to Britain. Rice exports from the Lower South exploded from less than half a million pounds in 1700 to eighty million pounds in 1770, nearly all of it grown by slaves. Exports of indigo also boomed. Together, rice and indigo made up three-fourths of exports from the Lower South, nearly two-thirds of them going to Britain and most of the rest to the West Indies, where sugar-growing slaves ate slave-grown rice.

Tobacco was by far the most important export from British North America. By 1770, it represented almost one-third of total colonial exports and three-fourths of all Chesapeake exports. Under the provisions of the Navigation Acts (see chapter 4), nearly all tobacco went to Britain, where the monarchy collected a lucrative tax on each pound. British merchants then re-exported more than 80 percent of the tobacco to the European continent, pocketing a nice markup for their troubles.

These products of slave labor made the southern colonies by far the richest in North America. The per capita wealth of free whites in the South was four times greater than that in New England and three times that in the middle colonies. At the top of the wealth pyramid stood the rice grandees of the Lower South and the tobacco gentry of the Chesapeake. These elite families commonly resided on large estates in handsome mansions adorned by luxurious gardens, all maintained and supported by slaves.

How did the British North American colonies change during the eighteenth century?

The vast differences in wealth among white southerners caused envy and occasional tension between rich and poor, but remarkably little open hostility. In private, the planter elite belittled humble whites, but in public, the planters claimed their lesser neighbors were equals in belonging to the superior—in their minds—white race. Looking upward, white yeomen and tenants (who owned neither land nor slaves) sensed the gentry's condescension and barely hidden contempt. But they also appreciated the gentry for granting favors, upholding white supremacy, and keeping slaves in their place. Although racial slavery made a few whites much richer than others, it also gave those who did not get rich a powerful reason to feel similar in race to those who were so different in wealth.

The slaveholding gentry dominated the politics and economy of the southern colonies. In Virginia, only adult white men who owned at least one hundred acres of unimproved land or twenty-five acres of land with a house could vote. This property-holding requirement prevented about 40 percent of white men in Virginia from voting for representatives to the House of Burgesses. In South Carolina, the property requirement was only fifty acres of land, and therefore most adult white men qualified to vote. In both colonies, voters elected members of the gentry to serve in the colonial legislature. The gentry passed elected political offices from generation to generation, almost as if they were hereditary. Politically, the gentry built a self-perpetuating oligarchy—rule by the elite few—with the votes of their many humble neighbors.

The gentry also set the cultural standard in the southern colonies. They entertained lavishly, gambled regularly, and attended Anglican (Church of England) services more for social than for religious reasons. Above all, they cultivated the leisurely pursuit of happiness. They did not condone idleness, however. Their many pleasures and responsibilities as plantation owners kept them busy. Thomas Jefferson, a phenomenally productive member of the gentry, recalled that his earliest childhood memory was of being carried on a pillow by a family slave—a powerful image of the slave hands supporting the gentry's leisure and achievement.

UNDERSTAND POINTS OF VIEW

Why did southern white yeomen and tenants support the political and economic power of wealthy slave owners?

QUICK REVIEW

How did slavery influence the society and economy of the southern colonies?

What unified colonists in British North America during the eighteenth century?

The societies of New England, the middle colonies, and the southern colonies became quite different from each other during the eighteenth century. But colonists throughout British North America also shared unifying experiences that set them apart from residents of the Spanish and French colonies. The first was economic. All three British colonial regions had their economic roots in agriculture. Colonists sold their products in markets that, in turn, offered a more or less uniform set of goods to consumers throughout British North America. Another unifying experience was a decline in the importance of religion. Some settlers called for a revival of religious intensity, but most people focused less on religion and more on the affairs of the world than they had in the seventeenth century. Also, white inhabitants throughout British North America became aware that they shared a distinctive identity as *British* colonists.

Thirteen different governments presided over these North American colonies, but all of them answered to the British monarchy. British policies governed not only trade but also military and diplomatic relations with the Indians, French, and Spanish along colonial borderlands. Royal officials who expected loyalty from the colonists often had difficulty obtaining obedience. The British colonists asserted their rights and privileges as British subjects to defend their own special colonial interests.

Commerce and Consumption

Eighteenth-century commerce whetted colonists' appetites to consume. Colonial products spurred the development of mass markets throughout the Atlantic world (**Figure 5.1**). Huge increases in the supply of colonial tobacco and sugar brought the prices of these small luxuries within the reach of most free whites. Colonial goods taught an important lesson of eighteenth-century commerce: Ordinary people, not just the wealthy elite, bought things that they desired, not just what they absolutely needed. Even news, formerly restricted mostly to a few people through face-to-face conversations or private letters, became an object of consumption with the innovation of newspapers and the rise in literacy among whites. With the ample supplies and low prices, market demand seemed nearly unlimited.

The Atlantic commerce that took colonial goods to markets in Britain brought objects of consumer desire back to the colonies. British merchants and manufacturers recognized that colonists made excellent customers, and the Navigation Acts gave British exporters privileged access to the colonial market. By midcentury, export-oriented industries in Britain were growing ten times faster than firms that catered to the home market.

When the colonists' eagerness to consume exceeded their ability to pay, British exporters extended credit, and colonial debts soared. Imported mirrors, silverware, spices, bed and table linens, clocks, tea services, wigs, books, and more found their way into parlors, kitchens, and bedrooms throughout the colonies. Despite the many differences among the colonists, the consumption of similar British exports built a certain uniformity of goods across region, religion, class, and status.

The dazzling variety of imported consumer goods also presented women and men with a novel array of choices. In many respects, the choices might appear trivial: whether to buy knives and forks, teacups, a mirror, or a clock. But such small choices confronted eighteenth-century consumers with a big question: What do you want? As colonial consumers defined and expressed their desires with greater frequency during the eighteenth century, they became accustomed to thinking of themselves as individuals who had the power to make decisions that influenced the quality of their lives.

Religion, Enlightenment, and Revival

Eighteenth-century colonists could choose from almost as many religions as consumer goods. Almost all of the many religious denominations represented some form of Christianity, nearly all of them Protestant. Slaves made up the largest group of non-Christians. A few slaves converted to Christianity in Africa or after they arrived in North America, but most continued to embrace their African religions. Roman Catholics concentrated in Maryland as they had since the seventeenth century, but even there they were far outnumbered by Protestants.

How did the British North American colonies change during the eighteenth century?

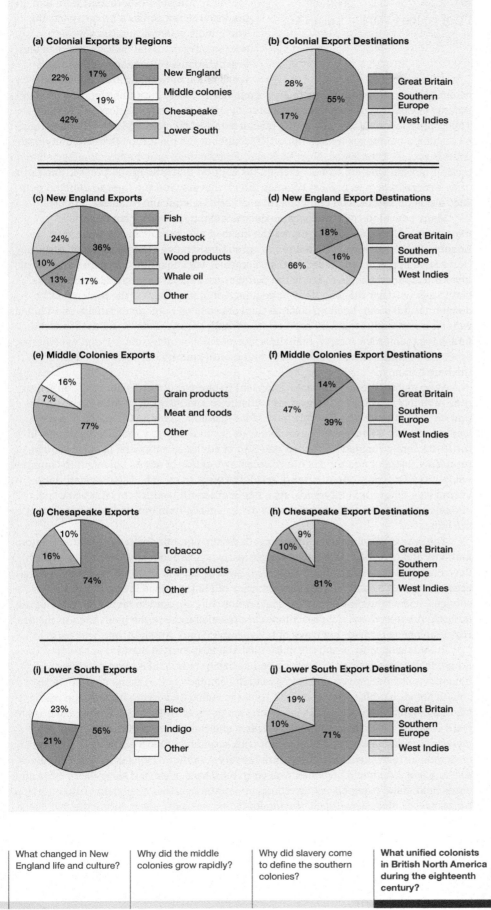

FIGURE 5.1 ◀ Colonial Exports, 1768–1772

These pie charts provide an overview of the colonial export economy in the 1760s. The first two show that almost two-thirds of colonial exports came from the South and that the majority of the colonies' exports went to Great Britain. The remaining charts illustrate the distinctive patterns of exports in each colonial region. What do these patterns reveal about regional variations in Britain's North American colonies? What do they suggest about Britain's economic interest in the colonies?

(a) Colonial Exports by Regions

- 17% New England
- 19%
- 42%
- 22%
- Middle colonies
- Chesapeake
- Lower South

(b) Colonial Export Destinations

- 55% Great Britain
- 17% Southern Europe
- 28% West Indies

(c) New England Exports

- 36% Fish
- 17% Livestock
- 13% Wood products
- 10% Whale oil
- 24% Other

(d) New England Export Destinations

- 18% Great Britain
- 16% Southern Europe
- 66% West Indies

(e) Middle Colonies Exports

- 77% Grain products
- 7% Meat and foods
- 16% Other

(f) Middle Colonies Export Destinations

- 14% Great Britain
- 39% Southern Europe
- 47% West Indies

(g) Chesapeake Exports

- 74% Tobacco
- 16% Grain products
- 10% Other

(h) Chesapeake Export Destinations

- 81% Great Britain
- 10% Southern Europe
- 9% West Indies

(i) Lower South Exports

- 56% Rice
- 21% Indigo
- 23% Other

(j) Lower South Export Destinations

- 71% Great Britain
- 10% Southern Europe
- 19% West Indies

| What changed in New England life and culture? | Why did the middle colonies grow rapidly? | Why did slavery come to define the southern colonies? | **What unified colonists in British North America during the eighteenth century?** | Conclusion: Why did British North American colonists develop a dual identity? |

> "A minister in Charleston observed that on the Sabbath 'the Taverns have more Visitants than the Churches.'"

The varieties of Protestant faith and practice ranged across a broad spectrum. The middle colonies and the southern backcountry included militant Baptists and Presbyterians. Huguenots who had fled persecution in Catholic France peopled congregations in several cities. In New England, old-style Puritanism splintered into strands of Congregationalism that differed over fine points of theological doctrine. The Congregational Church was the official established church in New England, and all residents paid taxes for its support. Throughout the plantation South and in urban centers such as Charleston, New York, and Philadelphia, prominent colonists belonged to the Anglican Church, which received tax support in the South. But dissenting faiths grew everywhere, and in most colonies their believers won the right to worship publicly, although established churches retained official legal and financial support.

Many educated colonists became deists, looking for God's plan in nature more than in the Bible. Deism shared the ideas of eighteenth-century European Enlightenment thinkers, who tended to agree that science and reason could disclose God's laws in the natural order. In the colonies as well as in Europe, **Enlightenment** ideas encouraged people to study the world around them, to think for themselves, and to ask whether the disorderly appearance of things masked the principles of a deeper natural order. Leading colonial thinkers such as Benjamin Franklin and Thomas Jefferson communicated with each other, seeking both to understand nature and to find ways to improve society. Franklin's interest in electricity, stoves, and eyeglasses typified the shift of focus among many eighteenth-century colonists from heaven to the here and now.

Enlightenment
An eighteenth-century philosophical movement that emphasized the use of reason to reevaluate previously accepted doctrines and traditions.

CONSIDER CAUSE AND EFFECT
Why did religious indifference develop in the colonies?

Most eighteenth-century colonists went to church seldom or not at all, although they probably considered themselves Christians. A minister in Charleston observed that on the Sabbath "the Taverns have more Visitants than the Churches." In the leading colonial cities, church members were a small minority. Anglican parishes in the South rarely claimed more than one-fifth of adults as members. In some regions of rural New England and the middle colonies, two-thirds of adults belonged to churches, while elsewhere only one-quarter of residents went to church. The dominant faith overall was religious indifference. As a late-eighteenth-century traveler observed, "Religious indifference is imperceptibly disseminated from one end of the continent to the other."

The spread of religious indifference, of deism, of rivalry among Protestant denominations, and of comfortable backsliding greatly concerned many Christians. A few despaired that, as one wrote, "religion . . . lay a-dying and ready to expire its last breath of life." To combat what one preacher called the "dead formality" of church services, some ministers set out to convert nonbelievers and to revive the piety of the faithful with a new style of preaching that appealed more to the heart than to the head. Historians have termed this wave of revivals the Great Awakening.

Great Awakening
Wave of revivals that began in Massachusetts and spread through the colonies in the 1730s and 1740s.

In Massachusetts during the mid-1730s, the fiery Puritan minister Jonathan Edwards reaped a harvest of souls by emphasizing traditional Puritan doctrines of humanity's utter depravity and God's vengeful omnipotence. A member of Edwards's church noted that his sermons caused "great moaning and crying through the whole [church]—What shall I do to be saved—oh I am going to Hell . . . the shrieks and cries were piercing and amazing." In Pennsylvania and New Jersey, William Tennent led revivals that dramatized spiritual rebirth with accounts of God's miraculous powers. The most famous revivalist in the eighteenth-century Atlantic world was George Whitefield. An Anglican, Whitefield preached well-worn messages of sin and salvation to large audiences in England using his spellbinding, unforgettable voice. Whitefield visited the North American colonies seven times, staying for more than three years during the mid-1740s

How did the British North American colonies change during the eighteenth century?

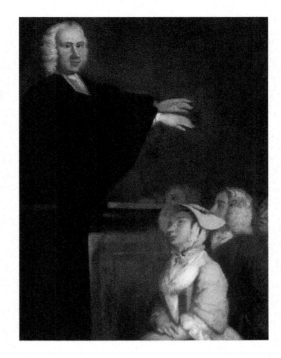

▶ **George Whitefield** An anonymous artist portrayed George Whitefield preaching, emphasizing the power of his sermons to transport his audience to a revived awareness of divine spirituality. The woman below his hands appears transfixed. Her eyes and Whitefield's do not meet, yet the artist's use of light suggests that she and Whitefield see the same core of holy Truth.

and attracting tens of thousands to his sermons, including Benjamin Franklin and Olaudah Equiano. Whitefield's preaching transported many in his audience to emotion-choked states of religious ecstasy, as he wrote, with "most lifting their eyes to heaven, and crying to God for mercy."

Whitefield's revivals spawned many lesser imitations. Itinerant preachers, many of them poorly educated, roamed the colonial back-country after midcentury. Bathsheba Kingsley, a member of Jonathan Edwards's flock, preached the revival message informally—as did an unprecedented number of other women throughout the colonies—causing Edwards's congregation to brand her a "brawling woman" who had "gone quite out of her place."

The revivals awakened and refreshed the spiritual energies of thousands of colonists struggling with the uncertainties and anxieties of eighteenth-century America. The conversions at revivals did not sub-stantially boost the total number of church members, however. After the revivalists moved on, the routines and pressures of everyday existence reasserted their priority in the lives of many converts. But the revivals expressed the important message that every soul mattered, that men and women could choose to be saved, that individuals had the power to make a decision for everlasting life or death. Colonial revivals expressed in religious terms many of the same democratic and egali-tarian values expressed in economic terms by colonists' patterns of consumption. One colonist noted the analogy by referring to itinerant revivalists as "Pedlars in divinity." Like consumption, revivals contributed to a set of common experiences that bridged colonial divides of faith, region, class, and status.

TRACE CHANGE OVER TIME

How did the Great Awakening change colonists' religious worship?

Trade and Conflict in the North American Borderlands

British power defended the inhabitants of its colonies from Indian, French, and Spanish enemies on their borders—as well as from foreign powers abroad. Royal officials warily eyed the small North American settlements of New France and New Spain for signs of threats to the British colonies.

Alone, neither New France nor New Spain jeopardized British North America, but with Indian allies, they could become a potent force that kept colonists on their guard (**Map 5.4**). Native Americans' desire to defend their territory from colonial tres-passing competed with their desire for trade, which tugged them toward the settlers. As a colonial official observed in 1761, "A modern Indian cannot subsist without Europeans. . . . [The European goods that were] only conveniency at first [have] now become necessity." To obtain such necessities as guns, ammunition, clothing, and iron tools manufactured largely by the British, Indians trapped beaver, deer, and other fur-bearing animals.

British, French, Spanish, and Dutch officials competed for the fur trade. Indians took advantage of this competition to improve their own prospects, playing one trader and empire off another. Indian tribes and confederacies also competed among themselves for favored trading rights with one colony or another, a competition colonists encouraged.

| What changed in New England life and culture? | Why did the middle colonies grow rapidly? | Why did slavery come to define the southern colonies? | **What unified colonists in British North America during the eighteenth century?** | Conclusion: Why did British North American colonists develop a dual identity? |

MAP 5.4 ▶ Zones of Empire in Eastern North America

The British zone, extending west from the Atlantic coast, was much more densely settled than the zones under French, Spanish, and Indian control. The comparatively large number of British colonists made them more secure than the relatively few colonists in the vast regions claimed by France and Spain or the settlers living among the many Indian peoples in the huge area between the Mississippi River and the Appalachian Mountains. Yet the British colonists were not powerful enough to dominate the French, Spanish, or Indians. Instead, they had to guard against attacks by powerful Indian groups allied with the French or Spanish.

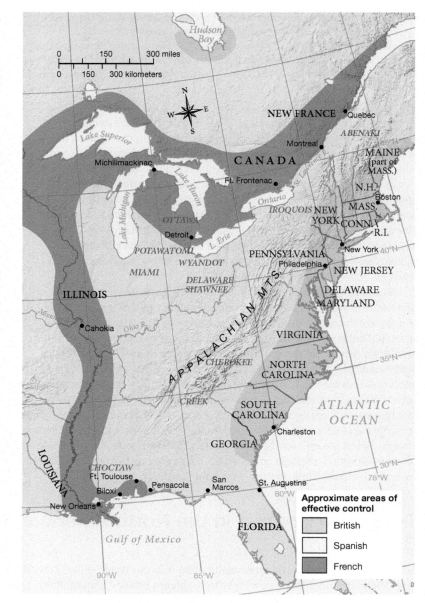

The shifting alliances and complex dynamics of the fur trade struck a fragile balance along the frontier. The threat of violence from all sides was ever present, and the threat became reality often enough for all parties to be prepared for the worst. In the Yamasee War of 1715, for example, the Yamasee and Creek Indians—with French encouragement—mounted a coordinated attack against colonial settlements in South Carolina. The Cherokee Indians, traditional enemies of the Creeks, refused to join the attack. Instead, they protected their access to British trade goods by allying with the colonists and turning the tide of battle, triggering a murderous rampage of revenge by the colonists against the Creeks and Yamasee.

Relations between Indians and colonists differed from colony to colony and from year to year. But the British colonists' nagging perceptions of menace on the frontier kept them continually hoping for help from the British to keep the Indians at bay and to maintain the essential flow of trade. In 1754, the British colonists' competition with the

How did the British North American colonies change during the eighteenth century?

▶ **Iroquois Warrior** This eighteenth-century engraving depicts a well-equipped Iroquois warrior much feared and respected by other Native Americans and by Euro-American colonists. This man's musket, tomahawk, beads, and textile clothing reflect Iroquois trade with colonists. His war club, headdress, moccasins, tattoos, and costume display features of Iroquois culture. British Library, London, UK / © British Library Board. All Rights Reserved / Bridgeman Images.

French flared into the Seven Years' War (also known as the French and Indian War), which would inflame the frontier for years (see chapter 6). Colonists agreed that Indians made deadly enemies, profitable trading partners, and powerful allies.

The Spanish kept an eye on the Pacific coast, where Russian hunters in search of the furs of seals and sea otters threatened to become a permanent presence on New Spain's northern frontier. To block Russian access to present-day California, officials in New Spain mounted a campaign to build forts (called **presidios**) and missions there. In 1769, an expedition headed by a military man, Gaspar de Portolá, and a Catholic priest, Junípero Serra, traveled north from Mexico to present-day San Diego, where they founded the first California mission, San Diego de Alcalá. They soon journeyed all the way to Monterey, which became the capital of Spanish California. There Portolá established a presidio in 1770 "to defend us from attacks by the Russians," he wrote. The same year, Serra founded Mission San Carlos Borroméo de Carmelo in Monterey to convert the Indians and recruit them to work to support the soldiers and other Spaniards in the presidio. By 1772, Serra had founded other missions along the path from San Diego to Monterey.

presidios
Spanish forts built to block Russian advance into California.

One Spanish soldier praised the work of the missionaries, writing that "with flattery and presents [the missionaries] attract the savage Indians and persuade them to adhere to life in society and to receive instruction for a knowledge of the Catholic faith, the cultivation of the land, and the arts necessary for making the instruments most needed for farming." Yet for the Indians, the Spaniards' California missions had horrendous consequences, as they had elsewhere in the Spanish borderlands. European diseases decimated Indian populations, Spanish soldiers raped Indian women, and missionaries beat Indians and subjected them to near slavery. Indian uprisings against the Spaniards occurred repeatedly, but the presidios and missions endured as feeble projections of the Spanish empire along the Pacific coast. **(See "Analyzing Historical Evidence: Spanish Priests Report on California Missions" on page 134.)**

Colonial Politics in the British Empire

The many different peoples, faiths, and communities that characterized the North American colonies arose from the somewhat haphazard policies of the eighteenth-century British empire. Unlike Spain and France—whose policies of excluding Protestants and foreigners kept the population of their North American colonial territories tiny—Britain kept the door to its colonies open to anyone. Tens of thousands of non-British immigrants settled in the British colonies and raised families. The open door did not extend to trade, however. The seventeenth-century Navigation Acts restricted colonial trade to British ships and traders. These policies evolved because they served the interests of the monarchy and of influential groups in Britain. The policies also gave the colonists a common framework of political expectations and experiences.

British attempts to exercise political power in their colonial governments met with success so long as British officials were on or very near the sea. Colonists

Spanish Missions in California

What changed in New England life and culture?	Why did the middle colonies grow rapidly?	Why did slavery come to define the southern colonies?	**What unified colonists in British North America during the eighteenth century?**	Conclusion: Why did British North American colonists develop a dual identity?

Spanish Priests Report on California Missions

Catholic missionaries sent regular reports to their superiors in Mexico City, New Spain's capital city. The reports described what the missionaries considered their successes in converting pagan Indians—whom they called gentiles—as well as the difficulties caused by the behavior of both Spaniards and Indians.

DOCUMENT 1

Father Luís Jayme Describes Conditions at Mission San Diego de Alcalá, 1772

Father Luís Jayme, a Franciscan missionary, reported on the deplorable behavior of some of the Spanish soldiers at Mission San Diego de Alcalá; they frequently raped Indian women, causing many Indians to resist the efforts of the missionaries.

With reference to the Indians, I wish to say that great progress [in converting Indians] would be made if there was anything to eat and the soldiers would set a good example. . . . As for the example set by the soldiers, no doubt some of them are good exemplars and deserve to be treated accordingly, but very many of them deserve to be hanged on account of the continuous outrages which they are committing in seizing and raping the women. There is not a single mission where all the gentiles have not been scandalized, and even on the roads. . . . Surely, as the gentiles themselves state, they [the soldiers] are committing a thousand evils, particularly of a sexual nature. . . .

At one of these Indian villages near this mission of San Diego . . . the gentiles therein many times have been on the point of coming here to kill us all, and the reason for this is that some soldiers went there and raped their women, and other soldiers who were carrying the mail to Monterey turned their animals into their fields and they ate up their crops. Three other Indian villages . . . [near] here have reported the same thing to me several times. For this reason on several occasions when . . . I have gone to see these Indian villages, as soon as they saw us they fled from their villages and fled to the woods or other remote places. . . . They do this so that the soldiers will

▲ **Mission Carmel** This eighteenth-century drawing portrays a reception for a Spanish visitor at Mission Carmel in what is now Carmel, California. Lines of mission Indians flank the entrance to the chapel where a priest and his assistants await the visitor. The Granger Collection, New York.

not rape their women as they have already done so many times in the past. . . .

Now [the Indians] all want to be Christians because they know that there is a God who created the heavens and earth and all things, that there is a Hell and Glory, that they have souls, etc. . . . [Now] they . . . do not have idols; they do not go on drinking sprees; they do not marry relatives; and they have but one wife. The married men sleep with their wives only. . . . Some of the first adults whom we baptized, when we pointed out to them that it was wrong to have sexual intercourse with

accepted British authority to collect customs duties, inspect cargoes, and enforce trade regulations—although they did not always follow the rules. But when royal officials tried to wield their authority in the internal affairs of the colonies, they invariably met colonial resistance. A governor appointed by the king in each of the nine royal colonies or by the proprietors in Maryland and Pennsylvania headed the government of each colony (Rhode Island and Connecticut selected their own governors). The British

How did the British North American colonies change during the eighteenth century?

a woman to whom they were not married, told me that they already knew that, and that among them it was considered to be very bad, and so they do not do so at all. "The soldiers," they told me, "are Christians and, although they know that God will punish them in Hell, do so, having sexual intercourse with our wives." . . . When I heard this, I burst into tears to see how these gentiles were setting an example for us Christians.

Source: Maynard Geiger, trans. and ed., *The Letter of Luís Jayme, O.F.M.: San Diego, October 17, 1772* (Los Angeles, 1979), 38–42. Courtesy of the Academy of American Franciscan History.

DOCUMENT 2

Father Junípero Serra Describes the Indian Revolt at Mission San Diego de Alcalá, 1775

Father Junípero Serra, the founder of many of the California missions, reported to his superiors in Mexico City that an Indian uprising had destroyed Mission San Diego de Alcalá. He recommended rebuilding and urged officials to provide additional soldiers to defend the missions, but not to punish the rebellious Indians.

I have just received [news] of the total destruction of the San Diego Mission, and of the death of the senior of its two religious ministers, called Father Luís Jayme, at the hand of the rebellious gentiles and of the Christian neophytes [Indians who lived in the mission]. All this happened . . . about one or two o'clock at night. The gentiles came together from forty rancherías [settlements] . . . and set fire to the church, after sacking it. They then went to the storehouse, the house where the Fathers lived, the soldiers' barracks, and all the rest of the buildings. They killed a carpenter . . . and a blacksmith. . . . They wounded with their arrows the four soldiers, who alone were on guard at the . . . mission. . . .

And now, after the Father has been killed, the Mission burned, its many and valuable furnishings destroyed, together with the sacred vessels, its paintings, its baptismal, marriage, and funeral records, and all the furnishings for the sacristy, the house, and the farm implements—now the forces [of soldiers] of both presidios [nearby] come together to set things right. . . . What happened was that before they set about reestablishing the Mission, they wanted to . . . lay hands on the guilty ones who were responsible for the burning of the Mission, and the death of the Fathers, and chastise them. The harassed Indians rebelled anew and became more enraged. . . . And so the soldiers there are gathered together in their presidios, and the Indians in their state of heathenism. . . .

But . . . what can be gained by campaigns [against the rebellious Indians]? Some will say to frighten them and prevent them from killing others. What I say is that, in order to prevent them from killing others, keep better guard over them than they did over the one who has been killed; and, as to the murderer, let him live, in order that he should be saved—which is the very purpose of our coming here, and the reason which justifies it.

Source: Antonine Tibesar, O.F.M., ed., *The Writings of Junípero Serra* (Washington, DC, 1956), 2:401–7. Courtesy of the Academy of American Franciscan History.

Questions for Analysis

ANALYZE THE EVIDENCE: How did the goals and activities of the Spanish soldiers compare with those of the Catholic missionaries?

RECOGNIZE VIEWPOINTS: In what ways did Jayme and Serra agree or disagree about the motivations of Indians in and around Mission San Diego de Alcalá? What might Spanish soldiers or Indians have said about these events? What might they have said about missionaries like Jayme and Serra?

CONSIDER THE CONTEXT: How did Indian resistance to the Spanish in missions compare to Native Americans' resistance to the British and French in the fur trade?

believed colonial governors were like mini-monarchs, able to exert influence in the colonies much as the king did in Britain. But colonial governors were not kings, and the colonies were not Britain.

Even the best-intentioned colonial governors had difficulty winning the trust and respect of influential colonists because their terms of office averaged just five years and could be terminated at any time. Colonial governors controlled few patronage

| What changed in New England life and culture? | Why did the middle colonies grow rapidly? | Why did slavery come to define the southern colonies? | **What unified colonists in British North America during the eighteenth century?** | Conclusion: Why did British North American colonists develop a dual identity? |

▶ **Ambush of Spanish Expedition** In 1720, the New Mexico governor sent forty-three Spanish soldiers and sixty Pueblo Indians to expel French intruders from New Spain's northern borderlands. The French and their Indian allies ambushed the expedition, killing thirty-three Spaniards and twelve Pueblos. Shortly afterward, an unknown artist recorded the event in this hide painting. Shown in the center of the painting is Father Juan Minguez of Albuquerque, and the Indian directly in front of him is Joseph Naranjo, leader of the Spaniards' Pueblo allies; both were killed in the ambush. MPI/Archive Photos/Getty Images.

positions in the colonies that would have allowed them to build political friendships. Obedient and loyal to their superiors in Britain, colonial governors fought with colonial assemblies. They battled over issues such as governors' vetoes of colonial legislation, removal of colonial judges, and dismissal of the representative assemblies. During the eighteenth century, the authority of governors declined as the assemblies gained the upper hand.

Since British policies did not clearly define the colonists' legal powers, colonial assemblies seized the opportunity to make their own rules. Gradually, the assemblies established a strong tradition of representative government similar in their eyes to the British Parliament. Voters often returned the same representatives to the assemblies year after year, building continuity in power and leadership that far exceeded that of the governor.

By 1720, colonial assemblies had won the power to initiate legislation, including tax laws and authorizations to spend public funds. Although all laws passed by the assemblies (except in Maryland, Rhode Island, and Connecticut) had to be approved by the governor and then by the Board of Trade in Britain, the difficulties in communication about complex subjects over long distances effectively ratified the assemblies' decisions. Years often passed before colonial laws were repealed by British authorities, and in the meantime the assemblies' laws prevailed.

The heated political struggles between royal governors and colonial assemblies that occurred throughout the eighteenth century taught colonists a common set of political lessons. They learned to employ traditionally British ideas of representative government to defend their own colonial interests. More important, they learned that power inside the British colonies rarely belonged to the British government.

CONSIDER CAUSE AND EFFECT

Why did colonial assemblies become more powerful than colonial governors during the eighteenth century?

> **QUICK REVIEW**
>
> How did culture, commerce, and consumption shape the identity of Britain's North American colonists in the eighteenth century?

How did the British North American colonies change during the eighteenth century?

Conclusion: Why did British North American colonists develop a dual identity?

During the eighteenth century, a society that was distinctively colonial and distinctively British emerged in North America. Tens of thousands of immigrants and slaves gave the colonies an unmistakably colonial complexion and contributed to the colonies' growing population and expanding economy. People of different ethnicities and faiths sought their fortunes in the colonies, where land was cheap, labor was dear, and work promised to be rewarding. Indentured servants and redemptioners risked temporary periods of bondage for the potential reward of better opportunities in the colonies than those found in the Old World. Slaves arrived in unprecedented numbers and endured lifelong servitude, which they neither chose nor desired, but from which their masters greatly benefited.

None of the European colonies could claim complete dominance of North America. The desire to expand and defend their territorial claims meant that the English, French, and Spanish colonies periodically fought one another, as well as the Indians upon whose land they encroached. In varying degrees, all colonists sought to influence or control Native Americans and their land, their military power, their trade, and even their souls. Spanish missionaries and soldiers sought to convert Indians on the West Coast and exploit their labor. French alliances with Indian tribes posed a formidable barrier to westward expansion of the British empire.

Yet despite attempts to secure their New World holdings, Spanish and French colonists did not develop societies that began to rival the European empires that sponsored and supported them. They did not participate in the cultural, economic, social, and religious changes experienced by their counterparts in British North America. Nor did they share in the emerging political identity of the British colonists.

Colonial products from New England, the middle colonies, and the southern colonies flowed to the West Indies and across the Atlantic. Back came unquestionably British consumer goods along with fashions in ideas, faith, and politics. The bonds of the British empire required colonists to think of themselves as British subjects and, at the same time, encouraged them to consider their status as colonists. By 1770, British colonists in North America could not imagine that their distinctively dual identity—as British and as colonists—would soon become a source of intense conflict.

STEP 1

EXPLAIN WHY IT MATTERS

Put your reading into practice. Identify each term below, and then explain why it matters in U.S. history.

TERM	WHO OR WHAT & WHEN	WHY IT MATTERS
natural increase (p. 112)		
partible inheritance (p. 114)		
Pennsylvania Dutch (p. 116)		
Scots-Irish (p. 117)		
redemptioners (p. 117)		
Middle Passage (p. 122)		
new Negroes (p. 123)		
Stono Rebellion (p. 124)		
task system (p. 125)		
Enlightenment (p. 130)		
Great Awakening (p. 130)		
presidios (p. 133)		

STEP 2

MOVE BEYOND THE BASICS

To demonstrate a more advanced understanding, consider the economy, society, culture, and politics of the major regions of British North America in 1700 and 1770. What accounts for the changes in each region?

Region	Economy (imports and exports, jobs, wealth)	Population (ethnicity, race, class)	Culture—Ways of Life, Values (including religious beliefs)	Colonial Politics
New England in 1700				
New England in 1770				
Middle Colonies in 1700				
Middle Colonies in 1770				
Southern Colonies in 1700				
Southern Colonies in 1770				

STEP 3

PUT IT ALL TOGETHER

Now, try to explain the big picture. Remember to use specific examples from the chapter in your answers.

NEW ENGLAND

• How did the economy of New England differ from that of other regions?

• Why did New England fail to attract as many immigrants as other areas?

MIDDLE COLONIES

• How did immigration shape the religious and ethnic diversity of the middle colonies?

• How did Atlantic commerce influence the middle colonies?

THE SOUTHERN COLONIES AND SPANISH CALIFORNIA

• How did slavery influence the social and economic development of the South?

• How did slaves try to retain some control within the limits of slavery?

• How did New Spain's establishment of presidios and missions affect Native Americans?

LOOKING BACKWARD, LOOKING AHEAD

• How did the relationship between the colonies and Britain change during the eighteenth century?

STEP 4

CONNECT THESE EVENTS

How did German and Scots-Irish immigration and the importation of African slaves shift the economic and class structures of eighteenth-century British North America?

STEP 5

CONNECT TO THE PRESENT

How does the religious and ethnic diversity of eighteenth-century colonial America continue to influence Americans today?

6

THE BRITISH EMPIRE AND THE COLONIAL CRISIS

1754–1775

Why did Britain's eighteenth century North American empire collapse? Chapter 6 explores the British government's efforts to tax and reform the colonies after the Seven Years' War. It traces the escalating colonial resistance, from political protest to open insubordination and—ultimately—to war.

This chapter will explore the following questions:

- How did the Seven Years' War lay the groundwork for colonial crisis?
- How did imperial authorities and British colonists differ about taxing the colonies?
- Why did the colonial crisis worsen after the repeal of the Stamp Act?
- How did British policy and colonial response to the repeal of the Townshend duties lead to rebellion?
- How did enslaved people in the colonies react to the stirrings of revolution?
- Conclusion: What changes did the American colonists want in 1775?

AN AMERICAN STORY

In 1771, Thomas Hutchinson became the royal governor of Massachusetts. Most governors were British aristocrats sent for short tours of duty. Hutchinson, by contrast, was fifth-generation American-born with a long record of public service. He lived in the finest mansion in Boston; wealth, power, and influence came to him easily. He prized his British identity and his fierce loyalty to his king. Alas, Hutchinson had the misfortune of being a loyal colonial leader during the tumultuous decades leading up to the American Revolution. He sought in vain to keep the interests of Britain and its colonies aligned. He promoted a plan of union to consolidate the colonies' Indian policy. After his plan failed, the Seven Years' War pitted Britain and its colonies against the French and their Indian allies. The war ended with a great British victory and the elimination of French claims in North America. The British empire's future had never looked so bright.

Hutchinson believed that the British government's plans to tax the colonies to help reimburse the war debt were perhaps unwise but legitimate. Many Bostonians disagreed. As angry crowds protested the tax policies enacted after 1763, Hutchinson maintained his loyalty to the empire. He was a measured and cautious man who believed in order and tradition.

Although he privately lamented the British tax policy, his sense of duty prevailed. He continued enforcing British law and became a villain to the growing revolutionary movement. "My temper does not incline to enthusiasm," he once wrote, even as disorder erupted around him.

When British troops occupied Boston in 1769, he wrote to a friend in England: "There must be an abridgement of what are called English liberties. . . . I doubt whether it is possible to project a system of government in which a colony three thousand miles distant from the parent state shall enjoy all the liberty of the parent state."

Thomas Hutchinson venerated the British empire, as did most English-speaking colonists in the 1750s. But the imperial policies following the Seven Years' War shook that affection, and eventually shattered it completely. From 1763 to 1773, British settlers raised profound questions about imperial governance. Many came to believe that a tyrannical Britain had embarked on a course to enslave the colonists by depriving them of their traditional liberties.

The colonists' invocation of terms like liberty, tyranny, and slavery inspired their passionate resistance in the 1760s and 1770s, but this rhetoric was a two-edged sword. The call to end slavery meant one thing when sounded by Boston merchants facing restrictions on commercial shipping; it meant something very different when sounded by African Americans locked in chattel slavery.

▼ **Thomas Hutchinson** A confident Thomas Hutchinson wears fashionable ruffles in this portrait. Painted in London when he was thirty years old, it is the only surviving portrait of the man who became governor of Massachusetts as revolution broke out. An angry crowd destroyed several family portraits when they sacked his Boston mansion in 1765. Hutchinson fled to Britain in 1775, only to realize how American he was. Massachusetts Historical Society, Boston, MA/Bridgeman Images.

How did the Seven Years' War lay the groundwork for colonial crisis?

1754
- Albany Congress convenes.

1755
- General Braddock defeated in western Pennsylvania.

1756
- Seven Years' War begins.

1757
- William Pitt fully commits to war.

1759–1760
- Quebec and Montreal fall to British; General Wolfe dies.

1763
- Treaty of Paris ends Seven Years' War.
- Pontiac's War begins.
- Royal Proclamation of 1763 forbids colonial settlements west of Appalachian Mountains.
- Paxton Boys massacre friendly Indians.

Seven Years' War
War (1756–1763) between Britain and France that shattered the French empire in North America. Known in America as the French and Indian War (fighting in America began and ended earlier than it did elsewhere in the world), it ended with the spectacular victory of Great Britain but planted the seeds of future imperial troubles.

From 1689 to 1815, Great Britain and France fought a succession of wars around the globe in a century-long effort to become the world's dominant power. The independence of Britain's North American colonies resulted at least in part from this great struggle, whose central turning point was the **Seven Years' War** (Americans called it the French and Indian War).

The global conflict began in 1754 in the distant Ohio Valley—land variously claimed by Virginia, Pennsylvania, the French empire, and more than a dozen Indian nations. In 1756, that backcountry struggle spread to encompass much of Europe, the Caribbean, and parts of Asia. By 1763, Great Britain had triumphed decisively over its enemy, defeating France in India, Europe, across the Caribbean, and permanently expelling French power from North America. It was the greatest victory the British empire had ever won, and it remade the island nation into a global power. But that victory came at great cost—in money, lives, and desire for revenge by the losers. Great Britain's triumph ultimately laid the groundwork for the imperial crisis of the 1760s and the collapse of the first British empire.

French-British Rivalry in the Ohio Country

For more than half a century, from their bases along the St. Lawrence valley and across the Great Lakes, French traders, missionaries, and officers had cultivated trade and diplomatic alliances with Indian peoples in the Ohio Country, who had migrated there in the wake of vicious wars and deadly epidemics. The French established a profitable exchange of manufactured goods for furs and other Native American exports. They supported their mostly Algonquian allies in their long struggle against the Iroquois people to the east (**Map 6.1**). Beginning in the 1740s, however, bold Pennsylvania traders began to infringe on the Ohio Valley, and on Franco-Indian trading relationships.

French and natives in the region could not tolerate these incursions. The Ohio Valley was, for the French, a crucial bridge connecting their strings of forts and settlements along the St. Lawrence and Mississippi rivers (**Map 6.2**). In response, French authorities sent a large contingent of French and Indian soldiers to build a series of military forts to secure their trade routes and to create a barrier against American expansion at the Appalachian Mountains (**Map 6.3**). These efforts alarmed both the British and their Iroquois allies. In 1753, the royal governor of Virginia, Robert Dinwiddie, dispatched a messenger to warn the French that they were trespassing on Virginia land. For this dangerous mission, he chose the twenty-one-year-old George Washington, a backwoods surveyor. Washington did not disappoint, returning with crucial intelligence that confirmed French military intentions. Impressed, Dinwiddie appointed the young man to lead a small military expedition west to assert Virginia's claim and chase the French away, but without attacking them.

In the spring of 1754, Washington set out with 160 Virginians and a contingent of Mingo Indians led by the Seneca chief Tanaghrisson. Their aims were identical: A year earlier, Tanaghrisson had similarly warned the French to leave the Ohio Country. As it would turn out, it was Washington's Native American allies—not the Virginians or the French—who would drive events. Early one morning, Tanaghrisson led a detachment of Washington's soldiers to a small French encampment in the woods. No one knows

How did the Seven Years' War lay the groundwork for colonial crisis?

142   CHAPTER 6
THE BRITISH EMPIRE AND THE COLONIAL CRISIS

who fired first, but in the ensuing battle fourteen Frenchmen were wounded. While a bewildered Washington looked on, Tanaghrisson and his men killed and then scalped thirteen of the wounded soldiers, including the French commander. Tanaghrisson probably hoped the battle would inflame hostilities between the French and the British colonists; if so, he had succeeded.

The massacre of French soldiers violated Dinwiddie's instructions and raised the stakes dramatically. Fearing retaliation, Washington ordered his men to throw together a makeshift "Fort Necessity" on the western side of the Appalachian Mountains. Several hundred Virginia reinforcements arrived to man the fort. Meanwhile, sensing disaster and displeased by Washington's leadership, the Mingos decamped. (Tanaghrisson later said, "The Colonel was a good-natured man, but had no experience; he took upon him to command the Indians as his slaves, [and] would by no means take advice from the Indians.") In July, six hundred French soldiers arrived, aided by one hundred Shawnee and Delaware warriors. They attacked Fort Necessity, killing or wounding a third of Washington's men. When Washington signed the articles of capitulation, it included an admission that he and his troops had "assassinated" the French commander in the initial fateful battle. "The volley fired by a young Virginian in the backwoods of America," the British politician Horace Walpole later wrote, "set the world on fire."

The Albany Congress

British leaders hoped to contain the conflict to the Ohio Country. One strategy was to strengthen the old partnership with the Mohawks of the Iroquois Confederacy, who since 1692 had joined with New York authorities in an alliance called the Covenant Chain to foster trade and mutual protection. Unscrupulous land speculators had caused the Mohawks to doubt British friendship, however. Authorities in London directed New York's royal governor to convene a colonial conference to repair trade relations and secure the Iroquois' help—or at least their neutrality—against the looming French threat. The conference convened at Albany in June and July 1754. All six nations of the Iroquois Confederacy attended, along with twenty-four delegates from seven colonies, making this an unprecedented intercolonial gathering.

Two delegates seized the occasion to present an additional proposal. Benjamin Franklin of Pennsylvania and Thomas Hutchinson of Massachusetts, both rising political stars, coauthored the Albany Plan of Union, a proposal for a unified colonial government with a president and a council to exercise sole authority over questions of war, peace, and trade with the Indians. No challenge to Parliament's authority was intended.

Delegates at the Albany Congress, alarmed by news of the Virginians' defeat at Fort Necessity, agreed to present the plan to their respective assemblies. To Franklin's surprise, not a single colony approved the Albany Plan. The Massachusetts assembly feared it was "a Design of gaining power over the Colonies," especially the power of taxation. Others objected that it would be impossible to agree on unified policies toward scores of quite different Indian nations. The British government never backed the Albany Plan; instead, it appointed two superintendents of Indian affairs, one for the northern and another for the southern colonies, each with exclusive powers to negotiate treaties, trade, and land sales with all tribes. This initiative centralized control of Indian policy with officials accountable to London rather than the colonial assemblies.

The Indians at the Albany Congress were no more impressed with the Albany Plan. The Covenant Chain alliance with the Mohawks was reaffirmed, but the other Iroquois nations left without pledging to fight with the British. Indeed, some of the Iroquois hoped that the French military presence around the Great Lakes would limit the westward push of American colonists, thus serving Indian interests.

▲ **Powder Horn from the Seven Years' War** To reload muskets, soldiers carried moisture-tight powder horns. Made from ox or bull horns, many became treasured objects memorializing significant moments in a soldier's life. Soldiers individualized them by carving names and dates, maps, or images. This horn from 1758 artfully charts the forts and river systems between New York City and Canada—a cherished object that also provided a map of unfamiliar territory. Mickael Almonds/The New York Historical Society/Getty Images.

ANALYZE EVIDENCE

What did the failure of the Albany Plan reveal about the colonies' relationship to each other?

| How did imperial authorities and British colonists differ about taxing the colonies? | Why did the colonial crisis worsen after the repeal of the Stamp Act? | How did British policy and colonial response to the repeal of the Townshend duties lead to rebellion? | How did enslaved people in the colonies react to the stirrings of revolution? | Conclusion: What changes did the American colonists want in 1775? |

MAP 6.1 ▲ European Areas of Influence and the Seven Years' War, 1756–1763

In the mid-eighteenth century, the French and Spanish empires had relatively few settlers on the ground, compared to the Anglo-American colonies. Among all empires, the actual amount of land controlled by European settlers was tiny relative to the land under Native American sovereignty.

The War and Its Consequences

By 1755, George Washington's frontier skirmish in the most distant reaches of European empires was turning into a global war. The British expected quick victories on three North American fronts. General Edward Braddock, recently arrived from England, marched his army toward Fort Duquesne in western Pennsylvania. Farther north, British troops moved toward Fort Niagara, critically located between Lakes Erie and Ontario. William Johnson, recently appointed superintendent of northern

How did the Seven Years' War lay the groundwork for colonial crisis?

MAP 6.2 ▲ Upper Ohio River Valley, 1753

It was in this hotly contested region of the Ohio Valley that Native American, French, and British powers confronted each other to begin the Seven Years' War. The English-allied Iroquois had long asserted their dominance over the Delaware and Shawnee, many of whom allied with the French, along with the Wyandot and Missisauga. This critical region connected the three great watersheds of the North American continent (see Map 6.3).

Indian affairs, led forces north toward Lake Champlain, intending to defend the border against the French in Canada (see Map 6.1).

Unfortunately for the British, the French and their Native American allies were prepared to fight. Braddock's army of 2,000 British soldiers marched west toward Fort Duquesne, carving a road through 125 miles of near-impenetrable Appalachian forest, and dragging cannons and heavy artillery across the mountains. On July 9, 1755, just twelve miles from their objective, Braddock's forces were attacked by 254 French and Canadian soldiers joined by a vast coalition of 600 to 700 disciplined and experienced

| How did imperial authorities and British colonists differ about taxing the colonies? | Why did the colonial crisis worsen after the repeal of the Stamp Act? | How did British policy and colonial response to the repeal of the Townshend duties lead to rebellion? | How did enslaved people in the colonies react to the stirrings of revolution? | Conclusion: What changes did the American colonists want in 1775? |

MAP 6.3 ▲ North America's Watersheds and River Systems Three North American watersheds drain into the Atlantic Ocean: the St. Lawrence, the Mississippi, and the Coastal Plain. At a time when water provided the principal means of accessing the continental interior, these river systems had an important influence on imperial rivalry in North America.

READING THE MAP: How do the geographic divisions depicted in this map relate to political divisions between French and British colonies and between Native American peoples portrayed in Map 6.1?

CONNECTIONS: How did geography help determine the placement of European forts? Why were the Six Iroquois Nations on such strategically located territory?

How did the Seven Years' War lay the groundwork for colonial crisis?

Native American warriors drawn from half the continent. It was one of the greatest defeats in British military history. In the bloody battle, nearly one thousand on the British side were wounded or killed, including General Braddock.

Although British forces vastly outnumbered the French, British leaders stumbled badly during the first years of the war, deploying inadequate numbers of undersupplied troops. What finally turned the war around was the rise to power in 1757 of William Pitt as Britain's prime minister, a man ready to commit massive resources to fight France and Spain, which had joined the war against Britain.

In America, British troops aided by American provincial soldiers at last captured Forts Duquesne, Niagara, and Ticonderoga, followed by the French cities of Quebec in 1759 and finally Montreal in 1760. By 1761, the war ended in North America but expanded globally, with battles in the Caribbean, Austria, Prussia, and India. The British captured the French sugar islands Martinique and Guadeloupe and then invaded Spanish Cuba with an army of some four thousand soldiers from New York and New England. France and Spain capitulated in 1762, and the Treaty of Paris was signed the following year.

VISUAL ACTIVITY

▲ **Death of General Wolfe** This epic painting depicts the death of General James Wolfe at the 1759 Battle of Quebec, the major turning point in the fall of New France. It became one of the most popular and famous images in Britain and its colonies; even George III ordered a copy. In reality, none of the figures depicted here were present at Wolfe's death. Private Collection/Phillips, Fine Art Auctioneers, New York, USA/Bridgeman Images.

READING THE IMAGE: What clues does the painting give to identify the origins of the figures watching Wolfe die? In what ways do they symbolize the British empire? How does the painting promote British nationalism?

CONNECTIONS: How did the defeat of New France change the relationship between Native Americans and the British empire?

| How did imperial authorities and British colonists differ about taxing the colonies? | Why did the colonial crisis worsen after the repeal of the Stamp Act? | How did British policy and colonial response to the repeal of the Townshend duties lead to rebellion? | How did enslaved people in the colonies react to the stirrings of revolution? | Conclusion: What changes did the American colonists want in 1775? |

▲ **Habit of an Ottawa** Images of Native Americans like this one circulated widely in European books and prints. This one shows an Odawa (or Ottawa) warrior in ceremonial dress. The Odawa were among the Anishinaabe people who lived around the Great Lakes, part of a vast web of native peoples all ed in diplomatic, trade, and military links to French power in North America. From the New York Public Library.

In the complex peace negotiations that produced the treaty, France ceded its North American empire, while British sovereignty was confirmed from the Atlantic coast to the Mississippi River. But French territory west of the Mississippi River, including New Orleans, was transferred to Spain, giving it a vast buffer zone for its lucrative Mexican colonies. Cuba was returned to Spain, and Martinique and Guadeloupe were returned to France.

It was a spectacular victory for Great Britain and for the British settlers in America. The French threat that had loomed on the northern flank of English settlements for over a century was now gone. An upsurge of patriotism washed across the colonies, as British settlers celebrated the glory of Great Britain and the fruits of their conquest. The Protestant British victory over its French Catholic enemies unleashed a wave of religious fervor; it seemed to presage the dawn of a new age. "Now commences the era of our quiet enjoyment of those liberties which our fathers purchased," proclaimed a Massachusetts clergyman. "Safe from the griping hand of arbitrary sway and cruel superstition; here shall be the late founded seat of peace and freedom . . . till time shall be no more."

But those hopes were soon dashed. The great victory planted the seeds of future downfall. The continental balance of power that had shaped diplomatic, economic, and cultural relations among native and European people was suddenly upended. The loss of a French counterweight to the British unshackled the restraints on settlers' ambitions in the west, raising their hopes for land and wealth that would soon be disappointed. Religious expectations, too, were dashed by the mundane realities of governance and political conflict. And perhaps most vexing of all, the enormous expense of the war—by 1763, Britain's national debt had doubled in just six years—posed a formidable challenge to British leaders. How would those war debts be paid?

Pontiac's War and the Proclamation of 1763

Although native peoples from the St. Lawrence valley to the Mississippi Delta had fought in the Seven Years' War, none were included or even consulted in the negotiations that led to the Treaty of Paris. As far as they were concerned, war had not ended. Minavavana, an Ojibwa chief of the Great Lakes region, put it succinctly to an English trader: "Englishman, although you have conquered the French, you have not yet conquered us! We are not your slaves. These lakes, these woods and mountains were left to us by our ancestors . . . and we will part

"Minavavana, an Ojibwa chief of the Great Lakes region, to an English trader: 'Englishman, although you have conquered the French, you have not yet conquered us! We are not your slaves.'"

with them to none." Furthermore, Minavavana noted, "your king has never sent us any presents, nor entered into any treaty with us, wherefore he and we are still at war."

Minavavana made an important point about the absence of British presents. In Indian diplomacy and trade, gifts cemented alliances, symbolizing honor and establishing obligation. Over many decades, the French had mastered the subtleties of this diplomacy, distributing goods on which their Native American allies had come to

How did the Seven Years' War lay the groundwork for colonial crisis?

depend, like weapons and manufactured items, and receiving fur, skins, slaves, and native goods like moccasins in return. British military leaders, new to Native American diplomacy, often discarded trade goods as trivial trinkets, insulting the very people they meant to court. "It is not my intention ever to attempt to gain the friendship of Indians by presents," Major General Jeffery Amherst declared. The native view was very different: In the ceremonial practices of diplomacy and trade, generosity expressed power and protection, not subordination.

France's former allies north of the Ohio River had cause for concern. As French officers turned their trading posts across the northwest over to the British, their former enemies turned them into military bases. Fort Duquesne, renamed Fort Pitt, gained new walls sixty feet thick at their base. This was no mere trading post.

Although the French king had abandoned North America, the transcontinental alliances the French had helped to forge, along with the experience of continent-wide fighting against the British, had fostered a greater sense of unity and even iden- tity among disparate Native American people. A renewed religious fervor began to spread across Indian country, magnifying feelings of antagonism toward the British. Decades of war and dislocation of native peoples across the trans-Appalachian West had set the stage for a religious revival. Onto this fertile ground stepped the Ottawa warrior Pontiac and the Delaware prophet Neolin, who preached a return to tradi- tional Indian ways, the formation of pan-Indian unity, and armed resistance to British power.

In May 1763, Ottawa, Potawatomi, and Huron warriors attacked Fort Detroit, launching **Pontiac's War**. Their objective was to keep British settlement and sovereignty out of Indian country. Six more attacks on forts followed within weeks, and soon settlements across the backcountry were under assault. By the fall, Pontiac's forces had captured every fort west of Detroit. More than four hundred British soldiers were dead and two thousand colonists killed or taken captive.

The pan-Indian unity west of the Appalachians found a counterpart in a growing anti-Indian racism among settlers to the east. Some exacted revenge. The most violent aggression occurred in late 1763, when some fifty Pennsylvania vigilantes known as the Paxton Boys descended on a peaceful village of friendly Conestoga Indians, murdering twenty. The vigilantes, now numbering five hundred, marched on Philadelphia to try to capture and murder some Christian Indians held in protective custody there. British troops prevented a further massacre, but the Paxton Boys escaped punishment for their murderous attack on the Conestoga village.

In early 1764, the uprising began to fade. The Indians, without their French allies, were short on ammunition, and the British were tired and broke. The British government recalled the imperious General Amherst, blaming him for mishandling the conflict (his own soldiers toasted his departure). A new military leader, Thomas Gage, reversed Amherst's unsuccessful policies and distributed gifts profusely among the Indians to cement new alliances.

▲ **Silver Medal to Present to Indians** After Pontiac's War, British officers distributed gifts among Native American nations in order to promote peaceful alliances. This 1766 silver medal shows King George III on the front and an Indian and a Briton smoking a peace pipe on the back. How would an English translator explain what HAPPY WHILE UNITED might mean? Courtesy of the American Numismatic Society.

Pontiac's War
The continued war of Native American peoples in the northwest after France capitulated at the end of the Seven Years' War. The war heightened Britain's determination to create a boundary between colonists and Indians, embodied in the Royal Proclamation of 1763.

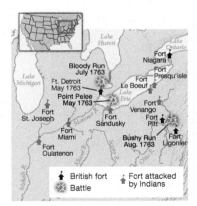

Pontiac's War, 1763

How did imperial authorities and British colonists differ about taxing the colonies?	Why did the colonial crisis worsen after the repeal of the Stamp Act?	How did British policy and colonial response to the repeal of the Townshend duties lead to rebellion?	How did enslaved people in the colonies react to the stirrings of revolution?	Conclusion: What changes did the American colonists want in 1775?

Royal Proclamation of 1763
A law that reserved lands to the west of the Appalachian Mountains as Native American territory. By forbidding colonial settlement and land purchases, the Proclamation helped to settle Pontiac's War, but it inflamed tensions between British settlers and the imperial government.

CONSIDER CAUSE AND EFFECT

How did Britain's victory in the Seven Years' War transform its North American empire and its relationship to Native Americans?

To contain the violence, the British government issued the Royal Proclamation of 1763, which protected the integrity of Indian territory by forbidding colonists to settle west of the Appalachian Mountains. But the Proclamation's language also took care not to identify western lands as belonging to the Indians. Instead, it spoke of lands that "are reserved to [Indians], as their Hunting Grounds." While the Proclamation of 1763 referred to American and even French colonists in Canada as "our loving subjects" entitled to English rights and privileges, it described native peoples more vaguely as "Tribes of Indians with whom We are connected." In fact, the British were not very well connected with most Indians, nor did they wish connections to form among the different nations. As William Johnson, the superintendent of northern Indian affairs, advised in 1764, "It will be expedient to treat with each nation separately . . . for could they arrive at a perfect union, they must prove very dangerous Neighbours."

If the Royal Proclamation calmed tensions with native peoples west of the Appalachians, it provoked angry reactions among British settlers and land speculators who had staked claims to huge tracts of western lands. Making matters worse, the boundary proved impossible to enforce. Surging population growth among British settlers had already sent hundreds west of the Appalachians, where they squatted on Indian lands. Violence periodically broke out, leaving settlers fearful, uncertain about their futures, and increasingly distrustful of British authority.

QUICK REVIEW

How did the Seven Years' War destabilize relations between colonists and British authorities?

How did imperial authorities and British colonists differ about taxing the colonies?

CHRONOLOGY

1760
- George III becomes British king.

1764
- Parliament enacts Sugar Act.

1765
- Parliament enacts Stamp Act.
- Virginia Resolves challenge Stamp Act.
- Sons of Liberty stage crowd actions.
- Stamp Act Congress meets.

1766
- Parliament repeals Stamp Act, passes Declaratory Act.

In 1760, George III, just twenty-two years old, became king of England. Timid and insecure, George struggled to gain his footing. He rotated through a succession of leaders, searching for a prime minister he could trust. A half dozen ministers in seven years took turns dealing with one basic underlying British reality: The huge war debt needed to be serviced. It seemed reasonable to British authorities to expect that British subjects in North America—who were, after all, principal beneficiaries of the great victory—should help pay the debt. To many American colonists, however, that proposition violated what they perceived as their rights and liberties as British subjects. Eventually, their resentment erupted in large-scale protests.

Grenville's Sugar Act

The first taxes were the work of Sir George Grenville, prime minister from 1763 to 1765. Searching for sources of revenue, he focused on the customs service, which monitored the shipping trades and collected all import and export duties. He found that the salaries of customs officers cost the government four times the revenue they collected. The shortfall was due in part to bribery and smuggling, so Grenville began to insist on more rigorous paperwork and stricter accounting. He also set about rationalizing

How did the Seven Years' War lay the groundwork for colonial crisis?

customs taxes. The hardest duty to enforce, he learned, resulted from the Molasses Act of 1733, which imposed a stiff tax on molasses imported to British colonies from outside the empire. Molasses was the central ingredient for rum, which British colonists drank in great quantities. Colonists had ignored the Molasses Act for decades, importing molasses from the French Caribbean islands, where it was much cheaper.

Grenville's solution was the Revenue Act of 1764, popularly dubbed the Sugar Act. It cut the duty on French molasses in half, making it more attractive for shippers to obey the law, and raised penalties for smuggling. Although the act appeared to be in the tradition of the Navigation Acts, which regulated trade (see chapter 4), its clear intent was to raise revenue. More ominously, the Sugar Act toughened enforcement policies, empowering British naval crews to board suspicious ships and seize illegal cargoes. Ship captains without proper paperwork would be prosecuted—not in a local court with a jury of peers, but in a vice-admiralty court located in distant Nova Scotia, where a crown judge presided without a jury.

Grenville's hopes for the Sugar Act did not materialize. Despite the decrease in duty, the tax was still too high to offset the profits to be made from smuggling. Meanwhile, the increased enforcement measures led to ugly confrontations in colonial port cities. From the perspective of British administrators, the Sugar Act was a reasonable effort to administer the colonies. To many colonists, however, the British law was a disturbing intrusion on colonial practices of self-taxation by elected colonial assemblies. It was the "exclusive Right of the People of the Colonies to tax themselves," one Bostonian wrote to Massachusetts's lobbyist in London, and they "ought not be deprived of a right they had so long enjoyed & which they held by Birth & by Charter."

The Stamp Act

In February 1765, Grenville expanded his revenue program with the Stamp Act, precipitating a major conflict between Britain and the colonies, and raising profound questions about the powers of Parliament over British settlers in America. The Stamp Act imposed a tax on paper used for official documents—newspapers, pamphlets, court documents, licenses, wills, ships' cargo lists, and more—requiring an affixed stamp to prove the tax had been paid. Unlike the Sugar Act, which regulated trade, the Stamp Act had only one purpose: to raise revenue. Although it affected anyone who used taxed paper, the Stamp Act's greatest impact fell on the business and legal communities, which used official paper in abundance. Anticipating that the stamp tax would be unpopular—Thomas Hutchinson had warned him—and not wanting the anger focused on imperial officers, Grenville delegated its enforcement to local stamp distributors. Each would earn 8 percent of the revenue collected.

English tradition held that only the people's representatives in Parliament could levy taxes. This view that taxation required the consent of the people rested on an essential concept of English political theory: that free people have the right to enjoy and use their property without fear of confiscation. The king could not demand taxes; only the House of Commons could grant them. But this traditional view did not address the place of settlers in British colonies, who did not elect representatives to Parliament. Could Parliament tax them?

Grenville agreed that taxation required the consent of the people, but he and his allies argued that the colonists benefited from virtual representation in Parliament. The House of Commons, he insisted, represented British subjects throughout the empire, whether or not they voted in parliamentary elections. Colonial leaders rejected this concept. They consented to local and provincial taxes, levied by their town, county, or colonial assemblies, which funded public expenses like local roads, schools, and poor relief. By contrast, they argued, the stamp tax was a departure, a fee-per-document tax levied by a distant Parliament on its colonies.

Sugar (Revenue) Act
1764 British law that decreased the duty on French molasses, making it more attractive for shippers to obey the law, and at the same time raised penalties for smuggling. The Sugar Act regulated trade but was also intended to raise revenue.

Stamp Act
1765 British law imposing a tax on all paper used for official documents, for the purpose of raising revenue. Widespread resistance to the Stamp Act led to its repeal in 1766.

virtual representation
The theory that all British subjects were represented in Parliament, whether they had elected representatives in that body or not. American colonists rejected the theory of virtual representation, arguing that only direct representatives had the right to tax the colonists.

| How did imperial authorities and British colonists differ about taxing the colonies? | Why did the colonial crisis worsen after the repeal of the Stamp Act? | How did British policy and colonial response to the repeal of the Townshend duties lead to rebellion? | How did enslaved people in the colonies react to the stirrings of revolution? | Conclusion: What changes did the American colonists want in 1775? |

Resistance: From Colonial Assemblies to Crowd Politics

When colonists learned of the Stamp Act in April 1765, seven months before it was to take effect, resistance began immediately. It centered first in colonial assemblies.

Virginia's assembly, the House of Burgesses, took the lead. At the end of its May session, after two-thirds of the members had left, Patrick Henry, a young political newcomer, presented a series of resolutions on the Stamp Act that became known as the Virginia Resolves. The first three stated the obvious: that Virginians were British citizens, that they enjoyed the same rights and privileges as other Britons, and that self-taxation was one of those rights. The fourth resolution noted that Virginians had always taxed themselves, through their representatives in the House of Burgesses. The fifth took a radical leap by pushing the other four unexceptional statements to one conclusion—that the Virginia assembly alone had the right to tax Virginians.

Two more fiery resolutions were debated as Henry pressed the logic of his case. The sixth resolution denied legitimacy to any tax law originating outside Virginia, and the seventh boldly called anyone who disagreed with these propositions an enemy of Virginia. This was too much for the other representatives. They voted down resolutions six and seven and later rescinded their vote on number five as well.

COMPARE AND CONTRAST

How did British authorities and colonists differ in their views of Parliament's right to tax the colonies? Were these differences based on English political traditions, or do they reflect an emerging American identity?

Their caution hardly mattered, however, because newspapers in other colonies printed all seven Virginia Resolves, creating the impression of a daring challenge to the Stamp Act. Consequently, other assemblies began considering even more radical questions: By what authority could Parliament legislate for the colonies without also taxing them? No one in 1765 disagreed that Parliament had legislative power over the colonists. They were, after all, British subjects. Several assemblies, however, began distinguishing between *external taxes*, imposed to regulate trade, and *internal taxes*, such as a stamp tax or a property tax, which could only be self-imposed.

If political debate about the Stamp Act began in legislative assemblies, it soon expanded to private sites like parlors and coffee shops, to public spaces like streets and docks, and into the printed pages of newspapers and pamphlets. Everyone whose livelihood required official paper had to decide whether to comply.

The first organized resistance to the Stamp Act began in Boston under the direction of town leaders, including Samuel Adams, John Hancock, and Ebenezer Mackintosh. Adams, in his forties, had shrewd political instincts and a gift for organizing. Hancock, not yet thirty, had inherited his uncle's shipping business and was one of the wealthiest merchants in Massachusetts. Mackintosh, a young shoemaker, was a highly experienced street activist. **(See "Spotlight: How Did a Shoemaker Influence the Revolution?" on page 154.)** Many other artisans, tradesmen, printers, tavern keepers, dockworkers, and sailors—the middling and lower orders—mobilized to oppose the Stamp Act, taking the name "Sons of Liberty."

The Boston protest called for a large street demonstration culminating in a mock execution designed to convince Andrew Oliver, the local stamp distributor, to resign. On August 14, 1765, a crowd of two to three thousand demonstrators, led by Mackintosh, hung an effigy of Oliver in a tree and then paraded it around town, before finally beheading and burning it. The royal governor, Francis Bernard, afraid of fueling public anger, took no action. The next day Oliver announced his resignation.

The demonstration provided lessons for everyone. Oliver learned that stamp distributors would be very unpopular. Governor Bernard, lacking a police force, learned the limitations of his power. The demonstration's leaders learned that street action could effect change. And thousands of ordinary people gained confidence in their ability to shape political events.

Two weeks later, a second crowd action showed how well these lessons had been learned. On August 26, a crowd visited the houses of three government officials,

How did the Seven Years' War lay the groundwork for colonial crisis?

▲ **Symbolic Death to Stamp Agents** Protesters across the colonies staged threatening demonstrations intended to intimidate stamp distributors, pressuring them to stop selling the hated stamps. In this contemporary cartoon, a dummy wearing a hat and waistcoat is being led to destruction. One protester carries a hangman's gallows, another a bundle of sticks to burn the dummy. Do you think the cartoonist sympathized with the demonstrators? The Granger Collection, New York.

breaking windows and raiding wine cellars. The crowd then moved on to the finest dwelling in Massachusetts—owned by Thomas Hutchinson, lieutenant governor of Massachusetts and the chief justice of the colony's highest court. Rumors abounded that Hutchinson had urged Grenville to adopt the Stamp Act. Although he had actually done the opposite, Hutchinson refused to set the record straight. "I am not obliged to give an answer to all the questions that may be put me by every lawless person," he insisted. The crowd attacked his house; by daybreak only the exterior walls were standing. Governor Bernard gave orders to call out the militia, but he was told that many militiamen were among the crowd.

The destruction of Hutchinson's house brought a temporary halt to protest in Boston. The town meeting issued a statement of sympathy for Hutchinson, but a large reward for the arrest and conviction of rioters failed to produce a single lead. Although Adams professed shock at the "truly mobbish Nature" of the violence, the opponents of the Stamp Act in Boston had triumphed. Crowd actions had succeeded where legislative protests had failed. No one replaced Oliver as distributor. When the act took effect on November 1, ships without stamped permits continued to clear the harbor. Since he could not bring the lawbreakers to court, Hutchinson, ever principled, resigned his office as chief justice. He remained lieutenant governor, however, and within five years became the royal governor.

Liberty and Property

Boston's crowd actions sparked similar eruptions in nearly fifty towns throughout the colonies by groups calling themselves Sons of Liberty. Facing widespread resistance and intimidation, stamp distributors everywhere resigned. A Connecticut crowd forced

UNDERSTAND POINTS OF VIEW

How did Thomas Hutchinson and the Bostonians gathered outside his mansion differ in their views about the kinds of people who can legitimately influence political events?

| How did imperial authorities and British colonists differ about taxing the colonies? | Why did the colonial crisis worsen after the repeal of the Stamp Act? | How did British policy and colonial response to the repeal of the Townshend duties lead to rebellion? | How did enslaved people in the colonies react to the stirrings of revolution? | Conclusion: What changes did the American colonists want in 1775? |

How Did a Shoemaker Influence the Revolution?

In August 1765, a little-known Boston shoemaker gained sudden prominence as the leader of crowd actions opposing the Stamp Act. Ebenezer Mackintosh boldly encouraged thousands of ordinary men in Massachusetts to assert their liberty against what they viewed as British tyranny. Mackintosh's story offers a glimpse into the experience of the man in the street during the decade of pre-Revolutionary turmoil. By 1776, this rhetoric of liberty would be a defining feature of the fledgling United States.

Although his ancestors had arrived in the Puritan migration of the 1630s, Ebenezer Mackintosh was born into poverty in 1737. Ebenezer's father, an orphan, owned no land and lacked a trade; he married and buried wives at least three times. The best he could do for young Ebenezer was to apprentice him to

a shoemaker so his son could learn a trade. During the Seven Years' War, Ebenezer joined the army to secure a signing bonus. He saw brief action and returned to Boston in 1758 to resume shoemaking. He was twenty-one.

A major fire in Boston in 1760 marked a dramatic change in Mackintosh's life. In the aftermath of the fire, the city looked to young, able-bodied men to reinvigorate its volunteer fire companies and picked Ebenezer to join a select firemen's association in the city's South End. In addition to fighting fires, fire clubs generated fraternal sociability, with firemen regularly meeting in taverns over pitchers of beer, cementing the collective spirit so critical to successful firefighting. Mackintosh proved to be a leader of men in times of emergency; he soon became head of the South End gang, which staged a mock battle once a year

▲ Skilled Boston fireman tapped water from underground water mains made from hollowed logs and pumped it vigorously by hand to douse fires. Demolition to halt the spread of fires was essential work. Mackintosh's fire-control skills transferred easily to anti–Stamp Act actions, whether rallying other men, burning effigies and small buildings, or destroying Thomas Hutchinson's house. The Granger Collection, New York.

one distributor to throw his hat and powdered wig in the air while shouting a cheer for "Liberty and property!" In Charleston, South Carolina, the stamp distributor resigned after crowds burned effigies and chanted "Liberty! Liberty!" Both fared better than another Connecticut stamp agent who was nearly buried alive. Only when the thuds of dirt sounded on his coffin did he scream out his resignation to his tormentors gathered above.

Some colonial leaders, disturbed by the increasingly aggressive crowds, sought to challenge the Stamp Act in more moderate ways. In October 1765, twenty-seven

How did the Seven Years' War lay the groundwork for colonial crisis?

against the rival North End gang. In this traditional street festival, Mackintosh gained experience managing rowdy crowds.

Expertise in fire and crowd control paved the way for Mackintosh's transition from community leader to community activist in 1765. Stamp Act protests erupted twice in August of that year. In the first event, Mackintosh presided over the mock hanging of a dummy representing Andrew Oliver, the stamp distributor, at a century-old elm tree known as the Liberty Tree. The shoemaker led several thousand protesters in a march on the new stamp office, which they pulled down and burned. Twelve days later, a smaller but far more destructive demonstration almost certainly led by Mackintosh demolished the mansion of Lieutenant Governor Thomas Hutchinson. Hutchinson ordered Mackintosh arrested, but no witnesses cared to identify him.

Hours later, the sheriff—a member of Mackintosh's fire company—released him, predicting worse trouble if he was kept in jail. The shoemaker continued to lead large demonstrations in November and December, forcing Oliver to repudiate his stamp distributor duties. In these protests, ordinary artisans, tradesmen, and workers like Mackintosh exerted a new authority and confidence, forcing their social betters to do their bidding.

In 1766, the Stamp Act was repealed, and Mackintosh went back to shoemaking. He married Elizabeth Maverick and had two children by 1769. Perhaps he took a break from activism; no record links him to protest activities when British troops came to town in 1769–1770, nor was his presence recorded at the Boston Massacre in March 1770. In 1773, he was apparently back at it, later bragging that he helped throw tea into Boston harbor.

In 1774, a rumor spread that a ship en route from London carried orders to arrest four rebellious subjects, most notably Samuel Adams and Mackintosh. Adams stayed put, but Mackintosh, whose wife had recently died, decided that flight was his best option. Carrying his two young children and his meager belongings, he walked one hundred fifty miles to a village in northern New Hampshire, where he set up shop as a shoemaker. He served locally and briefly as a soldier in the Revolution and then remarried and fathered four more children.

An especially telling clue to Mackintosh's commitment to ideals of liberty appears in the unusual name he gave his son born in 1769: Paschal Paoli Mackintosh. The boy was named in honor of Pasquale Paoli of Corsica, a freedom fighter who led his Mediterranean island's independence from Genoese rule, who drafted a constitution for the short-lived Corsican republic, and who became a celebrated figure among European writers and gained broad coverage in American newspapers in 1767–1769. (In those years, some scores of babies throughout the colonies were named Paschal.) Mackintosh lived to see liberty defined and enshrined in the foundational documents of the United States. Although his life ended in 1816 in obscurity, as it had begun, Mackintosh's activism in 1765 brought non-elite people to the forefront of national and imperial politics, and helped ensure that the thousands of people he mobilized learned to speak a political language of rights and liberties—a language that still resonates loudly today.

Questions for Analysis

RECOGNIZE VIEWPOINTS: Why would a twenty-eight-year-old shoemaker of low social status get upset about Britain's passage of the Stamp Act?

ASK HISTORICAL QUESTIONS: How did non-elite people like Mackintosh influence the course of the American Revolution? What did he gain in the Revolution? What stayed the same?

CONSIDER THE CONTEXT: How did international political events shape the course of events in North America in the 1760s and 1770s?

---

delegates representing nine colonial assemblies met in New York City as the Stamp Act Congress. For two weeks, they debated a petition addressed to the king and Parliament. Their statement closely resembled the first five Virginia Resolves, claiming that taxes were "free gifts of the people," which only elected representatives could grant. They dismissed the concept of virtual representation: "The people of these colonies are not, and from their local circumstances, cannot be represented in the House of Commons." At the same time, the delegates carefully affirmed their subordination to Parliament and monarch in deferential language. For all its moderation, the mere

ANALYZE EVIDENCE

How did the different modes of colonial protest— between crowd action and debate in legislative assemblies—suggest the existence of social tensions within colonial society?

| How did imperial authorities and British colonists differ about taxing the colonies? | Why did the colonial crisis worsen after the repeal of the Stamp Act? | How did British policy and colonial response to the repeal of the Townshend duties lead to rebellion? | How did enslaved people in the colonies react to the stirrings of revolution? | Conclusion: What changes did the American colonists want in 1775? |

existence of the Stamp Act Congress carried radical potential—of intercolonial political action that might challenge parliamentary authority.

The cry of "Liberty and property" made sense to colonists of many social ranks. Those terms came from a trinity of concepts—"life, liberty, property"—that had come to be regarded as the birthright of freeborn British subjects. Since at least the seventeenth century, a powerful tradition of British political thought affirmed these rights against abuse by royal authority. To many colonists, therefore, the Stamp Act seemed like a violation of their rights as British subjects.

Some colonists perceived a deeper plot behind these taxes: an effort by British leaders to enslave them. A Maryland writer warned that if the colonies lost "the right of exemption from all taxes without their consent," that loss would "deprive them of every privilege distinguishing freemen from slaves." In Virginia, a group of planters issued a document called the Westmoreland Resolves, claiming that the Stamp Act was an attempt "to reduce the people of this country to a state of abject and detestable slavery." If the opposed meanings of *liberty* and *slavery* seemed clear to white colonists, they stopped short of applying similar logic to the nearly half million blacks in actual slavery—people of African descent, who saw the contradiction quite clearly. When a crowd of black Charlestonians paraded with shouts of "Liberty!" just a few months after white Sons of Liberty had done the same, the town militia turned out to break up the demonstration.

Many people in Britain reacted with alarm to the colonial unrest. Merchants, in particular, feared trade disruptions and pressured Parliament to repeal the Stamp Act. By late 1765, a new minister, the Marquess of Rockingham, headed the king's cabinet and looked for a way to repeal the act without losing face. The solution came in March 1766: Parliament repealed the Stamp Act, but replaced it with the **Declaratory Act**, which asserted Parliament's right to legislate for the colonies "in all cases whatsoever." Perhaps the stamp tax had failed, but the power to tax—a prime legislative power—was stoutly upheld.

Declaratory Act
1766 law issued by Parliament to assert its unassailable right to legislate for its British colonies "in all cases whatsoever." The act put Americans on notice that Britain retained the power to govern the colonies despite repealing the Stamp Act.

QUICK REVIEW

Why did many British colonists see the Sugar Act and the Stamp Act as a violation of their rights?

Why did the colonial crisis worsen after the repeal of the Stamp Act?

Rockingham did not last long as prime minister. By the summer of 1766, George III had persuaded William Pitt to return to the office. Pitt appointed Charles Townshend as chancellor of the exchequer, the chief financial minister. Facing both the war debt and the cost of maintaining British troops in America, Townshend turned again to taxation. His plan to raise revenue touched off coordinated boycotts of British goods in 1768 and 1769. Women, too, became involved in the movement, increasingly politicized as self-styled "Daughters of Liberty." Boston once again led the opposition, prompting British authorities to send soldiers to assist the royal governor. The colonial resistance was gradually growing into a rebellion.

How did the Seven Years' War lay the groundwork for colonial crisis?

The Townshend Duties

Townshend proposed new taxes in the old form of a navigation act. Officially called the Revenue Act of 1767, and popularly known as the Townshend duties, it established new duties on tea, glass, lead, paper, and painters' colors imported into the colonies. A further reduction in the duty on French molasses had persuaded some American shippers to stop smuggling, and Britain was finally deriving a moderate revenue stream from its colonies. Townshend too hastily concluded that British colonists would accept external taxes.

The Townshend duties were not especially burdensome, but the principle they embodied—taxation through trade duties—looked more threatening to colonists in the wake of the Stamp Act crisis. Colonists' recent insistence on distinguishing between an external and an internal tax—one whose purpose was to direct the flow of trade, the other whose purpose was to raise revenue—was rendered irrelevant by an external tax meant only to raise money. John Dickinson, a Philadelphia lawyer, articulated this view in an essay titled *Letters from a Farmer in Pennsylvania*, which circulated widely in late 1767. "We are taxed without our consent," Dickinson wrote. "We are therefore—SLAVES." Dickinson expanded the colonists' argument against parliamentary taxation, claiming "a total denial of the power of Parliament to lay upon these colonies any 'tax' whatever."

A controversial provision of the Townshend duties directed some of the revenue generated to pay the salaries of royal governors. Previously, local assemblies set their officials' salaries, giving them significant influence over crown-appointed officeholders. With this new provision, Townshend aimed to curb the assemblies' independence.

Massachusetts again led the protests of the Townshend duties. Samuel Adams, now an elected member of the provincial assembly, argued that any form of parliamentary taxation was unjust. Further, he contended that the new way of paying governors' salaries subverted the relationship between the people and their rulers. The assembly circulated a letter with Adams's arguments to other colonial assemblies for their endorsement. As with the Stamp Act Congress of 1765, colonial assemblies started to coordinate their protests.

British officials did not look kindly on these actions. Lord Hillsborough, who was in charge of colonial affairs, instructed Massachusetts governor Bernard to dissolve the assembly if it would not repudiate Adams's letter. The assembly refused, by a vote of 92 to 17, and Bernard carried out his instruction. In the summer of 1768, its elected assembly suspended, Boston was in an uproar.

Nonconsumption and the Daughters of Liberty

Bostonians led the resistance to the Townshend duties by calling for nonconsumption agreements to boycott British-made goods. Dozens of other towns passed similar resolutions in 1767 and 1768. For example, New Haven, Connecticut, prohibited the purchase of carriages, furniture, hats, clothing, lace, clocks, and textiles, among other imported goods. The objective was to encourage home manufacture and to hurt trade, causing London merchants to pressure Parliament for a repeal of the duties.

Nonconsumption agreements were hard to enforce. With the Stamp Act, there was one hated item, a stamp, and a limited number of official distributors. In contrast, an agreement to boycott all British goods required widespread personal sacrifice and popular solidarity. A more direct blow to trade came from nonimportation agreements. But getting merchants to agree proved difficult because of fears that merchants in other colonies might not adhere and might thereby make handsome profits. Not until late 1768

CHRONOLOGY

1767
– Parliament enacts Townshend duties.

1768
– British station troops in Boston.

1768–1769
– Merchants sign nonimportation agreements.

1770
– Boston Massacre occurs.

Townshend duties
British law that established new duties on tea, glass, lead, paper, and painters' colors imported into the colonies. The Townshend duties led to boycotts and heightened tensions between Britain and the American colonies.

CONSIDER CAUSE AND EFFECT
How did British leaders' insistence on their right to tax the colonies radicalize the arguments and strategies of colonial protesters?

| How did imperial authorities and British colonists differ about taxing the colonies? | Why did the colonial crisis worsen after the repeal of the Stamp Act? | How did British policy and colonial response to the repeal of the Townshend duties lead to rebellion? | How did enslaved people in the colonies react to the stirrings of revolution? | Conclusion: What changes did the American colonists want in 1775? |

157

▶ **Edenton Tea Ladies** This cartoon mocks women who, like the Daughters of Liberty, resisted British imperial policies by boycotting tea and other consumer goods. Here, women in Edenton, North Carolina, who renounced British tea are shown in poses of wanton sexuality with neglected babies, urinating dogs, and mean-looking figures in the back. Library of Congress, 3g04617.

READING THE IMAGE: What does the satire in this cartoon tell us about contemporary ideals of female behavior? How are the women here violating those ideals?

CONNECTIONS: How did women's decision to refuse consuming British goods make them into political actors during the Revolution?

could Boston merchants agree to suspend trade for one year starting January 1, 1769. Sixty signed the nonimportation agreement. New York merchants soon followed suit, as did Philadelphia and Charleston merchants in 1769.

Many British products specified in nonconsumption agreements were household goods traditionally under women's control. By 1769, leaders of the boycott movement recognized that their cause depended on women's cooperation. Resistance to the Townshend duties thus created an unprecedented opening for women's participation in colonial politics. During the Stamp Act crisis, Sons of Liberty took to the streets in protest, expanding the range of political actors beyond the halls of legislative assemblies. During the protests of 1768 and 1769, the concept of Daughters of Liberty emerged to give shape to a new idea—that women were also political actors. Indeed, any woman could join the colonial protest by boycotting British-made goods. In Boston, more than three hundred women signed a petition to abstain from tea, "sickness excepted," in order to "save this abused Country from Ruin and Slavery."

The counterpart to nonconsumption was home manufacture—often by women. Quickly, homespun cloth became a prominent badge of patriotism. A young Boston girl learning to spin called herself "a daughter of liberty," noting that "I chuse to wear as much of our own manufactory as pocible." In the boycott period of 1768 to 1770, newspapers reported on spinning matches, or bees, in some sixty New England towns, in which women publicly came together to make yarn. Newspaper accounts variously called the spinners "Daughters of Liberty" or "Daughters of Industry."

How did the Seven Years' War lay the groundwork for colonial crisis?

This surge of public spinning further expanded the realm of colonial politics, infusing traditional women's work with new political purpose. But there were limits. Female spinners were not equivalents of the Sons of Liberty. The Sons marched in streets, burned effigies, threatened hated officials, and celebrated anniversaries of the movement with raucous drinking in taverns. The Daughters manifested their patriotism quietly, in actions marked by piety, industry, and charity. These differences were due in part to cultural ideals of gender, which prized masculine self-assertion and feminine selflessness, but they were also due to class. The Sons were a cross-class alliance, with leaders from the middling orders reliant on men and boys of the lower ranks to fuel their crowds. The Daughters dusting off spinning wheels and shelving their teapots were genteel ladies accustomed to buying British goods. The difference between the Sons and the Daughters also speaks to two views of how best to challenge authority: violent threats and street actions versus the self-disciplined, self-sacrificing boycott of consumer goods.

On the whole, the anti-British boycotts were a success. Imports fell by more than 40 percent; British merchants felt the sting and let Parliament know. In Boston, the Hutchinson family—whose fortune rested on British trade—endured substantial losses. But even more alarming to the lieutenant governor, Boston was overrun with anti-ministerial sentiment. The Sons of Liberty staged rollicking annual celebrations of the Stamp Act riot, and both Hutchinson and Governor Bernard concluded that British troops were needed to restore order.

Military Occupation and "Massacre" in Boston

In the fall of 1768, three thousand uniformed troops landed in Boston to pacify the city. The soldiers drilled conspicuously on the town Common, played loud music on the Sabbath, and in general grated on the nerves of Puritan Bostonians. Although the situation was often tense, no major troubles occurred that winter and through most of 1769. But as 1770 approached, marking the end of the nonimportation agreement, it was clear that some merchants—including Thomas Hutchinson's two sons—were ready to resume trade with Britain.

Trouble began in January, when a crowd smeared the door of the Hutchinson brothers' shop with excrement. In February, a crowd surrounded the house of a customs official, who panicked and fired a musket, accidentally killing a young boy passing on the street. The Sons of Liberty mounted a massive funeral procession to mark this first violent death in the imperial struggle.

For the next week, tension gripped Boston. The discord climaxed on the evening of March 5, 1770, when an angry crowd taunted eight British soldiers guarding the customs house. Onlookers threw snowballs and rocks and dared the soldiers to fire. Finally one did. After a short pause, someone yelled "Fire!" and the other soldiers shot into the crowd, hitting eleven men, killing five.

The Boston Massacre, as colonial protesters quickly labeled the event, was over in minutes. Hutchinson, now acting governor of the colony, courageously addressed the crowd from the statehouse balcony. He swiftly removed the regiments to an island in the harbor to prevent further bloodshed, and jailed army captain Thomas Preston and eight soldiers for their own protection, promising they would be held for trial.

In the wake of these events, the Sons of Liberty staged elaborate funeral rituals, turning the five victims into martyrs. Significantly, one nonwhite victim shared equally in the public's veneration: Crispus Attucks, the son of an African man and a Natick Indian woman. A slave in his youth, by 1770 he was a sailor and rope maker in his forties working on the Boston docks. Attucks was one of the first people to die in the colonial struggle with Britain, and certainly the first African American. Years later, he would become a powerful symbol for abolitionists seeking to highlight the participation of African Americans in the Revolution.

CONSIDER CAUSE AND EFFECT

How did the nonconsumption agreements change women's relationship to politics in the British colonies?

UNDERSTAND POINTS OF VIEW

How did the term "Boston Massacre" help promote the cause of colonial resistance to British authority? What other terms might have advanced a different perspective?

Boston Massacre
March 1770 incident in Boston in which British soldiers fired on an American crowd, killing five. The Boston Massacre became a rallying point for colonists who increasingly saw the British government as tyrannical and illegitimate.

How did imperial authorities and British colonists differ about taxing the colonies?

Why did the colonial crisis worsen after the repeal of the Stamp Act?

How did British policy and colonial response to the repeal of the Townshend duties lead to rebellion?

How did enslaved people in the colonies react to the stirrings of revolution?

Conclusion: What changes did the American colonists want in 1775?

▶ **Boston Massacre** This 1856 print of the "Boston Massacre" emphasizes the violence of the event. The action here focuses on Crispus Attucks, the son of an African man and a Natick woman, who died at the hands of British troops. In the 1850s, Attucks became a powerful symbol of the abolitionist movement—a black patriot who died for American liberty. American Antiquarian Society, Worcester, Massachusetts, USA/Bridgeman Images.

At trial in the fall of 1770, two Boston attorneys, John Adams and Josiah Quincy, ably defended the soldiers. While both supported the resistance, with direct ties to leaders of the Sons of Liberty, they believed that even unpopular defendants deserved a fair trial. Samuel Adams respected his cousin's decision to take the case, for there was a tactical benefit as well. It responded to images of Boston as a city of riotous crowds, casting its residents instead as lawful subjects defending traditional British rights.

The five-day trial resulted in acquittal for Preston and six soldiers; two others were convicted of manslaughter, branded on the thumbs, and released.

QUICK REVIEW

What were the major causes of the deepening colonial crisis from 1768 to 1770?

How did British policy and colonial response to the repeal of the Townshend duties lead to rebellion?

The very week that violence broke out in Boston, Lord Frederick North became Britain's prime minister. The seventh prime minister since George III became king a decade earlier, he would serve in that position for the next twelve turbulent years. A skillful politician, Lord North recognized the harmful impact of the boycott on trade and colonial relations and recommended repeal of the Townshend duties. Seeking peace with the colonies and prosperity for British merchants, Lord North persuaded Parliament to remove all the duties except the tax on tea, maintained as a face-saving symbol of parliamentary supremacy. For the next two years, colonial tensions ebbed. Then a series of incidents in 1772, followed by a renewed struggle over the tea tax in 1773, precipitated a full-scale crisis in the summer and fall of 1774. In response, representatives from nearly all the colonies gathered in a "Continental Congress" to debate the future of the British colonies.

How did the Seven Years' War lay the groundwork for colonial crisis?

The Calm before the Storm

The Townshend duties' repeal brought an end to the nonimportation agreements. Driven by the pent-up demand, trade boomed in 1770 and 1771. Meanwhile, the movement's leaders seemed to be losing influence. Samuel Adams, for example, ran for a minor local office and lost to a conservative merchant. Colonists once again seemed content as members of the British empire. Then, in 1772, several incidents brought the imperial conflict into sharp focus. One was the burning of the *Gaspée*, a Royal Navy ship pursuing suspected smugglers near Rhode Island. An investigating commission made no arrests but announced that it would send any suspects to Britain for trial on charges of high treason. This ruling seemed to fly in the face of the traditional English right to trial by a jury of one's peers.

When word of the *Gaspée* investigation spread, other colonies greeted the news with alarm. Patrick Henry, Thomas Jefferson, and Richard Henry Lee in the Virginia House of Burgesses proposed that a network of standing committees be established to better connect the colonies and share political news. By mid-1773, all but one colonial assembly had set up **committees of correspondence**.

Massachusetts, a continuing hotspot, developed its own rapid communications network. By spring 1773, more than half the towns in Massachusetts had set up committees of correspondence to receive, discuss, distribute, and act on the latest news. The first message to circulate came from Boston; it framed North's plan to pay judges with revenue from tea duties as the latest proof of an ongoing British conspiracy to undermine traditional liberties. First came taxation without consent, then military occupation and a massacre, and then a plot to subvert the justice system. Express riders swiftly distributed the message, which sparked ordinary townspeople to embrace a revolutionary language of rights and constitutional duties. Before long, the committees of correspondence would use this communications network to defend a countryside under attack.

The incident that ultimately shattered the calm of the early 1770s, however, was the **Tea Act of 1773**. After the nonimportation movement ended, colonists had resumed buying taxed British tea. But they were also importing much larger quantities of smuggled Dutch tea, undercutting the sales of Britain's East India Company. In response, Parliament lowered the tax on East India Company tea and, at the same time, allowed the company to sell tea directly to a few selected merchants, cutting out British middlemen. In an ironic twist, the Tea Act of 1773, unlike previous controversial duties, was not designed principally to raise revenue from the colonies; its intent was to shore up the flagging finances of the East India Company, which was then shouldering increased responsibilities in the new British possessions in India. The effect—which seemed benign to authorities in London—was to lower the retail price of the East India tea below that of smuggled Dutch tea, thus motivating colonists to obey the law. Unfortunately for British officials, colonists saw matters differently.

Tea in Boston Harbor

When news of the Tea Act reached the colonies, it struck many colonists as an insidious plot to trick colonists into buying duties tea. The real goal, some argued, was to reassert Britain's right to tax the colonies, increase revenue to pay the salaries of royal governors and judges, and shore up ministerial power in the colonies at the expense of local governance.

But how to resist the Tea Act? Nonimportation was not viable because the tea trade was too lucrative; even the most outraged merchants were unlikely to give it up willingly.

committees of correspondence
A communications network established among towns in Massachusetts and among colonial capital towns in 1772–1773. Providing for the rapid dissemination of important political news, these committees politicized ordinary townspeople, sparking a revolutionary language of rights.

Tea Act of 1773
British act that lowered the existing tax on tea to entice boycotting Americans to buy it. Resistance to the Tea Act led to the passage of the Coercive Acts and imposition of military rule in Massachusetts.

How did imperial authorities and British colonists differ about taxing the colonies?

Why did the colonial crisis worsen after the repeal of the Stamp Act?

How did British policy and colonial response to the repeal of the Townshend duties lead to rebellion?

How did enslaved people in the colonies react to the stirrings of revolution?

Conclusion: What changes did the American colonists want in 1775?

COMPARE AND CONTRAST

What did officials in London believe to be the purpose of the Tea Act, and how did their views differ from those of colonists in North America?

Consumer boycotts, meanwhile, would inevitably struggle against the difficulty of distinguishing between dutied and smuggled tea. The resistance thus focused on official tea agents—an echo of the Stamp Act distributors. The revived Sons of Liberty pressured them to resign, making it impossible to collect tea duties. Lacking agents, most governors acquiesced, landing cargoes of tea duty-free or sending them home.

Governor Hutchinson, however, refused to bend. In November 1773, three ships carrying tea arrived in Boston. Sensing extreme tension, their uneasy crews unloaded all the cargo except the tea. The ship captains wanted to return immediately to England, away from the conflict, but Hutchinson would not grant them clearance to leave without paying the tea duty. Adding to the pressure, a long-standing law imposed a twenty-day limit for the payment of duties, after which cargo would be confiscated. Hutchinson planned to enforce the law.

For twenty days, large crowds kept the pressure high. Then, on December 16, five thousand people gathered at Boston's Old South Meeting House to debate the next step. No solution emerged at the meeting, but when it ended one hundred to one hundred fifty men disguised as Mohawk Indians, wrapped in blankets with soot-darkened faces, boarded the ships and dumped over 90,000 pounds of tea into the harbor while a crowd of two thousand bystanders watched in eerie silence.

Everyone seemed aware that a new stage of the colonial resistance had begun. "This Destruction of the Tea is so bold, so daring, so firm, intrepid and inflexible," John Adams wrote in his diary, "and it must have so important Consequences."

The Coercive Acts

To imperial authorities, the colonists' actions seemed wildly excessive. Over the previous years, they had continually yielded to colonial sensibilities by abandoning revenue-generating measures—whose purpose, after all, was to pay the debt of a war that had greatly benefited them. Then, in the wake of a reduction in taxes, they had resorted to mob rule! Their actions could not be allowed to stand. "The crisis is come," declared General Gage, "when the provinces must be either British colonies, or independent and separate states." Lord North now decided to change tack, exchanging carrot for stick. He persuaded Parliament to issue the Coercive Acts, four laws intended to punish Massachusetts for destroying the tea. In America, those laws, along with a fifth, the Quebec Act, became known as the Intolerable Acts.

The first act, the Boston Port Act, closed Boston harbor to all shipping as of June 1, 1774, until the cost of the destroyed tea was repaid. The second act, the Massachusetts Government Act, altered the colony's charter by increasing the royal governor's powers. In addition to appointing his own council, the governor could now appoint all judges, sheriffs, and officers of the court. No town meeting beyond the annual spring election of town selectmen could be held without the governor's approval. This measure greatly expanded London's supremacy at the expense of local governance in Massachusetts.

The third Coercive Act, the Impartial Administration of Justice Act, stipulated that any royal official accused of a capital crime—for example, Captain Preston and his soldiers at the Boston Massacre—would be tried in a court in Britain. This act ominously suggested that more captains and soldiers might soon be firing into unruly crowds. The fourth act amended the 1765 Quartering Act, permitting military commanders to lodge soldiers wherever necessary, even in private households. To enforce the acts, Lord North appointed General Gage, the commander of the Royal Army in New York, as governor of Massachusetts, relieving the civilian Thomas Hutchinson of his duties. Military rule now returned to Boston.

The fifth act was unrelated to the four Coercive Acts, but it magnified colonists' fears. Also passed in 1774, the Quebec Act legalized French civil law and Catholicism

Coercive Acts

Four British acts of 1774 meant to punish Massachusetts for the destruction of three shiploads of tea. Known in America as the Intolerable Acts, they led to open rebellion in the northern colonies.

How did the Seven Years' War lay the groundwork for colonial crisis?

in the French territories won by Britain in the Seven Years' War. Granting civil rights to their longtime Catholic enemies struck Protestant New Englanders, who had just been denied their own representative government, as a shocking outrage. On a more material level, the act made the entire Ohio Valley part of the Province of Quebec, nullifying the land claims of the eastern colonies (and speculators whose ambitions rested on those claims), and excluding them from the lucrative fur trade in the region.

The five Intolerable Acts spread alarm throughout the colonies. **(See "Analyzing Historical Evidence: Reactions to the Boston Port Act outside of Massachusetts" on page 164.)** If Britain could subjugate Massachusetts—change its charter, suspend local government, inaugurate military rule, and on top of it all, give the Ohio Valley to Catholic Quebec—what liberties were secure? Meanwhile, royal governors in a half dozen colonies dismissed their sitting assemblies, adding to the sense of urgency. In response to all these measures, colonial leaders agreed to convene in Philadelphia in September 1774.

Beyond Boston: Rural New England

The Coercive Acts provoked New England to open insubordination. With a British general occupying the Massachusetts governorship and some three thousand troops controlling Boston, the center of protest shifted from urban radicals in Boston to rural farmers throughout the countryside, who launched dozens of spontaneous, dramatic showdowns. Some towns found creative ways to avoid the prohibition on town meetings, while others simply ignored the law. Governor Gage's call for elections for a new provincial assembly under his control sparked the formation of a competing unauthorized assembly that met in defiance of his orders. Throughout Massachusetts, crowds of armed men closed county courts run by crown-appointed jurists. No judges were physically harmed, but they were intimidated, forced to resign, and humiliated. By August 1774, farmers and artisans all over Massachusetts, in defiance of royal authority, had taken full control of local institutions.

New Englanders began planning for a showdown that now seemed inevitable. Towns stockpiled gunpowder "in case of invasion." Militia officers repudiated the official chain of command to the governor and drilled their units. Town after town withheld tax revenue from the crown and diverted it to military supplies. Governor Gage could do little in response. He wrote London, begging for troop reinforcements, and beefed up fortifications around Boston. But without more soldiers, his options were limited. Preventing stockpiles of gunpowder from falling into agitators' hands seemed like his best move.

An event known as the Powder Alarm showed how ready colonial settlers were to take up arms against the British government. Early on September 1, 1774, Gage sent troops to a town outside Boston to remove a store of gunpowder before it slipped from royal control. In the surprise of the mission, false rumors spread that troops had fired on defenders of the storehouse, killing six. Within twenty-four hours, thousands of armed men from Massachusetts, New Hampshire, and Connecticut descended on Boston to avenge the supposed deaths. At this moment, ordinary men became insurgents, willing to kill or die in the face of the British clampdown. Once the error was recognized and the crisis defused, everyone returned home peaceably. But Gage could no longer doubt the speed, numbers, and determination of the unruly colonists.

This vast mobilization had occurred without orchestration by Boston radicals, Gage reported. British leaders found that hard to believe. How could "a tumultuous Rabble," one official wrote, "without any Appearance of general Concert, or without any Head to advise, or Leader to conduct," rise up so effectively?

In the years to come, British authorities would repeatedly underestimate their opponents.

| How did imperial authorities and British colonists differ about taxing the colonies? | Why did the colonial crisis worsen after the repeal of the Stamp Act? | How did British policy and colonial response to the repeal of the Townshend duties lead to rebellion? | How did enslaved people in the colonies react to the stirrings of revolution? | Conclusion: What changes did the American colonists want in 1775? |

Reactions to the Boston Port Act outside of Massachusetts

As punishment for the destruction of the tea in Boston, Parliament closed Boston's port by naval blockade as of June 1, 1774, until the cost of the tea was paid. News of Parliament's action spurred discussion and action all around the American colonies.

DOCUMENT 1

George Washington Writes to George William Fairfax, 1774

Washington describes the transformation of the Virginia assembly, shut down by the royal governor, into a new legislative body meeting at a tavern. In one long, breathless sentence he voices his concerns about the Boston Port Act and the threats facing Virginia.

Williamsburg, June 10, 1774 . . . [The Assembly] Members convend themselves at the Raleigh Tavern & enterd into the Inclosd Association which being followed two days after by an Express from Boston accompanied by the Sentiments of some Meetings in our Sister Colonies to the Northwd the proceedings mentiond in the Inclos'd Papers were had thereupon & a general meeting requested of all the late Representatives in this City on the first of August when it is hopd, & expected that some vigorous measures will be effectually adopted to obtain that justice which is denied to our Petitions & Remonstrances; in short the Ministry may rely on it that Americans will never be tax'd without their own consent that the cause of Boston the despotick Measures in respect to it I mean now is and ever will be considerd as the cause of America (not that we approve their cond[uc]t in destroyg the Tea) & that we shall not suffer ourselves to be sacrificed by piecemeal though god only knows what is to become of us, threatned as we are with so many hoverg evils as hang over us at present; having a cruel & blood thirsty Enemy upon our Backs, the Indians, between whom & our Frontier Inhabitants many Skirmishes have happend, & with who(m) a general War is inevitable whilst those from whom we have a right to Seek protection are endeavouring by every piece of Art & despotism to fix the Shackles of Slavry upon us.

Source: George Washington to George William Fairfax, 10–15 June 1774, *The Papers of George Washington*, The University Press of Virginia. Copyright © 1995 by the Rector and Visitors of the University of Virginia.

DOCUMENT 2

An Anonymous Philadelphian Implores Boston to Pay for the Tea, 1774

A self-described "friend to the cause of America" argues that paying for the tea is in the best interests of justice and liberty, using repetition for effect.

To the Inhabitants on the Town of BOSTON, and Province of MASSACHUSETTS-BAY.

My Dear BRETHREN,

IN Messi'rs Mills and Hicks's Gazette of the 20th of June, I observed with great concern a paragraph with the signature of "Consideration," calculated to deter you from paying for the tea, a measure at this alarming juncture highly necessary and what every REAL friend to the cause of America must think your indispensible duty. While we contend for liberty, let us not destroy the idea of justice. A trespass has been committed on private property in consequence of the Resolves of your town. Restore to the sufferers the most ample compensation for the injury they have received—convince your enemies that their property is secure in every Port on the British Continent—Convince them that you do not regard the value of the article destroyed—that you only deny the right of taxation. Let not the annals of your history be sullied by a refusal—pay for the tea—it will rejoice your friends—it will convince your adversaries that the cause you are attach'd to is a righteous and just cause.

How did the Seven Years' War lay the groundwork for colonial crisis?

Convince them that you regard honesty as much as liberty, and that you detest libertinism and licentiousness. . . . Then can you with a degree of confidence call on your friends to stand by and protect you—your enemies, if any there be, you may defy to prejudice you. I beseech you, by every thing you hold dear—I conjure you, as you value a union of the colonies, pay for the tea; it is but justice, pay for it, let nothing retard it; it is an expedient, which ought to have been effected e'er this; we lament that it yet remains undone. . . .

These are the sentiments of the Pennsylvanians, and the anxious prayer of A PHILADELPHIAN.

Source: *The Massachusetts Gazette and the Boston Weekly News-Letter*, 14 July 1774, p. 2. Also at http://www.masshist.org/revolution/image-viewer .php?item_id=691

DOCUMENT 3

A New Hampshire Town Offers Sympathy and Support to Boston, 1774

Kingston, New Hampshire, was one of hundreds of towns to pledge assistance to Boston.

Sept. 14, 1774

Gentlemen,

The inhabitants of Kingston, in the Province of New Hampshire, see with deep concern the unhappy misunderstanding and disagreement that now subsists between Great Britain and these American Colonies, being fully sensible that the happiness of both countries depend on an union, harmony, and agreement to be established between them on a just, equitable, and permanent foundation. But when we consider the new, arbitrary, and unjust claims of our brethren in Great Britain, to levy taxes upon us at their sovereign will and pleasure, and to make laws to bind us in all cases, whatsoever, we view and consider ourselves and our posterity under the operations of these claims, as absolute slaves: for what is a slave, but one who is bound in all cases whatsoever by the will and command of another. And we look on the late unjust, cruel, hostile, and tyrannical Acts of the British

Parliament, respecting the Massachusetts Bay in general, and the Town of Boston in particular, as consequences of these unrighteous claims, and from them clearly see what the whole continent has to expect under their operation.

But when we consider the military forces, both by sea and land, sent in an hostile manner to enforce, with the point of the sword, and mouths of cannon, those acts and claims, we esteem it an high infringement of your rights and privileges, and an insult upon all North America, and are fully persuaded that unless there is a speedy alteration of those measures, a total disaffection will soon take place, and Britain, instead of being our best friend, will be looked upon as an enemy; and then a final separation in all respects will no doubt soon follow, the thoughts of which fill our minds with trouble, anxiety, and concern.

Source: "Correspondence in 1774 and 1775 between a Committee of the Town of Boston and Contributors of Donations for the Relief of Sufferers by the Boston Port Bill," in *Collections of the Massachusetts Historical Society*, vol. 4, 4th ser. (1858), pp. 74–76.

Questions for Analysis

RECOGNIZE VIEWPOINTS: Why does the Philadelphia correspondent urge that the tea must be paid for? How does his position on the destruction of the tea compare to Washington's? To the townsmen of Kingston?

ANALYZE THE EVIDENCE: Both Washington and the townsmen of Kingston invoke fears of slavery and enslavement. What do they mean? What connection is there, if any, to the institution of slavery that existed throughout the colonies?

ASK HISTORICAL QUESTIONS: Based on the evidence in these documents, do the colonists seek national independence from the British empire?

CONSIDER THE CONTEXT: Which of these three documents most clearly anticipates that a separation from Britain might lie in the future? Why?

First Continental Congress
September 1774 gathering of
colonial delegates in Philadelphia
to discuss the crisis precipitated by
the Coercive Acts. The congress
produced a declaration of rights
and an agreement to impose a
limited boycott of trade with Britain.

**CONSIDER CAUSE
AND EFFECT**

Why did Britain's imposition
of the Coercive Acts inspire
protest and resistance
in colonies beyond
Massachusetts?

The First Continental Congress

Twelve colonies sent delegates to the First Continental Congress in September 1774. The gathering in Philadelphia included notables such as Samuel Adams and John Adams from Massachusetts and George Washington and Patrick Henry from Virginia. Only Georgia was unrepresented. To moderate the most radical voices, a few colonies sent representatives who hoped to ease tensions with Britain, like Pennsylvania's Joseph Galloway.

Delegates discussed their liberties as British subjects and Parliament's powers over colonial settlers, and debated various responses to the Coercive Acts. Some wanted a total ban on trade with Britain, while others, especially southerners dependent on tobacco and rice exports, opposed such a dramatic measure. Samuel Adams and Patrick Henry advocated for a ringing denunciation of all parliamentary control. The conservative Joseph Galloway proposed a quickly defeated plan for a secondary parliament in America to assist the British Parliament in ruling the colonies.

After seven weeks of debate and discussion, the congress produced a declaration grounded in the delegates' idea of traditional English rights: "We ask only for peace, liberty and security. We wish no diminution of royal prerogatives, we demand no new rights." From the perspective of imperial officials, however, these constituted radical claims to new rights. British authorities particularly chafed at the idea that colonists were not represented in Parliament, and that colonial governments alone had the sole right to govern and tax. The colonists' only concession to parliamentary authority was a carefully worded statement that they would "cheerfully consent" to trade regulations for the larger good of the empire, so long as these were not intended to raise revenue.

To pressure British authorities, the delegates agreed to a gradually expanding trade boycott: imports prohibited the first year, exports the following, and rice totally exempted (to keep South Carolinians happy). To enforce the boycott, they called for a Continental Association, with chapters in each town variously called committees of public safety or inspection. These committees would monitor all commerce and punish suspected violators of the boycott (sometimes with a bucket of tar and a bag of feathers). Its work done, the congress disbanded with agreement to reconvene in May.

> "'We ask only for peace, liberty and security. We wish no diminution of royal prerogatives, we demand no new rights.'"

The committees of public safety, the committees of correspondence, the regrouped colonial assemblies, and the Continental Congress were all political bodies functioning defiantly without any constitutional authority. British officials did not recognize them as legitimate. But colonists angered by Parliament's actions instantly accepted them. Mostly composed of men who had held elective office before, these unauthorized governing bodies proved to be remarkably stable.

Parliament's harsh reaction to the Boston Tea Party radicalized colonists from New Hampshire to Georgia. It led them to see problems with British rule far beyond issues of taxation. The Coercive Acts violated traditional liberties and suppressed long-standing institutions of colonial self-government; they could not be ignored. With one colony already subject to military rule and a British army camped in Boston, the threat of a general war loomed.

QUICK REVIEW

Why did colonial responses to British actions become more radical after 1772?

How did the Seven Years'
War lay the groundwork
for colonial crisis?

How did enslaved people in the colonies react to the stirrings of revolution?

Before the Second Continental Congress could meet, violence broke out in Massachusetts. Fearing insurrection, General Thomas Gage sent his soldiers to capture an ammunition depot outside of Boston, and New England farmers mobilized against a power they feared would enslave them. Meanwhile, a variant of that story began unfolding to the south, as thousands of enslaved men and women seized on the growing challenge to government authority to mount an insurrection of their own—this one against the very planters crying out for liberty from the British.

Lexington and Concord

During the winter of 1774–75, British colonists continued their boycott. Optimists hoped for a repeal of the Coercive Acts; pessimists stockpiled arms and ammunition. In Massachusetts, militia units known as minutemen prepared to defend the countryside from the British troops in Boston.

Thomas Gage recognized the fragility of the imperial government's position. The people, Gage wrote Lord North, were "numerous, worked up to a fury, and not a Boston rabble but the freeholders and farmers of the country." He requested twenty thousand reinforcements. He also strongly advised repeal of the Coercive Acts, but this time leaders in London were unwilling to retreat. Instead, they doubled down on existing policy: In mid-April 1775, Gage was ordered to arrest the troublemakers.

Gage planned a surprise seizure of a suspected ammunition storage site at Concord, a village eighteen miles west of Boston. Near midnight on April 18, as Gage's troops crossed the Charles River, Bostonians Paul Revere and William Dawes raced ahead to alert the minutemen. When the British soldiers got to Lexington, five miles from Concord, they were met by some seventy armed men. The British commander barked out: "Lay down your arms, you damned rebels, and disperse." The militiamen hesitated and began to comply, but then someone fired. Nobody knows who began the fighting, but within two minutes, eight rebels were dead and ten were wounded.

The British units continued marching to Concord, any pretense of surprise now gone. Three companies of minutemen nervously occupied the town center but did not challenge the professional soldiers as they searched in vain for the ammunition. Finally, at the Old North Bridge in Concord, British troops and minutemen exchanged shots, killing two colonists and three British soldiers. As the British returned to Boston, thousands of men from local militia units repeatedly ambushed them. By the day's end, 273 British soldiers were wounded or dead; the toll for the colonists stood at about 95. It was April 19, 1775, and the war had begun.

Rebelling against Slavery

News of the battles of Lexington and Concord spread fast. In Virginia, Thomas Jefferson exclaimed that "a phrenzy of revenge seems to have seized all ranks of people." Lord Dunmore, the royal governor of Virginia, removed all gunpowder from the Williamsburg powder house to a ship out of the reach of angry Virginians. He also

CHRONOLOGY

1773
- Phillis Wheatley's *Poems on Various Subjects, Religious and Moral* published in London.

1775
- Battles of Lexington and Concord fought.
- Lord Dunmore promises freedom to defecting slaves.

ANALYZE EVIDENCE

What do the events at Lexington and Concord reveal about the popular support for the colonial insurrection in 1775?

| How did imperial authorities and British colonists differ about taxing the colonies? | Why did the colonial crisis worsen after the repeal of the Stamp Act? | How did British policy and colonial response to the repeal of the Townshend duties lead to rebellion? | How did enslaved people in the colonies react to the stirrings of revolution? | Conclusion: What changes did the American colonists want in 1775? |

threatened to arm slaves in response to the colonists' insurrection. The threat proved effective for several months.

In November 1775, as the crisis deepened, Dunmore made good on his threat. He issued a proclamation promising freedom to slaves who would fight for the British. Dunmore had no intention of abolishing slavery; indeed, as some observers noticed, he did not even free his own slaves. A Virginia barber named Caesar declared that "he did not know any one foolish enough to believe him [Dunmore], for if he intended to do so, he ought first to set his own free." Nonetheless, within a month some fifteen hundred slaves had joined Dunmore's "Ethiopian Regiment." Camp diseases quickly set in: dysentery, typhoid fever, and smallpox. When Dunmore sailed for England in mid-1776, he left with three hundred former slaves.

The association of freedom with the British authorities had been established, and during the war thousands more would flee American enslavement as the British army approached.

In the northern colonies, slaves took advantage of the evolving political struggle to claim their freedom. A twenty-one-year-old Bostonian highlighted the hypocrisy of local slave owners in a 1774 newspaper essay. "How well the Cry for Liberty, and the reverse Disposition for exercise of oppressive Power over others agree,—I humbly think it does not require the Penetration of a Philosopher to Determine," wrote Phillis Wheatley, a young enslaved woman who had already gained international recognition for her poetry. Wheatley's poems spoke of "Fair Freedom" as the "Goddess long desir'd" by Africans enslaved in America. Wheatley's owner freed the young poet in 1775.

From north to south, slaves pressed their case. Several enslaved Bostonians offered to fight for the British in exchange for freedom, but General Gage turned them down. In Maryland, a planter worried that blacks impatient for freedom had to be disarmed of about eighty guns along with some swords. In North Carolina, white suspicions about a planned slave uprising led to the arrest of scores of African Americans. The revolutionary committee of public safety ordered them to be punished by whipping.

As many as twenty thousand slaves had gained their freedom by fleeing to the British army by 1783, when the Revolution ended. About half succumbed to disease, especially

UNDERSTAND POINTS OF VIEW

Why did Lord Dunmore promise freedom to able-bodied slaves who would agree to fight alongside the British?

▶ **Phillis Wheatley's Frontispiece** African-born Phillis became the slave of John Wheatley in Boston at age seven. Remarkably gifted in English, she read the Bible and learned to write elegant poetry and essays. She traveled to London in 1773 and published a book of poems, gaining notice in British literary circles. Once freed, she briefly married and then worked in a Boston boardinghouse. She died in 1784. VCG Wilson/Corbis via Getty Images.

How did the Seven Years' War lay the groundwork for colonial crisis?

smallpox, in refugee camps. But some eight to ten thousand left America with the British army to start new lives of freedom in Canada's Nova Scotia or Africa's Sierra Leone.

QUICK REVIEW

What connection did slaves draw between the colonial rebellion against the British and their own rebellion against slavery?

Conclusion: What changes did the American colonists want in 1775?

In the aftermath of the Seven Years' War, the victors lost their spoils. Indeed, everyone seemed to come out the worse. France lost its North American empire. Indian land rights were increasingly violated. And Britain's huge war debt and subsequent revenue-generating policies set the stage for an imperial crisis.

For more than a century, British authorities had tolerated extensive colonial self-government—largely because they had no choice. Political power in distant lands necessarily rested on some level of consent, and over decades of innumerable local negotiations a delicate equilibrium had emerged that balanced the demands of settlers with the needs of the imperial state. It was only in the wake of the Seven Years' War—when the needs of the British state grew, triggering attempts at administrative reform—that the delicate balance was upended. "What can a governor do without the assistance of the govern'd?" exclaimed a Philadelphia customs official in 1770. "What can the magistrate do unless they are supported by their fellow citizens?"

Colonial resistance to imperial policy grew slowly but steadily. As British policies provoked anger in the colonies, officials in London looked across the Atlantic and increasingly saw rebellious colonists who needed to be brought to heel. Colonists, meanwhile, looking toward the imperial capital, increasingly saw in British policy a concerted effort to deprive them of their liberties. Neither view was correct at first, but as each side dug into its position, each brought its imagined fears about the other to reality. Britain did ultimately abrogate colonists' traditions of self-government and their right to live free of an occupying army, while colonists did ultimately rebel. None of these outcomes had been intended in 1763; by 1775, both had come to pass.

Meanwhile, African Americans experiencing actual slavery listened to shouts of "Liberty!" from white crowds and appropriated the language of revolution to their own circumstances. Defiance of authority was indeed contagious.

Even after the battles of Lexington and Concord, many colonists sought to avoid an expansion of the war. Long-standing imperial loyalties died hard. In the months ahead, American colonial leaders pursued peaceful as well as military solutions to the imperial crisis. By the end of 1775, however, reconciliation with the crown was fast slipping away.

| How did imperial authorities and British colonists differ about taxing the colonies? | Why did the colonial crisis worsen after the repeal of the Stamp Act? | How did British policy and colonial response to the repeal of the Townshend duties lead to rebellion? | How did enslaved people in the colonies react to the stirrings of revolution? | Conclusion: What changes did the American colonists want in 1775? |

STEP 1 — EXPLAIN WHY IT MATTERS

Put your reading into practice. Identify each term below, and then explain why it matters in U.S. history.

TERM	WHO OR WHAT & WHEN	WHY IT MATTERS
Seven Years' War (p. 142)		
Pontiac's War (p. 149)		
Royal Proclamation of 1763 (p. 150)		
Sugar (Revenue) Act (p. 151)		
Stamp Act (p. 151)		
virtual representation (p. 151)		
Declaratory Act (p. 156)		
Townshend duties (p. 157)		
Boston Massacre (p. 159)		
committees of correspondence (p. 161)		
Tea Act of 1773 (p. 161)		
Coercive Acts (p. 162)		
First Continental Congress (p. 166)		

STEP 2 — MOVE BEYOND THE BASICS

To demonstrate a more advanced understanding, describe the key pieces of British legislation aimed at the colonies between 1763 and 1774, the British rationale, and the colonial response.

Legislation	Provisions	British Rationale	Colonial Response
Royal Proclamation of 1763			
Sugar (Revenue) Act			
Stamp Act			
Townshend duties			
Tea Act of 1773			
Coercive Acts			

STEP 3

PUT IT ALL TOGETHER

Now, try to explain the big picture. Remember to use specific examples from the chapter in your answers.

THE SEVEN YEARS' WAR

• How did the outcome of the Seven Years' War change the balance of power in North America (including both European and native powers)?

• How did British and colonial views of the war and its consequences differ?

THE ESCALATION OF THE CONFLICT

• How did the British government's response to Native American resistance in 1763 spark the resentment of British settlers?

• Why was the Tea Act so provocative? How did some colonists protest its passage?

• How did the American response to British imperial policy alienate British authorities?

TAXING THE COLONIES

• How did the British justify their efforts to raise revenue?

• Why did some colonists see British efforts to tax the colonies as illegitimate?

LOOKING BACKWARD, LOOKING AHEAD

• How did the relationship between Britain and its North American colonies before 1763 differ from the relationship after 1763?

• Was war between Britain and the colonies inevitable after 1774? Why or why not?

STEP 4

CONNECT THESE EVENTS

How did British victory in the Seven Years' War lead to colonial crisis in the thirteen colonies?

STEP 5

CONNECT TO THE PRESENT

Can you think of any recent examples of when a war provoked radical disruptions in the political system of the victor? What are the parallels?

7

THE WAR FOR AMERICA

1775–1783

How did the United States gain its independence in the Revolution? Chapter 7 follows the course of the American Revolution from its outbreak in 1775, to its conclusion in 1783. It focuses not just on the war itself, and the factors that led to American success, but looks also at transformations on the home front.

This chapter will explore the following questions:

- What persuaded British North American colonists to support independence?
- How did the military objectives of each side shape the course of the war's early years?
- How did the war transform the home front?
- How did the American Revolution become a war among continental and global powers?
- What were the principal causes of the British defeat?
- Conclusion: Why did the British lose the American Revolution?

AN AMERICAN STORY

obert Shurtliff came late to the American Revolution. He enlisted in the Continental army after the battle at Yorktown in 1781, which ended the principal military campaigns in North America. New recruits were scarce in a country exhausted by war. Attracted by cash bounties, beardless young men who'd been mere children in 1775 now stepped forward. Claiming to be eighteen, Shurtliff was single, poor, and at loose ends. But he proved to be a talented soldier, and won assignment to an elite light infantry unit, part of Washington's army of ten thousand men stationed north of New York City.

That is, ten thousand men and one woman. "Robert Shurtliff" was actually Deborah Sampson, age twenty-three, from Massachusetts. For seventeen months, Sampson served as a man, marching through woods, skirmishing with the enemy, and enduring the monotony of military life. With privacy at a minimum, she faced constant risk of discovery. Why did she take the chance? A hard-luck childhood had left Sampson impoverished and unusually plucky. Placed in foster care at age five, Deborah became a servant in a succession of families. Along the way, she learned to plow a field and read and write—uncommon skills for a female servant. Next she became a weaver and then a teacher. Marriage should have been her following step, but the wartime shortage of men probably kept Deborah "masterless" and poor. The cash bounty enticed her to enlist.

When officials discovered Sampson's sex, she was immediately discharged. She only became famous by selling her tale to the public. In 1797, she told her life story (a blend of fact and fiction) in a short book. She then went on tour reenacting her wartime masquerade—once again crossing gender boundaries, since women normally avoided speaking in public.

Although Sampson's was an extreme case, many Americans experienced the disruptions of the revolutionary movement. Wartime shortages pushed women into typically male jobs. Soldiers fought for ideas, but they also fought for money. Hardship struck everywhere. Sampson's quest for personal independence—freedom from the constraints of female life—echoed the broader quest for national independence.

Despite the outcome, few people yearned for political independence in 1775. Some never yearned for it at all. Long after fighting began, the Continental Congress continued to seek reconciliation with Britain. It raised and financed an army, and sought alliances with foreign countries—all the while making diplomatic proposals for peace.

When King George III rejected all peace overtures, however, most Americans never looked back. The war moved into high gear. In part a classic war with professional armies, the Revolutionary War was also a civil war between rebels and loyalists. It had complex ethnic dimensions, pitting many Native American peoples allied with the British against some allied with the Americans, and providing unprecedented opportunities for enslaved African Americans to win freedom. And it was an international war, spreading far beyond North America, pulling in France, Spain, and other European powers, extending across multiple continents, and continuing for years after most fighting ended in North America.

▼ **Deborah Sampson** Deborah Sampson chose this portrait to illustrate *The Female Review*, a book about her extraordinary military career published in 1797. By then a wife and mother, the portrait displays her in feminine dress. Sampson the soldier had used a cloth band to compress her breasts; Sampson the matron wore a satin band to emphasize her bustline. Hulton Archive/Getty Images.

DEBORAH SAMPSON.
Published by H. Mann. 1797.

What persuaded British North American colonists to support independence?

CHRONOLOGY

1775
- Second Continental Congress convenes.
- Battle of Bunker Hill fought.
- Olive Branch Petition sent to British king.

1776
- *Common Sense* published.
- British evacuate Boston.
- Declaration of Independence written.

Second Continental Congress
Legislative body that governed the American colonies from May 1775 through the end of the war. It established an army, created its own money, and declared independence. It also conducted the nation's foreign policy, entering into a critical alliance with France.

O n May 10, 1775, nearly one month after the fighting at Lexington and Concord, the Second Continental Congress assembled in Philadelphia. It immediately set to work on two crucial but contradictory tasks: to raise an army and to pursue reconciliation with Britain. For the former, Congress needed soldiers and money. For the latter, it needed cautious diplomacy. But the king was not receptive, and as the war continued into 1776, hopes of reconciliation faded. British colonists began to ponder a future that only a few years earlier would have been unthinkable: national independence.

Assuming Political and Military Authority

The delegates to the Second Continental Congress were prominent local figures, but as the fighting began in Massachusetts they suddenly climbed onto a continental stage. The outbreak of war provoked sharp disagreement among them. The cousins John and Samuel Adams stood at the radical end of the spectrum, already favoring independence. John Dickinson of Pennsylvania, by contrast, made famous from his 1767 publication, *Letters from a Farmer*, hoped for reconciliation with Britain. Given the extraordinary stakes of the debate—any of the delegates could have been executed for treason—their general inexperience, and their divergent opinions, building consensus proved difficult.

Few delegates were yet prepared to break with Britain. Some maintained passionate loyalty to the monarchy, while others feared the risks of losing the British empire's protection against France and Spain. Almost all remained intensely attached to their identity as British subjects. Economic motivations also played a factor: Merchants and planters worried that independence would undermine the colonies' economy. Nor were such feelings limited to the delegates; few ordinary settlers envisioned complete independence at this stage. From the Stamp Act of 1765 to the Coercive Acts of 1774 (see chapter 6), the constitutional struggle with Britain had focused on questions of parliamentary power. Almost no one had challenged the monarchy itself.

The few men at the Continental Congress who favored independence were, not surprisingly, from Massachusetts. But they knew it was too soon to push for a break with Britain. As John Adams wrote his wife, Abigail, in June 1775: "America is a great, unwieldy body. Its progress must be slow. It is like a large fleet sailing under convoy. The fleetest sailors must wait for the dullest and slowest."

For all the disagreements about the ultimate course of events, the congress could not sit idly by; the events in Massachusetts demanded some reaction. Even moderates supported a military buildup in response to the British incursions. On June 14, the congress voted to create the Continental army, choosing George Washington as commander in chief. The choice of a Virginian to lead an army in defense of New England signaled continent-wide support for the effort.

Continental army
The army created in June 1775 by the Second Continental Congress to fight the British. Virginian George Washington, commander in chief, had the task of turning local militias and untrained volunteers into a disciplined force.

To pay for the military buildup, the congress authorized a currency issue of $2 million. Continental dollars were merely paper—not backed by gold or silver. Delegates naively expected that soldiers, farmers, munitions suppliers, and others would accept the new currency on good faith.

In just two months, the Second Continental Congress had created an army, gone to war, and issued its own currency. Although it had not declared independence, it had nonetheless assumed the principal functions of government.

Pursuing Both War and Peace

After the hostilities in Lexington and Concord, British troops retreated to the peninsula of Boston, leaving the insurgents in control of the countryside. In the months that followed, New England militia units fortified the hilly terrain of Charlestown, across the Charles River from the city. Thomas Gage, the military governor of Massachusetts, found himself besieged in Boston, and could only wait for reinforcements. When they finally arrived, he decided to take the offensive.

General William Howe, who had just arrived from Britain, insisted on a bold frontal attack with 2,500 soldiers. After three bloody assaults, the British took Bunker Hill. The **battle of Bunker Hill** was a British victory, but a costly one. British dead numbered 226, with more than 800 wounded; the insurgents suffered 140 dead, 271 wounded, and 30 captured. As another general remarked, "It was a dear bought victory; another such would have ruined us."

Instead of pursuing the fleeing insurgents, Howe retreated to Boston, unwilling to risk more raids into the countryside. If British commanders had grasped the weakness of the American units around Boston, they might have defeated the Continental army in its infancy. Instead, they remained in Boston, only to abandon it without a fight nine months later.

Howe used his time in Boston to inoculate his army against smallpox because a new epidemic was spreading across colonial port cities. Inoculation worked by producing a mild but real (and therefore risky) case of smallpox, followed by lifelong immunity. Howe made a wise decision: During the American Revolution, some 130,000 people on the continent, most of them Indians, died of smallpox.

General Washington arrived to take command of the new Continental army a week after Bunker Hill. He found enthusiastic but undisciplined troops. Washington attributed the disarray to the New England custom of letting militia units elect their own officers, which he believed undermined military authority. The Virginian moved quickly to impose more hierarchy and authority. "Be easy," he advised his newly appointed officers, "but not too familiar, lest you subject yourself to a want of that respect, which is necessary to support a proper command."

While military preparations moved forward, the Second Continental Congress pursued its second and contradictory objective: reconciliation with Britain. Delegates from the middle colonies (Pennsylvania, Delaware, and New York) still hoped for a peaceful resolution. In July 1775, congressional moderates led by John Dickinson engineered an appeal to the king called the Olive Branch Petition, affirming the colonists' loyalty to the monarchy and blaming the troubles on the king's ministers and on Parliament. As a solution to the crisis, it proposed that American colonial assemblies be recognized as individual parliaments under the monarchy. Unfortunately for the moderates, King George III rejected the Olive Branch Petition, condemning the insurgents as traitors. By undermining the position of those who still hoped for reconciliation with Britain, the defeat of the Olive Branch Petition advanced the case of delegates who favored independence.

Thomas Paine, Abigail Adams, and the Case for Independence

Pressure for independence started to mount in January 1776, when a pamphlet entitled *Common Sense* appeared in Philadelphia. Thomas Paine, its author, was an English artisan, radical, and coffeehouse intellectual who had sailed to America in the fall of 1774. He quickly launched himself into the movement for American independence, and wrote *Common Sense* to advance the cause.

Battle of Bunker Hill, 1775

battle of Bunker Hill
Early battle of the war, on June 17, 1775, involving a massive British attack on New England militia units on a hill facing Boston. The militiamen finally yielded the hill, but not before inflicting heavy casualties on the British.

Common Sense
A pamphlet written by Thomas Paine in 1776 that laid out the case for independence. In it, Paine rejected monarchy, urging its replacement with republican government based on the consent of the people. The wildly popular pamphlet influenced public opinion throughout the colonies.

How did the military objectives of each side shape the course of the war's early years?	How did the war transform the home front?	How did the American Revolution become a war among continental and global powers?	What were the principal causes of the British defeat?	Conclusion: Why did the British lose the American Revolution?

◀ **Thomas Paine** Thomas Paine's sensational pamphlet *Common Sense* advanced the cause of independence. Paine remained a provocative pamphleteer after the American Revolution, writing *The Rights of Man* in revolutionary France, followed by *The Age of Reason*, which many people denounced as an atheistic tract. In 1802, he returned to the United States. Spurned for his attacks on religion, he died in obscurity in 1809. American Antiquarian Society, Worcester, Massachusetts, USA/Bridgeman Images.

In simple yet forceful language, Paine portrayed the British monarchy as an absurd institution. Why, he asked, should one man have the power to rule by sheer accident of birth? "One of the strongest natural proofs of the folly of hereditary right in kings," Paine wrote, "is that nature disapproves it; otherwise she would not so frequently turn it into ridicule by giving mankind *an ass for a lion*." Calling the British king an ass broke through the deep well of deference most colonists still felt for the monarchy. Instead, Paine called for republican government based on the consent of the governed. Rulers, according to Paine, represented the people; the best form of government relied on frequent elections to keep rulers accountable.

Paine's pamphlet sold more than 150,000 copies in a matter of weeks. Newspapers reprinted it. Men read it aloud in taverns and coffeehouses. John Adams sent a copy to his wife, Abigail, who passed it around to her neighbors in Braintree, Massachusetts. Although many New Englanders already favored independence, settlers in other colonies remained cautious. Paine's pamphlet helped end the hesitation, pushing them to take the great leap of abandoning the British empire—and monarchy along with it.

Abigail Adams did not just yearn for independence. She also sought to broaden the movement by extending it beyond the ranks of white male colonists. In a series of letters to her husband, Adams highlighted the limitations of the intellectual ferment. "I have sometimes been ready to think that the passion for Liberty cannot be Equally strong in the Breasts of those who have been accustomed to deprive their fellow Creatures of theirs," Adams wrote of southern slave owners.

> "I desire you would Remember the Ladies, and be more generous and favourable to them than your ancestors," wrote Abigail Adams.

In another letter, she called for an expansion of women's legal rights: "In the new Code of Laws which I suppose it will be necessary for you to make I desire you would Remember the Ladies, and be more generous and favourable to them than your ancestors." Adams pointed to the legal dominion that men exercised over their wives. "Do not put such unlimited power into the hands of the Husbands," she warned. "Remember all Men would be tyrants if they could."

John dismissed his wife's concerns. But to another male politician, Adams reviewed the reasons for excluding women (and men who were black, or young, or lacking property) from political participation. Although he defended existing social hierarchies, Abigail's letter forced him to ponder the logic behind their exclusion, something few men—or women—did in 1776.

UNDERSTAND POINTS OF VIEW

How did John and Abigail Adams differ on their views of the scope and limits of the political movement? What distinguishes a movement for independence from a revolution?

The Declaration of Independence

One factor pushing the colonies toward independence was the prospect of an alliance with France. French authorities saw the brewing rebellion in Britain's colonies as an opportunity to strike a blow against their archrival by breaking up the British empire. They secretly provided money and supplies. But before they were willing to openly support the colonies, French officials wanted some assurance that the quarrel would end in independence, not reconciliation. News that British authorities were planning to hire German mercenary soldiers further boosted popular support for independence. By

What persuaded British North American colonists to support independence?

May 1776, all but four colonies were agitating for a declaration. Moderates were still hoping for reconciliation, but the political momentum was rapidly shifting away from them. An exasperated Virginian wrote to his friend in the congress, "For God's sake, why do you dawdle in the Congress so strangely? Why do you not at once declare yourself a separate independent state?"

In early June, the Virginia delegation introduced a resolution calling for independence. Moderates still commanded enough support to postpone a vote until July, however. In the meantime, the congress appointed a committee, which included Thomas Jefferson, John Adams, and Ben Franklin, to draft a document making the case.

On July 2, after intense debate, the Continental Congress voted for independence. Delegates then turned to the document Jefferson and his committee had drafted. It opened with a preamble that articulated radical philosophical principles about natural rights, equality, the right of revolution, and the doctrine that government derives its power from the consent of the governed. It then listed more than two dozen specific grievances against King George. Remarkably, given its radicalism, the preamble pro-voked little comment. Instead, the congress wrangled over the grievances, especially the issue of slavery. Jefferson had included an impassioned statement blaming the king for the existence of slavery in the colonies. Delegates from Georgia and South Carolina struck that section out, not wishing to denounce the labor system on which their wealth rested. But the congress let stand another of Jefferson's grievances, denouncing the king for mobilizing "the merciless Indian Savages" into bloody frontier warfare, a reference to

VISUAL ACTIVITY

▲ *La destruction de la statue royale a Nouvelle Yorck* This print, published in Paris, shows an artist's rendering of the destruction of a statue of King George III in New York on July 9, 1776, shortly after a public reading of the Declaration of Independence. The artist was obviously unfamiliar with life in the American colonies. The caption suggests that the print was intended for French and Dutch audiences. Library of Congress, 2004670213.

READING THE IMAGE: How does the artist portray New York? How does he portray slaves? What might these depictions tell us about European ideas of slavery and of the American colonies?
CONNECTIONS: Why was the destruction of a statue of the monarch such a powerful symbol in Europe in 1776? What effect might it have had on French audiences in particular?

| How did the military objectives of each side shape the course of the war's early years? | How did the war transform the home front? | How did the American Revolution become a war among continental and global powers? | What were the principal causes of the British defeat? | Conclusion: Why did the British lose the American Revolution? |

Pontiac's War (see chapter 6). The final, rousing paragraph declared the colonies "Free and Independent States," announcing their membership in the international community of nations. The United States was declaring itself into existence.

On July 4, the amendments to Jefferson's text were complete, and the congress formally adopted the Declaration of Independence. In August, the delegates gathered to sign the official parchment copy. Four men, including John Dickinson, declined to sign; several others "signed with regret . . . and with many doubts," according to John Adams. The document was then printed, widely distributed, and read aloud in celebrations everywhere.

Printed copies omitted the signers' names: They had committed treason, a crime punishable by death. On the day of signing, they indulged in gallows humor. When Benjamin Franklin paused for a moment, John Hancock of Massachusetts teased him, "Come, come, sir. We must be unanimous. No pulling different ways. We must all hang together." Franklin replied, "Indeed we must all hang together. Otherwise we shall most assuredly hang separately."

Declaration of Independence
A document containing philosophical principles and a list of grievances that declared and justified the colonies' independence from Britain. The Second Continental Congress adopted the Declaration on July 4, 1776, abandoning the moderates' policy of reconciliation and turning the rebellion into a revolution.

QUICK REVIEW

Why were so many British North American colonists initially reluctant to pursue independence from Britain?

How did the military objectives of each side shape the course of the war's early years?

CHRONOLOGY

1775
– Battle of Quebec fought.

1776
– Battle of Long Island fought.
– Washington captures German troops along Delaware River.

Both sides approached the war with uneasiness. The United States, with inexperienced militias made up mostly of farmers and artisans, had begun a war against the mightiest military power in the Atlantic world. With virtually no money, the upstart nation confronted the kingdom with the most sophisticated financial system of any global power. And notwithstanding the name of the new country, it lacked unity: Many Americans remained loyal to Britain. On the other hand, British forces faced serious obstacles as well: The logistics of supplying an army across three thousand miles of water with eighteenth-century technologies of travel and communication were daunting, to say the least. Moreover, the British goal was to regain popular allegiance, not to destroy and conquer, so victory could not be won on the battlefield alone. These patterns—undertrained American troops faced off against British troops reluctant to press their military advantage—played out repeatedly in the first year of war.

The American Military Forces

Defense in the colonies had long rested with militias composed of all able-bodied men over age sixteen. Militias, however, were best suited for local and limited engagements, for responding to slave rebellions, or for conflict with Native Americans. The United States now needed an army.

Congress initially set the term of enlistment at one year, which proved inadequate. Incentives produced longer commitments: a $20 bonus for three years of service, a hundred acres of land for enlistment until the war's end—a reward valid only if the United States won. Over the course of the war, some 230,000 men enlisted, totaling

What persuaded British North American colonists to support independence?

roughly one-quarter of the white male adult population. Women also served in the Continental army, cooking, washing, and nursing the wounded (and at least once, on the battlefield secretly dressed as a man). The British army established a ratio of one woman to every ten men; in the Continental army, the ratio was set at one woman to fifteen men. Close to twenty thousand "camp followers," as they were called, served during the war, many of them wives of men in service. Approximately twelve thousand children also tagged along, and babies were born in the camps. Some women helped during battles, supplying drinking water or ammunition to soldiers.

At first, the Continental army excluded African Americans. But as manpower needs increased, northern states welcomed free blacks into service, while slaves in some states could serve with their masters' permission. In all, about five thousand black men served the United States in the Revolutionary War. However much these men were inspired by the ideals of the Revolution—twenty-three gave "Liberty," "Freedom," and "Freeman" as their surnames at the time of enlistment—the number of black people serving in the American army paled in comparison to the numbers serving with British forces.

UNDERSTAND POINTS OF VIEW

What motivated African Americans who served on the rebel side of the Revolutionary War?

Military service helped politicize Americans during the early stages of the war. In 1776, independence was a risky, potentially treasonous idea. But as many people discovered, apathy had its dangers as well. Those who refused to serve risked being called traitors to the revolutionary cause. As the war continued, neutrality became more difficult to maintain, and military service offered a way of demonstrating political allegiance.

The American army was raw and inexperienced and often woefully undermanned. It never developed the precision and discipline of European professional armies. But it was not as ineffectual as British officers continually assumed.

The British Strategy

The American army did not have to win the war; it merely had to survive. As a consequence, American military objectives were straightforward—to repulse an invading army and avoid any catastrophic military defeats. The British strategy, on the other hand, was not as clear. Imperial authorities wanted to put down the rebellion and restore the crown's power in the colonies. But how? A decisive defeat of the Continental army was essential, but would not in itself end the rebellion; an armed and angry insurgent population would remain. Nor could the rebellion be defeated by an assault on some political nerve center. There were thirteen distinct political entities to capture, pacify, and then restore to the crown, stretching a thousand miles from New Hampshire to Georgia. Indeed, during the war British forces would capture and occupy every major port city. In a continent whose population was 95 percent rural, however, such victories mattered little. Charged with restoring the old governments, not destroying an enemy country, British generals could not win by ravaging the countryside or burning villages. Unwilling to confiscate food from Americans, the British needed hundreds of supply ships—and ports in which to land them. The British also depended on the support of Americans who remained loyal to the crown and would help the British war effort. It was therefore imperative not to alienate them.

British military strategy aimed to divide and conquer the colonies, focusing first on New York. In addition to having the greatest number of loyal subjects, New York offered an important geographic advantage. If British forces could control the Hudson River, they would isolate New England from the middle and southern colonies. Squeezed between a naval blockade along the coast and an army in the west, Massachusetts would be forced to surrender. New Jersey and Pennsylvania would then fall in line, British strategists hoped, as loyal British subjects took back power. Virginia posed a problem, but the British believed that loyalist support in the Carolinas would eventually help them isolate and subdue the colony.

PLACE EVENTS IN CONTEXT

Why did British military strategists decide to focus their initial efforts on controlling New York City?

| **How did the military objectives of each side shape the course of the war's early years?** | How did the war transform the home front? | How did the American Revolution become a war among continental and global powers? | What were the principal causes of the British defeat? | Conclusion: Why did the British lose the American Revolution? |

179

Quebec, New York, and New Jersey

In late 1775, the United States launched an expedition to capture the cities of Montreal and Quebec before British reinforcements could arrive (**Map 7.1**). The Americans hoped that the French Canadian population, only recently conquered by the British, would rise in support of their cause. A force of New York Continentals commanded by General Richard Montgomery took Montreal in September 1775 and then advanced on Quebec. Meanwhile, a second contingent of Continentals led by Colonel Benedict Arnold moved north through Maine to Quebec—a punishing trek through freezing rain with woefully inadequate supplies. Arnold showed heroic determination, but close to half of his men either died or turned back during the march. Arnold and Montgomery jointly attacked Quebec in December but failed to take the city. Worse yet, they experienced a smallpox epidemic, which killed more men than the battle did. Meanwhile, the French Canadian population, which had recently gained new civil rights under the Quebec Act of 1774 (see chapter 6), remained mostly neutral. The Canada expedition proved a costly failure for the United States.

The main action of the war's first year came not in Canada, however, but in New York. In August 1776, some forty-five thousand British troops (including eight thousand German mercenaries, called Hessians) commanded by General Howe landed south of New York City. General Washington had anticipated this move and marched his army of twenty thousand south from Massachusetts to meet them. The very green Continental army was no match for the well-trained British "redcoats" (slang referring to their red uniforms), however. Howe took the offensive in the **battle of Long Island**, inflicting many casualties and taking one thousand prisoners. A British general crowed, "If a good bleeding can bring those Bible-faced Yankees to their senses, the fever of independency should soon abate." Howe failed to press forward, however, perhaps remembering the terrible costs of his victory at Bunker Hill. Washington evacuated his troops from Long Island.

Washington withdrew to the north of Manhattan, to two forts on either side of the Hudson River. For two months, the armies engaged in limited skirmishing, but in November Howe captured Fort Washington and Fort Lee, taking another three thousand prisoners and very nearly defeating the Continental army. Washington retreated across New Jersey into Pennsylvania. Once again, Howe failed to press his advantage. Instead, he parked his German troops in winter quarters along the Delaware River. Perhaps he knew that many of the Continental soldiers' enlistment periods ended on December 31, and assumed that the Americans would not attack. He was wrong.

On the night of December 25, in an icy rain, Washington stealthily moved his army across the Delaware River. Early the next morning, he attacked the unsuspecting German soldiers, who were groggy from a night of Christmas revelry. The victory meant little in military terms, but after a series of humiliating defeats, the Continental army needed to boost the sagging morale of its troops and of the civilian population. For the next two weeks, Washington continued his offensive, capturing supplies in a clever attack on British units at Princeton. Soon he was safe in Morristown, in northern New Jersey, where he settled his army for the winter. Washington finally had time to administer mass smallpox inoculations and see his men through the abbreviated course of the disease.

All in all, in the first year of war, the rebellious Americans had a few proud moments but far more defeats. The inexperienced Continental army had barely survived the New York campaign. Washington had shown exceptional daring and admirable restraint, but what really saved the Americans was the repeated reluctance of British generals to press their military advantage to victory. Although it did not look promising, the cause of independence remained alive.

battle of Long Island
First major engagement of the new Continental army, which fought 45,000 British troops newly arrived on western Long Island (today Brooklyn). The Continentals retreated with high casualties and many taken prisoner.

QUICK REVIEW

> What were British military objectives, and how did they hinder Britain's early efforts to defeat the rebellion?

What persuaded British North American colonists to support independence?

MAP 7.1 ▲ The War in the North, 1775–1778 After battles in Massachusetts in 1775, rebel forces invaded Canada but failed to capture Quebec. The British army landed in New York in 1776, causing turmoil in New Jersey in 1777 and 1778. Burgoyne attempted to isolate New England, but he was stopped at Saratoga in 1777 in the decisive battle of the early war.

READING THE MAP: How did the availability of water routes affect British and American strategy? What were Burgoyne's objectives in his 1777 campaign? Why was the battle of Saratoga such a critical event?

CONNECTIONS: In what ways did the campaigns and military strategy in the American Revolution resemble that of the antagonists in the Seven Years' War? (See chapter 6.) What accounts for the differences?

How did the military objectives of each side shape the course of the war's early years?	How did the war transform the home front?	How did the American Revolution become a war among continental and global powers?	What were the principal causes of the British defeat?	Conclusion: Why did the British lose the American Revolution?

How did the war transform the home front?

CHRONOLOGY

1775
- **June**. Second Continental Congress declares all loyalists traitors.
- Mohawk leader Joseph Brant travels to England to pledge support for British side.

1776
- In New York City, loyalists sign "Declaration of Dependence."

1777
- British Parliament suspends habeas corpus.

1778
- Colonial committees of public safety fix prices on essential commodities.

1780
- Philadelphia Ladies Association raises money for soldiers.

Ladies Association
A women's organization in Philadelphia that collected donations in 1780 for Continental troops. A leader authored a declaration, "The Sentiments of an American Woman," to justify women's unexpected entry into political life.

loyalists
Colonists who remained loyal to Britain during the Revolutionary War, probably numbering around one-fifth of the population in 1776. Colonists supported Britain for many reasons, and loyalists could be found in every region of the country.

Battles alone did not win or lose the war. Struggles on the home front were just as important. Men who joined the army often left wives in charge of households. Some men and women remained loyal to Britain and opposed the war effort, while many others were undecided. Throughout the United States, supporters of the revolutionary cause used both persuasion and force to gain the allegiance of neutrals. An unstable wartime economy added to the domestic turbulence. The creative financing of the fledgling government brought hardships for many and opportunities for some, presenting Americans with new manifestations of virtue and corruption. As these changes spread through the former colonies, the colonial rebellion was gradually turning into a revolution.

Patriotism at the Local Level

Committees of correspondence, of public safety, and of inspection dominated the political landscape in patriot communities. These committees took on more tasks than local governance. They enforced boycotts, selected army draftees, and monitored suspected loyalists. They sometimes invaded homes to search for contraband goods such as British tea or textiles. These forceful demonstrations of power and even coercion dismayed loyalists. "Choose your committee or suffer it to be chosen by a half dozen fools in your neighborhood," a man in Westchester, New York, complained. "Open your doors to them—let them examine your tea-cannisters and molasses-jugs, and your wives' and daughters' petty coats—bow and cringe and tremble and quake—fall down and worship our sovereign lord the mob. . . . Should any pragmatical committee-gentleman come to my house and give himself airs, I shall show him the door." For all the tough talk, few people challenged the local committees. Their coercive powers pushed many middle-of-the-road citizens to side with the patriot forces, at least in public.

Another group new to political life—white women—demonstrated a capacity for patriotism as wartime hardships upended their lives. Many wives whose husbands left for military or political service took over traditionally masculine duties. As they managed farms and made business decisions, some even asserted themselves in political debates. Eliza Wilkinson managed a South Carolina plantation and talked revolutionary politics with her friends. "None were greater politicians than the several knots of ladies who met together," she remarked, alert to the sudden turn female conversations had taken. Women from prominent Philadelphia families took more direct action, forming the **Ladies Association** to collect money for Continental soldiers. Mrs. Esther DeBerdt Reed, wife of Pennsylvania's governor, published a broadside in 1780 titled "The Sentiments of an American Woman" to defend these new forms of female activism: "The time is arrived to display the same sentiments which animated us at the beginning of the Revolution, when we renounced the use of teas [and] when our republican and laborious hands spun the flax."

The Loyalists

Approximately one-fifth of the American population remained loyal to the crown in 1776, and another two-fifths tried to stay neutral, providing a significant base of popular support for the British. A broad and diverse group of Americans, **loyalists** opposed the revolution for a variety of reasons. Some cherished their identity as British subjects, and believed that the British empire was the freest, most liberal government

What persuaded British North American colonists to support independence?

in the world. Many believed in order and hierarchy, and saw the self-styled patriots as unscrupulous, violent men grabbing power for themselves and imposing a new form of democratic tyranny. Others saw the British empire as their best hope to maintain or achieve their liberty and autonomy. Pockets of loyalism existed everywhere (**Map 7.2**). The most visible loyalists (called Tories by their enemies) were royal officials like governors, local judges, and customs officers. Wealthy merchants gravitated toward loyalism to maintain the protections of navigation acts and the British navy. Conservative urban lawyers admired the stability of British law and order. Some colonists chose loyalism to oppose their political adversaries, like the backcountry Carolina farmers who resented the power of the pro-revolutionary elite. Southern slaves had their own resentments against the slave-owning class, and looked to Britain as the power that could bring their freedom. Even New England towns at the heart of the turmoil, such as Concord, Massachusetts, had a small and increasingly silenced core of loyalists. On occasion, fathers and sons and even brothers disagreed completely on the war. **(See "Analyzing Historical Evidence: Families Divide over the Revolution" on page 184.)**

Many Indian nations remained neutral at the war's start; they saw the conflict as a civil war between the English and Americans that did not concern them. Eventually, however, many were drawn into the war. From the perspective of most Native

UNDERSTAND POINTS OF VIEW

What different social groups composed the loyalist population, and what different motivations brought them to support the British side?

MAP 7.2 ◄ Loyalist Strength and Rebel Support

Although no count could have given exact numbers, this map shows the regions of loyalist strength on which the British relied—most significantly, the lower Hudson valley and the Carolina Piedmont. Commercialized port cities highly integrated into imperial trade tended to run more loyalist. The Mohawk Valley corridor—dominated by the Iroquois—proved to be one of the war's major hotspots.

Map labels:
Quebec, CANADA, NOVA SCOTIA, Halifax, Montreal, L. Huron, L. Ontario, VT., N.H., NEW YORK, MASS., Boston, Detroit, L. Erie, CONN., R.I., Newport (1776–78), Philadelphia (1777–78), PA., New York, N.J., MD., DEL., VIRGINIA, Norfolk, NORTH CAROLINA, Wilmington, SOUTH CAROLINA, Charleston, GEORGIA, Savannah, APPALACHIAN MTS., ATLANTIC OCEAN

0 75 150 miles
0 75 150 kilometers

Legend:
- Loyalist strongholds
- Indians: loyalist or neutral
- Strongly contested areas
- Patriot strongholds

How did the military objectives of each side shape the course of the war's early years?

How did the war transform the home front?

How did the American Revolution become a war among continental and global powers?

What were the principal causes of the British defeat?

Conclusion: Why did the British lose the American Revolution?

Families Divide over the Revolution

Generalizing about rebels versus loyalists is a complex historical task. Sometimes categorizing by class, race, and geographic descriptors helps explain the split. But sometimes the loyalist-patriot divide cut across families—and cut deeply. These documents reveal people pitted against loved ones over wartime allegiance.

DOCUMENT 1

Patriot Benjamin Franklin and Loyalist Son William Correspond, 1784

Benjamin Franklin, a leader of the Revolution, had a son who stayed loyal to the crown. Benjamin's illegitimate son, William, traveled to England with his father in 1757 during Benjamin's extended service as Pennsylvania's colonial agent. William acquired connections at court, and in 1762 he was appointed royal governor of New Jersey, a post he held until 1776. When the war began, he was placed under house arrest as a traitor to the patriot cause. Father and son did not communicate for the next nine years, even during the eight months when William was confined in a Connecticut prison. During this time, Benjamin took charge of William's oldest son, an illegitimate child born before William's legal marriage. After the war, William moved to England, and in 1784 he wrote to his father, then in Paris, asking for a meeting of reconciliation.

Dear and honored Father,

Ever since the termination of the unhappy contest between Great Britain and America, I have been anxious to write to you. . . . There are narrow illiberal Minds in all Parties. In that which I took, and on whose Account I have so much suffered, there have not been wanting some who have insinuated that my Conduct has been founded on Collusion with you, that one of us might succeed whichever Party should prevail. . . . The Falsity of such Insinuation in our Case you well know, and I am happy that I can with Confidence appeal not only to you but to my God, that I have uniformly acted from a strong Sense of what I conceived my Duty to my King, and Regard to my Country, required. If I have been mistaken, I cannot help it. It is an Error of Judgment what the maturest Reflection I am capable of cannot rectify; and I verily believe were the same Circumstances to occur again Tomorrow, my Conduct would be exactly similar to what it was heretofore.

The father replied:

Dear Son,

I . . . am glad to find that you desire to revive the affectionate Intercourse, that formerly existed between us. It will be very agreeable to me; indeed nothing has ever hurt me so much and affected me with such keen Sensations, as to find myself deserted in my old age by my only Son; and not only deserted, but to find him taking up Arms against me, in a Cause, wherein my good Fame, Fortune and Life were all at Stake. You conceived, you say, that your Duty to your King and regard for your Country requir'd this. I ought not to blame you for differing in Sentiment with me in Public Affairs. We are Men, all subject to errors. Our opinions are not in our own Power; they are form'd and govern'd much by Circumstances, that are often as inexplicable as they are irresistible. Your Situation was such that few would have censured your remaining Neuter, *tho' there are Natural Duties which preceded political ones, and cannot be extinguish'd by them.*

This is a disagreeable Subject. I drop it. And we will endeavor, as you propose mutually to forget what has

American peoples, the war pitted the land-hungry settlers against imperial officials, who had, at least on occasion, attempted to protect their interests. Choosing which side to support seemed obvious. The powerful Iroquois Confederacy, however, was divided: The Mohawk, Cayuga, Seneca, and Onondaga peoples lined up with the British; the Oneida and Tuscarora tribes aided Americans, betting on an American victory and preferring to side with the winners. One young Mohawk leader, Thayendanegea (known also by his English name, Joseph Brant), traveled to England in 1775 to complain to King George about land-hungry New York settlers. "It is very hard when we have let the King's subjects have so much of our lands for so little value," he wrote, "they should want to cheat us in this manner of the small spots we have left for our

What persuaded British North American colonists to support independence?

happened relating to it, as well as we can. I send your Son over to pay his Duty to you. . . . He is greatly esteem'd and belov'd in this Country, and will make his Way anywhere. . . . Wishing you Health, and more happiness than it seems you have lately experienced, I remain your affectionate father, B. Franklin

Source: Courtesy of the American Philosophical Society, http://www.amphilsoc.org.

DOCUMENT 2

Two Oneida Brothers Confront Their Different Allegiances, 1779

Mary Jemison was captured as a girl during the Seven Years' War and adopted into the Seneca tribe of western New York, where she remained for life. When she was eighty, her narrative was taken down and published. In this story from her narrative, she relates how some Oneida warriors siding with the British captured two Indians guiding General Sullivan's 1779 campaign of terror in central New York. One of the captors recognized his own brother.

Envy and revenge glared in the features of the conquering savage, as he advanced to his brother (the prisoner) in all the haughtiness of Indian pride, heightened by a sense of power, and addressed him in the following manner:

"Brother, you have merited death! The hatchet or the war-club shall finish your career! When I begged of you to follow me in the fortunes of war, you was deaf to my cries—you spurned my entreaties!

"Brother! You have merited death and shall have your deserts! When the rebels raised their hatchets to fight their good master, you sharpened your knife, you brightened your rifle and led on our foes to the fields of our fathers! You have merited death and shall die by our hands! When those rebels had drove us from the fields of our fathers to seek out new homes, it was you who could dare to step forth as their pilot, and conduct them even to the doors of our wigwams, to butcher our children and put us to death! No crime can be greater! But though you have merited death and shall die on this spot, my hands shall not be stained in the blood of a brother! *Who will strike?*" Little Beard, who was standing by, as soon as the speech was ended, struck the prisoner on the head with his tomahawk, and dispatched him at once.

Source: James E. Seaver, *A narrative of the life of Mrs. Mary Jemison, who was taken by the Indians, in the year 1755, when only about twelve years of age, and has continued to reside amongst them to the present time* (1824), chapter VII, Project Gutenberg, http://www.gutenberg.org/ebooks/6960 (accessed August 2, 2013).

Questions for Analysis

RECOGNIZE VIEWPOINTS: Does William regret or apologize for his loyalism? How does he explain his decision to remain loyal to the crown? What does Benjamin mean by the emphasized words "*Natural Duties*"? What position would Benjamin have wanted his son to have taken?

ANALYZE THE EVIDENCE: What three reasons did the Oneida warrior give to support his claim that his brother merited death? What does Mary Jemison's introduction to the warrior's speech tell us about her perspective on Native American culture?

CONSIDER THE CONTEXT: To what extent was the American Revolution a civil war? What was at stake for Native Americans in the war? What motivated those who supported Britain, and what motivated those who supported the American colonists?

women and children to live on." Brant pledged Indian support for the king in exchange for protection from encroaching settlers. In the Ohio Country, parts of the Shawnee and Delaware tribes started out pro-American, but shifted to the British side by 1779 in the face of repeated betrayals by American settlers and soldiers.

White loyalists were most vocal between 1774 and 1776, when a full-scale rebellion against Britain still seemed unlikely. They challenged the patriots' arguments in pamphlets and newspapers. In 1776 in New York City, 547 loyalists signed and circulated a broadside titled "A Declaration of Dependence" that rebutted the congress's July 4 declaration, denouncing the "most unnatural, unprovoked Rebellion that ever disgraced the annals of Time."

UNDERSTAND POINTS OF VIEW

Why did so many Indians who chose neutrality at the beginning of the Revolutionary War eventually support the British?

| How did the military objectives of each side shape the course of the war's early years? | **How did the war transform the home front?** | How did the American Revolution become a war among continental and global powers? | What were the principal causes of the British defeat? | Conclusion: Why did the British lose the American Revolution? |

◄ **Chief Joseph Brant** Thayendanegea, also known as Joseph Brant, was a prominent Mohawk leader who fought against the United States during the Revolution. This portrait was painted when Brant visited England after the war on a mission to secure land in Canada for his people. The painting was commissioned by Hugh Percy, the Duke of Northumberland, who had fought with Brant in the Revolution. The two remained lifelong friends and correspondents. VCG Wilson/Corbis via Getty Images.

READING THE IMAGE: How does the artist depict Brant? Is he portrayed negatively as savage? What might the clothing and regalia—which include a gorget given by King George—signify?

CONNECTIONS: Why did the Mohawks mostly side with the British in the American Revolution? How did the war affect the Iroquois Confederacy?

Who Is a Traitor?

In June 1775, the Second Continental Congress declared all loyalists to be traitors. Over the next year, state laws specified that acts such as provisioning the British army, saying anything that undermined patriot morale, and discouraging men from enlisting in the Continental army were treasonous. Punishments ranged from house arrest and suspension of voting privileges to confiscation of property and deportation. Sometimes self-appointed committees of Tory hunters bypassed the judicial process and terrorized loyalists, raiding their houses or tarring and feathering them.

Were wives of loyalists also traitors? When loyalist families fled the country, state governments typically confiscated their property. If the wife stayed, courts usually allowed her to keep one-third of the property, the amount due her if widowed, and confiscated the rest. Yet according to the laws of the time, a wife was not a political subject who made choices of her own; she was an extension of her husband's will. After the Revolution, some descendants of refugee loyalists filed lawsuits to regain property that had entered the family through the mother's inheritance. In one well-publicized Massachusetts case in 1805, the American son of loyalist refugee Anna Martin recovered her dowry property on the grounds that she had no independent will to be a loyalist.

To the loyalists, tarring and feathering, property confiscation, deportation, terrorism, and denials of liberty of conscience and of property rights proved the dangers of democratic tyranny. A Boston loyalist named Mather Byles aptly expressed this point: "They call me a brainless Tory, but tell me . . . which is better—to be ruled by one tyrant three thousand miles away, or by three thousand tyrants not a mile away?" Byles was soon sentenced to deportation.

Throughout the war, probably seven to eight thousand loyalists fled to England, and twenty-eight thousand eventually found refuge in Canada. Many stayed until the war's outcome became clear. In New Jersey, for example, three thousand felt protected (or scared) enough by the occupying British army in 1776 to swear an oath of allegiance to the king. But then the British drew back to New York City, leaving those loyalists to the mercy of local patriot committees—and highlighting the risks of openly declaring one's political allegiance. Despite the support of loyalists in 1776, British forces proved unable to build a winning strategy on their backs.

Financial Instability and Corruption

Wars cost money—for arms and ammunition, for food and uniforms, for soldiers' pay, and so much more. The Continental Congress printed money, but its value quickly deteriorated because no precious metals backed the currency. The paper money

PLACE EVENTS IN CONTEXT

Why were so many Americans unable to remain neutral?

What persuaded British North American colonists to support independence?

eventually bottomed out at one-fortieth of its face value. States, too, printed money to pay for wartime expenses, throwing more chaos into the wartime economy.

As the currency depreciated, the congress searched for other means to purchase supplies and labor. One method was to borrow hard money (gold or silver coins) from wealthy men in exchange for certificates of debt (public securities), promising repayment with interest. The certificates of debt functioned like present-day government bonds. To pay soldiers, the congress issued land-grant certificates, written promises of land usually located in frontier areas such as central Maine or north of the Ohio River. Both the public securities and the land-grant certificates would only have value in the event of a patriot victory. They became forms of negotiable currency, and soon depreciated as well.

Depreciating currency caused prices to rise: Sellers demanded more money as its value fell. The wartime economy of the late 1770s, with an unreliable currency and dramatic inflation, demoralized Americans everywhere. In 1778, local committees of public safety began to fix prices on essential goods such as flour. Inevitably, some turned this situation to their advantage. Money whose value was falling was better spent quickly; debts, meanwhile, could be repaid in devalued currency. A brisk black market sprang up in prohibited luxury imports, such as tea, sugar, textiles, and wines, even though these goods came from Britain. A New Hampshire delegate to the Continental Congress denounced the trade: "We are a crooked and perverse generation, longing for the fineries and follies of those Egyptian task masters from whom we have so lately freed ourselves."

From Rebellion to Revolution

As the war ground on, its influence extended into ever more aspects of American society. Although loyalists came from every social sector, some of the most prominent families of the political and economic life of the colonies sided with the empire. Their sudden exclusion from power opened up new opportunities for ambitious men supporting the patriot cause. The economic transformations unleashed by the war added to the turbulence, creating great new fortunes for some, even as policies of land confiscation or simple financial collapse brought down older dynasties. The active roles that women took in the revolutionary effort—in the boycott and homespun movements, for example, or in the Ladies Association—challenged prevailing gender norms, and created new ways for women to think of themselves in political and economic terms. The recruitment of blacks to the Continental Army and of former slaves to the British forces undermined the institution of slavery and challenged the racial ideologies on which slavery rested. Put together, these developments added up to a radical challenge to existing social hierarchies.

◄ Black Soldier Fighting for the Patriots
A French soldier who fought in the American Revolution painted this watercolor. It portrays several men in military uniform, including a black soldier who fought with the First Rhode Island Regiment. Some five thousand black soldiers served with United States forces, although many others chose to fight with the British after escaping American slavery. Anne S. K. Brown Military Collection, Brown University Library.

| How did the military objectives of each side shape the course of the war's early years? | **How did the war transform the home front?** | How did the American Revolution become a war among continental and global powers? | What were the principal causes of the British defeat? | Conclusion: Why did the British lose the American Revolution? |

None of these challenges had been intended by those who initially led the resistance to British imperial policy. But as the movement continued, it gained a momentum of its own, which eventually ran ahead of the political leadership. No one had a monopoly on the rhetoric of "liberty" and "slavery," of "tyranny" and "republicanism." Laborers, slaves, women, and many others began to appropriate the radical language that had become such common currency in the imperial struggle.

Although the American Revolution did not lead to wholesale social revolution in the former British colonies, it created a powerful new language of rights on which future generations would build. Over time, the republic governed by elite men established by the Revolution would become a raucous popular democracy. Women, blacks, workers, landless squatters, and many others would deploy the Revolution's rhetoric to claim their rights as citizens.

If such movements still lay in the future, one change came immediately and permanently. With the Declaration of Independence's proclamation that governments derive their just powers from the governed, the colonists who had long cherished their identity as subjects of the British king gave up their allegiance to monarchy and never looked back. Even as most claims to citizenship and democracy continued to be the subject of bitter contestation in American life, the question of monarchy was never seriously reconsidered. The United States was henceforth to be a republic, and no political movement ever emerged calling for a return to monarchy.

QUICK REVIEW

How did the revolutionary movement transform the former British colonies?

How did the American Revolution become a war among continental and global powers?

In early 1777, the Continental army's prospects looked bleak. With a mix of luck and skill, General Washington had avoided defeat. But the minor victories in New Jersey lent only faint optimism to the American side. Meanwhile, British troops moved south from Quebec, aiming to isolate New England by taking control of the Hudson River. Their presence drew the Continental army up into central New York, turning the Mohawk Valley into a bloody war zone and polarizing the tribes of the ancient Iroquois Confederacy. By 1779, Native American nations in the Ohio Valley were fully involved in the war, which for them had become a struggle to maintain their territory from settler encroachments. A major American victory at Saratoga led France to join the American struggle for independence, turning it into another global war for imperial dominance between Europe's two greatest military powers.

Burgoyne's Army and the Battle of Saratoga

In 1777, British general John Burgoyne began the northern squeeze on the Hudson River valley. His army of 8,400 troops, including some 400 Mohawk warriors, descended from Canada with the objective of capturing Albany, near the intersection of the Hudson

What persuaded British North American colonists to support independence?

and Mohawk rivers (see Map 7.1). Burgoyne's army did not travel light. In addition to 1,000 "camp followers" (cooks, laundresses, musicians) who followed along, Burgoyne's troops dragged a store of heavy artillery across a dense, roadless forest.

In July, Burgoyne captured Fort Ticonderoga. American troops spotted the approaching British and abandoned the fort without a fight. The British continued south, but they lost a month hacking their way through the forests. Supply lines back to Canada were severely stretched, and local militia units harassed British soldiers sent out to forage for food.

The next step in isolating New England should have been to send troops up the Hudson from New York City to meet Burgoyne. American surveillance indicated that General Howe in Manhattan was readying his men for a major move in August 1777. But Howe surprised everyone by sailing south to attack Philadelphia. It was a fateful decision.

To reinforce Burgoyne, British and Hessian troops from Montreal headed to Albany along the Mohawk River, aided by some thousand Mohawks and Senecas of the Iroquois Confederacy. At Fort Stanwix, one hundred miles west of Albany, they encountered American soldiers defending the approach. Hundreds of local patriot German militiamen and a number of Oneida Indians rushed to the Continentals' support. On August 6, 1777, Mohawk chief Joseph Brant led his large force of warriors in an ambush on the patriot fighters in a narrow ravine called Oriskany. It was one of the war's bloodiest battles: Of the eight hundred local militiamen, nearly four hundred were killed and another fifty wounded. Only ninety of Brant's warriors died. The defenders of Fort Stanwix ultimately repelled the British, who retreated north to Canada.

The deadly **battle of Oriskany** and battle of Fort Stanwix highlighted the ways in which the American Revolution was a complex and multiethnic civil war. They pitted German Americans against Hessian mercenaries, New York patriots against New York loyalists, English Americans against British soldiers, and Oneida Iroquois against Mohawk Iroquois. Indeed, the battles marked the beginning of the end of the Iroquois Confederacy, torn apart by lethal violence between members of its constituent tribes. By January 1779, the eternal flame of the council fire at Onondaga, which had symbolized the unity of the six confederated tribes of Iroquoia, was extinguished.

The British retreat at Fort Stanwix deprived General Burgoyne of critical reinforcements. Camped at the small village of Saratoga, isolated at the foot of the Adirondack Mountains, his food supplies dwindling and his men deserting, Burgoyne's position was desperate. Sensing opportunity, American general Horatio Gates began moving his army toward Saratoga. Burgoyne attacked first, and the British prevailed, but at the cost of six hundred dead or wounded. Three weeks later, a second American attack on Burgoyne's forces at the **battle of Saratoga** cost the British another six hundred men and most of their cannons. Isolated, without hope of reinforcements, General Burgoyne surrendered to the American forces on October 17, 1777. It was the first great victory for the Continental Army, sparking celebration throughout the colonies.

General Howe, meanwhile, succeeded in occupying Philadelphia in September 1777. Calculating that the capture of Philadelphia compensated for the loss at Saratoga, the British government proposed a negotiated settlement—not including independence— to end the war. No doubt the Continental Congress would have accepted the offer eighteen months earlier. But no longer: The Americans refused. Independence had now become the objective of the war, a cause they increasingly understood religiously, as bound up with a greater quest for human freedom.

If American spirits ran high after Burgoyne's defeat, supplies of arms and food ran precariously low. Washington moved his troops into winter quarters at Valley Forge, just west of Philadelphia. Quartered in drafty huts, the soldiers lacked blankets, boots, stockings, and food. Meanwhile, evidence of corruption and profiteering was abundant. Army suppliers too often provided defective food, clothing, and gunpowder. One shipment of bedding arrived with blankets one-quarter their customary size. Food supplies arrived

CHRONOLOGY

1777
- Ambush takes place at Oriskany; Americans hold Fort Stanwix.
- British occupy Philadelphia.
- British surrender at Saratoga.

1777–1778
- Continental army winters at Valley Forge.

1778
- France signs Treaty of Amity and Commerce with America.

1779
- Militias attack Cherokee settlements west of North Carolina.
- Americans destroy Iroquois villages in New York.
- Americans take Forts Kaskaskia and Vincennes.

battle of Oriskany
A punishing defeat for Americans in New York in August 1777. Mohawk and Seneca Indians ambushed German American militiamen and allied Oneida warriors, and four hundred on the revolutionary side were killed. It marked the beginning of bitter frontier warfare with sharp racial overtones.

battle of Saratoga
A two-stage battle in New York ending with the decisive defeat and surrender of British general John Burgoyne on October 17, 1777. This victory convinced France to ally with the American side in the war, turning the American Revolution into a global war.

| How did the military objectives of each side shape the course of the war's early years? | How did the war transform the home front? | **How did the American Revolution become a war among continental and global powers?** | What were the principal causes of the British defeat? | Conclusion: Why did the British lose the American Revolution? |

189

Battle of Saratoga, 1777

Map labels:
Fort Ticonderoga captured by British July 6
Fort Anne
Fort Edward
1st Battle, Sept. 19
2nd Battle, Oct. 7
Saratoga Burgoyne surrenders Oct. 17
Bennington
Albany

American forces / American victory
British forces / British victory

rotten. As one Continental officer said, "The people at home are destroying the Army by their conduct much faster than Howe and all his army can possibly do by fighting us."

Some two thousand men died of disease that terrible winter, while another two thousand deserted. "These are the times that try men's souls," wrote Thomas Paine in a pamphlet intended to shore up morale. "Heaven knows how to put a proper price upon its goods," he added, "and it would be strange indeed, if so celestial an article as FREEDOM should not be highly rated."

The War in the West: Indian Country

Between the fall of 1777 and the summer of 1778, the fighting on the Atlantic coast slowed. But in the American backcountry—the foothills and valleys on both sides of the Appalachian Mountains, including the Mohawk Valley, the Ohio Valley, and Kentucky—a war of Indians against the American rebels heated up. Native Americans in these regions fought to protect their sovereignty, their independence, and their traditional culture, in a mirror image of the Americans' quest for "life, liberty, and the pursuit of happiness." If the war in the east was a struggle for independence from empire, the war in the west was a struggle for imperial conquest.

The ambush and slaughter at Oriskany in August 1777 marked the beginning of three years of terror for the inhabitants of the Mohawk Valley. Loyalists and Indians raided patriot settlements throughout 1778. In retaliation, American militiamen destroyed Joseph Brant's village, killing several children. A month later, Brant's troops attacked the town of Cherry Valley, killing sixteen soldiers and thirty-two civilians. Brant called on Mohawk warriors "to defend their Lands & Liberty against the Rebels, who in a great measure begin this Rebellion to be sole Masters of this Continent."

In May 1779, General Washington ordered the "total destruction and devastation" of the Iroquois villages of central New York. "It will be essential to ruin their crops now in the ground and prevent their planting more," he added, ordering his commanders to "lay waste all the settlements around with instructions to do it in the most effectual manner, that the country may not be merely overrun but destroyed." General John Sullivan commanded 4,500 troops that launched the campaign of total war that summer and fall. The goal was to burn Indian villages and food and starve those the army did not kill. Forty Indian towns met with complete obliteration; Continental soldiers torched dwellings, cornfields, and orchards. In some towns, they slaughtered women and children, although inhabitants in most managed to escape. Thousands of Indian refugees, sick and starving, fled to Fort Niagara, where they remained for one of the most miserable winters on record.

By His EXCELLENCY

Joseph Reed, Esq. *President,*

And the SUPREME EXECUTIVE COUNCIL, *of the Commonwealth of* Pennsylvania.

A PROCLAMATION.

WHEREAS the Savages in Alliance with the King of *Great-Britain,* have attacked several of the Frontier Counties, and, according to the Custom of barbarous Nations, have cruelly murdered divers of the defenceless Inhabitants of this State: AND WHEREAS it has been found, by Experience, that the most effectual Mode of making War upon and repelling the Savage Tribes has been by Parties, consisting of small Numbers of vigorous, active Volunteers, making sudden irruptions into their Country, and surprising them in their Marches: WHEREFORE, for the Encouragement of those who may be disposed to chastise the Insolence and Cruelty of those Barbarians, and revenge the Loss of their Friends and Relations, WE HAVE thought fit, and do hereby offer a Reward of THREE THOUSAND DOLLARS for every *Indian* Prisoner, or Tory acting in Arms with them, and a Reward of TWO THOUSAND AND FIVE HUNDRED DOLLARS for every *Indian* Scalp, to be paid on an Order of the President or Vice-President in Council, to be granted on Certificate signed by the Lieutenant, or any two Sub-Lieutenants of the County, in Conjunction with any two Freeholders, of the Service performed. Such Reward to be in Lieu of all other Rewards or Emoluments to be claimed from the State.

GIVEN, by Order of the Council, under the Hand of His Excellency JOSEPH REED, *Esquire, President, and the Seal of the State, at Philadelphia, this Twenty-second Day of April, in the Year of our Lord One Thousand Seven Hundred and Eighty.*

JOSEPH REED, PRESIDENT.

Attest. T. MATLACK, *Secretary.*

GOD Save the PEOPLE

◀ **Proclamation** This proclamation issued by the State of Pennsylvania during the Revolution attacks Native Americans as "barbarous," "cruel," and "Savage." It offers a reward of $3,000 for every Indian prisoner and $2,500 for every Indian scalp. The war in the backcountry between the United States and native nations allied with Great Britain degenerated to horrific levels of violence. Library Company of Philadelphia.

What persuaded British North American colonists to support independence?

Farther west, a complex story of alliances and betrayals between American militiamen and Native Americans unfolded. Some 150,000 native people lived between the Appalachian Mountains and the Mississippi River, and by 1779, neutrality was no longer an option. Most sided with the British, but a portion of the Shawnee and Delaware nations first sought peace with the Americans. In mid-1778, the Delaware chief White Eyes negotiated a treaty at Fort Pitt, pledging his people's support for the American cause in exchange for supplies and trade goods. Escalating violence soon undermined the agreement. That fall, when American soldiers killed Cornstalk and Red Hawk, two friendly Shawnee chiefs, the Continental Congress hastened to apologize, as did the governors of Pennsylvania and Virginia. But the soldiers who stood trial for the murders were acquitted. Two months later, White Eyes died under mysterious circumstances, almost certainly murdered by militiamen who refused to distinguish between allied and enemy Indians. In these borderland areas, the Revolution was turning into a racial war of extermination.

West of North Carolina (today's Tennessee), American militias attacked Cherokee settlements in 1778, destroying thirty-six villages. The Cherokee responded by striking American settlements such as Boonesborough in present-day Kentucky (**Map 7.3**). In

MAP 7.3 ▲ The Indian War in the West, 1777–1782

Most Indian tribes supported the British. Iroquois Indians waged war on New York's Mohawk Valley throughout 1778, while the Continental army destroyed Iroquois villages throughout central New York. Shawnee and Delaware in western Pennsylvania fought against American militiamen in 1779, while tribes near Fort Detroit conducted raids on Kentucky settlers. Frontier fighting continued through 1782.

How did the military objectives of each side shape the course of the war's early years?	How did the war transform the home front?	**How did the American Revolution become a war among continental and global powers?**	What were the principal causes of the British defeat?	Conclusion: Why did the British lose the American Revolution?

retaliation, a young Virginian named George Rogers Clark led Kentucky militiamen into Illinois Country, attacking and taking the British fort at Kaskaskia. Although Clark's men wore native clothing—hunting shirts and breechcloths—their dress did not signal any solidarity with the Indians. When they attacked British-held Fort Vincennes in 1779, Clark's troops tomahawked Indian captives and threw their still-live bodies into the river in a gory spectacle witnessed by British troops. Clark vowed that "he would never spare Man, woman, or child of them on whom he could lay his hands."

By 1780, few Native Americans remained neutral. Violent raids by Americans drove Indians into the arms of the British at Forts Detroit and Niagara, or to the Spaniards, who controlled forts west of the Mississippi River. Rare as it was, Indian support for the American side occasionally emerged out of a strategic sense that the Americans were unstoppable in their westward pressure and that it was better to forge an alliance than to lose a war. But for most native peoples, it was gradually becoming clear that an American victory portended a grim future.

PLACE EVENTS IN CONTEXT

What accounts for the brutality of the American war against Indians after 1777?

The French Alliance

On their own, the Americans could not have won the war, especially as pressure from hostile Indians increased. But the military context changed dramatically after the Americans' victory at Saratoga: In February 1778, France recognized the United States as an independent nation in the **Treaty of Amity and Commerce**, promising full military and commercial support. The French treasury injected desperately needed funds for the American war effort. Most crucially, the French navy now joined the American war, challenging British sea power while providing essential supplies and troop reinforcements from across the Atlantic.

Well before 1778, the French had been covertly providing Americans with cannons, muskets, gunpowder, and military advisers. For French authorities, the rebellion in the British colonies provided an ideal opportunity to strike a crippling blow against the British empire. A victory would detach the lucrative colonial trade from Britain and reorient it to France, while also providing France with military bases on the American mainland and supplies for its immensely profitable Caribbean colonies. Even an American defeat would be a strategic victory for France if it drained Britain of men and money and weakened the British empire.

With the French alliance, the American Revolution expanded beyond a war for the independence of thirteen British colonies. It now became another global war in the century-long struggle between the French and British empires. At the prodding of French diplomats, Spain entered the war in 1779, fighting battles along the Gulf of Mexico and competing with Britain for the alliance of Native American nations in the southeastern backcountry. The Netherlands entered the fighting in 1782, when they formally recognized the United States at the cost of launching the fourth Anglo-Dutch War. By the time the fighting spread from the Caribbean to Europe and Asia, the American Revolution had long since ceased to concern just one country or even one continent.

Treaty of Amity and Commerce
Treaty between the United States and France signed on February 6, 1778. Along with the treaty of alliance, it provided French military and financial aid for the rebellious colonies, and mutual trade agreements to promote a permanent alliance. The U.S. promised not to make a separate peace with Britain.

CONSIDER CAUSE AND EFFECT

Why did the battle of Saratoga convince the French to join the war?

QUICK REVIEW

How did a war between settlers and their British government expand to encompass native and European powers?

What persuaded British North American colonists to support independence?

What were the principal causes of the British defeat?

When France entered the war, some British officials thought it was time to abandon the fight. "We are far from an anticipated peace, because the bitterness of the rebels is too widespread, and in regions where we are masters the rebellious spirit is still in them," one troop commander observed. "The land is too large, and there are too many people. The more land we win, the weaker our army gets in the field." The commander of the British navy agreed, as did Lord North, the prime minister. But the king could not tolerate the thought of losing his North American colonies. He pushed for a new strategy focusing on the southern colonies, thought to be more reliably loyalist. He had little idea of the depth of anger that deadly guerrilla warfare would produce between loyalists and patriots. The king's plan was shrewd but desperate and ultimately unsuccessful.

Georgia and South Carolina

The new strategy called for British forces to abandon New England to focus on the South. Georgia and the Carolinas appeared to hold large numbers of loyalists, providing a base of popular support on which to build the British war effort. British leaders also counted on the region's large slave population to push rebellious white southerners back into the arms of the empire.

Georgia, the first target, fell easily at the end of December 1778 (**Map 7.4**). With most of the Continental army in the North, while the French were fighting in the West Indies, British troops had a free hand. A small army of soldiers occupied Savannah and Augusta, installing a new royal governor and loyalist assembly. The British organized twenty loyal militia units, and 1,400 Georgians swore an oath of allegiance to the king. A joint Franco-American force, which included hundreds of troops of color from the French Caribbean colony of Saint Domingue (later Haiti), tried to retake Savannah in the fall of 1779. They failed after a bloody series of battles. Britain's southern strategy was off to a promising start.

Next came South Carolina. The Continental army sent ten regiments to Charleston to defend the port city from attack by British troops under the command of General Henry Clinton, who had replaced Howe as commander in chief. For five weeks in early spring 1780, the British laid siege to the city. They took it in May 1780, capturing 3,300 American soldiers.

Clinton began offering freedom to slaves owned by rebellious whites. Several thousand escaped to Charleston. Untrained in formal warfare, they served as guides to the countryside and as laborers building defensive fortifications. Freed slaves with boat-piloting skills were particularly valuable in navigating the inland rivers of the southern colonies.

Clinton returned to New York after the fall of Charleston, leaving the job of pacifying the rest of South Carolina to General Charles Cornwallis and four thousand troops. A bold commander, Lord Cornwallis quickly chased out the remaining Continentals and established military rule over South Carolina. He purged rebels from government office and disarmed rebel militias. Exports of rice, South Carolina's main crop, resumed, and pardons were offered to Carolinians willing to take up arms for the British.

CHRONOLOGY

1778
- British take Savannah, Georgia.

1780
- British lay siege to Charleston, South Carolina.
- French army arrives in Newport, Rhode Island.
- British win battle of Camden.
- Benedict Arnold exposed as traitor.
- Americans win battle of King's Mountain.

1781
- British forces invade Virginia.
- French blockade Chesapeake Bay.
- Cornwallis surrenders at Yorktown.

1783
- Treaty of Paris ends war.

How did the military objectives of each side shape the course of the war's early years? | How did the war transform the home front? | How did the American Revolution become a war among continental and global powers? | **What were the principal causes of the British defeat?** | Conclusion: Why did the British lose the American Revolution?

193

MAP 7.4 ▲ The War in the South, 1780–1781

After taking Charleston in May 1780, the British advanced into South and North Carolina, touching off a bloody civil war. An American loss at Camden was followed by victories at King's Mountain and Cowpens. The British then invaded Virginia but were trapped and overpowered at Yorktown in the fall of 1781 by joint French and American forces.

In August, American troops arrived from the North to strike back at Cornwallis. General Gates, the hero of Saratoga, led three thousand troops in an assault on Camden, South Carolina (see Map 7.4). Many of Gates's soldiers were newly recruited militiamen; they panicked at the sight of the approaching British cavalry and fled. When regiment leaders tried to regroup the next day, only seven hundred soldiers mustered for duty. The battle of Camden was a devastating defeat. American prospects had rarely looked worse.

Treason and Guerrilla Warfare

Britain's southern strategy was succeeding in part because of information about American troop movements provided by an American officer, Benedict Arnold. The hero of several American battles, Arnold was a vain and insecure man who never felt

What persuaded British North American colonists to support independence?

properly appreciated. Sometime in 1779, he opened secret negotiations with General Clinton in New York, trading information for money and hinting that he could deliver an even greater prize. When General Washington made him commander of West Point, a new fort on the Hudson River north of New York City, Arnold's plan crystallized. West Point controlled the Hudson; its capture by the British might finally lead them to victory.

Arnold's plot was foiled when American troops captured a spy carrying plans of the fort's defense. News of Arnold's treason created shock waves. Arnold symbolized the patriots' worst fears about themselves: driven by greed and self-interest, like the war profiteers; willing to abandon war aims, like that of turncoat southern Tories; apt to panic, like the terrified soldiers at Camden. Instead of demoralizing Americans, however, Arnold's treachery revived their commitment to the patriot cause. By demonizing Arnold, Americans could distance themselves from his deceitful conduct. His treachery renewed patriotism at a low point in the war.

Shock over Gates's defeat at Camden and Arnold's treason revitalized rebel support in western South Carolina. Cornwallis considered the area pacified and loyal. He was soon proven wrong, as the southern backcountry became the site of vicious guerrilla warfare. Fierce rebel militias confronted British-organized loyalist militia units throughout the region. In hit-and-run attacks, both sides burned and ravaged not only opponents' property but also the property of anyone claiming to be neutral. In South Carolina, some six thousand men became active partisans and fought at least twenty-six engagements. Guerrilla warfare soon spread to Georgia and North Carolina. Both sides committed atrocities and plundered property, leaving lasting scars among the population and the landscape.

Britain's southern strategy depended on loyalist support to hold reconquered territory as Cornwallis's army moved north. The backcountry civil war rendered this assumption false. The British might continue holding a few fortified outposts along the coast, but they could not conquer the vast countryside. The Americans won few major battles, but they succeeded by harassing British forces and preventing them from foraging for food. Cornwallis moved the war into North Carolina in the fall of 1780 because the North Carolinians were supplying the South Carolina rebels with arms and men (see Map 7.4). Then news of a massacre of loyalist units by 1,400 frontier riflemen at the battle of King's Mountain, in western South Carolina, sent him hurrying back. Without a secure base of loyalist support, the British were stretched too thin to hold even two colonies. How could they hope to hold a continent?

CONSIDER CAUSE AND EFFECT
What factors most account for the failure of Britain's southern strategy?

Surrender at Yorktown

By early 1781, Britain's hopes to hold its thirteen colonies were dimming. The brutal defeat at King's Mountain was quickly followed by a second major loss in South Carolina in January 1781. Cornwallis headed to North Carolina and then to Virginia, where he captured Williamsburg in June. A raiding party proceeded to Charlottesville, the seat of government, capturing members of the Virginia assembly but not Governor Thomas Jefferson, who fled just minutes before the British soldiers arrived. These victories led Cornwallis to believe that his campaign of raids in Virginia was succeeding. With some four thousand escaped slaves swelling the size of his army, a newly confident Cornwallis marched to Yorktown, near the mouth of the Chesapeake Bay. As the general waited for reinforcements by sea, smallpox and typhus began to set in among the black recruits.

| How did the military objectives of each side shape the course of the war's early years? | How did the war transform the home front? | How did the American Revolution become a war among continental and global powers? | **What were the principal causes of the British defeat?** | Conclusion: Why did the British lose the American Revolution? |

◀ **Lafayette at Yorktown, with James Armistead** In 1781, James Armistead, an enslaved Virginian, volunteered for service with Lafayette. During the Yorktown campaign, he played a daring role as a spy, feeding the British misinformation and bringing crucial intelligence to American forces. Lafayette helped secure Armistead's freedom after the war; his admiration of African Americans' wartime bravery pushed him to embrace abolitionism. Armistead later changed his name to James Armistead Lafayette. The Picture Art Collection/Alamy Stock Photo.

At this critical moment, the French-American alliance came into play. French regiments commanded by the Comte de Rochambeau had joined General Washington in Newport, Rhode Island, in mid-1780. In early 1781, warships under the Comte de Grasse had sailed from France to the West Indies. Washington, Rochambeau, and de Grasse now fixed their attention on Chesapeake Bay, and on Cornwallis's vulnerable army. De Grasse's fleet arrived at the mouth of the bay ahead of the British troop ships from New York. After a five-day battle, the French navy gained control of the Virginia coast, cutting off British reinforcements. Cornwallis's army was trapped.

With enemy forces at their front, and water at their back, General Cornwallis and his 7,500 troops faced a combined French and American army of 16,000 at the **battle of Yorktown**. For twelve days, the Franco-American force bombarded the British fortifications at Yorktown, as French military engineers methodically directed the siege of the British position. Cornwallis ran low on food and ammunition. He began to expel the black recruits, some of them sick and dying. A Hessian officer serving under Cornwallis later criticized this British action as disgraceful: "We had used them to good advantage, and set them free, and now, with fear and trembling, they had to face the reward of their cruel masters." Finally, Cornwallis was forced to confront the inevitable: Neither victory nor escape was possible. He surrendered on October 19, 1781. For all intents and purposes, American independence had been won.

battle of Yorktown
October 1781 battle that sealed American victory. French and American troops and the French navy trapped the British at army Yorktown, Virginia.

Siege of Yorktown, 1781

The Losers and the Winners

The surrender at Yorktown ended British hopes of keeping the thirteen rebellious colonies in the empire. Nonetheless, two more years of fighting continued across the continent and around the globe. Frontier areas in Kentucky, Ohio, and Illinois blazed with battles pitting American forces against Native American nations fighting to maintain control of their homelands. Meanwhile, war between France and Great Britain continued in the Caribbean and India, while the Spanish—who had joined the war alongside the French—fought to regain the strategic fort of Gibraltar, at the mouth of the Mediterranean Sea. The Netherlands, which had also entered the war against Britain, fought in Europe and India.

What persuaded British North American colonists to support independence?

The **Treaty of Paris**, also called the **Peace of Paris**, was two years in the making. Commissioners from America and Britain worked out the ten articles of peace, while a side treaty signed by Britain, France, Spain, and the Netherlands sealed related deals. **(See "Spotlight: Did France and Spain Accomplish Their Objectives in the American Revolution?" on page 198.)** The first article went to the heart of the cause: "His Britannic Majesty acknowledges the said United States to be free Sovereign and independent States." It was a catastrophic defeat for Britain, and a devastating personal blow for King George III. It marked a new era in the history of the British empire. Another article set the western boundary of the United States at the Mississippi River, overturning the boundaries that had been laid out in the Quebec Act of 1774 (see chapter 6), and blithely ignoring the territorial claims of Britain's Native American allies. Still another provision prohibited the British from "carrying away any Negroes or other property of the American inhabitants," although they, too, had fought as loyal subjects of the British empire. The treaty was signed on September 3, 1783.

If most white Americans celebrated news of the treaty, the thousands of self-liberated blacks who had joined the British under promise of freedom were horrified. South Carolinian Boston King, a refugee in New York City, recalled that the provision prohibiting evacuation of black refugees "filled us with inexpressible anguish and terror." King and others pressed the British commander in New York, Sir Guy Carleton, to honor pre-treaty British promises. Carleton obliged, issuing certificates of freedom for all refugees under British protection for more than a year—nullifying their status as "property" to be returned. More than four thousand blacks sailed out of New York for Nova Scotia, Boston King and his family among them. As Carleton coolly explained to a protesting George Washington, "the Negroes in question . . . I found free when I arrived at New York, I had therefore no right, as I thought, to prevent their going to any part of the world they thought proper." British commanders in Savannah and Charleston followed Carleton's lead and aided the emigration of perhaps ten thousand blacks from the United States.

> "As one American told the Shawnee people, 'Your Fathers the English have made Peace with use for themselves, but forgot you their Children, who Fought with them. . .'"

Emancipation had never been a war goal of Great Britain, whose colonies in the Caribbean ran on brutalizing slave labor. The British policy promising freedom to slaves of rebellious planters aimed to destabilize the patriot cause and gain necessary manpower. Had the British won the war, they might have tried to reenslave insurgent blacks to restore the profitable plantation economy of the South. For their part, slaves viewed British army camps as sites of refuge, not figuring on the devastations of epidemic diseases and food shortages. Although some came to venerate the British monarchy as a harbinger of liberty, for many others their loyalty to the British empire was essentially transactional.

The Treaty of Paris said nothing about Native American territorial rights. It was a great betrayal of Great Britain's Indian allies, who had played an essential role in the war but none in the treaty negotiations. As one American told the Shawnee people, "Your Fathers the English have made Peace with us for themselves, but forgot you their Children, who Fought with them, and neglected you like Bastards." The boundary lines drawn on maps in Europe did not change facts on the ground, however. Native American nations remained in firm control of their traditional homelands in the vast territory stretching from the Appalachian Mountains to the

Treaty (Peace) of Paris, 1783 September 3, 1783, treaty between the U.S. and Britain that ended the Revolutionary War. The treaty acknowledged America's independence, set its boundaries, and promised the quick withdrawal of British troops from American soil. It failed to recognize Indians as players in the conflict.

TRACE CHANGE OVER TIME
How and why did the British approach to slavery evolve over the course of its involvement in the South?

| How did the military objectives of each side shape the course of the war's early years? | How did the war transform the home front? | How did the American Revolution become a war among continental and global powers? | **What were the principal causes of the British defeat?** | Conclusion: Why did the British lose the American Revolution? |

197

Did France and Spain Accomplish Their Objectives in the American Revolution?

News of the decisive British defeat at Yorktown in late 1781 caused Britain's prime minister, Lord North, to stagger as though wounded and exclaim, "Oh, God, it is all over!" But in truth, it was far from over. A full year elapsed before the elements of a formal peace treaty could be worked out, and an additional year passed before the treaty was signed. The delay occurred in part because several European countries besides Britain had stakes in the war that had no connection to American independence.

As Europe's most powerful monarchy, the French crown had little sympathy for a republican revolution, even in the British colonies. France had entered the war mainly to weaken Britain, its traditional enemy. By snatching Britain's mainland colonies from its empire, French officials hoped to restore their imperial position after the devastating defeat in the Seven Years' War. An independent United States allied to France would not just weaken the British empire, however; it would also strengthen the French. France's primary colonial interests lay with their astonishingly lucrative, sugar-producing Caribbean colonies. (Recall that in the treaty negotiations of 1763 they had given up all of Canada in order to keep the island of Guadeloupe.) French officials believed an independent United States would provide bases for the French navy to support their Caribbean colonies, and provisions to feed Caribbean slaves in times of war and peace.

Spain joined the war in the form of a secret alliance with France in 1779. With vast colonies in the Americas,

▲ A British print of 1783 satirizes the diplomats who negotiated the Peace of Paris. The Indian declares, "I call this a free and Independent P—s" while the Frenchman (far right) gloats that "tho' we have wrangled you out of America you freely make P—s with us." Whom does the Indian figure represent? What is the point of view of this cartoon? Library of Congress, LC-DIG-ppmsca-10740.

Spanish officials abhorred the idea of an independent republic in North America. Nonetheless, they could not resist the opportunity to weaken the British empire, and

What persuaded British North American colonists to support independence?

most important, to oust the British from Gibraltar, a tiny three-square-mile territory dominated by a massive rock and situated at the southern end of the Iberian Peninsula. From this strategic location, Britain controlled the passage between the Atlantic and the Mediterranean, disrupting Spanish trade. Spain launched a siege that lasted more than three years and tied up scores of British ships and thousands of troops, military assets that were thus not available for the war in America. Another important interest for Spain was control of navigation rights on the Mississippi River. Since 1763, Spain had held the lands west of the river, and it hoped to gain the eastern bank—and thus fully control all navigation of that major river—as a prize for its contribution to defeating Britain.

The Continental Congress entrusted three distinguished Americans to negotiate the peace treaty. Benjamin Franklin, John Adams, and John Jay considered independence as the precondition for the talks to begin, so they were taken aback when the British negotiator showed up with credentials that pointedly addressed them as "the Commissioners of the Colonies." A month later, updated credentials referenced the three as representatives "of the Thirteen United States of America," a more satisfactory acknowledgment of their new standing. In September 1782, peace talks began in earnest. Lord Shelburne, Britain's new prime minister, conceded American independence and set his goal as the maintenance of favored trading status with the new country. He saw more clearly than his king that, although Britain's political dominance over its colonies had now ended, economic dominance might replace it.

The congress instructed its three diplomats to consult France at every step of the negotiation with Britain, a condition insisted on by the French minister to the United States. The 1778 treaty of alliance between France and the United States specifically stipulated that neither party would make an independent peace. But Jay and Adams had deep suspicions of the motives of the French foreign minister, the Count of Vergennes. They feared, with good reason, that Vergennes planned on placing their nation's western boundary some distance east of the Mississippi River, to meet the demands of Spain and preserve the United States in a state of dependence on France. So the Americans ignored their instructions and secretly negotiated a separate peace with Britain.

By January 1783, France, Britain, and Spain had produced their own treaties, involving lands in India, Africa, and the Mediterranean. In September of that year, all the treaties were officially approved and signed. Franklin wrote to a friend in Massachusetts, "We are now Friends with England and with all Mankind. May we never see another War! for in my Opinion, there never was a good War, or a bad Peace."

Questions for Analysis

SUMMARIZE THE ARGUMENT: What was at stake for France and Spain in the American Revolution? Why did they support American independence? How were those goals reflected in the Treaty of 1783?

RECOGNIZE VIEWPOINTS: Why did American diplomats ignore their instructions and their treaty obligations to negotiate a separate peace with Britain?

CONSIDER THE CONTEXT: Many Indian tribes fought valiantly with their British allies in the Revolution. Why did they not participate in the treaty making in Paris? How was their strategic position affected by the outcome of the Treaty of 1783?

| How did the military objectives of each side shape the course of the war's early years? | How did the war transform the home front? | How did the American Revolution become a war among continental and global powers? | **What were the principal causes of the British defeat?** | Conclusion: Why did the British lose the American Revolution? |

199

Mississippi River; the Treaty of Paris brought no peace to those regions. "As we were not partys," warned a Creek leader, "so we are determined to pay no attention to the Manner in which the British Negotiators has drawn out the Lines." If the colonists had won their struggle for independence from Britain, Native Americans would continue fighting an ongoing war for their own independence from American settler encroachments for years to come.

With the treaty finally signed, the British began evacuating New York, Charleston, and Savannah, a process complicated by the sheer numbers involved—soldiers, loyalists, and escaped slaves by the thousands. In New York City, more than 27,000 soldiers and 30,000 loyalists sailed on hundreds of ships for England in the fall of 1783. In a final act of mischief, the losing side raised the British flag at the southern tip of Manhattan, cut the ropes used to hoist it, greased the flagpole, and sailed away.

QUICK REVIEW

What factors were most critical to the British defeat in the American Revolution?

Conclusion: Why did the British lose the American Revolution?

The British began the war for America convinced they could not lose. They had the best-trained army and navy in the world; they knew the landscape; their Native American allies dominated the backcountry; and they easily captured every port city of consequence in America. A majority of colonists were either neutral or loyal to the crown. Why, then, did the Americans win?

Difficult supply lines were one continuing problem. British forces depended on a steady stream of ships from across the Atlantic Ocean, and insecurity about food helps explain their reluctance to pursue the Continental army aggressively. A second obstacle was their continual misuse of loyalist energies. Any plan to pacify the colonies required the cooperation of the loyalists, but the British repeatedly left them to the mercy of vengeful rebels.

French intervention also explains the British defeat. Even before the formal alliance, French artillery, ammunition, and money proved vital to the Continental army. After 1780, the French army fought alongside the Americans, and the French navy made the Yorktown victory possible. Finally, the British abdicated civil power in the colonies in 1775 and 1776, when royal officials fled to safety, and they never regained it. The basic British goal—to turn back the clock to imperial rule—receded into impossibility as the war dragged on.

The Revolution profoundly disrupted the lives of all Americans. It was a war for colonial independence from Britain, to be sure, but it was also more. It was a global

What persuaded British North American colonists to support independence?

war among Europe's most powerful empires. For Native Americans, it was a central event in their ongoing struggle to retain control of their territories. For the former British colonists, it was also a social revolution. It required men and women to think about politics and the legitimacy of authority. The rhetoric employed to justify the war against Britain put the words *liberty*, *tyranny*, *slavery*, *independence*, and *equality* into common usage. These terms carried far deeper meanings than a mere complaint over taxation without representation. The Revolution unleashed a dynamic of equality and liberty that was largely unintended and unwanted by many of the political leaders of 1776. But that dynamic emerged as a potent force in American life in the decades to come.

| How did the military objectives of each side shape the course of the war's early years? | How did the war transform the home front? | How did the American Revolution become a war among continental and global powers? | What were the principal causes of the British defeat? | **Conclusion: Why did the British lose the American Revolution?** |

201

STEP 1 — EXPLAIN WHY IT MATTERS

Put your reading into practice. Identify each term below, and then explain why it matters in U.S. history.

TERM	WHO OR WHAT & WHEN	WHY IT MATTERS
Second Continental Congress (p. 174)		
Continental army (p. 174)		
battle of Bunker Hill (p. 175)		
Common Sense (p. 175)		
Declaration of Independence (p. 178)		
battle of Long Island (p. 180)		
Ladies Association (p. 182)		
loyalists (p. 182)		
battle of Oriskany (p. 189)		
battle of Saratoga (p. 189)		
Treaty of Amity and Commerce (p. 192)		
battle of Yorktown (p. 196)		
Treaty (Peace) of Paris, 1783 (p. 197)		

STEP 2 — MOVE BEYOND THE BASICS

To demonstrate a more advanced understanding, describe the most important turning points in the war and why they mattered.

Period	Key Events	Major Battles/Victories
June 1775–December 1776		
January 1777–February 1778		
March 1778–1783		

STEP 3 — PUT IT ALL TOGETHER

Now, try to explain the big picture. Remember to use specific examples from the chapter in your answers.

DECLARING INDEPENDENCE

- Why were so many Americans divided about the question of independence from Britain?

- What factors contributed to the decision by the Continental Congress to declare independence in July 1776?

THE FIRST TWO YEARS OF WAR

- What challenges did the Americans face in the first year of war? How successfully did they meet them?

- What caused the French to ally with the United States, and how did the alliance change the course of the war?

- What were the Native Americans' goals in the war, and what impact did they have on its course?

AMERICAN VICTORY

- Why did the British switch to the southern strategy? Why did it fail?

- Is it more accurate to say that the Americans won the Revolutionary War or that the British lost it? Why?

LOOKING BACKWARD, LOOKING AHEAD

- When did the chain of events that culminated in the establishment of an independent United States begin? In 1763? In 1776? In 1783? At another date? Present evidence to support your answer.

- What challenges did the United States face as it emerged victorious from the Revolutionary War?

STEP 4 — CONNECT THESE EVENTS

How did the Declaration of Independence in 1776 change the war's objectives, strategy, and character?

STEP 5 — CONNECT TO THE PRESENT

What distinguishes a rebellion from a revolution? Can you think of any recent historical events that have similarities to the American Revolution?

8

BUILDING A REPUBLIC
1775–1789

What led to the formulation and ratification of the U.S. Constitution? Chapter 8 explores the momentous challenges the United States confronted after the Revolution. It examines the process that led to the abandonment of the Articles of Confederation and the adoption of the Constitution.

This chapter will explore the following questions:

- What kind of government did the Articles of Confederation create?
- How was republican government implemented?
- Why did the Articles of Confederation fail?
- How did the Constitution change the nation's form of government?
- Why did so many Americans object to the Constitution?
- Conclusion: What was the "republican remedy"?

AN AMERICAN STORY

James Madison graduated from Princeton College in 1771, still undecided about his future. Returning to his father's plantation in Virginia held little appeal: He preferred books to farming. Fluent in Greek, Latin, French, and mathematics, he enjoyed reading and discussing great thinkers, both ancient and modern. He stayed in Princeton as long as he could.

Still adrift, he returned home in 1772. He studied law, but it held little appeal. While Madison was struggling for direction in Virginia, powerful political winds were swirling throughout the continent. A trip north to deliver his brother to boarding school in Philadelphia put Madison in the eye of the storm just as the spectacular news broke: Britain had shut down the port of Boston.

Turbulent protests over the Coercive Acts turned the aimless young man into a committed revolutionary. Back in Virginia, Madison joined his father on the committee of public safety. He took up musket practice but proved a poor shot. Realizing that his study of political theory might prove useful, he gained election in 1776 to the Virginia Convention, a new Revolutionary assembly. The convention's main task was to hammer out a state constitution with republican innovations such as frequent elections and limited executive power. Young and shy, Madison stayed on the sidelines at first, but Virginia's elder statesmen noted his thoughtful contributions. When Madison lost reelection, he was appointed to the governor's council, where he spent the next two years.

In 1780, Madison served in the Continental Congress as a representative of Virginia. His years in Philadelphia acquainted him with a network of leading revolutionaries and the challenges of wartime governance. Madison flourished in this setting. His negotiating skills broke the long deadlock over the ratification of the Articles of Confederation by arranging for the cession of Virginia's vast western land claims, soon called the Northwest Territory. For all his skill, however, Madison's congressional service proved frustrating. He came to believe that the central government lacked essential powers, chief among them the power to tax.

Madison returned to the Virginia assembly in 1784, but he did not retreat to the point of view held by other state politicians. The economic hardships created by the heavy postwar tax burdens that were rapidly undermining the new United States—they led to a full-fledged rebellion in Massachusetts—spurred Madison to pursue a stronger national government.

Madison helped organize a convention in May 1787, where delegates created an entirely new and much stronger national government. True to form, Madison spent the months before the Philadelphia convention feverishly studying the great thinkers he'd read in college, searching for clues about republican government. His lifelong passion for study, seasoned by a dozen years of political experience, paid off handsomely. Madison was one of the most important figures behind the new United States Constitution.

By the end of the 1780s, James Madison had mastered the dynamics of local, state, confederation, and, finally, national politics. He even observed the first U.S.-Indian treaty negotiations carried out in 1784. Not yet forty, he'd transformed himself from an aimless and solitary young man into one of the leading political actors of Revolutionary America. His career under the new U.S. Constitution had only just begun.

▼ **Articles of Confederation** This title page of a pamphlet of the Articles of Confederation printed in 1777 emphasizes a "Union between the States," and lists each one. The 1787 U.S. Constitution, which replaced the Articles of Confederation, begins differently: as an agreement among "We the People." Granger Collection, New York.

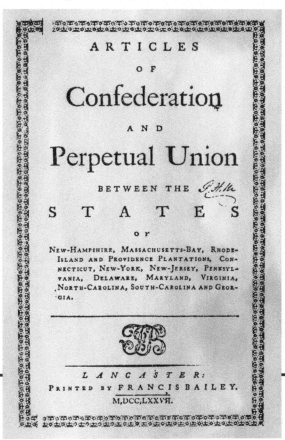

ARTICLES
OF
Confederation
AND
Perpetual Union
BETWEEN THE
STATES
OF

NEW-HAMPSHIRE, MASSACHUSETTS-BAY, RHODE-ISLAND AND PROVIDENCE PLANTATIONS, CONNECTICUT, NEW-YORK, NEW-JERSEY, PENESYL-VANIA, DELAWARE, MARYLAND, VIRGINIA, NORTH-CAROLINA, SOUTH-CAROLINA AND GEORGIA.

LANCASTER:
PRINTED BY FRANCIS BAILEY.
M,DCC,LXXVII.

What kind of government did the Articles of Confederation create?

CHRONOLOGY

1777
– Articles of Confederation sent to states.

1781
– Articles of Confederation ratified.
– Executive departments created.

Articles of Confederation
The written document defining the structure of the government during and after the Revolution. Under the Articles, the Union was a confederation of equal states, with no president and with limited powers, existing mainly to foster a common defense.

Creating and approving a written plan of government for the new confederation took five years, as delegates and states sought agreement on fundamental principles. With monarchy rejected, where did sovereignty lie? What was the nature of representation? Who held the power to tax? Because the thirteen states could not agree on answers to these questions, the Articles of Confederation were surprisingly difficult to implement. Once the Articles were ratified and the war began drawing to a close, the congressional politics faded in importance relative to politics in the individual states.

Confederation and Taxation

Only after declaring independence did the Continental Congress turn its attention to writing a document specifying its powers and the authority on which they were grounded. Delegates agreed about the key government powers: pursuing war and peace, conducting foreign relations, regulating trade, and running a postal service. Beyond that, however, consensus proved elusive. Because the congress's first priority was the war, it took a year to reach agreement on the Articles of Confederation.

Having launched a revolution against central imperial authority and unrepresentative taxation policies, the congress was suspicious of both. As a result, the new compact between the states did not provide for a national executive (that is, a president) or a judiciary. The congress, consisting of delegates selected annually by state legislatures, was the sole governing agency. Much like today's United Nations, each state had a single vote. Delegates representing the states faced term limits of three years to ensure frequent rotation. Routine decisions required a simple majority of seven states, whereas momentous decisions, such as declaring war, required a two-thirds majority of nine. To approve or amend the Articles required the unanimous consent of the states—giving any state veto power over changes. Finally, the Articles gave the national government no power of direct taxation.

Congress's inability to raise revenue through taxation was a crippling weakness. All governments—especially those fighting a war—require money. To finance the Revolutionary War, the confederation congress first issued interest-bearing bonds purchased by French and Dutch bankers as well as middling to wealthy Americans. But revenue was necessary to repay these loans. Other routine government functions required money too: Trade regulation required salaried customs officers; a postal system required postmen, horses and wagons, and well-maintained roads; the western lands required surveyors; and Indian diplomacy (or war) added further large costs.

The Articles of Confederation provided a delicate two-step solution. The congress would request money to be paid into the common treasury, and each state legislature would then levy taxes within its borders to pay the requisition. The Articles called for state contributions assessed in proportion to the property values, so that populous states paid more than did sparsely populated states. Because only state legislatures could pass actual tax bills, the Articles upheld the Revolution's principle of taxation only by direct representation. The essential flaw, however, was the absence of any mechanism compelling states to pay.

A weak confederation government was exactly what many people wanted in the late 1770s. A league of states with rotating personnel, no executive branch, no power

What kind of government did the Articles of Confederation create?

of direct taxation, and a requirement of unanimity for any major change would keep the dangers of centralized government authority in check. But had the congress gone too far in restricting its own powers? Ominously, ratification itself required unanimous agreement, and even that proved difficult to secure.

The Problem of Western Lands

The primary obstacle to ratification lay in the west. According to their original colonial charters, several colonies (now states) had no western boundary; they extended across the Appalachian Mountains all the way to the Mississippi River, if not beyond. These old charters were vague and conflicted with each other, with the land claims of other European empires, and with the sovereignty of Native Americans. Most vexingly of all, from the perspective of the unity of the thirteen states, only eight states claimed western land. Disagreements about these western land claims delayed ratification of the Articles for years, forcing the United States to wage the Revolution without an official constitution. Would future land sales between the Appalachian Mountains and the Mississippi River benefit the states with claims or the entire nation? The five states without claims insisted that those western lands must be granted to the national domain (**Map 8.1**). As one Rhode Island delegate said, "The western world opens an amazing prospect as a national fund; it is equal to our debt."

The eight land-claiming states were ready to sign the Articles of Confederation in 1777. Three states without claims—Rhode Island, Pennsylvania, and New Jersey—eventually capitulated and signed, "not from a Conviction of the Equality and Justness of it," said a New Jersey delegate, "but merely from an absolute Necessity there was of complying to save the Continent." But Delaware and Maryland held out, insisting on a national domain policy. In 1779, the states finally compromised: Any land a state voluntarily relinquished would become the national domain. When James Madison and Thomas Jefferson ceded Virginia's huge land claim in 1781, the Articles of Confederation were at last unanimously approved—barely six months before the battle of Yorktown.

The controversy over western lands demonstrated the deep divisions among the thirteen states. The temporary unity of purpose inspired by the war covered yawning cracks in the new confederation.

UNDERSTAND POINTS OF VIEW

Why was the issue of western land so important to Delaware and Maryland that their delegates refused to sign the Articles of Confederation?

Running the New Government

No fanfare greeted the new government's long-delayed inauguration. The congress continued to sputter along. Lack of a quorum—defined as two men from seven states, or fourteen men—often hampered day-to-day business. State legislatures were slow to select delegates. Many officials preferred to devote their energies to state governments when the congress seemed so ineffective.

It did not help that the congress had no permanent home. During the war, when the British army threatened Philadelphia, the congress relocated to small Pennsylvania towns such as Lancaster and York and then to Baltimore. After hostilities ceased, the congress moved from Trenton to Princeton to Annapolis to New York City. Many delegates were reluctant to travel far, especially if they had wives and children. Consequently, some of the most committed delegates were young bachelors, such as James Madison, or men in their fifties and sixties who no longer had responsibility for their children, such as Samuel Adams.

CONSIDER CAUSE AND EFFECT

Why did American political leaders tend to focus on state and local affairs, rather than national ones, after the war's end?

How was republican government implemented?	Why did the Articles of Confederation fail?	How did the Constitution change the nation's form of government?	Why did so many Americans object to the Constitution?	Conclusion: What was the "republican remedy"?

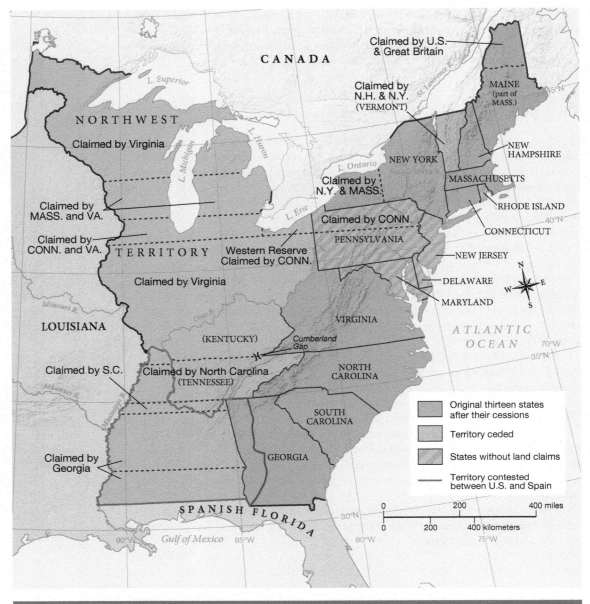

MAP ACTIVITY

MAP 8.1 ▲ Western Land Claims, ca. 1783 Parts of the region between the Appalachian Mountains and the Mississippi River were claimed by various Native American peoples, who controlled most of the area; by the United States; by eight of thirteen states; and by the Spanish and British empires. The United States needed that land—and the revenue its sale would generate—to have any hope of survival.

READING THE MAP: How did the various native, U.S., and European land claims intersect? Where did they intersect most significantly?

CONNECTIONS: In what ways did British, Spanish, and Native American claims to the west threaten the U.S. hold on the region? What were the United States' most significant challenges to retaining the territory?

In 1781, the congress created executive departments of war, finance, and foreign affairs to handle purely administrative functions. When the department heads were ambitious—most notably Robert Morris, a wealthy Philadelphia merchant who served as superintendent of finance—they exercised considerable executive power.

What kind of government did the Articles of Confederation create?

The Articles of Confederation had deliberately refrained from setting up an executive branch, but necessity was causing one to come into existence.

QUICK REVIEW

What were the confederation government's most severe limitations?

republicanism
A political philosophy founded on the principle of government by the consent of the people. It embraced representative institutions (as opposed to monarchy) and required a citizenry willing to put the public good ahead of its private interests.

How was republican government implemented?

Because of the decentralized nature of the confederation government, the thirteen states became the arena for testing various republican innovations. Each state implemented a constitution and determined voter qualifications, expanding suffrage for those who met property requirements and drawing new exclusionary lines. As the states committed themselves to republican ideals, they came face-to-face with the problem of slavery, an issue that would plague the nation for decades to come.

The State Constitutions

In rejecting monarchy, Americans embraced the founding principle of republicanism. Republicanism meant different things to different people, however. For some, it implied a system of government led by virtuous citizens capable of putting the public good above private interests. For others, it signified direct democracy, with nothing standing in the way of the people's will. Drawing on the examples of ancient Greek history, many Americans believed that republics could succeed only on a small scale, when they remained close to the people they served. For everyone, republicanism meant that governments were grounded on the consent of the governed, and therefore required some electoral system and representative institutions.

It fell to the individual states to put this vague but powerful principle into practice. In May 1776, the congress recommended that all states draw up constitutions based on "the authority of the people." By 1778, ten states had done so, and three more (Connecticut, Massachusetts, and Rhode Island) had updated their original colonial charters. All the new state constitutions rested on the principle that government required the consent of the governed. North Carolina's constitution of 1776, for instance, opened with the statement "That all political power is vested in and derived from the people only." Eleven states continued the colonial practice of a two-chamber assembly but augmented the powers of the lower house. Pennsylvania and Georgia abolished their upper house altogether, and most states limited the powers of the governor.

Real power thus resided with the lower houses—the ones most responsive to the will of majorities because annual elections and term limits guaranteed frequent rotation in office. If a representative displeased his constituents, they could vote him out of office in a matter of months. James Madison learned this lesson when he lost reelection to the Virginia assembly in 1777. Ever shy, he attributed the loss to his reluctance to socialize at taverns and glad-hand his constituents in the traditional Virginia style. His political posts from 1778 to 1787 all came by appointment, not popular election.

CHRONOLOGY

1776
- Declaration of Independence adopted.
- Virginia adopts state bill of rights.

1778
- State constitutions completed.

1780
- Pennsylvania institutes gradual emancipation.

1781
- Several Massachusetts slaves sue for freedom.

1783
- Massachusetts enfranchises taxpaying free blacks.

1784
- Gradual emancipation laws passed in Rhode Island and Connecticut.

1799
- Gradual emancipation law passed in New York.

1804
- Gradual emancipation law passed in New Jersey.

| How was republican government implemented? | Why did the Articles of Confederation fail? | How did the Constitution change the nation's form of government? | Why did so many Americans object to the Constitution? | Conclusion: What was the "republican remedy"? |

Six of the state constitutions included bills of rights—lists of individual liberties that government could not abridge. Virginia passed the first in June 1776. It asserted that "all men are by nature equally free and independent, and have certain inherent rights, of which, when they enter into a state of society, they cannot by any compact deprive or divest their posterity; namely, the enjoyment of life and liberty, with the means of acquiring and possessing property, and pursuing and obtaining happiness and safety." These inherent rights carried more specific rights to freedom of speech, freedom of the press, and trial by jury.

Who Are "the People"?

When the Continental Congress called for state constitutions based on "the authority of the people," or when the Virginia bill of rights granted "all men" certain rights, who did they mean by "the people"? Who were the citizens of this new country, and how far would the principle of democratic government extend? People answered these questions differently, but certain limits to political participation became clear through the 1770s.

Property constituted the first important limit. Nearly every state imposed property qualifications of some kind on voters and political candidates. In Maryland, candidates for governor had to possess the large sum of £5,000, while voters had to own fifty acres of land or £30. Pennsylvania, by far the most democratic state, extended the right to vote or hold office to any property taxpayer, large or small. Non-taxpayers were still excluded. According to the dominant political theory, only property owners possessed the necessary independence to make wise political choices. Are not propertyless men, asked John Adams, "too little acquainted with public affairs to form a right judgment, and too dependent upon other men to have a will of their own?"

> "'Every poor man has a life, a personal liberty, and a right to his earnings; and is in danger of being injured by government in a variety of ways.'"

Property qualifications probably disfranchised from one-quarter to one-half of adult white males in the United States. Not all of them accepted their nonvoter status quietly. One Maryland man wondered what was so special about being worth £30, his state's threshold for voting: "Every poor man has a life, a personal liberty, and a right to his earnings; and is in danger of being injured by government in a variety of ways." Others noted that propertyless men were fighting and dying in the Revolutionary War: Surely they had legitimate political concerns. A few radical voices challenged the notion that wealth correlated with good citizenship; indeed, some wondered if the opposite might be truer. But such ideas fell outside the mainstream. The writers of the new constitutions, themselves men of property, believed that the right to own and preserve property was a central principle of the Revolution.

Women's exclusion from voting was so ingrained that only a handful of well-placed women thought to question it. For them, the Revolution's proclamations of rights seemed to conflict with laws that barred married women from owning property—and the privileges that came with it. Abigail Adams wrote to her husband, John,

◀ **A Possible Voter in Essex County, New Jersey** Mrs. Annis Boudinot Stockton, widow of a New Jersey politician, frequently entertained members of the Continental Congress. George Washington became a close friend and long-term correspondent. The wealthy Mrs. Stockton would have been eligible to vote in state elections under New Jersey's unique enfranchisement of property-holding women. She died in 1801, before suffrage was redefined to become the exclusive right of males. Princeton University Art Museum/Art Resource, NY.

What kind of government did the Articles of Confederation create?

in 1782, "Even in the freest countrys our property is subject to the controul and disposal of our partners, to whom the Laws have given a sovereign Authority. Deprived of a voice in Legislation, obliged to submit to those Laws which are imposed upon us, is it not sufficient to make us indifferent to the publick Welfare?"

So powerful was the assumption that only men could vote, only three states bothered to specify that voters had to be male. The New Jersey state constitution of 1776 enfranchised all free inhabitants worth more than £50, language that in theory opened the door to free blacks and unmarried women who met the property requirement. (By law, married women's husbands held title to their property.) Sure enough, in the 1780s, small numbers of white women and some free blacks began to go to the polls. Little fanfare accompanied this radical shift, and historians have debated whether the law intentionally included unmarried women and blacks, or whether it was an oversight. But New Jersey was an exception: In most states, women and free blacks, no matter how big or small their numbers, never gained the right to vote.

However limited its immediate impact on voting rights, the Revolution opened the door to previously unthinkable possibilities. John Adams urged the framers of the Massachusetts constitution to stick with traditional property qualifications. If suffrage is brought up for debate, he warned, "there will be no end of it. New claims will arise; women will demand a vote; lads from twelve to twenty-one will think their rights not enough attended to; and every man who has not a farthing, will demand an equal voice with any other." These fears—or these hopes—would largely set the terms of political debate in the decades to come.

CONSIDER CAUSE AND EFFECT

To what extent did the republican ideology of the American Revolution affect the legal status of women according to the new state constitutions?

Equality and Slavery

In these various state bills of rights, the Revolution thrillingly proclaimed a set of natural freedoms for all individuals. And yet several hundred thousand slaves lived and toiled amidst the soaring rhetoric. British settlers had long seen slavery as a natural part of the social order. The various proclamations of rights, however, cast a harsh new light on the legitimacy of the institution.

The author of the Virginia bill of rights was George Mason, a planter who owned 118 slaves. When he wrote that "all men are by nature equally free and independent," Mason did not have slaves in mind. He was claiming that white Americans were the equals of the British and entitled to equal liberties. Other Virginia legislators, worried how their words might be interpreted, added a qualifying phrase: that all men "when they enter into a state of society" have inherent rights. As one legislator insisted, "Slaves, not being constituent members of our society, could never pretend to any benefit from such a maxim." One month later, the Declaration of Independence used nearly the same phrase about equality—this time without a modifying clause. Thomas Jefferson, its primary author, owned hundreds of slaves at the very moment he penned those words. Two state constitutions, Pennsylvania and Massachusetts, also asserted that all men were created equal. In Massachusetts, one town suggested rewording the draft constitution to read "All men, whites and blacks, are born free and equal." Stated this bluntly, the claim went too far. The suggestion fell on deaf ears. **(See "Spotlight: A Slave Sues for Her Freedom" on page 212.)**

The obvious contradiction between the Revolution's egalitarian ideals and the widespread existence of slavery brought new attention to the morality of slaveholding, and threatened to destabilize the institution. Often, enslaved blacks led the challenge. In 1777, several Massachusetts slaves petitioned for their "natural & unalienable right to that freedom which the great Parent of the Universe hath bestowed equally on all mankind." They asked for freedom for their children at age twenty-one and were turned down. In 1779, similar petitions in Connecticut and New Hampshire met with no success. Seven Massachusetts free men, including the mariner brothers Paul and John Cuffe, refused to

| How was republican government implemented? | Why did the Articles of Confederation fail? | How did the Constitution change the nation's form of government? | Why did so many Americans object to the Constitution? | Conclusion: What was the "republican remedy"? |

A Slave Sues for Her Freedom

The stirring language about liberty, equality, and freedom that inspired revolutionaries in the 1770s began to appear in many state constitutions in the 1780s. Few whites seemed to notice the implications it might have on the institution of slavery.

Fewer than four thousand slaves lived in Massachusetts—less than 2 percent of the population. State law had long allowed slaves to bring lawsuits against whites. Before 1780, some thirty Massachusetts slaves had sued for freedom, but their cases had turned on individual circumstances, such as an owner's unfulfilled promise to emancipate. Then, amidst the revolutionary enthusiasm, a new state constitution of 1780 boldly declared: "all men are born free and equal." Although its framers had little intention of outlawing slavery, the new constitution opened the door to legal challenges to the institution. The first such case was brought by Elizabeth Freeman, known as "Mum Bett," a slave living in the Massachusetts town of Sheffield.

Born of African parents in the early 1740s, Freeman grew up as a slave in Claverack, New York. At some point, she and her sister were sold to Colonel John Ashley of Sheffield, Massachusetts. A town tax list of 1771 shows Ashley as the richest man in Sheffield and owner of five slaves. He was a supporter of the Revolution.

In 1773, Freeman was, according to one report, "keepin' still and mindin' things" while she served refreshments to a dozen men meeting with Colonel Ashley to draft anti-British resolutions. The first read, "Resolved, That mankind in a state of nature are equal, free, and independent of each other, and have a right to the undisturbed enjoyment of their lives, their liberty and property." Their discussion did not escape Freeman's notice.

One day, Mrs. Ashley became enraged with Freeman's sister and heaved a hot kitchen shovel at her. Freeman

▲ After winning her freedom suit, Elizabeth Freeman worked for the family of her lawyer, Theodore Sedgwick. A Sedgwick son later wrote, "If there could be a practical refutation of the imagined superiority of our race to hers, the life and character of this woman would afford that refutation. She had . . . an air of command which conferred a degree of dignity." Portrait of Elizabeth "Mumbet" Freeman (c. 1742–1829), 1811 (w/c on ivory)/ Sedgwick, Susan Anne Livingston Riley (fl. 1811)/ MASSACHUSETTS HISTORICAL SOCIETY/© Massachusetts Historical Society, Boston, MA, USA/Bridgeman Images.

pay taxes on the grounds that they could not vote and so were not represented. The Cuffe brothers went to jail in 1780 for tax evasion, but their petition to the Massachusetts legislature led to the extension of suffrage to taxpaying free blacks in 1783.

Another strategy for slaves to claim their freedom was to sue in court. In 1781, an enslaved woman named Elizabeth Freeman (also known as Mum Bett) won her freedom suit in a Massachusetts court, basing her case on the just-passed state constitution that declared "all men are born free and equal." Another Massachusetts slave, Quok Walker, charged his master with assault and battery, arguing that he was a free man under that same constitutional phrase. Walker won and was set free, a decision confirmed in an appeal to the state's superior court in 1783. Several similar cases followed, and by 1789 a series of judicial decisions had effectively abolished slavery in Massachusetts.

What kind of government did the Articles of Confederation create?

interceded and sustained a burn on her arm that left a lifelong scar. She left the Ashleys and refused to return. Freeman contacted Theodore Sedgwick, Sheffield's representative in the state legislature. "I heard that paper read yesterday that says, 'all men are born equal, and that every man has a right to freedom,'" Sedgwick's daughter later recalled Freeman telling her father. "Won't the law give me my freedom?"

Sedgwick filed a writ arguing that Freeman and another slave named Brom were illegally held in bondage. The case, officially called *Brom and Bett v. J. Ashley, Esq.*, went to trial. The brief records do not reveal the legal arguments presented in court, but Freeman and Sedgwick are believed to have grounded the case on the Massachusetts constitution, an argument that had the potential to free not just the petitioners but all enslaved blacks in Massachusetts. The jury agreed that Freeman and Brom were entitled to freedom and ordered Ashley to pay each plaintiff damages and court costs.

It was then that the woman known as Mum Bett chose a new name to go with her new status: Elizabeth Freeman. She left Colonel Ashley's and became a paid housekeeper in the Sedgwick family, raising the children when their mother became incapacitated by illness. "Her spirit spurned slavery," Sedgwick's daughter later wrote, offering this quotation from Freeman as evidence: "Anytime, anytime while I was a slave, if one minute's freedom had been offered to me, and I had been told I must die at the end of that minute, I would have taken it—just to stand one minute on God's earth a free woman—I would."

According to Sedgwick family lore, Freeman played an active role protecting the Sedgwick home during Shays's Rebellion in 1786. Because Sedgwick represented the legal elite of the county, he was a target of hostile crowd action. Freeman was home alone when insurgents, searching for Sedgwick and for valuables to plunder, demanded entry. Freeman allegedly hid the family's silver among her possessions, following the dissidents around the house with a large shovel and threatening to flatten anyone who damaged property. When Freeman died in 1829, she was buried in the Sedgwick family plot, with a gravestone inscription that ended "Good mother, farewell."

Freeman's lawsuit of 1781 inspired others to sue, and in a case in 1783 the judge of the Massachusetts Supreme Court declared that "slavery is in my judgment as effectively abolished as it can be by the granting of rights and privileges" in the state constitution. It took several more legal challenges and additional time for that news to trickle out, but the erosion of slavery in Massachusetts gradually picked up speed as blacks demanded manumission or wages for work, or simply walked away from their owners. In 1790, the federal census listed 5,369 "other free persons" (that is, nonwhites) in the state and not a single slave.

Questions for Analysis

CONSIDER THE CONTEXT: What events prompted Freeman to sue for her freedom?

ANALYZE THE EVIDENCE: Freeman left no firsthand account of her thoughts. What evidence is presented here, and how do we use it to learn about freeman's views?

ASK HISTORICAL QUESTIONS: How did the American Revolution create opportunities for enslaved people to challenge the institution of slavery? Where were they most successful?

State legislatures acted more slowly. Pennsylvania enacted a **gradual emancipation** law in 1780. It freed no one immediately, but put the state on the course toward freedom by providing that children born to an enslaved mother after March 1, 1780, would become free at age twenty-eight. Pennsylvania did not fully abolish slavery until 1847, but slaves did not wait for such slow implementation. Untold numbers ran away. One estimate holds that more than half of young slave men in Philadelphia joined the ranks of free blacks, and by 1790, free blacks outnumbered slaves in Pennsylvania two to one.

Rhode Island and Connecticut adopted gradual emancipation laws in 1784; New York waited until 1799 and New Jersey until 1804 to enact theirs. These last were the two northern states with the largest number of slaves: In 1800, New York had 20,000

gradual emancipation
Laws passed in five northern states that provided a multistage process for freeing slaves. Gradual emancipation laws were seen as a middle path, balancing enslaved peoples' rights to liberty with slave owners' rights to "property": two fundamental rights enshrined by the Revolution.

| How was republican government implemented? | Why did the Articles of Confederation fail? | How did the Constitution change the nation's form of government? | Why did so many Americans object to the Constitution? | Conclusion: What was the "republican remedy"? |

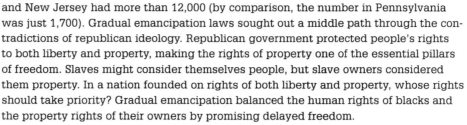

▲ **Black Loyalists in Canada: Passport to Freedom** This black woodcutter in Nova Scotia was one of three thousand black loyalists who moved to Canada between 1783 and 1785. The inset shows a passport issued by the British high command to Cato Rammsay, permitting him to leave New York in 1783. Very few of the Nova Scotia refugees were able to acquire land, forcing most to become laborers for whites. Low wages created dissatisfaction, and in 1791–1792 nearly a third left for Sierra Leone in West Africa. Sketch: Library and Archives Canada, Acc. No. 1970-188-1090, W. H. Coverdale Collection of Canadiana; Passport of Cato Rammsay to emigrate to Nova Scotia, 21 April 1783: Nova Scotia Archives, Gideon White family fonds, MG 1 vol. 948 no. 196 (microfilm no. 14960).

Legal Changes to Slavery, 1777–1804

and New Jersey had more than 12,000 (by comparison, the number in Pennsylvania was just 1,700). Gradual emancipation laws sought out a middle path through the contradictions of republican ideology. Republican government protected people's rights to both liberty and property, making the rights of property one of the essential pillars of freedom. Slaves might consider themselves people, but slave owners considered them property. In a nation founded on rights of both liberty and property, whose rights should take priority? Gradual emancipation balanced the human rights of blacks and the property rights of their owners by promising delayed freedom.

South of Pennsylvania, in Delaware, Maryland, and Virginia, where slavery was critical to the economy, emancipation bills failed. All three states, however, made individual acts of emancipation easier under new manumission laws passed in 1782 (Virginia), 1787 (Delaware), and 1790 (Maryland). By 1790, close to 10,000 newly freed Virginia slaves had formed free black communities complete with schools and churches.

In the deep South—the Carolinas and Georgia—most whites could not imagine a society in which slaves gained their freedom. But cracks in that worldview were beginning to show. Several thousand slaves had defected to British lines during the war, and between 3,000 and 4,000 left with the British. Including northern blacks

What kind of government did the Articles of Confederation create?

evacuated from New York City in 1783, the number of emancipated slaves who left the United States probably totaled between 8,000 and 10,000. Some went to Canada, some to England, and some to Sierra Leone on the west coast of Africa. Many hundreds took refuge with the Seminole and Creek Indians, becoming permanent members of their communities in Spanish Florida and western Georgia.

Although these instances of emancipation were gradual, small, and incomplete, their symbolic importance was enormous. Every state from Pennsylvania north acknowledged that slavery was fundamentally inconsistent with Revolutionary ideology. "All men are created equal" was beginning to acquire force as a basic principle.

COMPARE AND CONTRAST

How did the manumission laws of the three middle states differ from the gradual emancipation laws of states in the North? Which plan led to more immediate freedom for some blacks?

QUICK REVIEW

How did the various states expand and limit the scope of citizenship?

Why did the Articles of Confederation fail?

In 1783, the confederation government faced three interrelated concerns: paying down the large war debt, making peace with the Indians, and creating a plan for western settlement. Because the congress lacked the power to raise tax revenue, the sale of western lands offered the most promising solution to the nation's fiscal pressures, but Native American power in the territory northwest of the Ohio River made American settlement impossible. From 1784 to 1786, the congress struggled mightily with these three issues. Many Americans believed the Articles of Confederation were too weak to address these pressing problems. Others defended the Articles as the best guarantee of republican liberty. A major outbreak of civil disorder in western Massachusetts crystallized the debate and propelled the critics of the Articles toward decisive and far-reaching action.

The War Debt and the Newburgh Conspiracy

For nearly two years—as war between Britain, France, and Spain continued in other parts of the world—the Continental army camped at Newburgh, some sixty miles north of British-occupied New York. As the bored and restless soldiers waited for news of a peace treaty, they grew angrier about the congress's inability to pay their salaries. An earlier promise of generous pensions (half pay for life), made in 1780 in a desperate effort to retain the officers, seemed increasingly doubtful. In December 1782, these frustrations boiled over, as officers petitioned the congress for immediate back pay for their men. The petition darkly hinted that failure to pay the men "may have fatal effects."

Instead of rejecting the petition outright, several members of the congress saw an opportunity to pressure the states to grant the confederation government greater taxation powers. One of these was Robert Morris, a Philadelphia merchant with a gift for financial dealings. As the congress's superintendent of finance, Morris kept the books and wheedled loans from European bankers using his own substantial fortune as collateral. To forestall total insolvency, Morris led an effort in 1781 and again in 1786 to

CHRONOLOGY

1783
- Newburgh Conspiracy exposed.

1784
- Treaty of Fort Stanwix signed.

1785
- Ordinance of 1785 passed.
- Congress calls for $3 million requisition.

1786
- Shays's Rebellion begins.

1787
- Shays's Rebellion suppressed.
- Northwest Ordinance passed.

| How was republican government implemented? | **Why did the Articles of Confederation fail?** | How did the Constitution change the nation's form of government? | Why did so many Americans object to the Constitution? | Conclusion: What was the "republican remedy"? |

amend the Articles to allow collection of a 5 percent impost (an import tax). Each time it failed by one vote, illustrating the difficulty of achieving unanimity and highlighting the confederation government's weakness. The officers' petition offered new prospects to make the case for taxation.

The result was a plot called the **Newburgh Conspiracy**. Morris and several other congressmen encouraged the officers to march the army on the congress to demand its pay. The plot's leaders did not envision a real coup; they wanted to augment the congress's power of taxation. But the risks were extraordinary. For the plan to succeed, most soldiers and officers could not know the plot was a ruse. What if they took the coup to heart?

General George Washington, sympathetic to the plight of unpaid soldiers and officers, had approved the initial petition. But the plotters, aware of his reputation for integrity, kept him in the dark about their collusion with congressional leaders. When the general learned of these developments in March 1783, he delivered an emotional speech to a meeting of five hundred officers. Reminding them in stirring language of honor, heroism, and sacrifice, he denounced the plotters as "subversive of all order and discipline." "Let me conjure you," Washington implored, "as you value your own sacred honor, as you respect the rights of humanity, and as you regard the military and national character of America, to express your utmost horror and detestation of the man, who wishes, under any specious pretences, to overturn the liberties of our country." His audience was left speechless and tearful. Washington—who might have chosen to march his army on the capital, overthrow the congress, and install himself at the head of the nation—ended the plot instead. Few could now doubt his virtue, and his fame grew to new heights.

Morris continued to try to find money to pay the soldiers. But the trickle of money from a few states was too little and too late, coming after the army began to disband. For its part, the congress voted to endorse a plan to commute, or transform, the lifetime pension promised the officers into a lump-sum payment of full pay for five years. But no lump sum was available. Instead, the officers were issued "commutation certificates" promising future payment with interest, which quickly depreciated in value.

In 1783, the soldiers' pay and officers' pensions added some $5 million to the growing public debt. With ever-larger requisitions to the states falling on deaf ears, the confederation government turned to its one remaining source of untapped wealth: the extensive western territories inhabited by Indians.

Newburgh Conspiracy
A threatened coup planned by Continental army officers and leaders in the Continental Congress in 1782–1783. General Washington defused the threat by appealing to the officers' commitment to republicanism and their sense of honor. As a result, his fame grew to new heights.

MAP 8.2 ▲ Fort Stanwix Treaty Region
The 1784 Treaty of Fort Stanwix between U.S. and Iroquois negotiators led to the cession of Iroquois lands in large parts of western New York and Pennsylvania. By the end of the 1790s, the mighty Iroquois—who had dominated this part of the continent for centuries, and fought with the British in the American Revolution—had lost most of their territory.

The Treaty of Fort Stanwix

Native Americans had not participated in the negotiations leading to the Treaty of Paris of 1783, and had not made peace with the United States. The confederation government hoped to formalize treaties ending hostilities between Indians and settlers and securing land cessions. The congress first turned its attention to western New York, inhabited by the Iroquois Confederacy, long-standing allies of the British empire (**Map 8.2**).

What kind of government did the Articles of Confederation create?

► **Cornplanter** Cornplanter, whose Seneca name was Kaintwakon ("what one plants"), served as a negotiator of the Treaty of Fort Stanwix in 1784. He reluctantly agreed to the treaty, and was bitterly denounced afterward. The son of a prominent Seneca woman and a Dutch fur trader, he moved with his family and his followers to the banks of the Allegheny River in western Pennsylvania in 1785. Portrait of Ki-on-twong-ky, 1796 (oil on canvas)/Bartoli, F. (fl. 1796)/ New York Historical Society/Collection of the New-York Historical Society, USA/Bridgeman Images.

During the war, four of the six Iroquois nations had fought with the British, while two, the Oneida and Tuscarora, had sided with the United States. The fighting had been particularly bitter. (See chapter 7.) Feelings ran hot after the war. Making matters even more complicated, land-hungry speculators were already trying to negotiate land cessions to New York State, although the Articles of Confederation quite clearly gave the responsibility for managing "all affairs with the Indians" to the congress, "not members of any of the States."

United States commissioners arrived in Fort Stanwix, New York, in October 1784. Divided and demoralized, the Iroquois negotiators were at a disadvantage. Several prominent leaders, including Joseph Brant, did not attend. The U.S. negotiators, meanwhile, came with a detachment of troops to intimidate the Iroquois leaders who did. The Iroquois negotiators tried vainly to secure an equitable peace. "We are free, and independent," declared a Mohawk chief. Unlike the British, the Iroquois had not been defeated in war. The U.S. negotiators disagreed. "It is not so. You are a subdued people; you have been overcome in a war which you entered into with us, not only without provocation, but in violation of most sacred obligations." The United States would treat the Iroquois as a defeated people. "We shall now, therefore declare to you the condition, on which alone you can be received into the peace and protection of the United States."

The **Treaty of Fort Stanwix** forced the Iroquois to cede Seneca lands in western New York, including a strip of land from Fort Niagara due south, which established U.S.-held territory adjacent to the border with Canada. A later treaty with Pennsylvania dispossessed the Iroquois of all their lands in that state. The Iroquois also surrendered their claims to the Ohio Valley—which came as a surprise to the Delaware, Mingo, and Shawnee Indians who lived there. Several of the negotiators were taken hostage until American captives taken during the war could be returned. While the Oneida and Tuscarora allies of the United States fared better at Fort Stanwix, within a decade they would be dispossessed of their lands too.

After their return, the negotiators were denounced by their fellow Iroquois, who disavowed the treaty, increasing political disunity and hampering efforts at continued resistance. Cornplanter, the Seneca negotiator, moved with his followers to a village along the Allegheny River at the Pennsylvania/New York border. Brant chose to move his Mohawk followers into Canadian territory.

Treaty of Fort Stanwix
A 1784 treaty between the United States and the Iroquois Confederacy that resulted in large land cessions in western New York and northwestern Pennsylvania. Tribes not present at Fort Stanwix disavowed the treaty.

The Northwest Territory

Once the states ceded their western land claims in the ratification fight over the Articles of Confederation, the territory northwest of the Ohio River emerged as the most promising region for land sales. But how would the territory be organized?

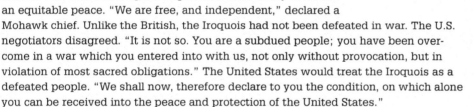

How was republican government implemented?	**Why did the Articles of Confederation fail?**	How did the Constitution change the nation's form of government?	Why did so many Americans object to the Constitution?	Conclusion: What was the "republican remedy"?

▲ **Jefferson's Map of the Northwest Territory** In the map on the left, drawn in 1784, Thomas Jefferson proposed nine states for the territory north of the Ohio River. His vision imposed straight lines on the map, ignoring geographic features and native land claims. The 1783 map on the right, by contrast, carefully notes the location of Native American territories and geographic features like mountains and mines. Map: William L Clements Library, University of Michigan; Detail: Library of Congress, Geography and Map Division.

READING THE IMAGE: How do the two maps differ? What is present and what is absent in each? How do maps help shape political visions and territorial claims?

CONNECTIONS: Why was the formation of new states in the west a matter of such importance to the United States?

Congressman Thomas Jefferson, charged with drafting a policy, proposed dividing the territory north of the Ohio River and east of the Mississippi—the Northwest Territory—into nine future states with evenly spaced east-west boundaries and townships ten miles square. He advocated giving, not selling, the land to settlers, arguing that future property taxes on the improved land would be payment enough. Jefferson's aim was to encourage rapid and democratic settlement and discourage land speculation. In order to attract settlers, he drafted plans for republican governments in the new states. It was a momentous decision: The new states would not become colonies of the older states but would be equals in every respect, with eventual membership in the United States. Finally, and perhaps most consequentially, Jefferson's draft prohibited slavery in the nine new states.

Jefferson's plan provided the basis for a series of laws passed by the confederation government that extended republican government into the west. The first two ordinances, passed in 1784 and 1785, established the rectangular grid pattern for laying out the western states, and called for three to five new states. These new states were divided into townships six miles square, and further divided into thirty-six

What kind of government did the Articles of Confederation create?

MAP 8.3 ▲ The Northwest Territory and Ordinance of 1785

Surveyors ventured into the eastern edge of the Northwest Territory in the 1780s and produced this first map (right) showing neat six-mile-square townships, each subdivided into one-mile squares containing sixteen 40-acre farms. Jefferson got his straight lines and right angles after all; compare this map to Jefferson's map of the Northwest Territory. Plat Map © TNGenNet Inc. 2002.

sections of 640 acres, each section to be subdivided further into family farms (**Map 8.3**). Reduced to easily mappable squares, the land would be sold at public auction for a minimum of one dollar an acre. In order to raise the maximum amount of revenue as fast as possible, the congress decreed a minimum purchase of 640 acres, with payment in hard money or in certificates of debt from Revolutionary days. Because such sums were far beyond the means of average settlers, the law meant that prosperous speculators would dominate initial land purchases with the intention of reselling them. The commodification of land had been taken to a new level.

A third land act, the Northwest Ordinance of 1787, set forth a three-stage process by which settled territories would advance to statehood. First, the congress would appoint officials for a sparsely populated territory who would adopt a legal code and appoint local magistrates to administer justice. When the male population of voting age and landowning status (fifty acres) reached five thousand, the territory could elect its own legislature and send a nonvoting delegate to the congress. When the population of voting citizens reached sixty thousand, the territory could write a state constitution and apply for full admission to the Union.

The Northwest Ordinance of 1787 was perhaps the most important legislation passed by the confederation government. It ensured that the new United States, so recently released from colonial dependency, would not reproduce the European model

Northwest Ordinance
Land act of 1787 that established a three-stage process by which settled territories would become states. It also banned slavery in the Northwest Territory. The ordinance guaranteed that new states joining the United States would not become colonial dependencies.

How was republican government implemented?

Why did the Articles of Confederation fail?

How did the Constitution change the nation's form of government?

Why did so many Americans object to the Constitution?

Conclusion: What was the "republican remedy"?

▲ **A Newly Cleared Frontier Farm** It took tremendous muscle and sweat to turn the densely wooded land of the Northwest Territory into farmland. Men with axes and oxen chopped down trees and dragged the logs, transforming them into log cabins and wooden fences. Women's labor was equally essential, preparing food, spinning textiles, and caring for children. Note the smoke: When burned, wood provided the major energy source for settlers. The Granger Collection, New York.

COMPARE AND CONTRAST

In what ways was the Northwest Ordinance a colonization plan, and it what ways was it anticolonial?

Northwest Confederacy
Coalition of Native American nations defending their territory situated between the Ohio River and the Great Lakes from U.S. expansion. With the assistance of British officers in forts along the Great Lakes, it fought to preserve a zone of Native American sovereignty.

of settler colonialism. Instead, settlers moving west would become citizens of new states, and eventually gain equal status with the thirteen original states. It established a mechanism for the colonization of the continent in republican form.

In the tradition of colonial laws and boundaries, the Northwest Ordinance ignored social reality. Tens of thousands of Native Americans lived in the region between the Appalachian Mountains and the Mississippi River; they had no intention of ceding their lands to the expansionist Americans. Low-level fighting had continued since 1783 in the region between the Ohio River and the Great Lakes, as bands of Native American nations harassed American attempts at surveying and settlement.

Over the course of the 1780s, diverse Native American nations, including some members of the Iroquois Confederacy, along with the Huron, Ottawa, Shawnee, Cherokee, Delaware, Chippewa, Potawatomie, Miami, and Wabash nations, came together to form the **Northwest Confederacy** to resist American expansion. Long-standing allies of the British, the Northwest Confederacy continued receiving the material and logistical support of British officers who retained possession of key forts along the Great Lakes. Many of these officers had been shocked by the British government's decision to abandon their Indian allies in 1783. In 1786, a council of the Northwest Confederacy gathered near Detroit. While proclaiming its desire for peace with the United States, it insisted that "any cession of our lands should be made in the most public manner, and

What kind of government did the Articles of Confederation create?

by the united voice of the confederacy," and warned "your surveyors and others, that mark out lands, to cease from crossing the Ohio."

The Northwest Ordinance acknowledged the Indian presence, and promised that "the utmost good faith shall always be observed towards the Indians; their lands and property shall never be taken from them without their consent; and, in their property, rights, and liberty, they shall never be invaded or disturbed, unless in just and lawful wars authorized by Congress." The 1787 ordinance further pledged that "laws founded in justice and humanity, shall from time to time be made for preventing wrongs being done to them." Such promises may have indicated noble intentions, but the dynamics in the northwest were far more powerful than any pledges of good faith on the East Coast. With land-hungry settlers and a U.S. government starved for revenue on one side and Native Americans determined to protect their territories and control the pace of land cessions on the other, the stage was set for years of conflict.

The 1787 ordinance enacted Jefferson's plan to prohibit slavery in the Northwest Territory, which the congress had voted down in 1784. **(See "Analyzing Historical Evidence: The Northwest Ordinance's Slavery Clause" on page 222.)** To appease the interests of slaveholders, the prohibition was paired with a fugitive slave provision promising that escaped slaves caught north of the Ohio River would be returned south. The ordinance thus acknowledged and supported slavery in one region even as it barred it from another. North-South sectionalism based on slavery was slowly taking shape.

PLACE EVENTS IN CONTEXT
How did the Northwest Ordinance of 1787 reflect the values and ideology of the American Revolution?

The Requisition of 1785 and Shays's Rebellion, 1786–1787

Still lacking the power to tax, with public land sales yet unrealized, the confederation government had not solved its essential dilemma: how to pay its debts. In 1785 the government requested $3 million from the states—an amount four times greater than the previous year's levy. Of this sum, 30 percent would pay the government's operating costs, while another 30 percent would reimburse debts owed to foreign lenders, who insisted on payment in gold or silver. The remaining 40 percent was intended for American bondholders, who held IOUs of the Revolutionary years. A significant slice of that 40 percent represented the interest (but not the principal) owed to army officers for their recently issued "commutation certificates." The government's revenue needs had reached a critical point.

With its huge 1785 requisition, the Continental Congress had poked a hornet's nest. Although they had the power to tax, the states were no more solvent than the federal government. They were struggling to fund their own governments and pay their own wartime debts, and were already pressing higher tax bills onto their citizens in order to retire state debts. In nearly every state, the requisition of 1785 spawned some combination of crowd protests, demands for inflationary paper money, and anger at state authorities and greedy speculators. Once again, Americans seemed to be rising up in resistance to new taxes levied to pay off wartime debt.

States like New Jersey and Connecticut without major ports (and the import duties that ports generated) simply ignored the confederation's requisition. In New Hampshire, where financial pressures on the populace were reaching a breaking point, town meetings voted to refuse the requisition. The state legislature took notice when two hundred armed insurgents surrounded the New Hampshire capitol to protest state taxes in 1786. Although an armed militia drove the insurgents off, the assemblymen backed off from an earlier order to haul delinquent taxpayers into courts. Rhode Island, North Carolina, and Georgia responded to their own protests by issuing paper money and allowing the payment of taxes in depreciated currency.

| How was republican government implemented? | **Why did the Articles of Confederation fail?** | How did the Constitution change the nation's form of government? | Why did so many Americans object to the Constitution? | Conclusion: What was the "republican remedy"? |

The Northwest Ordinance's Slavery Clause

Given the central importance of the ban in U.S. history, the reasons the Continental Congress prohibited slavery in the Northwest Territory remain remarkably elusive.

A committee presented an early draft of the ordinance to the congress in April 1787. The lack of a quorum sidelined the draft. A second committee revised the plan extensively that summer—at the very time the constitutional convention was meeting in Philadelphia. Its members included two men from Virginia and one each from South Carolina, New York, and Massachusetts. The congress considered this draft on July 11 and 12. No draft up to that point mentioned slavery.

On July 13, at the third and final reading, article 6 made its first appearance. The records are silent about what debate, if any, occurred in response. The final document passed unanimously, the eight states present all voting in favor: Massachusetts, New York, New Jersey, Delaware, Virginia, North Carolina, South Carolina, and Georgia.

DOCUMENT 1

Northwest Ordinance of 1787

In the 1784 ordinance, Thomas Jefferson had suggested prohibiting slavery. The congress voted no. The fugitive slave provision, entirely new to the confederation government, would also appear in the U.S. Constitution, ratified in 1788.

Art. 6. There shall be neither slavery nor involuntary servitude in the said territory, otherwise than in the punishment of crimes whereof the party shall have been duly convicted: Provided, always, That any person escaping into the same, from whom labor or service is lawfully claimed in any one of the original States, such fugitive may be lawfully reclaimed and conveyed to the person claiming his or her labor or service as aforesaid.

Source: *Journals of the Continental Congress,* ed. Roscoe R. Hill (Washington, DC: Government Printing Office, 1936), 32:339, 343, http://memory.loc.gov /ammem/amlaw/lwjc.html.

DOCUMENT 2

Two Letters by Delegates in Congress

Nathan Dane of Massachusetts served on both drafting committees. Rufus King was a Massachusetts politician. Virginian William Grayson chaired the congress in July 1787. James Monroe of Virginia had headed a 1786 committee to draft the ordinance. Newspapers printed the full ordinance, but no discussion of article 6 resulted. No further commentary on the subject has come to light in private correspondence.

Nathan Dane to Rufus King, New York, July 16, 1787
Dear Sir

. . . We have been much engaged in business for ten or twelve days past for a part of which we have had 8 States. . . . We have been employed about several objects—; the principal ones of which have been the Government inclosed [the Northwest Ordinance] and the Ohio purchase. . . . we met several times and at last agreed on some principles. . . . When I drew the ordinance which passed (in a few words excepted) as I originally formed it, I had no idea the States would agree to the sixth Art. prohibiting Slavery—; as only Massa[chusetts] of the Eastern States was present—; and therefore omitted it in the draft—; but finding the House favourably disposed on this subject, after we had completed the other parts I moved the art[icle]—; which was agreed to without opposition. . . .

William Grayson to James Monroe, New York, August 8, 1787
Dear Sir,

. . . Congress has passed the Ordnance for the government of the Western country, in a manner some thing different from the one which you drew, though I expect the departure is not so essential but that it will meet your approbation. . . . The clause respecting slavery was agreed to by the Southern members for the purpose of preventing Tobacco & Indigo from being made on the N.W. side of the Ohio, as well as for sevl. other political reasons.

Source: *Letters of Delegates to Congress, 1774–1789,* ed. Paul H. Smith (Washington, DC: Library of Congress, 1976), 24:358–59, 394, http://memory .loc.gov/ammem/amlaw/lwdglink.html.

What kind of government did the Articles of Confederation create?

DOCUMENT 3

Early Residents Petition the U.S. Congress

Territorial populations in the early 1790s consisted largely of longtime French residents in Illinois Country, some of whom owned slaves, and new migrants from Virginia and Kentucky. Several groups sent petitions to the federal government to narrow article 6, arguing that slaves who were residents before 1787 (and their offspring) should continue as slaves, to preserve slave owners' property rights. This petition of 1796 took aim at the whole article, but the federal government offered no reply.

Your petitioners humbly hope that they will not be thought presumptuous in venturing to disapprove of the article concerning slavery in toto, as contrary not only to the interest, but almost to the existence of the country they inhabit, where laborers can not be procured to assist in cultivating the grounds under one dollar per day. . . . Your petitioners do not wish to increase the number of slaves already in the dominions of the United States; all they hope for or desire is, that they may be permitted to introduce from any of the United States such persons, and such only, as by the laws of such States are slaves therein.

Source: Jacob Piatt Dunn, *Slavery Petitions and Papers* (Indianapolis: Bowen-Merrill, 1894), 6, http://catalog.hathitrust.org/Record/000317559.

DOCUMENT 4

Indenture Record of Jacob, 1805

Indiana's indenture law of 1805 allowed two parties to voluntarily enter a service contract. One of forty-seven such contracts in Knox County, Indiana, involved Eli Hawkins from South Carolina and his onetime slave Jacob, age sixteen. Before a court clerk they . . .

. . . determined and agreed among themselves . . . that said Jacob shall and will serve the said Eli Hawkins and his assigns for term of Ninety years . . . the said Eli Hawkins and his assigns providing the said Jacob with necessary and sufficient provisions and clothing, washing and lodging, according to his degree and state . . . after the expiration

of said term the said Jacob shall be free to all intents and purposes.

Source: Daniel Owen, "Circumvention of Article VI of the Ordinance of 1787," *Indiana Magazine of History* 36 (1940): 115, http://scholarworks.iu.edu/journals/index.php/imh/article/view/7219/8151.

DOCUMENT 5

Territorial and Federal Censuses

Indiana and Illinois together formed the Indiana Territory in 1800. They became separate states in 1816 and 1818. Study the census data below. Does the enumeration of slaves seem surprising? Where would the indentured Jacob be counted?

	Total Population	Free Blacks	Slaves
1800	5,000	163	135
1810	24,500	393	237
1820 Indiana	147,000	1,230	190
Illinois	55,000	457	917

Data source for 1800 and 1810: "Slavery in Indiana Territory," www.in.gov/history/2492.htm. Data source for 1820: Historical Census Browser, http://mapserver.lib.virginia.edu/.

Questions for Analysis

ASK HISTORICAL QUESTIONS: Did article 6, when it was passed, seem like a significant matter to the congressmen who debated and voted on it? Why did Nathan Dane initially leave the clause out and only introduce it later? Was slavery in fact abolished by article 6?

RECOGNIZE VIEWPOINTS: What explanation is given for the support of article 6 by Virginia? Why did existing settlers in Illinois Country oppose it, and what remedies did they propose? Do you think young Jacob in Document 4 considered it a success?

CONSIDER THE CONTEXT: Why is the abolition of slavery in the Northwest Territory a significant event? What might have been different had article 6 never been introduced?

▶ **Two Rebel Leaders** A Boston almanac of 1787 portrayed Daniel Shays (on the left) with another rebel leader, Job Shattuck. Both were ringleaders in the rebellion against taxation in Massachusetts. It is unlikely the artist ever saw either man. This particular almanac series was pro-Constitution in 1788, so the artist was not likely to sympathize with the Shaysites. Art Collection 2/ Alamy Stock Photo.

UNDERSTAND POINTS OF VIEW

What political and economic grievances drove rebels like Daniel Shays to protest? Which grievances were most threatening to the government?

Attack by Shays's followers

Encounter between Shays's and government forces

Shays's Rebellion, 1786–1787

But nowhere did tensions grow to such heights as in Massachusetts. For four years in a row, a fiscally conservative legislature, dominated by the eastern commercial centers, had passed tough tax laws to pay state creditors in hard money, rather than cheap paper. Already farmers in the western parts of the state, where hard money was nearly impossible to obtain, were facing bankruptcies and foreclosure over their inability to pay existing taxes. Then, in March 1786, the legislature in Boston loaded the federal requisition onto the bill. The response was almost immediate. In June, farmers in southeastern Massachusetts marched on a courthouse—the local symbol of state authority—in an effort to close it down. Angry petitions denouncing oppressive taxation poured in from the western two-thirds of the state. When the legislature ignored the complaints and adjourned that July, dissidents held a series of conventions and called for revisions to the state constitution.

In the fall of 1786, several thousand armed men shut down courthouses in six counties; sympathetic local militias refused to intervene. The insurgents were not predominantly poor or debt-ridden farmers; they included veteran soldiers and officers in the Continental army as well as town leaders. One was a farmer and onetime army captain, Daniel Shays.

The governor of Massachusetts, James Bowdoin, who had only recently protested British taxes, now characterized the western dissidents as rebels. A Boston newspaper claimed that Shays planned to burn Boston to the ground and overthrow the government. Another former radical, Samuel Adams, now argued that "the man who dares rebel against the laws of a republic ought to suffer death." These aging revolutionaries insisted that popularly elected representatives, unlike monarchs, were by definition fair and just. They could not see how the legislature had attended to the interests of coastal merchants at the expense of backcountry farmers.

The Massachusetts insurgency was the most dramatic of the various uprisings throughout the United States. It seemed to be rapidly spinning out of control. In October, the congress attempted to triple the size of the federal army, but fewer than one hundred men enlisted. So Governor Bowdoin raised a private army, gaining the services of some three thousand men with pay provided by wealthy Boston merchants.

In January 1787, the insurgents learned of the army marching west from Boston. In an echo of the hostilities in Concord and Lexington that had launched the Revolution, 1,500 of them moved to capture a federal armory in Springfield to obtain weapons. But a militia band loyal to the state government beat them to the weapons facility and

What kind of government did the Articles of Confederation create?

met their attack with gunfire; four rebels were killed and another twenty wounded. The final encounter came at Petersham, where Bowdoin's army surprised the rebels and took several hundred of them prisoner. In the end, two men were executed for rebellion; sixteen more sentenced to hang were reprieved at the last moment on the gallows. Some four thousand men gained leniency by confessing their misconduct and swearing an oath of allegiance to the state.

Shays's Rebellion provoked alarm throughout the country. With angry farmers protesting taxes and resisting unpopular governments, the American Revolution seemed to be repeating itself. Panicked Massachusetts newspapers wrote about mob rule spreading to other states. New York lawyer John Jay fretted to George Washington, "Our affairs seem to lead to some crisis, some revolution—something I cannot foresee or conjecture. I am uneasy and apprehensive; more so than during the war." Benjamin Franklin, in his eighties, shrewdly observed that in 1776 Americans had feared "an excess of power in the rulers" but now the problem was perhaps "a defect of obedience" in the subjects. The fledgling United States seemed on the verge of disintegration. With such fears looming, the nation's leaders now set themselves on one last, desperate effort.

Shays's Rebellion
Uprising (1786–1787) led by farmers centered in western Massachusetts. Dissidents protested tax policies of the eastern elites who controlled the state's government. Shays's Rebellion caused leaders throughout the country to worry about the confederation's ability to handle civil disorder.

QUICK REVIEW

What were the most important factors in the failure of the Articles of Confederation?

How did the Constitution change the nation's form of government?

Shays's Rebellion provoked an odd mixture of fear and hope that the government under the Articles of Confederation was losing its grip on power. A small circle of Virginians decided to try one last time to increase the powers granted to the government by the Articles. They called for a meeting to discuss trade regulation, which led them to scrap the Articles and write an entirely new constitution.

From Annapolis to Philadelphia

Spooked by the protests erupting across the country, a group of Virginians led by James Madison convinced the confederation congress to try again to revise the trade regulation powers of the Articles. Only five states participated at the first meeting at Annapolis, Maryland, in the fall of 1786. The delegates planned a second for Philadelphia the following May. The congress reluctantly endorsed the Philadelphia meeting but limited its scope to "the sole and express purpose of revising the Articles of Confederation." A few men had more ambitious plans, however.

The fifty-five men who assembled at Philadelphia in May 1787 had already concluded that the Articles of Confederation were fatally weak. Patrick Henry, author of the Virginia Resolves in 1765 and former state governor, refused to attend the convention, saying he "smelled a rat." Rhode Island declined to send delegates.

| How was republican government implemented? | Why did the Articles of Confederation fail? | **How did the Constitution change the nation's form of government?** | Why did so many Americans object to the Constitution? | Conclusion: What was the "republican remedy"? |

225

Two men sent by New York's legislature to check the influence of fellow delegate Alexander Hamilton left in dismay in the middle of the convention, leaving Hamilton as the state's sole representative. This gathering of white men included no artisans, day laborers, or ordinary farmers. Two-thirds of the delegates were lawyers. Half had been officers in the Continental army. The majority had served in the confederation congress and knew its weaknesses. Seven men had been governors of their states and knew firsthand the frustrations of thwarted executive power. A few elder statesmen attended, such as Benjamin Franklin and George Washington, but on the whole the delegates were young, like Madison and Hamilton.

The Virginia and New Jersey Plans

The convention worked in total secrecy, which allowed the delegates to deliberate freely and explore ideas without concern for public opinion. Once the convention decided to scrap the Articles and draft a new constitution, the debate began.

The Virginia delegation first presented a fifteen-point plan that repudiated the principle of a confederation of states. Largely the work of Madison, the Virginia Plan proposed a three-branch government composed of a two-chamber legislature, a powerful executive, and a judiciary. It sharply reduced the power of smaller states by pegging representation in both houses of the congress to population. The theory was that this new government would be a compact among the people, not the states. Among the expansive powers assigned to the congress were the rights to veto state legislation and to coerce states to obey national laws. To prevent the congress from wielding absolute power, the executive and judiciary could jointly veto its actions.

In mid-June, delegates from New Jersey, Connecticut, Delaware, and New Hampshire—all small states—unveiled an alternative proposal. The New Jersey Plan maintained the existing single-house congress of the Articles of Confederation in which each state had one vote. Acknowledging the need for an executive, it created a plural presidency to be held by three men elected by the congress from among its membership. It departed from the existing government in the sweeping powers it gave to the new congress: the right to tax, regulate trade, and use force on unruly state governments. Like the Virginia Plan, it favored national power over states' rights. But the New Jersey Plan retained the principle that the national government should be a confederation of states, not of people.

For two weeks, delegates debated the two plans. The small-state delegates compromised by allowing one of the two legislative houses to be apportioned by population. But they would not concede for both houses, fearing their loss of power in the central government. Madison was equally vehement that congressional representation should not be determined by state, which he viewed as the fundamental flaw in the Articles.

The debate seemed deadlocked, and for a while the convention was "on the verge of dissolution, scarce held together by the strength of a hair," according to one delegate. Only in mid-July did the so-called Great Compromise break the stalemate and produce the basic structural features of the United States Constitution. Delegates agreed on a bicameral legislature: Population would determine representation in the lower house, the House of Representatives, while each state would get an equal vote in the upper house, the Senate. By thus appeasing the smaller states worried about their loss of power in national decision making, the delegates succeeded in brokering a compromise and creating a new government for the United States. Unlike the Articles of Confederation, which had been a compact among thirteen sovereign states, the new Constitution could truly claim, as it did in its opening words, to be a compact among "We the People" of the United States.

Virginia Plan
Plan drafted by James Madison proposing a powerful three-branch government, with representation in both houses of the congress tied to population. This plan eclipsed the voice of small states in national government.

New Jersey Plan
Alternative plan drafted by delegates from small states, retaining the confederation's single-house congress with one vote per state. Like the Virginia Plan, it proposed enhanced congressional powers, including the right to tax, regulate trade, and use force on unruly state governments.

United States Constitution
The document written in 1787 and subsequently ratified by the original thirteen states that laid out the governing structure of the United States in separate legislative, executive, and judicial branches.

What kind of government did the Articles of Confederation create?

But the new foundational concept for the nation left some important matters undefined. Who were "the people"? Were slaves, for example, people or property? As people, they would add weight to the southern delegations in the House of Representatives, giving those states an obvious incentive to include them in the population count. And yet, as northern delegates were quick to point out, the ideology of slavery held that slaves were property. What emerged was the compromise known as the three-fifths clause: All free persons plus "three-fifths of all other Persons" constituted the population count for apportioning representatives in the House.

The term "all other Persons" suggests the delegates' reluctance to recognize slavery in the Constitution. The words *slave* and *slavery* appear nowhere in the original document, although it regulated the institution in several ways. The new government's power to regulate trade included the slave trade, which the Constitution euphemistically described as "the Migration or Importation of such Persons as any of the States now shall think proper to admit." Another provision governed the return of fugitive slaves using clumsy prose: "No person, held to Service or Labour in one State, under the Laws thereof, escaping into another, shall, in Consequence of any Law or Regulation therein, be discharged from such Service or Labour but shall be delivered up on Claim of the party to whom such Service or Labour may be due." If the text itself left slavery unnamed—as though it could evade the growing moral doubts about the institution by hiding its presence in awkward phrasing—the Constitution nonetheless recognized, protected, and perpetuated the institution.

three-fifths clause
A clause in the Constitution stipulating that all free persons plus "three-fifths of all other Persons" would constitute the numerical base for apportioning both representation and taxation. The clause tacitly acknowledged the existence of slavery in the United States, and gave extra representation to slaveholding states.

Checks and Balances

With the new constitution grounded on "We the People," the delegates in Philadelphia confronted a dilemma: For most political thinkers of the eighteenth century, pure democracy was dangerous. As a Massachusetts delegate said, "The evils we experience flow from the excess of democracy." Although the delegates remained committed to republican government, they created a constitutional system that would check the people's voice through a variety of mechanisms.

First were protections against direct election. The people elected only representatives in the House. Senators, by contrast, were elected not by direct popular vote but by state legislatures, and served for six years, as opposed to the two-year terms in the House. Their longer terms and their indirect election shielded them from the will of democratic majorities.

Similarly, the Constitution isolated the powerful new presidency it created from the reach of direct democracy. The Constitution established an electoral college that selected the president and vice president. Each state's legislature would choose the electors, whose number was determined by the sum of representatives and senators for the state. The president thus would owe his office not to Congress, the states, or the people but to a temporary assemblage of distinguished citizens who could vote their own judgment on the candidates. The president served a term of four years without any limitation on reelection. As for the judges who would compose the new federal judiciary, they were appointed by the president and confirmed by the Senate, and thus would never be subject to election in any form.

In addition to these protections against direct democracy, the framers of the Constitution devised a government with limits and checks on all three of its branches. They created a powerful president who could veto legislation passed in Congress, but gave Congress the power to override presidential vetoes. They established a national judiciary to settle disputes between states and citizens of different states. They separated the branches of government not only by functions and by reciprocal checks but also by deliberately basing the election of each branch on different bodies—voting

How was republican government implemented? | Why did the Articles of Confederation fail? | **How did the Constitution change the nation's form of government?** | Why did so many Americans object to the Constitution? | Conclusion: What was the "republican remedy"?

227

citizens (the House), state legislators (the Senate), and the electoral college (the presidency).

The convention carefully specified the powers of the president and of Congress. The president initiated policy, proposed legislation, and vetoed acts of Congress; he commanded the military and directed foreign policy; and he appointed the entire judiciary, subject to Senate approval. Congress held the purse strings: the power to levy taxes, to regulate trade, and to coin money and control the currency. States could no longer issue paper money. Congress also had the sole power to declare war. Two more congressional powers—to "provide for the common defence and general Welfare" of the country and "to make all laws which shall be necessary and proper" for carrying out its powers—provided elastic language that potentially granted sweeping powers to the new government.

While no one was entirely satisfied with every line of the Constitution, only three delegates refused to sign it. The Constitution specified a mechanism for ratification that avoided the dilemma faced earlier by the confederation government: Nine states, rather than all thirteen, had to ratify it; and special conventions elected only for that purpose, rather than state legislatures, would make the crucial decision.

QUICK REVIEW

In what ways did the Constitution drafted at the Philadelphia convention limit direct democracy?

Why did so many Americans object to the Constitution?

CHRONOLOGY

1787
– Pro-Constitution essays called *The Federalist Papers* begin to be published.

1788
– U.S. Constitution ratified.

Federalists
Originally the term for the supporters of the ratification of the U.S. Constitution in 1787–1788. In the 1790s, it became the name for one of the two dominant political groups that emerged during that decade.

Had a popular vote been taken on the Constitution in the fall of 1787, it probably would have been rejected. Having just fought a war against a distant imperial government they viewed as tyrannical, many Americans did not want to grant vast new powers to a distant national government that might eventually become tyrannical. In the three most populous states—Virginia, Massachusetts, and New York—substantial majorities opposed the new Constitution. North Carolina and Rhode Island refused to call ratifying conventions. Seven of the eight remaining states were easy victories for partisans of the Constitution, but securing the approval of the ninth proved difficult. Pro-Constitution forces, called Federalists, had to strategize shrewdly to defeat anti-Constitution forces, called Antifederalists.

The Federalists

Calling themselves Federalists, supporters of the Constitution moved swiftly. They secured agreement from an uneasy confederation congress to defer a vote and instead send the Constitution to the states for their consideration. It was thus on the state level that Federalists would confront Antifederalists, in special ratifying conventions called for the sole purpose of debating the new Constitution.

What kind of government did the Articles of Confederation create?

MAP 8.4 ▲ Ratification of the Constitution, 1788–1790

Populated areas cast votes for delegates to state ratification conventions. This map shows Antifederalist strength generally concentrated in backcountry, noncoastal, and non-urban areas, but with significant exceptions (for example, Rhode Island).

Merchants, lawyers, and urban artisans generally favored the Constitution, as did large landowners and slaveholders. Antifederalists tended to be rural, western, and noncommercial—men whose access to news was limited and whose participation in state government was tenuous. To gain momentum, Federalists began the voting in states most likely to support the Constitution.

Delaware ratified in early December, before the Antifederalists had even begun their campaign. Pennsylvania, New Jersey, and Georgia followed within a month (**Map 8.4**). Delaware and New Jersey were small commercial states; to them, a central government that would regulate trade and set taxes was an attractive proposition. Georgia sought the protection that a stronger national government would afford against hostile Indians to the west, Spanish Florida to the south, and slaves who made up 35 percent of the population. "If a weak State with the Indians on its back and the Spaniards on its flank does not see the necessity of a General Government there must I think be wickedness or insanity in the way," commented George Washington. Another three easy victories came in Connecticut, Maryland, and South Carolina.

| How was republican government implemented? | Why did the Articles of Confederation fail? | How did the Constitution change the nation's form of government? | **Why did so many Americans object to the Constitution?** | Conclusion: What was the "republican remedy"? |

▶ **Massachusetts, the Sixth Pillar** The debate over the U.S. Constitution spilled beyond the ratification assemblies into newspapers and even political cartoons. One set of images that circulated widely represented each state that ratified the Constitution as a neoclassical column. This print, labeled "United they stand—divided fall," was published on January 16, 1788, as Massachusetts debated whether to ratify the Constitution. Library of Congress, 3a45780.

READING THE IMAGE: What elements of this image make an argument for ratification of the Constitution? Where does the hand raising the Massachusetts pillar come from? What might that mean?

CONNECTIONS: How did the U.S. Constitution establish its authority as the nation's governing law?

Massachusetts was the first state to seriously challenge the Federalists. The selection of delegates to the ratifying convention favored the Antifederalists, whose strength lay in the state's western areas, home to Shays's Rebellion. One delegate from rural Worcester County voiced widely shared suspicions: "These lawyers and men of learning and money men that talk so finely, and gloss over matters so smoothly, to make us poor illiterate people swallow down the pill, expect to get into Congress themselves; they expect to be the managers of the Constitution and get all the power and all the money into their own hands, and then they will swallow up all us little folks." But another western farmer said he knew "the worth of good government by the want of it." He urged his fellow farmers to work with the elite leaders; "they are all embarked on the same cause with us, and we must swim or sink together. . . . We shall never have another opportunity." By such arguments and by a vigorous Federalist newspaper campaign, the Antifederalists' initial lead gradually eroded. In the end, the Federalists won in Massachusetts, but only by a slim margin and with promises that the first Congress would consider a set of constitutional amendments based on the Antifederalists' objections.

> "'We must swim or sink together. . . . We shall never have another opportunity.'"

By May 1788, eight states had ratified; only one more was needed for the Constitution to come into effect. North Carolina and Rhode Island were hopeless for the Federalist cause, and New Hampshire seemed nearly as bleak. More worrisome was the failure to win over the large and economically critical states of Virginia and New York. Could nine other states survive as a nation without them?

The Antifederalists

Antifederalists
Opponents of the ratification of the Constitution. Antifederalists feared that a powerful and distant central government would be out of touch with the needs of citizens. They also complained that the Constitution failed to guarantee individual liberties in a bill of rights.

The **Antifederalists** were a broad coalition of groups united in their objection to the Constitution. At its core, the Antifederalist position rested on the fear that distant power would infringe on people's liberties.

Although their political strength most rested on backcountry regions long suspicious of eastern elites, Antifederalists came from a variety of social levels. Some, like the Massachusetts merchant Elbridge Gerry or the Virginia planter Patrick Henry,

What kind of government did the Articles of Confederation create?

sprang from the highest ranks of American society. Like the Federalists, they believed in a society run by a virtuous elite; unlike the Federalists, they thought that the elite should govern locally through institutions like militias, juries, or state legislatures. Other Antifederalists came from the middling orders—yeoman farmers, tavern keepers, artisans—who believed in economic mobility and popular leadership. Still others hailed from the lowest social orders—subsistence farmers, landless squatters, the urban poor—and had a more radically egalitarian political outlook. They favored crowd actions, and attacked an economic aristocracy they believed was trying to consolidate its power through the Constitution.

Because the Federalists had moved so fast, the Antifederalists faced an uphill battle. Moreover, their name made them sound defensive and negative, and lacking a program of their own. Even so, their fear of distant and excessively powerful government resonated widely. "The difficulty, if not impracticability, of exercising the equal and equitable powers of government by a single legislature over an extent of territory that reaches from the Mississippi to the western lakes, and from them to the Atlantic ocean, is an insuperable objection to the adoption of the new system," wrote Mercy Otis Warren.

The new government was indeed distant. In the proposed House of Representatives, the Constitution's only directly elected body, each member represented some thirty thousand people. Could that member really know or communicate with his whole constituency? One Antifederalist essayist contrasted the Constitution's structure with the intimacy of state-level representation: "The members of our state legislature are annually elected—they are subject to instructions—they are chosen within small circles—they are sent but a small distance from their respective homes. Their conduct is constantly known to their constituents." Some Antifederalists worried that only elites would serve as national representatives, "ignorant of the sentiments of the middling and much more of the lower class of citizens, strangers to their ability, unacquainted with their wants, difficulties, and distress," as one Maryland man wrote.

Most Federalists agreed that national elections would favor the elite. Indeed, it was one of the Constitution's objectives. "Fools and knaves have voice enough in government already," joked one. Federalists like Alexander Hamilton claimed that mechanics and laborers preferred to have their social betters represent them. Antifederalists, of course, disagreed: "In reality, there will be no part of the people represented, but the rich. . . . It will literally be a government in the hands of the few to oppress and plunder the many."

The most widespread Antifederalist objection focused on the Constitution's lack of a bill of rights, like those contained in many state constitutions. During the ratification debates, Federalists conceded the point, and promised to amend the Constitution to add a bill of rights. In the end, a small state—New Hampshire—provided the decisive ninth vote for ratification, following an intensive and successful lobbying effort by Federalists.

Although the Antifederalists lost their struggle to defeat the Constitution, they won in other ways. Most concretely, their concerns about the absence of specified rights in the Constitution led to the first ten amendments, known today as the Bill of Rights. On a more abstract level, the vigorous debate they waged changed the practice of American politics. Where Federalists had debated their Constitution in a gathering of elite men behind closed doors, Antifederalists forced them into public. In this way, they expanded the scope of American political life by making newspaper articles, speeches, and other forms of public debate the forum for decisions of momentous significance. And finally, Antifederalists' arguments against the power of elites brought a robust populist language into the center of American politics, where it would remain for centuries to come.

| How was republican government implemented? | Why did the Articles of Confederation fail? | How did the Constitution change the nation's form of government? | **Why did so many Americans object to the Constitution?** | Conclusion: What was the "republican remedy"? |

The Federalist Persuasion

Although the Constitution came into force with the ratification of New Hampshire, four states still held out. New York was perhaps the most crucial. Once, the British had thought to defeat the rebellious colonies by conquering the state and dividing New England from the middle Atlantic and south. Could the United States survive without New York?

Although New York voters leaned Antifederalist, the state was home to some of the most brilliant and persuasive Federalist leaders. Starting in October 1787, Alexander Hamilton collaborated with James Madison and New York lawyer John Jay on a series of eighty-five essays on the political philosophy of the new Constitution. Published in New York newspapers, and later republished as *The Federalist Papers*, the essays brilliantly set out the failures of the Articles of Confederation and offered an analysis of the complex nature and advantages of the Constitution. In one of the most compelling essays, number 10, Madison challenged the Antifederalists' heartfelt conviction that republican government could flourish only on a small scale. To the contrary, Madison argued, a large and diverse population was the best guarantee against tyranny. In a national government, no single faction could ever grow large enough to subvert the freedom of other groups. "Extend the sphere, and you take in a greater variety of parties and interests; you make it less probable that a majority of the whole will have a common motive to invade the rights of other citizens," Madison asserted. He called it "a republican remedy for the diseases most incident to republican government."

At New York's ratifying convention, Antifederalists predominated, but impassioned debate and lobbying—plus the dramatic news that Virginia, the largest of the thirteen states, had finally ratified—tipped the balance to the Federalists. Even so, the Antifederalists' approval of the document came with a list of twenty-four individual rights and thirty-three structural changes they wanted made to the Constitution. New York's ratification ensured the viability of the new government, yet it took another year and a half for Antifederalists in North Carolina to assent. Though it was the smallest of the thirteen states, fiercely independent Rhode Island held out until May 1790, ratifying by a two-vote margin.

In less than twelve months, the U.S. Constitution had been written and ratified. The Federalists had faced a formidable task, but with savvy strategy and the promise of a bill of rights, they carried the day.

QUICK REVIEW

Why did Antifederalists oppose the Constitution?

Conclusion: What was the "republican remedy"?

Thus ended one of the most intellectually tumultuous and creative periods in American history.

The confederation government's requirement of unanimity was crippling. In a large and fractious republic with divergent interests, consensus was illusory. Divisions on western lands, an impost, and taxation in a republican state ran too deep for perfect harmony. The new Constitution offered a different approach, loosening

What kind of government did the Articles of Confederation create?

the grip of an impossible unanimity and embracing the ideas of a divided public life and a carefully balanced government. James Madison's great insight was to see that diversity of opinion in a republic was not just an unavoidable reality but a hidden strength. This was the "republican remedy" he invoked in Federalist essay number 10.

Madison's optimism notwithstanding, Americans' bitter political differences worried many people. The Federalists still hoped for a society in which leaders of exceptional wisdom would govern in the public interest. They looked backward to a society of hierarchy, rank, and benevolent rule by an enlightened aristocracy of talent, but they created a government with forward-looking checks and balances to moderate a democratic political culture. The Antifederalists also looked backward, but to an order of small-scale direct democracy and local control. They feared a national government led by distant, corruptible leaders. In the 1790s, these two conceptions of republicanism and of leadership would clash with each other, and neither would survive.

| How was republican government implemented? | Why did the Articles of Confederation fail? | How did the Constitution change the nation's form of government? | Why did so many Americans object to the Constitution? | Conclusion: What was the "republican remedy"? |

233

STEP 1

EXPLAIN WHY IT MATTERS

Put your reading into practice. Identify each term below, and then explain why it matters in U.S. history.

TERM	WHO OR WHAT & WHEN	WHY IT MATTERS
Articles of Confederation (p. 206)		
republicanism (p. 209)		
gradual emancipation (p. 213)		
Newburgh Conspiracy (p. 216)		
Treaty of Fort Stanwix (p. 217)		
Northwest Ordinance (p. 219)		
Northwest Confederacy (p. 220)		
Shays's Rebellion (p. 225)		
Virginia Plan (p. 226)		
New Jersey Plan (p. 226)		
United States Constitution (p. 226)		
three-fifths clause (p. 227)		
Federalists (p. 228)		
Antifederalists (p. 230)		

STEP 2

MOVE BEYOND THE BASICS

To demonstrate a more advanced understanding, fill in the chart below with the powers and responsibilities of the various branches of government under the Articles of Confederation and under the Constitution. What were the important differences?

	Powers and Responsibilities under Articles of Confederation	Powers and Responsibilities under U.S. Constitution
Congress		
Executive Branch		
Federal Judiciary		
States		

STEP 3   PUT IT ALL TOGETHER

Now, try to explain the big picture. Remember to use specific examples from the chapter in your answers.

THE ARTICLES OF CONFEDERATION AND POSTWAR INSTABILITY

- Why did many people see the Articles of Confederation as flawed?

- How did postwar state governments implement republican government?

- What were the gravest threats to the nation's political and economic stability after 1783?

- Why were western lands so important to the United States after 1783?

THE NEW CONSTITUTION

- What were the principal differences between the Articles of Confederation and the 1787 Constitution?

- What political compromises were embodied in the Constitution?

THE FIGHT FOR RATIFICATION

- Why did Antifederalists oppose the new Constitution? Where was their support the strongest? Why?

- Why did the Federalists ultimately prevail over the Antifederalists? What were the Federalists' most important weapons in the debate over the Constitution?

LOOKING BACKWARD, LOOKING AHEAD

- How did pre-revolutionary experiences with colonial legislatures and the British government shape the Articles of Confederation? The U.S. Constitution?

- What issues were left unresolved by the framers of the Constitution? Why?

STEP 4   CONNECT THESE EVENTS

How did the social disorder affecting the nation after the Revolution shape the U.S. Constitution?

STEP 5   CONNECT TO THE PRESENT

How do you think the constitutional debates and compromises of the 1780s have affected our present politics in the twenty-first century?

9

THE NEW NATION TAKES FORM

1789–1800

How did the United States overcome the domestic and international challenges it faced in the 1790s? Chapter 9 examines the efforts to achieve political stability in Constitution's first years. It explores Alexander Hamilton's plans to stabilize government finances; wars in the west and on the Atlantic; and partisan divisions that emerged in response to the turmoil.

This chapter will explore the following questions:

- What were the sources of political stability in the 1790s?
- Why did Hamilton's economic policies provoke such controversy?
- What threats did the United States face in the west?
- What threats did the United States face in the Atlantic world?
- How did partisan rivalries shape the politics of the late 1790s?
- Conclusion: Why did the United States form political parties?

AN AMERICAN STORY

By the 1790s, Alexander Hamilton—who brilliantly unified the pro-Constitution Federalists of 1788 and then headed the new government's Treasury Department—had become the country's most polarizing figure.

Hamilton grew up on a small Caribbean island. His parents were not married; his father abandoned the family when he was young and his mother died when he was eleven. His childhood struggles would stoke the fires of a ferocious ambition. After serving an apprenticeship, Hamilton made his way to New York City, where he gained entry to college. During the American Revolution, he served as General George Washington's aide. The two became close. In the 1780s, Hamilton practiced law in New York and participated in the constitutional convention in Philadelphia. He served a critical role in the ratification process.

Handsome and well-connected, Hamilton married into one of New York's wealthiest and most powerful families. His magnetic charm attracted both men and women; at social gatherings, he shone. Late-night revelry, however, never interfered with Hamilton's prodigious capacity for work.

As Washington's first treasury secretary, Hamilton took bold action. A government "confident of its own powers," he remarked, "is the surest way to inspire the same confidence in others." He tackled the country's Revolutionary War debt, producing a complex plan to pump millions of dollars into the economy. He instituted a national banking system and proposed a system of government subsidies and tariffs to promote manufacturing.

Hamilton was a gifted man endowed with remarkable political instincts. He also excelled at making enemies. The "founding fathers" who had allied in the 1770s and 1780s to fight a revolution and write a constitution became bitter rivals in the 1790s as deep ideological fissures pulled the nation apart.

James Madison, now a representative in Congress, led the opposition to Hamilton's economic program. John Adams, Washington's vice president, privately called Hamilton "the bastard brat of a Scotch pedlar," driven by "disappointed Ambition and unbridled malice and revenge." Years later, when asked why he had deserted Hamilton, Madison coolly replied: "Colonel Hamilton deserted me."

Hamilton and his allies assumed that government was most stable when in the hands of "the rich, the wise, and the good"—by which he meant America's commercial elite. By contrast, Jefferson, Madison, and their supporters clung to agrarian values, and looked suspiciously on finance and manufacturing. The turbulent international events of the period—including the French and Haitian Revolutions and the explosion of extraordinarily destructive warfare throughout Europe and its colonies—dramatically inflamed American divisions.

The political antagonisms of these first years left their mark on the young country. No one predicted the intense polarization over economic and foreign policy. By 1800, the two opposing camps had crystallized into political parties—the Federalists and the Republicans. At their heart, the two parties reflected opposing ideas about the meaning of republicanism, the limits of federal power, and the nation's role on the global stage. To most Americans of that day, this was an unhappy development—one the Constitution had not foreseen.

▼ *Alexander Hamilton,* by John Trumbull Hamilton posed for this portrait in 1792, at the age of thirty-seven. He was then secretary of the treasury. Born of an unwed mother who died when he was still a boy, Hamilton ascended to the heights of power and status. Everett Collection Historical/Alamy.

What were the sources of political stability in the 1790s?

CHRONOLOGY

1789
- George Washington inaugurated as first president.
- First Congress meets.

1790
- Judith Sargent Murray publishes "On the Equality of the Sexes."

1791
- States ratify Bill of Rights.

PLACE EVENTS IN CONTEXT

What popular fears did Washington have to overcome in establishing the institution of the presidency?

After the turbulence of the 1780s, the new government's most urgent task was to establish stability and heal the lingering divisions between Federalists and Antifederalists. The election of George Washington as president offered a good start. People trusted him with the presidency's expansive powers. Congress had important work as well in fleshing out the new government and amending the Constitution. It quickly agreed on the Bill of Rights, which answered the concerns of many Antifederalists.

Beyond politics, changing meanings of gender enhanced political stability. The private virtue of women was mobilized to bolster the public virtue of male citizens and to promote political stability. Republicanism forced a rethinking of women's relation to the state.

Washington Inaugurates the Government

George Washington was elected president in February 1789 by a unanimous vote of the electoral college. (John Adams, with half as many votes, became vice president.) Washington embodied the republican ideal of disinterested, public-spirited leadership. He cultivated that image through dramatic ceremonies like the surrender of his sword to the Continental Congress at the Revolution's end—enacting the subservience of military power to the law and instilling faith among Americans in his commitment to republican government. According to one delegate, the president's powers under the Constitution would not have been so extensive "had not many of the members cast their eyes toward General Washington as President; and shaped their Ideas of the Powers to be given to a President, by their opinions of his Virtue."

Once in office, Washington acted cautiously, aware that every step set a precedent and any misstep could endanger the fragile government. Congress debated a title for Washington, ranging from "His Highness" to "His Majesty, the President"; Washington favored "His High Mightiness." In the end, republican simplicity prevailed. "President of the United States of America" became the executive's title, and the established form of address became "Mr. President," a restrained yet dignified title.

Washington's success in launching the presidency lay in his ability to extend his personal reputation to the public office. In the political language of the day, he was "virtuous," meaning that he put the public good over his private interest and personal ambition. Most Americans were confident he would resist taking power for himself. Despite his genuine commitment to republican values, he occasionally indulged in ostentation to endow the office with respect, traveling with six horses to pull his coach, hosting formal balls, and surrounding himself with uniformed servants. He held weekly levees, as European monarchs did, hour-long audiences granted to distinguished visitors, male and female, at which he appeared attired in black velvet with a feathered hat and a polished sword. The president and his guests bowed, avoiding the egalitarian familiarity of a handshake. Ultimately, he succeeded in endowing the office with respect while avoiding the royal splendor of a monarch.

Washington chose talented men to lead the newly created Departments of War, State, and the Treasury. For the Department of War, Washington selected General Henry Knox, former secretary of war in the confederation government. For the Treasury—an especially tough job in view of the revenue crisis that sparked the drafting of the Constitution—the president appointed Alexander Hamilton. To lead

What were the sources of political stability in the 1790s?

the State Department, which ran foreign policy, Washington chose Thomas Jefferson, who had served as minister to France in the 1780s. For attorney general, Washington picked Edmund Randolph, a Virginian who had attended the constitutional convention but had turned Antifederalist during ratification. For chief justice of the Supreme Court, Washington appointed John Jay, a New York lawyer who had helped write *The Federalist Papers.*

Soon Washington began holding regular meetings with these men, establishing the precedent of a presidential cabinet. (Vice President John Adams was not included; his only official duty, to preside over the Senate, he found "a punishment." To his wife he complained: "My country has in its wisdom contrived for me the most insignificant office.") No one anticipated the party turbulence that would soon divide this brilliant group into rival camps.

The Bill of Rights

The First Congress began meeting in 1789. Its most pressing business was to pass a Bill of Rights. Seven states had ratified the Constitution with the demand of amendments to specify protected individual rights and limitations on federal power. The framers of the Constitution had thought such a list unnecessary. After the divisions of the ratification controversy, however, it seemed likely to promote national unity, and "to extinguish from the bosom of every member of the community," as Congressman James Madison put it, "any apprehensions that there are those among his countrymen who wish to deprive them of the liberty for which they valiantly fought and honorably bled."

Drawing on existing state constitutions, the proposed amendments enumerated rights to freedom of speech, press, and religion; the right to petition and assemble; and the right to freedom from unwarranted searches and seizures. One amendment guaranteed the right to keep and bear arms in support of a "well-regulated militia," to which Madison added, "but no person religiously scrupulous of bearing arms, shall be compelled to render military service in person." That provision for what a later century would call "conscientious objector" status failed to gain acceptance in Congress.

In September 1789, Congress approved a set of twelve amendments and sent them to the states for approval; by 1791, ten were ratified. The First through Eighth dealt with individual liberties, and the Ninth and Tenth addressed the boundary between federal and state authority.

Not everyone was satisfied. State ratifying conventions had submitted some eighty proposed amendments. Congress never considered proposals to change structural features of the new government. It had no appetite to reopen debates about the length of the president's term, for example, or the power to levy excise taxes. Although the Bill of Rights ignored the status of enslaved people, some activists capitalized on the First Amendment's right to petition to force the First Congress to debate the issue.

Significantly, no one pointed to a striking omission in the Bill of Rights: the right to vote. Voting was seen as a fundamental right only decades later. The Constitution left the definition of eligible voters to the states because of the wide variation in local voting practices. Most of these were based on property qualifications, although some touched on religion.

Bill of Rights
The first ten amendments to the Constitution, officially ratified by 1791. The First through Eighth Amendments dealt with individual liberties, and the Ninth and Tenth concerned the boundary between federal and state authority.

The Republican Wife and Mother

The exclusion of women from formal politics did not eliminate them from all civic roles. To the contrary, a growing chorus of voices argued that American women had special obligations. A republic, it was believed, required virtuous citizens to survive.

| Why did Hamilton's economic policies provoke such controversy? | What threats did the United States face in the west? | What threats did the United States face in the Atlantic world? | How did partisan rivalries shape the politics of the late 1790s? | Conclusion: Why did the United States form political parties? |

▲ **Republican Womanhood: Judith Sargent Murray** Judith Sargent Murray became known in the 1790s as America's foremost spokeswoman for woman's equality. She argued that women had "natural powers" of mind fully the equal of men's. George Washington and John Adams each bought a copy of her collected essays. John Singleton Copley (1738–1815). Portrait of Mrs. John Stevens (Judith Sargent, later Mrs. John Murray). 1770–1772. Oil on canvas, 50 x 40 in. Daniel J. Terra Art Acquisition Endowment Fund, 2000.6. Terra Foundation for American Art, Chicago / Art Resource, NY.

republican motherhood
Ideology emphasizing the importance of female education to equip women to raise educated and enlightened male citizens. Even as it opened pathways for women's education, the ideology reinforced existing hierarchies of gender.

CONSIDER CAUSE AND EFFECT

How did the Revolutionary ideal calling for a virtuous citizenry affect ideas about the role of women in the new republic?

Who would foster that virtue? According to more and more people, that task fell to women. "The solidity and stability of the liberties of your country rest with you; since Liberty is never sure, 'till Virtue reigns triumphant," wrote one author to female audiences. "While you thus keep our country virtuous, you maintain its independence."

Until the late eighteenth century, public virtue was strictly a masculine quality—the prerogative of the male, landowning, independent head of the household. But another kind of virtue now grew in importance: feminine sexual chastity. Essayists of the 1790s explicitly advised young women to use their private sexual virtue to increase public virtue in men. "Love and courtship . . . invest a lady with more authority than in any other situation that falls to the lot of human beings," one essayist proclaimed.

Republican ideals also cast motherhood in a new light. Throughout the 1790s, advocates for female education argued that educated women would make better mothers, who would in turn produce better male citizens. Historians call this the concept of **republican motherhood**. Benjamin Rush, a Pennsylvania physician and educator, called for female education because "our ladies should be qualified . . . in instructing their sons in the principles of liberty and government."

Massachusetts writer Judith Sargent Murray favored education that would remake women into self-confident, rational beings. She boldly titled her first essay, published in 1790, "On the Equality of the Sexes." In a subsequent essay on education, however, she reassured readers that educated women would retain their "characteristic trait" of sweetness—thus reaffirming older stereotypes of women as compliant.

Although women's obligations as wives and mothers carried new political meanings, they did not amount to a revolution in gender relations. **(See "Spotlight: France, Britain, and Woman's Rights in the 1790s" on page 242.)** The analogy between motherhood and republican government succeeded because the term *virtue* implied that both men and women should subordinate their private interests. Men should put the public good first, just as women must put their husbands and families first. Women might gain literacy and knowledge, but the objective was to create better male citizens. Nor did ideas of republican motherhood extend to black women; that they might also have the capacity for virtue eluded most writing at the time. In Federalist America, wives and citizens should feel affection for and trust in their rulers, but neither should ever rebel.

QUICK REVIEW

How did political leaders in the 1790s attempt to overcome the divisions of the 1780s?

What were the sources of political stability in the 1790s?

Why did Hamilton's economic policies provoke such controversy?

Compared to the instability of the 1780s, the 1790s brimmed with opportunity. Trade, transportation, and banking sectors all boomed. In 1790, the nation's capital moved to Philadelphia, the nation's largest city, where Treasury Secretary Alexander Hamilton launched his ambitious plans to strengthen government finances. His proposals to fund the national debt, set up a national bank, promote manufacturing, and raise revenue with a whiskey tax met with intense political opposition.

Agriculture, Transportation, and Banking

A sharp rise in international grain prices in the 1790s drove American farmers to increase agricultural production and exports. From the Connecticut River valley to the Chesapeake, wheat production generated profits for farmers, and new jobs for millers, coopers, dockworkers, and shipbuilders.

Cotton production also boomed, spurred by demand from British textile manufacturers and a new mechanical invention. For nearly a century, planters had grown long staple cotton with slave labor in coastal areas of the South. But this variety of cotton did not prosper in the continent's vast inland regions. Short staple cotton grew well inland, but its rough seeds stuck to the cotton fibers and took hours of labor to remove. In 1793, Yale graduate Eli Whitney devised a machine called a gin that separated out the seeds. Suddenly—just as Native Americans were losing their vast territories to American settlers—short staple cotton could be profitably grown. Production soared, contributing to the growing transatlantic trade with Britain, whose factories processed the raw cotton into cloth.

A surge of roadbuilding further stimulated the economy. Before 1790, one road connected Maine to Georgia. With the establishment of the U.S. Post Office in 1792, road mileage increased sixfold. Private companies also built toll roads, such as the Lancaster Turnpike west of Philadelphia, the Boston-to-Albany turnpike, and a road from Virginia to Tennessee. By 1800, a network of dirt, gravel, and plank roadways connected towns in southern New England and the Middle Atlantic states, expanding the number of commercial stage companies and reducing travel times between major cities (**Map 9.1**).

During the 1790s, commercial banking grew dramatically. The number of banks nationwide multiplied tenfold, from three to twenty-nine. Banks drew in money chiefly through the sale of stock. They then made loans in the form of banknotes—paper currency backed by gold and silver from stock sales. By issuing two or three times as much money in banknotes as they held in hard money, they expanded the money supply and helped spur the economy.

The U.S. population expanded along with the economic development. As measured by the first two federal censuses in 1790 and 1800, the population grew from 3.9 million to 5.3 million, an extraordinary increase of 35 percent.

The Public Debt and Taxes

The upturn in the economy, along with the government's new taxation powers, meant that the United States might soon pay off its wartime debt. But Hamilton had a different objective: He wanted to make the new country creditworthy rather than debt-free. His 1790 *Report on Public Credit* recommended that the debt be funded—but not

CHRONOLOGY

1790
- Congress approves Hamilton's debt plan.
- National capital moves to Philadelphia.

1791
- Bank of the United States chartered.
- Hamilton issues *Report on Manufactures*.

1793
- Eli Whitney invents cotton gin.

Major Roads in the 1790s

Report on Public Credit
Hamilton's 1790 report recommending that the national debt be funded at full value, but not repaid immediately. Hamilton's goal was to make the new country creditworthy, not debt-free, and tie the interests of wealthy bondholders to the new government. Critics complained that it would benefit speculators.

Why did Hamilton's economic policies provoke such controversy?	What threats did the United States face in the west?	What threats did the United States face in the Atlantic world?	How did partisan rivalries shape the politics of the late 1790s?	Conclusion: Why did the United States form political parties?

France, Britain, and Woman's Rights in the 1790s

During the 1770s and 1780s, no one in the United States wondered publicly about rights for women. Boycotts by the Daughters of Liberty before the Revolution did not challenge gender hierarchy, nor did New Jersey's handful of women voters (see "Who Are 'the People'?" in chapter 8). It took radical ideas from France and Britain to spark serious challenges to women's inferior status in American society.

In France between 1789 and 1793, by contrast, the revolution against monarchy enlarged ideas about citizenship. It led some women to call themselves *citoyennes*, female citizens. Women's political clubs sent petitions, gave speeches to the National Assembly demanding education and voting rights, and generally challenged patriarchal powers of men over women. In 1791, Frenchwoman Olympe de Gouges rewrote the revolutionaries' document *The Declaration of the Rights of Man* into the *Declaration of the Rights of Woman and the Female Citizen*. It asserted that "all women are born free and remain equal to men in rights." Another prominent woman, Anne Josèphe Théroigne de Méricourt, maintained a political salon (intellectual gathering), marched around Paris in masculine riding attire, and addressed crowds engaged in violent street actions. Her vision went beyond political rights to the social customs that enforced women's subordination: "It is time for women to break out of the shameful incompetence in which men's ignorance, pride, and injustice have so long held us captive."

Although the National Assembly—composed exclusively of men—never approved voting rights for French women, it did reform French civil and family law. Marriage became a secular contract, removed from church control. Divorce was legalized, and the age of majority for women (when females qualified as adults) was lowered. A major change in inheritance law required the division of a man's estate among all his children, regardless of age, sex, and even legitimacy. By contrast, most

FRONTISPIECE.

Publish'd at Philad.ª *Dec.ʳ 1.ˢᵗ 1792.*

▲ This engraving accompanied excerpts from Mary Wollstonecraft's *A Vindication of the Rights of Woman*. The kneeling woman holds out a paper entitled "Rights of Woman" to Lady Liberty, imploring her to embrace this new concept. Notice the objects below Lady Liberty. What do they suggest about the artist's interpretation of the "rights of woman"? Library of Congress, LC-DIG-ppmsca-02951.

repaid immediately. Old certificates of debt would be converted into new bonds, which would earn interest for several years before being fully paid off. In the meantime, the bonds would circulate, injecting millions of dollars of new money into the economy. Equally important, from Hamilton's perspective, holders of the country's bonds would develop a direct financial stake in the government's success. "A national debt if not excessive will be to us a national blessing," he wrote. "It will be a powerful cement of our union."

What were the sources of political stability in the 1790s?

American states adopted traditional English family law virtually unchanged.

French feminism traveled across the Channel to Britain to inspire the brilliant writer Mary Wollstonecraft. Born into a respectable but downwardly mobile family, Wollstonecraft worked as a governess before establishing herself as a writer in London. There she fell in with a circle of radical thinkers that included Thomas Paine, the philosopher William Godwin, and other leading artists and intellectuals. In 1792, she published *A Vindication of the Rights of Woman*, building on Paine's 1791 book *The Rights of Man*. Paine wrote about property and politics as fundamental rights but never considered women. Wollstonecraft argued that women, too, had inherent rights. She spoke forcefully about the intellectual equality of the sexes, and called for female education. She championed women's economic independence, and most radically, suggested that traditional marriage at its worst was legalized prostitution.

Wollstonecraft's book created a sensation in the United States. Excerpts appeared in periodicals, and bookstores stocked the London edition; by 1795, there were three American reprints. Some women readers responded cautiously. A sixty-year-old Philadelphian, Elizabeth Drinker, reflected in her diary that Wollstonecraft "speaks my mind" on some issues but not others; "I am not for quite so much independence." A youthful Priscilla Mason delivered a commencement address at her academy and, inspired by Wollstonecraft, condemned "the high and mighty lords" (men) who denied women education and professional opportunities. "Happily, a more liberal way of thinking begins to prevail," Mason predicted.

Male readers also responded in a variety of ways. Aaron Burr, a senator from New York, called Wollstonecraft's book "a work of genius." A Fourth of July speaker in New Jersey in 1793 proclaimed that "the Rights of Woman are no longer strange sounds to an American ear" and called for revisions in state laws. But critics of Wollstonecraft were not in short supply. A New York orator on that same July Fourth argued that a woman's rights really meant her duty "to submit to the control of that government she has voluntarily chosen"—the government of a husband.

The keen interest in woman's rights faded fast, however. The unhappy fate of de Gouges, guillotined in France in 1794, was soon followed by news of Wollstonecraft's death in childbirth in 1797. Soon after, William Godwin, father of her infant daughter, published details of her unconventional personal life: love affairs, two children conceived out of wedlock, and two suicide attempts. "Her licentious practice renders her memory odious to every friend of virtue," declared a prominent American minister in 1801. Public admiration of Wollstonecraft and her ideas about women had been successfully suppressed.

Questions for Analysis

SUMMARIZE THE ARGUMENT: How did French ideas about woman's rights go beyond existing American debates, and how did they influence discussion on the topic in the United States?

ANALYZE THE EVIDENCE: What arguments did opponents of Mary Wollstonecraft use to criticize her ideas?

ASK HISTORICAL QUESTIONS: How do the radical ideas of Mary Wollstonecraft contrast with the more moderate concept of "republican motherhood," which sums up the expectations for American women's contributions to civil society and family life?

Funding the debt in full was controversial because speculators had bought most debt certificates at a sharp discount when it appeared they would never be repaid. Hamilton compounded the controversy with his proposal that the federal government take on another $25 million of state debt. During the war, states had obtained supplies by issuing IOUs to farmers, merchants, and moneylenders. Some states, such as Virginia and New York, had paid these debts off entirely. Others, such as Massachusetts, had partially paid them off through heavy taxation of the people. About half the states had

| Why did Hamilton's economic policies provoke such controversy? | What threats did the United States face in the west? | What threats did the United States face in the Atlantic world? | How did partisan rivalries shape the politics of the late 1790s? | Conclusion: Why did the United States form political parties? |

243

MAP 9.1 ▶ Travel Times from New York City in 1800

Traveling along waterways—oceans and rivers—was much faster than traveling over land; from New York, travel extended over a much greater distance in the first week than in subsequent weeks. It took less time to get from New York to New Orleans, though it was 1,170 miles away, than it did to get to St. Louis, only 873 miles away.

made little headway. Hamilton called for the federal government to assume these state debts and combine them with the federal debt.

Congressman James Madison strenuously objected to a plan that provided windfall profits to wealthy speculators—while the soldiers and farmers who had earned the debt certificates by their struggles and sacrifice received a fraction of the money they were promised. He instead proposed a complex scheme to pay both the original holders of the federal debt and the speculators, each in fair proportion. Madison also objected to assumption of the states' debts. First, he thought the plan unfair to those states that had struggled to pay off their debt. Furthermore, he believed a large debt was dangerous because it would inevitably lead to high taxation. Jefferson shared Madison's concerns: "This exactly marks the difference between Colonel Hamilton's views and mine," he wrote. "That I would wish the debt paid tomorrow; he wishes it never to be paid, but always to be a thing where with to corrupt and manage the legislature."

To resolve the impasse, Jefferson invited Hamilton and Madison to dinner. Over good food and wine, Madison pledged his support for Hamilton's plan. In return, Hamilton agreed to endorse the relocation of the nation's capital city to the South, along the Potomac River—an outcome sure to please Virginians. In early July 1790, Congress voted for the Potomac site, and in late July, Congress passed the debt package, assumption and all.

UNDERSTAND POINTS OF VIEW

Why did Alexander Hamilton believe that funding the public debt would be more beneficial to the United States than eliminating it? Why did Madison and Jefferson object?

What were the sources of political stability in the 1790s?

◀ **William Russell Birch, *Bank of the United States*** As part of his controversial plan for building the U.S. financial system, Alexander Hamilton proposed a Bank of the United States, modeled on the Bank of England. This building, completed in 1797, became the bank's first permanent home. How does the building reinforce the authority of the federal government and emphasize the stability of government finances? Library of Congress, 3b52049.

The First Bank of the United States and the *Report on Manufactures*

The second and third elements of Hamilton's economic plan recommended a national bank of the United States and support for domestic manufacturing. Arguing that banks were "nurseries of national wealth," Hamilton modeled his proposed bank on the Bank of England, which he believed had advanced Britain's economic and military power in the eighteenth century. According to Hamilton's plan, the central bank would be capitalized at $10 million, a sum larger than all the hard money in the entire nation. The federal government would hold 20 percent of the bank's stock; the bank would receive and administer government revenues from import duties, land sales, and various other taxes. Private investors would subscribe to the other 80 percent of the bank's capital, buying stock with either hard money (silver or gold) or the recently issued federal securities. Because of its size and its status as national bank, the Bank of the United States would help stabilize the economy by exerting prudent control over credit, interest rates, and inflation.

> "'The tailor who has made thousands in one day, tho' he has lost them the next, can never again be content with the slow and moderate earnings of his needle,' said Jefferson."

Concerned that a few rich bankers might gain excessive influence over the economy, Madison tried to block the plan in Congress. Jefferson advised President Washington that the Constitution did not permit Congress to charter banks. Hamilton countered that Congress possessed explicit powers to regulate commerce and a broad mandate "to make all laws which shall be necessary and proper for carrying into execution the foregoing powers." Washington sided with Hamilton and signed the Bank of the United States into law in February 1791, giving it a twenty-year charter.

When the bank's stock went on sale a few months later, it sold out in a few hours. Calling the spectacle "a mere scramble for so much public plunder," a discouraged Madison reported that in New York "the Coffee House is in an eternal buzz with the gamblers." The intense speculation pained Jefferson, too. "The spirit of gaming, when once it has seized a subject, is incurable. The tailor who has made thousands in one

Why did Hamilton's economic policies provoke such controversy?	What threats did the United States face in the west?	What threats did the United States face in the Atlantic world?	How did partisan rivalries shape the politics of the late 1790s?	Conclusion: Why did the United States form political parties?

day, tho' he has lost them the next, can never again be content with the slow and moderate earnings of his needle."

Hamilton proposed the final element of his economic plan in his December 1791 *Report on Manufactures*. With the production of American-made goods in its infancy, Hamilton hoped to support domestic manufacturers by imposing moderate tariffs on imports. His plan targeted iron goods, arms and ammunition, coal, textiles, wood products, and glass. Among the benefits of manufacturing, he included the new employment opportunities that would open to children and unmarried young women, who he believed were underutilized in agricultural societies.

Hamilton's *Report on Manufactures* went a step too far, however. Congress never approved or even voted on the plan. Many agriculturalists in Congress believed that industry was a curse rather than a blessing; they wanted a nation of landowning farmers, not wage-working laborers. Madison and Jefferson also objected to stretching the "general welfare" clause of the Constitution to include public subsidies to private businesses.

Report on Manufactures
Hamilton's 1791 proposal to encourage the production of American-made goods by subsidizing manufacturers and imposing tariffs on imports. Its vision of a future manufacturing society broke sharply from the nation's agrarian economy. Congress rejected the measure.

QUICK REVIEW

What were Hamilton's principal economic policies, and why were they controversial?

What threats did the United States face in the west?

Conflicts over economic policy were not the only threats to the nation's stability. Other pressures originated on the country's western periphery, where discontented settlers threatened rebellion against the federal government. Meanwhile, Native Americans continued to battle U.S. sovereignty in the region between the Appalachian Mountains and the Mississippi River. To the southwest, the Washington administration engaged principally in diplomatic negotiations to extend U.S. sovereignty. To the northwest, however, the army waged a bitter war to conquer Native American territory.

Western Discontent and the Whiskey Rebellion

For more than a century, settlers along the western edge of colonial settlement had distrusted centralized authority. Their resentment had periodically boiled over: in Bacon's Rebellion in the seventeenth century (see chapter 3), in resistance to the Royal Proclamation of 1763 (see chapter 6), and in Shays's Rebellion in 1787 (see chapter 8). In regions west of the Appalachian Mountains, resentment continued to seethe. In part for geographic reasons, in part a response to feelings of federal neglect, tensions between eastern and western regions threatened the stability of the United States in the 1790s.

For land-hungry settlers, victory in the American Revolution signaled an invitation to occupy the west. Kentucky was the first front. With an insignificant settler presence in 1780, the region's white population exploded: from under 74,000 in 1790 to over 220,000 in 1800. As settlers pushed into Indian territories, they unleashed a fierce resistance among Native Americans dedicated to protecting their lands. Exhausted from the Revolution, the army could barely muster a defense against native attacks.

The federal government's inability to protect them from Indian assaults angered many settlers. Even worse, from their perspective, federal power chased squatters off public lands as often as it protected them from attacks. "Choose lands for a settlement that are near those of the navigable waters that *run towards* the Atlantick ocean," read

What were the sources of political stability in the 1790s?

one piece of advice published in newspapers in 1789. Magnifying western settlers' distrust of eastern authorities were the derogatory terms often used by government officials: "a parcel of banditti, who will bid defiance to all authority," as George Washington once put it. "Our *own* white Indians," a Connecticut official muttered.

In the mid-1790s, anger toward the federal government boiled over, this time in response to Hamilton's tax policies. His economic plan required revenue to pay the interest on the large national debt. In deference to the eastern merchants, Hamilton did not propose an increase in import duties. Nor did he propose land taxes, which would have fallen hardest on the nation's wealthy landowners in the East. Instead, he convinced Congress in 1791 to pass a 25 percent tax on whiskey, which fell disproportionately on western farmers bringing grain to the distillery.

The whiskey tax was deeply unpopular. In 1791, farmers in Kentucky and the western parts of Pennsylvania, Virginia, Maryland, and the Carolinas forcefully expressed their resentment. "If this is not an oppressive tax," wrote one farmer, "I am at a loss to describe what is." Discontent only grew in the following years, as crowds threatened to tar and feather tax collectors. It finally exploded in western Pennsylvania in July 1794, when a stubborn tax collector named John Neville along with a federal marshal served legal documents to several distillers.

The Whiskey Rebellion began the next day, when a crowd of five hundred burned Neville's house while the marshal fled to Pittsburgh. On August 1, seven thousand Pennsylvania farmers gathered to protest the tax. A group of them issued a letter calling on "citizen[s] of the western country" to join the protesters "with as many volunteers as you can raise." Echoing the American Revolution, this resistance to an unpopular tax seemed ready to spread across the Ohio Valley from Pennsylvania, Maryland, and Virginia to Kentucky and Ohio—areas where the popular loyalties to the distant central government were thinnest.

Recognizing the threat to his new government, President Washington nationalized the Pennsylvania militia. With Hamilton at his side, he rode out at the head of thirteen thousand soldiers. A Philadelphia newspaper criticized the massive mobilization: "Shall torrents of blood be spilled to support an odious excise system?" But no blood spilled; the massive show of force quashed the rebellion. By the time Washington and his army arrived in late September, the demonstrators had dispersed. No battles were fought, and no shots were exchanged. Twenty men were charged with high treason, but only two were convicted, and Washington pardoned both.

Had the federal government overreacted? Thomas Jefferson thought so. The rebel farmers agreed: They felt entitled to protest oppressive taxation. Hamilton and Washington, however, thought that laws passed by a republican government, as opposed to those of an unrepresentative Parliament, demanded strict obedience. For them, the Whiskey Rebellion presented an opportunity for the new federal government to flex its muscles and stand up to civil disorder.

Whiskey Rebellion
July 1794 uprising by farmers in western Pennsylvania in response to enforcement of an unpopular tax on whiskey. Fearing it might spark a revolution against the new government in the west, President Washington responded with overwhelming force to quash the rebellion and avoid bloodshed.

ANALYZE EVIDENCE

What did the Whiskey Rebellion and government officials' responses to it reveal about the political and geographic divisions in the United States in the 1790s?

Creeks in the Southwest

If Washington's response to the Whiskey Rebellion muted resentment among western settlers, at least for the time being, it did nothing to appease the anger of Native Americans at the continual encroachment on their lands. Some twenty thousand Indians of loosely affiliated Creek villages occupied the territory extending from Georgia into what is now Mississippi. Border skirmishes with land-hungry Georgians were growing in frequency. To help keep American squatters off their lands, Creek leaders cultivated alliances with Spanish authorities in Louisiana. The U.S. government was in a bind: It needed to take charge of Indian affairs without alienating the settlers whose loyalties it needed, and without getting embroiled in a costly war. Washington and his secretary of war, Henry Knox, singled out the Creek chief Alexander McGillivray to negotiate a treaty.

Why did Hamilton's economic policies provoke such controversy?	**What threats did the United States face in the west?**	What threats did the United States face in the Atlantic world?	How did partisan rivalries shape the politics of the late 1790s?	Conclusion: Why did the United States form political parties?

◀ **Alexander McGillivray, 1790** Artist John Trumbull approached the Creek delegation in New York City for treaty negotiations and asked them to sit for individual portraits. They "possessed a dignity of manner, form, countenance and expression, worthy of Roman Senators," Trumbull recalled. They all declined, and the artist was forced to make five drawings "by stealth" instead. McGillivray here wears an American military coat, a present from President Washington. The New York Public Library/Art Resource, NY.

Like others of mixed European and native ancestry, McGillivray played an important role as a broker between cultures and mediator in trade and diplomacy. His French-Creek mother conferred a claim to Creek leadership, while his Scottish fur-trading father gave him exposure to British diplomacy. Fluent in English and conversant in Spanish, McGillivray spoke several Creek languages and had even studied Greek and Latin. In the 1770s, he worked for the British distributing gifts to various southern tribes; in the 1780s, he gained renown for brokering negotiations with the Spanish in Florida.

Secretary Knox invited McGillivray to New York to meet with the president. McGillivray arrived in a triumphal procession of Creek chiefs and was accorded the honors of a head of state. The delegation was met with the largest crowds since Washington's inauguration. Their negotiations resulted in the 1790 Treaty of New York. The United States guaranteed Creek tribal lands, promising that its federal troops would protect the boundary against land-seeking settlers. U.S. authorities also committed to annual payments to the Creek people in money and trade goods. In return, the Creeks promised to accept the United States as its sole trading partner, shutting Spain out.

Both sides had made promises they could not keep. McGillivray believed the best way to advance the Creeks' interests was by fostering competition between American and Spanish officials for Creek alliances and trade. By 1792, he had signed an agreement with the Spanish governor of New Orleans, each side pledging to resist encroachments by Georgia settlers. As for U.S. authorities, they were in no position to prohibit intrusions into Creek lands. They lacked the military power and the political will to fight their own citizens. Nor did they wish to inflame the anger of settlers in the Southwest and risk another rebellion. By the time Alexander McGillivray died in 1793, the Treaty of New York joined the list of treaties never implemented.

In dealing with the Creeks, Washington and Knox had sought a different approach to Indian affairs, one rooted more in British than in American experience. But a republican government required popular consent—all the more so in border regions, where national loyalties were so tenuous. This imperative meant that confrontation with the native population was all but inevitable. As Washington wrote in 1796, "I believe scarcely any thing short of a Chinese Wall, or line of Troops will restrain Land Jobbers, and the encroachment of Settlers, upon Indian Territory."

PLACE EVENTS IN CONTEXT

In what ways did the republican nature of U.S. politics make the nation's government less able to meet the demands of Native Americans?

Ohio Indians in the Northwest

Native people between the Ohio River and the Great Lakes were even less willing to negotiate with the new federal government. By the 1790s Shawnee, Delaware, Miami, and other groups forming the Northwest Confederacy (see chapter 8) had been fighting to control their lands for nearly half a century, playing European powers off each other in a complex game of trade and diplomacy. They refused to recognize the 1783 Treaty of Paris (see chapter 7), in which the British had ceded their lands to the United States without their consent. They continued to fight for their homelands. They were in direct confrontation with U.S. ambitions to settle the region.

What were the sources of political stability in the 1790s?

MAP 9.2 ▲ Western Expansion and Indian Land Cessions to 1810 By the first decade of the nineteenth century, intense U.S. warfare against Native Americans had resulted in major land cessions to the United States.

READING THE MAP: Where did most of the Native American land cessions occur between 1759 and 1783, and where did they occur most intensely after 1783?

CONNECTIONS: How did the explosive population growth of the United States affect relations between Native Americans and settlers in the west?

Guided by the Northwest Ordinance (see chapter 8), the federal government started to survey and map eastern Ohio in preparation to sell the land. Fort Washington, on the Ohio River at the site of present-day Cincinnati, became the command post for three major invasions of Indian country (**Map 9.2**). This American offensive met a determined Native American resistance, strengthened by support from British forts along the Great Lakes and in the Ohio Valley. These forts protected the fur trade between British traders and Indians, supplied weapons to the Northwest Confederacy, and sustained native claims to the land.

The first U.S. campaign began in the fall of 1790, when General Josiah Harmar marched with 1,400 men into northwest Ohio, burning Indian villages. Miami and

Why did Hamilton's economic policies provoke such controversy?	**What threats did the United States face in the west?**	What threats did the United States face in the Atlantic world?	How did partisan rivalries shape the politics of the late 1790s?	Conclusion: Why did the United States form political parties?

Shawnee Indians led by their chiefs, Little Turtle and Blue Jacket, ambushed Harmar's inexperienced troops and chased them out.

Harmar's defeat prompted a second effort. In the fall of 1791, General Arthur St. Clair, military governor of the Northwest Territory, led two thousand men (and two hundred women camp followers) deep into Indian country, where they constructed two forts. The show of military might did not intimidate native forces, however. They attacked at the headwaters of the Wabash River, leaving 55 percent of the Americans dead or wounded; only three women escaped alive. "The savages seemed not to fear anything we could do," an officer later wrote. "The ground was literally covered with the dead." With more than nine hundred lives lost, it was the worst American defeat in the history of Indian wars.

After St. Clair's defeat, Washington doubled the U.S. military presence in Ohio and appointed a new commander, General Anthony Wayne of Pennsylvania. About the Ohio peoples, Wayne wrote, "I have always been of the opinion that we never should have a permanent peace with those Indians until they were made to experience our

VISUAL ACTIVITY

▲ **Treaty of Greenville, 1795** This contemporary painting allegedly depicts the signing of the Treaty of Greenville. General Anthony Wayne stands at the center. Little Turtle, the great Miami chief, talks to General Wayne, while a kneeling officer interprets and transcribes the Indian's speech. Although Indians from a dozen Ohio tribes gathered at the signing ceremony, this picture shows very few. The Treaty of Greenville on August 3, 1795 (oil on canvas),

1805/American School (19th century)/CHICAGO HISTORY MUSEUM/Chicago History Museum, USA/Bridgeman Images.

READING THE IMAGE: How likely is it that the artist actually witnessed the signing of the treaty? Are there clues in the painting that offer evidence?

CONNECTIONS: How did the Jay Treaty (page 253) influence the Northwest Confederacy's willingness to capitulate to an unfavorable treaty with the U.S. government?

What were the sources of political stability in the 1790s?

superiority." Throughout 1794, Wayne's army engaged in skirmishes with the Northwest Confederacy's forces. Chief Little Turtle of the Miami tribe urged his allies to negotiate; in his view, Wayne's army looked overpowering. But Blue Jacket of the Shawnees counseled war, and prevailed.

> "'This liquor that they introduce into our country is more to be feared than the gun and tomahawk,' said Chief Little Turtle."

The decisive battle came in August 1794 at Fallen Timbers, near the Maumee River southwest of Lake Erie. Eight hundred warriors of the Northwest Confederacy ambushed the American forces without adequate weaponry. Unable to defeat the Americans, they withdrew and sought refuge at nearby Fort Miami, still held by the British. But the British commander locked the gate and refused protection. British forces stood by as their former allies were defeated, and their ranks decimated.

The defeat at Fallen Timbers marked the end of the Northwest Confederacy. It shattered the native coalition that had successfully resisted American encroachment into the Ohio Valley for over a decade, and signaled the arrival of U.S. sovereignty in the northwest. In 1795, about a thousand Indians representing nearly a dozen nations met with Wayne and other American emissaries to negotiate the **Treaty of Greenville**. The Americans offered treaty goods (calico shirts, axes, knives, blankets, kettles, mirrors, ribbons, thimbles, and abundant wine and liquor casks) worth $25,000 and promised annual shipments going forward. In exchange, the Indians ceded most of Ohio to the United States. Only the northwest part of the territory was reserved to the Indians.

If the treaty brought temporary peace to the region, it generated new forms of discontent among many native peoples. The annual allowance from the United States too often came in the form of liquor. "More of us have died since the Treaty of Greenville than we lost by the years of war before, and it is all owing to the introduction of liquor among us," said Chief Little Turtle in 1800. "This liquor that they introduce into our country is more to be feared than the gun and tomahawk." Frustration about a decline of supposedly traditional Indian ways of life would help provoke renewed war in the following decade. In the meantime, however, U.S. settlement in the region would grow exponentially.

Treaty of Greenville
1795 treaty between the United States and nations of the Northwest Confederacy. The United States gave Native Americans treaty goods valued at $25,000. In exchange, the Indians ceded most of Ohio. The treaty brought only temporary peace to the region.

PLACE EVENTS IN CONTEXT

How did the European presence in North America shape the U.S. war against Native Americans in the west?

QUICK REVIEW

How did the U.S. government respond to the varied threats to its sovereignty in the west?

What threats did the United States face in the Atlantic world?

If discontented settlers and war with Native Americans threatened the sovereignty of the United States on its western borders, epic events in the Atlantic world threatened the nation's very existence. In Europe, the outbreak of the French Revolution and renewed war between France and Great Britain pushed Americans to take sides. Desperate to avoid getting pulled into another war, the Washington and Adams administrations had to navigate bitter domestic and diplomatic divisions.

| Why did Hamilton's economic policies provoke such controversy? | What threats did the United States face in the west? | **What threats did the United States face in the Atlantic world?** | How did partisan rivalries shape the politics of the late 1790s? | Conclusion: Why did the United States form political parties? |

CHRONOLOGY

1789
– French Revolution begins.

1791
– Haitian Revolution begins.

1793
– War between Great Britain and France begins.
– Washington issues Neutrality Proclamation.

1794
– France abolishes slavery in all its colonies.

1795
– Congress approves Jay Treaty.

UNDERSTAND POINTS OF VIEW

Why did American public opinion split in response to the French Revolution?

Meanwhile, to the south, an unprecedented revolution of enslaved people in the Caribbean's most important colony raised racial fears and exposed the dangers of the nation's growing reliance on slave labor.

France and Britain: Toward Neutrality

In 1789, revolution broke out in France. To many Americans, it seemed as though the French—who had helped secure their independence—were now following their example. "Since the commencement of your revolution our attention has been drawn, with no small anxiety, almost to France alone," President Washington wrote his former comrade in arms, Lafayette. "How great! How important . . . is the part, which the actors in this momentous scene have to perform! Not only the fate of millions of the present day depends upon them, but the happiness of posterity is involved in their decisions." Americans up and down the coast organized celebrations and parades, sang French revolutionary songs, and proudly displayed French patriotic garb. Dozens of pro-French political clubs, called Democratic-Republican Societies, sprang up around the country, many of them establishing correspondence with revolutionary clubs in France, and avowing their solidarity with the French Republic. "Let us unite with France and stand or fall together," declared one Virginia speaker.

If most Americans celebrated the French Revolution in its early years, opinion began to divide in 1792 with its radicalization. After the French king was executed in January 1793, and Great Britain declared war on France, American popular opinion split sharply. Pro-French partisans, thrilled to see an absolutist monarchy overthrown and a sister republic emerge in the heart of Europe, enthusiastically threw their support behind the French cause. To them, the American and French Revolutions were two branches of a single movement for worldwide republicanism. Meanwhile, those shaken by reports of the massacres of thousands of French aristocrats concluded that the French Revolution had spun out of control. They feared its effect on the United States, and denounced the Democratic-Republican Societies as dangerous manifestations of popular unrest. To them, the American Revolution was distinct from the French, the former succeeding where the latter had failed.

▶ **Revolutionary Solidarity** In 1792–1793, Americans thrilled to news of the French Revolution. Many wore tricolor cockades—bows made of red, white, and blue ribbons. Women in the United States wore Parisian revolutionary fashions, as shown in this French picture. Such clothing, along with long, loose hair, made a bold partisan statement, inserting women into the political sphere. The New York Public Library/Art Resource, NY.

What were the sources of political stability in the 1790s?

War between Britain and France meant war in the Caribbean, right on the United States' doorstep. Large sections of the U.S. economy—shipbuilding, exports, finance, and more—depended on trade with the lucrative Caribbean islands. Although the United States was bound by the 1778 Treaty of Amity and Commerce to support France (see chapter 7), President Washington believed the country could not risk a renewed war with Great Britain. In May 1793, he issued the Neutrality Proclamation in an effort to stay out of the European war.

The Jay Treaty

Neutrality was more easily proclaimed than preserved. Taking advantage of its naval superiority, the British government issued a policy imposing a total blockade of France and its colonies, authorizing British vessels to "stop and detain all ships" trading with France or its islands. Before Americans had even learned of the policy, armed British privateers began seizing American ships, harassing their captains, impounding their cargoes, and forcing their sailors into service. In all, British forces detained more than 250 American ships. For all of Washington's efforts to keep the United States out of war, war seemed to be imposing itself upon him.

In a desperate attempt to maintain peace, Washington sent John Jay, the chief justice of the Supreme Court, to negotiate a new treaty with Great Britain. Jay sailed off with ambitious instructions. He was to establish commercial relations in the British West Indies, secure compensation for the seized American ships, address southerners' demands for reimbursement for the slaves who left with the British during the American Revolution, and end the British occupation of frontier forts and their continuing support of the Northwest Confederacy in its war against the United States.

Jay returned from his diplomatic mission with a humiliating agreement. The Jay Treaty accomplished only one of its objectives: the evacuation of frontier forts by the British. Meanwhile, the treaty failed to address the captured cargoes or the escaped slaves, and did not recognize American neutrality. It called for repayment with interest of debts that American planters owed to British firms dating from the Revolutionary War, and it secured trading rights to British Caribbean islands on terms so limited that the Senate struck them out. Meanwhile, American shipping to the Caribbean would still be subject to seizure, and American sailors still subject to harassment. With almost no concessions, British negotiators had secured the same commercial rights for their country as those granted to France. It looked to many Americans like a shameful capitulation to their former British monarchical enemy, and a disgraceful betrayal of their French republican ally.

When newspapers published the terms of the treaty, public outrage erupted. Thousands of protesters gathered in Philadelphia and Charleston to burn copies of the treaty and throw stones at the houses of its most prominent supporters. Jay was burned in effigy in Boston, Philadelphia, and New York, and even as far west as Lexington, Kentucky; he joked that he could travel from one end of the seaboard to the other by the light of his burning effigies. "Damn John Jay," read some graffiti on the side of one New York building. "Damn everyone that won't damn John Jay. Damn everyone that won't put up lights in the windows and sit up all night damning John Jay." For six weeks, hardly a day passed without some protest. When the Senate voted on the treaty it passed by a vote of 20 to 10—the bare minimum of the two-thirds majority required.

The yearlong struggle over the Jay Treaty revealed the emerging role of public opinion in political debates—voiced by an aroused citizenry and often managed and shaped by newspaper editors and political clubs. It built on the Hamilton-Jefferson split over economic policy, further dividing Americans into two rival partisan camps. The boisterous republicanism emerging on the ground was looking very different from that imagined by the nation's founding fathers.

Jay Treaty
1795 treaty between the United States and Britain negotiated by John Jay. It secured limited trading rights in the West Indies but failed to accomplish most other U.S. objectives. Bitterly denounced by its opponents, it sharply divided Americans and hastened the formation of political parties.

Why did Hamilton's economic policies provoke such controversy?

What threats did the United States face in the west?

What threats did the United States face in the Atlantic world?

How did partisan rivalries shape the politics of the late 1790s?

Conclusion: Why did the United States form political parties?

The Haitian Revolution

In addition to wars on the western front and across the Atlantic, a growing conflict to the south raised bleaker fears about the nation's future. It took place in the French colony of Saint Domingue, which had experienced extraordinary economic growth over the eighteenth century. By the time the French Revolution broke out in 1789, it was the richest, most productive colony of any European empire, exporting vast amounts of sugar, coffee, indigo, and cotton to markets in North America and Europe. All of it rested on the unstable foundation of slavery.

Beginning in 1791, the colony exploded in a revolution that eventually led to the creation of the Republic of Haiti in 1804. The Haitian Revolution, like the French and American Revolutions that preceded it, expressed radical ideas of liberty and equality. Unlike the other two, it extended that equality to people of African descent.

Extreme social tensions preceded the revolution. At the top of the social order stood some 30,000 whites who dominated the colony. Alongside them were approximately 28,000 free people of African descent (*gens de couleur*), who owned one-third of the island's plantations and nearly one-quarter of the slave labor force. Despite their economic power, the *gens de couleur* had gradually been excluded from most sectors of the island's civil life over the previous two decades, including local political offices and militia service, and they were increasingly resentful. Finally, vastly outnumbering both groups were some 465,000 brutally oppressed slaves who produced the island's extravagant wealth.

When the French Revolution broke out, white colonists divided between those supporting the French monarchy and others favoring reforms. Many took the opportunity to demand the elimination of imperial trade restrictions, pitting them against colonial authorities in France. The *gens de couleur*, meanwhile, saw the French Revolution's rhetoric of liberty and equality as an opportunity to abolish racist laws on the island. Whites were unwilling to give up their racial privileges, however, and before long armed warfare broke out between the *gens de couleur* and recalcitrant whites. All of these tensions grew as hundreds of thousands of slaves groaned under some of the most brutal slavery the world had ever known.

In August 1791, some two thousand slaves in the island's rich northern plantations rose up, killing plantation owners and their families, and setting fire to the immense fields of sugarcane. By September, roughly fifty thousand slaves were in armed insurrection. "The noble plain adjoining the Cape was covered with ashes, and the surrounding hills, as far as the eye could reach, and every where presented to us ruins still smoking," wrote a Jamaican planter who sailed into Cap-Français that month. "It was a sight more terrible than the mind of any man, unaccustomed to such a scene, can easily conceive." Smoke and dust blocked the sky for days.

The outbreak of war between France, Britain, and Spain in 1793 complicated the uprising, adding an imperial war to the existing divisions between royalists and republicans, whites and *gens de couleur,* free and slave. Led by former slave Toussaint Louverture, slaves and free blacks in alliance with Spain occupied the northern regions of the island. Desperate to retain their most important colony, French authorities on the island offered freedom to slaves willing to fight on their side. Thousands responded to the call. In June 1793, the colony's principal port, Cap-Français, was burned to ruins.

Thousands of white and mixed-race planters, along with some of their slaves, fled to Spanish Louisiana and port cities in the United States. In 1794, driven by events in Saint Domingue, the French revolutionary government in Paris abolished slavery in all its colonies. Ten years later, after repelling both British and Spanish invasions and successfully resisting a brutal French attempt to restore slavery to the island, the former slaves proclaimed the creation of the Republic of Haiti. It was the first and only slave revolution to result in the creation of an independent nation.

Haitian Revolution

Uprising in the French colony of Saint Domingue that began in 1791 and led to the creation of the Republic of Haiti in 1804. Unlike the French and American Revolutions, the Haitian Revolution committed itself to the liberty of slaves and equality for people of African descent. It fueled fears of slave insurrections in the United States.

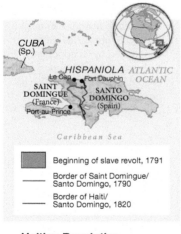

Haitian Revolution, 1791–1804

What were the sources of political stability in the 1790s?

◀ **Toussaint Louverture** Numbers of lithographs and paintings depicted Toussaint Louverture in styles and poses familiar to those of venerated European military leaders. In this image, he looks like a Haitian version of Napoleon, the general who became emperor of France in 1804. Images like this one countered racist views of black people as passive or weak by emphasizing the martial heroism of the Haitian revolutionaries. Schomburg Center, NYPL/Art Resource, NY.

White Americans closely followed the revolution through newspapers and refugees' accounts. A few sympathized with the slaves' struggle for liberty, but many more feared that violence might spread to the United States. Most condemned the violence, unwilling or unable to see the similarities between the American and Haitian Revolutions, between whites in North America fighting for their freedom and slaves in the Caribbean fighting for theirs. Most black Americans, however, saw matters differently. They found inspiration in the epic revolution and the creation of the first black republic in the Americas.

Among white southerners, the Haitian Revolution provoked naked fears of slave insurrection. A tortured Jefferson wrote another Virginia slaveholder in 1797 that "if something is not done, and soon done," about slavery in the United States, "we shall be the murderers of our own children." New Englanders generally did not share Jefferson's cataclysmic fears. Massachusetts politician Timothy Pickering would later chastise Jefferson for supporting French revolutionaries while condemning black Haitians only because they had "a skin not colored like our own."

COMPARE AND CONTRAST

In what ways did the Haitian Revolution resemble the American Revolution, and in what ways was it different?

QUICK REVIEW

How did international events contribute to the intensification of political divisions in the United States?

Why did Hamilton's economic policies provoke such controversy?	What threats did the United States face in the west?	**What threats did the United States face in the Atlantic world?**	How did partisan rivalries shape the politics of the late 1790s?	Conclusion: Why did the United States form political parties?

How did partisan rivalries shape the politics of the late 1790s?

Federalists

Originally the term for supporters of the Constitution in 1787–1788. In the 1790s, it became the name for one of the two political parties. Federalists supported Britain in foreign policy and commercial interests at home. Prominent Federalists included George Washington, Alexander Hamilton, and John Adams.

Republicans

Sometimes called Democratic-Republicans, they emerged as a political party in the 1790s in opposition to the Federalists. Republicans supported the revolutionaries in France and agrarian interests at home. Prominent Republicans included Thomas Jefferson and James Madison.

Despite a broadly shared distrust of political parties, two rival political groups had emerged by Washington's second presidential term. After his retirement and the election of John Adams, party strife accelerated over failed diplomacy in France, bringing the United States to the brink of war. Pro-war and antiwar antagonism created a major crisis over political free speech, militarism, and fears of sedition and treason.

Federalists and Republicans

During the 1790s, polarization over Hamilton's economic program, the French Revolution, and the Jay Treaty created two distinct parties: **Federalists** and **Republicans**. Federalists supported Hamilton's economic program and sought closer diplomatic and economic ties with Britain. They condemned the excesses of the French Revolution and accused Republicans of imitating bloodthirsty French revolutionaries. Republicans, on the other hand, opposed Hamilton's economic program, and sought closer ties with the French republic. They continued supporting the revolution in France, and accused Federalists of wanting to turn the United States into a monarchy.

Washington struggled to stay above party politics amidst the bitter division that raged around him. But the effort wore him down. In 1796, he decided to retire rather than seek a third term, announcing the decision in his Farewell Address. Warning Americans "in the most solemn manner against the baneful effects of the Spirit of Party," Washington stressed the importance of a "unity of government." He warned against "*Geographical* discriminations—*Northern* and *Southern*—*Atlantic* and *Western*," urging Americans to unite as "an indissoluble community of Interest as *one Nation*." Finally, he cautioned his countrymen against "a passionate attachment of one nation for another." He urged the nation to "steer clear of permanent alliances with any portion of the foreign world." As a nationalist text that stressed the importance of political and geographic unity, the Farewell Address would go on to become one of the country's most important documents, recited at patriotic occasions like Washington's birthday or July 4.

Vice President John Adams of Massachusetts was elected the nation's second president, while his chief opponent, Thomas Jefferson, became vice president. (Because the Constitution did not anticipate political parties, the top vote-getter became president, and the next-highest assumed the vice presidency. The Twelfth Amendment, adopted in 1804, corrected this procedural flaw.) Although his views mostly aligned with those of Federalists, Adams too sought to govern above party. His inaugural speech pledged neutrality in foreign affairs and respect for the French people, which made Republicans hopeful. To please Federalists, Adams retained three cabinet members from Washington's administration—the secretaries of state, treasury, and war. Adams was not an adept politician, however, and his prickly personality alienated potential allies. Nor could his ambition to govern without party allegiance survive the bitter quarrels of the 1790s.

The XYZ Affair

From the start, Adams's presidency was in crisis. France retaliated for the British-friendly Jay Treaty by abandoning its 1778 alliance with the United States. French privateers—armed private vessels—started detaining American ships carrying British

What were the sources of political stability in the 1790s?

▲ **John and Abigail Adams** The artist Gilbert Stuart began these portraits in 1800, but did not finish them until 1815. The portrait of John represents him as he looked in 1815; Abigail, by contrast, is portrayed as she was in 1800, at the age of 56. Their son, John Quincy Adams, called it "so excellent a likeness" of his mother that he continued pestering the artist until he finally completed the pair. When she saw the completed portrait in 1815, Abigail wrote that it "serves only to remind me of the ravages of time and the decays of Nature." National Gallery of Art, Washington, DC. Gift of Mrs. Robert Homans.

goods; by March 1797, they had seized more than three hundred American vessels. Federalists started speaking openly about war with France. Resisting Federalist pressure, Adams dispatched a three-man commission to France in the fall of 1797 to negotiate a resolution.

When the American commissioners arrived in Paris, French officials refused to receive them. Instead, the French minister of foreign affairs sent three French agents—unnamed and later known to the American public as X, Y, and Z—to the American commissioners, informing them that a $250,000 bribe might grease the wheels of diplomacy. A $12 million loan to the French government, the agents added, would be the price of a peace treaty. Incensed, the commissioners brought news of the French demands to the president.

Americans reacted to the **XYZ affair** with shock and anger. Even staunch pro-French Republicans began to reevaluate their allegiance. The Federalist-dominated Congress appropriated money for an army of ten thousand soldiers and repealed all prior treaties with France. In 1798, twenty naval warships launched the United States into its first undeclared war, called the Quasi-War by historians to underscore its uncertain legal status. The main scene of action was the Caribbean, where more than one hundred French ships were captured.

Antagonism between Federalists and Republicans intensified. Because the chance of a land invasion by France was vanishingly remote, some Republicans began to fear that Federalist demands for an enlarged army were intended to suppress domestic dissent. Partisanship grew to a frenzy. Republican newspapers denounced Adams as "a person without patriotism, without philosophy, and a mock monarch." Pro-French mobs roamed the streets of Philadelphia, the capital.

Adams, fearing for his safety, stocked weapons in his presidential quarters. Federalists, too, went on the offensive. In Newburyport, Massachusetts, they lit a huge bonfire and burned issues of the state's Republican newspapers. Officers in a New York militia unit drank a toast on July 4, 1798: "One and but one party in the United States." A Federalist editor ominously declared that "he who is not for us is against us."

XYZ affair
A 1797 incident in which French officials demanded bribes from the United States as the price for peace negotiations. American diplomats refused. News of the incident caused widespread outrage in the United States, and led to an undeclared war with France, known as the Quasi-War.

COMPARE AND CONTRAST
Compare and contrast the views of Federalists and Republicans in the 1790s. What political positions did each group articulate, and how did each view the other?

| Why did Hamilton's economic policies provoke such controversy? | What threats did the United States face in the west? | What threats did the United States face in the Atlantic world? | **How did partisan rivalries shape the politics of the late 1790s?** | Conclusion: Why did the United States form political parties? |

The Crisis of 1798: Sedition

With war against France looming, Republican newspaper editors criticized President John Adams with such venomous insults that Federalists in Congress criminalized seditious words. Republicans just redoubled their opposition.

DOCUMENT 1

Abigail Adams Complains of Sedition, 1798

A beleaguered Abigail Adams called repeatedly in letters to her sister for a sedition law to silence Benjamin Bache, editor of the Philadelphia Aurora.

(April 26): . . . Yet dairingly do the vile incendaries keep up in Baches paper the most wicked and base, voilent & caluminiating abuse. . . . But nothing will have an Effect until congress pass a Sedition Bill. . . . (April 28): . . . We are now wonderfully popular except with Bache & Co who in his paper calls the President old, querilous, Bald, blind, cripled, Toothless Adams. . . . (May 10): . . . This Bache is cursing & abusing daily. If that fellow . . . is not surpressd, we shall come to a civil war. . . . (May 26): . . . I wish the Laws of our Country were competant to punish the stirer up of sedition, the writer and Printer of base and unfounded calumny. . . . (June 19): . . . In any other Country Bache & all his papers would have been seazd and ought to be here, but congress are dilly dallying about passing a Bill enabling the President to seize suspisious persons, and their papers.

Source: Excerpts from *New Letters of Abigail Adams, 1788–1801*, edited by Stewart Mitchell. Copyright © 1947 by The American Antiquarian Society. Copyright © renewed 1974 by The American Antiquarian Society. Reprinted by permission of Houghton Mifflin Harcourt Publishing Company. All rights reserved.

DOCUMENT 2

The Sedition Act of 1798

On July 14, Congress made sedition with malicious intent a federal crime.

SECTION 1. . . . if any persons shall unlawfully combine or conspire together, with intent to oppose any measure or measures of the government of the United States . . . , or to intimidate or prevent any person holding . . . office in or under the government of the United States, from undertaking, performing or executing his trust or duty, and if any person or persons, with intent as aforesaid, shall counsel, advise or attempt to procure any insurrection, riot, unlawful assembly . . . , he or they shall be deemed guilty of a high misdemeanor, and on conviction . . . shall be punished by a fine not exceeding five thousand dollars, and by imprisonment during a term not less than six months nor exceeding five years. . . .

SEC. 2. . . . If any person shall write, print, utter or publish . . . , any false, scandalous and malicious writing or writings against the government of the United States, or either house of the Congress of the United States, or the President of the United States, with intent to defame the said government . . . or to bring them . . . into contempt or disrepute; or to excite against them . . . the hatred of the good people of the United States . . . , then such person, being thereof convicted . . . shall be punished by a fine not exceeding two thousand dollars, and by imprisonment not exceeding two years.

Source: Excerpted text from congressional bill, July 14, 1798.

DOCUMENT 3

Matthew Lyon Criticizes John Adams, 1798

Matthew Lyon, congressman from Vermont, criticized Adams and was charged with sedition. Handed a four-month sentence and a fine of $1,000, Lyon ran for reelection from his cell—and won.

The Alien and Sedition Acts

With tempers so high, out of a persistent belief that political dissent was equivalent to treason, Federalist leaders moved to silence the opposition. Perceiving a threat "to overturn and ruin the government by publishing the most shameless falsehoods against the representatives of the people," they resorted to extreme measures. In mid-1798, Congress passed the Sedition Act, which criminalized speech or words that

What were the sources of political stability in the 1790s?

. . . Whenever I shall, on the part of the Executive, see every consideration of the public welfare swallowed up in a continual grasp for power, in an unbounded thirst for ridiculous pomp, foolish adulation, or selfish avarice; when I shall behold men of real merit daily turned out of office for no other cause but independence of sentiment; when I shall see men of firmness, merit, years, abilities, and experience, discarded on their application for office, for fear they possess that independence; . . . when I shall see the sacred name of religion employed as a State engine to make mankind hate and persecute one another, I shall not be their humble advocate.

Source: Matthew Lyon, Letter in *Spooner's Vermont Journal*, July 31, 1798, pp. 1–2. Courtesy, American Antiquarian Society.

DOCUMENT 4

The Virginia Resolution, December 24, 1798

James Madison drafted the Virginia Resolution and had a trusted ally present it to the Virginia legislature, dominated by Republicans. (Jefferson did the same for Kentucky.) The document denounces the Alien and Sedition Acts and declares that states have the right to "interpose" to stop unconstitutional actions by the federal government.

RESOLVED . . . That this assembly most solemnly declares a warm attachment to the Union of the States, to maintain which it pledges all its powers; and that for this end, it is their duty to watch over and oppose every infraction of those principles which constitute the only basis of that Union, because a faithful observance of them, can alone secure its existence and the public happiness.

That this Assembly doth explicitly and peremptorily declare, that it views the powers of the federal government, as resulting from the compact, to which the states are parties; as limited by the plain sense and intention of the instrument constituting the compact; . . . and that in case of a deliberate, palpable, and

dangerous exercise of other powers, not granted by the said compact, the states who are parties thereto, have the right, and are in duty bound, to interpose for arresting the progress of the evil, and for maintaining within their respective limits, the authorities, rights and liberties appertaining to them. . . .

That the General Assembly doth particularly protest against the palpable and alarming infractions of the Constitution, in the two late cases of the "Alien and Sedition Acts" . . . ; the first of which exercises a power no where delegated to the federal government . . . ; and the other . . . exercises in like manner, a power not delegated by the constitution, but on the contrary, expressly and positively forbidden by one of the amendments thereto; a power, which more than any other, ought to produce universal alarm, because it is levelled against that right of freely examining public characters and measures, and of free communication among the people thereon, which has ever been justly deemed, the only effectual guardian of every other right.

Source: Avalon Project, Yale Law School, 1996. http://www.yale.edu. © 1996–2007 The Avalon Project at Yale Law School.

Questions for Analysis

ANALYZE THE EVIDENCE: Why did the Federalists believe that the Sedition Act was necessary? What exactly was the threat, according to Abigail Adams? What threat is implied in the wording of the act? How does the Virginia Resolution justify its resistance to the Sedition Act?

RECOGNIZE VIEWPOINTS: Does Matthew Lyon's criticism of President Adams rise to the level of threat that the Federalists feared? How do you explain Lyon's guilty verdict? His reelection to Congress?

ASK HISTORICAL QUESTIONS: What political or personal issues created the deep polarization between Federalists and Republicans that led to the Alien and Sedition Acts? What precedent did the Virginia Resolution set?

defamed the president or Congress. In all, twenty-five men, almost all Republican newspaper editors, were charged with sedition; twelve were convicted. **(See "Analyzing Historical Evidence: The Crisis of 1798: Sedition" above.)**

Congress also passed two Alien Acts. The first extended the period for an immigrant to acquire citizenship to fourteen years, from five, and required all foreigners to register with the federal government. The second empowered the president in time of war to deport or imprison without trial any foreigner suspected of being a danger to the United States.

| Why did Hamilton's economic policies provoke such controversy? | What threats did the United States face in the west? | What threats did the United States face in the Atlantic world? | **How did partisan rivalries shape the politics of the late 1790s?** | Conclusion: Why did the United States form political parties? |

Alien and Sedition Acts

1798 laws passed to suppress political dissent. The Sedition Act criminalized conspiracy and criticism of government leaders. The two Alien Acts extended the waiting period for citizenship and empowered the president to deport or imprison without trial any foreigner deemed a danger.

Virginia and Kentucky Resolutions

1798 resolutions condemning the Alien and Sedition Acts submitted to the federal government by the Virginia and Kentucky state legislatures. The resolutions advanced the idea that state legislatures could judge the constitutionality of federal laws and nullify them.

Republicans strongly opposed the Alien and Sedition Acts, but did not have the votes to block them in Congress. Nor could they count on the federal judiciary, dominated by Federalist judges, to challenge laws that conflicted with the Bill of Rights. Jefferson and Madison therefore turned to the state legislatures to press their opposition. Each man anonymously drafted a set of resolutions condemning the acts and convinced the legislatures of Virginia and Kentucky to present them to the federal government. The 1798 Virginia and Kentucky Resolutions argued that state legislatures have the right to nullify federal laws that violate the Constitution. Although the resolutions made little dent in the Alien and Sedition Acts, the idea that a state could nullify federal law did not disappear. It would resurface several times in decades to come, most notably in a major tariff dispute in 1832 and in the sectional arguments that led to the Civil War.

Amid the war hysteria and sedition fears of 1798, President Adams regained his balance. He showed uncharacteristic restraint in pursuing opponents under the Sedition Act. Most significantly, he refused to declare war on France. He shrewdly realized that France—still embroiled in ferocious warfare with Great Britain—did not want a war with the United States, and that a peaceful settlement might be possible.

VISUAL ACTIVITY

▲ **Cartoon of the Lyon-Griswold Fight in Congress** Political tensions ran high in 1798. On the floor of Congress, Federalist Roger Griswold called Republican Matthew Lyon a coward. Lyon responded with some well-aimed spit. Griswold then raised his cane to strike Lyon, whereupon Lyon grabbed fire tongs to defend himself. Madison later commented that the two should have dueled, the honorable way to avenge insults. Library of Congress, 3a05342.

READING THE IMAGE: How does this image portray the Griswold-Lyon fight? How do the other members of Congress react to the brawl? What does the image tell us about contemporary views of the fight?
CONNECTIONS: Why did divisions between Federalists and Republicans become so bitter in 1798?

What were the sources of political stability in the 1790s?

In January 1799, French authorities signaled that diplomatic channels were open, and that new peace commissioners would be welcomed. Adams appointed new negotiators. By late 1799, the Quasi-War with France had subsided, and in 1800 diplomats agreed on a treaty declaring "a true and sincere friendship" between the United States and France.

The election of 1800 pitted Adams against Thomas Jefferson in the bitterest election of the country's brief history. Faced with this choice, Hamilton abandoned Adams: "If we must have an enemy at the head of government, let it be one whom we can oppose, and for whom we are not responsible." Having lost his Federalist allies, Adams lost the election.

When President Jefferson mounted the inaugural platform in 1800, he attempted to unite Americans across the yawning partisan divide, announcing: "We are all republicans, we are all federalists." If the harmonious rhetoric was appropriate to an inaugural address, it also perpetuated the denial of party politics as a legitimate feature of political life—a denial that ran deep in the founding generation.

QUICK REVIEW

How did the unexpected emergence of two political parties in the 1790s manifest itself in political conflicts during the Adams administration?

Conclusion: Why did the United States form political parties?

American political leaders launched the new government in 1789 hoping to unify the country and overcome factionalism. The great public reservoir of trust in President Washington was the central foundation for those hopes, and Washington did not disappoint. He became a model Mr. President, with a blend of integrity and authority. The easy passage of the Bill of Rights (to appease Antifederalists) further added to the stability, as did attention to cultivating a citizenry of virtuous men supported by republican womanhood. Yet the optimism of that honeymoon period soon turned to worry and then fear as major political disagreements blazed.

On the domestic front, the principal source of political conflict concerned economic policy. Hamilton's economic program, brilliant as it was, rested on a vision of the future that much of the country opposed. Hamilton and his allies wanted a powerful federal government overseeing a robust financial system and the development of manufacturing. Jefferson, Madison, and their allies hoped for a nation of small landowning farmers trading peacefully with the rest of the world. These disagreements about political economy might not have led to such bitter partisanship had the international context been more peaceful, but it was not. The Constitution's first decade took place in the face of Native Americans' determination to maintain their lands, bitter violence on the nation's western front, and on the Atlantic Ocean, some of the most intense warfare the world had ever experienced.

The United States could not avoid being dragged into the conflicts. As the radical ideas articulated in the American Revolution echoed across the Atlantic and in the Caribbean, questions about the connected fates of liberty, equality, race, and republicanism pressed insistently on the nation's emerging institutions.

| Why did Hamilton's economic policies provoke such controversy? | What threats did the United States face in the west? | What threats did the United States face in the Atlantic world? | How did partisan rivalries shape the politics of the late 1790s? | **Conclusion: Why did the United States form political parties?** |

STEP 1 — EXPLAIN WHY IT MATTERS

Put your reading into practice. Identify each term below, and then explain why it matters in U.S. history.

TERM	WHO OR WHAT & WHEN	WHY IT MATTERS
Bill of Rights (p. 239)		
republican motherhood (p. 240)		
Report on Public Credit (p. 241)		
Report on Manufactures (p. 246)		
Whiskey Rebellion (p. 247)		
Treaty of Greenville (p. 251)		
Jay Treaty (p. 253)		
Haitian Revolution (p. 254)		
Federalists (p. 256)		
Republicans (p. 256)		
XYZ affair (p. 257)		
Alien and Sedition Acts (p. 260)		
Virginia and Kentucky Resolutions (p. 260)		

STEP 2 — MOVE BEYOND THE BASICS

To demonstrate a more advanced understanding, assess the positions and policies of the Federalists and the Republicans. Is it accurate to describe them as political parties? Why or why not?

	FEDERALISTS	REPUBLICANS
States' Rights		
Views and Policies Related to Economic Development		
Social and Political Hierarchy		
Relations with Britain		
Relations with France		
Views of the Haitian Revolution		

STEP 3

PUT IT ALL TOGETHER

Now, try to explain the big picture. Remember to use specific examples from the chapter in your answers.

DOMESTIC AFFAIRS

• What important precedents did George Washington set? How did he use the presidency to bring political stability to the country?

• How did Hamilton's vision for the nation conflict with Jefferson's?

NATIONAL SECURITY

• What were the most important threats to America's national security in the 1790s?

• How did the Washington and Adams administrations respond to those threats?

FEDERALISTS AND REPUBLICANS

• What led to the polarization of American politics in the 1790s?

• How did the French Revolution contribute to the split between Federalists and Republicans in the United States?

LOOKING BACKWARD, LOOKING AHEAD

• How did the government Washington headed differ from the government created by the Articles of Confederation?

• Do you think the creation of political parties made the country more or less stable in the long run?

STEP 4

CONNECT THESE EVENTS

How did the creation of a more powerful federal government under the Constitution of 1787 affect the nation's response to the challenges of the 1790s?

STEP 5

CONNECT TO THE PRESENT

Do the partisan divisions of the 1790s seem more serious than the partisanship today? Explain.

REPUBLICANS IN POWER

1800–1828

How did the United States give meaning to republican government, institutions, and traditions in the early nineteenth century?

Chapter 10 follows the country's explosive growth from the election of Thomas Jefferson to the presidency of John Quincy Adams. It examines the violent loss of Native American land; new educational opportunities for white women; and the expansion of voting rights for whites and their restriction for blacks.

This chapter will explore the following questions:

- What was the revolution of 1800?

- How did the Louisiana Purchase affect the United States?

- What led to the War of 1812?

- How did the civil status of free American women and men differ in the early Republic?

- Why did partisan conflict increase during the administrations of Monroe and Adams?

- Conclusion: How did republican simplicity become complex?

AN AMERICAN STORY

The name Tecumseh translates as "Shooting Star," a fitting name for the Shawnee chief who reached meteoric heights of fame across Indian country. He was by all accounts a charismatic leader. Graceful, eloquent, brilliant, Tecumseh was all these and more, a gifted natural commander, equal parts politician and warrior.

The Ohio Country, where Tecumseh was born in 1768, was home to some dozen Indian peoples. During the Revolutionary War, the region became a battleground. Tecumseh lost his father and two brothers to the violence. The Revolution's end in 1783 brought no peace to Indian country, however. The youthful Tecumseh fought at the devastating defeat of Fallen Timbers, and watched as eight treaties ceded much of Ohio to the Americans between 1795 and 1805. Some Native Americans resigned themselves to accommodation, taking up farming, trade, and intermarriage with white settlers. Others found refuge in alcohol. Tecumseh's younger brother Tenskwatawa led an embittered life of idleness and drink. But Tecumseh rejected accommodation and instead campaigned for a return to ancient ways. Donning traditional animal-skin clothing, he traveled around the Great Lakes region persuading tribes to join his pan-Indian confederacy. The territorial governor of Indiana, William Henry Harrison, admired and feared Tecumseh, calling him "one of those uncommon geniuses which spring up occasionally to produce revolutions."

Even Tecumseh's dissolute brother was born anew. After a near-death experience in 1805, Tenskwatawa recounted a startling vision of meeting the Master of Life. Renaming himself the Prophet, he urged his many Indian followers to regard whites as children of the Evil Spirit, destined for destruction.

President Thomas Jefferson worried about the Indian confederacy and its potential for a renewed alliance with the British in Canada. His worries became a reality as the threat of war with Britain reemerged, and the Indian-British alliance rematerialized along the Canadian-U.S. border. In the end, the War of 1812 settled little between the United States and Britain. Its effect on Indian country, by contrast, was transformative. Eight hundred warriors led by Tecumseh helped defend Canada against U.S. attacks, but the British did not reciprocate when the Indians came under threat. Tecumseh died on a Canadian battlefield in the fall of 1813. No Indian leader with his star power would emerge again east of the Mississippi. When the war between Britain and the United States ended, so did the dream of any substantial territory controlled by native peoples in between the two countries.

Tecumseh's ability to unite disparate Native American peoples had no counterpart in the young Republic's confederation of states. Widespread unity behind a single leader proved impossible. Bitter partisan conflict continued during the Jefferson and Madison administrations, but Federalists doomed their party by opposing the War of 1812. The next two presidents, James Monroe and John Quincy Adams, congratulated themselves on the Federalist Party's demise, but divisions within their own party persisted. Wives of politicians increasingly inserted themselves into this dissonant mix, managing their husbands' politicking and enabling them to maintain the fiction of nonpartisanship. That it was a fiction had become sharply apparent by the time John Quincy Adams ascended to the presidency in 1825.

▼ **Tecumseh** This 1848 engraving was adapted from an earlier drawing of Tecumseh made in a live sitting by a French fur trader in 1808. The engraver has given Tecumseh a British army officer's uniform, showing that he fought on the British side in the War of 1812. Notice the head covering and the medallion around Tecumseh's neck, marking his Indian identity. Courtesy of Toronto Public Library.

What was the revolution of 1800?

The first presidential election of the new century provoked all-out partisan war. A panicky Federalist newspaper in Connecticut predicted that a victory by Thomas Jefferson would lead to civil war and "murder, robbery, rape, adultery and incest." Apocalyptic fears gripped parts of the South, where some whites predicted a slave uprising if Jefferson won. Nothing nearly so dramatic occurred. True, Jefferson later called his election the "revolution of 1800," but the reality of Jeffersonian government was more complicated. While Jefferson cherished republican simplicity in principle, events required decisive and sometimes expensive government action, including war overseas to protect American shipping.

Turbulent Times: Election and Rebellion

The election of 1800 was historic for many reasons. One is that it was the first to be decided by the House of Representatives. Probably by mistake, voters in the electoral college gave Jefferson and his running mate, Senator Aaron Burr of New York, an equal number of votes. (To fix this problem, the Twelfth Amendment to the Constitution, adopted in 1804, separated the votes for president and vice president.) Since the vote resulted in a tie, the House had to choose between those two men. The Federalist candidate, John Adams, was eliminated.

Although he was the Republican candidate for vice president, Burr declined to concede. It thus fell to the Federalist-dominated House of Representatives, in its waning days in early 1801, to choose the Republican president. Some Federalists preferred Burr, believing that his character flaws made him susceptible to Federalist pressure. But the influential Alexander Hamilton, though no friend of Jefferson, believed that the vain and ambitious Burr would be more dangerous in the presidency. Jefferson might be a "contemptible hypocrite" in Hamilton's opinion, but at least he could be counted on to put the nation's interests ahead of his own. In 1804, Burr would shoot and kill Hamilton in a duel. **(See "Spotlight: How Could a Vice President Get Away with Murder?" on page 268.)**

Thirty-six ballots and six days later, Jefferson won the presidency. Jefferson's victory marked a second historic feature of the election of 1800: For the first time, a sitting president was defeated, and governmental control passed from one party to its opposition. This peaceful transfer of power was extraordinary for the time; it had few precedents in history.

As the country struggled over this crisis in political leadership, a twenty-four-year-old blacksmith named Gabriel plotted rebellion in Virginia. Inspired by the Haitian Revolution, Gabriel was said to be organizing a thousand slaves to march on the state capital and take the governor, James Monroe, hostage. On the appointed day, however, a few nervous slaves confessed the news of Gabriel's rebellion to authorities. Within days, scores of implicated conspirators were jailed and put on trial.

One of the rebels compared himself to the most venerated icon of the early Republic: "I have nothing more to offer than what General Washington would have had to offer, had he been taken by the British and put to trial by them." The specter of a black George Washington terrified white Virginians. That example could only go so far. In the fall of 1800 twenty-six men, including Gabriel, were hanged for allegedly taking part in the rebellion. In a letter to Jefferson, Governor Monroe wondered "where to arrest the hand of the Executioner."

Gabriel's rebellion
Planned rebellion organized by an enslaved blacksmith named Gabriel and inspired by the Haitian Revolution. When the alleged conspiracy was revealed, the accused slaves defended themselves by comparing their violent resistance to slavery with the American Revolution.

What was the
revolution of 1800?

"There is a strong sentiment that there has been hanging enough," Jefferson wrote back. "The world at large will forever condemn us if we indulge a principle of revenge."

The Jeffersonian Vision of Republican Government

Once elected, Thomas Jefferson set out to roll back Federalist government. The first president inaugurated in the new District of Columbia, Jefferson spurned elaborate ceremony and dressed in everyday clothing to emphasize his republican simplicity. He even walked to the Capitol for his modest swearing-in ceremony. As president, he dramatically reduced the size of the federal government, and slashed the budget.

Jefferson was no Antifederalist; he had supported the Constitution in 1788. But he worried that the executive branch had grown too powerful, jeopardizing the Constitution's careful balance and threatening the nation's republican character. He had opposed Hamiltonian policies to refinance the public debt, establish a national bank, and foster commercial ties with Britain. In Jefferson's eyes, these policies

▲ **George Washington (Lansdowne Portrait), by Gilbert Stuart, and Thomas Jefferson, by Rembrandt Peale** The portrait of George Washington on the left was painted in 1796, at the end of his two terms in office. The portrait of Thomas Jefferson on the right was painted in 1800, just before Thomas Jefferson's election as president. Painted just four years apart, each offers an iconic portrait of a president. Both of them were widely reproduced for appreciative audiences. George Washington: GraphicaArtis/Getty Images; Thomas Jefferson: Michael Ochs Archives/Getty Images.

READING THE IMAGE: What are the principal differences between the two presidential portraits? How do these differences represent the so-called "revolution of 1800"?

MAKING CONNECTIONS: How did Thomas Jefferson change the exercise of presidential power after his election? How did his understanding of presidential power differ from that of Federalists?

How did the Louisiana Purchase affect the United States?	What led to the War of 1812?	How did the civil status of free American women and men differ in the early Republic?	Why did partisan conflict increase during the administrations of Monroe and Adams?	Conclusion: How did republican simplicity become complex?

How Could a Vice President Get Away with Murder?

On July 11, 1804, Vice President Aaron Burr shot Alexander Hamilton. The setting was a duel staged on the cliffs of Weehawken, New Jersey, across the Hudson River from New York City. A bullet tore through Hamilton's rib, demolished his liver, and splintered his spine. He died the next day in agonizing pain.

How did a sitting vice president and one of the nation's most famous leaders put themselves at such risk? Two eminent attorneys, skilled in negotiations, each fired .54-caliber weapons at ten paces. How could no one have stopped them?

Burr challenged Hamilton in late June after learning about a newspaper report that Hamilton "looked upon Mr. Burr to be a dangerous man, and one who ought not be trusted with the reins of government." Burr knew of Hamilton's low opinion of him, but now his private disparagement had made its way into print. Burr believed that Hamilton's remark had lost him the election to become governor of New York.

He may have been right. Suspecting that Jefferson would dump him from the federal ticket in the 1804 election, Burr decided to focus his political ambitions on New York. He appeared to have the support of New York's Federalist leadership—until Hamilton's remark circulated.

On June 18, Burr challenged Hamilton to a duel if he did not disavow his comment. For three weeks, the men exchanged letters clarifying the nature of the insult to Burr. Hamilton the lawyer evasively quibbled over words, but he could neither deny the insult nor spurn the challenge without damaging his reputation. Both Burr and Hamilton were locked in a highly ritualized cultural institution central to a gentleman's code of honor that had begun among officers in the Revolution and spread across the country. Although state legislatures had begun to outlaw duels, laws could not so easily change cultural norms.

▲ These dueling pistols belonged to Hamilton's brother-in-law, who had once fought a duel with Aaron Burr without injury. Hamilton's son Philip had borrowed them for his own fatal duel in 1799. During a cleaning in 1884, a hidden hair trigger came to light, which allowed for a more rapid firing with one-twentieth the force of pull on the trigger. Hamilton, alas, gained no advantage from it. Courtesy JPMorgan Chase History Program.

In accord with the code of dueling, each man had a trusted "second" to deliver the letters and assist at the duel. Only a handful of close friends knew of the challenge. No one tried to stop it. Hamilton did even not tell his wife. He wrote her a tender farewell letter, to be opened in the event of his death. He knew the pain dueling brought, for three years earlier his nineteen-year-old son Philip had been killed in a duel. His father was about to inherit the sins of the son.

COMPARE AND CONTRAST

How did Thomas Jefferson's economic vision for the United States differ from Alexander Hamilton's? What, if anything, did they have in common?

favored the interests of greedy speculators and merchants over honest citizens, and would inevitably lead to the government's corruption. He believed that republican liberty could flourish only in a nation of virtuous, independent farmers who owned and worked their land. Although his own economic situation hardly conformed to his political vision—Jefferson owned hundreds of slaves and lived from the profits of their exploited labor—many Americans shared his views.

As president, Jefferson set about systematically dismantling Federalist innovations. He cut the military budget in half. Favoring militias over standing armies, he reduced the size of the army by a third, and cut the navy back to six ships, from

What was the revolution of 1800?

When Hamilton's wife was called to his deathbed, she was first told he had a sudden illness. Women were excluded from the world of dueling, a world in which men spoke to each other through ritualized violence.

News of Hamilton's death spread quickly. The funeral shut New York down, and the city council declared a six-week mourning period. Burr fled to Philadelphia, fearing retribution by crowds of mourners.

Northern newspapers expressed outrage over the illegal duel; not so in the South, where dueling was more widely accepted as a remedy for insult. Laws in northern states treated a challenge as a misdemeanor and a dueling death as a homicide. Even in death, the loser of an illegal duel could endure a range of humiliations—being buried without a coffin, having a stake driven through the body, being strung up in public until the body rotted, or being donated to medical students for dissection. Hamilton's body was spared such dishonor. But two ministers in succession refused to administer last rites before a third relented.

A coroner's jury in New York indicted Burr on misdemeanor charges for issuing a challenge, and a grand jury in New Jersey indicted him for murder. By that time, Burr was hiding out in South Carolina.

But not for long. Amazingly, he returned to Washington, D.C., in November 1804 to resume his duties as vice president of the United States. He continued presiding over sessions of the Senate until his term ended in March 1805. Federalists snubbed him, but eleven Republican senators petitioned New Jersey to drop its indictment on the grounds that "civilized nations" do not treat dueling deaths as "common murders." New Jersey did not pursue the murder charge. Burr freely visited New Jersey and

New York for three more decades, paying no penalty for killing Hamilton.

Few would doubt that Burr was a scoundrel, albeit a brilliant one. A few years later, he was indicted for treason for a plot to break off part of the United States and start his own country in the Southwest. (He dodged that bullet, too.) Hamilton certainly held Burr in contempt, and when that opinion reached print, Burr had cause to defend his honor under the etiquette of dueling. The accuracy of Hamilton's charge was of no account. Dueling redressed questions of honor, not questions of fact.

Dueling held sway in the South for several more decades, but in the North the custom became extremely rare by the 1820s, discouraged by the tragedy of Hamilton's death and by the rise of a legalistic society that now preferred evidence, interrogation, and monetary judgments to avenge injury.

Questions for Analysis

SUMMARIZE THE ARGUMENT: Why did Burr challenge Hamilton to a duel? Why did Hamilton accept?

ANALYZE THE EVIDENCE: Why was Burr never brought to trial for killing Hamilton in a duel?

CONSIDER THE CONTEXT: How might differences between the North and the South—economic, social, cultural, racial—possibly explain why dueling was a dying custom in the North but continued to be tolerated in the South?

thirty. With Congress's consent, he abolished internal federal taxes, dramatically shrinking government revenue, which would now be derived solely from customs duties and the sale of western land.

Jefferson similarly rolled back Federalist attempts to create a national elite and endow the federal government with symbols of authority. Martha Washington and Abigail Adams had received the wives of government officials at weekly teas, cementing social relations among the governing class. But Jefferson, a longtime widower, disdained such gatherings and abandoned George Washington's formal receptions. Instead, he hosted small dinner parties with carefully chosen guests. He sold the

<table>
<tr><td>How did the Louisiana Purchase affect the United States?</td><td>What led to the War of 1812?</td><td>How did the civil status of free American women and men differ in the early Republic?</td><td>Why did partisan conflict increase during the administrations of Monroe and Adams?</td><td>Conclusion: How did republican simplicity become complex?</td></tr>
</table>

coaches and horses and silver harnesses that President Adams had used, keeping only a one-horse market cart. He dressed casually, and was even said to greet guests at the White House in his slippers.

ANALYZE EVIDENCE

Do the changes Thomas Jefferson implemented support the argument that his election amounted to a "revolution"?

A federal government limited to its proper size, according to Jefferson, maintained a postal system, federal courts, and coastal lighthouses; it collected customs duties and conducted the census. He believed it should do little else. The president had one private secretary, a young man named Meriwether Lewis, whom he paid out of his own pocket. The Department of State employed eight people: Secretary James Madison, six clerks, and a messenger. The Treasury Department was by far the largest, with seventy-three revenue commissioners, auditors, and clerks, plus two watchmen. The payroll of the entire executive branch amounted to just one hundred thirty people in 1801. By the end of his first term, Jefferson had dramatically reduced the national debt.

However, 217 government workers lay beyond Jefferson's command—judicial and military appointments made just days before Jefferson took office. Jefferson repudiated the appointment of those "midnight judges." One disappointed job seeker, William Marbury, sued the new secretary of state, James Madison, for refusing to deliver his commission. This suit gave rise to the 1803 Supreme Court decision *Marbury v. Madison*. The Court found that the grounds of Marbury's suit, resting in the Judiciary Act of 1789, conflicted with the Constitution. For the first time, the Court invalidated a federal law on the grounds that it was unconstitutional. Interestingly, the Supreme Court's authority to overturn laws of Congress—the principle known as "judicial review"—is nowhere mentioned in the text of the Constitution.

Marbury v. Madison
1803 Supreme Court case that established the concept of judicial review in finding that parts of the Judiciary Act of 1789 were in conflict with the Constitution. The Supreme Court assumed legal authority to overrule acts of other branches of the government.

Dangers Overseas: The Barbary Wars

Jefferson's ambition to reduce the size of the federal government and the military met a severe test in the western Mediterranean Sea. For more than a century, the states of Morocco, Algiers, Tunis, and Tripoli—situated along the Mediterranean coast of Africa, and called the Barbary States by Americans—demanded large annual payments (called "tribute") for the safe passage of ship traffic along their coastlines. Countries refusing to pay risked the seizure of their ships and crews. With its independence, the United States lost the protection of the British empire, and during the 1790s, several hundred American crew members were taken captive and held in slavery. Eventually, the United States agreed to pay $50,000 a year in tribute to secure safe passage for its ships.

In May 1801, when the monarch of Tripoli failed to secure a large increase in his tribute, he declared war on the United States. Jefferson considered such payments extortion, and sent four warships to the Mediterranean to protect U.S. shipping. From 1801 to 1803, U.S. frigates engaged in skirmishes with North African privateers.

Then, in late 1803, the USS *Philadelphia* ran aground near Tripoli's harbor and was captured along with its three-hundred-man crew. Early the next year, a U.S. naval ship commanded by Lieutenant Stephen Decatur sailed into the harbor after dark, guided by an Arabic-speaking pilot to fool harbor sentries. Decatur's crew set the *Philadelphia* on fire, rendering it useless to the Tripoli monarch. Later in 1804, a small force of U.S. ships attacked the harbor and damaged or destroyed nineteen Tripolitan ships and bombarded the city. Yet the sailors from the *Philadelphia* remained in captivity.

In 1805, William Eaton, an American officer stationed in Tunis, requested a thousand Marines to invade Tripoli. Secretary of State James Madison rejected the plan. On his own, Eaton assembled a force of four hundred men (mostly Greek and Egyptian mercenaries plus eight Marines) and marched them over five hundred miles of desert for a surprise attack on Tripoli's second-largest city. Amazingly, he succeeded. The monarch of Tripoli yielded, released the prisoners taken from the *Philadelphia*, and negotiated a treaty with the United States.

What was the revolution of 1800?

Periodic attacks by Algiers and Tunis continued to plague American ships during Jefferson's second term of office and into his successor's. The Second Barbary War ended in 1815 when the hero of 1804, Stephen Decatur, sailed to the northern coast of Africa with a fleet of twenty-seven ships. By show of force, he engineered three treaties that put an end to the tribute system and provided reparations for damages to U.S. ships.

QUICK REVIEW

How did Jefferson's election and the Republican victory in 1800 change the American government?

How did the Louisiana Purchase affect the United States?

In 1803, an unanticipated opportunity presented itself when France offered to sell its territory west of the Mississippi River to the United States. President Jefferson set aside his usually cautious exercise of federal power and quickly accepted. He soon launched four expeditions into the prairie and mountains to explore this huge acquisition. The powerful Osage of the Arkansas River Valley responded to overtures for an alliance and were soon lavishly welcomed by Jefferson in Washington City, but the even more powerful Comanche of the southern Great Plains stood their ground against all invaders. Meanwhile, the expedition by Lewis and Clark, the longest and northernmost trek of the four launched by Jefferson, mapped U.S. terrain all the way to the Pacific Ocean, boosting expansionist aspirations.

The Louisiana Purchase

In 1763, at the end of the Seven Years' War, France had transferred its imperial claims on the vast territory between the Mississippi River and the Rocky Mountains to Spain. Whatever the lines drawn on maps in European capitals might have indicated, however, the territory was never very Spanish. Centered on the Great Plains, it was home to numerous Indian peoples, most notably the powerful and expansionist Comanche nation.

New Orleans was Spain's principal stronghold, a city of French origins and population situated on the Mississippi River near its outlet at the Gulf of Mexico. An essential geographic fact made it the single most strategic city in North America: All the major rivers between the Appalachian and Rocky mountains—including the Ohio River basin, which the United States had fought a series of wars to control—drained down the Mississippi past New Orleans. Whatever power controlled New Orleans thus exercised an outsized influence on the commerce of the northwest territories, along with Kentucky, Tennessee, and western Pennsylvania. Since the 1780s, Spain had earned modest revenues from taxes it imposed on the agricultural products shipped downriver from American farms.

Spanish officials recognized that their sparse population could not withstand the westward movement of Americans and that their best hope lay in maintaining an expensive network of Indian alliances. Under pressure from the French emperor Napoleon, whose armies had conquered much of Europe, Spain ceded the Louisiana

CHRONOLOGY

1803
– Louisiana Purchase approved by Congress.

1804
– Jefferson meets with Osage Indians.

1804–1806
– Lewis and Clark expedition explores west.

1807
– United States establishes trade with Comanche Indians.

| **How did the Louisiana Purchase affect the United States?** | What led to the War of 1812? | How did the civil status of free American women and men differ in the early Republic? | Why did partisan conflict increase during the administrations of Monroe and Adams? | Conclusion: How did republican simplicity become complex? |

271

A VIEW of NEW ORLEANS TAKEN FROM THE PLANTATION OF MARIGNY

VISUAL ACTIVITY

▲ **View of New Orleans** This engraving of New Orleans was dedicated to Thomas Jefferson by John L. Bosquet de Woiseri, a geographer and engineer. Woiseri advertised the print as "displaying all the principal and most remarkable buildings" and highlighting "all that is necessary to be known" about the city. Art Collection 2/Alamy Stock Photo.

READING THE IMAGE: What elements of the city does the artist emphasize here? How does this scene offer a vision of the future of New Orleans in the United States?

MAKING CONNECTIONS: Why was it important to the United States to control New Orleans at the mouth of the Mississippi River? (See Map 6.3)

Territory to France. Spanish officials hoped that a French Louisiana would provide a buffer zone between Spain's valuable holdings in northern Mexico and the land-hungry Americans. The French emperor Napoleon agreed to Spain's condition that France could not sell Louisiana to anyone without Spanish permission.

From the U.S. perspective, Spain had proved a weak neighbor, one it could confidently expect to displace one day. But France was another story: As one of Europe's greatest powers, its armies had just conquered most of Europe, while its navy controlled large parts of the Caribbean. The rumored transfer alarmed Jefferson. Whatever his sympathies for France, Jefferson recognized the danger a French Louisiana posed to the United States. "There is on the globe one single spot, the possessor of which is our natural & habitual enemy," he wrote. "It is New Orleans, through which the produce of three eighths of our territory must pass to market." He instructed Robert R. Livingston, America's minister in France, to try to purchase the city. In the negotiations, Livingston hinted that the United States might seize New Orleans if buying was not an option.

The prospect of war in North America did not appeal to Napoleon. On the verge of war with Britain, France needed both money and neutrality from the United States. In addition, the recent devastating loss of Haiti, its most valuable Caribbean possession, made a French presence in New Orleans far less desirable. The French offered to sell the entire Louisiana Territory to the United States. To his astonishment, Livingston secured the vast territory for the bargain price of $15 million (**Map 10.1**).

With such an extraordinary prize dangling before him, Jefferson set aside his scruples about the scope of federal power. Although he had no constitutional authority to make such a purchase, the prospect was too good to pass up. Jefferson gained congressional approval for the Louisiana Purchase, but without the votes of Federalist New England, which feared that a vast national expansion would weaken

UNDERSTAND POINTS OF VIEW

Why was Thomas Jefferson so alarmed by the prospect of France's control of the Louisiana Territory?

Louisiana Purchase
1803 purchase of French territory west of the Mississippi River that stretched from the Gulf of Mexico to Canada. The Louisiana Purchase nearly doubled the size of the United States and opened the way for future American expansion west.

What was the revolution of 1800?

MAP 10.1 ▲ **Jefferson's Expeditions in the West, 1804–1806** The Louisiana Purchase of 1803 vastly increased the size of the United States. But the new territory lacked clear boundaries. Jefferson sent four scientific expeditions to explore the region and assess the potential antagonism from Indian inhabitants.

READING THE MAP: How did the size of the newly acquired territory compare to the existing American states and territories? What natural features of the land might have suggested boundaries for the Louisiana Purchase? Did those natural features coincide with existing patterns of human settlement?

CONNECTIONS: What international events created the opportunity for the United States to purchase Louisiana? How did the acquisition of Louisiana affect Spain's territory in North America?`

the Federalist Party. In late 1803, the American army took formal control of the Louisiana Territory, and the United States nearly doubled in size—at least on paper.

The Lewis and Clark Expedition

Jefferson quickly launched four government-financed expeditions up the river valleys of the new territory to establish relationships with Indian peoples and determine the extent of European influence. The first, in 1804, set out toward the upper reaches of the Missouri River. Jefferson appointed his twenty-eight-year-old secretary, Meriwether Lewis, as its head. He instructed Lewis to investigate Indian cultures, collect plant and animal specimens, and chart the geography of the West. Congress asked the expedition to scout locations for military posts, negotiate fur trade agreements, and identify river routes to the West (**Map 10.1**).

| How did the Louisiana Purchase affect the United States? | What led to the War of 1812? | How did the civil status of free American women and men differ in the early Republic? | Why did partisan conflict increase during the administrations of Monroe and Adams? | Conclusion: How did republican simplicity become complex? |

For his co-leader, Lewis chose Kentuckian William Clark, a veteran of the 1790s Indian wars. They recruited a crew of forty-five, including expert rivermen, gunsmiths, hunters, interpreters, a cook, and Clark's slave, York. Leaving St. Louis in the spring of 1804, they traveled northwest, up the Missouri River. They camped for the winter at a Mandan village in what is now central North Dakota. There, they entered a world of long-standing trade and diplomatic alliances between native peoples and with French and Métis traders, many of whom had married into Indian families and served as important links to European markets. These established trading networks stretched west to the Pacific Ocean, north to Hudson's Bay, and east across the Atlantic to Europe. Americans were newcomers to that world.

The following spring, the explorers headed west, accompanied by a sixteen-year-old Shoshoni woman named Sacajawea. Kidnapped by Mandans at about age ten, she had been sold to a French trapper as a slave/wife. Hers was not a unique story among Indian women; such women, often fluent in several languages, served as cultural brokers, translators, and mediators. Sacajawea and her new baby allowed the American expedition to appear peaceful to suspicious tribes. As Lewis wrote in his journal, "No woman ever accompanies a war party of Indians in this quarter."

Lewis and Clark expedition
1804–1806 expedition led by Meriwether Lewis and William Clark that explored the trans-Mississippi West for the U.S. government. The expedition's mission was scientific, political, and geographic.

The **Lewis and Clark expedition** reached the Pacific Ocean at the mouth of the Columbia River in November 1805. When the two leaders returned home the following year, Americans greeted them as national heroes. They had established relations with dozens of Indian tribes; they had collected invaluable information on the peoples, soils, plants, animals, and geography of the West; and they had inspired a nation of restless explorers and solitary imitators.

Osage and Comanche Indians

Three additional expeditions set forth between 1804 and 1806 to explore the contested southwestern border of the Louisiana Purchase. The first left from Natchez, Mississippi, and ascended the Red River to the Ouachita River, ending in present-day Arkansas. Two years later, the second group followed the Red River west into eastern Texas. The third embarked from St. Louis and traveled west, deep into the Rockies. This last group, led by Zebulon Pike, had gone too far, in the view of the Spaniards: Pike and his men were arrested, taken to northern Mexico, and released.

"'Commerce is the great engine by which we are to coerce them,' Jefferson wrote, 'not war.'"

Of the scores of Indian peoples in this lower Great Plains region, two in particular dominated their territories. The Osage ruled the land between the Missouri and the lower Arkansas rivers, while the Comanche controlled the territory from the upper Arkansas River to the Rockies and south into Texas. Both were formidable powers that had proved equal to the Spaniards. The Osage asserted themselves through careful diplomacy and periodic shows of strength, the Comanche by expert horsemanship, a brisk trade in guns and captives, and a readiness to employ deadly force.

In 1804, Jefferson invited Osage leaders to Washington City, where he greeted them with ceremonies and gifts. He positioned the Osage as equals of the Americans: "The great spirit has given you strength & has given us strength, not that we might hurt one another, but to do each other all the good in our power." Jefferson wanted to introduce new agricultural tools to the Osage: hoes and plows for the men; spinning wheels and looms for the women. They implied a departure from the native gender system in which women tended crops while men hunted game. If the Osage became an agricultural people, Jefferson believed, men would give up the hunt and therefore need less land. "Commerce is the great engine by which we are to coerce them," Jefferson wrote, "not war."

What was the revolution of 1800?

◀ **Comanche Feats of Horsemanship, 1834**
Pennsylvania artist George Catlin toured the Great Plains and captured Comanche equestrian warfare in training. "Every young man," he wrote, learned "to drop his body upon the side of his horse." Thus protected, "he will hang whilst his horse is at fullest speed, carrying with him his bow and his shield, and also his long lance . . . which he will wield upon his enemy as he passes." Smithsonian American Art Museum, Washington, DC/Art Resource, NY.

In exchange, the Osage asked for protection against Indian refugees dispossessed by American settlers and pushed into their lands. Jefferson's Osage alliance proved to be expensive, driven up by the costs of providing defense, brokering treaties, and giving gifts.

These peace initiatives were short-lived. By 1808, warfare was on the rise, and the governor of the Louisiana Territory declared that the U.S. government no longer had an obligation to protect the Osage from Native American refugees displaced by American expansion. Jefferson's presidency was near its end, and soon the United States returned to its practice of whittling away Indian lands through coercive treaties, so familiar to men like Tecumseh. Four treaties between 1808 and 1839 dramatically shrank the Osage lands. By the 1860s the Osage were relocated to present-day Oklahoma.

The Comanche, by contrast, forcefully resisted U.S. expansion. Over the previous decades, they had established their dominance of a vast region known as Comanchería, which stretched across much of New Spain and now straddled the border with the Louisiana Territory. In 1807, a newly appointed U.S. Indian agent invited Comanche leaders to Natchitoches in Louisiana, where he proclaimed an improbable solidarity with the Comanche: "It is now so long since our Ancestors came from beyond the great Water that we have no remembrance of it. We ourselves are Natives of the Same land that you are, in other words white Indians, we therefore Should feel & live together like brothers & Good Neighbours." Trade relations flourished, with American traders allowed to enter Comanchería to attend local market fairs, selling weapons, cloth, and household metal goods in exchange for horses, bison, and furs. No matter what the map of the United States looked like, on the ground Comanchería remained under the control of the Comanche and off-limits to American settlement—a dynamic that would not change until much later in the nineteenth century (see Map 10.1).

COMPARE AND CONTRAST
Compare and contrast the Osage and Comanche Indians' experiences with the United States in the first decades after the Louisiana Purchase. What factors account for the differences in the tribes' standing at the end of that time?

QUICK REVIEW

What impact did the Louisiana Purchase have on U.S. relations with Spain and the Indian nations within the territory?

| How did the Louisiana Purchase affect the United States? | What led to the War of 1812? | How did the civil status of free American women and men differ in the early Republic? | Why did partisan conflict increase during the administrations of Monroe and Adams? | Conclusion: How did republican simplicity become complex? |

What led to the War of 1812?

When Jefferson was reelected in 1804, the threat of war loomed. Hoping to avoid a costly and dangerous confrontation, Jefferson tried a novel tactic: an embargo. His successor, James Madison, continued the policy, but domestic dissent grew. In 1812, the United States declared war on Britain and on Tecumseh's Indian confederacy. The two-year war cost the young nation its White House and its Capitol, but ended in a triumphant, if symbolic, victory.

Impressment and Embargo

After a brief truce, warfare between France and Britain resumed in 1803. Maintaining the policy George Washington had first established with his Neutrality Proclamation of 1793 (see chapter 9), Jefferson continued to insist on a U.S. right to trade with all nations. That objective became increasingly unattainable. As war engulfed Europe, both Britain and France expanded their campaigns to the commercial realm. Napoleon, in control of most of continental Europe, imposed a blockade on trade with Britain, including trade with neutral powers. British authorities responded with their own order forbidding trade with France. The United States was stuck in the middle.

Both Britain and France stopped U.S. ships and seized their cargoes. But Britain took the policy a step further, seizing suspected deserters from the British navy. Many of those seized were not British deserters but Americans: In an age before passports with photographs or standardized citizenship laws, asserting U.S. citizenship was much harder. Ultimately, the British forced 2,500 U.S. citizens to man their ships at war with France. In retaliation for the impressment of American sailors, Congress passed a nonimportation law, banning particular British-made goods.

One event particularly provoked U.S. popular opinion. In June 1807, a British frigate policing the Chesapeake Bay—in U.S. territory—stopped the American ship *Chesapeake*, ordering the Americans to turn over British deserters on board. When the *Chesapeake* refused, the British opened fire, killing three Americans. "Never, since the battle of Lexington, have I seen this country in such a state of exasperation as at present," Jefferson wrote a friend, adding: "and even that did not produce such unanimity." In response, Congress passed the **Embargo Act of 1807**, prohibiting U.S. ships from sailing to any foreign port or place. Using economic pressure to force the British into concessions, the drastic measure brought an immediate halt to all overseas trade.

The Embargo Act was a disaster. From 1790 to 1807, U.S. exports had increased fivefold; the embargo brought them to a standstill. Unemployment soared in New England, the heart of the shipping industry. Grain plummeted in value, river traffic halted, tobacco rotted in the South, and cotton went unpicked. Federal government revenues plunged as import duties collapsed. Protest petitions flooded Washington. The Federalist Party, in danger of fading away after its showing in the election of 1804, began to revive.

Federalist popularity did not grow enough to win the presidency in 1808, however. Secretary of State James Madison succeeded Jefferson, maintaining the Republican hold on the office. Support for the Federalists remained centered in New England, whose economy was most reliant on foreign shipping, while Republicans held the balance of power nationwide.

Embargo Act of 1807
Act of Congress that prohibited U.S. ships from traveling to foreign ports and effectively banned overseas trade in an attempt to deter Britain from halting U.S. ships at sea. The embargo caused grave hardships for Americans engaged in overseas commerce.

PLACE EVENTS IN CONTEXT

What does the British treatment of American shipping suggest about U.S. military and economic power relative to that of European nations?

What was the revolution of 1800?

Tecumseh and Tippecanoe

Madison inherited the international tensions stemming from the impressment and embargo controversies when he became president. But they were not the only foreign crises to fall in his lap, for nowhere was the threat of war greater than on the United States' western front.

After the 1795 Treaty of Greenville (see chapter 9), the U.S. settler population north of the Ohio River had grown dramatically, putting intense pressure on the remaining native lands in the northwest. The 1810 census counted some 230,000 Americans in Ohio, while another 40,000 inhabited the territories of Indiana, Illinois, and Michigan. The Native American population of the same area was probably about 70,000.

Since the collapse of the Northwest Confederacy in 1794, Native Americans had divided over the best strategy for retaining their autonomy. On the one hand were those, like the Miami leader Little Turtle, who sought some form of accommodation with the United States to protect their peoples' lands. Confronting the tide of settlers and native refugees pouring into the Ohio Valley, they believed the best approach to retaining their lands was to abandon traditional hunting practices and adopt European methods of agriculture. Often privileging their tribal loyalties over the interests of Native Americans as a whole, they negotiated the best deals they could and redistributed the revenues to their people. On the other hand were those who, drawing on decades of resistance to European encroachment, believed that Indian lands belonged to native peoples in common and could not be sold. These militants rejected the accommodationist tactics of their opponents. "No tribe has the right to sell [these lands], even to each other, much less to strangers," proclaimed Tecumseh, who emerged as the leader of the militant faction. "Sell a country! Why not sell the air, the great sea, as well as the earth? Didn't the Great Spirit make them all for the use of his children?"

For a decade after the Treaty of Greenville, Indiana's territorial governor, William Henry Harrison, shrewdly exploited those divisions. He negotiated a series of treaties that extracted great tracts of Indian lands. When Tecumseh and his brother Tenskwatawa rose to power, however, Harrison's strategy began to falter. Faced with the loss of Native American territory, Tecumseh consolidated a confederacy of Indian nations to resist further land cessions, and renewed alliances with the British in Canada.

Meanwhile, his brother Tenskwatawa, after experiencing a set of visions in 1805, became the most important Native American prophet of the period, leading a pan-Indian religious movement to purify Native American culture. He bemoaned what he saw as a decline in Native American manners, morals, and traditions, particularly the consumption of alcohol, and sought to unite Indian people in resistance to whites. In response to the catastrophes rained down upon Indian peoples by war, illness, and dispossession, Tenskwatawa advanced an idea of a shared Indian identity that would overcome persistent tribal and familial loyalties.

In 1809, while Tecumseh was away recruiting allies, Harrison assembled the leaders of the Potawatomi, Miami, and Delaware nations to negotiate the Treaty of Fort Wayne. After promising—falsely—that this was the last land cession the United States would seek, Harrison secured three million acres at about two cents per acre.

The Treaty of Fort Wayne was the last straw. It advanced the militants' opposition to accommodation, fostered the idea of a pan-Indian resistance, and consolidated Tecumseh's leadership. Tecumseh renewed the old military alliance with the British in Canada in preparation for war. Leaving his brother in charge at Prophetstown on the Tippecanoe River, the Shawnee chief left to seek allies among

Indian Lands Ceded in the Northwest Territory before 1810

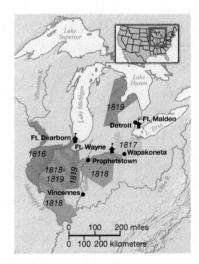

Indian Lands Ceded in the Northwest Territory between 1815–1820

COMPARE AND CONTRAST

How did the views of Tecumseh and Tenskwatawa differ from those of "accommodationist" Indian leaders?

How did the Louisiana Purchase affect the United States?

What led to the War of 1812?

How did the civil status of free American women and men differ in the early Republic?

Why did partisan conflict increase during the administrations of Monroe and Adams?

Conclusion: How did republican simplicity become complex?

▶ **Ten-squat-a-way** George Catlin painted this portrait of Tenskwatawa in 1830, calling him "one of the most remarkable men, who has flourished on these frontiers for some time past." Beginning in 1805, Tenskwatawa led a pan-Indian religious movement that advanced a shared Indian identity and sought to restore an imagined cultural purity. His movement paralleled a growing anti-Indian racism among white Americans in the years before the War of 1812. Smithsonian American Art Museum, Washington, DC/Art Resource, NY.

battle of Tippecanoe
An attack on Shawnee Indians at Prophetstown on the Tippecanoe River in 1811 by American forces headed by William Henry Harrison, Indiana's territorial governor. Tenskwatawa, the Prophet, fled with his followers. Tecumseh, his brother, deepened his resolve to make war on the United States.

War Hawks
Young men newly elected to the Congress of 1811 who were eager for war against Britain in order to end impressments, fight Indians, and expand into neighboring British territory. Leaders included Henry Clay of Kentucky and John C. Calhoun of South Carolina.

Cherokees and Choctaws in the South. In November 1811, while Tecumseh was away, Harrison attacked Prophetstown with one thousand men, killing forty Indians. The Americans won the **battle of Tippecanoe** in November 1811, but war on the western front had begun.

The Indian conflicts in the old Northwest soon merged into the wider conflict with Britain, now known as the War of 1812. In 1809, Congress had replaced Jefferson's embargo with the Non-Intercourse Act. It limited trade prohibitions to Britain and France and their colonies, opening up other trade routes and alleviating the distress of American shippers, farmers, and planters. Nonetheless, Britain and France continued to attack U.S. ships. By 1811, the country was seriously divided and on the verge of war.

In March 1811, several dozen young Republicans from the West and South ascended to Congress. They would be known as the **War Hawks**. Led by thirty-four-year-old Henry Clay from Kentucky and twenty-nine-year-old John C. Calhoun from South Carolina, they believed a war with Britain would consolidate the U.S. hold on the northwest and finally end the impressment of Americans. Many were expansionists, looking to invade Spanish Florida and Canada. Clay was elected Speaker of the House, an extraordinary honor for a newcomer, and Calhoun won a seat on the Foreign Relations Committee. The War Hawks approved major military expenditures, and the army soon quadrupled in size.

In June 1812, Congress declared war on Great Britain. The vote divided along sectional lines: New England and some Middle Atlantic states opposed the war, fearing its effect on commerce, while the South and West strongly favored it. Ironically, Britain had just announced that it would stop the search and seizure of American ships. The war momentum would not be slowed, however. The Foreign Relations Committee issued an elaborate justification titled *Report on the Causes and Reasons for War*, written mainly by Calhoun and containing extravagant language about Britain's "lust of power," "unbounded . . . tyranny," and "mad ambition." **(See "Analyzing Historical Evidence: The Nation's First Formal Declaration of War" on page 280.)**

The War Hawks proposed an invasion of Canada, confidently predicting victory in four weeks. Instead, the war lasted two and a half years, and Canada never fell. The invasion turned into a series of blunders that revealed the country's weakness against the powerful British and Indian forces (**Map 10.2**). By the fall of 1812, the outlook was grim.

What was the revolution of 1800?

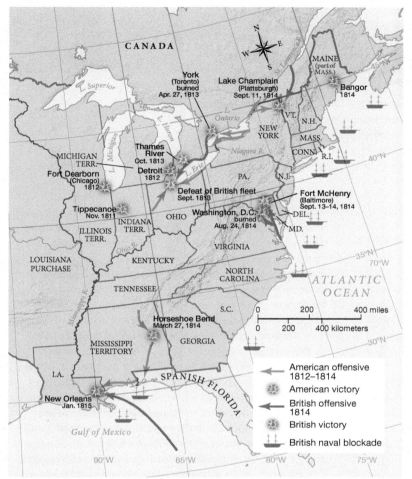

MAP 10.2 ◀ The War of 1812

During the War of 1812, battles were fought along the Canadian border and in the Chesapeake region. The most important American victory came in New Orleans two weeks after a peace agreement had been signed in England.

Worse, a powerful current of dissent to the war emerged in New England. States delayed raising troops, while many New England merchants traded illegally with Britain. In the election of 1812, not a single New England state voted for Madison, except Vermont.

In late 1812 and early 1813, the tide began to turn. The United States won several naval victories. In April 1813, the Americans attacked York (now Toronto) and burned it. A few months later, Commodore Oliver Hazard Perry defeated the British fleet at the western end of Lake Erie. Emboldened, General Harrison drove an army into Canada from Detroit and defeated the British and Indians at the battle of the Thames in October 1813, where Tecumseh was killed.

Creek Indians in the South who had allied with Tecumseh's confederacy were also plunged into war. Some 10,000 living in the Mississippi Territory fought valiantly against U.S. forces for ten months. But the Creek War ended suddenly in March 1814 when a general named Andrew Jackson led 2,500 Tennessee militiamen in a bloody attack at the Battle of Horseshoe Bend. More than 550 Indians were killed, and several hundred more died trying to escape. Later that year, General Jackson forced the defeated tribe to cede thousands of square miles of their land.

CONSIDER CAUSE AND EFFECT

What factors explain the regional conflicts within the United States that emerged over the War of 1812?

Creek War
Part of the War of 1812 involving the Creek nation in the Mississippi Territory and Tennessee militiamen. General Andrew Jackson's forces defeated the Creeks at the Battle of Horseshoe Bend in 1814, forcing them to sign away much of their land.

| How did the Louisiana Purchase affect the United States? | **What led to the War of 1812?** | How did the civil status of free American women and men differ in the early Republic? | Why did partisan conflict increase during the administrations of Monroe and Adams? | Conclusion: How did republican simplicity become complex? |

The Nation's First Formal Declaration of War

War fever gripped the United States in the spring of 1812. On June 1, President Madison sent Congress a list of British insults. On June 5, the House voted 79 to 49 to declare war. Two weeks later the Senate did likewise, 19 to 13. No Federalist voted for war, while 81 percent of Republicans supported it.

DOCUMENT 1

Federalist Boston Protests the War

On June 15, 1812, the Boston town meeting approved a lengthy report denouncing the House of Representatives' vote.

. . . Believing, as we do, that an immense majority of the people are invincibly averse from a conflict equally unnecessary, and menacing ruin to themselves and their posterity . . . we cannot but trust that a general expression of the voice of the people would satisfy Congress that those of their Representatives who have voted in favor of war, have not truly represented the wishes of their constituents. . . .

From the commencement of the system of Commercial restrictions [the embargo], the Inhabitants of this Town (inferior we trust to none in ardent patriotism and attachment to the Union) have [deplored] . . . the utter inefficacy, destructive operation, and ultimate tendency of this unprecedented and visionary scheme. They could discern in it nothing but a deliberate sacrifice of their best interests, and a conformity to the views of France . . . and hostility to Britain. . . .

Had the policy of Government been inclined towards resistance to the pretensions of the belligerents, by open war, there could be neither policy, reason, or justice in singling out Great Britain as the exclusive object of hostility. If the object of war is merely to vindicate our honor, why is it not declared against the first aggressor? If the object is defence and success, why is it to be waged against the adversary most able to annoy, and least likely to yield? . . .

Tho' we cannot discern the least reason for this discrimination in favor of France . . . , still in a war with [England] there might have been found some consolation had our country been in any measure prepared. . . . But under the present circumstances, there will be . . . no chance for success, no hope of national glory . . . and in the end an inglorious peace, in which [France will join Britain] to shackle & restrain the commerce of our infant empire, by regulations in which they will find a common interest. . . .

Resolved, that it is the true policy and duty of this nation to adhere to an impartial neutrality; to abandon commercial restrictions; . . . to indemnify itself against the losses to which its commerce is exposed in the present European war. . . . That to abstain from efforts of impotent resentment, blind rage, or desperate policy is not to be deemed submission to any foreign power, but a conformity to necessities imposed on our country by an overruling Providence, for which our courage and patriotism is not responsible. That we should endeavor to ride out the storm which we cannot direct, and that to plunge into the present war would be a wanton and impious rejection of the advantages with which the Almighty has blessed our country.

Voted, That a suitable number of copies of the foregoing report be printed . . . [and transmitted] to each Town in this Commonwealth.

Source: *A Volume of Records Relating to the Early History of Boston, Containing Boston Town Records, 1796 to 1813* (Boston: Municipal Print Office, 1905), 316–20, http://catalog.hathitrust.org/Record/011718472.

Washington City Burns: The British Offensive

In August 1814, British ships sailed into Chesapeake Bay, landing 5,000 troops and throwing the capital into a panic. Families evacuated, banks hid their money, and government clerks carted away boxes of important papers. James Madison's wife, Dolley, fled with her husband's papers, while servants rescued a portrait of George Washington. As the cook related, "When the British did arrive, they ate up the very

What was the revolution of 1800?

DOCUMENT 2

Congress Declares War

In early June 1812, the House Foreign Relations Committee, chaired by John C. Calhoun, produced a seventeen-page "Manifesto" justifying war. It went public on June 18, the day after the formal congressional declaration of war.

The period has now arrived, when the United States must support their character and station among the nations of the earth, or submit to the most shameful degradation. . . . The mad ambition, the lust of power and commercial avarice of Great Britain, arrogating to herself the complete dominion of the ocean, and exercising over it an unbounded and lawless tyranny, have left to neutral nations an alternative only between the base surrender of their rights, and a manly vindication of them.

[The manifesto devotes a dozen pages to maritime provocations by Great Britain stretching back to 1805.]

Under the pretext of impressing British seamen . . . our Citizens are wantonly snatched from their Country . . . ; doomed to an ignominious and slavish bondage; compelled to fight the battles of a foreign Country and often to perish in them. . . . While this practice is continued, it is impossible for the United States to consider themselves an independent Nation. . . .

It is known that symptoms of British hostility towards the United States have never failed to produce corresponding symptoms among those tribes [on the frontiers]. . . . [Furthermore] abundant supplies of the ordinary munitions of war have been afforded by the agents of British commercial companies . . . wherewith they were enabled to commence that system of savage warfare on our frontiers.

. . . From this review of the multiplied wrongs of the British government since the commencement of the present war, it must be evident to the impartial world that the contest which is now forced on the United States, is radically a contest for their sovereignty and independence. . . . The control of our commerce by G. Britain in regulating . . . and expelling it almost from the ocean; the oppressive manner in which these regulations have been carried into effect, by seizing . . . such of our vessels, with their cargoes, as were said to have violated her edicts, often without previous warning . . . ; the impressment of our citizens from on board our own vessels on the high seas . . . are encroachments of that high and dangerous tendency, which could not fail to produce that pernicious effect. . . . The proof which so complete and disgraceful a submission to its [Great Britain's] authority would afford of our degeneracy, could not fail to inspire confidence, and there was no limit to which its usurpations, and our degradation, might not be carried.

Source: House Foreign Relations Committee, *Report, or Manifesto of the Causes and Reasons of War with Great Britain* (Washington, DC: A. & G. Way, 1812), 3–4, 10–12, 16–17, https://archive.org/details/cihm_51537.

Questions for Analysis

RECOGNIZE VIEWPOINTS: Why do the Boston Federalists oppose the war? Why do Republicans in Congress support it?

ANALYZE THE EVIDENCE: Why does the Boston town meeting compare the problem of British threats to a bad storm that has to be endured? What does that comparison suggest about the limits of U.S. power? On what grounds do Republicans in Congress believe a military response is necessary?

CONSIDER THE CONTEXT: In what ways do debates about the War of 1812 echo those that led to the American Revolution, and in what ways are they different?

dinner, and drank the wines, &c., that I had prepared for the President's party." Then the British torched the White House, the Capitol, a newspaper office, and a well-stocked arsenal. Instead of holding the city, the British headed north and attacked Baltimore, where the Maryland militia successfully defended the city.

In another offensive that month, British troops marched from Canada into New York State. After losing a naval skirmish at Plattsburgh on Lake Champlain, they retreated. Five months later, a large British army landed in lower Louisiana. In early

| How did the Louisiana Purchase affect the United States? | **What led to the War of 1812?** | How did the civil status of free American women and men differ in the early Republic? | Why did partisan conflict increase during the administrations of Monroe and Adams? | Conclusion: How did republican simplicity become complex? |

281

January 1815, it encountered General Andrew Jackson and his militia just outside New Orleans in the war's final battle. Jackson's forces won a tremendous victory in the **battle of New Orleans**. The British suffered between 2,000 and 3,000 casualties, the Americans fewer than 80. Jackson instantly became a national hero. No one in the United States knew that negotiators in Europe had signed a peace agreement two weeks earlier. The news had not yet crossed the Atlantic.

The Treaty of Ghent, signed in December 1814, settled few of the issues that had led to war between Britain and the United States. Neither country emerged victorious, and no land changed hands. The Americans dropped their demand for an end to impressment, which subsided when war between Britain and France finally ended in 1815. They also gave up any claim to Canada. The British agreed to stop all aid to Indians in the northwest. Nothing was said about shipping rights, the ostensible cause of the war. The most concrete result was a plan for a future commission to determine the boundary between the United States and Canada.

Antiwar Federalists in New England could not gloat over the war's ambiguous conclusion, however. In an ill-timed move, the region's leaders had convened a secret meeting in Hartford, Connecticut. They discussed a series of proposals to reduce the South's power and break Virginia's hold on the presidency. Delegates to the **Hartford Convention** proposed abolishing the Constitution's three-fifths clause; requiring a two-thirds vote (instead of a simple majority) for imposing embargoes, admitting new states, or declaring war; limiting the president to one term; and prohibiting the election of successive presidents from the same state. They even discussed secession from the Union. Although the proposals were reasonable, the timing could not have been worse: December 1814, the very month U.S. diplomats signed the Treaty of Ghent. By its meeting, the Federalist Party looked unpatriotic, even treasonous. It never recovered. Within a few years the party disappeared entirely.

Although the United States did not exactly win the War of 1812, Americans celebrated as though they had. Only thirty years from its independence, the United States had fought its former colonial master, Europe's greatest power, to a draw. (Admittedly, British forces were tied down in Europe in the incomparably bigger and more significant Napoleonic Wars against France.) The war—which many saw as a second American Revolution—gave rise to a new spirit of American nationalism. Lingering fears about the nation's fragility began to wane.

If the United States did not exactly win the War of 1812, there could be little doubt that Native Americans in the West lost it. Tecumseh was dead, his brother the Prophet discredited. Once again, British negotiators abandoned their Native American allies in European peace negotiations. The prospects for an Indian confederacy were dashed, and with them any last hope of an internationally recognized Native American homeland with borders protected from U.S. settlement. Further south, the Creeks lost millions of acres of their land, and vast areas of the Southwest—the future cotton belt—now opened to a frenzied U.S. expansion. The consequences would prove devastating for Native Americans, for slaves, and eventually for the nation's very integrity.

QUICK REVIEW

What caused the War of 1812, and what were its most significant outcomes?

What was the revolution of 1800?

How did the civil status of free American women and men differ in the early Republic?

olley Madison pioneered the role of "presidentress," hosting social events at the White House and creating an active role for elite women in political affairs. But as with the 1790s ideal of republican motherhood (see chapter 9), Mrs. Madison and her female circle engaged in politics to further men's careers. There was little talk of the "rights of woman." Indeed, from 1800 to 1825, key institutions shaping women's lives—the legal system, marriage, and religion—proved stubbornly resistant to change. Nonetheless, the increased commitment to female education that began in the 1780s continued into the nineteenth century.

CHRONOLOGY

1790–1820
– In era of religious ferment, small number of women openly engage in preaching.

1821
– Emma Willard founds Troy Female Seminary in New York.

1822
– Catharine Beecher founds Hartford Seminary in Connecticut.

Dolley Madison and Social Politics

Although women could not vote or hold office, the female relatives of Washington politicians played an important role in the nation's political life. They networked through dinners, balls, receptions, and the intricate custom of "calling," in which men and women paid brief visits at each other's homes. Webs of friendship and influence in turn facilitated female political lobbying.

Dolley Madison built elaborate social networks during Jefferson's presidency that flourished during her husband's administration. Called by some the "presidentress," Mrs. Madison struck a balance between queenliness and republican openness. She dressed in resplendent clothes, and opened three elegant rooms in the executive mansion for a weekly open-house party called "Mrs. Madison's crush" or "squeeze."

In contrast to George and Martha Washington's stiff, brief receptions, the Madisons' parties went on for hours. They became indispensable events for the scores or even hundreds of guests who milled about, trading information and establishing relationships over food and drink. Members of Congress, cabinet officers, distinguished guests, envoys from foreign countries, and their wives all orbited around Mrs. Madison's salons.

In 1810 to 1811, the executive mansion acquired its present name, the White House. Dolley Madison, a major asset to her shy husband, understood how the White House could enhance the power and legitimacy of the presidency, and how her social events could advance his political agenda.

Women and the Law

Whatever part elite women like Mrs. Madison played in the political life of the young Republic, the broader legal context sharply limited most women's public roles. In English common law, the legal doctrine of *feme covert* (covered woman) held that a wife had no legal or political personhood independent of her husband. A wife was obligated to obey her husband: Her property belonged to him, as did her domestic and sexual services, and even their children. Wives had no right to make contracts, keep their wages, or sue or be sued. Even as they redrafted other British laws to make them more republican, American state legislatures largely left the laws of domestic relations untouched. The unequal power relations at the heart of marriage seemed natural to most Americans.

The one aspect of family law that changed in the early Republic was divorce. Before the Revolution, only New England jurisdictions recognized a limited right to divorce; by 1820, every state except South Carolina did. A mutual wish to terminate a marriage

feme covert
Legal doctrine grounded in British common law that held that a wife's civic life was subsumed by her husband's. Married women lacked independence to own property, make contracts, or keep wages earned. The doctrine shaped women's status in the early Republic.

| How did the Louisiana Purchase affect the United States? | What led to the War of 1812? | **How did the civil status of free American women and men differ in the early Republic?** | Why did partisan conflict increase during the administrations of Monroe and Adams? | Conclusion: How did republican simplicity become complex? |

283

◀ **Dolley Madison, by Gilbert Stuart** Dolley Payne Todd married James Madison in 1794, while Madison served in the House of Representatives. When James became secretary of state in 1801, Dolley presided over Washington's most important social gatherings, helping to advance her husband's political career. Painted in 1804, this portrait displays Mrs. Madison in fashionable French style, wearing a high-waisted, low-cut dress, her hair pulled up in neoclassical style. Historic Images/Alamy Stock Photo.

was never sufficient grounds for a legal divorce, however. Many states required a petition to the legislature for a divorce, a daunting obstacle for most people. A New York judge affirmed that "it would be aiming a deadly blow at public morals to decree a dissolution of the marriage contract merely because the parties requested it." Marriage, according to the law, protected people deemed naturally dependent (women and children) and regulated the use and inheritance of property. Only certain reasons could justify its dissolution. Legal enforcement of marriage and *feme covert* helped maintain gender inequality in the nineteenth century.

Single adult women had more legal rights. They could own and convey property, make contracts, initiate lawsuits, and pay taxes. But their civil status remained limited, too: They could not vote (except in New Jersey before 1807), serve on juries, or practice law. Social customs further restricted single women's economic status. Job prospects were few and low-paying. Unless they inherited property or lived with married siblings, single adult women in the early Republic were usually poor.

None of the laws that structured white gender relations applied to slaves. As property, enslaved people had no legal ability to consent to contractual obligations, including marriage. Enslaved men and women thus lacked the protections of state-sponsored unions. Because they were not recognized by law, and could be torn apart at any moment by sale or the whim of a slave owner, slave marriages and family relations developed different customs, dynamics, and meanings than did those among whites. Extended networks of kinship powerfully shaped slaves' worlds, providing emotional sustenance and even structuring forms of property ownership on plantations in ways that lay completely outside the formal legal system.

Women and Church Governance

In most Protestant denominations around 1800, white women made up the majority of congregants. Although leadership generally rested in men's hands, some exceptions existed. In Baptist congregations in New England, women served on church governance committees, deciding on the admission of new members, voting on hiring ministers, and even debating doctrinal points. Quakers, too, had a history of giving power to women. Some achieved the status of minister, capable of leading and speaking in Quaker meetings.

Between 1790 and 1820, a small number of women ascended to positions of open spiritual leadership. Most came from Freewill Baptist groups in New England and upstate New York, others from small Methodist sects, while some lacked any formal religious affiliation. Probably fewer than a hundred such women existed, but several dozen traveled beyond their communities, creating converts and controversy. They

PLACE EVENTS IN CONTEXT

How did the republican culture of the early United States influence Americans' religious practices?

What was the revolution of 1800?

▶ **Women and the Church: Jemima Wilkinson** In this engraving, Jemima Wilkinson, "the Publick Universal Friend," wears a clerical collar and robe, as a male minister would wear, in keeping with the claim that the former Jemima was now without gender. Wilkinson's hair is swept back from the forehead and curled at the neck in the style of men's powdered wigs of the 1790s. History and Directory of Yates County by Stafford C. Cleveland, 1873.

The Universal Friend.

spoke without prepared speeches, often exhibiting trances and claiming to exhort (counsel or warn) rather than to preach.

The best-known exhorting woman was Jemima Wilkinson, who called herself "the Publick Universal Friend." After a near-death experience from high fever, Wilkinson proclaimed her body no longer female or male but the incarnation of the "Spirit of Light." She dressed in men's clothes, wore her hair in a masculine style, shunned gender-specific pronouns, and preached openly in Rhode Island and Philadelphia. In the early nineteenth century, Wilkinson established a town called New Jerusalem in western New York with some 250 followers. Periodic newspaper articles kept her in the public eye, feeding curiosity about her cross-dressing and her unfeminine forcefulness.

The decades from 1790 to the 1820s were a period of remarkable confusion, ferment, and creativity in American religion. New denominations blossomed. Fervent religious passion gripped adherents, while a burgeoning religious press popularized extraordinary theological and institutional innovations. In this climate, the most radically democratic churches contested entrenched traditions of gender subordination. But male religious authority withstood the challenge. Denominations that accepted women's participation in church governance eventually began to pull back, reinstating patterns of hierarchy along gender lines.

Female Education

Because an educated citizenry was deemed essential to a republic, states and localities began investing in public schools. Young girls attended district schools along with boys; by 1830, they had made rapid gains. In many places, female literacy rates approached those of males. If educational opportunities broadened dramatically in this period, however, they were not universal. Most schools were located in northern states, and few addressed the needs of free black children, whether male or female.

More advanced female education came from a growing number of private academies. In 1800, Judith Sargent Murray, the Massachusetts author who had called for equality of the sexes a decade earlier, predicted "a new era in female history" from the "female academies [that] are everywhere establishing." Some dozen were founded in the 1790s; by 1830, the number had grown to nearly two hundred. Students between twelve and sixteen years old came from elite families as well as middling families with intellectual aspirations. They studied ornamental arts, like drawing, needlework, or French conversation, as well as more academic subjects such as English grammar, literature, history, the natural sciences, geography, and elocution (the art of effective public speaking). Unlike theological seminaries that trained men for the clergy, many female academies prepared their students to teach. Author Harriet Beecher Stowe, educated at an academy where she later taught, shared the widely held view that women made better teachers than men. "If men have more knowledge they have less talent at communicating it. Nor have

"Harriet Beecher Stowe wrote, 'If men have more knowledge they have less talent at communicating it. Nor have they the patience, the long-suffering, and gentleness necessary to superintend the formation of character.'"

◄ **Frontispiece for Thomas Branagan's *Penitential Tyrant*** This image from an 1807 antislavery book portrays a mournful lady liberty seated under neoclassical columns marked with "Liberty," "Virtue," and "Independence" while African slaves are marched off ships in the background. The author wanted "to demonstrate the hypocrisy and villainy of professing to be votaries of liberty, while, at the same time, we encourage, or countenance, the most ignoble slavery." The Library Company of Philadelphia.

they the patience, the long-suffering, and gentleness necessary to superintend the formation of character."

The most immediate value of female academies came from the self-cultivation and confidence they fostered. Following the model of male colleges, female graduation exercises featured speeches performed in front of family, friends, and local notables. Elocution, a common subject in the academies, taught the young women the art of persuasion along with correct pronunciation and the skill of public speaking. Bowing to the widespread hostility toward learned woman, however, academies took care to promote female modesty.

Advanced education was limited to a tiny subset of the population—fewer than one percent of their age group. Nonetheless, by the mid-1820s the total annual enrollment at female academies equaled the enrollment at the nearly six dozen male colleges in the United States. Male students generally became ministers, lawyers, judges, and political leaders, while most female graduates in time married and raised families. Before getting married, however, many women taught at academies and district schools. A large number also became authors, contributing essays and poetry to newspapers, editing periodicals, and publishing novels. If it was not exactly revolutionary, this attention to training female minds laid the foundation for major transformations in the gender system as girls of the 1810s matured into adult women of the 1830s.

UNDERSTAND POINTS OF VIEW

How did ideas of innate differences between men and women both restrict and open educational opportunities for women in the early nineteenth century?

QUICK REVIEW

In what ways did women take on public roles in the early Republic?

Why did partisan conflict increase during the administrations of Monroe and Adams?

After the War of 1812, the men called War Hawks took up the banner of the Republican Party and carried it in new directions. These young politicians favored trade, western expansion, internal improvements, and the development of new markets. Virginians continued their hold on the presidency with the election of James Monroe in 1816. The collapse of the Federalist Party ushered in an

What was the revolution of 1800?

apparent period of one-party rule; in 1820, Monroe won reelection with all but one electoral vote. But politics remained highly partisan. At the state level, increasing political engagement sparked a drive for universal white male suffrage. At the national level, bitter feelings emerged in response to a sectional crisis over the admission of Missouri to the Union. Controversies over Latin American independence and European involvement in the region animated sharp disagreements as well. Four candidates vied for the presidency in 1824 in an election decided by the House of Representatives. One-party rule was far from harmonious.

From Property to Democracy

In the 1780s, twelve of the original thirteen states enacted property qualifications based on the theory that only male freeholders—landowners, as distinct from tenants or servants—had sufficient economic independence to be entrusted with the vote. Over the course of the next generation, this idea of suffrage collapsed as U.S. political life was radically democratized.

In the 1790s, Vermont became the first state to enfranchise all adult males. Meanwhile, four other states broadened suffrage by allowing all male taxpayers to vote. As new states in the west joined the Union, most extended voting rights to all free white men. Pressure grew for eastern states to broaden their suffrage laws.

Not everyone favored expanded suffrage; propertied elites tended to support the status quo. But they found themselves on the defensive as the American Revolution's ideological assault on monarchy extended to ever more elements of the country's political life. Under pressure, state legislatures called new constitutional conventions to debate questions of suffrage, balloting procedures, apportionment, and representation.

By 1820, half a dozen states had reformed their voting laws. Some enacted universal manhood suffrage, while others tied the vote to tax status or militia service. Eighteenth-century ideas of republican government gradually turned into nineteenth-century ideas of democratic government. The disfranchised no longer accepted the idea that landowners had greater independence or superior virtue. "More integrity and more patriotism are generally found in the labouring class of the community than in the higher orders," argued one delegate to New York's constitutional convention. Owning land was no more predictive of wisdom and good character than it was of a person's height or strength, said another observer.

Both sides of the debate generally agreed that character mattered, as did maintaining an electorate of sufficient wisdom. The exclusion of paupers and felons convicted of "infamous crimes" found favor in many states. The exclusion of women provoked no discussion in constitutional conventions, so firm was the legal principle of *feme covert* subjugating married women to their husbands. In one exceptional moment, at the Virginia constitutional convention in 1829, a delegate wondered aloud why unmarried women older than twenty-one could not vote. He was silenced with the argument that all women lacked the necessary "free agency and intelligence."

The voting rights of free black men was another story. It generated extensive discussion at all the conventions. Under freehold qualifications, a small number of propertied black men could vote; universal or taxpayer suffrage would inevitably enfranchise many more. Many delegates at various state conventions spoke against that extension, claiming that blacks as a race lacked virtue, independence, and education. With the exception of New York, which retained the existing property qualification for black voters as it removed it for whites, most states expanded suffrage for whites while restricting it for blacks.

CHRONOLOGY

1816
– James Monroe elected president.

1819
– Adams-Onís Treaty negotiated.

1820
– Missouri Compromise approved by Congress.

1823
– Monroe Doctrine asserted.

1825
– John Quincy Adams elected president by House of Representatives.

CONSIDER CAUSE AND EFFECT

What were the connections between the expansion of voting rights for white men and their restriction for black men?

| How did the Louisiana Purchase affect the United States? | What led to the War of 1812? | How did the civil status of free American women and men differ in the early Republic? | **Why did partisan conflict increase during the administrations of Monroe and Adams?** | Conclusion: How did republican simplicity become complex? |

The Missouri Compromise

Monroe's first term in office saw one of the most significant political crises of the early nineteenth century. Since 1815, four states had joined the Union (Indiana, Mississippi, Illinois, and Alabama), bringing the total number to twenty-two. All had followed the orderly blueprint laid out by the Northwest Ordinance of 1787 (see chapter 8): States north of the Ohio River entered the Union as free states, while those south of the river entered as slave states. Then, in February 1819, Missouri—a territory recently taken from the Osage Indians—applied for statehood.

Missouri posed a problem. The Northwest Ordinance said nothing about the territory west of the Mississippi River, and geography provided no obvious solution. Positioned just to the west of the free state of Illinois, most of its territory lay north of the latitude of the Ohio River's mouth. And yet Missouri's population already included ten thousand slaves brought there by southern planters. What to do? New York congressman James Tallmadge Jr. proposed a solution, offering two amendments to the statehood bill. The first stipulated that slaves born in Missouri after statehood would be free at age twenty-five, and the second declared that no new slaves could be imported into the state. Tallmadge's proposal was not particularly radical. Based on New York's emancipation law of 1799 (see chapter 8), it put forward a gradual abolition scheme that would not strip slave owners of their property. Over time, however, it would make Missouri a free state.

Tallmadge's amendments generated a firestorm of opposition that threatened to tear the political system apart. Until that point, the number of states in which slavery was legal matched the number in which it had either been abolished or been put on the road to extinction. Indeed, since the Union began admitting new states, Congress had continuously maintained a sectional balance. "Kentucky to the Union given— / Vermont will make the balance even," read a playful verse printed in newspapers in 1790. "Still Pennsylvania holds the scales, / and neither South or North prevails." By 1820, the Union comprised twenty-two states, half of them "free," and the other half "slave." Although the free-state population exceeded that of the slave states, southern political power drew extra strength because of the three-fifths rule. In 1820, the South owed seventeen of its seats in the House of Representatives to its slave population. The Tallmadge amendments threatened to upset that delicate balance.

They passed in the House by a close and sharply sectional vote that pitted North against South. The ferocious debate led a Georgia representative to observe that the question had started "a fire which all the waters of the ocean could not extinguish. It can be extinguished only in blood." The Senate, with an even number of slave and free states, voted down the amendments.

The Missouri Compromise of 1820 broke the impasse. In a set of complex negotiations brokered by Kentucky's Henry Clay, Maine, once part of Massachusetts, applied for statehood as a free state, thus preserving a balance between free and slave states. So that the issue would not return with each new state admission, the Senate agreed that the southern boundary of Missouri—latitude 36°30′—would become the permanent line dividing slave from free states as the country expanded west (**Map 10.3**).

The split over Missouri threatened to realign the country's political geography. The vote was not grounded in the familiar ideological division between Federalist and Republican parties, but by a sectional division between North and South that endangered the nation's very integrity. Faced with this specter, most of the country's political leaders retreated. They agreed that the split between free and slave states was too dangerous a fault line. When new parties developed in the 1830s, their leaders took pains to bridge geography, each party developing a presence in the North and South.

If the Missouri fight did not lead to crisis in 1820, it worried many Americans to the core. "This momentous question, like a fire bell in the night, awakened and filled

Missouri Compromise
1820 congressional compromise engineered by Henry Clay that paired Missouri's entrance into the Union as a slave state with Maine's entrance as a free state. The compromise also established Missouri's southern border as the permanent line dividing slave states from free states.

UNDERSTAND POINTS OF VIEW

Why did the admission of Missouri generate such controversy among northern and southern politicians?

What was the revolution of 1800?

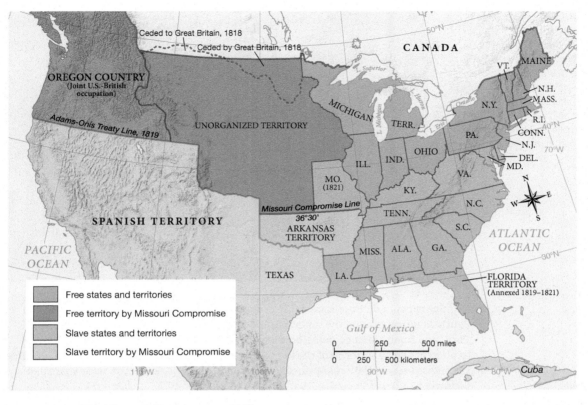

MAP 10.3 ▲ The Missouri Compromise, 1820

After a difficult battle in Congress, Missouri entered the Union in 1821 as part of a package of compromises. Maine was admitted as a free state to balance slavery in Missouri, and a line drawn at latitude 36°30′ put most of the rest of the Louisiana Territory off-limits to slavery in the future.

me with terror," Jefferson wrote a correspondent in 1820. "I considered it at once as the knell of the Union. It is hushed indeed for the moment. But this is a reprieve only, not a final sentence."

The Monroe Doctrine

Even as Congress struggled with the future of slavery, foreign relations generated new controversies. In 1816, U.S. troops led by General Andrew Jackson invaded Spanish Florida in search of Seminole Indians harboring escaped slaves. Jackson declared himself the commander of northern Florida, and demonstrated his power in 1818 by executing two British men he accused of aiding his enemies. These were acts of extreme provocation against both Spain and Great Britain. President Monroe considered court-martialing Jackson, but decided that Jackson's popularity as the hero of the battle of New Orleans made this course of action impossible.

Instead, John Quincy Adams, the secretary of state, negotiated the Adams-Onís Treaty with Spain, which delivered Florida to the United States in 1819 and settled the disputed borders of the Louisiana Purchase. In exchange, the United States abandoned any claims on Texas or Cuba. Although the Adams-Onís Treaty extended U.S. borders to the south, opening future lands for the expansion of slavery, the treaty's concession angered many southerners. With many at the leadership of the country's foreign policy, they harbored ambitions for the nation's expansion not just west across the continent but also south into the Caribbean and Mexico.

How did the Louisiana Purchase affect the United States?	What led to the War of 1812?	How did the civil status of free American women and men differ in the early Republic?	**Why did partisan conflict increase during the administrations of Monroe and Adams?**	Conclusion: How did republican simplicity become complex?

► **Morse, House of Representatives**
Samuel F. B. Morse began this monumental painting (measuring more than seven by twelve feet) of debates in the House of Representatives the year after debate over the Missouri Compromise split the country's political life. Morse prepared individual studies of each figure in the painting. Failing to earn money in a traveling exhibit, Morse gave up painting and turned to science. He later invented the telegraph. DEA Picture Library/Getty Images.

Spain could do little to resist U.S. aggression in Florida because its colonies in South America were in the midst of rebellion. In the early 1820s, Chile, Colombia, Peru, and finally Mexico declared themselves independent. U.S. popular opinion exulted at the emergence of these new republics in the Americas. In support, Monroe formulated a declaration of principles on South America, known in later years as the **Monroe Doctrine**.

In 1823, the president warned that "the American Continents, by the free and independent condition which they have assumed and maintain, are henceforth not to be considered as subjects for future colonization by any European power." Any European attempt to interfere in the Western Hemisphere would be considered as "the manifestation of an unfriendly disposition towards the United States." In exchange for noninterference by Europeans, Monroe pledged that the United States would stay out of European struggles. Although couched in diplomatic language, the Monroe Doctrine was a clear assertion of U.S. sovereignty not just in North America but across the entire Western Hemisphere.

Monroe Doctrine
Declaration warning European powers not to intervene in the Western Hemisphere, and pledging American non-interference in European events. Named after President James Monroe, who issued it in 1823, after Latin American countries' independence from Spain.

The Election of 1824

Monroe's nonpartisan administration was the last of its kind, a throwback to eighteenth-century ideals—as was Monroe himself, the last president to wear a powdered wig and knee breeches. Monroe's cabinet contained men of sharply different political views who all called themselves Republicans. Secretary of State John Quincy Adams represented the urban Northeast and believed in social reform and a robust federal government. South Carolinian John C. Calhoun spoke for the planter aristocracy as secretary of war, promoting internal improvements, tariffs, and an aggressive foreign policy. William H. Crawford of Georgia, secretary of the treasury, was a proponent of Jeffersonian states' rights and limited federal power. Even before the end of Monroe's first term, these men and many others began looking ahead to the election of 1824.

Political wives played key roles in their husbands' ambitions, accomplishing some of the work of modern campaign managers by courting men and women of influence. Louisa Catherine Adams threw a weekly Washington party for guests that regularly

What was the revolution of 1800?

numbered in the hundreds. The somber Adams lacked the charm increasingly necessary to political life—"I am a man of reserved, cold, austere, and forbidding manners," he once wrote—but his wife more than compensated. She made frequent social calls, sometimes as many as two dozen in a morning, and counted sixty-eight members of Congress as her regular guests.

John Quincy and Louisa Catherine Adams were not the only ones with ambitions on the presidency. Others included Henry Clay, Speaker of the House of Representatives, who promoted a package of protective tariffs to encourage manufacturing and federal expenditures for internal improvements such as roads and canals that he dubbed the "American System." Treasurer William Crawford was a favorite of Republicans from Virginia and New York. Calhoun was another serious contender, with experience in Congress and several cabinets.

The final candidate was an outsider and a latecomer—General Andrew Jackson of Tennessee. Jackson had far less political experience than the others, but he enjoyed great celebrity from his military career. In 1824, on the anniversary of the battle of New Orleans, the Adamses threw a spectacular ball in his honor, hoping to claim some of Jackson's star power. Neither yet thought of Jackson as a rival. Not long after, however, Jackson's supporters put his name forward for the presidency. Voters in the West and South reacted with enthusiasm. Adams was dismayed. Calhoun dropped out of the race and shifted his attention to winning the vice presidency.

The election of 1824 was the first to have a popular vote tally for the presidency. As they democratized the vote, eighteen states (out of twenty-four) had put the power to choose members of the electoral college directly in the hands of voters, as opposed to state legislatures. Jackson dominated his rivals, winning 153,544 votes, compared to Adams's 108,740. Clay won 47,136 votes, and Crawford 46,618. Although the turnout probably amounted to just over one-quarter of adult white males, the election of 1824 launched a new era in the country's political history that would be marked by intense partisanship and an energized electorate.

In the electoral college, Jackson received 99 votes, Adams 84, Crawford 41, and Clay 37 (**Map 10.4**). Because Jackson lacked a majority, the House of Representatives decided the election once again. Each congressional delegation had one vote. According to the Constitution's Twelfth Amendment passed in 1804, only the top three candidates joined the runoff. Henry Clay was therefore out of the race, and in a position to bestow his support on another candidate. It proved decisive. With Clay's support, Adams won by one vote in the House in February 1825.

Jackson's allies called the election of 1824 the "corrupt bargain." Clay's support made sense on several levels, however. Despite strong mutual dislike, he and Adams agreed on issues such as federal funding for roads and canals. Moreover, Jackson's volatile temperament and unknown political views troubled Clay. What made his support look "corrupt" was President Adams's subsequent appointment of Clay as secretary of state, the traditional stepping-stone to the presidency.

Jackson and his supporters believed the election had been stolen. "The Judas of the West," he wrote of Clay, "has closed the contract and will receive the thirty pieces of silver." The charge would motivate Jackson, who thrived on anger, while haunting Adams throughout his brief presidency.

Candidate*	Electoral Vote	Popular Vote	Percent of Popular Vote
John Q. Adams	84	108,740	30.5
Andrew Jackson	99	153,544	43.1
Henry Clay	37	47,136	13.2
W. H. Crawford	41	46,618	13.1

*No distinct political parties

Note: Because no candidate garnered a majority in the electoral college, the election was decided in the House of Representatives. Although Clay was eliminated from the running, as Speaker of the House he influenced the final decision in favor of Adams.

MAP 10.4 ▲ The Election of 1824

How did the Louisiana Purchase affect the United States?

What led to the War of 1812?

How did the civil status of free American women and men differ in the early Republic?

Why did partisan conflict increase during the administrations of Monroe and Adams?

Conclusion: How did republican simplicity become complex?

The Adams Administration

John Quincy Adams, like his father, was a one-term president. He had built his career on diplomacy, not electoral politics. His wife's rich endowments in political skills could not make up for his lack of them. Like his father before him, Adams welcomed his opposition into his cabinet. He asked Crawford to stay on in the Treasury. He retained an openly pro-Jackson postmaster general, although the position controlled thousands of patronage appointments across the nation. He even asked Jackson to become secretary of war. Crawford and Jackson declined.

Adams had lofty ambitions for his presidency. He presented a sweeping plan to Congress that called for federally funded roads, canals, and harbors. He proposed a national university in Washington and government-sponsored scientific research. He wanted to build observatories to advance astronomical knowledge and promote precision in timekeeping, and he backed a decimal-based system of weights and measures. Adams saw himself pursuing the legacy of Jefferson and Madison, using the government's powers to advance knowledge. But his opponents saw him as a latter-day Hamilton, deploying federal power illegitimately to advance commercial interests.

CONSIDER CAUSE AND EFFECT

How did the democratization of suffrage affect the presidential election of 1824?

But Adams was neither a Hamilton nor a Jefferson, and he failed to implement most of his programs. He scorned the idea of courting voters or using patronage to advance his political aims. He often used appointments to posts such as customs collectors to placate enemies, rather than to reward friends. The story of a toast offered to the president may well have been invented, but it came to summarize Adams's feeble political skills. A dignitary raised a glass and said, "May he strike confusion to his foes," to which another voice scornfully chimed in, "as he has already done to his friends."

QUICK REVIEW

How did the collapse of the Federalist Party influence the administrations of James Monroe and John Quincy Adams?

Conclusion: How did republican simplicity become complex?

With the election of 1800, the Jeffersonian Republicans worked to undo much of what the Federalists had accomplished in the 1790s. But the promise of a simpler government gave way to the complexities of domestic and foreign politics. The Louisiana Purchase and the Barbary Wars required energetic government responses, and the threats posed by Britain on the seas finally drew the country into war once again. The War of 1812, waged against Native American nations and the British, proved longer and more divisive than anyone imagined.

What was the revolution of 1800?

The war also elevated General Andrew Jackson to national prominence. His popularity with voters in the 1824 election set the era of one-party rule of Republicans hurtling to a close. John Quincy Adams had barely assumed office in 1825 before the election campaign of 1828 had begun. Reformed suffrage laws ensured that appeals to the mass of white male voters would become the hallmark of future elections.

Many Americans, notably free black men and all women, had no place in government. Legislatures maintained women's *feme covert* status, keeping wives dependent on husbands. A few women found greater personal autonomy through religion, while many others benefited from expanded female schooling in schools and academies. These substantial gains in education would blossom into a major transformation in the 1830s and 1840s.

Two other developments proved momentous in later decades. In the political realm, the bitter debate over slavery that surrounded the Missouri Compromise opened divisions between northern and southern states that would expand in the decades to come. In the economic realm, Jefferson's long embargo followed by Madison's war boosted American manufacturing. When peace returned in 1815, economic development burst forth into a period of sustained growth that continued nearly unabated into the middle of the century.

| How did the Louisiana Purchase affect the United States? | What led to the War of 1812? | How did the civil status of free American women and men differ in the early Republic? | Why did partisan conflict increase during the administrations of Monroe and Adams? | Conclusion: How did republican simplicity become complex? |

293

CHAPTER 10 STUDY GUIDE

STEP 1

EXPLAIN WHY IT MATTERS

Put your reading into practice. Identify each term below, and then explain why it matters in U.S. history.

TERM	WHO OR WHAT & WHEN	WHY IT MATTERS
Gabriel's rebellion (p. 266)		
Marbury v. Madison (p. 270)		
Louisiana Purchase (p. 272)		
Lewis and Clark expedition (p. 274)		
Embargo Act of 1807 (p. 276)		
battle of Tippecanoe (p. 278)		
War Hawks (p. 278)		
Creek War (p. 279)		
battle of New Orleans (p. 282)		
Hartford Convention (p. 282)		
feme covert (p. 283)		
Missouri Compromise (p. 288)		
Monroe Doctrine (p. 290)		

STEP 2

MOVE BEYOND THE BASICS

To demonstrate a more advanced understanding, assess the positions and policies of the early-nineteenth-century presidents. What core assumptions and beliefs informed each president's policies and positions? How did each successive president change the presidency?

Aspects and Developments	Jefferson	Madison	Monroe	J. Q. Adams
Power of the Presidency				
Expansion of the Nation				
Domestic Affairs				
Foreign Affairs				
Difficulties				
Successes				

STEP 3

PUT IT ALL TOGETHER

Now, try to explain the big picture. Remember to use specific examples from the chapter in your answers.

JEFFERSON AND REPUBLICANISM

- What steps did Jefferson take in the aftermath of the Louisiana Purchase to help facilitate western expansion of the United States?

- How did international issues shape the Jefferson presidency?

MADISON AND THE WAR OF 1812

- Where was support for the War of 1812 strongest? Where was it weakest? Why?

- How did the status of women change in the early decades of the nineteenth century? In what ways did some women exert political influence?

MONROE, ADAMS, AND PARTISANSHIP

- What led to the expansion of voting rights in the early nineteenth century?

- In what ways did the election of 1824 mark a turning point in American politics?

LOOKING BACKWARD, LOOKING AHEAD

- How did the partisanship of the 1820s differ from the partisanship of the 1790s? What explains the changes?

- What problems were solved by the Missouri Compromise? What tensions and conflicts were left unresolved?

STEP 4

CONNECT THESE EVENTS

How did Jefferson's election in 1800 spur changes that democratized American politics and society?

STEP 5

CONNECT TO THE PRESENT

Is there any modern-day equivalent of the decline and death of the Federalist Party? Why or why not?

11

THE EXPANDING REPUBLIC

1815–1840

How did rapid economic changes interact with political and social developments in the years after 1815 to reshape the nation? Chapter 11 explores the nation's dizzying economic expansion; examines the extraordinary eruption of religious and reform movements; and surveys the complex legacies of Andrew Jackson's presidency.

This chapter will explore the following questions:

- What economic developments reshaped the U.S. economy after 1815?
- How did new practices of party politics shape Andrew Jackson's election and agenda?
- What was Andrew Jackson's impact on the presidency?
- What were the most significant social and cultural changes in the 1830s?
- What political and economic events dominated Martin Van Buren's presidency?
- Conclusion: The Age of Jackson or the era of reform?

AN AMERICAN STORY

In 1837, audiences throughout Massachusetts witnessed an astonishing spectacle: two sisters from a wealthy southern family giving fiery speeches denouncing slavery. Women lecturers were rare in the 1830s, but Sarah and Angelina Grimké were on a mission. "Whilst in the act of speaking," Angelina explained, "I am favored to forget little 'I' entirely & to feel altogether hid behind the great cause I am pleading." In their seventy-nine speaking engagements that year, forty thousand women and men came to hear them.

Little in their family background predicted the sisters' radicalism. They grew up among the elite of Charleston, South Carolina. Their father was chief justice of the state supreme court. Nonetheless, they developed independent minds and a hatred of slavery. In the 1820s, both sisters moved to Philadelphia and joined the Quakers' Society of Friends.

The abolitionist movement was still in its infancy in the 1830s. In 1835, Angelina Grimké wrote to William Lloyd Garrison, editor of the Boston *Liberator*, describing herself as a white southern exile from slavery. Garrison published her letter, which caused a stir and propelled her into her new career.

The sisters' 1837 tour of Massachusetts doubled the membership of northern antislavery societies. Newspapers and religious leaders fiercely debated the Grimkés' boldness in presuming to lecture to men. The sisters defended their stand: "Whatever is morally right for a man to do is morally right for a woman to do," Angelina wrote. "I recognize no rights but human rights." Sarah produced a set of essays titled *Letters on the Equality of the Sexes* (1838), the first American treatise asserting women's equality with men.

The Grimké sisters' radicalism emerged from the vibrant, contested public life that developed in the 1830s. This decade—often called the Age of Jackson, after the president—saw rapid economic, political, and social change. Old social hierarchies eroded. Ordinary men dreamed of success and fortune. Advances in transportation and economic productivity fueled these dreams, sending thousands of people west. Urban growth and technological changes spread exhilarating new ideas through an expanding periodical press.

Expanded communication dramatically transformed politics. Sharp disagreements arose over questions of individual liberty, economic opportunity, and national prosperity. These fights shaped the political parties that reemerged in the early 1830s, attracting large numbers of white male voters into their ranks. Religion became democratized as well. An extraordinary evangelical revival brought its adherents the certainty that salvation was available to all.

It all came at a steep cost, however. Steamboats blew up, banks and businesses periodically collapsed, and alcoholism soared. New opportunities for whites resulted from the murder of Indians and the theft of their lands. Much of the economy, in the South as well as the North, rested on the foundation of a brutalized slave labor force. The brash confidence that turned some people into rugged, self-promoting individuals inspired others to think about the human costs of rapid economic expansion, and about how to reform society. The common denominator was a faith that people and societies could shape their own destinies.

▼ **Grimké Sisters** Sarah and Angelina Grimké sat for these portraits around 1840, at ages 48 and 35. Day caps were typical indoor wear for older women and for Quaker women of all ages, signaling modesty in contrast to fancily coiffed or loose hair. For these sisters advancing radical antislavery ideas in public, such self-presentation might be particularly important. Sarah Grimké: Library of Congress, 3a03340; Angelina Grimké: Library of Congress, 3a03341.

What economic developments reshaped the U.S. economy after 1815?

The return of peace in 1815 unleashed powerful forces that transformed the economy. Innovations in transportation facilitated the movement of commodities, information, and people. Textile mills and other factories in new industries created thousands of wage-earning jobs. Innovations in banking, legal practices, and tariff policies promoted rapid economic growth. If these changes did not amount to an industrial revolution, they accelerated the pace of economic activity and the number of people pulled into national and international markets. This new economy carried serious risks, however, as periodic economic crashes revealed.

Improvements in Transportation

Before 1815, transportation in the United States was slow and expensive; it cost as much to ship a crate over thirty miles of domestic roads as it did to send it across the Atlantic Ocean. A stagecoach took four days to travel from Boston to New York. Between 1815 and 1840, networks of roads, canals, steamboats, and finally railroads dramatically raised the speed and lowered the cost of travel (**Map 11.1**).

Improved transportation moved goods into wider markets. It moved passengers, too, allowing people to take up new employment in cities or factory towns. Transportation facilitated the flow of political information: The U.S. mail offered bargain postal rates for newspapers, periodicals, and books. Infrastructure like roads and canals was expensive, however, and produced uneven economic benefits. Presidents from Jefferson to Monroe resisted funding it with federal dollars. Instead, private investors pooled resources and chartered transport companies, receiving significant subsidies and monopoly rights from state governments. Turnpike and roadway mileage increased substantially after 1815. Stagecoach companies proliferated, and travel times on main routes were cut in half, even as costs fell sharply.

▶ **The Erie Canal at Lockport** The Erie Canal, completed in 1825, was an engineering marvel not only for its length of 350 miles but also for its elevation, which required eighty-three locks. The biggest construction challenge came at Lockport, twenty miles northeast of Buffalo, where the canal cut through a steep slate bluff. Work crews—mostly immigrant Irishmen—used gunpowder and grueling physical labor to blast the artificial gorge shown here. Department of Rare Books and Special Collections, Rush Rhees Library, University of Rochester.

What economic developments reshaped the U.S. economy after 1815?

CHAPTER 11
THE EXPANDING REPUBLIC

298

MAP ACTIVITY

MAP 11.1 ◀ **Routes of Transportation in 1840** Transportation advances cut travel times and reduced shipping costs. The trip from New York City to Buffalo, a two-week journey by road, took four days via the Erie Canal. Steamboats cut travel time from New York to New Orleans from four weeks by road to less than two weeks by river.

READING THE MAP: In what parts of the country were canals built most extensively? Were most limited within a single state's borders, or did they encourage interstate travel and shipping?

CONNECTIONS: What impact did the Erie Canal have on the development of New York City? How did improvements in transportation affect urbanization elsewhere?

Water travel was similarly transformed. In 1807, Robert Fulton's steam-propelled boat, the *Clermont*, churned up the Hudson River from New York City to Albany, touching off a steamboat craze. By the early 1830s, more than seven hundred steamboats operated along the Ohio and Mississippi rivers alone.

Steamboats were not benign, however. The urge to cut travel time led to over-stoked furnaces, sudden boiler explosions, and mass fatalities. An investigation of an accident near Cincinnati that killed 150 passengers in 1838 concluded: "Such disasters have their foundation in the present mammoth evil of our country, an inordinate love of gain. We are not satisfied with getting rich, but we must get rich in a day. We are not satisfied with traveling at a speed of ten miles an hour, but we must fly." By the mid-1830s, nearly three thousand Americans had died in steamboat accidents, prompting the first federal attempt to regulate safety on vessels in interstate commerce. Environmental costs also intensified: Steamboats had to load fuel—"wood up"—every twenty miles or so. Mass deforestation resulted. By the 1830s, the banks of many rivers were denuded of trees, and forests miles back from the rivers fell to the ax. The smoke from wood-burning steamboats created America's first significant air pollution.

Canals were another major innovation of the period. Canal boats powered by mules moved slowly—less than five miles per hour—but the low-friction water enabled one mule to pull a fifty-ton barge. Several states launched major government-sponsored canal enterprises, the most impressive being the **Erie Canal**, finished in 1825. It stretched 350 miles between Albany and Buffalo and linked the Hudson River with the entire Great Lakes region.

Wheat and flour moved east, household goods and tools moved west, and passengers went in both directions. By the 1830s, the cost of shipping by canal fell to

Erie Canal
Canal finished in 1825, covering 350 miles between Albany and Buffalo and linking the port of New York City with the entire Great Lakes region. The canal turned New York City into the country's premier commercial city.

| How did new practices of party politics shape Andrew Jackson's election and agenda? | What was Andrew Jackson's impact on the presidency? | What were the most significant social and cultural changes in the 1830s? | What political and economic events dominated Martin Van Buren's presidency? | Conclusion: The Age of Jackson or the era of reform? |

▲ **Cotton Textile Mill, 1840** New England textile factories ran on water power. A complex series of belts and wheels delivered the river's energy to the factory's floors. This room contains "spinning frames," which turned cleaned cotton into yarn for textile weaving. Mary Evans Picture Library/age fotostock.

READING THE IMAGE: Study the women workers shown here. Does this image suggest stressful or dangerous work? What might be the political or ideological uses of such an image in 1840?

CONNECTIONS: Why was the antebellum textile industry located primarily in New England? Consider the geography and climate as well as demographic factors.

less than one-tenth the cost of overland transport. New York City, at the mouth of the Hudson, blossomed into the premier commercial city in the United States.

In the 1830s, private railroad companies heavily subsidized by state legislatures began to compete with canals. The nation's first railroad, the Baltimore and Ohio, laid thirteen miles of track in 1829; by 1840, workers had built three thousand more miles of track nationwide. Rail lines in the 1830s were generally short—on the order of twenty to one hundred miles. They did not yet provide an efficient distribution system for goods. But passengers flocked to experience the marvelous speeds of fifteen to twenty miles per hour. Railroads and other advances in transportation began to unify the country culturally and economically.

Factories, Workingwomen, and Wage Labor

With transportation advances expanding the market for goods, manufacturing boomed after 1815. The two leading industries, textiles and shoes, altered methods of production and labor relations. The development of water-driven machinery along

> **What economic developments reshaped the U.S. economy after 1815?**

rivers spurred textile production. Shoe manufacturing, still using the power and skill of human hands, saw a reorganization of production. Both industries pulled young women into wage-earning labor for the first time.

An English immigrant built the first textile factory in the United States in Pawtucket, Rhode Island. By 1815, nearly 170 spinning mills stood along New England rivers. British manufacturers generally hired entire families for mill work. American factory owners changed this model by hiring young single women. They assumed female labor was cheaper, because women had limited employment options and generally left to get married after a few years of work. The association of spinning as women's work also made it more acceptable to hire young women.

In 1821, a group of Boston entrepreneurs founded the town of Lowell on the Merrimack River. It offered a new model of cloth manufacturing by centralizing all aspects of production: combing, shrinking, spinning, weaving, and dyeing. By 1836, the eight **Lowell mills** employed more than five thousand young women, who lived in carefully managed company-owned boardinghouses. Company rules at the Lowell mills required church attendance and prohibited drinking and unsupervised courtship. Dorms were locked at 10 p.m. A typical mill worker earned $2 to $3 for a seventy-hour week, more than a seamstress or domestic servant could earn, but less than a man's wages.

Despite the long hours, young women embraced factory work as a means to earn spending money and build savings before marriage. Several banks in town held the nest eggs of thousands of workers. Many of these young workers relished the freedom of living in an all-female social space, away from parents and liberated from domestic chores. In the evening, the women could engage in self-improvement activities, like public lectures. In 1837, 1,500 mill girls crowded Lowell's city hall to hear Angelina and Sarah Grimké speak about the evils of slavery.

In the mid-1830s, worldwide competition in the cotton market forced mill owners to speed up work and reduce wages. The workers protested. The communal living arrangements fostered solidarity, while the workers' relative independence as temporary employees encouraged their boldness. In 1834 and again in 1836, hundreds of women at Lowell went on strike. **(See "Analyzing Historical Evidence: Mill Girls Stand Up to Factory Owners, 1834" on page 302.)**

The labor unrest spread. In 1834, mill workers in Dover, New Hampshire, denounced their owners for trying to turn them into "slaves." In the end, however, the ease of replacing these relatively unskilled workers undermined their bargaining power. Surprised by the women's assertiveness, owners in the 1840s began to shift to immigrant families as their primary labor source.

The shoe manufacturing industry centered in eastern New England also experimented with new forms of labor. Manufacturers reorganized production by hiring women, including married women, as shoebinders. Male shoemakers still cut the leather and made the soles in shops, but female shoebinders working from home now stitched the upper parts of the shoes. Working from home meant that wives could contribute to family income—unusual for most wives in that period—and still perform their domestic chores.

In the economically turbulent 1830s, shoebinder wages fell. Unlike mill workers, female shoebinders worked in isolation, hindering their ability to organize collectively. In Lynn, Massachusetts, a major shoemaking center, women used female church networks to organize resistance, communicating via religious newspapers. The Lynn shoebinders who demanded higher wages in 1834 expressed a collective understanding of themselves not just as workers, but as female workers. "Equal rights should be extended to all—to the weaker sex as well as the stronger," they proclaimed.

In the end, the Lynn shoebinders' protests failed to increase wages. At-home workers all over New England continued to accept low wages. Even in Lynn, many women shied away from organized protest. They preferred to situate their work in the context of family duty (helping their husbands finish the shoes) instead of market relations.

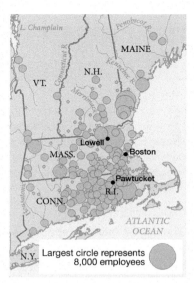

Cotton Textile Industry, ca. 1840

Largest circle represents 8,000 employees

Lowell mills
Water-powered textile mills constructed along the Merrimack River in Lowell, Massachusetts, that pioneered the extensive use of female laborers. By 1836, the eight mills there employed more than five thousand young women, who lived in boardinghouses under close supervision.

COMPARE AND CONTRAST
What did female textile workers have in common with female shoebinders? How and why did their experiences differ?

| How did new practices of party politics shape Andrew Jackson's election and agenda? | What was Andrew Jackson's impact on the presidency? | What were the most significant social and cultural changes in the 1830s? | What political and economic events dominated Martin Van Buren's presidency? | Conclusion: The Age of Jackson or the era of reform? |

301

Mill Girls Stand Up to Factory Owners, 1834

Lowell's first large "turn out" by mill girls came in February 1834, when factory owners announced a 15 percent wage cut. Newspapers played up the spectacle of allegedly docile young women taking to the streets in protest. After four days, the strike failed when the inexperienced workers realized that the owners could easily replace them. But workingwomen learned important lessons, and a later Lowell "turn out," in 1836, continued for several months.

DOCUMENT 1

The *Lowell Journal* Reports the Strike, February 18, 1834

A town newspaper favorable to the factory owners characterized the work stoppage as a delusional farce led by a small number of "wicked and malicious girls."

The Factory Girls.—It has become known, from rumor, that a considerable number of the girls employed in the mills of this town turned out on Friday last, to prevent a reduction in wages. . . . It was proposed, some time since, to make a very small reduction in the wages of all of the hands on the first of March, and notices to that effect were posted in the mills. . . .

Upon this, several wicked and malicious girls . . . undertook to get up a turn out, with a view to threaten the agents with an entire stoppage of the works, in order to exact the higher rates of wages. . . . On Friday and Saturday from 800 to 1000 girls revolted under the most laughable delusions, that mischief could invent. The first day, processions were formed of about 700 girls, who listened to sundry stimulative exhortations, . . . and marched through the streets, ankle-deep in mud. . . . Saturday became a day of repentance to many; and they would gladly have returned to their business, but for a pledge, cunningly devised, that each who did so, should forfeit five dollars to the rebels. The Sabbath afforded opportunity for a little more cool reflection, and on Monday morning, a large concourse attended by a parcel of idle men and boys, heard another speech. . . . The result of the whole matter is, that a few of the ring-leaders are refused entrance into the mills, and most of the disaffected, having learned the truth, and becoming sensible of the wicked misrepresentations of which they had nearly been the victims, are returning to their work, ready to take a diminished price, and continue to labor at wages which will give them from one and a half, to two and a half dollars per week, more than their board.—This, to be sure, is not so much as they have had in past times, nor so much as we hope they will soon have again, but it is more than they can get in any other occupation in New England.

Source: The *Lowell Journal*, February 18, 1834, as reprinted in the *New-York Spectator*, March 6, 1834. Gale Database, "Nineteenth-Century U.S. Newspapers."

DOCUMENT 2

Anonymous Mill Girls, "Union Is Power"

A position paper, quickly drafted, framed the strikers' goals in terms of "rights" and appealed to the patriotic spirit of the American Revolution to justify their actions.

Our present object is to have union and exertion, and we remain in possession of our own unquestionable rights. We circulate this paper, wishing to obtain the names of all who imbibe the spirit of our patriotic ancestors, who preferred privation to bondage, and parted with all that renders life desirable—and even life itself—to procure independence

Bankers and Lawyers

Entrepreneurs like the Lowell factory owners relied on innovations in the banking system to finance their ventures. In just two years, between 1814 and 1816, the number of state-chartered banks in the United States more than doubled: from fewer than 90 to 208. By 1830, there were 330, and by 1840, hundreds more. Banks stimulated the economy by making loans to merchants and manufacturers and by enlarging the money supply. Borrowers received loans in the form of banknotes—certificates unique

What economic developments reshaped the U.S. economy after 1815?

for their children. The oppressing hand of avarice would enslave us; and to gain their object, they very gravely tell us of the pressure of the times; this we are already sensible of, and deplore it. If any are in want of assistance, the Ladies will be compassionate, and assist them; but we prefer to have the disposing of our charities in our own hands; and as we are free, we would remain in possession of what kind Providence has bestowed upon us, and remain daughters of freemen still.

All who patronize this effort, we wish to have discontinue their labors until terms of reconciliation are made.

Resolved, That we will not go back into the mills to work unless our wages are continued to us as they have been.

Resolved, That none of us will go back unless they receive us all as one.

Source: Printed in *The Man*, February 22, 1834. Published in New York City by G. H. Evans. American Periodicals Series Online.

DOCUMENT 3

A Strike Leader Speaks Out, Mid-March 1834

A month later, one of the leaders explained that reduced wages as well as anger at the insolence of wealthy factory owners had caused the strike. Her remarks were published in The Man, *a New York paper friendly to workingmen's issues.*

The Lowell Girls have been censured in no measured terms by the Federal press of the east, for the "turn out." . . . One of the girls has turned round on her accusers, and while she does not outstep the modesty of her sex, her spirit would do credit to any parentage in these or other days. Hear the yankee girl:

"We do not estimate our *Liberty* by dollars and cents; consequently it was not the reduction of *wages* alone which

caused the excitement, but that *haughty, overbearing disposition—* that *purse proud insolence*, which was becoming more and more apparent—that spirit of tyranny so manifest at present among the *avaricious* and wealthy manufacturers of this and the old country.

"I have only to add, that if the proprietors and agents are not satisfied with alluring us from our homes—from the peaceful abodes of our childhood, under the false promises of a great reward, and then casting us upon the world, . . . merely because we would not be slaves— . . . let them bring down upon us the whole influence of the *rich* and *noble*, the *proud* and the *mighty*, all piled upon the *United States Bank—steep* us in poverty to the very dregs, but we beseech them not to asperse our characters, or *stigmatize* us as *disorderly* persons. Grant us this favor, and give us the privilege of breathing the air of freedom in its *purity*, and we will be content."

Source: *The Man*, March 20, 1834. Published in New York City by G. H. Evans. American Periodicals Series Online.

Questions for Analysis

ANALYZE THE EVIDENCE: How does the *Lowell Journal* explain the motivations of female workers in the street protests? In what ways do the strikers use the history of the American Revolution to justify their cause?

RECOGNIZE VIEWPOINTS: Do these young women feel subordinate and deferential to the factory owners? Do the factory owners seem to take their views seriously?

CONSIDER THE CONTEXT: How does the strike leader's explanation for the causes of the strike manifest Jacksonian political rhetoric?

to each bank—that were used as money. Neither federal nor state governments issued paper money, so banknotes issued by hundreds of individual banks became the country's currency. Constant uncertainty about the true worth of a banknote created substantial risk for the economy, since it was hard to know how stable any particular bank might be. The sheer variety of notes in circulation also created ideal conditions for counterfeiters.

Bankers exercised great power over the economy by deciding who would get loans at what interest rate. The most powerful bankers sat on the board of directors

| How did new practices of party politics shape Andrew Jackson's election and agenda? | What was Andrew Jackson's impact on the presidency? | What were the most significant social and cultural changes in the 1830s? | What political and economic events dominated Martin Van Buren's presidency? | Conclusion: The Age of Jackson or the era of reform? |

303

second Bank of the
United States

National bank chartered in 1816.
Intended to help regulate the
economy, the bank became a
major issue in Andrew Jackson's
1832 reelection campaign.

CONSIDER CAUSE
AND EFFECT

What legal and political
factors shaped the
emerging capitalist
economy in the first half of
the nineteenth century, and
what effect did they have?

for the second Bank of the United States, headquartered in Philadelphia with eighteen branches across the country. The twenty-year charter of the first Bank of the United States had expired in 1811. After surprisingly little debate, the second Bank of the United States opened for business in 1816 under another twenty-year charter. The rechartering of this second bank would become a major issue in the 1832 presidential campaign.

Lawyers and politicians significantly shaped the early U.S. economy by refashioning commercial law to increase private investment. In 1811, states began to rewrite their laws of incorporation. The number of corporations exploded, from about twenty in 1800 to eighteen hundred by 1817. Incorporation protected individual investors from liability for corporate debts. State lawmakers also wrote laws of eminent domain, empowering states to buy land for roads and canals, even from unwilling sellers. These new laws created the foundation for a market economy that facilitated risk taking, encouraged innovation, and promoted economic development.

Not everyone applauded these developments. Andrew Jackson, a skillful lawyer turned politician, spoke for a large segment of the population when he warned about the potential abuses of power "which the moneyed interest derives from a paper currency which they are able to control [and] from the multitude of corporations with exclusive privileges." Jacksonians believed that abolishing government-granted privileges was the surest path to individual liberty and economic opportunity.

Booms and Busts

As the economy made more room for risk taking, periodic financial collapses resulted. The exhilarating boom years from 1815 to 1818 led to the first sharp, large-scale economic downturn in U.S. history. Americans called it a "panic." Some blamed the panic of 1819 on the second Bank of the United States for inflating an economic bubble and then suddenly contracting the money supply. A financial crisis in Europe in the spring of 1819 accelerated the downturn.

Overseas, prices for American cotton, tobacco, and wheat plummeted by more than 50 percent. As confidence collapsed, so did banks' willingness to extend credit. When they began to call in their outstanding loans, debtors in the commodities trade found themselves unable to pay. Business and personal bankruptcies skyrocketed, creating more debtors unable to pay their loans, leading to more bank failures. It was a vicious cycle. Because of this intricate web of credit and debt relationships, the panic affected almost everyone connected to the new commercial economy. Thousands of Americans lost their savings and property. An estimated half a million people lost their jobs.

Recovery took several years. Unemployment declined, but bitterness lingered, waiting to be stirred up by politicians in the decades to come. The dangers of a system dependent on credit had become clear. In one folksy formulation that circulated around 1820, a farmer compared credit to "a man pissing in his breeches on a cold day to keep his arse warm—very comfortable at first but I dare say . . . you know how it feels afterwards."

By the mid-1820s, the economy was growing once again, driven by productivity increases, consumer demand, and international trade. Despite the panic of 1819, credit continued to fuel the system, and the network of credit and debt relations grew denser still. Confidence in continued growth supported the elaborate system, but a single business failure could produce panic, and many victims. Long after the panic of 1819 had ended, an undercurrent of anxiety about rapid economic change still troubled many Americans.

QUICK REVIEW

What role did state governments and private businesses play in the economic developments after 1815?

What economic
developments reshaped
the U.S. economy after
1815?

How did new practices of party politics shape Andrew Jackson's election and agenda?

Just as the years after 1815 saw the emergence of a new market economy, the years of Andrew Jackson's presidency (1829–1837) saw the emergence of a new style of party politics. Like the new economy, the birth of this second party system was slow and uneven. Not until 1836 would political parties have distinct names and consistent programs transcending the individuals running for office. Over those years, more men could and did vote, expanding the scope of American democracy.

Popular Politics and Partisan Identity

The election of 1828, which pitted Andrew Jackson against John Quincy Adams, was the first presidential contest in which the popular vote determined the outcome. In twenty-two out of twenty-four states, voters—not state legislatures—designated the number of electors committed to a particular candidate. The Adams-Jackson rematch generated intense political interest. More than a million voters participated—three times the number in 1824, nearly half the free male population. But it was only the beginning of the era's intense partisanship. Throughout the 1830s, as property qualifications tumbled, voter turnout continued to rise, reaching 70 percent in some localities.

The 1828 election also inaugurated a new style of campaigning. For the first time, state-level candidates routinely gave speeches at rallies, picnics, and banquets. Adams and Jackson held to an older tradition, declining such appearances as undignified. But Henry Clay of Kentucky, campaigning for Adams, earned the nickname "the Barbecue Orator." Campaign rhetoric became more informal. The Jackson camp established Hickory Clubs, trading on Jackson's popular nickname, "Old Hickory," from a common Tennessee tree associated with resilience and toughness.

Growing numbers of partisan newspapers shaped issues and publicized political personalities as never before. Improved printing technology and rising literacy rates drove the expansion of newspapers as well as other kinds of popular printed materials (**Table 11.1**). Party leaders subsidized newspapers or provided other favors for editors, even in remote towns and villages. Political news traveled swiftly in the mail, reprinted in allied newspapers. Presidential campaigns were now coordinated in a national arena.

Whigs
Political party that evolved out of the National Republicans after 1834. With a northeastern power base, the Whigs supported federal action to promote commercial development and generally looked favorably on the reform movements associated with the Second Great Awakening.

TABLE 11.1 The Growth of Newspapers, 1820–1840

	1820	1830	1835	1840
U.S. population (in millions)	9.6	12.8	15.0	17.1
Number of newspapers published	500	800	1,200	1,400
Daily newspapers	42	65	—	138

Democrats
Political party that evolved out of the Democratic Republicans after 1834. Strongest in the South and West, the Democrats embraced Andrew Jackson's vision of limited government, expanded political participation for white men, and the promotion of an ethic of individualism.

At first, politicians identified themselves as Jackson or Adams men, honoring the fiction of Republican Party unity. By 1832, however, the terminology had evolved to National Republicans, who favored federal action to promote commercial development, and Democratic Republicans, who promised fidelity to the majority. Between 1834 and 1836, National Republicans came to be called Whigs, while Jackson's party became the Democrats.

| How did new practices of party politics shape Andrew Jackson's election and agenda? | What was Andrew Jackson's impact on the presidency? | What were the most significant social and cultural changes in the 1830s? | What political and economic events dominated Martin Van Buren's presidency? | Conclusion: The Age of Jackson or the era of reform? |

305

The Election of 1828 and the Character Issue

Perhaps because it was the first popularly decided presidential election, the campaign of 1828 was also the first to center on claims about morality, honor, and discipline. It was also the first dominated by scandal and questions of personal character. In the run-up to the election, Jackson and Adams came to represent two dramatically different styles of manhood.

John Quincy Adams's opponents vilified him as an elitist, a bookish academic, even a monarchist. They attacked his "corrupt bargain" of 1824—the alleged deal between Adams and Henry Clay that led to Adams's election in the House of Representatives (see chapter 10).

Adams's supporters countered by playing on Jackson's fatherless childhood to portray him as the illegitimate son of a prostitute. Playing on the cloudy circumstances around his marriage to Rachel Donelson Robards in 1791, Jackson's enemies peddled the claim that he was a seducer and an adulterer, and had married a woman not legally divorced from her first husband.

Pro-Adams newspapers played up Jackson's impulsive and violent temper, as seen in his many duels, brawls, and canings. Jackson's supporters used the same stories to paint Old Hickory as a tough frontier hero who knew how to command obedience. Pro-Adams editors portrayed their candidate as pious, learned, and virtuous. Jackson's supporters responded that their candidate's rough frontier education gave him a "natural sense," as a Boston editor wrote, that "can never be acquired by reading books—it can only be acquired, in perfection, by reading men."

Jackson won a sweeping victory, with 56 percent of the popular vote and 178 electoral votes to Adams's 83 (**Map 11.2**). Jackson took most of the South and West and carried Pennsylvania and New York as well; Adams carried the remainder of the East. Jackson's vice president was John C. Calhoun, who had just served as vice president under Adams, but had broken with Adams's policies.

After 1828, national politicians no longer deplored the existence of political parties. In this new, increasingly democratic society, parties came to be seen as an inevitable feature of the nation's political life. Indeed, many Americans began to believe that political parties might even carry some advantages. They mobilized and delivered voters, organized coalitions of interest groups, and created a framework in which political and ideological differences could be settled mostly peacefully.

But modern political parties had not quite taken on their fully developed form. In 1832 and 1836, they still turned on the sharply defined characters of Adams and Jackson. On the one hand were the Whigs, a moralistic party more comfortable with hierarchy and top-down forms of political action. On the other hand were the Democrats, a contentious, energetic party that embraced liberty-loving individualism and promoted a radically egalitarian society for white men.

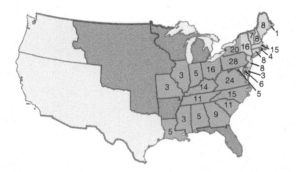

Candidate	Electoral Vote	Popular Vote	Percent of Popular Vote
Andrew Jackson (Democratic Republican)	178	647,286	56
John Q. Adams (National Republican)	83	508,064	44

MAP 11.2 ▲ The Election of 1828

COMPARE AND CONTRAST

How did the Democratic and Whig parties differ from each other?

Jackson's Democratic Agenda

Before the inauguration in March 1829, Rachel Jackson died. Certain that the ugly campaign had hastened his wife's death, the president went into deep mourning. His health deteriorated due to constant pain from a bullet still lodged in his chest from an 1806 duel, and due to mercury poisoning from the medicines he took. At sixty-two, Jackson carried only 140 pounds on his six-foot-one frame. His adversaries doubted that he would live to a second term.

His supporters, however, went wild at his March 1829 inauguration. Thousands cheered his ten-minute inaugural address, the shortest in history. An open reception at the White House turned riotous as well-wishers jammed the premises, used windows

What economic developments reshaped the U.S. economy after 1815?

as doors, stood on furniture for a better view of the new president, and broke thousands of dollars' worth of china and glasses.

For Jackson's opponents, the chaos symbolized the disorder of this new democratic order coming into being. But Jackson was not discouraged. During his presidency, he offered unprecedented hospitality to the public. Committed to his image as president of the "common man," Jackson continued to hold audiences with unannounced visitors throughout his two terms.

Since George Washington's administration, presidents had tried to reduce party conflict by including men of different political views in their cabinets. Jackson broke with this tradition by appointing only party loyalists to his cabinet, a practice most presidents have followed ever since. For secretary of state, he tapped New Yorker Martin Van Buren, one of the shrewdest politicians of the day. Throughout the federal government, from postal clerks to ambassadors, Jackson replaced civil servants with party loyalists. Jackson's opponents called these appointments a "spoils system," after a Democratic politician coined the slogan "to the victor belong the spoils."

Jackson soon began implementing his agenda, built on a Jeffersonian view of limited federal government. Believing that intervention in the economy inevitably favored some groups at the expense of others, Jackson opposed federal support for transportation, and grants of monopolies and charters. Like Jefferson, he championed the rapid settlement of the country's interior, where widespread landholding would foster a democratic culture among settlers. Removing Indians from their lands was therefore among his highest priorities. Compared to other presidents, Jackson more freely used his veto power over Congress. In 1830, he vetoed a highway project in Maysville, Kentucky, Henry Clay's home state. The Maysville Road veto symbolized Jackson's belief that public money should be spent on projects of a "general, not local" character. In all, Jackson vetoed twelve bills; all previous presidents combined had exercised that power a total of nine times.

QUICK REVIEW

In what ways was Andrew Jackson's defeat of John Quincy Adams a pivotal moment in U.S. political history?

What was Andrew Jackson's impact on the presidency?

In his two terms as president, Andrew Jackson set about implementing his vision for the country: a nation of opportunity for all white men. That vision, however, was built on the violent expulsion of Indians from their lands. To accomplish his objectives, Jackson forcibly relocated tens of thousands of Indian people still living

| How did new practices of party politics shape Andrew Jackson's election and agenda? | **What was Andrew Jackson's impact on the presidency?** | What were the most significant social and cultural changes in the 1830s? | What political and economic events dominated Martin Van Buren's presidency? | Conclusion: The Age of Jackson or the era of reform? |

1828
– So-called Tariff of Abominations passes.

1830
– Indian Removal Act passes.

1832
– Hundreds of Sauk and Fox Indians massacred.
– *Worcester v. Georgia* decided.
– Jackson vetoes charter renewal of Bank of the United States.

1833
– South Carolina nullifies federal tariffs.

1838
– Cherokee Trail of Tears migration kills thousands.

UNDERSTAND POINTS OF VIEW

How did Andrew Jackson justify his policy of seizing Indian land as being in their best interest?

Indian Removal Act of 1830 Act that directed the forced relocation of eastern tribes to territory west of the Mississippi. Jackson insisted that his goal was to save the Indians. Indians resisted the controversial act, but in the end most were forced to comply.

east of the Mississippi River. A fervent nationalist, he dramatically confronted the state of South Carolina when it tried to nullify the tariff of 1828. Disapproving of government-granted privilege, Jackson fought against the second Bank of the United States. In all these actions and more, he greatly enhanced the power of the presidency.

Indian Policy and the Trail of Tears

Probably nothing defined Jackson's presidency more than his efforts to solve what he saw as the "Indian problem." Indeed, it was one of the central threads of his career. Jackson had first gained fame in his battles with the Creek and Seminole nations in the 1810s. For all their forced land cessions, however, thousands of Indians still lived in the South, where they held millions of acres. In addition, many other Native Americans remained in the old Northwest, New England, and New York. Jackson's presidency would change all that.

In his first message to Congress in 1829, Jackson announced his ambition to remove Indians to territory west of the Mississippi. It was, he declared, the only way to save them. White civilization had destroyed Indian "resources," he claimed, dooming them to waste away. "That this fate surely awaits them if they remain within the limits of the states does not admit of a doubt. Humanity and national honor demand that every effort should be made to avert so great a calamity." Thus could Jackson—who had fought Indians in the Southwest from the beginning of his career and now determined to seize their remaining land—position himself not as their tormentor but as their savior.

Prior administrations had adopted different Indian policies. Starting in 1819, Congress funded missionary associations eager to "civilize" native peoples by converting them to Christianity and pushing them to adopt Euro-American agricultural practices. From the perspective of U.S. authorities, persuading Native Americans to farm and raise domestic animals rather than hunt meant they would need far less land. It also meant that Indians would abandon their traditional way of life. The federal government had also coerced many tribes into signing harsh treaties.

In contrast to previous administrations, however, which viewed Indian peoples as foreign nations, Jackson saw them as subjects of the United States (neither foreigners nor citizens). At his urging, Congress passed the Indian Removal Act of 1830. It authorized the removal of Native Americans from approximately one hundred million acres of their homeland, reallocating it for eventual white settlement (**Map 11.3**).

The Indian Removal Act generated widespread controversy. Newspapers, public lecturers, and local clubs debated the expulsion law. Many people, especially in the North, passionately denounced the policy. "One would think that the guilt of African slavery was enough for the nation to bear, without the additional crime of injustice to the aborigines," one writer declared in 1829. Thousands of northern white women signed antiremoval petitions, arguing that sovereign peoples on the road to Christianity were entitled to their land.

Many northern tribes, diminished by years of war, had already begun to migrate west. Not all of them went quietly, however. Black Hawk, a leader of the Sauk and Fox Indians who had fought with Tecumseh in the War of 1812 (see chapter 10), resisted the movement. In 1832, volunteer militias attacked and chased his followers from western Illinois into Wisconsin. After several skirmishes and a deadly battle (later called the Black Hawk War), Black Hawk was captured. U.S. soldiers and local militiamen massacred some four hundred of his people.

The large southern tribes—the Creek, Chickasaw, Choctaw, Seminole, and Cherokee— also resisted U.S. policy. Cherokees in Georgia had worked to assimilate to American culture.

"'One would think that the guilt of African slavery was enough for the nation to bear, without the additional crime of injustice to the aborigines.'"

What economic developments reshaped the U.S. economy after 1815?

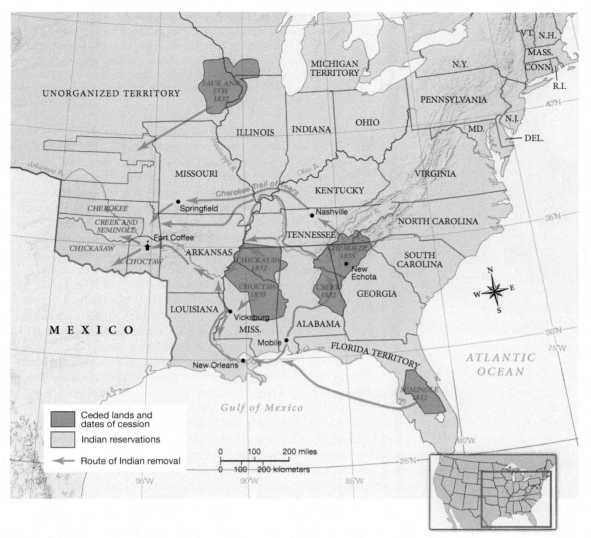

MAP 11.3 ▲ Indian Removal and the Trail of Tears

The federal government under President Andrew Jackson pursued a violent policy of Indian removal in the 1830s, forcibly moving native peoples west to land known as Indian Territory (present-day Oklahoma). In 1838, as many as one-quarter of the Cherokee refugees died on the route known as the Trail of Tears.

They had adopted written laws—including, in 1827, a constitution modeled on the U.S. Constitution. Wealthy Cherokee men had intermarried with Americans, adopting their styles of housing, dress, and cotton agriculture, including the ownership of slaves. They developed a written alphabet and published a newspaper and Christian prayer books in their language. These elements of their society made their cause attractive to northerners who petitioned the government on their behalf.

When Georgia announced its plans to seize all Cherokee property in 1831, the tribal leadership took its case to the U.S. Supreme Court. In *Worcester v. Georgia* (1832), the Court upheld the territorial sovereignty of the Cherokee people, recognizing their existence as "a distinct community, occupying its own territory, in which the laws of Georgia can have no force." An angry President Jackson ignored the decision

COMPARE AND CONTRAST

How did Jackson's views of Native Americans' legal status differ from those articulated by the Supreme Court? Why did Jackson's views ultimately prevail?

| How did new practices of party politics shape Andrew Jackson's election and agenda? | **What was Andrew Jackson's impact on the presidency?** | What were the most significant social and cultural changes in the 1830s? | What political and economic events dominated Martin Van Buren's presidency? | Conclusion: The Age of Jackson or the era of reform? |

John Ross, Principal Cherokee Chief, 1843 John Ross was elected Principal Chief of the Cherokees from 1828 to 1866. His mission schooling, bilingual skills, and brilliant legal mind helped advance Cherokee interests. Despite a decade of lobbying trips to Washington, Ross could not stop the Cherokee expulsion. His wife, Quatie, died on the Trail of Tears. Library of Congress, LC-DIG-pga-07513.

and demanded that the Cherokee move west. "If they now refuse to accept the liberal terms offered, they can only be liable for whatever evils and difficulties may arise. I feel conscious of having done my duty to my red children."

The Cherokee tribe remained on their lands for two more years without major violence. Then in 1835, a small, unauthorized faction signed a treaty selling all the tribal lands to the state, which rapidly resold them to whites. Chief John Ross, backed by several thousand Cherokees, unsuccessfully petitioned the U.S. Congress to ignore the bogus treaty. Most Cherokees refused to move. In May 1838, the deadline set for voluntary removal, federal troops arrived. Driven out at gunpoint by U.S. soldiers, the Cherokees embarked on a 1,200-mile journey west that became known as the Trail of Tears. Nearly one-quarter of the Cherokees died during the forced migration. Survivors joined the fifteen thousand Creek, twelve thousand Choctaw, five thousand Chickasaw, and several thousand Seminole Indians also forcibly relocated to Indian Territory (which became the state of Oklahoma in 1907).

Trail of Tears
Forced westward journey of Cherokees from their lands in Georgia to present-day Oklahoma in 1838. Despite a Supreme Court decision in their favor, federal troops forced the Cherokees on a grueling 1,200-mile march. Nearly one-quarter died en route.

In his farewell address to the nation in 1837, Jackson insisted on the humanitarian benefits of Indian removal: "This unhappy race . . . are now placed in a situation where we may well hope that they will share in the blessings of civilization and be saved from the degradation and destruction to which they were rapidly hastening while they remained in the states." Perhaps Jackson genuinely believed their removal was necessary for American democracy to flourish.

The Tariff of Abominations and Nullification

During the Jacksonian era, economic policy was a central topic of political debate. The most heated controversies erupted over tariffs, or taxes on imports. In the 1830s, a fight over tariffs turned into a constitutional crisis pitting federal against state power.

In order to shelter American manufacturers from foreign competition, Congress had passed steep federal tariffs on imports such as textiles and iron goods in 1816 and again in 1824. Many southern congressmen opposed the tariffs. Their states, reliant on exports of agricultural crops like cotton, gained nothing from the support for manufacturing, which was heavily concentrated in the North. By reducing foreign trade, however, tariffs hurt southern economies. In 1828, Congress passed a revised tariff that came to be known as the Tariff of Abominations. A bundle of conflicting duties, some as high as 50 percent, the legislation contained provisions that pleased and angered every economic and sectional interest.

nullification
Theory asserting that states could nullify acts of Congress that exceeded its constitutional powers. South Carolina advanced the theory of nullification in 1828 in response to an unfavorable federal tariff. A show of force by Andrew Jackson, combined with tariff revisions, ended the crisis.

South Carolina particularly suffered from the 1828 tariff. Worldwide prices for cotton had declined in the late 1820s, squeezing the southern economy, and the tariffs made a bad situation worse. In response, a group of South Carolina politicians headed by John C. Calhoun advanced a doctrine called nullification. They argued that states had the right to nullify federal law when Congress overstepped

What economic developments reshaped the U.S. economy after 1815?

its constitutional powers. As precedents, they pointed to the Virginia and Kentucky Resolutions of 1798, intended to invalidate the Alien and Sedition Acts (see chapter 9). They argued that Congress had acted unconstitutionally in using tariff policy to benefit specific industries. Tariffs, they claimed, could be used only to raise revenue.

On assuming the presidency in 1829, Jackson ignored the South Carolina statement of nullification. He excluded Calhoun, his vice president, from influence or power. Tariff revisions in 1832 brought little relief to the South. Sensing futility, Calhoun resigned the vice presidency and became a U.S. senator. In November 1832, South Carolina leaders took the radical step of declaring federal tariffs null and void in their state as of February 1, 1833. The constitutional crisis had begun.

In response, Jackson sent armed ships to Charleston harbor and threatened to invade the state. He pushed the Force Bill through Congress, which defined South Carolina's stance as treason and authorized military action to collect federal tariffs. Meanwhile, Congress passed a revised tariff that was more acceptable to the South, reducing tariffs to their 1816 level. On March 1, 1833, Congress passed both the new tariff and the Force Bill at once. South Carolina withdrew its nullification of the old tariff—and then nullified the Force Bill. It was a symbolic gesture since federal force was no longer required.

The constitutional question about the scope of federal power relative to states' rights was far from settled, however. To the contrary, it had only grown. Could a state refuse to follow federal law it determined to be unconstitutional? The question applied not just to tariffs, but also to the question of slavery. As antislavery voices in the North grew louder, many white southerners began to wonder if a northern-dominated federal government might try to end slavery in the South. Could federal law be nullified in that case?

The Bank War and Economic Boom

President Jackson's third major political battle concerned the second Bank of the United States. Since its recharter in 1816, the bank had played an important role in the growing U.S. economy. Expanded to twenty-nine branches, it handled the federal government's deposits, extended credit and loans, and issued banknotes. Since the United States still lacked a federal currency, notes from the bank had become the country's most stable currency by 1830. Jackson, however, opposed the bank because it concentrated great economic power in the hands of a few private individuals.

National Republican (Whig) senators Daniel Webster and Henry Clay decided to force the issue. They convinced the bank to apply for charter renewal in 1832, even though the existing charter ran until 1836. It seemed like a smart political strategy. Convinced of the bank's popularity, they believed Jackson would not dare veto the bank and face an angry public on the eve of an election. But if he did veto the bill, they reasoned that the bank would survive on an override vote by a new Congress swept into power on the anti-Jackson tide. "Should Jackson veto it," Clay declared, "I will veto him!"

At first, the plan seemed to work. The bank applied for rechartering, and Congress voted to renew. Jackson, angry at being manipulated, issued his veto. But Clay and Webster had radically misjudged the bank's popularity. Jackson wrote a brilliant veto message, appealing directly to public opinion, and positioning himself as the champion of the democratic masses against the moneyed power. "When the laws undertake. . . to grant titles, gratuities, and exclusive privileges, to make the rich richer and the most potent more powerful," Jackson wrote, "the humble members of society—the farmers, mechanics, and laborers—who have neither the time nor the

| How did new practices of party politics shape Andrew Jackson's election and agenda? | **What was Andrew Jackson's impact on the presidency?** | What were the most significant social and cultural changes in the 1830s? | What political and economic events dominated Martin Van Buren's presidency? | Conclusion: The Age of Jackson or the era of reform? |

311

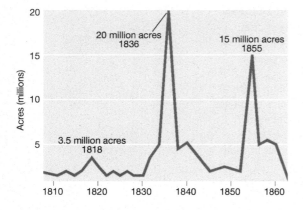

FIGURE 11.1 ◄ Western Land Sales, 1810–1860

Land sales peaked in the 1810s, 1830s, and 1850s, as Americans launched into frenzied speculation in lands seized from Native Americans. The surges in 1818 and 1836 demonstrate the volatile, speculative economy that suddenly collapsed in the panics of 1819 and 1837.

means of securing like favors to themselves, have a right to complain of the injustice of their Government."

Clay and his supporters found Jackson's economic ideas and his rhetoric of class antagonism so absurd that they distributed thousands of copies of the bank veto as campaign material for their own party. A confident Henry Clay headed his party's ticket for the presidency. But their political strategy backfired spectacularly. The language of deep social antagonism resonated with many Americans. Forced to choose "between the Aristocracy and the People," read one set of state resolutions, Jackson "stands by the people." He won the election easily, gaining 55 percent of the popular vote and 219 electoral votes to Clay's 49. Jackson's party still controlled Congress, so no override was possible.

Jackson had won his epic battle against the bank. As one newspaper put it, Jackson had saved "the people from becoming enslaved by the corruptions of a moneyed aristocracy."

But the war was not yet over. Wanting to destroy the bank immediately, Jackson ordered the sizable federal deposits removed from the bank's vaults and placed into Democratic-allied state banks. In retaliation, the Bank of the United States raised interest rates and called in loans. This action caused a brief economic crisis in 1833, but it supported Jackson's claim that the bank was too powerful for the country's good.

Unleashed and unregulated, the economy moved into high gear. By coincidence, an excess of silver from Mexican mines had recently made its way into American banks, giving bankers license to print more banknotes. From 1834 to 1837, inflation soared; prices of basic goods rose more than 50 percent. States chartered hundreds of new private banks, each issuing its own banknotes. Entrepreneurs borrowed and invested money. The webs of credit and debt relationships that characterized the American economy grew denser yet. Western land sales boomed. In 1834, about 4.5 million acres of the public domain had been sold, the highest annual volume since 1818. By 1836, the total reached an astonishing 20 million acres (**Figure 11.1**).

In one respect, the economy attained an admirable goal: The national debt was paid off. For the only time in its history, the U.S. government had a monetary surplus between 1835 and 1837. Much of that surplus, however, consisted of questionable bank currencies—"bloated, diseased" currencies, in Jackson's vivid terminology. As would so often be the case in American history, as long as the boom continued, few people paused to worry about what would happen when the bust eventually came.

PLACE EVENTS IN CONTEXT

What elements of American political culture did Jackson use to turn the bank veto to his advantage?

QUICK REVIEW

How did Jackson alter the power and role of the federal government and the presidency in American life?

What economic developments reshaped the U.S. economy after 1815?

What were the most significant social and cultural changes in the 1830s?

The country's booming economy and rapidly democratizing politics transformed its social and cultural life. For many families in the 1830s, especially in the commercialized Northeast, standards of living rose, consumption patterns changed, and the nature and location of work shifted in subtle but significant ways. These developments resulted in new cultural ideas about men, women, and children's education. Extraordinary new religious and reform movements burgeoned from this fertile mix. The revival of evangelical religion known as the Second Great Awakening revolutionized religious life in the country and inspired far-reaching social movements championing temperance, moral reform, and abolition.

Separate Spheres

In agricultural and artisanal settings, work and home life were largely inseparable. Families worked together in a mostly cashless economy. The economic changes after 1815 increasingly brought cash to the household, especially in the manufacturing and urban Northeast. Farmers and tradesmen sold products in a market, and bankers, bookkeepers, shoemakers, and canal diggers earned regular salaries or wages. Many men now worked at an office or a store, while women in the growing middle classes stayed at home. By the 1830s, the increased separation between work and home provoked profound changes in ideas about gender.

The concept of separate spheres rested on the idea that husbands found their status and authority in the new world of work, leaving wives to tend to home and family. Sermons, advice books, periodicals, and novels reinforced this idea that men and women inhabited separate public and domestic realms. The home became defined as a feminine private space, sharply distinct from the masculine sphere of work. "To woman it belongs . . . to elevate the intellectual character of her household [and] to kindle the fires of mental activity in childhood," wrote Mrs. A. J. Graves in a popular book titled *Advice to American Women.*

Women's experiences were more complicated than such cultural prescriptions indicated. Although the vast majority of married white women did not hold paying jobs, their homes required time-consuming labor. But the advice books treated housework as a loving familial duty, making it invisible in an economy that valued work by the cash it generated. What was more, many wives contributed to family income by taking in boarders or sewing for pay. Wives in the poorest classes, including most free black wives, did not have the luxury of husbands earning adequate wages; for them, work as a servant or a laundress was a necessary part of family income.

The idea of separate spheres did not gain such cultural power because it was so true, however, but rather because it was so useful to the society's economic, political, and cultural life. In the emerging capitalist economy of the nineteenth century, "the absorbing passion for gain, and the pressing demands of business," as Graves wrote, took up men's "whole attention." But was not a passion for gain traditionally known as avarice? And were not values of competition and acquisitiveness traditionally deemed to be sinful? Here is where the concept of separate spheres came to the rescue. Because women were believed to have special endowments of private virtues—piety, benevolence, sentiment, morality—they could make the home into a refuge from the cruel and competitive world of market relations. The home, now understood as

CHRONOLOGY

1817
– American Colonization Society founded.

1826
– American Temperance Society founded.

1829
– David Walker publishes *An Appeal . . . to the Coloured Citizens of the World*.

1830–1831
– Charles Grandison Finney preaches in Rochester, New York.

1831
– William Lloyd Garrison starts *Liberator*.

1832
– New England Anti-Slavery Society founded.

1833
– New York and Philadelphia antislavery societies founded.
– New York Female Moral Reform Society founded.

1836
– American Temperance Union founded.

separate spheres
Ideology that posited a sharp separation between the masculine, public sphere of the workplace and the feminine, domestic sphere of the home. Both consequence and facilitator of the rapid economic changes of the early nineteenth century, it transformed gender and family relations.

| How did new practices of party politics shape Andrew Jackson's election and agenda? | What was Andrew Jackson's impact on the presidency? | **What were the most significant social and cultural changes in the 1830s?** | What political and economic events dominated Martin Van Buren's presidency? | Conclusion: The Age of Jackson or the era of reform? |

▲ **The Otis Family at Home, 1836** Between 1832 and 1838, artist Joseph H. Davis traveled through Maine and New Hampshire painting family portraits. In this portrait, Daniel Otis sits on one side of the table reading the Great Falls *Journal*, published in a mill town in southeastern New Hampshire, while his wife Betsy and daughter Polly sit opposite. Metropolitan Museum of Art, Gift of Edgar William and Bernice Chrysler Garbisch, 1972.

READING THE IMAGE: How are gender distinctions established in this image? How do these associations relate to the ideology of separate spheres?
CONNECTIONS: How did the heightened attention to gender differences connect to the changing economy and politics of Jacksonian America?

the exclusive domain of women, became the source of intimacy, love, and safety—of domesticity.

This formulation of gender difference helped smooth the path for Americans experiencing rapid and disorienting economic changes. Both men and women of the middle classes benefited. Men were set free to pursue wealth, while women gained moral authority within the home. Although they had broad cultural power, these new gender ideals had limited relevance beyond white families of the middle and upper classes. Nor did they emerge unchallenged. Radical voices like those of the Grimké sisters, for instance, questioned whether "virtue" and "duty" had separate masculine and feminine manifestations at all.

The ideology of separate spheres could also open up a few new opportunities for women outside the home. By the 1830s, especially in the North, state-supported public school systems had become the norm. They produced pupils of both sexes able to read, write, and calculate and thus participate in the growing market economy. Literacy rates for white females climbed dramatically, rivaling the rates for white males for the first time. Building on older ideas that it was women's role to educate their children, as seen in the concept of republican motherhood (see chapter 9), school districts often hired female teachers. "Heaven has plainly appointed females as the natural instructors of young children," wrote the Connecticut Board of Education, "and endowed them with those qualities of mind and disposition, which preeminently fit them for

What economic developments reshaped the U.S. economy after 1815?

◀ **Women Graduates of Oberlin College, Class of 1855** Oberlin College, founded by abolitionists in the 1830s, admitted African American men and women. In the early years, black students were all male, and women students were all white. By 1855, black women had integrated the Ladies' Department. Each student wears a dark dress with a detachable lace collar. Note the uniform hairstyles, parted down the middle, with locks coiled over the ears. Oberlin College Archives.

such a task." An added advantage, from the perspective of legislatures wincing at the price of public school systems, was that women could be hired more cheaply.

The vast majority of male youths left public school at age fourteen to apprentice in trades or embark on business careers by seeking entry-level clerkships in the growing urban centers. Many young women, meanwhile, headed for mill towns or cities to work in the expanding service sector as seamstresses and domestic servants. For the first time, large numbers of young people escaped the watchful eyes of their parents, transforming the institution of the family.

The Second Great Awakening and Moral Reform

As the economy reshaped gender and family relations, a newly invigorated evangelical Protestantism gained momentum in the 1820s and 1830s. Among the most serious adherents were men and women of the new merchant classes, whose self-discipline in pursuing market ambitions meshed with the message of self-discipline in pursuit of spiritual perfection. The outburst of evangelical fervor animated enormous campaigns to eliminate alcohol abuse and eradicate sexual sin. Millions of Americans took the temperance pledge to abstain from alcohol, and thousands became involved in efforts to end prostitution.

"'At one time I saw at least five hundred swept down in a moment as if a battery of a thousand guns had been opened upon them, and then immediately followed shrieks and shouts that rent the very heavens.'"

The earliest manifestations of this fervent piety, which historians call the **Second Great Awakening**, appeared in 1801 in Kentucky, when a crowd of ten thousand people camped out on a hillside at Cane Ridge for a revival meeting that lasted several weeks. By the 1810s and 1820s, camp meetings had spread across the Atlantic seaboard states. The gatherings attracted women and men hungry for an emotional, even ecstatic spiritual experience. One eyewitness reported that "some of the people were singing, others praying, some crying for mercy. . . . At one time I saw at least five hundred swept down in a moment as if a battery of a thousand guns had been opened upon them, and then immediately followed shrieks and shouts that rent the very heavens."

Second Great Awakening Unprecedented religious revival in the 1820s and 1830s that promised access to salvation. It was a major impetus for reform movements of the era, inspiring efforts to combat drinking, sexual sin, and slavery.

| How did new practices of party politics shape Andrew Jackson's election and agenda? | What was Andrew Jackson's impact on the presidency? | **What were the most significant social and cultural changes in the 1830s?** | What political and economic events dominated Martin Van Buren's presidency? | Conclusion: The Age of Jackson or the era of reform? |

◀ **"Signing the Pledge" in the 1840s** This lithograph celebrates a hard-won moment in the life of a poor family. A temperance worker convinces the father to sign an oath to abstain from alcohol, while his wife exhibits prayerful gratitude. The temperance pledge was a major tool of anti-alcohol advocates. It drew on the power of religious oaths in a society infused with religious belief. The Granger Collection, New York.

From 1800 to 1820, church membership doubled in the United States, much of it among the evangelical denominations. Methodists, Baptists, and Presbyterians formed the core of the movement. Women served as its spiritual foot soldiers. Drawn in great numbers, wives and mothers typically recruited husbands and sons to join them.

A notable leader of the Second Great Awakening was a lawyer turned minister named Charles Grandison Finney. Finney lived in western New York, where the completion of the Erie Canal in 1825 intensely altered the social and economic landscape. Rapid industrialization and commercialization came with other side effects, however, such as prostitution, drinking, and gaming. Finney saw New York canal towns as ripe for evangelical awakening. In Rochester, he launched a revival in 1830 that lasted six months and generated thousands of converts.

Finney's message, directed primarily at the business classes, promoted a public-spirited outreach. Evangelicals supported Sunday schools to bring piety to children; they battled to honor the Sabbath by ending mail delivery, stopping public transport, and closing shops on Sundays. Many women formed missionary societies that distributed millions of Bibles and religious tracts. Through such avenues, evangelical religion further expanded women's spheres of influence. Finney adopted the tactics of Jacksonian-era politicians—publicity, argumentation, rallies, and speeches—to sell his cause. His object, he said, was to get Americans to "vote in the Lord Jesus Christ as the governor of the Universe."

Not content with individual perfection, many evangelical reformers sought to perfect society as well. The first target was alcohol consumption, which had grown among all social classes in the decades up to 1830. A lively saloon culture fostered drink and camaraderie among laborers, while after-dinner whiskey or sherry was common in elite homes. Colleges before 1820 routinely served students a pint of ale with meals, and the military included rum in the daily ration.

Organized opposition to drinking first emerged in the 1810s among health and religious reformers. In 1826, Lyman Beecher, a Connecticut minister of an "awakened" church, founded the **American Temperance Society**. It maintained that drinking led to poverty, idleness, crime, and family violence. Temperance lecturers spread the word, and middle-class drinking began a steep decline. One powerful tool of persuasion was the temperance pledge, which many business owners began to require of employees.

In 1836, leaders of the temperance movement regrouped into a new society, the American Temperance Union, which demanded total abstinence from its adherents. The campaign against alcohol moved beyond individual moral persuasion into the realm of politics. Reformers began trying to deny taverns liquor licenses. By 1845, temperance advocates had succeeded in dramatically reducing alcohol consumption. In just fifteen years, per capita consumption had fallen by 75 percent.

CONSIDER CAUSE AND EFFECT

What might the temperance and moral reform movements and the institutionalization of education have had to do with the economic changes of the early nineteenth century?

American Temperance Society

Organization founded in 1826 by Lyman Beecher that linked drinking with poverty, idleness, ill health, and violence. The temperance movement had considerable success, contributing to a sharp drop in American alcohol consumption.

What economic developments reshaped the U.S. economy after 1815?

More controversial than temperance was a social movement called "moral reform." It first aimed at public morals in general, but quickly narrowed to target sexual sin. In 1833, a group of Finneyite women started the **New York Female Moral Reform Society**. Its members insisted that uncontrolled male sexuality, manifested in seduction and prostitution, posed a serious threat to society. Within five years, more than four thousand auxiliary groups of women had sprung up, mostly in New England, New York, Pennsylvania, and Ohio. **(See "Spotlight: Who Scorned Temperance and Moral Reform?" on page 318)**

In its conviction that women had a duty to speak out, the Moral Reform Society pushed the limits of female public expression. But these women did not regard themselves as radicals. They were pursuing the logic of a gender system that defined home protection and morality as women's special sphere and a spiritual conviction that called for the eradication of sin.

New York Female Moral Reform Society
An organization of religious women inspired by the Second Great Awakening to eradicate sexual sin and male licentiousness. Formed in 1833, it spread to hundreds of auxiliaries across the country.

Organizing against Slavery

The campaign to eradicate sin was not limited to drink and prostitution. In the 1830s, the decades-old abolitionist movement entered a new chapter. This second wave built on several important foundations. First was a powerful tradition of organizing and militancy against slavery among African Americans, both free and slave. Second was the transatlantic antislavery movement that began in the eighteenth century centered in Great Britain. It succeeded in abolishing the Atlantic slave trade in 1807, and then slavery itself throughout the British empire in 1834.

The most immediate trigger for the new wave of abolition, however, was opposition to the American Colonization Society (ACS). Founded in 1817 by Maryland and Virginia planters, the ACS promoted the gradual emancipation of slaves followed by their removal, or "colonization," to Africa. Seen to advocate a moderate position between the growing defense of slavery and the mounting call for its abolition, the ACS counted the country's most eminent political figures in its ranks. Few slaves or free African Americans supported the movement, however. To the contrary, their insistent demands for slavery's immediate abolition began to gain attention among northern whites.

In 1829, a Boston printer named David Walker published a fiery pamphlet entitled *An Appeal . . . to the Coloured Citizens of the World*. Condemning racism and invoking the egalitarian language of the Declaration of Independence, Walker hinted at racial violence if slavery did not end soon. In 1830, at the inaugural National Negro Convention in Philadelphia, forty African Americans from nine states discussed the racism of American society and proposed emigration to Canada. In 1832 and 1833, a twenty-eight-year-old black woman named Maria Stewart delivered rousing public lectures on slavery and racial prejudice to black audiences in Boston. Her message gained broader circulation when a Boston newspaper published her lectures.

Founded in 1831, the *Liberator* took antislavery agitation to new heights. Its founder and editor, William Lloyd Garrison, denounced moderation in response to the existence of slavery, demanding its immediate abolition instead. "On this subject, I do not wish to think, or speak, or write, with moderation. No! No! Tell a man whose house is on fire to give a moderate alarm; tell him to moderately rescue his wife from the hands of the ravisher; tell the mother to gradually extricate her babe from the fire into which it has fallen—but urge me not to use moderation in a cause like the present."

In 1832, Garrison's supporters started the New England Anti-Slavery Society. Activists in Philadelphia and New York organized similar groups in 1833. Soon a dozen antislavery newspapers and scores of antislavery lecturers were spreading the word and inspiring the formation of new local societies. By 1837, thirteen hundred antislavery organizations existed across the North, with a membership totaling a quarter of a million men and women.

How did new practices of party politics shape Andrew Jackson's election and agenda?

What was Andrew Jackson's impact on the presidency?

What were the most significant social and cultural changes in the 1830s?

What political and economic events dominated Martin Van Buren's presidency?

Conclusion: The Age of Jackson or the era of reform?

Who Scorned Temperance and Moral Reform?

The movements to curb alcohol use and stigmatize illicit sexual expression that burgeoned in the 1830s grew directly out of new ideals of middle-class domesticity and the religious fervor of the Second Great Awakening. But of course not everyone was won over. Considerable portions of one segment of the population in particular—young single men living away from home—embraced alcohol consumption and free sexual expression as central features of their youthful camaraderie.

Historians point to several features of 1830s society that contributed to this boisterous subculture among disorderly young men. More than ever before, adolescent boys left their native farming villages to take jobs far from home. They moved to commercial hubs and became shop clerks, secretaries, and typesetters. They delayed marriage into their middle twenties, waiting for sufficient economic stability to support a family. This delay extended their time free from the responsibilities of family life.

Unlike earlier eras, when apprentices lived with watchful masters in a familial environment, young men now worked for wages and congregated in boardinghouses, often with minimal adult supervision. Long work hours heightened the appeal of leisure entertainments. Taverns and saloons provided a space for male friends to gather. Theaters, dance halls, and brothels were additional options for those living in cities. All of these venues served alcohol to patrons, loosening inhibitions and promoting sociability.

▲ Male patrons of a well-known Manhattan saloon called the Pewter Mug blow smoke and lift mugs as they read the latest issue of the *Weekly Rake*. All are wearing the business suit of the day; this is not a working-class bar. This self-celebratory lithograph appeared in the *Weekly Rake*, which offered its readers salacious commentary on sex and the city. American Antiquarian Society, Worcester, Massachusetts, USA/Bridgeman Images.

Recent discoveries of scores of scurrilous newspapers, stored uncatalogued for years in venerable historical societies or found in attics by surprised descendants, have given historians a window into this masculine subculture. This new genre of publications began to appear in the mid-1830s, promoting a distinctive oppositional voice to the standard newspapers of the day. They carried names such as the *Owl* and the *Hawk and Buzzard* (suggesting overhead flights that peer into private places); the *Microscope*, the *Gleaner*, the *Paul Pry*, the *Censor*, and the

Many white northerners reacted with fury at the abolitionists. Even if they were theoretically opposed to slavery, most thought the call for immediate abolition unwise. They viewed abolitionists as radical agitators who threatened the nation's unity. From 1834 to 1838, more than a hundred episodes of mob violence erupted against abolitionists and free blacks. On one occasion, crowds burned antislavery headquarters in Philadelphia and a black church and orphanage to the ground. In another incident, a rioting crowd killed Illinois abolitionist editor Elijah Lovejoy and destroyed his printing press. When the Grimké sisters lectured in 1837, some authorities tried to intimidate them and deny them meeting space. The following year, rocks shattered windows when Angelina Grimké

What economic developments reshaped the U.S. economy after 1815?

Whip (words conveying punishing exposure); and the *Blade*, the *Satirist*, the *Loafer*, the *Flash*, and the *Rake* (humorous self-descriptive labels). They appeared in cities like Boston; Albany, New York; Philadelphia; Baltimore; and Washington, D.C.; and in smaller towns like Rochester, New York, and Manchester, New Hampshire. No doubt they were published in other places too. This journalistic craze erupted around 1835, generated a fierce blaze of excitement, and then burned out around 1845. The editors were nearly all young men in their early twenties.

The salacious weeklies combined humor, gossip, and scandal in varying proportions. They featured profiles of well-known sporting men or prostitutes and commentary on the local social, theatrical, and sports scenes. They often devoted extensive space to reader communications, a feature not found in more traditional newspapers. A recurring "wants to know" column posted dozens of readers' brief gossipy questions: Who was that climbing into Miss B's bedroom window on State Street last Thursday? Who was doing what in a shed on Cooper's alley at 10 p.m. last Saturday? Pickpockets and cheating clerks in stores received scathing treatment, as did unpleasant work supervisors and men who failed to pay their tavern debts. Letters from readers detailed the bawdy social action in their neighborhoods or in nearby towns, naming scoundrels by their initials. The more successful of these papers had wide regional distributions, as shown by their far-flung correspondents.

Editors of these publications piously asserted that they were shaming the immoral by exposing their transgressions. The Boston *Blade*'s masthead proclaimed, "We hold it evident, that truth should be published as villainy stalks abroad, so wide." The New York *Owl* vowed that "the reformation of the rising generation has been our unceasing endeavor." They and everyone else knew such declarations were a joke, especially when the papers detailed exact addresses of brothels and obscene booksellers. Even so, when editors were hauled into court on obscenity charges, they claimed to be high-minded critics of vice, no more guilty of obscenity than the good ladies agitating in print for moral reform. Skeptical judges most often sentenced them to jail.

Not all young men participated in this subculture, of course. Historians have mapped out competing subcultures, from the highly religious or economically ambitious youth cultivating personal restraint, to a "martial manhood" attracted to service as soldiers, firemen, or policemen, and a working-class "jolly fellow" tavern culture that made a high art of comical and practical jokes.

The raunchy weeklies shone a light on the presence of hidden enclaves of vice that had long existed in American cities. They provided a guide to the sexual underworld, making that realm visible and navigable to the new throngs of young men on the loose. Their unique interactive quality helped to create and define an oppositional youth culture that thumbed its nose at the moralists, who now grasped, better than ever, how difficult it would be to curb a decade of visible dissolution.

Questions for Analysis

SUMMARIZE THE ARGUMENT: What evidence does the essay provide to explain why an urban sexual underworld developed in the United States in the 1830s? Can you think of additional factors?

ANALYZE THE EVIDENCE: How did historians discover the outlines of this male subculture? What can the names, unusual format, and details in the newspapers tell us about this largely hidden world?

CONSIDER THE CONTEXT: What role did the rapid economic changes of the era play in the development of this particular subculture of masculinity? In what ways was this subculture oppositional to more visible and dominant movements of the era?

spoke at a female antislavery convention in Philadelphia. After the women fled the building, a mob burned it to the ground.

Despite the physical dangers, large numbers of northern women played a role in the movement. Most notable were the antislavery petitions they presented to the U.S. Congress with tens of thousands of signatures. At first, women framed the petitions as respectful memorials about the evils of slavery. Later, they demanded an end to slavery in the District of Columbia, which was under Congress's jurisdiction. With such tactics, antislavery women asserted their claim to speak on political issues independently of their husbands and fathers.

▶ **Controversy over Abolitionism** Violence regularly erupted in response to abolitionist speakers. This 1837 poster from Poughkeepsie, New York, blasts out inflammatory language that often sparked riots. Antislavery societies raised money to support lecture tours. The weekly pledge was one method of fund-raising. This contribution box is inscribed with biblical passages and the iconic image of a kneeling slave in chains, pleading for liberty.

Poster: Library of Congress, Rare Book and Special Collections Division; Box: Boston Public Library/Rare Books Department—Courtesy of the Trustees.

Before long, women's activism on behalf of antislavery led them to write and speak about woman's rights. Some began to see the oppression of slaves and of women as related issues. "The denial of our duty to act, is a bold denial of our right to act," Angelina Grimké declared, in response to those who tried to silence her and her sister. "And if *we* have no right to act, then may we well be termed 'the white slaves of the North'—for, like our brethren in bonds, we must seal our lips in silence and despair."

If the abolitionists did not secure an immediate end to slavery in the 1830s, they succeeded in making their cause the nation's central political issue by the close of the decade. The movement grew at least in part from the larger social and intellectual currents of the era. Millions of men and women in the 1830s found their initial inspiration in evangelical Protestantism's dual message: Salvation was open to all, and society needed to be perfected. The growing scope of the movement, and its insistence that changing public opinion was the means to abolish slavery, emerged from the democratized political culture of the Jacksonian era. And abolitionists' activist mentality squared well with the interventionist tendencies of the Whig Party.

PLACE EVENTS IN CONTEXT

How did the emerging woman's rights movement relate to the abolitionist movement of the 1830s and 1840s?

QUICK REVIEW

What connections did the social reform movements of the 1830s have to each other, and to the political and economic changes of the period?

What political and economic events dominated Martin Van Buren's presidency?

By the mid-1830s, a tumultuous democratic political culture governed American life. Andrew Jackson, too ill to stand for a third term, made way for his vice president, Martin Van Buren. Van Buren was a skilled politician, but soon after his inauguration the country's economy collapsed. A devastating panic in 1837, followed by another in 1839, brought the country to its knees.

What economic developments reshaped the U.S. economy after 1815?

Meanwhile, as the institution of slavery continued to grow, so did its status as the country's preeminent political conflict.

The Politics of Slavery

Martin Van Buren of New York was known as "the Little Magician" for his consummate political talents. First a senator and then governor, he became Jackson's secretary of state and then his running mate in 1832. Perhaps his greatest political achievement lay in building a sophisticated Democratic Party organization.

Jackson favored Van Buren for the nomination in 1836. But starting in 1832, political parties chose their candidates through nominating conventions. In 1835, Van Buren won the convention balloting unanimously. His rival, the South Carolinian John C. Calhoun, sought to discredit Van Buren among southern Democrats. Van Buren spent months assuring southerners that he was a "northern man with southern principles." It was a credible argument. His Dutch family hailed from the Hudson River counties in New York where slavery had once flourished. His own family had owned slaves as late as the 1810s.

Calhoun succeeded in making trouble for Van Buren because white southerners were growing ever more alarmed by the rise of northern antislavery sentiment. When activists tried to circulate a million abolitionist pamphlets through the South in 1835, a bag of their mail was hijacked at the post office in Charleston, South Carolina. Crowds burned the pamphlets along with effigies of leading abolitionists. President Jackson condemned the theft but instructed postmasters to use their judgment when deciding whether to allow such mail into the South. Southern censorship of the mail became a political issue in the North.

Abolitionists did not fear escalating sectional tensions. To the contrary, it was one of the movement's objectives. When hundreds of antislavery petitions inundated Congress, southern congressmen responded by passing a gag rule that prohibited entering the documents into the public record. They argued that a congressional act abolishing slavery was unconstitutional, a violation of white southerners' property rights. Abolitionists like the Grimké sisters, on the other hand, saw the gag rule as a violation of their rights of free speech. Southerners' fear of the petitions suggested how effective they were. "The South already turns pale at the number sent," exulted Angelina Grimké.

Van Buren shrewdly seized on the issues of mail censorship and the gag rule to affirm his prosouthern sympathies. Abolitionists were "fanatics," he claimed, possibly under the influence of "foreign agents" (British abolitionists). He promised that, as president, he would not allow any interference in southern "domestic institutions."

Elections and Panics

If the first presidential elections were relatively staid affairs negotiated among gentlemanly elites, Jackson's charismatic personality shaped the elections of 1824, 1828, and 1832. The nation's democratic institutions entered a new stage in 1836. Van Buren, an exceptional backroom politician, was the first president to win the presidency through the new party system—an apparatus made up of local and state committees throughout the country, and more than four hundred partisan newspapers.

The Whigs had also built a network of state-level organizations and loyal newspapers. Lacking a contender with nationwide support, three regional candidates opposed Van Buren: Senator Daniel Webster of Massachusetts; Hugh Lawson White of Tennessee; and General William Henry Harrison of Ohio. No single one of the three candidates could win the presidency alone, but together they nearly denied Van Buren a majority. Van Burenites saw the three-Whig strategy as a plot to move the election to the House of Representatives.

CHRONOLOGY

1835
- Abolitionist literature burned in Charleston, South Carolina.

1836
- Martin Van Buren elected president.
- Congress institutes "gag rule" against antislavery petitions.

1837
- Major financial panic disrupts economy.

1839
- Financial panic recurs.

1840
- William Henry Harrison elected president.

ANALYZE EVIDENCE

What does Congress's passage of the gag rule in 1836 suggest about abolitionists' effect on public opinion and on American political institutions?

| How did new practices of party politics shape Andrew Jackson's election and agenda? | What was Andrew Jackson's impact on the presidency? | What were the most significant social and cultural changes in the 1830s? | **What political and economic events dominated Martin Van Buren's presidency?** | Conclusion: The Age of Jackson or the era of reform? |

In the end, Van Buren won with 170 electoral votes; the other three received a total of 113. But Van Buren's victories came from narrow majorities, far below those Jackson had commanded. Van Buren successfully assembled a national Democratic Party with wins in both North and South. But he did so at a steep cost, by committing northern Democrats to a southern proslavery agenda. Meanwhile, the three regional Whig candidates helped usher in victories at the state level.

When Van Buren took office in March 1837, financial markets were already quaking. A month later, the country was plunged into crisis. The panic of 1837 had multiple causes, some of them global. Bad harvests in Europe and a large trade imbalance between Britain and the United States caused the Bank of England to call in loans to American merchants. Meanwhile, a downturn in international cotton prices fed the growing disaster. Lacking access to credit, cotton merchants in the South could no longer meet their obligations.

New York firms that had lent money to southern merchants and planters began to fail—ninety-eight of them in March and April of 1837 alone. Frightened citizens overwhelmed banks, trying to withdraw their money. Businesses rushed to sell their assets to pay off debts. Prices of stocks, bonds, and real estate all collapsed. The dynamic of the panic of 1819 unfolded again, with terrifying speed. Credit markets, which had seemed so stable, suddenly tumbled like a house of cards. Newspapers used the language of emotional states—excitement, anxiety, terror, panic—to describe the collapse. Such terms focused on human reactions to the crisis, rather than on structural features of the economy.

Lacking a sophisticated understanding of economic forces, few people could see the bigger picture: an interlinked capitalist world system coming into existence. To explain the crisis, Americans turned instead to politics, religion, or individual character. Some Whig leaders pointed to Jackson's antibank and hard-money policies. New Yorker Philip Hone, a wealthy Whig, called the Jackson administration "the most disastrous in the annals of the country" for its "wicked interference" in banking and monetary matters. Others framed the devastation as divine retribution for the frenzy of speculation that had gripped the nation. A religious periodical in Boston hoped that Americans would abandon their sinful greed: "We were getting to think that there was no end to the wealth," read one article, "that economy was not needed, that prudence was weakness."

The panic of 1837 subsided by 1838. But in 1839, another run on banks and wave of business failures further deflated the economy, creating a second panic. President Van Buren called a special session of Congress to consider an independent treasury system that could perform some of the functions of the former Bank of the United States. Such a system, funded by government deposits, would moderate inflation rates and stabilize credit markets. But Van Buren met strong resistance in Congress. His treasury system finally won approval in 1840, but by then Van Buren's chances of winning a second term in office had vanished.

In 1840, the Whigs settled on William Henry Harrison to oppose Van Buren. The campaign mobilized voters as no presidential campaign ever had. This time, Whigs borrowed tricks from the Democrats. They portrayed Harrison as a common man born in a log cabin (in reality, he was born on a Virginia plantation). Campaign parades even featured toy log cabins. They emphasized his experience fighting Indians to give him a Jacksonian aura. Whigs staged boisterous rallies around the country, drumming up mass appeal with parades and shows. Women participated in rallies as never before. Some 78 percent of eligible voters cast ballots—the highest percentage ever in American history.

Harrison took 53 percent of the popular vote and won a resounding 234 electoral college votes to Van Buren's 60 votes. A Democratic editor lamented, "We have taught them how to conquer us!"

panic of 1837
Major economic crisis that led to several years of hard times in the United States from 1837 to 1841. Sudden bankruptcies, contraction of credit, and runs on banks led to hardships nationwide. The causes were multiple and global and not well understood.

TRACE CHANGE OVER TIME
How did the elections of 1836 and 1840 demonstrate the changing nature of American politics?

What economic developments reshaped the U.S. economy after 1815?

QUICK REVIEW

What were the most significant issues of Martin Van Buren's presidency?

Conclusion: The Age of Jackson or the era of reform?

Harrison's election closed a decade that brought democracy and the figure of the common man to the center of American politics. Economic transformations help explain the rapid changes of the 1830s. Transportation advances accelerated the circulation of goods and people. Water-powered manufacturing began to change the nature of labor. Great waves of land auctions redistributed territory violently seized from Indians. Slavery expanded into vast new territories of the Southwest. Trade and banking mushroomed, pulling ever-expanding parts of the continent into an increasingly interlinked global economic system. Two sharp economic downturns—the panic of 1819 and the panics of 1837 and 1839—offered sobering lessons about speculative fever.

Andrew Jackson symbolized this age of opportunity more than any single figure. His fame—as an aggressive general, victorious Indian fighter, champion of the common man, tormentor of the moneyed interests, and defender of slavery—attracted growing numbers of voters to the Democratic Party. Democrats emerged as the champions of personal liberty, free competition, and egalitarian opportunity for all white men.

A vocal segment of the population challenged the Jacksonian vision. Inspired by the Second Great Awakening, evangelical reformers targeted personal vices (illicit sex and alcohol consumption) and social problems (prostitution, poverty, and slavery). They joined forces with wealthy lawyers and merchants, in the North and South, who favored a national bank and protective tariffs. The Whigs became the party of activist moralism and state-sponsored entrepreneurship. Voters were male, of course, but thousands of reform-minded women expanded the political sphere by mobilizing the ideology of separate spheres to insert themselves as moral voices in national politics. They engaged in reform activities and disseminated petitions on the issues of Indian removal and slavery. A few exceptional women, like Sarah and Angelina Grimké, even became famous in their own right.

National politics in the 1830s were more divided than at any time since the 1790s. With the great expansion of the suffrage, the new party system of Democrats and Whigs reached much deeper into the electorate than had the first party system of Federalists and Republicans. Politics acquired immediacy and excitement, causing nearly four out of five white men to cast ballots in 1840.

All these changes laid the groundwork for the political and social trends of the 1840s and 1850s. Continued urban growth, westward expansion, and industrialization sustained the Democrat-Whig split in politics but they created new divisions as well. In particular, the spectacular growth of slavery—from 681,000 slaves in 1790 to 2.5 million by 1840, heading to 4 million in 1860—would raise profound questions about the nature of American democracy even as it seemed to stand at the vanguard of the new liberal societies of the Atlantic world. Ultimately, slavery would prove to be a problem that the political system, for all its resiliency, could not solve.

| How did new practices of party politics shape Andrew Jackson's election and agenda? | What was Andrew Jackson's impact on the presidency? | What were the most significant social and cultural changes in the 1830s? | What political and economic events dominated Martin Van Buren's presidency? | **Conclusion: The Age of Jackson or the era of reform?** |

323

STEP 1 · EXPLAIN WHY IT MATTERS

Put your reading into practice. Identify each term below, and then explain why it matters in U.S. history.

TERM	WHO OR WHAT & WHEN	WHY IT MATTERS
Erie Canal (p. 299)		
Lowell mills (p. 301)		
second Bank of the United States (p. 304)		
Whigs (p. 305)		
Democrats (p. 305)		
Indian Removal Act of 1830 (p. 308)		
Trail of Tears (p. 310)		
nullification (p. 310)		
separate spheres (p. 313)		
Second Great Awakening (p. 315)		
American Temperance Society (p. 316)		
New York Female Moral Reform Society (p. 317)		
panic of 1837 (p. 322)		

STEP 2 · MOVE BEYOND THE BASICS

To demonstrate a more advanced understanding, consider change over time as it affected the American economy, politics, society, and culture. What was the relationship between each of the sectors?

	1815	1830–1840
Transportation		
Industry and Labor		
Economy		
Politics		
Social Reform and Cultural Developments		

STEP 3

PUT IT ALL TOGETHER

Now, try to explain the big picture. Remember to use specific examples from the chapter in your answers.

ECONOMIC TRANSFORMATIONS

- How did industrialization change workers' lives and the meaning of work itself?

- In what ways did economic transformations after 1815 change women's status in the country?

THE AGE OF JACKSON

- What does Andrew Jackson's rise to the presidency tell us about popular politics in the 1820s and 1830s?

- How did Andrew Jackson change the relationship among the president, Congress, and the courts?

THE ERA OF REFORM

- How did the Second Great Awakening lead to a variety of social reform movements? What impact did these reform movements have on politics and society in the 1830s?

- What role did women play in the reform movements of the early nineteenth century?

LOOKING BACKWARD, LOOKING AHEAD

- How did the second American party system differ from the first party system?

- How do the reform movements of the 1820s and 1830s help explain the sectional tensions that would dominate the 1840s and 1850s?

STEP 4

CONNECT THESE EVENTS

How did the economic transformations of the period from 1815 to 1840 affect meanings of gender, reform movements, and political life in the United States?

STEP 5

CONNECT TO THE PRESENT

Compare the goal of abolishing slavery in the 1830s to the goal of curbing global warming today. Are there similarities? Differences?

12

THE NORTH AND WEST

1840–1860

How did the economy and society of the North and West change during the 1840s and 1850s?

This chapter discusses American economic growth, territorial expansion, political debate, and social reform during the 1840s and 1850s. It also examines the ideal of free labor common in the North and West.

This chapter will explore the following questions:

- Why did "industrial evolution" occur?

- How did the free-labor ideal explain economic inequality?

- What spurred westward expansion?

- Why did the United States go to war with Mexico?

- What changes did social reformers seek in the 1840s and 1850s?

- Conclusion: How did the free-labor ideal contribute to economic growth?

AN AMERICAN STORY

Early in November 1842, Abraham Lincoln and his new wife, Mary, moved into their first home in Springfield, Illinois, a small rented room on the second floor of the Globe Tavern. It was the worst place Mary had ever lived. She grew up in Lexington, Kentucky, attended by slaves in the elegant home of her father, a prosperous merchant and banker. In contrast, the room was the nicest place Abraham had ever lived. Nineteen years later, the Lincolns moved into the presidential mansion in Washington, D.C.

Abraham Lincoln climbed from the Globe Tavern to the White House by work, ambition, and talent. Lincoln and many others celebrated his rise from backwoods poverty as an example of the opportunities available in the free-labor economy of the North and West. They believed his spectacular ascent came from his individual qualities. They tended to ignore the help he received from Mary and many other people.

Born in a Kentucky log cabin in 1809, Lincoln grew up on small, struggling farms as his family migrated west. His father, Thomas Lincoln, born in Virginia, never learned to read. As Abraham recalled, Thomas "never did more in the way of writing than to bunglingly sign his own name." Lincoln's mother, Nancy, could neither read nor write. In 1816, Thomas Lincoln moved his young family from Kentucky to the Indiana wilderness where "there was absolutely nothing to excite ambition for education," Lincoln wrote. Unlike Lincoln, Mary Todd spent ten years in Lexington's best private schools for young women.

In 1830, Thomas Lincoln moved to central Illinois. When he moved again a year later, Abraham set out on his own, a "friendless, uneducated, penniless boy," as he described himself.

By constant striving, Abraham Lincoln gained an education and the respect of his Illinois neighbors, although he did not earn a steady income for years. After he got married, Lincoln received help from Mary's father. He gave the couple eighty acres of land and a yearly allowance of about $1,100 for six years. That helped them move out of their room above the Globe Tavern and into their own home. Abraham eventually built a thriving law practice in Springfield, Illinois, and served in the state legislature and in Congress. Mary helped him in many ways, rearing their sons, tending their household, and integrating him into her wealthy and influential family in Illinois and Kentucky. Mary also shared Abraham's keen interest in politics and ambition for power. With her support, Abraham became the first president born west of the Appalachian Mountains.

Like Lincoln, millions of Americans believed they could make something of themselves, whatever their origins, so long as they were willing to work. Individuals who were lazy, undisciplined, or foolish had only themselves to blame if they failed, advocates of free-labor ideology declared. Work was a requirement for success, not a guarantee. This emphasis on work highlighted the individual efforts of men and tended to overlook the many crucial contributions women and family members made to the successes of men like Lincoln. In addition, the rewards of work tilted toward white men and away from women and free African Americans, as antislavery and woman's rights reformers pointed out. Still, the promise of rewards for work spurred efforts that shaped the contours of America. Plowing new fields and building railroads pushed the boundaries of the nation westward to the Pacific Ocean. The nation's economic, political, and geographic expansion raised the question of whether slavery should also move west. Lincoln and other Americans confronted that question following the Mexican-American War, yet another outgrowth of the nation's westward movement.

▼ **Abraham and Mary Todd Lincoln** About five years after they got married, Abraham and Mary Todd Lincoln posed for these daguerreotypes. The clothing worn by Abraham reflects his rise from log-cabin poverty to respectability as a lawyer and budding politician by age 37. Mary, ten years younger, wore a fine dress and jewelry that suggests her privileged upbringing as well as the social and political ambitions she shared with her husband. Library of Congress, 3g02439 and 3g06189.

Why did "industrial evolution" occur?

During the 1840s and 1850s, Americans experienced impressive economic growth. Since 1800, the total output of the U.S. economy had multiplied twelvefold. Four developments in American society fueled this remarkable economic growth. First, millions of Americans moved from farms to towns and cities, Abraham Lincoln among them. Second, factory workers (mainly in towns and cities) increased to about 20 percent of the labor force. Third, a shift from waterpower to steam as a source of energy raised productivity, especially in factories and transportation. Railroads harnessed steam power, speeding transport and cutting costs. Fourth, agricultural productivity nearly doubled during Lincoln's lifetime, spurring the nation's economic growth more than any other factor.

Historians often refer to this cascade of changes as an industrial revolution. However, these changes did not cause a total revolution in America's economy or society, which remained overwhelmingly agricultural. Old methods of production continued alongside new ones. A better term for the changes in the American economy during the 1840s and 1850s is "industrial evolution."

Agriculture and Land Policy

Agriculture was the foundation of the United States' economic growth. A French traveler noted that Americans had "a general feeling of hatred against trees." Trees limited agricultural productivity because farmers had to spend time and energy clearing them to make fields open to sunlight and cultivation. When farmers pushed westward looking for cheap land, like Lincoln, they came to the Midwest's comparatively treeless prairie, where they could spend less time clearing land and more time with a plow and hoe. Rich prairie soils yielded bumper crops, enticing farmers to migrate to the Midwest by the tens of thousands between 1830 and 1860. The populations of Indiana, Illinois, Michigan, Wisconsin, and Iowa exploded tenfold between 1830 and 1860, much faster than the growth of the nation as a whole.

Laborsaving improvements in farm implements also boosted agricultural productivity. Inventors tinkered to craft stronger, more efficient plows. In 1837, John Deere made a strong, smooth steel plow that sliced through prairie soil so cleanly that farmers called it the "singing plow." Deere's company produced more than ten thousand plows a year by the late 1850s. Human and animal muscles provided the energy for plowing, but Deere's plows permitted farmers to break more ground and plant more crops.

Improvements in wheat harvesting also increased farmers' productivity. In 1850, most farmers harvested wheat by hand, cutting two or three acres a day. In the 1840s, Cyrus McCormick and others experimented with designs for a **mechanical reaper**, and by the 1850s, a McCormick reaper that cost between $100 and $150 allowed a farmer to harvest twelve acres a day. Improved reapers and plows, usually powered by horses or oxen, allowed farmers to cultivate more land, doubling the corn and wheat harvests between 1840 and 1860.

Federal land policy made possible the leap in agricultural productivity. Up to 1860, the United States continued to be land-rich and labor-poor. The nation became much richer in land with the Louisiana Purchase (see chapter 10) and with the vast territory acquired following the Mexican-American War (discussed later in this chapter). The federal government made most of this land available for purchase in order to attract settlers and to generate money for government expenses. Millions of ordinary farmers bought federal land for $1.25 an acre, or $50 for a forty-acre farm that could support a family. Millions of other

mechanical reaper
Machine that allowed farmers to harvest up to twelve acres of wheat a day.

Why did "industrial evolution" occur?

VISUAL ACTIVITY

▲ **Mechanical Reaper Advertisement** This advertisement for the mechanical reaper manufactured by the Lagonda Agricultural Works in Ohio illustrates the labor saved—and the labor still required—to harvest wheat. The revolving reel pulled the stalks of wheat toward a cutter and piled the cut grain on a platform. One man pushed the cut wheat onto the ground and another man bound it into sheaves. Library of Congress, LC-DIG-pga-02032.

READING THE IMAGE: What kinds of labor are represented by the two men standing on each side of the oval picture of the reaper? What kinds of labor did the mechanical reaper save, and what kinds were required?

CONNECTIONS: How did reapers and other improvements increase agricultural productivity?

---

farmers squatted on unclaimed federal land, as Thomas Lincoln did, and carved out farms. By making land available on relatively easy terms, federal land policy boosted agricultural productivity, which in turn fueled the nation's economic growth.

Manufacturing and Mechanization

Changes in manufacturing arose from the nation's land-rich, labor-poor economy. In Europe's land-poor, labor-rich economies, few opportunities in agriculture created plenty of factory workers and kept wages low. In the United States, western expansion and government land policies supported agriculture, keeping millions of people on the farm—80 percent of the nation's 31 million people lived in rural areas in 1860. The large agricultural workforce limited the supply of workers for manufacturing and in turn elevated wages. Because of the relative shortage of workers, American manufacturers searched constantly for ways to save labor and reduce their costs.

PLACE EVENTS IN CONTEXT

How did manufacturing contribute to the increase in agricultural productivity?

How did the free-labor ideal explain economic inequality?	What spurred westward expansion?	Why did the United States go to war with Mexico?	What changes did social reformers seek in the 1840s and 1850s?	Conclusion: How did the free-labor ideal contribute to economic growth?

Mechanization allowed manufacturers to produce more with less labor. In general, factory workers produced twice as much (per unit of labor) as agricultural workers. Some manufacturers began making interchangeable parts and then assembling them into more or less uniform products. This process became known as the American system. It started in gun-making and spread to other industries. Standardized parts made by machine also allowed manufacturers to employ unskilled workers, who were much cheaper than highly trained craftsmen. A visitor to a Massachusetts gun factory noted that standardized parts made the trained gunsmith's "skill of the eye and hand, [previously] acquired by practice alone, . . . no longer indispensable." Despite mechanization, factories remained small. Even in heavily mechanized industries, factories rarely employed more than twenty or thirty workers.

Manufacturing and agriculture meshed into a dynamic national economy. New England led the nation in manufacturing, shipping goods such as guns, clocks, plows, and axes west and south. Southern and western states sent commodities such as wheat, pork, whiskey, tobacco, and cotton north and east. Between 1840 and 1860, coal production in Pennsylvania, Ohio, and elsewhere multiplied eightfold, cutting coal prices in half and powering the many coal-fired steam engines. Even so, by 1860 coal accounted for less than a fifth of the nation's energy consumption. Even in manufacturing, muscles provided thirty times more energy than steam did.

American manufacturers specialized in producing for the huge domestic market rather than for export. British goods dominated the international market, and they were usually cheaper and better than American-made products. U.S. manufacturers supported tariffs to raise prices on British goods, but their best protection from British competitors came from pleasing their American customers, most of whom were farmers. The developing economy was accelerated by railroads, which linked farmers and factories in new ways.

Railroads: Breaking the Bonds of Nature

Railroads captured Americans' imagination because they seemed to break the bonds of nature. When canals and rivers froze in winter or became impassable during summer droughts, trains steamed ahead, averaging more than twenty miles an hour during the 1850s. Above all, railroads gave cities not blessed with canals or navigable rivers a way to compete for rural trade.

In 1850, trains steamed along 9,000 miles of track, almost two-thirds of it in New England and the Middle Atlantic states. By 1860, several railroads spanned the Mississippi River, connecting frontier farmers to the nation's 30,000 miles of track, approximately as much as in all of the rest of the world combined (**Map 12.1**). In 1857, for example, France had only 3,700 miles of track, while England and Wales had 6,400 miles. The massive expansion of American railroads helped catapult the nation to the world's second greatest industrial power, after Great Britain.

In addition to speeding transportation, railroads propelled the growth of other industries, such as iron and communications. Iron production grew five times faster than the population during the decades up to 1860, in part to meet railroads' demand. Railroads also stimulated the emerging telegraph industry. In 1844, Samuel F. B. Morse demonstrated the potential of his telegraph by transmitting an electronic message between Washington, D.C., and Baltimore. By 1861, more than fifty thousand miles of telegraph wire stretched across the continent to the Pacific Ocean, often alongside railroad tracks, accelerating communications of all sorts.

Private corporations built and owned almost all American railroads, in contrast to the government-owned railroads in other industrial nations. But privately owned American railroads received massive government aid, especially federal land grants. Up to 1850, the federal government had granted a total of seven million acres of federal land to various turnpike, highway, and canal projects. In 1850, Congress approved a grant to railroads of six square miles of federal land for each mile of track laid. By 1860, Congress had granted

Why did "industrial evolution" occur?

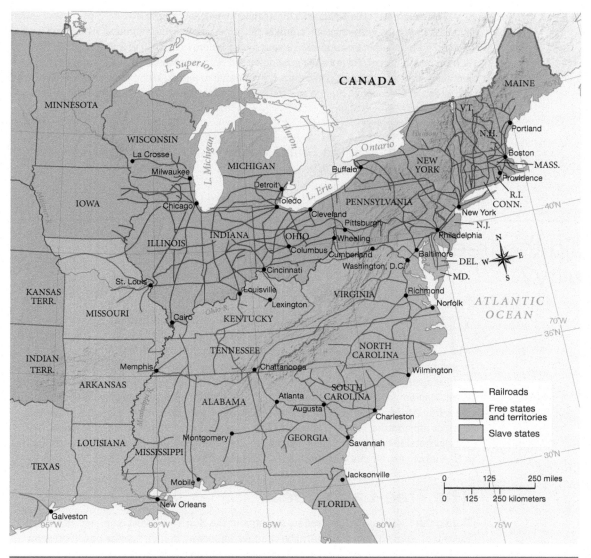

MAP 12.1 ▲ Railroads in 1860 Railroads were a crucial component of the revolutions in transportation and communications that transformed nineteenth-century America. The railroad system reflected the differences in the economies of the North and South.

READING THE MAP: Which sections of the country had most of the railroad track by the mid-nineteenth century? What cities served as the busiest railroad hubs?

CONNECTIONS: How did the expansion of railroad networks affect the American economy? Why was the U.S. government willing to grant more than twenty million acres of public land to the private corporations that ran the railroads?

---

railroads more than twenty million acres of federal land. These land grants supported railroad construction costs and promoted the expansion of the rail network, the settlement of federal land, and the integration of the domestic market.

The railroad boom of the 1850s demonstrated the growing industrial might of the American economy. Like other industries, railroads succeeded because they served both farms and cities. But transportation was not revolutionized overnight. Most Americans in 1860 were still far more familiar with horses than with locomotives. Even by 1875, trains carried only about one-third of the mail; most of the rest still went by horseback or stagecoach.

UNDERSTAND POINTS OF VIEW

Why did the federal government give private railroad companies huge grants of federal land?

| How did the free-labor ideal explain economic inequality? | What spurred westward expansion? | Why did the United States go to war with Mexico? | What changes did social reformers seek in the 1840s and 1850s? | Conclusion: How did the free-labor ideal contribute to economic growth? |

The economy of the 1840s and 1850s linked an expanding, westward-moving population in farms and cities with muscles, animals, machines, steam, and railroads. Abraham Lincoln planted corn and split fence rails as a young man before he moved to Springfield, Illinois, and became a successful attorney who defended railroad corporations, among others. His mobility—westward, from farm to city, from manual to mental labor, and upward—illustrated the direction of economic change and the opportunities that beckoned enterprising individuals.

QUICK REVIEW

Why did the United States become a leading industrial power by the 1850s?

How did the free-labor ideal explain economic inequality?

The nation's impressive economic performance did not reward all Americans equally. Native-born white men tended to do better than immigrants. With few exceptions, women were excluded from opportunities open to men. Tens of thousands of women worked as seamstresses, laundresses, domestic servants, factory hands, and teachers, but they had little opportunity to aspire to higher-paying jobs. In the North and West, slavery was slowly eliminated in the half century after the American Revolution, but most free African Americans had dead-end jobs as laborers and servants. Discrimination against immigrants, women, and free black people did not trouble most white men. With certain notable exceptions, they considered discrimination proper and just, the outcome of a free-labor system that rewarded hard work and, ideally, education.

The Free-Labor Ideal

During the 1840s and 1850s, leaders throughout the North and West emphasized a set of ideas that seemed to explain why the changes underway in their society benefited some people more than others. They referred again and again to the advantages of what they termed *free labor*. (The word *free* referred to laborers who were not slaves. It did not mean laborers who worked for nothing.) By the 1850s, free-labor ideas described a social and economic ideal that accounted for both the successes and the shortcomings of the economy and society taking shape in the North and West.

"'I had no books in my house we didn't think about books—papers —We worked—had to live.'"

Spokesmen for the free-labor ideal celebrated hard work, self-reliance, and independence. They proclaimed that the door to success was open not just to those who inherited wealth or high status but also to self-made men, such as Abraham Lincoln. Free labor, Lincoln argued, was "the just and generous, and prosperous system, which opens the way for all—gives hope to all, and energy, and progress, and improvement of condition to all." Free labor permitted farmers and artisans to enjoy the products of their own labor, and it also benefited wageworkers. "The prudent, penniless beginner in the world," Lincoln declared, "labors for wages awhile, saves a surplus with which to buy tools or land, for himself; then labors on his own account another while, and at length hires another new beginner to help him." Wage labor, Lincoln claimed, was the first rung on the ladder that reached upward to self-employment and eventually to hiring others.

Why did "industrial evolution" occur?

The free-labor ideal proclaimed a democratic vision of human potential. Lincoln and other spokesmen stressed the importance of universal education to permit "heads and hands [to] cooperate as friends." Throughout the North and West, communities supported public schools to make learning available to young children. In rural areas, where the labor of children was difficult to spare, schools typically enrolled no more than half the school-aged children. One farm woman recalled, "I had no books in my house we didn't think about books—papers—We worked—had to live."

Textbooks and teachers—most of whom were young women—drummed into students the lessons of the free-labor system: self-reliance, discipline, and, above all else, hard work. "Remember that all the ignorance, degradation, and misery in the world is the result of indolence and vice," one textbook intoned. Both in and outside school, free-labor ideology emphasized labor as much as freedom.

Economic Inequality

The free-labor ideal made sense to many Americans in the North and West who believed it described their own experiences. Money seemed to many the best measure of success. An English visitor observed that he had never "overheard Americans conversing without the word DOLLAR being pronounced." Lincoln frequently referred to his lowly origins as a hired laborer and invited his listeners to consider how far he had come. In 1860, his assets of $17,000 easily placed him in the wealthiest 5 percent of the population. Few men became much richer. Most Americans, however, measured success in more modest terms. The average wealth of adult white men in the North in 1860 barely topped $2,000. Nearly half of American men had no wealth at all. About 60 percent owned no land. Women had far less wealth than men, because the property of married women was typically controlled by their husbands. Free African Americans had still less; 90 percent of them had none. **(See "Spotlight: How Did the American Economy Compare to the Rest of the World?" on page 334.)**

Free-labor spokesmen considered these economic inequalities a natural outgrowth of freedom—the inevitable result of some individuals being luckier, more able, and more willing to work. The inequalities also demonstrate the gap between the promise and the performance of the free-labor ideal. Economic growth permitted many men to move from being landless squatters to landowning farmers and from being hired laborers to independent, self-employed producers. But many more Americans remained behind, landless and working for wages. Even those who realized their aspirations often had a precarious hold on their independence. Bad debts, falling prices, crop failure, sickness, or death could quickly eliminate a family's gains.

Americans' pursuit of free-labor ideals created restless social and geographic mobility. While fortunate people such as Abraham Lincoln rose far beyond their social origins, others shared the misfortune of a merchant who, an observer noted, "has been on the sinking list all his life." In search of better prospects, roughly two-thirds of the rural population moved every decade, and population turnover in cities was even greater.

Immigrants and the Free-Labor Ladder

The risks and uncertainties of free labor did not deter millions of immigrants from entering the United States during the 1840s and 1850s. Almost 4.5 million immigrants arrived between 1840 and 1860, six times more than had come during the previous two decades (**Figure 12.1**).

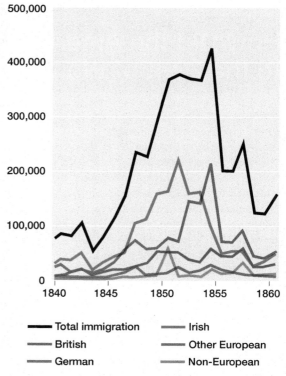

FIGURE 12.1 ▲ Antebellum Immigration, 1840–1860
Immigration shot up in the mid-1840s. Between 1848 and 1860, nearly 3.5 million immigrants entered the United States.

ANALYZE EVIDENCE
How did the free-labor ideal influence white women's experiences?

How did the free-labor ideal explain economic inequality?	What spurred westward expansion?	Why did the United States go to war with Mexico?	What changes did social reformers seek in the 1840s and 1850s?	Conclusion: How did the free-labor ideal contribute to economic growth?

How Did the American Economy Compare to the Rest of the World?

By the 1850s, the U.S. economy had achieved a remarkable economic transformation. In 1801, when president-elect Thomas Jefferson rode horseback 180 miles from his home in Monticello, Virginia, to Washington, D.C., he had to swim his horse across several rivers that lacked bridges or ferries. In 1861, when president-elect Abraham Lincoln traveled more than 1,000 miles to Washington from his home in Springfield, Illinois, he did not need to get wet swimming across rivers. He rode the entire way on railroads. The changes that made Lincoln's journey possible created an American economy that produced more goods and services per capita than any other country in the world, except one— Great Britain.

In the 1850s, some countries in the world produced more total goods and services than the United States. But since they had much larger populations than the United States, they produced much less per capita. For example, China produced roughly four times more than the United States. But since the Chinese population was about twenty times greater than that of the United States, the per capita production of China was only about one-fifth that of the United States.

In other words, if all the goods and services in China and the United States in 1850 had been shared equally by the people who lived in each country, each person in China would have had only one-fifth as much as each person in the United States.

▲ The prosperous couple entering the door brings blankets and parcels probably containing food to this poverty-stricken family living in a barren attic. The charity provided by the benevolent couple offered a small measure of temporary relief, but it did not promise a long-term solution to the poor family's plight. The clothing and bodily postures in the painting highlight the contrast between poverty and prosperity in the mid-nineteenth century. The Granger Collection, New York.

Of course, all goods and services were never shared equally in either country (or in any other country for that matter). Rich people had more than poor people; landowners had more than laborers; slave owners had more than slaves; and so on. Still, per capita production can serve as an imperfect but revealing indicator of the general prosperity of a country's economy.

Nearly three-fourths of the immigrants who arrived between 1840 and 1860 came from either Germany or Ireland. The majority of the 1.4 million Germans who entered during these years were skilled tradesmen and their families. Roughly one-quarter were farmers, many of whom settled in Texas. German Americans were often Protestants. They usually were the kind of independent producers celebrated by free-labor spokesmen. Relatively few worked as wage laborers or domestic servants.

Why did "industrial evolution" occur?

Like China, African countries were about one-fifth as prosperous as the United States. India, Japan, Mexico, and Brazil had somewhat more prosperous economies, with per capita production about one-third that of the United States. European countries such as Russia, Spain, and Italy were about half as prosperous as the United States. Overall, more than 90 percent of the people in the world in 1850 lived in countries whose economies produced half or less (much less, for most people) per capita than did the economy of the United States. In other words, the vast majority of the global population was, in general, much poorer than people in the United States.

The American economy surpassed even the two largest countries of western continental Europe, France and Germany. Both countries, like the United States, had started to industrialize, making them far more prosperous than most of the world. But they lagged behind the United States in per capita production. Germany's per capita production was about 80 percent of the United States; France's was about 90 percent.

Great Britain, the most prosperous country in the world in 1850, surpassed the per capita production of the United States by 30 percent. With a population of 21 million, slightly fewer than the 23 million residents of the United States, Britain produced a whopping 45 percent of the world's manufactured goods.

Three factors were especially important in Britain's economic leadership. First, most people in Britain had moved to towns and cities by 1850. Rural folks made up only 22 percent of Britain's population, compared to 85 percent of the U.S. population. Many urban dwellers worked in industries that, in general, were more productive than agriculture, boosting British output. Second, wages were relatively high in Britain, giving manufacturers a big incentive to replace costly labor with machinery. Although machinery required capital outlays to set up and maintain, it was far more efficient and tireless than wageworkers.

Manufacturers in both Britain and the United States had similar incentives to industrialize, but British producers did so first and with far greater effectiveness than those in the United States. An important reason was Britain's cheap and nearly inexhaustible source of energy—coal, which was the third crucial factor in Britain's economic leadership. Britain had huge deposits of coal that could be mined relatively easily, making coal prices much lower than in the rest of the world. Low coal prices gave manufacturers a cheap energy source, making it less costly for them to adopt innovative industrial techniques that boosted production such as steam power. In 1850, coal consumption in Britain was ten times greater than in France and seven times greater than in Germany and the United States. Britain's unique combination of cheap energy, high wages, and a large urban population helped make it the most productive and prosperous country in the world in 1850.

Questions for Analysis

SUMMARIZE THE ARGUMENT: In 1850, how did U.S. prosperity compare to that of the rest of the world?

ANALYZE THE EVIDENCE: Why did Britain have the world's leading economy in 1850? What accounted for Britain's success compared to the United States?

CONSIDER THE CONTEXT: What does the pattern of global prosperity and poverty in 1850 suggest about the motivations for immigration to the United States?

RECOGNIZE VIEWPOINTS: To what extent is per capita production a misleading measure of prosperity? Can you think of better measures?

ASK HISTORICAL QUESTIONS: How did the comparative economic prosperity of the United States influence the experiences and ideas of Americans during the 1850s?

Irish immigrants, in contrast, entered at the bottom of the free-labor ladder and struggled to climb up. Nearly 1.7 million Irish immigrants arrived between 1840 and 1860, nearly all of them desperately poor and often weakened by hunger and disease. Potato blight caused a deadly famine in Ireland in 1845, and it returned repeatedly year after year. Many Irish people crowded into ships and sailed to America, where they settled in northeastern cities. As one immigrant group declared, "All we want is to get out of Ireland; we must be better anywhere than here."

How did the free-labor ideal explain economic inequality?	What spurred westward expansion?	Why did the United States go to war with Mexico?	What changes did social reformers seek in the 1840s and 1850s?	Conclusion: How did the free-labor ideal contribute to economic growth?

▶ **A German Immigrant in New York** This 1855 painting depicts a German immigrant in New York City asking directions from an African American man cutting firewood. Like many other German immigrants, the man shown here appears fairly well off. Unlike most Irish immigrants, who arrived without family members, his daughter and son accompany the German immigrant. North Carolina Museum of Art, Raleigh, purchased with funds from the State of North Carolina (52.9.2).

READING THE IMAGE: How does the clothing of the German immigrant compare to that of the black man cutting wood and the white laborer on the right? What racial attitudes are illustrated by the painting?

CONNECTIONS: How did mid-nineteenth-century immigrants compare to native-born Americans?

Roughly three out of four Irish immigrants worked as wage laborers or domestic servants. Irish men dug canals, loaded ships, laid railroad track, and did odd jobs. Irish women worked in the homes of others—cooking, washing, ironing, minding children, and cleaning house. Almost all Irish immigrants were Catholic, which set them apart from the overwhelmingly Protestant native-born Americans. Many Americans regarded the Irish as hard-drinking, unruly, half-civilized folk. Job announcements commonly stated, "No Irish need apply." One immigrant recalled that Irish laborers were thought of as "nothing . . . more than dogs . . . despised and kicked about." Despite such prejudices, Americans hired Irish immigrants because they accepted low pay and worked hard.

In America's labor-poor economy, Irish laborers could earn more in one day than in several weeks in Ireland. In America, one immigrant explained in 1853, there was "plenty of work and plenty of wages plenty to eat and no land lords thats enough what more does a man want." But many immigrants also craved respect and decent working conditions.

The opportunities for immigrants and native-born laborers often did not live up to the optimistic vision outlined by the free-labor ideal. Many wage laborers could not realistically aspire to become independent, self-sufficient property holders, despite the claims of Abraham Lincoln and other free-labor proponents.

UNDERSTAND POINTS OF VIEW

Why did the free-labor ideal appeal to Americans?

QUICK REVIEW

How did the free-labor ideal explain economic and social inequality?

Why did "industrial evolution" occur?

What spurred westward expansion?

Beginning in the 1840s, the nation's expanding population, booming economy, and boundless confidence propelled a new era of rapid westward migration. Under the banner of manifest destiny, Americans moved west of the Mississippi River, where they encountered Native Americans, who inhabited the plains, deserts, and rugged coasts of the West; the British, who claimed the Oregon Country; and the Mexicans, whose flag flew over the vast expanse of the Southwest. Nevertheless, by 1850, the United States stretched to the Pacific and included the Utah Territory with its Mormon settlement.

Frontier settlers took the land and then, with the exception of the Mormons, lobbied the federal government to acquire the territory they had settled. The human cost of expansion was high. The young Mexican nation lost a war and half of its territory. Two centuries of Indian wars, which ended east of the Mississippi during the 1830s, continued for another half century in the West.

Manifest Destiny

Most Americans believed that their superior institutions and white skin bestowed on them a God-given right to spread across the continent. They imagined the West as a howling wilderness, empty and undeveloped. If they recognized Indians and Mexicans at all, they dismissed them as primitives who would have to be redeemed, shoved aside, or extermi-nated. The West provided young men especially an arena in which to "show their man-hood." Most Americans believed that the West needed the civilizing power of the hammer and the plow, the ballot box and the pulpit, which had transformed the East.

In 1845, a New York magazine edited by John L. O'Sullivan coined the term *manifest destiny* to justify white settlers taking the land they wanted. O'Sullivan called on Americans to resist any effort to thwart "the fulfillment of our manifest destiny to overspread the continent allotted by Providence for the free development of our yearly multiplying millions . . . [and] for the development of the great experiment of liberty and federative self-government entrusted to us." Almost overnight, the magic phrase *manifest destiny* swept the nation, providing a defense for conquering the West.

As important as national pride and racial arrogance were to manifest destiny, land hunger drew hundreds of thousands of Americans westward. Some politicians believed that national prosperity depended on capturing the rich trade of Asia. To trade with the Far East, the United States needed the Pacific coast ports that stretched from San Diego to Puget Sound. The United States and Asia must "talk together, and trade together," Missouri senator Thomas Hart Benton declared. "Commerce is a great civilizer." In the 1840s, American economic expansion came wrapped in talk of uplift and civilization.

Oregon and the Overland Trail

American expansionists and the British competed for the Oregon Country—a vast region bounded on the west by the Pacific Ocean, on the east by the Rocky Mountains, on the south by the forty-second parallel, and on the north by Russian Alaska. In 1818, the United States and Great Britain decided on "joint occupation" that would leave Oregon "free and open" to settlement by both countries. By the 1820s, a handful of American fur traders and "mountain men" roamed the region.

In the late 1830s, settlers began to trickle along the Oregon Trail (**Map 12.2**). The first wagon trains headed west in 1841, and by 1843 about 1,000 emigrants a year set out from Independence, Missouri. By 1869, when the first transcontinental railroad was completed, approximately 350,000 migrants had traveled west in wagon trains.

CHRONOLOGY

1836
- Battle of the Alamo fought.
- Texas declares independence from Mexico.

1841
- First wagon trains head west on Oregon Trail.

1845
- Term *manifest destiny* coined.

1846
- Bear Flag Revolt movement raised in California.

1847
- Mormons settle in Utah.

1850
- Utah Territory annexed.

1851
- Fort Laramie conference marks beginning of Indian concentration.

1857
- Mormon War reasserts U.S. authority in Utah.

manifest destiny
Term coined in 1845 by journalist John L. O'Sullivan to justify American expansion.

Oregon Trail
Route from Independence, Missouri, to Oregon traveled by American settlers starting in the late 1830s.

| How did the free-labor ideal explain economic inequality? | **What spurred westward expansion?** | Why did the United States go to war with Mexico? | What changes did social reformers seek in the 1840s and 1850s? | Conclusion: How did the free-labor ideal contribute to economic growth? |

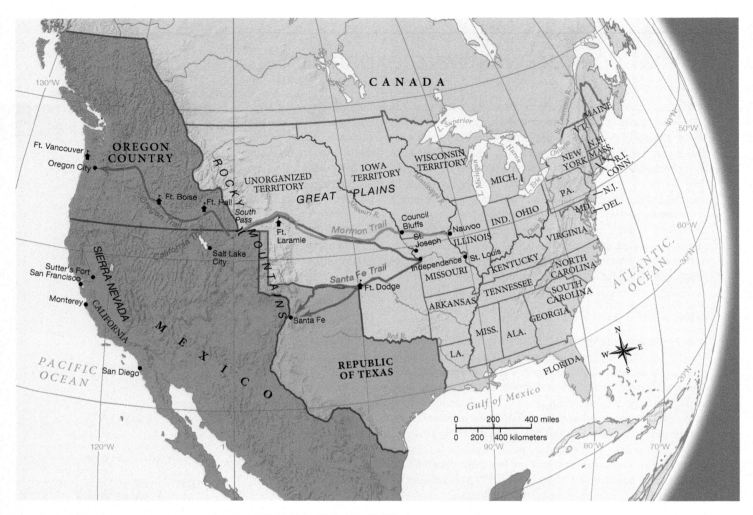

MAP 12.2 ▲ Major Trails West

In the 1830s, wagon trains began snaking their way to the Southwest and the Pacific coast. Deep ruts, some of which can still be seen today, soon marked the most popular routes.

Emigrants encountered the Plains Indians, a quarter of a million Native Americans scattered over the area between the Mississippi River and the Rocky Mountains. Some were farmers who lived peaceful, settled lives, but a majority—the Sioux, Cheyenne, Shoshoni, and Arapaho of the central plains, and the Kiowa, Wichita, and Comanche of the southern plains—were horse-mounted, nomadic, nonagricultural peoples whose warriors symbolized the "savage Indian" in the minds of whites.

Horses, which had been brought to North America by Spaniards in the sixteenth century, permitted the Plains tribes to become highly mobile hunters of buffalo. They came to depend on buffalo for nearly everything—food, clothing, shelter, and fuel. Competition for buffalo led to war between the tribes. Young men were introduced to warfare early, learning to ride ponies at breakneck speed while firing off arrows and, later, rifles with astounding accuracy. "A Comanche on his feet is out of his element," observed western artist George Catlin, "but the moment he lays his hands upon his horse, his *face* even becomes handsome, and he gracefully flies away like a different being."

The Plains Indians struck fear in the hearts of whites on the wagon trains. But Native Americans had far more to fear from whites. Indians killed fewer than four hundred emigrants on the trail between 1840 and 1860, while whites brought alcohol and deadly epidemics, and white hunters slaughtered buffalo for the international hide market and sometimes just for sport.

CONSIDER CAUSE AND EFFECT

What did westward migration in the 1840s and 1850s mean for Native Americans who lived west of the Mississippi River?

Why did "industrial evolution" occur?

◀ **Members of the Sioux Dakota Tribe, by George Catlin, 1854** Beginning in the 1830s, artist George Catlin, convinced that Indian cultures would soon disappear, roamed the West painting Native Americans in their own environments. Here Catlin pictures a warrior, women, and children of the Dakota Sioux, who were a farming people driven westward into the Great Plains, where they became a feared horse-riding society. bpk Bildagentur/Ethnologisches Museum, Staatliche Museen, Berlin/Gisela Oestreich/Art Resource, NY.

The government constructed a chain of forts along the Oregon Trail (see Map 12.2) and adopted a new Indian policy: "concentration." In 1851 at the Fort Laramie conference, the government persuaded the Plains Indians to sign agreements that cleared a wide corridor for wagon trains by restricting Native Americans to specific areas that whites promised they would never violate. This policy of concentration became the seedbed for the subsequent policy of reservations. But whites would not keep out of Indian territory, and Indians would not easily give up their traditional ways of life. Struggle for control of the West meant warfare for decades to come.

Still, Indians threatened emigrants less than life on the trail did. Emigrants could count on at least six months of hard travel. With nearly two thousand miles to go and making no more than fifteen miles a day, the pioneers endured parching heat, drought, treacherous rivers, disease, physical and emotional exhaustion, and, if the snows closed the mountain passes before they got through, freezing and starvation. Women faced the ordeal of trailside childbirth. It was said that a person could walk from Missouri to the Pacific stepping only on the graves of those who had died heading west.

Men usually found Oregon "one of the greatest countries in the world." From "the Cascade mountains to the Pacific, the whole country can be cultivated," declared one eager farmer. When women reached Oregon, they found that things were in a "primitive state." "I had all I could do to keep from asking George to turn around and bring me back home," one woman wrote to her mother in Missouri. Work seemed unending. "I am a very old woman," declared twenty-nine-year-old Sarah Everett. "My face is thin sunken and wrinkled, my hands bony withered and hard." Another settler observed, "A woman that can not endure almost as much as a horse has no business here." Yet despite the ordeal of the trail and the difficulties of starting from scratch, emigrants kept coming.

Plains Indians and Trails West in the 1840s and 1850s

The Mormon Exodus

Not every wagon train heading west was bound for the Pacific Slope. One remarkable group of religious emigrants halted near the Great Salt Lake in what was then Mexican territory. After years of persecution in the East, the Mormons fled west to find religious freedom and communal security.

Mormons
Members of the Church of Jesus Christ of Latter-Day Saints founded by Joseph Smith in 1830.

How did the free-labor ideal explain economic inequality?	**What spurred westward expansion?**	Why did the United States go to war with Mexico?	What changes did social reformers seek in the 1840s and 1850s?	Conclusion: How did the free-labor ideal contribute to economic growth?

▶ **Mormon Family** Most of America found the Mormon practice of polygamy deeply offensive. In 1890, the Mormons officially abandoned plural marriages, but in this photograph from Salt Lake City in the 1850s, a husband, his three wives, and their five children sit for a family portrait.

READING THE IMAGE: How would you describe the family's attitude about their unusual family constellation—at ease and proud or uneasy and embarrassed?

CONNECTIONS: Why would most Americans find the Mormon practice of plural marriage so disturbing?

In the 1820s, an upstate New York farm boy named Joseph Smith Jr. said that he was visited by an angel who led him to golden tablets buried near his home. With the aid of magic stones, he translated the mysterious language on the tablets to produce *The Book of Mormon*, which he published in 1830. It told the story of an ancient Hebrew civilization in the New World and predicted the appearance of an American prophet who would reestablish Jesus Christ's kingdom in America. Converts, attracted to the promise of a pure faith in the midst of antebellum America's social turmoil and runaway materialism, flocked to the new Church of Jesus Christ of Latter-Day Saints (the Mormons).

Neighbors branded Mormons heretics and drove Smith and his followers from New York to Ohio, then to Missouri, and finally in 1839 to Nauvoo, Illinois, where they built a prosperous community. But after Smith sanctioned "plural marriage" (polygamy), non-Mormons arrested Smith and his brother. On June 27, 1844, a mob stormed the jail and shot both men dead.

The embattled church turned to an extraordinary new leader, Brigham Young, who oversaw a great exodus. In 1846, traveling in 3,700 wagons, twelve thousand Mormons made their way to Iowa and then on to their new home beside the Great Salt Lake. Young described the region as a barren waste, "the paradise of the lizard, the cricket and the rattlesnake." Within ten years, however, the Mormons developed an irrigation system that made the desert bloom. Under Young's stern leadership, the Mormons built a thriving community using cooperative labor, not the individualistic and competitive enterprise common among most emigrants.

In 1850, the United States annexed the Mormon kingdom as the Utah Territory. Shortly afterward, Brigham Young announced that many Mormons practiced polygamy. Although only one Mormon man in five had more than one wife (Young had twenty-three), Young's statement caused an outcry that forced the U.S. government to establish its authority in Utah. In 1857, 2,500 U.S. troops invaded Salt Lake City in what was known as the Mormon War. The bloodless occupation illustrated that most Americans viewed the Mormons as a threat to American morality and institutions.

Why did "industrial evolution" occur?

The Mexican Borderlands

In the Mexican Southwest, westward-moving Anglo-American pioneers confronted northern-moving Spanish-speaking frontiersmen. On this frontier as elsewhere, national cultures and interests collided. Mexico won its independence from Spain in 1821 (**Map 12.3**), but the young nation was plagued by civil wars, economic crises, quarrels with the Roman Catholic Church, and devastating raids by the Comanche, Apache, and Kiowa. Mexico found it increasingly difficult to defend its sparsely populated northern provinces, especially when faced with a neighbor convinced of its superiority and bent on territorial acquisition.

The American assault began quietly. In the 1820s, Anglo-American traders drifted into Santa Fe, a remote outpost in the northern province of New Mexico. The traders made the long trek southwest along the Santa Fe Trail (see Map 12.2) with wagons crammed with inexpensive American manufactured goods and returned home with Mexican silver, furs, and mules.

The Mexican province of Texas attracted a flood of Americans who had settlement, not long-distance trade, on their minds (see Map 12.3). Wanting to populate and develop its northern territory, the Mexican government granted the American Stephen F. Austin a huge tract of land along the Brazos River. In the 1820s, when Austin offered land at only ten cents an acre, thousands of Americans poured across the border. Most were Southerners who brought cotton and slaves with them.

By the 1830s, settlers had established a thriving plantation economy in Texas. Americans numbered 35,000, while the *Tejano* (Spanish-speaking) population was less than 8,000. Few Anglo-American settlers were Roman Catholic, spoke Spanish, or cared about assimilating into Mexican culture. Afraid of losing Texas to the new arrivals, the Mexican government in 1830 banned further emigration from the United States and outlawed the introduction of additional slaves. Anglo-Americans in Texas

Texas War for Independence, 1836

MAP 12.3 ◀ Texas and Mexico in the 1830s

As Americans spilled into lightly populated and loosely governed northern Mexico, Texas and then other Mexican provinces became contested territory.

How did the free-labor ideal explain economic inequality?	**What spurred westward expansion?**	Why did the United States go to war with Mexico?	What changes did social reformers seek in the 1840s and 1850s?	Conclusion: How did the free-labor ideal contribute to economic growth?

COMPARE AND CONTRAST
How was the settling of the Utah Territory similar to and different from the settling of Texas?

made it clear that they wanted to be rid of the "despotism of the sword and the priesthood" and to govern themselves.

When the Texan settlers rebelled, General Antonio López de Santa Anna ordered the Mexican army to San Antonio. The rebels, commanded by Colonel William B. Travis from Alabama and including the Tennessee frontiersman Davy Crockett and the Louisiana adventurer James Bowie as well as a handful of Tejanos, had occupied a former Franciscan mission known as the Alamo. In February 1836, Santa Anna sent wave after wave of his 2,000-man army crashing against the walls until the attackers finally broke through and killed all 187 rebels. A few weeks later, outside the small town of Goliad, Mexican forces captured and executed almost 400 Texans as "pirates and outlaws." In April 1836, at San Jacinto, General Sam Houston's army adopted the massacre of Goliad as a battle cry and crushed Santa Anna's troops in a surprise attack. The Texans had succeeded in establishing the Lone Star Republic, and the following year the United States recognized the independence of Texas from Mexico.

Lone Star Republic
Independent republic, also known as the Republic of Texas, that was established by a rebellion of Texans against Mexican rule.

Earlier, in 1824, seeking to increase Mexican migration to the province of California, the Mexican government granted *ranchos*—huge estates devoted to cattle raising—to new settlers. *Rancheros* ruled over near-feudal empires worked by Indians whose condition sometimes approached that of slaves. In 1834, *rancheros* persuaded the Mexican government to confiscate the Franciscan missions and make their vast lands available to new settlement.

Despite the efforts of the Mexican government, California in 1840 had a population of only 7,000 Mexican settlers. Non-Mexican settlers numbered only 380, but among them were Americans who championed manifest destiny. They convinced some American emigrants who were traveling the Oregon Trail to head southwest on the California Trail (see Map 12.2). The first overland party arrived in California in 1841. As a New York newspaper observed in 1845, "Let the tide of emigration flow toward California and the American population will soon be sufficiently numerous to play the Texas game." Few Americans in California wanted a war, but many dreamed of living again under the U.S. flag.

In 1846, American settlers in the Sacramento Valley took matters into their own hands. Encouraged by John C. Frémont, a former army captain and explorer who had arrived with a party of sixty buckskin-clad frontiersmen, the Californians raised an independence movement known as the Bear Flag Revolt. By then, James K. Polk, a champion of expansion, sat in the White House.

QUICK REVIEW

Why did westward migration expand dramatically in the mid-nineteenth century?

Why did the United States go to war with Mexico?

Although emigrants acted as the advance guard of American empire, there was nothing automatic about the U.S. annexation of territory in the West. Acquiring territory required political action. In the 1840s, expansion became entangled with sectionalism and the slavery question. Texas, Oregon, and the Mexican borderlands also thrust the United States into dangerous diplomatic crises with Great Britain and Mexico.

Aggravation between Mexico and the United States escalated to open antagonism in 1845 when the United States annexed Texas. Absorbing territory still claimed by Mexico set

Why did "industrial evolution" occur?

the stage for war. But it was President James K. Polk's insistence on having Mexico's other northern provinces that made war certain. The war was not as easy as Polk anticipated, but it ended in American victory and the acquisition of a new American West. The discovery of gold in one of the nation's new territories, California, prompted a massive wave of emigration that nearly destroyed Native American and *Californio* societies.

The Politics of Expansion

Texans had sought admission to the Union almost since winning their independence from Mexico in 1836. But any suggestion of adding another slave state to the Union outraged most Northerners, who applauded westward expansion but imagined the expansion of liberty, not slavery.

John Tyler, who became president in April 1841 when William Henry Harrison died one month after taking office, understood that Texas was a dangerous issue because of slavery. Adding to the danger, Great Britain began sniffing around Texas, apparently contemplating adding the young republic to its growing empire. In 1844, Tyler, who was a passionate expansionist, decided to risk annexing the Lone Star Republic. Predictably, howls of protest erupted across the North. Future Massachusetts senator Charles Sumner deplored the "insidious" plan to annex Texas and carve from it "great slaveholding states." The Senate soundly rejected the annexation treaty.

During the election of 1844, the Whig nominee for president, Henry Clay, in an effort to woo northern voters, came out against annexation of Texas. "Annexation and war with Mexico are identical," he declared. But the Democratic nominee, Tennessean James K. Polk, vigorously backed annexation. To make annexation acceptable to Northerners, the Democrats cleverly yoked the annexation of Texas to the annexation of Oregon, thus tapping the desire for expansion in the free states of the North as well as in the slave states of the South. The Democratic platform called for the "reannexation of Texas" and the "reoccupation of Oregon." The statement that the United States was merely reasserting existing rights was poor history but good politics.

When Clay finally recognized the popularity of expansion, he waffled, hinting that he might accept the annexation of Texas after all. His retreat succeeded only in alienating antislavery opinion in the North. James G. Birney, the candidate of the new Liberty Party, denounced Clay as "rotten as a stagnant fish pond" and picked up the votes of thousands of disillusioned Clay supporters. In the November election, Polk won a narrow victory.

In his inaugural address on March 4, 1845, Polk defended America's manifest destiny. "This heaven-favored land," he proclaimed, enjoyed the "most admirable and wisest system of well-regulated self-government . . . ever devised by human minds." He asked, "Who shall assign limits to the achievements of free minds and free hands under the protection of this glorious Union?"

The nation did not have to wait for Polk's inauguration to see results from his victory. One month after the election, President Tyler announced that the triumph of the Democratic Party provided a mandate for the annexation of Texas "promptly and immediately." In February 1845, after a fierce debate between antislavery and proslavery forces, Congress approved a joint resolution offering the Republic of Texas admission to the United States. Texas entered as the fifteenth slave state.

While Tyler delivered Texas, Polk had promised Oregon, too. Westerners particularly demanded that the new president make good on the Democratic pledge "Fifty-four forty or Fight"—that is, all of Oregon, right up to Alaska (54° 40' was the southern latitude of Russian Alaska). But Polk was close to war with Mexico and could not afford a war with Britain over U.S. claims in Canada. He renewed an old offer to divide Oregon along the forty-ninth parallel. Westerners cried betrayal, but when Britain accepted the compromise, the nation gained an enormous territory peacefully. When the Senate approved the treaty in June 1846, the United States and Mexico were already at war.

CHRONOLOGY

1841
- Vice President John Tyler becomes president when William Henry Harrison dies.

1844
- James K. Polk elected president.

1845
- Texas enters Union as slave state.

1846
- Congress declares war on Mexico.
- United States and Great Britain divide Oregon Country.

1848
- Treaty of Guadalupe Hidalgo signed.

1849
- California gold rush begins.

TRACE CHANGE OVER TIME
How did American political leaders accomplish the annexation of Texas?

How did the free-labor ideal explain economic inequality?	What spurred westward expansion?	**Why did the United States go to war with Mexico?**	What changes did social reformers seek in the 1840s and 1850s?	Conclusion: How did the free-labor ideal contribute to economic growth?

The Mexican-American War, 1846–1848

From the day he entered the White House, Polk craved Mexico's remaining northern provinces: California and New Mexico, land that today makes up California, Nevada, Utah, most of New Mexico and Arizona, and parts of Wyoming and Colorado. Since the 1830s, Indians had attacked Mexican ranches and towns, killing thousands, and Polk pointed to Mexico's inability to control its northern provinces to undermine its claims to them. The president hoped to buy the territory, but when the Mexicans refused to sell, he concluded that military force would be needed to realize the United States' manifest destiny.

Polk ordered General Zachary Taylor to march his four-thousand-man army 150 miles south from the Nueces River, the southern boundary of Texas according to the Mexicans, to the banks of the Rio Grande, the boundary claimed by Texans (**Map 12.4**). Lieutenant George G. Meade, who would later command troops at

MAP 12.4 ▲ The Mexican-American War, 1846–1848

American and Mexican soldiers skirmished across much of northern Mexico, but the major battles took place between the Rio Grande and Mexico City.

Why did "industrial evolution" occur?

Gettysburg, admitted, "I hope for a war and a speedy battle." Viewing the American advance as aggression, Mexican cavalry on April 25, 1846, attacked a party of American soldiers, killing or wounding sixteen.

On May 11, the president told Congress, "Mexico has passed the boundary of the United States, has invaded our territory, and shed American blood upon American soil." Thus "war exists, and, notwithstanding all our efforts to avoid it, exists by the act of Mexico herself." Congress passed a declaration of war and began raising an army. The U.S. Army was pitifully small, only 8,600 soldiers. Faced with the nation's first foreign war, against a Mexican army that numbered more than 30,000, Polk called for volunteers. More than 30,000 Tennesseans competed for the state's 3,000 allotted positions. Eventually, more than 112,000 white Americans (40 percent were immigrants; blacks were banned) joined the army to fight in Mexico.

Despite the flood of volunteers, the war divided the nation. Northern Whigs in particular condemned the war. The Massachusetts legislature claimed that the war was being fought for the "triple object of extending slavery, of strengthening the slave power, and of obtaining control of the free states." On January 12, 1848, a gangly freshman Whig representative from Illinois rose in the House of Representatives and likened the president's views to the "half-insane mumbling of a fever dream." He proclaimed Polk a "bewildered, confounded, and miserably perplexed man." Before Abraham Lincoln sat down, he had questioned Polk's intelligence, honesty, and sanity. The president ignored the upstart representative, but antislavery, antiwar Whigs kept up the attack throughout the conflict.

President Polk expected a short war in which U.S. armies would occupy Mexico's northern provinces and defeat the Mexican army in a decisive battle or two, after

UNDERSTAND POINTS OF VIEW

How persuasive were Polk's arguments for war with Mexico?

▲ *Batalla del Sacramento*, **by Julio Michaud y Thomas** Artists from the United States created most images of the Mexican-American War, but Mexicans also recorded the war. In this hand-colored lithograph, Mexican artist Julio Michaud y Thomas depicts the February 1847 battle in which 1,100 American troops engaged 3,000 Mexicans on the banks of the Sacramento River near Chihuahua. Beinecke Rare Book and Manuscript Library, Yale University.

How did the free-labor ideal explain economic inequality?	What spurred westward expansion?	**Why did the United States go to war with Mexico?**	What changes did social reformers seek in the 1840s and 1850s?	Conclusion: How did the free-labor ideal contribute to economic growth?

which Mexico would sue for peace and the United States would keep the territory its armies occupied.

At first, Polk's strategy seemed to work. In May 1846, Zachary Taylor's troops drove south from the Rio Grande and routed the Mexican army, first at Palo Alto, then at Resaca de la Palma (see Map 12.4). "Old Rough and Ready," as Taylor's troops called him, became an instant war hero. Polk rewarded Taylor for his victories by making him commander of the Mexican campaign.

A second prong of the campaign centered on Colonel Stephen Watts Kearny, who led a 1,700-man army from Missouri into New Mexico. Without firing a shot, U.S. forces took Santa Fe in August 1846. Kearny then marched to San Diego, where he encountered a major Mexican rebellion against American rule. In January 1847, after several clashes and severe losses, U.S. forces occupied Los Angeles. California and New Mexico were in American hands.

By then, Taylor had driven deep into the interior of Mexico. In September 1846, after house-to-house fighting, he had taken the city of Monterrey. Taylor pushed his 5,000 troops southwest, where the Mexican hero of the Alamo, General Antonio López de Santa Anna, was concentrating an army of 21,000. On February 23, 1847, Santa Anna's troops attacked Taylor at Buena Vista. The Americans won the day but suffered heavy casualties. The Mexicans suffered even greater losses (some 3,400 dead, wounded, and missing, compared with 650 Americans). During the night, Santa Anna withdrew his battered army.

> "'I can assure you that fighting is the least dangerous & arduous part of a soldier's life,' one young man declared."

Uninterrupted victories in northern Mexico fed the American troops' sense of invincibility. "No American force has ever thought of being defeated by any amount of Mexican troops," one soldier declared. The Americans worried about other hazards, however. "I can assure you that fighting is the least dangerous & arduous part of a soldier's life," one young man declared. Letters home told of torturous marches across deserts alive with tarantulas, scorpions, and rattlesnakes. Others recounted dysentery, malaria, smallpox, cholera, and yellow fever. Of the 13,000 American soldiers who died (some 50,000 Mexicans perished), fewer than 2,000 fell to Mexican bullets and shells. Disease killed most of the others. Medicine was so primitive that, as one Tennessee man observed, "nearly all who take sick die."

Victory in Mexico

Despite heavy losses on the battlefield, Mexico refused to trade land for peace. One American soldier captured the Mexican mood: "They cannot submit to be deprived of California after the loss of Texas, and nothing but the conquest of their Capital will force them to such a humiliation." President Polk had arrived at the same conclusion. While Taylor occupied the north, Polk ordered General Winfield Scott to land an army on the Gulf coast of Mexico and march 250 miles inland to Mexico City. The plan entailed enormous risk because Scott would have to cut himself off from supplies and lead his men deep into enemy country against a much larger army.

An amphibious landing on March 9, 1847, near Veracruz put some 10,000 American troops ashore. After furious shelling, Veracruz surrendered. In April 1847, after gathering 9,300 wagons, 17,000 pack mules, 500,000 bushels of oats and corn, and 100 pounds of blister ointment, Scott's forces moved westward, following the path blazed more than three centuries earlier by Hernán Cortés to "the halls of Montezuma" (see chapter 2).

After the defeat at Buena Vista, Santa Anna had returned to Mexico City, where he rallied his ragged troops and marched them east to set a trap for Scott in the mountain pass at Cerro Gordo. Knifing through Mexican lines, the Americans almost captured

Why did "industrial evolution" occur?

Santa Anna, who fled the field on foot. So complete was the victory that Scott gloated to Taylor, "Mexico no longer has an army." But Santa Anna again rallied the Mexican army. Some 30,000 troops took up defensive positions on the outskirts of Mexico City and began melting down church bells to cast new cannons.

In August 1847, Scott began his assault on the Mexican capital. The fighting proved the most brutal of the war. Santa Anna backed his army into the city, fighting each step of the way. At the battle of Churubusco, the Mexicans took 4,000 casualties in a single day and the Americans more than 1,000. At the castle of Chapultepec, American troops scaled the walls and fought the Mexican defenders hand to hand. After Chapultepec, Mexico City officials persuaded Santa Anna to evacuate the city to save it from destruction, and on September 14, 1847, Scott rode in triumphantly.

On February 2, 1848, American and Mexican officials signed the **Treaty of Guadalupe Hidalgo** in Mexico City. Mexico agreed to give up all claims to Texas north of the Rio Grande and to cede the provinces of New Mexico and California—more than 500,000 square miles—to the United States (see Map 12.4). The United States agreed to pay Mexico $15 million and to assume $3.25 million in claims that American citizens had against Mexico. Some Americans clamored for all of Mexico, but the treaty gave the president all he wanted. In March 1848, the Senate ratified the treaty. Polk had his Rio Grande border, his Pacific ports, and all the land that lay between.

The American triumph had enormous consequences. Less than three-quarters of a century after its founding, the United States had achieved its self-proclaimed manifest destiny to stretch from the Atlantic to the Pacific (**Map 12.5**). It would enter the industrial age with vast new natural resources and a two-ocean economy, while Mexico faced a sharply diminished economic future.

Treaty of Guadalupe Hidalgo
February 1848 treaty that ended the Mexican-American War.

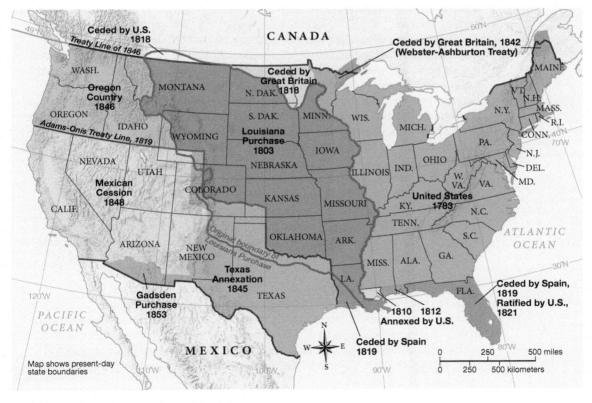

MAP 12.5 ▲ Territorial Expansion by 1860

Less than a century after its founding, the United States spread from the Atlantic seaboard to the Pacific coast. War, purchase, and diplomacy had gained a continent.

| How did the free-labor ideal explain economic inequality? | What spurred westward expansion? | **Why did the United States go to war with Mexico?** | What changes did social reformers seek in the 1840s and 1850s? | Conclusion: How did the free-labor ideal contribute to economic growth? |

Golden California

California gold rush
Mining rush initiated by James Marshall's discovery of gold in the foothills of the Sierra Nevada in 1848.

Another consequence of the Mexican defeat was that California gold poured into American, not Mexican, pockets. In January 1848, James Marshall discovered gold in the American River in the foothills of the Sierra Nevada. His discovery set off the **California gold rush**, one of the wildest mining stampedes in the world's history. Between 1849 and 1852, more than 250,000 "forty-niners," as the miners were known, descended on the Golden State. In less than two years, Marshall's discovery transformed California from foreign territory into a state.

Gold fever quickly spread around the world. A flood of men of various races and nationalities poured into California, where they remade the quiet world of Mexican ranches into a roaring mining-town economy. Only a few struck it rich, and life in the goldfields was nasty, brutish, and often short. The prospectors who filled Hangtown, Hell's Delight, Gouge Eye, and a hundred other crude mining camps faced cholera and scurvy, exorbitant prices, deadly encounters with claim jumpers, and endless backbreaking labor. **(See "Analyzing Historical Evidence: The Gold Rush" on page 350.)**

By 1853, San Francisco had grown into a raw city of 50,000 that depended as much on gold as did the mining camps inland. Enterprising individuals learned that there was money to be made tending to the needs of miners. Hotels, saloons, restaurants, laundries, brothels, and stores of all kinds exchanged goods and services for miners' gold dust and nuggets. Violent crime was so common that in 1851, the Committee of Vigilance determined to bring order to the city. Members pledged that "no thief, burglar, incendiary or assassin shall escape punishment, either by the quibbles of the law, the insecurity of prisons, the carelessness or corruption of the police, or a laxity of those who pretended to administer justice." Lynchings proved the committee meant business.

Establishing civic order was made more difficult by California's diversity and Anglo bigotry. The Chinese attracted special scrutiny. By 1851, 25,000 Chinese lived in California, and their religion, language, dress, queues (long pigtails), eating habits, and use of opium convinced many Anglos that they were not fit citizens of the Golden State. In 1850, the California legislature passed the Foreign Miners' Tax Law, which levied high taxes on non-Americans to drive them from the goldfields, except as hired laborers. The Chinese were restricted to certain residential areas and occupations and, along with blacks and Indians, denied public education and the right to testify in court.

Opponents demanded a halt to Chinese immigration, but Chinese leaders in San Francisco fought back. Admitting deep cultural differences, they insisted that "in the important matters we are good men. We honor our parents; we take care of our children; we are industrious and peaceable; we trade much; we are trusted for small and large sums; we pay our debts; and are honest, and of course must tell the truth." Their protests offered little protection, however, and racial violence grew.

Anglo-American prospectors asserted their dominance over other groups, including the Californios, Spanish and Mexican settlers who had lived in California for decades. Despite the U.S. government's pledge to protect Mexican and Spanish land titles, Americans took the land of the *rancheros* and through discriminatory legislation pushed Hispanic professionals, merchants, and artisans into the ranks of unskilled labor. Mariano Vallejo, a leading Californio, said of the forty-niners, "The good ones were few and the wicked many."

California's Indians would have agreed; for them, the gold rush was a disaster. Numbering some 150,000 when the gold rush began, the Indian population dropped

Why did "industrial evolution" occur?

to less than 30,000 by 1860. Forty-niners killed many. One observer described white behavior toward Indians during the gold rush as "one of the last human hunts of civilization, and the basest and most brutal of them all." The government of California sanctioned "a war of extermination . . . until the Indian race becomes extinct."

Some developments were unplanned, even unintended, but they were nevertheless deadly. So many miners poured into California, for example, that they destroyed the Indians' food supply. Malnourishment weakened resistance to disease, and epidemics of measles and chickenpox ravaged Indian societies. California Indians resisted in many ways, but they were unable to save their homelands, societies, and often themselves.

The forty-niners created dazzling wealth: In 1852, 81 million ounces of gold, nearly half of the world's production, came from California. However, most miners never struck it rich and eventually took up farming, opened small businesses, or worked for wages for the corporations that took over the mining industry. Other Americans traded furs, hides, and lumber and engaged in whaling and the China trade in tea, silk, and porcelain.

▲ **Miners, Auburn Ravine, California, 1852** More than a sluice box separates the three white miners on the left of the photograph from the Chinese miners on the right. Whites welcomed Chinese into gold country as hired laborers, not as independent miners like themselves. Fotosearch/Getty Images.

How did the free-labor ideal explain economic inequality?	What spurred westward expansion?	**Why did the United States go to war with Mexico?**	What changes did social reformers seek in the 1840s and 1850s?	Conclusion: How did the free-labor ideal contribute to economic growth?

The Gold Rush

The discovery of gold in California fired imaginations around the world. But getting to gold country was not easy. Americans in the East could sail 18,000 miles around the tip of South America; or sail to the Atlantic side of the Isthmus of Panama, slog through the jungle to the Pacific, and wait for a ship to San Francisco; or walk overland across the continent. Nothing got easier when they arrived in California. The West presented emigrants with unprecedented challenges and only occasionally with fulfillment.

DOCUMENT 1

James Marshall, Account of His Discovery of Gold, 1848

On January 24, 1848, while building a sawmill on the American River for Swiss rancher John Sutter, James Marshall found gold. Marshall gave several accounts of his discovery, but this is probably his first. Marshall never benefited from his discovery and died bitter and penniless.

One morning in January—it was a clear, cold morning; I shall never forget that morning—as I was taking my usual walk along the race after shutting off the water, my eye was caught with the glimpse of something shining in the bottom of the ditch. There was about a foot of water running then. I reached my hand down and picked it up; it made my heart thump, for I was certain it was gold. The piece was about half the size and of the shape of a pea. Then I saw another piece. . . .

When I returned to our cabin for breakfast I showed the two pieces to my men. They were all a good deal excited, and had they not thought that the gold only existed in small quantities they would have abandoned everything and left me to finish my job alone. However, to satisfy them, I told them that as soon as we had the mill finished we would devote a week or two to gold hunting and see what we could make out of it.

. . . We thought it our best policy to keep it as quiet as possible till we should have finished our mill. But there was a great number of disbanded Mormon soldiers in and about the fort, and when they came to hear of it, why it just spread like a wildfire, and soon the whole country was in a bustle. . . .

Source: James W. Marshall, "Marshall's Own Account of the Gold Discovery," *Century Illustrated Magazine*, no. 4 (Feb. 1891): 537–39.

DOCUMENT 2

Sarah Royce, Memoir of the Journey to California in 1849

In 1849, Sarah Royce, with her husband and two-year-old daughter, left New York for California. Her memoir of their journey westward by covered wagon recounts the family's encounters with Indians, cholera, thirst, and hunger. Thirty years later she wrote her memories, and in 1932, her son published them. Here she describes traveling through a desert southwest of Salt Lake City.

There was no moon yet, but by starlight we had for some time seen, only too plainly, the dead bodies of cattle lying here and there on both sides of the road. As we advanced they increased in numbers, and presently we saw two or three wagons. At first we thought we had overtaken a company but, coming close, no sign of life appeared. . . . Everything indicated a complete break down, and a hasty flight. Some animals were lying nearly in front of a wagon, apparently just as they had dropped down, while loose yokes and chains indicated that part of the teams

Still, as one observer noted, California was separated "by thousands of miles of plains, deserts, and almost impossible mountains" from the rest of the Union. Some dreamers imagined a railroad that would someday connect the Golden State with the thriving agriculture and industry of the East. Others imagined a country transformed not by transportation but by progressive individual and institutional reform.

QUICK REVIEW

What were the most significant consequences of the U.S. war with Mexico?

Why did "industrial evolution" occur?

had been driven on, laden probably with some necessaries of life; for the contents of the wagons were scattered in confusion, the most essential articles alone evidently having been thought worth carrying. . . . It was not a very encouraging scene but our four oxen still kept their feet; we would drive on a little farther, out of this scene of ruin, bait them, rest ourselves, and go on. We did so, but soon found that what we supposed an exceptional misfortune must have been the common fate of many companies; for at still shortening intervals, scenes of ruin similar to that just described kept recurring till we seemed to be but the last, little, feeble struggling band at the rear of a routed Army.

Source: Sarah Royce, *A Frontier Lady* (New Haven, CT: Yale University Press, 1932), 51–53.

DOCUMENT 3

Daniel B. Woods, Life of a California Miner, 1849

Daniel B. Woods, a Philadelphia schoolteacher, reached the diggings in California in 1849. He soon discovered that mining was very hard work, and he suspected that he would never get rich. He poured his frustration and disillusionment into his diary and after sixteen months quit gold country.

July 9th [1849]. To-day we have made $20 each. One of the conclusions at which we are rapidly arriving is that the "chances of our making a fortune in the old mines are about the same as those in favor of our drawing a prize in a lottery." No kind of work is so uncertain.

July 10th. We made three dollars each to-day. This life of severe hardship and exposure has affected my health. Our diet consists of hard bread, flour, which we eat half-cooked, and salt pork, with occasionally a salmon which we purchase of the Indians. Vegetables are not to be procured. Our feet

are wet all day, while a hot sun shines down upon our heads, and the very air parches the skin like the hot air of an oven. Our drinking water comes down to us thoroughly impregnated with the mineral substances washed through a thousand cradles above us.

After our days of labor, exhausted and faint, we *retire—if* this word may be applied to the simple act of lying down in our clothes—robbing our feet of their boots to make a pillow of them, and wrapping blankets about us, on a bed of pine boughs, or on the ground, beneath the clear, bright stars of night. . . .

Aug. 23d. After all our preparations and hopes, our toil early and late, toil of the most laborious kind, digging down in the channel of the river till the water was up to our knees, giving ourselves barely time to eat, we have made but $4 each. We sat down on the rocks, and looked at the small ridge of gold in the pan, and at each other. One fell to swearing, another to laughing.

Source: Daniel B. Woods, *Sixteen Months at the Gold Diggings* (New York: Harper & Brothers, 1851), 57–63.

Questions for Analysis

RECOGNIZE VIEWPOINTS: What was James Marshall's primary concern after he discovered gold?

ANALYZE THE EVIDENCE: What was Sarah Royce's initial understanding of her nighttime encounter? How well did Sarah Royce's and Daniel Woods's previous experiences prepare them for the gold rush?

CONSIDER THE CONTEXT: How did the realities of gold rush California fit with the promises of manifest destiny?

What changes did social reformers seek in the 1840s and 1850s?

While manifest destiny, the Mexican-American War, and the California gold rush transformed the nation's boundaries, many Americans sought personal and social reform. The emphasis on self-discipline and individual effort at the core of the free-labor ideal led Americans to believe that lack of self-control caused the major social problems of the era. Evangelical Protestants struggled to

| How did the free-labor ideal explain economic inequality? | What spurred westward expansion? | Why did the United States go to war with Mexico? | **What changes did social reformers seek in the 1840s and 1850s?** | Conclusion: How did the free-labor ideal contribute to economic growth? |

CHRONOLOGY

1840s
- Fourierist communities founded.

1848
- Oneida community organized.
- Seneca Falls convention held.

1849
- Harriet Tubman escapes from slavery and becomes leader of underground railroad.

control individuals' propensity to sin. Temperance advocates exhorted drinkers to control their taste for alcohol. Only about one-third of Americans belonged to a church in 1850, but the influence of evangelical religion reached far beyond church members.

Most reformers possessed an evangelical temperament—a belief that righteousness, energy, self-discipline, and faith could improve the world. However, a few activists pointed out that certain widespread injustices involved more than individual self-control. Transcendentalists and utopians believed that social reform required rejecting the competitive, individualistic values of mainstream society. Woman's rights activists sought to overcome the subordination of women. Abolitionists aimed to eliminate slavery and end racial discrimination. These reformers faced the difficult challenge of overturning widespread beliefs in male supremacy and white supremacy and changing the institutions of family and slavery that reinforced those beliefs.

The Pursuit of Perfection: Transcendentalists and Utopians

A group of New England writers, who came to be known as transcendentalists, believed that individuals should not conform to the demands of the everyday world or to the dogmas of formal religion. Instead, Americans should look within themselves for truth and guidance. The leading transcendentalist, Ralph Waldo Emerson—an essayist, poet, and lecturer—proclaimed that the power of the solitary individual was nearly limitless. The novelist Herman Melville ridiculed transcendentalism's inward gaze as "oracular gibberish" and "self-conceit" that was less an alternative to mainstream values than an extreme form of the individualism of the era.

Unlike transcendentalists, who sought to turn inward, a few reformers tried to change the world by organizing utopian communities as alternatives to the existing society. Although these communities never attracted more than a few thousand people, their members tried to realize their visions of social perfection.

Some communities set out to become models that would point the way toward a better life for everyone. During the 1840s, more than two dozen communities organized themselves around the ideas of Charles Fourier. Members of these Fourierist phalanxes, as these communities were called, believed that individualism and competition were evils that denied the basic truth that "men . . . are brothers and not competitors." Phalanxes aspired to replace competition with harmonious cooperation based on communal ownership of property. But Fourierist communities failed to realize their lofty goals, and few survived more than two or three years.

Oneida community
Utopian community organized by John Humphrey Noyes in New York in 1848.

The Oneida community went beyond the Fourierist notion of communalism. John Humphrey Noyes, the leader of Oneida, believed that American society's commitment to private property made people greedy and selfish. Noyes claimed that the root of private property lay in marriage, in husbands' conviction that their wives were their exclusive property. With support from a sizable inheritance, Noyes organized the Oneida community in New York in 1848 to abolish marital property rights by permitting sexual intercourse between any consenting man and woman in the community. He also required all members to relinquish their economic property to the community. Most of their neighbors considered Oneidans dangerous adulterers. The practices that set Oneida apart from its mainstream neighbors strengthened the community, and it survived long after the Civil War. But it did not change the institutions of marriage and private property in America at large.

Why did "industrial evolution" occur?

Woman's Rights Activists

Women participated in the many reform activities that grew out of evangelical churches. Women church members outnumbered men two to one and worked to put their religious ideas into practice by joining peace, temperance, antislavery, and other societies. Involvement in reform organizations gave a few women activists practical experience in such political arts as speaking in public, running a meeting, drafting resolutions, and circulating petitions. The abolitionist Lydia Maria Child pointed out that "those who urged women to become missionaries and form tract societies . . . have changed the household utensil to a living energetic being and they have no spell to turn it into a broom again."

In 1848, about three hundred reformers led by Elizabeth Cady Stanton and Lucretia Mott gathered at Seneca Falls, New York, for the first national woman's rights convention in the United States. As Stanton recalled, "The general discontent I felt with women's portion as wife, mother, housekeeper, physician, and spiritual guide, [and] the wearied anxious look of the majority of women impressed me with a strong feeling that some active measure should be taken to right the wrongs of society in general, and of women in particular." The Seneca Falls Declaration of Sentiments set an ambitious agenda to demand civil liberties for women and to right the wrongs of society. The declaration proclaimed that "the history of mankind is a history of repeated injuries and usurpations on the part of man toward woman, having in direct object the establishment of an absolute tyranny over her." In the style of the Declaration of Independence, the Seneca Falls declaration demanded that women "have immediate admission to all the rights and privileges which belong to them as citizens of the United States," particularly the "inalienable right to the elective franchise."

Nearly two dozen other woman's rights conventions assembled before 1860, repeatedly calling for suffrage and an end to discrimination against women. But women had difficulty receiving a respectful hearing, much less achieving legislative action. Even so, the Seneca Falls declaration served as a pathbreaking manifesto of dissent against male supremacy and of support for woman suffrage. The declaration inspired many women to challenge the barriers that limited their opportunities.

Stanton and other activists sought fair pay and expanded employment opportunities for women by appealing to the free-labor ideal. One woman's rights advocate urged Americans to stop discriminating against able and enterprising women: "Let [women] . . . open a Store, . . . learn any of the lighter mechanical Trades, . . . study for a Profession, . . . be called to the lecture-room, [and] . . . the Temperance rostrum . . . [and] let her be appointed [to serve in the Post Office]." Some women pioneered in these and many other occupations during the 1840s and 1850s. Woman's rights activists also succeeded in protecting married women's rights to their own wages and property in New York in 1860. But discrimination against women remained very strong because most men believed in and practiced male supremacy.

COMPARE AND CONTRAST
How did the reforms sought by woman's rights activists compare to those of utopian communities?

Seneca Falls Declaration of Sentiments
Declaration issued in 1848 at the first national woman's rights convention in the United States, which was held in Seneca Falls, New York.

▲ **Who Rules the Family?** This 1855 print, "The Discord," satirizes the challenge to male supremacy by woman's rights activists. The man pulling on the pants declares he'd "Rather die! than let my wife have *my* pants. A man ought always to be the ruler." The man's wife pulling on the other side of the pants responds that "Woman is born to rule and not to obey those contemptible creatures called men!" The pantless man on the left has already lost this struggle, while the woman on the right cheers on the wife and exclaims, "Stick to them, it is only us, which ought to rule and to whom the pants fit the best." Collection of the New-York Historical Society, USA/ Bridgeman Images.

| How did the free-labor ideal explain economic inequality? | What spurred westward expansion? | Why did the United States go to war with Mexico? | **What changes did social reformers seek in the 1840s and 1850s?** | Conclusion: How did the free-labor ideal contribute to economic growth? |

Abolitionists and the American Ideal

During the 1840s and 1850s, abolitionists continued to struggle to focus the nation's attention on the plight of slaves and the need for emancipation. Former slaves Frederick Douglass, Henry Bibb, and Sojourner Truth lectured to reform audiences throughout the North about the cruelties of slavery. Abolitionists published newspapers, held conventions, and petitioned Congress, but they never attracted a mass following among white Americans. Many white Northerners became convinced that slavery was wrong, but they still believed that blacks were inferior. Many other white Northerners shared the common view of white Southerners that slavery was necessary and even desirable. The westward extension of the nation during the 1840s offered abolitionists an opportunity to link their unpopular ideal to a goal that many white Northerners found much more attractive—limiting the geographic expansion of slavery, an issue that moved to the center of national politics during the 1850s (see chapter 14).

Black leaders rose to prominence in the abolitionist movement during the 1840s and 1850s. African Americans had actively opposed slavery for decades, but a new generation of leaders arose in these years. Frederick Douglass, Henry Highland Garnet, William Wells Brown, Martin R. Delany, and others became impatient with white abolitionists' appeals to the conscience of the white people. In 1843, Garnet urged slaves to choose "Liberty or Death" and rise in insurrection against their masters, an idea that alienated almost all white people and had little influence among slaves. To express their own uncompromising ideas, black abolitionists founded their own newspapers and held their own antislavery conventions, although they still cooperated with sympathetic whites.

The commitment of black abolitionists to battling slavery grew out of their own experiences with white supremacy. The 250,000 free African Americans in the North and West made up less than 2 percent of the total population in 1860. They faced the humiliations of racial discrimination in nearly every arena of daily life. Only Maine, Massachusetts, New Hampshire, and Vermont—where few African Americans lived—permitted black men to vote. New York imposed a special property-holding requirement on black—but not white—voters, effectively excluding most black men from the ballot box. Widespread racial discrimination both handicapped and energized black abolitionists.

Some cooperated with the efforts of the **American Colonization Society** to send freed slaves and other black Americans to Liberia in West Africa. Others sought to move to Canada, Haiti, or elsewhere. As an African American from Michigan wrote, "It is impracticable, not to say impossible, for the whites and blacks to live together, and upon terms of social and civil equality, under the same government." Most black American leaders, however, refused to support emigration. Instead, they insisted that they deserved the same rights as white Americans. They worked against racial prejudice in their own communities, organizing campaigns against segregation, particularly in transportation and education. Their most notable success came in

CONSIDER CAUSE AND EFFECT

How did manifest destiny and westward expansion influence abolitionism in the 1840s and 1850s?

American Colonization Society
Organization that sent freed slaves and other black Americans to Liberia in West Africa.

▲ **Abolitionist Meeting** This rare daguerreotype portrays an abolitionist meeting in New York in 1850. Frederick Douglass, who had escaped from slavery in Maryland, is seated on the platform next to the woman at the table. One of the nation's most eloquent abolitionists, Douglass also supported equal rights for women. The man behind Douglass is Gerrit Smith, a wealthy and militant abolitionist whose funds supported many reform activities. Digital image courtesy of the Getty's Open Content Program.

Why did "industrial evolution" occur?

1855 when Massachusetts integrated its public schools. Elsewhere, uncompromising white supremacy reigned.

Outside the public spotlight, free African Americans in the North and West contributed to the antislavery cause by quietly aiding fugitive slaves. Harriet Tubman escaped from slavery in Maryland in 1849 and repeatedly risked her freedom and her life to return to the South to escort slaves to freedom. When the opportunity arose, free blacks in the North provided fugitive slaves with food, a safe place to rest, and a helping hand. This **underground railroad** ran mainly through black neighborhoods, black churches, and black homes. It grew from the belief in abolition and opposition to white supremacy that unified nearly all African Americans in the North and West.

underground railroad
Network consisting mainly of black homes, churches, and neighborhoods that helped slaves escape to the North.

QUICK REVIEW

Why were women especially prominent in many nineteenth-century reform efforts?

Conclusion: How did the free-labor ideal contribute to economic growth?

During the 1840s and 1850s, a cluster of changes—population growth, steam power, railroads, and the growing mechanization of agriculture and manufacturing—meant greater economic productivity, a burst of output from farms and factories, and prosperity for many. Diplomacy with Great Britain and war with Mexico handed the United States 1.2 million square miles and more than 1,000 miles of Pacific coastline. One prize of manifest destiny, California, almost immediately rewarded its new owners with tons of gold. Most Americans believed that the new territory and vast riches were appropriate rewards for the nation's stunning economic progress and superior institutions.

To Americans in the North and West, industrial evolution confirmed the choice they had made to promote free labor as the key to independence, equality, and prosperity. Like Abraham Lincoln, millions of Americans could point to their personal experiences as evidence of the practical truth of the free-labor ideal. But millions of others knew that poverty and wealth continued to rub shoulders in the free-labor system. Free-labor enthusiasts denied that the problems lay in the country's social and economic systems. Instead, they argued, inequality sprang from individual failures. Some reformers focused on personal self-control and discipline, such as avoiding sin and alcohol. Other reformers agitated for woman's rights and the abolition of slavery. They challenged male supremacy and black inferiority but did not overcome the prevailing free-labor ideal based on individualism, racial prejudice, and male superiority.

By the 1850s, the North and West had economic interests, cultural values, and political aims that differed from those of the South. Each region celebrated its self-image and increasingly criticized the other's. Not even the victory over Mexico could bridge the deepening divide between the North and West on one side and the South on the other side.

| How did the free-labor ideal explain economic inequality? | What spurred westward expansion? | Why did the United States go to war with Mexico? | What changes did social reformers seek in the 1840s and 1850s? | **Conclusion: How did the free-labor ideal contribute to economic growth?** |

STEP
1

EXPLAIN WHY IT MATTERS

Put your reading into practice. Identify each term below, and then explain why it matters in U.S. history.

TERM	WHO OR WHAT & WHEN	WHY IT MATTERS
mechanical reaper (p. 328)		
American system (p. 330)		
manifest destiny (p. 337)		
Oregon Trail (p. 337)		
Mormons (p. 339)		
Lone Star Republic (p. 342)		
Treaty of Guadalupe Hidalgo (p. 347)		
California gold rush (p. 348)		
Oneida community (p. 352)		
Seneca Falls Declaration of Sentiments (p. 353)		
American Colonization Society (p. 354)		
underground railroad (p. 355)		

STEP
2

MOVE BEYOND THE BASICS

How did economic developments described in the chapter contribute to industrial change? How did agriculture and manufacturing complement each other?

	Key Developments	Consequences/Who Benefited
Agricultural Technology		
Federal Land Policy		
Mechanization and Energy Sources		
Railroads		

STEP 3 — PUT IT ALL TOGETHER

Now, explain the big picture. Remember to use specific examples from the chapter in your answers.

INDUSTRIAL DEVELOPMENT AND WESTWARD EXPANSION

- What were the social consequences of American industrial development in the 1840s and 1850s?

- What role did American nationalism and economic opportunity play in promoting westward expansion?

THE MEXICAN-AMERICAN WAR

- Where was support for war with Mexico strongest? Where was there the least support? Why?

- How did victory in the Mexican-American War contribute to rising tensions over slavery?

REFORM

- What shared concerns linked the reform movements of the 1840s and 1850s?

- What reforms did abolitionists and women activists seek in the 1840s and 1850s?

LOOKING BACKWARD, LOOKING AHEAD

- How did America's economy and society changed between 1800 and 1860?

- How did American expansion and industrial development contribute to the sectional conflicts that culminated in the Civil War?

STEP 4 — CONNECT THESE EVENTS

How did the free-labor ideal contribute to westward expansion and the Mexican-American War?

STEP 5 — CONNECT TO THE PRESENT

How do the basic assumptions of the free-labor ideal shape our understanding of success today?

13

THE SLAVE SOUTH

1820–1860

How did slavery shape the institutions and values of the antebellum South? Chapter 13 explores the emergence and development of a distinctive slave society in the American South. It examines the cotton economy, the social world of the plantation, the lives of nonslaveholding whites and free blacks, and the impact of slavery on southern politics.

This chapter will explore the following questions:

- Why did the South become so different from the North?
- What was plantation life like for slave masters and mistresses?
- What was plantation life like for slaves?
- How did nonslaveholding southern whites work and live?
- What place did free blacks occupy in the South?
- How did slavery shape southern politics?
- Conclusion: How did slavery come to define the South?

AN AMERICAN STORY

Nat Turner was born a slave in Southampton County, Virginia, in October 1800. His parents said that the special marks on his body were signs that he was "intended for some great purpose." His master said that he learned to read without being taught. As an adolescent, he became a devoted Christian and fasted. In his twenties, he said he received visits from the "Spirit," the same spirit that had spoken to the ancient prophets. In time, Nat Turner began to interpret these things to mean that God had appointed him an instrument of divine vengeance for the sin of slaveholding.

On the morning of August 22, 1831, he set out with six friends—Hark, Henry, Sam, Nelson, Will, and Jack—to punish slave owners. Turner struck the first blow, an ax to the head of his master, Joseph Travis. The rebels killed all of the white men, women, and children they encountered. By noon, they had visited eleven farms and slaughtered fifty-seven whites. Along the way, they had added fifty or sixty men to their army. Word spread quickly, and soon the militia and hundreds of local whites gathered. They quickly captured or killed all of the rebels except Turner, who hid out for about ten weeks before being captured in nearby woods. Within a week, he was tried, convicted, and executed. By then, forty-five slaves had stood trial, twenty had been convicted and hanged, and another ten had been banished from Virginia. Frenzied whites had killed another hundred or more blacks—insurgents and innocent bystanders—in their counterattack against the rebellion.

White Virginians blamed the rebellion on outside agitators. In 1829, David Walker, a freeborn black man living in Boston, had published his *An Appeal . . . to the Coloured Citizens of the World*, an invitation to slaves to rise up in bloody revolution, and copies had fallen into the hands of Virginia slaves. On January 1, 1831, the Massachusetts abolitionist William Lloyd Garrison had published the first issue of the *Liberator*, his fiery newspaper calling for the overthrow of slavery.

In the months following the insurrection, the Virginia legislature reaffirmed the state's determination to preserve slavery by passing laws that strengthened the institution and further restricted free blacks. A professor at the College of William and Mary, Thomas R. Dew, published a vigorous defense of slavery that became the bible of Southerners' proslavery arguments. More than ever, the nation was divided along the Mason-Dixon line, the surveyors' mark that in colonial times had established the boundary between Maryland and Pennsylvania but half a century later divided the free North and the slave South. Black slavery increasingly molded the South into a distinctive region.

In the decades after 1820, Southerners, like Northerners, raced westward; but unlike Northerners, who spread small farms, manufacturing, and free labor, Southerners spread slavery, cotton, and plantations. Geographic expansion reinvigorated slavery and made it more profitable than ever. As it embraced more people, it increased the South's political power. Antebellum Southerners sometimes found themselves at odds with one another—not only slaves and free people but also women and men; Indians, Africans, and Europeans; and aristocrats and common folk. Nevertheless, beneath this diversity, a distinctively southern society and culture were forming. The South became a slave society, and most white Southerners were proud of it.

▼ *Horrid Massacre in Virginia* No contemporary images of Nat Turner are known to exist. This woodcut imagines the rebellion as a nightmare in which black brutes took the lives of innocent whites. Although there was never another rebellion as large as Turner's, images of black violence continued to haunt white imaginations. Library of Congress, 3a33960.

Why did the South become so different from the North?

CHRONOLOGY

1808
- External slave trade outlawed.

1820s–1830s
- Southern legislatures enact slave codes.
- Southern intellectuals fashion systematic defense of slavery.

1830
- Southern slaves number approximately two million.

1836
- Arkansas admitted to Union as slave state.

1840
- Cotton accounts for more than 60 percent of nation's exports.

1845
- Texas and Florida admitted to Union as slave states.

1860
- Southern slaves number nearly four million, one-third of South's population.

Mason-Dixon line
A surveyor's mark that had established the boundary between Maryland and Pennsylvania in colonial times. By the 1830s, the boundary divided the free North and the slave South.

From the earliest settlements, inhabitants of the southern colonies had shared a great deal with northern colonists. Most whites in both sections were British and Protestant, spoke a common language, and celebrated their victorious revolution against British rule and the creation of the new nation under the Constitution in 1789. The beginnings of a national economy fostered economic interdependence and communication across regional boundaries. White Americans everywhere praised the prosperous young nation, and they looked forward to its seemingly boundless future.

Despite these national similarities, Southerners and Northerners grew increasingly different. The French political observer Alexis de Tocqueville believed he knew why. "I could easily prove," he asserted in 1831, "that almost all the differences which may be noticed between the character of the Americans in the Southern and Northern states have originated in slavery." And a quarter of a century after Tocqueville, neither Northerners nor Southerners liked the society that had developed on the other side of the Mason-Dixon line. "On the subject of slavery," the *Charleston Mercury* declared, "the North and South . . . are not only two Peoples, but they are rival, hostile Peoples." Slavery made the South different, and it was the differences between the North and South, not the similarities, that increasingly shaped antebellum American history.

Cotton Kingdom, Slave Empire

In the first half of the nineteenth century, millions of Americans migrated west. In the South, the stampede began after the Creek War of 1813–1814, which cost the Creek Indians 24 million acres and initiated the government campaign to remove Indian people living east of the Mississippi River. Hard-driving slaveholders seeking virgin land for new plantations, ambitious farmers looking for patches for small farms, striving herders and drovers pushing their hogs and cattle toward fresh pastures—everyone felt the pull of western land.

More than anything, however, it was cotton that propelled Southerners westward. South of the **Mason-Dixon line**, climate and geography were ideally suited for the cultivation of cotton. And by the 1830s, cotton fields stretched from the Atlantic seaboard to central Texas. Heavy migration led to statehood for Arkansas in 1836 and for Texas and Florida in 1845. Cotton production soared to nearly 5 million bales in 1860, when the South produced three-fourths of the world's supply. The South—especially that tier of states from South Carolina west to Texas called the Lower South—had become the **cotton kingdom** (**Map 13.1**).

The cotton kingdom was also a slave empire. The South's cotton boom rested on the backs of slaves. As cotton agriculture expanded westward, whites shipped more than a million enslaved men, women, and children from the Atlantic coast westward in what has been called the "Second Middle Passage," a massive deportation that dwarfed the transatlantic slave trade to North America. Victims of this brutal domestic slave trade marched hundreds of miles southwest to the Lower South, where they literally cut new plantations from the forests. Cotton, slaves, and plantations moved west together.

| Why did the South become so different from the North? | What was plantation life like for slave masters and mistresses? |

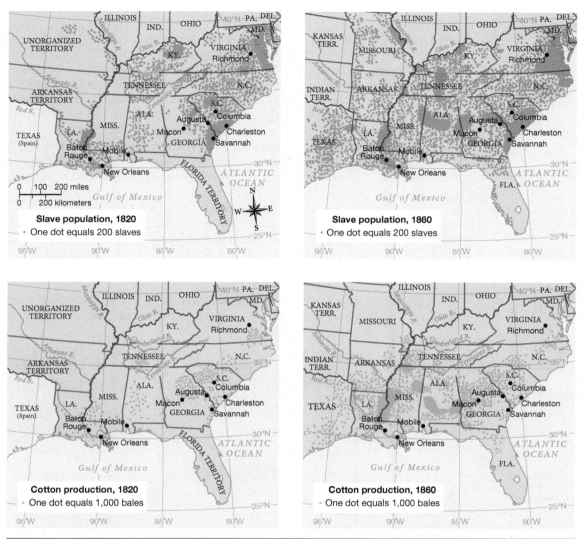

MAP 13.1 ▲ Cotton Kingdom, Slave Empire: 1820 and 1860 As the production of cotton soared, the slave population increased dramatically. Slaves continued to toil in tobacco and rice fields, but in Alabama, Mississippi, and Texas, they increasingly worked on cotton plantations.

READING THE MAP: Where was slavery most prevalent in 1820? In 1860? How did the spread of slavery compare with the spread of cotton?

CONNECTIONS: How much of the world's cotton was produced in the American South in 1860? How did the number of slaves in the American South compare with that in the rest of the world? What does this suggest about the South's cotton kingdom?

The slave population grew enormously. Southern slaves numbered fewer than 700,000 in 1790, about 2 million in 1830, and almost 4 million by 1860. By 1860, the South contained more slaves than all the other slave societies in the New World combined. The extraordinary growth was not the result of the importation of slaves, which the federal government outlawed in 1808. Instead, the slave population grew through natural reproduction; by midcentury, the great majority of U.S. slaves were native-born Southerners.

cotton kingdom
Term that reflected the dominance of cotton in the southern economy. Cotton was particularly important in the tier of states from South Carolina west to Texas. Cotton cultivation was the key factor in the growth of slavery.

What was plantation life like for slaves?	How did nonslaveholding southern whites work and live?	What place did free blacks occupy in the South?	How did slavery shape southern politics?	Conclusion: How did slavery come to define the South?

The South in Black and White

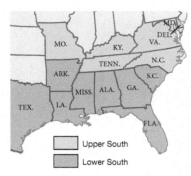

The Upper and Lower South

Upper South
Lower South

By 1860, one in every three Southerners was black (approximately 4 million blacks to 8 million whites). In the Lower South states of Mississippi and South Carolina, blacks constituted the majority (**Figure 13.1**). The contrast with the North was striking: In 1860, only one Northerner in seventy-six was black (about 250,000 blacks to 19 million whites).

The presence of large numbers of African Americans had profound consequences for the South. Southern culture—language, food, music, religion, and even accents—was in part shaped by blacks. But the most direct consequence of the South's biracialism was southern whites' commitment to white supremacy. Northern whites believed in their racial superiority, too, but their dedication to white supremacy lacked the intensity and urgency increasingly felt by white Southerners who lived among millions of slaves who had every reason to strike back.

After 1820, attacks on slavery—from slaves in the South and from northern abolitionists—caused white Southerners to make extraordinary efforts to strengthen slavery. State legislatures constructed **slave codes** (laws) that required the total submission of slaves. As the Louisiana code stated, a slave "owes his master . . . a respect without bounds, and an absolute obedience." The laws also underlined the authority of all whites, not just masters. Any white could "correct" slaves who did not stay "in their place."

Intellectuals joined legislators in the campaign to strengthen slavery. The South's professors, writers, and clergy constructed every imaginable defense. They argued that

slave codes
Laws enacted in southern states to strengthen the institution of slavery that required the total submission of slaves.

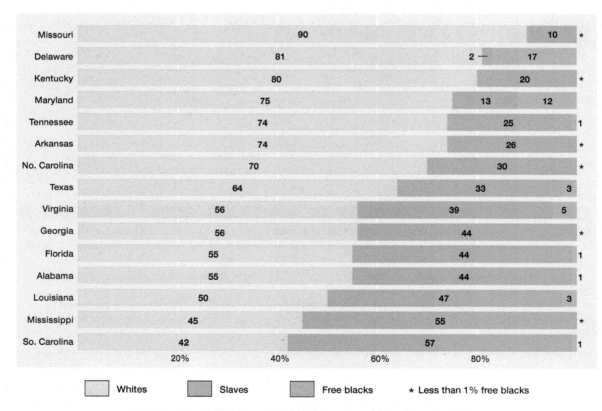

FIGURE 13.1 ▲ **Black and White Populations in the South, 1860**

Blacks represented a much larger fraction of the population in the South than in the North, but considerable variation existed from state to state. Only one Missourian in ten, for example, was black, while Mississippi and South Carolina had black majorities. States in the Upper South were "whiter" than states in the Lower South, despite the Upper South's greater number of free blacks.

| Why did the South become so different from the North? | What was plantation life like for slave masters and mistresses? |

PRACTICAL AMALGAMATION (Musical Soirée.)

▲ **Practical Amalgamation (Musical Soirée)** In this lithograph from 1839, Edward W. Clay of Philadelphia attacked abolitionists by imagining the social mixing across racial lines that would follow emancipation. Clay gives the African American men cartoon features meant to ridicule and implies that miscegenation (sexual mixing, also known as "amalgamation") might be the next step. American Antiquarian Society, Worcester, Massachusetts, USA / Bridgeman Images.

READING THE IMAGE: How does the artist signal racial danger in his depiction of a simple social event?
CONNECTIONS: In the opinion of abolitionists, who was responsible for miscegenation, and why?

slaves were legal property, and wasn't the protection of property the bedrock of American liberty? History also endorsed slavery, they claimed. Weren't the great civilizations—such as those of the Hebrews, Greeks, and Romans—slave societies? They argued that the Bible, properly interpreted, also sanctioned slavery. Old Testament patriarchs owned slaves, they observed, and in the New Testament, Paul returned the runaway slave Onesimus to his master. Proslavery spokesmen claimed that the freeing of slaves would lead to the sexual mixing of the races, or miscegenation.

George Fitzhugh of Virginia defended slavery by attacking the North's free-labor economy and society. He claimed that behind the North's grand slogans of freedom and individualism lay a heartless philosophy: "Every man for himself, and the devil take the hindmost." Gouging capitalists exploited wageworkers unmercifully, Fitzhugh declared,

miscegenation
Interracial sex. Proslavery spokesmen argued that abolition would lead to miscegenation. In reality, slavery led to considerable sexual abuse of black women by their white masters.

What was plantation life like for slaves?	How did nonslaveholding southern whites work and live?	What place did free blacks occupy in the South?	How did slavery shape southern politics?	Conclusion: How did slavery come to define the South?

Defending Slavery

White Southerners who defended slavery were rationalizing their economic interests and racial privileges, of course, but they also believed what they said about slavery being just, necessary, and godly. Whatever their specific arguments, they agreed with the *Charleston Mercury* that without slavery, the South would become a "most magnificent jungle."

DOCUMENT 1

John C. Calhoun, Speech before the U.S. Senate, 1837

When abolitionists began to denounce slavery as sinful and evil, John C. Calhoun, the South's leading proslavery politician, rose to defend the institution as "a positive good." Calhoun devoted part of his speech to the argument that enslavement benefited the slaves themselves.

Be it good or bad, it [slavery] has grown up with our society and institutions, and is so interwoven with them, that to destroy it would be to destroy us as a people. But let me not be understood as admitting, even by implication, that the existing relations between the two races in the slaveholding States is an evil: far otherwise; I hold it to be a good. . . . I appeal to facts. Never before has the black race of Central Africa, from the dawn of history to the present day, attained a condition so civilized and so improved, not only physically, but morally and intellectually. It came to us in a low, degraded, and savage condition, and in the course of a few generations, it has grown up under the fostering care of our institutions, reviled they have been, to its present comparatively civilized condition. This, with the rapid increase of numbers, is conclusive proof of the general happiness of the race, in spite of all the exaggerated tales to the contrary. . . .

I hold that in the present state of civilization, where two races of different origin, and distinguished by color, and other physical differences, as well as intellectual, are brought

together, the relation now existing in the slaveholding States between the two, is, instead of an evil, a good—a positive good. . . .

I may say with truth, that in few countries so much is left to the share of the laborer, and so little exacted from him, or where there is more kind attention paid to him in sickness or infirmities of age. Compare his condition with the tenants of the poor houses in the more civilized portions of Europe—look at the sick, and the old and infirm slave, on one hand, in the midst of his family and friends, under the kind superintending care of his master and mistress, and compare it with the forlorn and wretched condition of the pauper in the poor house.

Source: John C. Calhoun, "Speech on the Reception of Abolition Petitions, Delivered in the Senate, February 6th, 1837," in *Speeches of John C. Calhoun, Delivered in the House of Representatives and in the Senate of the United States,* edited by Richard K. Cralle (Appleton, 1853), 625–33.

DOCUMENT 2

William Harper, *Memoir on Slavery*, 1837

William Harper—judge, politician, and academic—defended slavery by denouncing abolitionists, particularly the "atrocious philosophy" of "natural equality and inalienable rights" that they used to support their attacks on slavery.

All men are born free and equal. Is it not palpably nearer the truth to say that no man was ever born free, and that no two men were ever born equal? . . . Wealth and poverty, fame or

and he contrasted the North's vicious free-labor system with the humane relations that he said prevailed between masters and slaves. Slaves were protected, he said, because they were valuable capital that masters sought to protect. As evidence, John C. Calhoun, an influential southern politician, argued that in the states where slavery had been abolished, "the condition of the African, instead of being improved, has become worse," while in the slave states, the Africans "have improved greatly in every respect."

At the heart of the defense of slavery, however, lay the claim of black inferiority. Black enslavement was necessary, proslavery champions argued, because Africans were lesser beings. Rather than exploitative, slavery was a mass civilizing effort that lifted lowly blacks from African barbarism and savagery, taught them disciplined work,

| Why did the South become so different from the North? | What was plantation life like for slave masters and mistresses? |

obscurity, strength or weakness, knowledge or ignorance, ease or labor, power or subjection, make the endless diversity in the condition of men. . . .

It is the order of nature and of God, that the being of superior faculties and knowledge, and therefore of superior power, should control and dispose of those who are inferior. It is as much in the order of nature, that men should enslave each other, as that other animals should prey upon each other.

Moralists have denounced the injustice and cruelty which have been practiced towards our aboriginal Indians, by which they have been driven from their native seats and exterminated.

. . . No doubt, much fraud and injustice has been practiced in the circumstances and manner of their removal. Yet who has contended that civilized man had no moral right to possess himself of the country? That he was bound to leave this wide and fertile continent, which is capable of sustaining uncounted myriads of a civilized race, to a few roving and ignorant barbarians? Yet if any thing is certain, it is certain that there were no means by which he could possess the country, without exterminating or enslaving them. Savage and civilized man cannot live together, and the savage can only be tamed by being enslaved or by having slaves.

Source: William Harper, *Memoir on Slavery* (J. S. Burges, 1838).

DOCUMENT 3

Thornton Stringfellow, "The Bible Argument: or, Slavery in the Light of Divine Revelation," 1856

The Reverend Thornton Stringfellow, a Baptist minister from Virginia, defended human bondage based on his reading of the Bible. He makes a case that Jesus himself approved of the relationship between master and slave.

Jesus Christ recognized this institution [slavery] as one that was lawful among men, and regulated its relative duties. . . . I affirm

then, first, (and no man denies,) that Jesus Christ has not abolished slavery by a prohibitory command: and second, I affirm, he has introduced no new moral principle which can work its destruction, under the gospel dispensation; and that the principle relied on for this purpose, is a fundamental principle of the Mosaic law, under which slavery was instituted by Jehovah himself. . . .

To the church at Colosse . . . Paul in his letter to them, recognizes the three relations of wives and husbands, parents and children, servants and masters, as relations existing among the members . . . and to the servants and masters he thus writes: "Servants obey in all things your masters, according to the flesh: not with eye service, as men pleasers, but in singleness of heart, fearing God: and whatsoever you do, do it heartily, as to the Lord and not unto men; knowing that of the Lord ye shall receive the reward of the inheritance, for ye serve the Lord Christ. . . . Masters give unto your servants that which is just and equal, knowing that you also have a master in heaven."

Source: *Slavery Defended: The Views of the Old South* by Eric L. McKitrick, editor. Published by Prentice-Hall, 1963. Reprinted with permission. *Cotton Is King and Pro-Slavery Arguments* by Thornton Stringfellow (Pritchard, Abbott & Loomis, 1860), 459–546.

Questions for Analysis

SUMMARIZE THE ARGUMENT: How do the authors' proslavery convictions shape their arguments?

ANALYZE THE EVIDENCE: The authors of these documents build their defenses of slavery on three different kinds of evidence. What are they?

CONSIDER THE CONTEXT: What did William Harper hope to gain by interjecting Americans' treatment of Indians into his defense of slavery?

and converted them to soul-saving Christianity. According to Virginian Thomas R. Dew, most slaves were grateful. He declared that "the slaves of a good master are his warmest, most constant, and most devoted friends." **(See "Analyzing Historical Evidence: Defending Slavery" above.)**

African slavery encouraged southern whites to unify around race rather than to divide by class. The grubbiest, most tobacco-stained white man could proudly proclaim his superiority to all blacks and his equality with the most refined southern planter. Georgia attorney Thomas R. R. Cobb observed that every white Southerner "feels that he belongs to an elevated class. It matters not that he is no slaveholder; he is not of the inferior race; he is a freeborn citizen." Consequently, the "poorest meets the richest as an equal; sits at his

TRACE CHANGE OVER TIME

How did white Southerners try to strengthen the institution of slavery between 1820 and 1860?

What was plantation life like for slaves?	How did nonslaveholding southern whites work and live?	What place did free blacks occupy in the South?	How did slavery shape southern politics?	Conclusion: How did slavery come to define the South?

table with him; salutes him as a neighbor; meets him in every public assembly, and stands on the same social platform." In the South, Cobb boasted, "there is no war of classes." By providing every white Southerner membership in the ruling race, slavery helped whites bridge vast differences in wealth, education, and culture.

The Plantation Economy

planter
A substantial landowner who tilled his estate with twenty or more slaves. Although small in number, planters dominated the economic, social, and political world of the South.

plantation
Large farm worked by twenty or more slaves. Although small farms were far more numerous, plantations produced more than 75 percent of the South's export crops.

As important as slavery was in unifying white Southerners, only about one-quarter of the white population lived in slaveholding families. Most slaveholders owned fewer than five slaves. Only about 12 percent of slaveholders owned twenty or more, the number of slaves that historians consider necessary to distinguish a **planter** from a farmer. Despite their small numbers, planters dominated the southern economy. In 1860, 52 percent of the South's slaves lived and worked on **plantations**, where they produced more than 75 percent of the South's cotton and other export crops, the backbone of the region's economy. While slavery was dying elsewhere in the New World (only Brazil and Cuba still had slaves by midcentury), slave plantations increasingly dominated southern agriculture.

The South's major cash crops—tobacco, sugar, rice, and cotton—grew on plantations (**Map 13.2**). Tobacco, the original plantation crop in North America, had shifted westward in the nineteenth century from the Chesapeake to Tennessee and Kentucky.

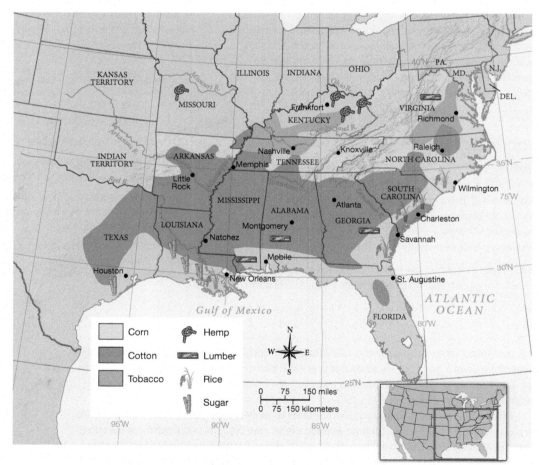

MAP 13.2 ▲ The Agricultural Economy of the South, 1860
Cotton dominated the South's agricultural economy, but the region grew a variety of crops and was largely self-sufficient in foodstuffs.

Why did the South become so different from the North?

What was plantation life like for slave masters and mistresses?

Large-scale sugar production began in 1795, when Étienne de Boré built a modern sugar mill in what is today New Orleans, and sugar plantations were confined almost entirely to Louisiana. Commercial rice production began in the seventeenth century, and like sugar, rice was confined to a small geographic area, a narrow strip of coast stretching from the Carolinas into Georgia.

By the nineteenth century, cotton reigned as king of the South's plantation crops. Cotton became commercially significant in the 1790s after the invention of a new cotton gin by Eli Whitney (see chapter 9). Cotton was relatively easy to grow and took little capital to get started—just enough for land, seed, and simple tools. Thus, small farmers as well as planters grew cotton. But planters, whose extensive fields were worked by gangs of slaves, produced three-quarters of the South's cotton, and cotton made planters rich.

Plantation slavery also enriched the nation. By 1840, cotton accounted for more than 60 percent of American exports. Most of the cotton was shipped to Great Britain, the world's largest manufacturer of cotton textiles. **(See "Spotlight: Cotton's Global Empire" on page 368.)** Much of the profit from the sale of cotton overseas returned to planters, but some went to northern middlemen who bought, sold, insured, warehoused, and shipped cotton to the mills in Great Britain. As one New York merchant observed, "Cotton has enriched all through whose hands it has passed." As middlemen invested their profits in the expanding northern economy, industrial development received a burst of much-needed capital. Furthermore, southern plantations benefited northern industry by providing an important market for textiles, agricultural tools, and other manufactured goods.

The economies of the North and South steadily diverged. While the North developed a mixed economy—agriculture, commerce, and manufacturing—the South remained overwhelmingly agricultural. Year after year, planters funneled the profits they earned from land and slaves back into more land and more slaves. With its capital flowing into agriculture, the South did not develop many factories. By 1860, only 10 percent of the nation's industrial workers lived in the South. Some cotton mills sprang up, but the region that produced 100 percent of the nation's cotton manufactured less than 7 percent of its cotton cloth.

Without significant economic diversification, the South developed fewer cities than the North and West. In 1860, it was the least urban region in the country. Whereas nearly 37 percent of New England's population lived in cities, less than 12 percent of Southerners were urban dwellers. Because the South had so few cities

PLACE EVENTS IN CONTEXT

What was the relationship between the North's economic transformation in this period and cotton agriculture in the South?

◀ **Steamships Moored in the Docks at New Orleans, Louisiana, 1862** In this chaotic scene, cotton waits to be loaded on ships jostling for a birth at the South's busiest port. A few years earlier, an awed visitor reported: "It must be seen to be believed; and even then, it will require an active mind to comprehend acres of cotton bales standing upon the levee." Otto Herschan/Getty Images.

| What was plantation life like for slaves? | How did nonslaveholding southern whites work and live? | What place did free blacks occupy in the South? | How did slavery shape southern politics? | Conclusion: How did slavery come to define the South? |

Cotton's Global Empire

Long before T-shirts and jeans became our everyday wear, cotton had already changed the world. Before cotton, people wore wool and linen, materials that were expensive, scratchy, and—because they were nearly unwashable—smelly. The world welcomed cotton because it was cheap, comfortable, and washable. But before we could dress in cotton, planters in the American South, merchants on both sides of the Atlantic, and manufacturers in Britain had to link America's plantations with the textile factories of Great Britain. Once they did, the world was never the same.

Before 1793, when Eli Whitney devised a new machine to clean raw cotton, no North American cotton whatsoever reached Britain. Following Whitney's invention, American cotton production exploded as a "cotton rush" carried cotton, cotton gins, plantations, and slaves westward across land taken from the Indians. U.S. cotton began to arrive in Liverpool in 1795. By 1802, the United States had become the single most important supplier of cotton to Britain, and Britain had become the world's dominant manufacturer of cotton cloth. By the 1850s, the South supplied 77 percent of the 800 million pounds that each year fed Britain's cotton-hungry textile factories.

Wool had previously been basic to English manufacturing and trade, but cotton quickly displaced wool in northwestern England's manufacturing districts. Because cotton could not be grown in the cold, rainy climate of Europe, manufacturers had to import every pound. Traders bought the American cotton crop and shipped it across the Atlantic to English mills, where it was spun into yarn, woven into cloth, and carried to customers around the world. The production of cotton cloth became the world's first mechanized and industrialized business. New machines, new sources of power, and a new labor system revolutionized the making of cotton cloth and made mass production possible.

American slaves grew cotton, but cotton was made into cloth by a new British army of wage laborers. The explosion of textile factories meant that people from the countryside crowded into the cities of Manchester and Liverpool, into housing that was "offensive, dark, damp, and incommodious." For at least twelve hours a day, six days a week, textile workers operated the machines that turned raw cotton into cloth. The insatiable demand for labor swept up huge numbers of women and children. In 1833, Parliament revealed the degree of exploitation when it barred children from working in the spinning mills before the age of nine and required that those between nine and thirteen work only nine hours a day. An 1833 report observed, "The consequence of this excess of toil is that the growth of the body is checked, and the limbs become weak, and sometimes horribly distorted."

and industrial jobs, it attracted fewer European immigrants. Seeking economic opportunity, not competition with slaves (whose labor would keep wages low), immigrants steered northward. In 1860, 13 percent of all Americans were born abroad. But in nine of the fifteen slave states, only 2 percent or less of the population was foreign-born.

Northerners claimed that slavery was a backward labor system, and compared with Northerners, Southerners invested less of their capital in industry, transportation, and public education. But few Southerners perceived economic weakness in their region. Indeed, planters' pockets were never fuller than in the 1850s, thanks to the South's near monopoly on cotton, the hottest commodity in the international marketplace. Planters' decisions to reinvest in cotton ensured the continuation of the plantation economy and the political and social relationships rooted in it.

QUICK REVIEW

Why did the nineteenth-century southern economy remain primarily agricultural?

Why did the South become so different from the North?

What was plantation life like for slave masters and mistresses?

Cotton manufacturing became the center of the British economy and caused extraordinary changes in British society. British factories produced two-thirds of the world's cotton cloth, and Manchester became the most industrialized city in the world. By 1860, nearly 500,000 laborers worked in Britain's cotton industry, where they experienced radically new ways of working and living as well as unprecedented poverty and misery.

Manufacturers elsewhere tried to follow the path that Manchester had blazed. Cotton mills sprang up in France, Germany, Russia, Switzerland, the Netherlands, and Belgium, each hoping to reproduce the success achieved in Britain. In each case, the American South's slave-grown cotton fed the mills. For example, 90 percent of the 192 million pounds used in France came from the United States. Beginning in the 1810s, the United States began building its own cotton factories, and those factories depended entirely on southern cotton. By 1860, cotton textiles were the most important manufacturing industry in the United States in terms of capital invested and workers employed.

Cotton stood at the center of the first modern manufacturing industry and the world's first global economy. When cotton linked two major nineteenth-century developments — the westward expansion of plantation slavery in the United States and the rise of the factory and wage labor in Europe — it created a global web of agriculture, trade, and industrial production. The repercussions from the industrialization of cotton resonated across nations and continents. Mass production put comfortable cotton clothes within reach of common people. Because British cotton manufacturing proved to be the first step of what is called the industrial revolution, raw cotton — grown by American slaves — played an essential role in international industrialization.

Questions for Analysis

ANALYZE THE EVIDENCE: What evidence supports the contention that American cotton played an essential role in the industrialization of cotton cloth?

CONSIDER THE CONTEXT: What advantages did cotton have that caused it to quickly supplant wool?

RECOGNIZE VIEWPOINTS: How might cotton manufacturers and cotton workers — on both sides of the Atlantic — have viewed the industrialization of cotton cloth differently?

What was plantation life like for slave masters and mistresses?

Nowhere was the contrast between northern and southern life more vivid than on the plantations of the South. A plantation typically included a "big house," where the plantation owner and his family lived, and a slave quarter. Near the big house were the kitchen, storehouse, smokehouse (for curing and preserving meat), and hen coop. More distant were the barns, toolsheds, artisans' workshops, and overseer's house. Large plantations sometimes had a rude hospital and a chapel for slaves. Depending on the crop, there was also a tobacco shed, a rice mill, a sugar refinery, or a cotton gin house. Lavish or plain, plantations everywhere had an underlying similarity (**Figure 13.2**).

The plantation was the home of masters, mistresses, and slaves. A hierarchy of rigid roles and duties governed their relationships. Presiding was the master, who by law ruled his wife, children, and slaves as dependents under his authority and protection.

| What was plantation life like for slaves? | How did nonslaveholding southern whites work and live? | What place did free blacks occupy in the South? | How did slavery shape southern politics? | Conclusion: How did slavery come to define the South? |

Savannah River

Brick Wall

Legend

1 **Mansion**
2 **Kitchen**
3 **Smokehouse**
4 **Stables**
5 **Coach House**
6 **Lot**
7 **Sunken Garden**
8 **Overseer's House**
9 **Hospital**
10 **Slave Huts**

paternalism
The theory of slavery that emphasized reciprocal duties and obligations between masters and their slaves. Whites employed the concept of paternalism to deny that the slave system was brutal and exploitative.

FIGURE 13.2 ◀ A Southern Plantation
Slavery determined how masters laid out their plantations and where they situated their big houses and slave quarters. This model of the Hermitage, the mansion built in 1830 for Henry McAlpin, a Georgia rice planter, shows the overseer's house poised halfway between the owner's mansion and the slave huts. Original illustration property of the Historic American Buildings Survey, a division of the National Park Service. Library of Congress, Prints & Photographs Division, Reproduction number HABS GA,26-SAV.V,1-(sheet 1 of 3).

Paternalism and Male Honor

Whereas smaller planters supervised the labor of their slaves themselves, larger planters hired overseers who went to the fields with the slaves, leaving the planters free to concentrate on marketing, finance, and the general affairs of the plantation. Planters also found time to escape to town to discuss cotton prices, to the courthouse and legislature to debate politics, and to the woods to hunt and fish.

Increasingly, planters characterized their mastery in terms of what they called "Christian guardianship" and what historians have called paternalism. The concept of paternalism denied that the form of slavery practiced in the South was brutal and exploitative. Instead, paternalism claimed that plantations benefited all. In exchange for the slaves' work and obedience, masters provided basic care and necessary guidance for a childlike, dependent people. In 1814, Thomas Jefferson captured the essence of the advancing ideal: "We should endeavor, with those whom fortune has thrown on our hands, to feed & clothe them well, protect them from ill usage, require such reasonable labor only as is performed voluntarily by freemen, and be led by no repugnancies to abdicate them, and our duties to them." A South Carolina rice planter insisted, "I manage them as my children."

Paternalism was part propaganda and part self-delusion. But it was also economically shrewd. Masters increasingly recognized slaves as valuable assets, particularly after the nation closed its external slave trade in 1808 and the cotton boom stimulated the demand for slaves. The expansion of the slave labor force could come only from natural reproduction. As one slave owner declared in 1849, "It behooves those who own them to make them last as long as possible."

One consequence of this economic self-interest was a small improvement in slaves' welfare. Diet improved, although nineteenth-century slaves still ate mainly fatty pork and cornmeal. Housing improved, although the cabins still had cracks large enough, slaves said, for cats to slip through. Clothing improved, although slaves seldom received much more than two crude outfits a year and perhaps a pair of cheap shoes. While most planters offered a rest period in the heat of the day and ceased the colonial practice of punishing slaves by branding and mutilation, workdays remained long, from sunup to sundown.

Paternalism should not be mistaken for "Ol' Massa's" kindness and goodwill. It encouraged better treatment because it made economic sense to provide at least minimal care for valuable slaves. But paternalism did not require that planters put down their whips. They could whip and still claim that they were only fulfilling their responsibilities as guardians of their naturally lazy and at times insubordinate black dependents. State laws gave masters nearly "uncontrolled authority over the body" of the slave, according to one North Carolina judge, and whipping remained planters' basic form of coercion.

Why did the South become so different from the North?

What was plantation life like for slave masters and mistresses?

Ex-slaves remembered the whipping. In testimony given after the war, they gave gruesome evidence of the cruelty of slavery. "You say how did our Master treat his slaves?" asked one woman. "Scandalous, they treated them just like dogs!" She was herself whipped "till the blood dripped to the ground." Another slave never personally felt the sting of the lash, but he recalled hearing slaves on other farms "hollering when they get beat." He added, "They beat them till it a pity." Most planters believed they whipped their slaves no more than was necessary to get the work done. But that meant that on most plantations the whip fell on someone's back every few days.

Paternalism never won universal acceptance among planters, but by the nineteenth century it had become a kind of communal standard. With its notion that slavery imposed on masters a burden and a duty, paternalism provided slaveholders with a means of rationalizing their rule. But it also provided some slaves with leverage in controlling the conditions of their lives. Slaves learned to manipulate the slaveholder's need to see himself as a good master. To avoid a reputation as a cruel tyrant, planters sometimes negotiated with slaves, rather than just resorting to the whip. Masters sometimes granted slaves small garden plots in which they could work for themselves after working all day in the fields, or they gave slaves a few days off and a dance when they had gathered the last of the cotton.

Virginia statesman Edmund Randolph argued that slavery created in white southern men a "quick and acute sense of personal liberty" and a "disdain for every abridgment of personal independence." Indeed, prickly individualism and aggressive independence became crucial features of the southern concept of honor. Social standing, political advancement, and even self-esteem rested on an honorable reputation. Defending honor became a male passion. Andrew Jackson's mother reportedly told her son, "Never tell a lie, nor take what is not your own, nor sue anybody for slander or assault and battery. *Always settle them cases yourself.*"

Among planters, such advice sometimes led to dueling, a ritual that had arrived from Europe in the eighteenth century. It died out in the North, but in the South, even after legislatures banned it, gentlemen continued to defend their honor with pistols at ten paces. Duels were fought by Andrew Jackson, whose wife one foolish man slandered, as well as by two South Carolina college students who happened at dinner to reach simultaneously for the last piece of trout.

Southerners also expected an honorable gentleman to be a proper patriarch. Nowhere in America was masculine power more apparent. Planters allowed no opposition from any of their dependents, black or white. The master's power sometimes led to miscegenation. Laws prohibited interracial sex, but as long as slavery gave white men extraordinary power, slave women were forced to submit to the sexual demands of the men who owned them.

In time, as the white children of one elite family married the white children of another, ties of blood and kinship, as well as ideology and economic interest, linked planters to one another. Aware of what they shared as slaveholders, planters worked together to defend their common interests. The values of the big house—slavery, honor, male domination—washed over the boundaries of plantations and flooded all of southern life.

▲ **Gordon** This photograph of Gordon, a runaway slave from Baton Rouge, Louisiana, was taken on April 2, 1863. Frederick W. Mercer, an assistant surgeon with the 47th Massachusetts Regiment, examined four hundred other runaways and found many "to be as badly lacerated." Publication of Gordon's photograph in the popular *Harper's Weekly* made him a symbol of slavery's terrible brutality. © Massachusetts Historical Society, Boston, MA/Bridgeman Images.

PLACE EVENTS IN CONTEXT
Why didn't paternalism mean gentle treatment for slaves?

| What was plantation life like for slaves? | How did nonslaveholding southern whites work and live? | What place did free blacks occupy in the South? | How did slavery shape southern politics? | Conclusion: How did slavery come to define the South? |

The Southern Lady and Feminine Virtues

Like their northern counterparts, southern ladies were expected to possess the feminine virtues of piety, purity, chastity, and obedience within the context of marriage, motherhood, and domesticity. Countless toasts praised the southern lady as the perfect complement to her husband, the commanding patriarch. She was physically weak, "formed only for the less laborious occupations," and thus dependent on male protection. To gain this protection, she exhibited modesty and delicacy, possessed beauty and grace, and cultivated refinement and charm. The lady, southern men said proudly, was an "ornament."

Chivalry—the South's romantic ideal of male-female relationships—glorified the lady while it subordinated her. Chivalry's underlying assumptions about the weakness of women and the protective authority of men resembled the paternalistic defense of slavery. Just as the slaveholder's mastery was written into law, so too were the superior rights of husbands. Married women lost almost all their property rights to their husbands. Women throughout the nation found divorce difficult, but southern women found it almost impossible.

Daughters of planters confronted chivalry's demands at an early age. At their private boarding schools, they learned to be southern ladies, reading literature, learning languages, and studying the appropriate drawing-room arts. Elite women began courting young and married early. Kate Carney exaggerated only slightly when she despaired in her diary: "Today, I am seventeen, getting quite old, and am not married." Yet marriage meant turning their fates over to their husbands and making enormous efforts to live up to the South's lofty expectations. Caroline Merrick of Louisiana told a friend in 1859, "We owe it to our husbands, children, and friends to represent as nearly as possible the ideal which they hold so dear."

chivalry
The South's romantic ideal of male-female relationships. Chivalry's underlying assumptions about the weakness of white women and the protective authority of men resembled the paternalistic defense of slavery.

▶ **Black Woman Holding White Child,**
ca. 1855 Most of the white children who grew up in the big house had slave nurses, or nannies. The fact that this nanny is included in the portrait of the child indicates her importance in the white household. Library of Congress, 3g05251.

| Why did the South become so different from the North? | **What was plantation life like for slave masters and mistresses?** |

◀ **Varina Howell Davis, 1849** Elite plantation women often had expensive lockets like this, in which their portraits were painted in miniature on ivory. In 1845, eighteen-year-old Varina Howell married Jefferson Davis, a man twice her age and the future president of the Confederate States of America. National Portrait Gallery, Smithsonian Institution; gift of Varina Webb Stewart. Conserved with funds from the Smithsonian Women's Committee.

Proslavery advocates claimed that slavery freed white women from the drudgery of housework. Surrounded "by her domestics," declared Thomas R. Dew, "she ceases to be a mere beast of burden" and "becomes the cheering and animating center of the family circle." In reality, however, having servants required the plantation mistress to work long hours. She managed the big house, directly supervising sometimes more than a dozen slaves. One slaveholder remembered that his boyhood home had "two cooks, two washer-women, one dining room servant, two seamstresses, one house girl, one house boy, one carriage driver, one hostler [stableman], one gardener, [and] one errand boy." He added, "they were all under the supervision of my mother." But unlike her husband, the mistress had no overseer. All house servants answered directly to her. She assigned them tasks each morning, directed their work throughout the day, and punished them when she found fault.

Whereas masters used their status as slaveholders as a springboard into public affairs, the plantation restricted mistresses' lives. Masters left when they pleased, but mistresses had heavy responsibilities at home, and besides they needed chaperones to travel. When they could, they went to church, but women spent most days at home, where they often became lonely. In 1853, Mary Kendall wrote how much she enjoyed her sister's letter: "For about three weeks I did not have the pleasure of seeing one white female face, there being no white family except our own upon the plantation."

As members of slaveholding families, mistresses lived privileged lives. But they also had grounds for discontent. No feature of plantation life generated more anguish among mistresses than miscegenation. Mary Boykin Chesnut of Camden, South Carolina, confided in her diary, "Ours is a monstrous system, a wrong and iniquity. Like the patriarchs of old, our men live all in one house with their wives and their concubines; and the mulattos one sees in every family partly resemble the white children. Any lady is ready to tell you who is the father of all the mulatto children in everybody's household but her own. Those, she seems to think drop from the clouds."

CONSIDER CAUSE AND EFFECT

How did the concepts of chivalry and paternalism shape the experiences of white plantation mistresses in the South?

| What was plantation life like for slaves? | How did nonslaveholding southern whites work and live? | What place did free blacks occupy in the South? | How did slavery shape southern politics? | Conclusion: How did slavery come to define the South? |

But most planters' wives, including Chesnut, accepted and defended slavery. After all, the privileged life of a mistress rested on slave labor as much as a master's did. Mistresses enjoyed the rewards of their class and race. But these rewards came at a price. Still, the heaviest burdens of slavery fell not on those who lived in the big house, but on those who toiled to support them.

QUICK REVIEW

Why did the ideology of paternalism gain currency among planters in the nineteenth century?

What was plantation life like for slaves?

On most plantations, only a few hundred yards separated the big house and the slave quarter. But the distance was great enough to provide slaves with some privacy. Out of eyesight and earshot of the big house, slaves drew together and built lives of their own. They created families, worshipped God, and developed an African American community and culture. Individually and collectively, slaves found ways to resist their bondage.

Despite the rise of plantations, almost half of the South's slaves lived and worked elsewhere. Most labored on small farms, where they wielded a hoe alongside another slave or two and perhaps their master. But by 1860, almost half a million slaves (one in eight) did not work in agriculture at all. Some lived in towns and cities, where they worked as domestics, day laborers, bakers, barbers, tailors, and more. Other slaves, far from urban centers, toiled as fishermen, lumbermen, railroad workers, and deckhands on riverboats. Slaves could also be found in most of the South's factories. Nevertheless, a majority of slaves (52 percent) counted plantations as their workplaces and homes.

Work

Whites enslaved blacks for their labor, and all slaves who were able worked. Former slave Carrie Hudson recalled that children who were "knee high to a duck" were sent to the fields to carry water to thirsty workers or to protect ripening crops from hungry birds. Others helped in the slave nursery, caring for children younger than themselves, or in the big house, where they swept floors or shooed flies in the dining room. When slave boys and girls reached the age of eleven or twelve, masters sent most of them to the fields. After a lifetime of hard work, old women left the fields to care for the small children and spin yarn, and old men moved on to mind livestock and clean stables.

The overwhelming majority of plantation slaves worked as field hands. Planters sometimes assigned men and women to separate gangs, the women working at lighter tasks and the men doing the heavy work of clearing and breaking the land. But women also did heavy work. "I had to work hard," Nancy Boudry remembered, and "plow and go and split wood just like a man." The backbreaking labor and the monotonous routines caused one ex-slave to observe that the "history of one day is the history of every day."

A few slaves (about one in ten) became house servants. Nearly all of those (nine out of ten) were women. They cooked, cleaned, babysat, washed clothes, and did the dozens of other tasks the master and mistress required. House servants were constantly on call, with

Why did the South become so different from the North?

What was plantation life like for slave masters and mistresses?

▲ **Slaves Working** Although carefully staged, this photograph of cotton pickers at harvesttime captures the fact that all hands—men, women, and children—were pressed into the fields during this crucial phase of cotton production. Yale Collection of American Literature, Beinecke Rare Book and Manuscript Library.

no time that was entirely their own. Since no servant could please constantly, most bore the brunt of white frustration and rage. Ex-slave Jacob Branch of Texas remembered, "My poor mama! Every washday old Missy give her a beating."

Even rarer than house servants were skilled artisans. In the cotton South, no more than one slave in twenty (almost all men) worked in a skilled trade. Most were blacksmiths and carpenters, but slaves also worked as masons, mechanics, millers, ginsmiths, and shoemakers. Skilled slave fathers took pride in teaching their crafts to their sons. "My pappy was one of the black smiths and worked in the shop," John Mathews remembered. "I had to help my pappy in the shop when I was a child and I learnt how to beat out the iron and make wagon tires, and make plows."

Rarest of all slave occupations was that of slave driver. Probably no more than one male slave in a hundred worked in this capacity. These men were well named, for their primary task was driving other slaves to work harder in the fields. In some drivers' hands, the whip never rested. Ex-slave Jane Johnson of South Carolina called her driver the "meanest man, white or black, I ever see." But other drivers showed all the restraint they could. "Ole Gabe didn't like that whippin' business," West Turner of Virginia remembered. "When Marsa was there, he would lay it on 'cause he had to. But when old Marsa wasn't lookin', he never would beat them slaves."

Normally, slaves worked from what they called "can to can't," from "can see" in the morning to "can't see" at night. Even with a break at noon for a meal and rest, it made for a long day. For slaves, Lewis Young recalled, "work, work, work, 'twas all they do."

COMPARE AND CONTRAST

What do the experiences of enslaved men and enslaved women tell us about how slave owners' assumptions about womanhood varied by race?

What was plantation life like for slaves?	How did nonslaveholding southern whites work and live?	What place did free blacks occupy in the South?	How did slavery shape southern politics?	Conclusion: How did slavery come to define the South?

Family and Religion

From dawn to dusk, slaves worked for their master, but at night and all day Sunday and usually Saturday afternoon, slaves were left largely to themselves. Bone tired perhaps, they nonetheless used the time to develop what mattered most to them. Over the generations, they created a community and a culture of their own that sustained them.

Slavery was a severe assault on the slave family. Between 1820 and 1860, some one million slaves entered the interstate slave trade that fed labor to the booming cotton South, and perhaps twice as many slaves were sold locally. Every slave dreaded the appearance of a slave trader at the gate of the plantation. Falling into the hands of a trader meant separation from family, probably for life, and a new existence under an unknown master.

"Abream Scriven wrote, 'My dear wife for you and my children my pen cannot express the griffe I feel to be parted from you all. I remain your truly husband until Death.'"

Though severely battered, the black family survived slavery. Young men and women in the quarter fell in love, married, and set up housekeeping in cabins of their own. But no laws recognized slave marriage, and therefore no master was legally obligated to honor the bond. While some slave marriages were long-lasting, the massive deportation associated with the Second Middle Passage and local sales destroyed hundreds of thousands of slave families.

In 1858, a slave named Abream Scriven wrote to his wife, who lived on a neighboring plantation in South Carolina. "My dear wife," he began, "I take the pleasure of writing you . . . with much regret to inform you I am Sold to man by the name of Peterson, a Treader and Stays in New Orleans." Before he left for Louisiana, Scriven asked his wife to "give my love to my father and mother and tell them good Bye for me. And if we do not meet in this world I hope to meet in heaven. . . . My dear wife for

▶ **Family outside Cabin, 1862** On a plantation just outside Beaufort, South Carolina, this poor, proud, but unnamed family includes at least four generations. Because of slavery's assault on the family life of slaves, very few blacks could gather as many generations. Library of Congress, LC-DIG-ppmsc-00057.

| Why did the South become so different from the North? | What was plantation life like for slave masters and mistresses? |

you and my children my pen cannot express the griffe I feel to be parted from you all."
He closed with words no master would have permitted in a slave's marriage vows: "I
remain your truly husband until Death." The letter makes clear Scriven's love for and
commitment to his family; it also demonstrates slavery's massive assault on family life
in the quarter.

Masters sometimes permitted slave families to work on their own, "overwork,"
as it was called. In the evenings and on Sundays, they tilled gardens, raised pigs and
fowl, and chopped wood, selling the products in the market for a little pocket change.
"Den each fam'ly have some chickens and sell dem and de eggs and maybe go huntin'
and sell de hides and git some money," a former Alabama slave remembered. "Den us
buy what am Sunday clothes with dat money, sech as hats and pants and shoes and
dresses." Slave children remembered the extraordinary efforts their parents made to
sustain their families, and they held them in high esteem.

Religion also provided slaves with a refuge and a reason for living. In the nineteenth century, evangelical Baptists and Methodists had great success in converting
slaves from their African beliefs. Planters promoted Christianity in the quarter because
they believed that the slaves' salvation was part of the obligation of paternalism; they
also hoped that religion would make slaves more obedient. South Carolina slaveholder
Charles Colcock Jones, the leading missionary to the slaves, instructed them "to
count their Masters 'worthy of all honour,' as those whom God has placed over them
in this world." But slaves laughed up their sleeves at such messages. "That old white
preacher just was telling us slaves to be good to our masters," one ex-slave said with
a chuckle. "We ain't cared a bit about that stuff he was telling us 'cause we wanted to
sing, pray, and serve God in our own way."

Meeting in their cabins or secretly in the woods, slaves created an African
American Christianity that served their needs, not the masters'. Laws prohibited
teaching slaves to read, but a few could read enough to struggle with the Bible. Rather
than obedience, their faith emphasized justice. Slaves believed that God kept score
and that the accounts of this world would be settled in the next. "God is punishing
some of them old suckers and their children right now for the way they use to treat
us poor colored folks," one ex-slave declared. But the slaves' faith also spoke to
their experiences in this world. In the Old Testament, they discovered Moses, who
delivered his people from slavery, and in the New Testament, they found Jesus, who
offered salvation to all. Jesus' message of equality provided a powerful rebuttal to the
planters' claim that blacks were an inferior people whom God condemned to slavery.

Christianity did not entirely drive out traditional African beliefs. Even slaves who
were Christians sometimes continued to believe that conjurers and witches possessed
the power to injure and protect. Slaves' Christian music and preaching reflected the
influence of Africa, as did many of their secular activities, such as wood carving,
quilt making, dancing, and storytelling. But by the mid-nineteenth century, black
Christianity had assumed a central place in slaves' quest for freedom. In the words of
one spiritual, "O my Lord delivered Daniel / O why not deliver me too?"

Resistance and Rebellion

Slaves did not suffer slavery passively. They were, as whites said, "troublesome property."
Slaves understood that accommodation to what they could not change was the price of
survival, but in a hundred ways they protested their bondage. Supposedly, the master
was all-powerful and the slave powerless. But sustained by their families, religion, and
community, slaves engaged in day-to-day resistance against their enslavers.

The spectrum of slave resistance ranged from mild to extreme. Telling a pointed
story by the fireside in a slave cabin was probably the mildest form of protest.

What was plantation life like for slaves?	How did nonslaveholding southern whites work and live?	What place did free blacks occupy in the South?	How did slavery shape southern politics?	Conclusion: How did slavery come to define the South?

When the weak got the better of the strong, as they did in tales of Br'er Rabbit and Br'er Fox (*Br'er* is a contraction of *Brother*), listeners could imagine such a victory over their own masters. Protest in the fields was riskier and included putting rocks in their cotton bags before having them weighed, feigning illness, and pretending to be so thickheaded that they could not understand the simplest instruction. Slaves broke so many hoes that owners outfitted the tools with oversized handles. Slaves so mistreated the work animals that masters switched from horses to mules, which could absorb more abuse. Although slaves worked hard in the master's fields, they also sabotaged his interests.

Running away was a common form of protest, but except along the borders with northern states and with Mexico, escape to freedom was almost impossible. Most runaways could hope only to escape for a few days. They sought temporary respite from hard labor or avoided punishment, and their "lying out," as it was known, usually ended when the runaway, worn out and ragged, gave up or was finally chased down by slave-hunting dogs.

Although resistance was common, outright rebellion—a violent assault on slavery by large numbers of slaves—was very rare. Conditions gave rebels almost no chance of success. By 1860, whites in the South outnumbered blacks two to one and were heavily armed. Also, communication between plantations was difficult, and the South provided little protective wilderness into which rebels could retreat and defend themselves. Rebellion was virtual suicide.

Steady resistance did not mean that slaves had the power to end their bondage. Centuries of slavery thwarted their hopes and aspirations. It broke some and crippled others. But slavery's destructive power had to contend with the power of the human spirit. Slaves fought back physically, culturally, and spiritually. Not only did they survive bondage, but they also created in their quarter a vibrant African American culture that buoyed them up during long hours in the fields and brought them joy and hope in the few hours they had to themselves.

UNDERSTAND POINTS OF VIEW

How were enslaved African Americans able to find some comfort and express their humanity within the oppressive institution of slavery?

QUICK REVIEW

Why did slaves resist often but rebel rarely?

How did nonslaveholding southern whites work and live?

Most whites in the South did not own slaves, not even one. In 1860, more than six million of the South's eight million whites lived in slaveless households. Some slaveless whites lived in cities and worked as artisans, mechanics, and traders. Others lived in the country and worked as storekeepers, parsons, and schoolteachers. But most "plain folk" were small farmers. Perhaps three out of four were **yeomen**, small farmers who owned their own land. As in the North, farm owner-ship provided a family with an economic foundation, social respectability, and political standing. Unlike their northern counterparts, however, southern yeomen lived in a region whose economy and society were increasingly dominated by slavery.

In an important sense, the South had more than one white yeomanry. The South was huge and provided space enough for two yeoman societies, separated roughly

yeomen
Farmers who owned and worked on their own small plots of land. Yeomen living within the plantation belt were more dependent on planters than were yeomen in the upcountry, where small farmers dominated.

Why did the South become so different from the North?

What was plantation life like for slave masters and mistresses?

along geographic lines. Yeomen throughout the South had much in common, but the life of a small farm family in the cotton belt—the flatlands that spread from South Carolina to Texas—differed from the life of a family in the upcountry—the area of hills and mountains. Some rural slaveless whites were not yeomen at all; they owned no land and were sometimes desperately poor.

Plantation-Belt Yeomen

Plantation-belt yeomen lived within the orbit of the planter class. Even in the plantation belt, small farms outnumbered plantations, but they were dwarfed in importance. Small farmers grew mainly food crops, particularly corn, but they also produced a few 400-pound bales of cotton each year. Large planters measured their crop in hundreds of bales. Small farmers' cotton tied them to planters. Unable to afford cotton gins or baling presses of their own, they relied on slave owners to gin and bale their cotton. With no link to merchants in the port cities, plantation-belt yeomen also turned to better-connected planters to ship and sell their cotton.

A network of relationships connected small farmers and planters. Planters hired out surplus slaves to ambitious yeomen who wanted to expand cotton production. They sometimes chose the sons of local farm families as overseers. Plantation mistresses occasionally nursed ailing neighbors. Family ties could span class lines, making planter and yeoman kin as well as neighbors. Yeomen helped police slaves by riding in slave patrols, which nightly rode country roads to make certain that no slaves were moving about without permission. On Sundays, plantation dwellers and plain folk came together in church to worship.

Plantation-belt yeomen may have envied, and at times even resented, wealthy slaveholders, but small farmers learned to accommodate. Planters made accommodation easier by going out of their way to behave as good neighbors and avoid direct exploitation of slaveless whites in their community. As a consequence, rather than raging at the oppression of the planter regime, the typical plantation-belt yeoman sought entry into it. He dreamed of adding acreage to his farm, buying a few slaves of his own, and retiring from exhausting field work.

Upcountry Yeomen

By contrast, the hills and mountains of the South resisted the spread of slavery and plantations. In the western parts of Virginia, North Carolina, and South Carolina, in northern Georgia and Alabama, and in eastern Tennessee and Kentucky, the higher elevation, colder climate, rugged terrain, and poor transportation made it difficult for commercial agriculture to make headway. As a result, planters and slaves were scarce. Geographically isolated, the upcountry was a yeoman stronghold.

All members of the upcountry farm family worked, their tasks depending on their sex and age. Husbands labored in the fields, and with their sons, they cleared, plowed, planted, and cultivated primarily food crops—corn, wheat, beans, sweet potatoes, and perhaps some fruit. Wives and their daughters labored in and about the cabin. One upcountry farmer remembered that his mother "worked in the house cooking, spinning, weaving [and doing] patchwork." Women also tended the vegetable garden, kept a cow and some chickens, preserved food, cleaned their homes, fed their families, and cared for their children. Male and female tasks were equally crucial to the farm's success, but as in other white southern households, the male patriarch ruled the domestic sphere.

The typical upcountry yeoman also grew a little cotton or tobacco, but food production was more important than cash crops. Not much currency changed hands

plantation belt
Flatlands that spread from South Carolina to east Texas and were dominated by large plantations.

The Cotton Belt

Upcountry of the South

upcountry
The hills and mountains of the southern interior whose higher elevation, colder climate, rugged terrain, and poor transportation made the region less hospitable than the flatlands to slavery and plantations.

| What was plantation life like for slaves? | **How did nonslaveholding southern whites work and live?** | What place did free blacks occupy in the South? | How did slavery shape southern politics? | Conclusion: How did slavery come to define the South? |

in the upcountry. Barter was common. A yeoman might trade his small cotton or tobacco crop to a country store owner for a little salt, bullets, needles, and nails, or swap extra sweet potatoes for a plow from a blacksmith or for leather from a tanner. Networks of exchange and mutual assistance tied individual homesteads to the larger community. Farm families joined together in logrolling, house and barn raising, and cornhusking.

Even the hills had some plantations and slaves, but the few upcountry folks who owned slaves usually had only two or three. As a result, slaveholders had much less social and economic power, and yeomen had more. But the upcountry did not oppose slavery. As long as plain folk there were free to lead their own lives, they defended slavery and white supremacy just as staunchly as other white Southerners.

UNDERSTAND POINTS OF VIEW

Why did southern yeomen defend slavery even though they did not own any slaves?

Poor Whites

The majority of slaveless white Southerners were hardworking, landholding small farmers, but Northerners held a different image of nonslaveholding whites. They believed that slavery had condemned most whites to poverty and backwardness. One antislavery advocate charged that the South harbored three classes: "the slaves on whom devolves all the regular industry, the slaveholders who reap all the fruits, and an idle and lawless rabble who live dispersed over vast plains little removed from absolute barbarism." Critics called this third class a variety of derogatory names: hillbillies, crackers, rednecks, and poor white trash. According to critics, poor whites were not just whites who were poor. They were also supposedly ignorant, diseased, and degenerate.

Contrary to northern opinion, only about one in four nonslaveholding rural white men was landless and very poor. Some worked as tenants, renting land and struggling to make a go of it. Others survived by herding pigs and cattle. And still others worked for meager wages, ditching, mining, logging, and laying track for railroads.

Some poor white men earned reputations for crime and violence. One visitor claimed that a "bowie-knife was a universal, and a pistol a not at all unusual companion." Edward Isham, an illiterate transient, spent about as much time fighting as he did working. When he was not engaged in ear-biting, eye-gouging free-for-alls, he gambled, drank, stole, had run-ins with the law, and in 1860 murdered a respected slaveholder, for which he was hanged.

Unlike Isham, most poor white men did not engage in ferocious behavior but worked hard and dreamed of becoming yeomen. The Lipscomb family illustrates the possibility of upward mobility. In 1845, Smith and Sally Lipscomb and their children abandoned their worn-out land in South Carolina for Benton County, Alabama. "Benton is a mountainous country but ther is a heep of good levil land to tend in it," Smith wrote back to his brother. Alabama, Smith said, "will be better for the rising generation if not for ourselves but I think it will be the best for us all that live any length of time."

Because the Lipscombs had no money to buy land, they squatted on seven unoccupied acres. With the help of neighbors, they built a cabin and two stables. In the first year, Smith and his sons produced several bales of cotton and enough food for the table. The women worked just as hard in the cabin, and Sally contributed to the family's income by selling homemade shirts and socks. In time, the Lipscombs bought land and joined the Baptist church, completing their transformation to respectable yeomen.

Many poor whites succeeded in climbing the economic ladder, but in the 1850s, upward mobility slowed. The cotton boom of that decade caused planters to expand their operations, driving the price of land beyond the reach of poor families. Whether they gained their own land or not, however, poor whites shared common cultural traits with yeoman farmers.

Why did the South become so different from the North?

What was plantation life like for slave masters and mistresses?

The Culture of the Plain Folk

The lives of most plain folk revolved around farms, family, a handful of neighbors, the local church, and perhaps a country store. Work occupied most hours, but plain folk still found time for pleasure. "Dancing they are all fond of," a visitor to North Carolina discovered, "especially when they can get a fiddle, or bagpipe." But the most popular pastimes of men and boys were fishing and hunting. A traveler in Mississippi recalled that his host sent "two of his sons, little fellows that looked almost too small to shoulder a gun," for food. "One went off towards the river and the other struck into the forest, and in a few hours we were feasting on delicious venison, trout and turtle."

Plain folk did not have much "book learning." Public schools were scarce, and private academies charged fees that yeomen could not afford. "Education is not extended to the masses here as at the North," observed a northern visitor. Although most people managed to pick up the "three R's," approximately one southern white man in five was illiterate in 1860, and the rate for white women was even higher. "People here prefer talking to reading," a Virginian remarked. Telling stories, reciting ballads, and singing hymns were important activities in yeoman culture.

Plain folk spent more hours in revival tents than in classrooms. Preachers spoke day and night to save souls, and by midcentury, Baptists and Methodists had become the South's largest religious groups. By emphasizing free choice and individual worth, the plain folk's religion was hopeful and affirming. Hymns and spirituals provided guides to right and wrong—praising humility and steadfastness, condemning drunkenness and profanity. Above all, hymns spoke of the eventual release from worldly sorrows and the assurance of eternal salvation.

COMPARE AND CONTRAST
How did the lives of nonslaveholding whites in the South compare to those of white workers and small farmers in the North during this time?

QUICK REVIEW

Why did the lives of plantation-belt yeomen and upcountry yeomen diverge?

What was plantation life like for slaves?	**How did nonslaveholding southern whites work and live?**	What place did free blacks occupy in the South?	How did slavery shape southern politics?	Conclusion: How did slavery come to define the South?

What place did free blacks occupy in the South?

CHRONOLOGY

1820s–1830s
– Southern legislatures restrict free blacks.

1822
– Denmark Vesey executed.

1860
– Some 260,000 free blacks live in South.

free black
An African American who was not enslaved. State legislatures stemmed the growth of the free black population and shrank the liberty of free blacks.

UNDERSTAND POINTS OF VIEW

Why were southern whites so threatened by the presence of free blacks?

All white Southerners—slaveholders and slaveless alike—considered themselves superior to all blacks. But not every black Southerner was a slave. In 1860, some 260,000 (approximately 6 percent) of the region's 4.1 million African Americans were free. What is surprising is not that their numbers were small, but that they existed at all. According to proslavery thinking, blacks were supposed to be slaves; only whites were supposed to be free. Blacks who were free stood out, and whites made them targets of oppression. But a few found success despite the restrictions placed on them by white Southerners.

Precarious Freedom

The population of **free blacks** expanded after the Revolutionary War, when the natural rights philosophy of the Declaration of Independence, the egalitarian message of evangelical Protestantism, and a depression in the tobacco economy of the Upper South led to a brief flurry of emancipation—the act of freeing from slavery. The rising numbers of free blacks worried white Southerners, who, because of the cotton boom, wanted more slaves, not more blacks who were free.

In the 1820s and 1830s, state legislatures slowed the growth of the free black population and shrank the liberty of those blacks who had gained their freedom. New laws denied masters the right to free their slaves. Other laws subjected free blacks to special taxes, prohibited them from interstate travel, denied them the right to have schools, prohibited voting, and required them to carry "freedom papers" to prove they were not slaves. Increasingly, whites subjected free blacks to the same laws as slaves. Free blacks could not testify under oath in a court of law or serve on juries. Free blacks were forbidden to strike whites, even to defend themselves. "Free negroes belong to a degraded caste of society," a South Carolina judge said in 1848. "They are in no respect on a perfect equality with the white man. . . . They ought, by law, to be compelled to demean themselves as inferiors."

Laws confined most free African Americans to poverty and dependence. Typically, free blacks were rural, uneducated, unskilled agricultural laborers and domestic servants who had to scramble to survive. Opportunities of any kind—for work, education, or community—were slim. Planters believed that free blacks set a bad example for slaves, subverting the racial subordination that was the essence of slavery.

Whites feared that free blacks might lead slaves in rebellion. In 1822, whites in Charleston accused Denmark Vesey, a free black carpenter, of conspiring with slaves to slaughter Charleston's white inhabitants. The authorities rounded up scores of suspects, who, prodded by torture and the threat of death, implicated others in a "plot to riot in blood, outrage, and rapine." Although the city fathers never found any weapons and Vesey and most of the accused steadfastly denied the charges of conspiracy, officials hanged thirty-five black men, including Vesey, and banished another thirty-seven blacks from the state.

Achievement despite Restrictions

Despite increasingly harsh laws and stepped-up persecution, free African Americans made the most of the advantages their status offered. Unlike slaves, free blacks could legally marry and pass on their heritage of freedom to their children. Freedom also

Why did the South become so different from the North?

What was plantation life like for slave masters and mistresses?

TEARING UP FREE PAPERS.

In the Southern States every colored person is presumed to be a slave, till proved to be free; and they are often robbed of the proof.

▲ **"Tearing Up Free Papers," 1838** This engraving portrays every free black's worst nightmare: the loss of his or her freedom papers. Here a white man destroys the only proof that this black woman has that she is legally free. Without documents, every black person was presumed to be a slave. © Boston Athenaeum, USA/Bridgeman Images.

meant that they could choose occupations and own property. For most, however, these economic rights proved only theoretical, for a majority of the South's free blacks remained propertyless.

Still, some free blacks escaped the poverty and degradation whites thrust on them. Particularly in the South's cities, a free black elite emerged. Consisting of light-skinned African Americans, this group worked at skilled trades, as tailors, carpenters, mechanics, and the like. Their customers were prominent whites—planters, merchants, and judges—who appreciated their able, respectful service. Urban whites enforced many of the restrictive laws only sporadically, allowing free blacks room to maneuver. They operated schools for their children and traveled in and out of their states, despite laws forbidding both activities. They worshipped with whites (in separate seating) and lived scattered about in white neighborhoods, not in ghettos. And some owned slaves. Of the 3,200 black slaveholders (barely 1 percent of the free black population), most owned only a few family members whom they could not legally free. Others owned slaves in large numbers and exploited them for labor.

One such free black slave owner was William Ellison of South Carolina. Born a slave in 1790, Ellison bought his freedom in 1816 and set up business as a cotton gin maker, a trade he had learned as a slave. His business grew with the cotton boom, and by 1835 he was prosperous enough to purchase the home of a former governor of the state. By the time of his death in 1861, he had become a cotton planter, with sixty-three slaves and an 800-acre plantation.

Most free blacks neither became slaveholders like Ellison nor sought to raise a slave rebellion, as whites accused Denmark Vesey of doing. Rather, most free blacks simply tried to preserve their freedom, which was under increasing attack. Unlike

CONSIDER CAUSE AND EFFECT

Why could some free blacks get ahead despite harsh laws?

| What was plantation life like for slaves? | How did nonslaveholding southern whites work and live? | **What place did free blacks occupy in the South?** | How did slavery shape southern politics? | Conclusion: How did slavery come to define the South? |

blacks in the North whose freedom was secure, free blacks in the South clung to a precarious freedom by seeking to impress whites with their reliability, economic contributions, and good behavior.

QUICK REVIEW

Why did many state legislatures pass laws restricting free blacks' rights in the 1820s and 1830s, and what were the results?

How did slavery shape southern politics?

By the mid-nineteenth century, all southern white men—planters and plain folk—and no southern black men, even those who were free, could vote. But even after the South's politics became democratic for white males, political power remained unevenly distributed. The nonslaveholding white majority wielded less political power than their numbers suggested. The slaveholding white minority wielded more. With a well-developed sense of class interest, slaveholders engaged fully in party politics, elections, and officeholding, and as a result they received significant benefits from state governments. Nonslaveholding whites were concerned mainly with preserving their liberties and keeping their taxes low. They asked government for little of an economic nature, and they received little.

Slaveholders sometimes worried about nonslaveholders' loyalty to slavery, but most whites accepted the planters' argument that the existing social order served *all* Southerners' interests. Slavery rewarded every white man—no matter how poor—with membership in the South's white ruling race. It also provided the means by which nonslaveholders might someday advance into the ranks of the planters.

White men in the South argued furiously about many things, but they agreed that they should take land from Indians, promote agriculture, uphold white supremacy and masculine privilege, and defend slavery from its enemies.

"In the South, it seemed, 'everyone talked about politics everywhere,' even the 'illiterate and shoeless.'"

The Democratization of the Political Arena

In the first half of the nineteenth century, Southerners eliminated the wealth and property requirements that had once restricted political participation. By the 1850s, every state had extended the right to vote to all adult white males. Most southern states also removed the property requirements for holding state offices. To be sure, undemocratic features lingered. Plantation districts still wielded disproportionate power in several state legislatures. Nevertheless, southern politics took place within an increasingly democratic political structure, as it did elsewhere in the nation.

White male suffrage ushered in an era of vigorous electoral competition in the South. Eager voters rushed to the polls to exercise their new rights. Candidates

Why did the South become so different from the North?

What was plantation life like for slave masters and mistresses?

crisscrossed their electoral districts, treating citizens to barbecues and bands, rum and races, as well as stirring speeches. In the South, it seemed, "everybody talked politics everywhere," even the "illiterate and shoeless."

As politics became aggressively democratic, it also grew fiercely partisan. From the 1830s to the 1850s, Whigs and Democrats battled for the electorate's favor. Both parties presented themselves as the plain white folk's best friend. All candidates declared their allegiance to republican equality and pledged themselves to defend the people's liberty. And each party sought to portray the other as a collection of rich, snobbish, selfish men who had antidemocratic designs up their silk sleeves.

Planter Power

Whether Whig or Democrat, southern officeholders were likely to be slave owners. The master's power over slaves did not translate directly into political authority over whites, however. In the nineteenth century, political power could only be won at the ballot box, and almost everywhere nonslaveholders were in the majority. Yet year after year, proud and noisily egalitarian common men elected wealthy slaveholders.

By 1860, the percentage of slave owners in state legislatures ranged from 41 percent in Missouri to nearly 86 percent in North Carolina (**Table 13.1**). Legislators not only tended to own slaves; they often owned large numbers. The percentage of planters (individuals

TABLE 13.1 Percent of Slaveholders and Planters in Southern Legislatures, 1860

Legislature	Slaveholders	Planters*
North Carolina	85.8%	36.6%
South Carolina	81.7	55.4
Alabama	76.3	40.8
Mississippi	73.4	49.5
Georgia	71.6	29.0
Virginia	67.3	24.2
Tennessee	66.0	14.0
Louisiana	63.8	23.5
Kentucky	60.6	8.4
Florida	55.4	20.0
Texas	54.1	18.1
Maryland	53.4	19.3
Arkansas	42.0	13.0
Missouri	41.2	5.3

*Planters: Owned 20 or more slaves.

Data from Ralph A. Wooster, *The People in Power: Courthouse and Statehouse in the Lower South, 1850–1860,* page 40. Copyright © 1975 by Ralph A. Wooster. Courtesy of the University of Tennessee Press.

| What was plantation life like for slaves? | How did nonslaveholding southern whites work and live? | What place did free blacks occupy in the South? | **How did slavery shape southern politics?** | Conclusion: How did slavery come to define the South? |

with twenty or more slaves) in southern legislatures in 1860 ranged from 5.3 percent in Missouri to 55.4 percent in South Carolina. Even in North Carolina, where only 3 percent of the state's white families belonged to the planter class, more than 36 percent of state legislators were planters. Clearly, plain folk did not throw the planters out of office.

Upper-class dominance of southern politics reflected the elite's success in persuading the yeoman majority that what was good for slaveholders was also good for plain folk. In reality, the South had, on the whole, done well by common white men. Most had farms of their own. They participated as equals in a democratic political system. They enjoyed an elevated social status, above all blacks and in theory equal to all other whites. They commanded patriarchal authority over their households. And as long as slavery existed, they could dream of joining the planter class. Slaveless white men found much to celebrate in the slave South.

Most slaveholders took pains to win the plain folk's trust and to nurture their respect. One nonslaveholder told his wealthy neighbor that he had a bright political future because he never thought himself "too good to sit down & talk to a poor man." Mary Boykin Chesnut of South Carolina complained about the fawning attention her husband, a U.S. senator, showed to poor men, including one who had "mud sticking up through his toes." But smart candidates found ways to convince wary plain folk of their democratic convictions and egalitarian sentiments, whether they were genuine or not. Walter L. Steele, who ran for a seat in the North Carolina legislature in 1846, detested campaigning for votes, but he learned, he said, to speak with a "candied tongue."

Georgia politics illustrate how well planters protected their interests in state legislatures. In 1850, about half of the state's revenues came from taxes on slaves, the principal form of planter wealth. However, the tax rate on slaves was puny, only about one-fifth the rate on land. Planters benefited from public spending far more than other groups did. Financing railroads—which carried cotton to market—was the largest state expenditure. The legislature also established low tax rates on land, the principal form of yeoman wealth, which meant that the typical yeoman's annual tax bill was small. Still, relative to their wealth, large slaveholders paid less than did other whites. Relative to their numbers, they got more. Slaveholding legislators protected planters' interests and gave the impression of protecting the small farmers' interests as well.

In addition to politics, slaveholders defended slavery in other ways. In the 1830s, Southerners decided that slavery was too important to debate. "So interwoven is [slavery] with our interest, our manners, our climate and our very being," one man declared in 1833, "that no change can ever possibly be effected without a civil commotion from which the heart of a patriot must turn with horror." Powerful whites dismissed slavery's critics from college faculties, drove them from pulpits, and hounded them from political life. Sometimes antislavery Southerners fell victim to vigilantes and mob violence. One could defend slavery; one could even delicately suggest mild reforms. But no Southerner could any longer safely call slavery evil or advocate its destruction.

In the South, therefore, the rise of the common man occurred alongside the continuing, even growing, power of the planter class. Rather than pitting slaveholders against nonslaveholders, elections remained an effective means of binding the region's whites together. Elections affirmed the sovereignty of white men, whether planter or plain folk, and the subordination of African Americans. Those twin themes played well among white women as well. Though unable to vote, white women supported equality for whites and slavery for blacks. In the antebellum South, the politics of slavery helped knit together all of white society.

CONSIDER CAUSE AND EFFECT

How did slave owners use their political power to protect their interests?

QUICK REVIEW

How did planters retain political power in a democratic system?

| Why did the South become so different from the North? | What was plantation life like for slave masters and mistresses? |

Conclusion: How did slavery come to define the South?

By the early nineteenth century, northern states had either abolished slavery or put it on the road to extinction, while southern states were building the largest slave society in the New World. Regional differences increased over time, not only because the South became more and more dominated by slavery, but also because developments in the North rapidly propelled it in a very different direction.

By 1860, one-third of the South's population was enslaved. Bondage saddled blacks with enormous physical and spiritual burdens: hard labor, harsh treatment, broken families, and most important, the denial of freedom itself. Although degraded and exploited, they were not defeated. Out of African memories and New World realities, blacks created a life-affirming African American culture that sustained and strengthened them. Their families, religion, and community provided defenses against white racism and power. Defined as property, they refused to be reduced to things. Perceived as inferior beings, they rejected the notion that they were natural slaves.

The South was not merely a society with slaves; it had become a slave society. Slavery shaped the region's economy, culture, social structure, and politics. Whites south of the Mason-Dixon line believed that racial slavery was necessary and just. By making all blacks a subordinate class, all whites gained a measure of equality and harmony.

Many features of southern life helped to confine class tensions among whites: the wide availability of land, rapid economic mobility, the democratic nature of political life, the patriarchal power among all white men, and, most of all, slavery and white supremacy. All stress along class lines did not disappear, however, and anxious slave-holders continued to worry that yeomen would defect from the proslavery consensus. But during the 1850s, white Southerners' acceptance of slavery would increasingly unite them in political opposition to their northern neighbors.

| What was plantation life like for slaves? | How did nonslaveholding southern whites work and live? | What place did free blacks occupy in the South? | How did slavery shape southern politics? | **Conclusion: How did slavery come to define the South?** |

387

STEP 1 — EXPLAIN WHY IT MATTERS

Put your reading into practice. Identify each term below, and then explain why it matters in U.S. history.

TERM	WHO OR WHAT & WHEN	WHY IT MATTERS
Mason-Dixon line (p. 360)		
cotton kingdom (p. 360)		
slave codes (p. 362)		
miscegenation (p. 363)		
planter (p. 366)		
plantation (p. 366)		
paternalism (p. 370)		
chivalry (p. 372)		
yeomen (p. 378)		
plantation belt (p. 379)		
upcountry (p. 379)		
free black (p. 382)		

STEP 2 — MOVE BEYOND THE BASICS

To demonstrate a more advanced understanding, assess the key characteristics and trends in the North (see chapter 12) and the South in the nineteenth century.

Key Characteristics and Trends	North	South
Agriculture		
Urbanization/Industrialization		
White Racial Attitudes		
Economic Diversity/Labor		
Population/Immigration		

STEP 3

PUT IT ALL TOGETHER

Now, explain the big picture. Remember to use specific examples from the chapter in your answers.

REGIONAL DIVERGENCE

• How and why did the economies of the North and South steadily diverge over the course of the first half of the nineteenth century?

• How did the presence of large numbers of African Americans shape southern culture?

SOUTHERN SOCIETY AND POLITICS

• How did southern yeomen see themselves and their place in southern society, and how did slavery affect their sense of themselves?

• How did slavery shape southern politics?

PLANTATION LIFE

• How did plantation owners see the relationship between master and slave? How did slavery shape other social relationships in the antebellum South?

• In what ways did slaves create communities for themselves and develop methods to resist their bondage?

LOOKING BACKWARD, LOOKING AHEAD

• How did southern slave societies change from the eighteenth to nineteenth centuries?

• Why did many white Southerners come to believe that slavery had to be preserved at any cost? How might that have influenced national politics?

STEP 4

CONNECT THESE EVENTS

How did slavery help shape the economy, social structure, and politics of the South in the first half of the nineteenth century?

STEP 5

CONNECT TO THE PRESENT

To what extent do the distinctive features of the antebellum South continue to make the South different today?

14

THE HOUSE DIVIDED

1846–1861

How did the issue of slavery drive the United States toward civil war in the mid-nineteenth century? Chapter 14 explores the politics of slavery in the years leading up to the Civil War. It examines how the issue of the expansion of slavery into newly acquired territories deepened sectional divisions, undermined existing political parties, helped create new ones, and finally led to secession and civil war.

This chapter will explore the following questions:

- Why did the acquisition of land from Mexico contribute to sectional tensions?
- What upset the balance between slave and free states?
- How did the party system change in the 1850s?
- Why did northern fear of the "Slave Power" intensify in the 1850s?
- Why did some southern states secede immediately after Lincoln's election?
- Conclusion: Why did political compromise fail?

AN AMERICAN STORY

Grizzled, gnarled, and fifty-nine years old, John Brown had for decades lived like a nomad, hauling his large family of twenty children across six states as he tried farming, raising sheep, selling wool, and running a tannery. But failure dogged him. Failure, however, had not budged his conviction that slavery was wrong and ought to be destroyed. In the wake of the fighting that erupted over the future of slavery in Kansas in the 1850s, his beliefs turned violent. On May 24, 1856, he led an eight-man antislavery posse in the midnight slaughter of five allegedly proslavery men at Pottawatomie, Kansas. He told Mahala Doyle, whose husband and two oldest sons he killed, that if a man stood between him and what he thought right, he would take that man's life as calmly as he would eat breakfast.

After the killings, Brown slipped out of Kansas and reemerged in the East, where he begged money to support his vague plan for military operations against slavery. On the night of October 16, 1859, Brown took his war against slavery into the South. With only twenty-one men, including five African Americans, he invaded Harpers Ferry, Virginia. His band seized the town's armory and rifle works, but the invaders were immediately surrounded. When Brown refused to surrender, federal troops under Colonel Robert E. Lee charged with bayonets. Although a few of Brown's raiders escaped, federal forces killed ten of his men (including two of his sons) and captured seven, among them Brown.

Months before the raid, Brown had claimed, "When I strike, the bees will begin to swarm." As the slaves arrived, Brown said he would arm them and fight a war of liberation. Brown, however, neglected to inform the slaves when he had arrived in Harpers Ferry, and the few who knew of his arrival wanted nothing to do with his enterprise. "It was not a slave insurrection," Abraham Lincoln observed. "It was an attempt by white men to get up a revolt among slaves, in which the slaves refused to participate. In fact, it was so absurd that the slaves, with all their ignorance, saw plainly enough it could not succeed." White Southerners viewed Brown's raid as proof that Northerners actively incited slaves in bloody rebellion. Sectional tension was as old as the Constitution, but hostility had escalated with the outbreak of war with Mexico in May 1846 (see "The Mexican-American War, 1846–1848" in chapter 12). National expansion and the slavery issue intersected when Representative David Wilmot introduced a bill to prohibit slavery in any territory that might be acquired as a result of the war. After that, the problem of slavery in the territories became the principal wedge that divided the nation.

"Mexico is to us the forbidden fruit," South Carolina senator John C. Calhoun declared at the war's outset. "The penalty of eating it [is] to subject our institutions to political death." For a decade and a half, the slavery issue intertwined with the fate of former Mexican land, poisoning the national political debate. Slavery proved powerful enough to transform party politics into sectional politics. Rather than Whigs and Democrats confronting one another across party lines, Northerners and Southerners eyed one another hostilely across the Mason-Dixon line. As the nation lurched from crisis to crisis, southern disaffection and alienation mounted, and support for compromise eroded. The era began with a crisis of union and ended with the Union in even graver peril. As Abraham Lincoln predicted in 1858, "A house divided against itself cannot stand."

▼ **John Brown** In this 1859 photograph, John Brown appears respectable, but contemporaries debated his mental state and moral character, and the debate still rages. Critics argue that he was a bloody terrorist, a religious fanatic who believed that God had touched him for a great purpose. Admirers see a selfless hero, a shrewd political observer who recognized that only violence would end slavery in America. Library of Congress, 3a06152.

Why did the acquisition of land from Mexico contribute to sectional tensions?

CHRONOLOGY

1846
– Wilmot Proviso introduced.

1847
– Wilmot Proviso defeated in Senate.
– "Popular sovereignty" compromise offered.

1848
– Free-Soil Party founded.
– Zachary Taylor elected president.

1849
– California gold rush begins.

1850
– Taylor dies; Vice President Millard Fillmore becomes president.
– Compromise of 1850 becomes law.

Wilmot Proviso
Proposal put forward by Representative David Wilmot of Pennsylvania in August 1846 to ban slavery in territory acquired from the Mexican-American War.

free labor
Term referring to work conducted free from constraint and according to a voluntary contract between employer and laborer. The ideal of free labor lay at the heart of the North's argument that slavery should not be extended into the western territories.

Victory in the Mexican-American War brought vast new territories in the West into the United States. The gold rush of 1849 transformed the sleepy frontier of California into a booming economy (see chapter 12). The 1850s witnessed new "rushes," for gold in Colorado and silver in Nevada. It quickly became clear that Northerners and Southerners had very different visions of the West, particularly the place of slavery in its future. Politicians battled over whether to ban slavery from former Mexican land or permit it to expand to the Pacific. In 1850, Congress patched together a plan that Americans hoped would last. This plan for expansion envisioned stability only for the Anglo-Americans, however. Native Americans in the West would soon see their traditional way of life assaulted.

The Wilmot Proviso and the Expansion of Slavery

Most Americans agreed that the Constitution left the issue of slavery to the individual states to decide. Northern states had done away with slavery, while southern states had retained it. But what about slavery in the nation's territories? The Constitution states that "Congress shall have power to . . . make all needful rules and regulations respecting the territory . . . belonging to the United States." The debate about slavery, then, turned toward Congress.

The spark for the national debate appeared in August 1846 when a Democratic representative from Pennsylvania, David Wilmot, proposed that Congress bar slavery from all lands acquired in the war with Mexico. The Mexicans had abolished slavery in their country, and Wilmot declared, "God forbid that we should be the means of planting this institution upon it."

Regardless of party affiliation, Northerners lined up behind the Wilmot Proviso. They supported free soil, by which they meant territory in which slavery would be prohibited, for several reasons. Some wanted to preserve the West for free labor, for hardworking, self-reliant free men, not for slaveholders and slaves. But support also came from those who were simply anti-South. New slave territories would eventually mean new slave states. Wilmot himself said his proposal would blunt "*the power* of slaveholders" in the national government.

Additional support for free soil came from Northerners who were hostile to blacks and wanted to reserve new land for whites. Wilmot himself blatantly encouraged racist support when he declared, "I would preserve for free white labor a fair country, a rich inheritance, where the sons of toil, of my own race and own color, can live without the disgrace which association with negro slavery brings upon free labor." It is no wonder that some called the Wilmot Proviso the "White Man's Proviso."

The thought that slavery might be excluded in the territories outraged white Southerners. Like Northerners, they regarded the West as a ladder for economic and social opportunity. They also believed that the exclusion of slavery was a slap in the face to southern veterans of the Mexican-American War. "When the war-worn soldier returns home," one Alabaman asked, "is he to be told that he cannot carry his property to the country won by his blood?" In addition, southern leaders sought to maintain equal political strength with the North to protect the South's interests, especially slavery. The need seemed especially urgent in the 1840s, when the North's population

Why did the acquisition of land from Mexico contribute to sectional tensions?

and wealth were booming. James Henry Hammond of South Carolina predicted that ten new states would be carved from the acquired Mexican land. If free soil won, the North would "ride over us roughshod" in Congress, he claimed. "Our only safety is in *equality* of power."

Foes of slavery's expansion and foes of slavery's exclusion squared off in the nation's capital. Because Northerners had a majority in the House, they easily passed the Wilmot Proviso. In the Senate, however, where slave states outnumbered free states fifteen to fourteen, Southerners defeated it in 1847. Senator John C. Calhoun of South Carolina even denied that Congress had the constitutional authority to exclude slavery from the nation's territories. He argued that because the territories were the "joint and common property" of all the states, Congress could not bar citizens of one state from migrating with their property (including slaves) to the territories. Whereas Wilmot demanded that Congress slam shut the door to slavery, Calhoun declared that Congress must hold the door wide open.

Senator Lewis Cass of Michigan offered a compromise. He proposed the doctrine of **popular sovereignty**, by which the people who settled the territories would decide for themselves slavery's fate. This solution, Cass argued, sat squarely in the American tradition of democracy and local self-government. It also offered a lack of clarity about the precise moment when settlers could determine slavery's fate. That gave popular sovereignty an advantage. Northern advocates believed that the decision on slavery could be made as soon as the first territorial legislature assembled. With free-soil majorities likely because of the North's greater population, they would shut the door to slavery immediately. Southern supporters believed that popular sovereignty guaranteed that slavery would be unrestricted throughout the entire territorial period. Only when settlers in a territory drew up a constitution and applied for statehood could they decide the issue of slavery. By then, slavery would have sunk deep roots. As long as the matter of timing remained vague, popular sovereignty gave hope to both sides.

When Congress ended its session in 1848, no plan had won a majority in both houses. Northerners who demanded no new slave territory anywhere, ever, and Southerners who demanded entry for their slave property into all territories, or else, staked out their positions. Unresolved in Congress, the territorial question naturally became an issue in the presidential election of 1848.

The Election of 1848

When President Polk, worn out and ailing, chose not to seek reelection, the Democratic convention nominated Lewis Cass of Michigan, the man most closely associated with popular sovereignty. The Whigs nominated a Mexican-American War hero, General Zachary Taylor, a man who had never voted and who had no known political opinions. The Whigs declined to adopt a party platform, betting that the combination of a military hero and total silence on the slavery issue would unite their divided party. Georgia politician Robert Toombs hailed Taylor, who owned more than one hundred slaves on plantations in Mississippi and Louisiana, as a "Southern man, a slaveholder, a cotton planter."

Antislavery Whigs balked. Senator Charles Sumner called for a major political realignment, "one grand Northern party of Freedom." In the summer of 1848, antislavery Whigs and antislavery Democrats founded the Free-Soil Party, nominating a Democrat, Martin Van Buren, for president and a Whig, Charles Francis Adams, for vice president. The platform boldly proclaimed, "Free soil, free speech, free labor, and free men."

In the November election, Free-Soilers did not carry a single state. Taylor won the all-important electoral vote 163 to 127, carrying eight of the fifteen slave states and seven of

Mexican Cession, 1848

popular sovereignty
The idea that government is subject to the will of the people. Applied to the territories, popular sovereignty meant that the residents of a territory should determine, through their legislature, whether to allow slavery.

CONSIDER CAUSE AND EFFECT

Why did the Missouri Compromise, which had resolved disputes over the status of slavery in the western territories in 1820, fail to resolve them in the 1840s?

What upset the balance between slave and free states?	How did the party system change in the 1850s?	Why did northern fear of the "Slave Power" intensify in the 1850s?	Why did some southern states secede immediately after Lincoln's election?	Conclusion: Why did political compromise fail?

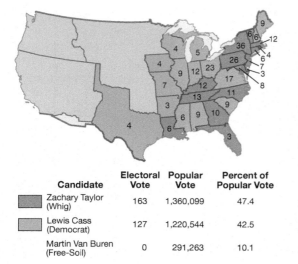

Candidate	Electoral Vote	Popular Vote	Percent of Popular Vote
Zachary Taylor (Whig)	163	1,360,099	47.4
Lewis Cass (Democrat)	127	1,220,544	42.5
Martin Van Buren (Free-Soil)	0	291,263	10.1

MAP 14.1 ▲ The Election of 1848

the fifteen free states (**Map 14.1**). (Wisconsin had entered the Union earlier in 1848 as the fifteenth free state.) Northern voters were not yet ready for Sumner's "one grand Northern party of Freedom," but the struggle over slavery in the territories had shaken the major parties badly.

Debate and Compromise

When Zachary Taylor entered the White House in March 1849, the new slaveholding president shocked the nation by championing a free-soil solution to the Mexican cession. Believing that he could avoid further sectional strife if California and New Mexico skipped the territorial stage, Taylor encouraged the settlers to apply for admission to the Union as states. Predominantly antislavery, the settlers began writing free-state constitutions. "For the first time," Mississippian Jefferson Davis lamented, "we are about permanently to destroy the balance of power between the sections."

Congress convened in December 1849, beginning one of the most contentious sessions in its history. President Taylor urged Congress to admit California as a free state immediately and to admit New Mexico, which lagged behind a few months, as soon as it applied. Southerners exploded. A North Carolinian declared that Southerners who would "consent to be thus degraded and enslaved, ought to be whipped through their fields by their own negroes."

Into this rancorous scene stepped Senator Henry Clay of Kentucky, the architect of Union-saving compromises in the Missouri and nullification crises (see chapters 10 and 11). Clay offered a series of resolutions meant to answer and balance "all questions in controversy between the free and slave states, growing out of the subject of slavery." Admit California as a free state, he proposed, but organize the rest of the Southwest without restrictions on slavery. Require Texas to abandon its claim to parts of New Mexico, but compensate it by assuming its preannexation debt. Abolish the domestic slave trade in Washington, D.C., but confirm slavery itself in the nation's capital. Affirm Congress's lack of authority to interfere with the interstate slave trade, and enact a more effective fugitive slave law.

Both antislavery advocates and "fire-eaters" (as radical Southerners who urged secession from the Union were called) savaged Clay's plan. Senator Salmon P. Chase of Ohio ridiculed it as "sentiment for the North, substance for the South." Senator Henry S. Foote of Mississippi denounced it as more offensive to the South than the speeches of abolitionists William Lloyd Garrison, Wendell Phillips, and Frederick Douglass combined. The most frightening response came from Calhoun, who argued that the fragile political unity of North and South depended on continued equal representation in the Senate, which Clay's plan for a free California destroyed. "As things now stand," he said in February 1850, the South "cannot with safety remain in the Union."

◀ **Henry Clay Offering His California Compromise to the Senate on 5 February 1850** Artist Peter F. Rothermel captures the high intensity of the seventy-three-year-old Kentuckian's last significant political act. Citizens who packed the galleries of the U.S. Senate had come to hear the renowned orator explain that his package of compromises required mutual concessions from both North and South but no sacrifice of "great principle" from either. Friends called his performance the "crowning grace to his public life." The Granger Collection, New York.

Why did the acquisition of land from Mexico contribute to sectional tensions?

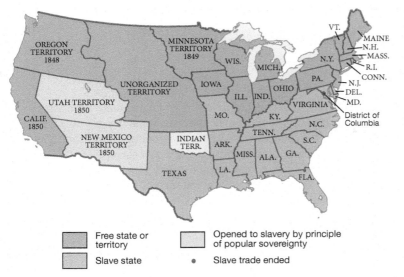

MAP 14.2 ◀ **The Compromise of 1850**
The patched-together sectional agreement was both clumsy and unstable. Few Americans—in either North or South—supported all five parts of the Compromise.

Legend:
- ▨ Free state or territory
- ▨ Slave state
- ☐ Opened to slavery by principle of popular sovereignty
- • Slave trade ended

Like Clay, Massachusetts senator Daniel Webster defended compromise. He told Northerners that the South had legitimate complaints, but he told Southerners that secession from the Union would mean civil war. He argued that the Wilmot Proviso's ban on slavery in the territories was reckless and unnecessary because the harsh climate effectively prohibited the expansion of cotton and slaves into the Southwest. Why, then, "taunt" Southerners with the proviso? "I would not take pains uselessly to reaffirm an ordinance of nature, nor to reenact the will of God," Webster declared.

Free-soil forces recoiled from what they saw as Webster's desertion. Senator William H. Seward of New York responded that Webster's and Clay's compromise with slavery was "radically wrong and essentially vicious." Seward rejected Calhoun's argument that Congress lacked the constitutional authority to exclude slavery from the territories. In any case, he said, there was a "higher law than the Constitution"—the law of God—to ensure freedom in all the public domain. Claiming that God was a Free-Soiler did nothing to cool the superheated political atmosphere.

In May 1850, the Senate considered a bill that joined Clay's resolutions into a single comprehensive package. Clay bet that a majority of Congress wanted compromise and that the members would vote for the package, even though it contained provisions they disliked. But the strategy backfired. Free-Soilers and proslavery Southerners voted down the comprehensive plan. Fortunately for those who favored a settlement, Senator Stephen A. Douglas, a rising Democratic star from Illinois, broke the bill into its parts and skillfully ushered each through Congress. The agreement Douglas won in September 1850 was very much the one Clay had proposed in January. California entered the Union as a free state. New Mexico and Utah became territories where popular sovereignty would decide slavery's fate. Texas accepted its boundary with New Mexico and received $10 million from the federal government. Congress ended the slave trade in the District of Columbia but enacted a more stringent fugitive slave law. In September, Millard Fillmore, who had become president when Zachary Taylor died in July, signed into law each bill, collectively known as the Compromise of 1850 (**Map 14.2**). The nation breathed a sigh of relief, for the Compromise preserved the Union and peace, for the moment.

PLACE EVENTS IN CONTEXT

What did each faction concede and gain in the Compromise of 1850, and which stood to benefit most from its terms?

Compromise of 1850
Laws passed in 1850 meant to resolve disputes about the place of slavery in the nation. Key elements included the admission of California as a free state and the Fugitive Slave Act.

QUICK REVIEW

How might the Compromise of 1850 have eased sectional tensions, and at what cost?

| What upset the balance between slave and free states? | How did the party system change in the 1850s? | Why did northern fear of the "Slave Power" intensify in the 1850s? | Why did some southern states secede immediately after Lincoln's election? | Conclusion: Why did political compromise fail? |

What upset the balance between slave and free states?

CHRONOLOGY

1852
- *Uncle Tom's Cabin* published.
- Franklin Pierce elected president.

1853
- Gadsden Purchase negotiated.

1854
- Kansas-Nebraska Act passes.

The Compromise of 1850 began to come apart almost immediately. Surprisingly, the cause was not slavery in the territories, the crux of the disagreement, but runaway slaves in New England, a neglected part of the settlement. The implementation of the Fugitive Slave Act brought the horrors of slavery into the North. Millions of Northerners who never saw a runaway slave confronted slavery through Harriet Beecher Stowe's *Uncle Tom's Cabin*, a novel that vividly depicts the brutality of the South's "peculiar institution." Congress did its part to undo the Compromise as well. Four years after Congress put the sectional compromise together, it undid it. With the Kansas-Nebraska Act in 1854, it again raised the question of slavery in the territories, the deadliest of all sectional issues.

The Fugitive Slave Act

The issue of runaway slaves was as old as the Constitution, which contained a provision for the return of any "person held to service or labor in one state" who escaped to another. In 1793, a federal law gave muscle to the provision by authorizing slave owners to enter other states to recapture their slave property. Proclaiming the 1793 law a license to kidnap free blacks, northern states in the 1830s began passing "personal liberty laws" that provided fugitives with some protection.

Some northern communities also formed vigilance committees to help runaways. Each year, a few hundred slaves escaped into free states and found friendly northern "conductors" who put them aboard the underground railroad, which was not a railroad at all but a series of secret "stations" (hideouts) on the way to Canada. Harriet Tubman, an escaped slave from Maryland, returned more than a dozen times and guided more than three hundred slaves to freedom in this way.

Furious about northern interference, Southerners in 1850 insisted on the stricter fugitive slave law that was part of the Compromise. According to the **Fugitive Slave Act**, to seize an alleged slave, a slaveholder simply had to appear before a commissioner and swear that the runaway was his. The commissioner earned $10 for every individual returned to slavery but only $5 for those set free. Most galling to Northerners, the law expected all citizens to assist officials in apprehending runaways. That required Northerners to become slave catchers.

In Boston in February 1851, an angry crowd overpowered federal marshals and snatched a runaway named Shadrach from a courtroom, put him on the underground railroad, and whisked him off to Canada. Three years later, when another Boston crowd rushed the courthouse in a failed attempt to rescue runaway Anthony Burns, a guard was shot dead. Martha Russell was among the angry crowd that watched Burns being escorted to the ship that would return him to Virginia. "Did you ever feel every drop of blood in you boiling and seething, throbbing and burning, until it seemed you should suffocate?" she asked. "I have felt all this today. I have seen that poor slave, Anthony Burns, carried back to slavery."

Fugitive Slave Act
A law included in the Compromise of 1850 to strengthen provisions for capturing runaway slaves in the North.

"'We went to bed one night old fashioned, conservative, Compromise Union Whigs & waked up stark mad abolitionists.'"

To white Southerners, the "fanatics of the higher law creed" had whipped Northerners into a frenzy of massive resistance. Actually, the overwhelming majority of fugitives claimed by slaveholders were reenslaved

Why did the acquisition of land from Mexico contribute to sectional tensions?

▶ **Fugitive Ellen Craft in Disguise** In 1848, William and Ellen Craft, a slave couple from Macon, Georgia, executed a daring escape. Light-skinned, Ellen disguised herself as a sickly southern gentleman who was traveling to Philadelphia for medical treatment. She carried her arm in a sling to explain why she couldn't sign travel documents. William acted as her personal servant as they anxiously made their way by train to Savannah, then on to Philadelphia by boat and train. The Crafts told their daring story throughout the North until the Fugitive Slave Act of 1850 drove them to Britain, where adoring crowds greeted them as celebrities. Mary Evans Picture Library/Everett Collection.

ELLEN CRAFT.
The fugitive Slave.

peacefully. But brutal enforcement of the unpopular law had a radicalizing effect in the North, particularly in New England. Textile mill owner Amos A. Lawrence said that "we went to bed one night old fashioned, conservative, Compromise Union Whigs & waked up stark mad abolitionists." He exaggerated, but to Southerners, Northerners had betrayed the Compromise and the Constitution. "The continued existence of the United States as one nation," warned the *Southern Literary Messenger*, "depends upon the full and faithful execution of the Fugitive Slave Bill."

Uncle Tom's Cabin

The spectacle of shackled African Americans being herded south seared the conscience of every Northerner who witnessed such a scene. But far more Northerners were turned against slavery by a novel. Harriet Beecher Stowe, a white Northerner who had never set foot on a plantation, made the South's slaves into flesh-and-blood human beings almost more real than life.

A member of a famous clan of preachers, teachers, and reformers, Stowe despised the slave catchers and wrote to expose the sin of slavery. Published as a book in 1852, *Uncle Tom's Cabin, or Life among the Lowly* became a blockbuster hit, selling 300,000 copies in its first year and more than 2 million copies within ten years. Stowe's characters leaped from the page. Here was the gentle slave Uncle Tom, a Christian saint who forgave those who beat him to death; the courageous slave Eliza, who fled with her child across the frozen Ohio River; and the fiendish overseer Simon Legree, whose Louisiana plantation was a nightmare of torture and death.

Stowe aimed her most powerful blows at slavery's destructive impact on the family. Her character Eliza succeeds in keeping her son off the auction block, but other mothers are not so fortunate. When told that her infant has been sold, Lucy drowns herself. Driven half-mad by the sale of a son and daughter, Cassy decides "never again [to] let a child live to grow up!" She gives her third child an opiate and watches as "he slept to death." Northerners shed tears and sang praises to *Uncle Tom's Cabin*. What Northerners accepted as truth, Southerners denounced as slander. A Virginian proclaimed Stowe a member of the "Woman's Rights" and "Higher Law" schools and dismissed the novel as a work of "intense fanaticism." A New Orleans newspaper called Stowe "part quack and part cutthroat," a fake physician who came with arsenic in one hand and a pistol in the other to treat diseases she had "never witnessed." Although it is impossible to measure precisely the impact of a novel on public opinion, *Uncle Tom's Cabin* helped to crystallize northern sentiment against slavery and to confirm white Southerners' suspicion that they no longer received any sympathy in the free states.

Uncle Tom's Cabin
Enormously popular antislavery novel written by Harriet Beecher Stowe and published in 1852. It helped to solidify northern sentiment against slavery and to confirm white Southerners' sense that no sympathy remained for them in the free states.

PLACE EVENTS IN CONTEXT

How did the social reform movements of the nineteenth century shape Harriet Beecher Stowe's novel and Northerners' strong response to it?

| What upset the balance between slave and free states? | How did the party system change in the 1850s? | Why did northern fear of the "Slave Power" intensify in the 1850s? | Why did some southern states secede immediately after Lincoln's election? | Conclusion: Why did political compromise fail? |

Other writers—ex-slaves who knew life in slave cabins firsthand—also produced stinging indictments of slavery. Solomon Northup's compelling *Twelve Years a Slave* (1853) sold 27,000 copies in two years, and the powerful *Narrative of the Life of Frederick Douglass, as Told by Himself* (1845) eventually sold more than 30,000 copies. But no work touched the North's conscience as did the novel by a free white woman. A decade after its publication, when Stowe visited Abraham Lincoln at the White House, he reportedly said, "So you are the little woman who wrote the book that made this great war."

The Kansas-Nebraska Act

As the 1852 election approached, the Democrats and Whigs sought to close the sectional rifts that had opened within their parties. For their presidential nominee, the Democrats turned to Franklin Pierce of New Hampshire. Pierce's well-known sympathy with southern views caused his northern critics to include him among the "doughfaces," northern men malleable enough to champion southern causes. The Whigs chose another Mexican-American War hero, General Winfield Scott of Virginia. But the Whigs' northern and southern factions were hopelessly divided, and the Democrat Pierce carried twenty-seven states to Scott's four and won the electoral college vote 254 to 42 (**Map 14.4**). The Free-Soil Party lost almost half of the voters who had turned to it in the tumultuous political atmosphere of 1848.

Eager to leave the sectional controversy behind, the new president turned swiftly to foreign expansion. Manifest destiny remained robust. Pierce's major objective was Cuba, which was owned by Spain and in which slavery flourished, but when antislavery Northerners blocked Cuba's acquisition to keep more slave territory from entering the Union, Pierce turned to Mexico. In 1853, diplomat James Gadsden negotiated a $10 million purchase of some 30,000 square miles of land in present-day Arizona and New Mexico. The Gadsden Purchase furthered the dream of a transcontinental railroad to California and Pierce's desire for a southern route through Mexican territory. Talk of a railroad ignited rivalries in cities from New Orleans to Chicago as they maneuvered to become the eastern terminus. Inevitably in the 1850s, the contest for a transcontinental railroad became a sectional struggle over slavery.

Gadsden Purchase, 1853

Illinois's Democratic senator Stephen A. Douglas badly wanted the transcontinental railroad for Chicago. Any railroad that ran west from Chicago would pass through a region that Congress in 1830 had designated a "permanent" Indian reserve (see chapter 11). Douglas proposed giving this vast area between the Missouri River and the Rocky Mountains an Indian name, Nebraska, and then throwing the Indians out. Once the region achieved territorial status, whites could survey and sell the land, establish a civil government, and build a railroad.

Nebraska lay within the Louisiana Purchase and, according to the Missouri Compromise of 1820, was closed to slavery (see chapter 10). Douglas needed southern votes to pass his Nebraska legislation, but Southerners had no incentive to create another free territory or to help a northern city win the transcontinental railroad. Southerners, however, agreed to help if Congress organized Nebraska according to popular sovereignty. That meant giving slavery a chance in Nebraska Territory and reopening the dangerous issue of slavery expansion. In January 1854, Douglas introduced his bill to organize Nebraska Territory, leaving to the settlers themselves the decision about slavery. At southern insistence, and even though he knew it would "raise a hell of a storm," Douglas added an explicit repeal of the Missouri Compromise. Free-Soilers branded Douglas's plan "a gross violation of a sacred pledge" and an "atrocious plot" to transform free land into a "dreary region of despotism, inhabited by masters and slaves."

Undaunted, in 1854 Douglas skillfully shepherded the explosive bill through Congress. Nine-tenths of the southern members (Whigs and Democrats) and half of

UNDERSTAND POINTS OF VIEW

What motivated Stephen Douglas, who had played a significant role in enacting the Compromise of 1850, to risk the fragile sectional accord it had achieved?

Why did the acquisition of land from Mexico contribute to sectional tensions?

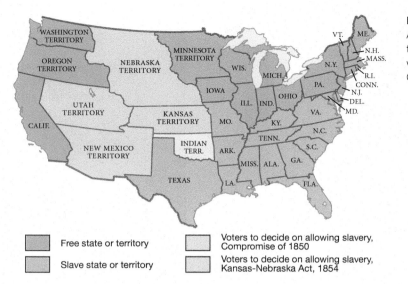

MAP 14.3 ◀ The Kansas-Nebraska Act, 1854
Americans hardly thought twice about dispossessing the Indians of land guaranteed them by treaty, but many worried about the outcome of repealing the Missouri Compromise and opening up the region to slavery.

Free state or territory

Slave state or territory

Voters to decide on allowing slavery, Compromise of 1850

Voters to decide on allowing slavery, Kansas-Nebraska Act, 1854

the northern Democrats cast votes in favor of the bill. Like Douglas, most northern supporters believed that popular sovereignty would make Nebraska free territory. The **Kansas-Nebraska Act** divided the huge territory in two: Nebraska and Kansas (**Map 14.3**). With this act, the government pushed the Plains Indians farther west, making way for farmers and railroads.

Kansas-Nebraska Act
1854 law that divided Indian Territory into Kansas and Nebraska, repealed the Missouri Compromise, and left the new territories to decide the issue of slavery on the basis of popular sovereignty.

QUICK REVIEW

Why did the Compromise of 1850 fail to achieve sectional peace?

How did the party system change in the 1850s?

Since the early 1830s, Whigs and Democrats had organized and channeled political conflict in the nation. This party system dampened sectionalism and strengthened the Union. To achieve national political power, the Whigs and Democrats had to retain strength in both the North and South. Strong northern and southern wings required that each party compromise and find positions acceptable to both sections.

The Kansas-Nebraska controversy shattered this stabilizing political system. In place of two national parties with bisectional strength, the mid-1850s witnessed the development of one party heavily dominated by one section and another party entirely limited to the other section. Rather than "national" parties, the country had what one critic disdainfully called "geographic" parties, a development that thwarted political compromise between the sections.

CHRONOLOGY

1854
– American (Know-Nothing) Party emerges.
– Republican Party founded.

1856
– James Buchanan elected president.

The Old Parties: Whigs and Democrats

As early as the Mexican-American War, members of the Whig Party had clashed over the future of slavery in annexed Mexican lands. By 1852, the Whig Party could please its

What upset the balance between slave and free states?	**How did the party system change in the 1850s?**	Why did northern fear of the "Slave Power" intensify in the 1850s?	Why did some southern states secede immediately after Lincoln's election?	Conclusion: Why did political compromise fail?

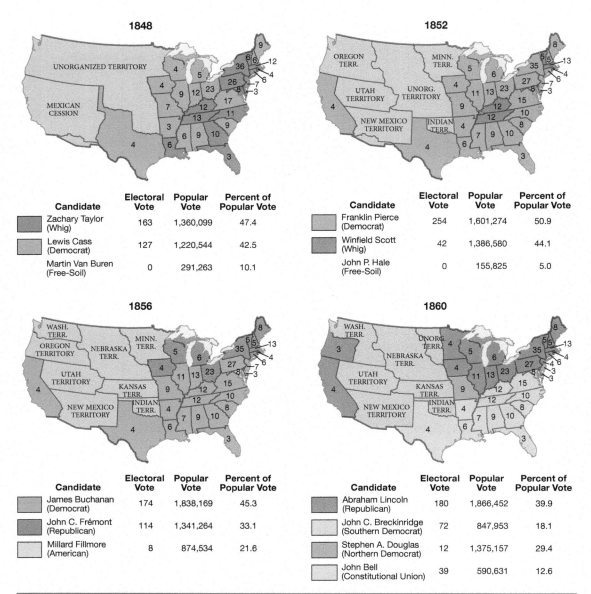

1848

Candidate	Electoral Vote	Popular Vote	Percent of Popular Vote
Zachary Taylor (Whig)	163	1,360,099	47.4
Lewis Cass (Democrat)	127	1,220,544	42.5
Martin Van Buren (Free-Soil)	0	291,263	10.1

1852

Candidate	Electoral Vote	Popular Vote	Percent of Popular Vote
Franklin Pierce (Democrat)	254	1,601,274	50.9
Winfield Scott (Whig)	42	1,386,580	44.1
John P. Hale (Free-Soil)	0	155,825	5.0

1856

Candidate	Electoral Vote	Popular Vote	Percent of Popular Vote
James Buchanan (Democrat)	174	1,838,169	45.3
John C. Frémont (Republican)	114	1,341,264	33.1
Millard Fillmore (American)	8	874,534	21.6

1860

Candidate	Electoral Vote	Popular Vote	Percent of Popular Vote
Abraham Lincoln (Republican)	180	1,866,452	39.9
John C. Breckinridge (Southern Democrat)	72	847,953	18.1
Stephen A. Douglas (Northern Democrat)	12	1,375,157	29.4
John Bell (Constitutional Union)	39	590,631	12.6

MAP ACTIVITY

MAP 14.4 ▲ Political Realignment, 1848–1860 In 1848, slavery and sectionalism began taking their toll on the country's party system. The Whig Party was an early casualty. By 1860, national parties—those that contended for votes in both the North and South—had been replaced by regional parties.

READING THE MAP: Which states did the Democrats pick up in 1852 compared to 1848? Which of these states did the Democrats lose in 1856? Compare the general geographic location of the states won by the Republicans in 1856 versus those won in 1860.

CONNECTIONS: In the 1860 election, which party benefited the most from the western and midwestern states added to the Union since 1848? Why do you think these states chose to back this party?

proslavery southern wing or its antislavery northern wing but not both. The Whigs' miserable showing in the election of 1852 made it clear that they were no longer a strong national party. By 1856, after more than two decades of contesting the Democrats, they were hardly a party at all (see Map 14.4).

> Why did the acquisition of land from Mexico contribute to sectional tensions?

The collapse of the Whig Party left the Democrats as the country's only national party. Popular sovereignty provided a doctrine that many Democrats could support. Even so, popular sovereignty very nearly undid the party. When Stephen Douglas applied the doctrine to the part of the Louisiana Purchase where slavery had been barred, he divided northern Democrats and destroyed the dominance of the Democratic Party in the free states. After 1854, the Democrats were a southern-dominated party. Still, gains in the South more than balanced Democratic losses in the North, and during the 1850s Democrats elected two presidents and won majorities in Congress in almost every election.

The breakup of the Whigs and the disaffection of many northern Democrats set millions of Americans politically adrift. Americans found that the death of the old party system created a multitude of fresh political harbors.

TRACE CHANGE OVER TIME

Around what issues did the Whigs organize as a political party in 1834, and how did the party's agenda and constituency change during its twenty-year life span?

The New Parties: Know-Nothings and Republicans

Dozens of new political organizations vied for voters' attention. Out of the confusion, two emerged as true contenders. One grew out of the slavery controversy, a coalition of indignant antislavery Northerners. The other arose from an entirely different split in American society, between native Protestants and Roman Catholic immigrants.

The wave of immigrants that arrived in America from 1845 to 1855 produced a nasty backlash among Protestant Americans, who feared that the Republic was about to drown in a sea of Roman Catholics from Ireland and Germany (see Figure 12.1 on page 333). Nativists (individuals who were anti-immigrant) began to organize, first into secret societies and then in 1854 into a political party. Recruits swore never to vote for either foreign-born or Roman Catholic candidates and not to reveal any information about the organization. When questioned, they said, "I know nothing." Officially, they were the American Party, but most Americans called them Know-Nothings.

The Know-Nothings enjoyed dazzling success in 1854 and 1855. They captured state legislatures throughout the nation and claimed dozens of seats in Congress. Democrats and Whigs described the Know-Nothings' phenomenal record as a "tornado," a "hurricane," and "a freak of political insanity." But by 1855, an observer might reasonably have concluded that the Know-Nothings had emerged as the successor to the Whigs.

The Know-Nothings were not the only new party making noise, however. One of the new antislavery organizations provoked by the Kansas-Nebraska Act called itself the Republican Party. The Republicans attempted to unite all those who opposed the extension of slavery into any territory of the United States.

Republican Party
Antislavery party formed in 1854 following passage of the Kansas-Nebraska Act. The Republicans attempted to unite all those who opposed the extension of slavery into any territory of the United States.

VISUAL ACTIVITY

◀ **Know-Nothing Cartoon** This cartoon underscores the Know-Nothing contention that hard-drinking Irish and German immigrants were stealing elections and polluting American democracy. In addition to the Irishman's whiskey and the German's beer, the artist completes the negative stereotypes by giving the Irishman his shillelagh (club) and the German his pipe. The Granger Collection, New York.

READING THE IMAGE: What is taking place behind the Irishman and German, and how does it spell danger for the Republic?
CONNECTIONS: In what parts of the nation would you suppose the Know-Nothing message had its greatest appeal?

What upset the balance between slave and free states?	**How did the party system change in the 1850s?**	Why did northern fear of the "Slave Power" intensify in the 1850s?	Why did some southern states secede immediately after Lincoln's election?	Conclusion: Why did political compromise fail?

"A Purse of Her Own": Petitioning for the Right to Own Property

In the early Republic, as today, having money and deciding how to spend it was a fundamental aspect of independent adulthood. Yet antebellum married women were denied this privilege, because of the laws of *coverture*, which placed wives under the full legal control of their husbands (see "Women and the Law" in chapter 10). By law, husbands made all the financial decisions in a household. Even money that a wife earned or brought into a marriage was not hers to control as long as she remained married. Ernestine Potowsky Rose of New York City thought that was wrong, and she became the first woman in the United States to take action to change the law.

Born in Poland in 1810, Ernestine Potowsky was the daughter of a rabbi, which meant that her destiny was fixed: an arranged marriage, many children, and a life strictly governed by religious law. Ernestine rejected this fate and left home for London, where at age nineteen she married William Rose. The couple migrated to the United States and settled in New York City, where William, a jeweler, started a business.

Ernestine soon learned of a bill presented in 1837 in the New York assembly proposing that married women, "equally with males and unmarried females, possess the rights of *life*, *liberty*, and PROPERTY, and are equally entitled to be protected in all three." But, predictably, the bill failed to pass.

▶ Ernestine Rose, in her midforties when this photograph was taken, managed to hold a smile for the several minutes required to capture her image on a photographic plate. Fotosearch/Getty Images.

The Republican creed tapped into the basic beliefs and values of Northerners. Slavery, Republicans believed, degraded the dignity of white labor by associating work with blacks and servility. As evidence, they pointed to the South, where, one Republican claimed, nonslaveholding whites "retire to the outskirts of civilization, where they live a semi-savage life, sinking deeper and more hopelessly into barbarism with every succeeding generation." Republicans warned that the insatiable slaveholders of the South, whom antislavery Northerners called the "Slave Power," were conspiring through their control of the Democratic Party to expand slavery, subvert liberty, and undermine the Constitution.

Only by restricting slavery to the South, Republicans believed, could free labor flourish elsewhere. In the North, one Republican declared in 1854, "every man holds his fortune in his own right arm; and his position in society, in life, is to be tested by his own individual character." Without slavery, western territories would provide

Why did the acquisition of land from Mexico contribute to sectional tensions?

The devastating panics of 1837 and 1839, and the resulting bankruptcies, soon changed some traditionalists' minds about wives and property. Men in several state legislatures crafted laws that shielded a wife's inherited property from creditors collecting debts from her husband. By 1848, eighteen states had modified property laws in the name of family protection.

In New York, as support for such a law grew, Ernestine Rose mobilized women around the argument that married women should be able to own and control property. She circulated petitions and spoke from public platforms, often joined by Elizabeth Cady Stanton, a young wife from western New York. In April 1848, three months before the Seneca Falls woman's rights convention, the New York assembly finally awarded married women sole authority over property they brought to a marriage.

Rose welcomed the new law but recognized its key shortcoming: It made no provision for wages earned by a married woman. Nor did it alter inheritance laws that limited a widow's share of her husband's estate. Speaking at every national woman's rights convention from 1850 to 1860, Rose argued for women's economic independence.

Of particular concern to Rose was the plight of poor wives. She and Susan B. Anthony encountered women trapped in marriages with husbands who failed to support their dependents. Anthony, herself a lifelong single woman, recalled that "as I passed from town to town I was made to feel the great evil of women's utter dependence on man. . . . Woman must have a purse of her own."

Rose's efforts paid off. In 1860, New York amended its law to include a wife's wages as her own, but only if she earned the money outside the household. Money earned selling eggs or caring for boarders still went directly into the husband's pocket. Perhaps the most significant beneficiaries of this law were women whose husbands were incompetent to support them or who had deserted them. These husbands now had no right to their wives' hard-gained earnings.

The revised New York law made other important changes to coverture. A wife could now sue (or be sued), make legal contracts of her own, and serve as joint guardian of her children, "with equal powers, rights and duties in regard to them." These changes, adopted in many states after 1860, began the long (and still ongoing) process of elevating women to equality with men.

Questions for Analysis

RECOGNIZE VIEWPOINTS: What do the laws of coverture reveal about how most men viewed married women in antebellum America?

ANALYZE THE EVIDENCE: Why, according to women activists like Ernestine Rose, did a woman need "a purse of her own"?

CONSIDER THE CONTEXT: What do you suppose there was about women's condition that drew some northern women to the antislavery campaign?

vast economic opportunity for free men. Powerful images of liberty and opportunity attracted a wide range of Northerners to the Republican cause.

Women as well as men rushed to the new Republican Party. Indeed, three women helped found the party in Ripon, Wisconsin, in 1854. Although they could not vote and suffered from other legal handicaps, women nevertheless participated in politics by writing campaign literature, marching in parades, giving speeches, and lobbying voters. Women's antislavery fervor attracted them to the Republican Party, and participation in party politics in turn nurtured the woman's rights movement. Susan B. Anthony, who attended Republican meetings throughout the 1850s, found that her political activity made her disfranchisement all the more frustrating. She and other women in the North worked on behalf of antislavery and woman suffrage and the right of married women to control their own property. **(See "Spotlight: 'A Purse of Her Own': Petitioning for the Right to Own Property" above.)**

COMPARE AND CONTRAST
What did the Republican Party and the Know-Nothing Party have in common, and how did they differ?

| What upset the balance between slave and free states? | **How did the party system change in the 1850s?** | Why did northern fear of the "Slave Power" intensify in the 1850s? | Why did some southern states secede immediately after Lincoln's election? | Conclusion: Why did political compromise fail? |

► **John and Jessie Frémont Poster** The election of 1856 marked the first time a candidate's wife appeared on campaign items. Jessie Benton Frémont helped plan her husband's campaign, coauthored his election biography, and drew northern women into political activity as never before. "What a shame that women can't vote!" declared abolitionist Lydia Maria Child. "We'd carry 'our Jessie' into the White House on our shoulders, wouldn't we."

The Election of 1856

The election of 1856 revealed that the Republicans had become the Democrats' main challenger, and slavery in the territories, not immigration, was the election's principal issue. When the Know-Nothings insisted on a platform that endorsed the Kansas-Nebraska Act, most Northerners walked out. The few Know-Nothings who remained nominated ex-president Millard Fillmore.

The Republican platform focused mostly on "making every territory free." When they labeled slavery a "relic of barbarism," they signaled that they had written off the South. For president, they nominated the soldier and California adventurer John C. Frémont. Frémont lacked political credentials, but his wife, Jessie Frémont, the daughter of Senator Thomas Hart Benton of Missouri, knew the political map well. Though careful to maintain a proper public image, the energetic young mother and antislavery defender helped attract voters and draw women into politics.

The Democrats, successful in 1852 in bridging sectional differences by nominating a northern man with southern principles, chose another "doughface," James Buchanan of Pennsylvania. They portrayed the Republicans as extremists ("Black Republican Abolitionists") whose support for the Wilmot Proviso risked pushing the South out of the Union.

The Democratic strategy carried the day for Buchanan, who won 174 electoral votes against Frémont's 114 and Fillmore's 8 (see **Map 14.4**). But the big news was that the Republicans, campaigning under the banner "Free soil, Free men, Frémont," carried all but five of the states north of the Mason-Dixon line. Sectionalism had fashioned a new party system, one that spelled danger for the Democrats and the nation. Indeed, war had already broken out between proslavery and antislavery forces in the distant Kansas Territory.

QUICK REVIEW

Why did the Whig Party disintegrate in the 1850s?

Why did the acquisition of land from Mexico contribute to sectional tensions?

Why did northern fear of the "Slave Power" intensify in the 1850s?

Events in Kansas Territory in the mid-1850s underscored the Republicans' contention that the slaveholding South presented a profound threat to American freedoms. Kansas reeled with violence that Republicans argued was southern in origin. Republicans also pointed to the brutal beating by a Southerner of a respected northern senator on the floor of Congress. Even the Supreme Court, in the Republicans' view, reflected the South's drive toward minority rule and tyranny. Then, in 1858, the issues dividing North and South received an extraordinary hearing in a senatorial contest in Illinois, when the nation's foremost Democrat debated an up-and-coming Republican (**Figure 14.1**).

"Bleeding Kansas"

Three days after the House of Representatives approved the Kansas-Nebraska Act in 1854, Senator William H. Seward of New York declared: "Come on then, Gentlemen of the Slave States, since there is no escaping your challenge, I accept it in behalf of the cause of freedom. We will engage in competition for the virgin soil of Kansas, and God give the victory to the side which is stronger in numbers as it is in right." Because of Stephen Douglas, popular sovereignty would determine whether Kansas became slave or free. Free-state and slave-state settlers each sought a majority at the ballot box, claimed God's blessing, and kept their rifles ready.

CHRONOLOGY

1856
- "Bleeding Kansas" pits anti- versus proslavery advocates.
- "Sack of Lawrence" orchestrated.
- Pottawatomie massacre kills five in Kansas.

1857
- *Dred Scott* decision announced.
- Congress rejects Lecompton constitution.
- Panic of 1857 ripples throughout economy.

1858
- Lincoln and Douglas debate; Douglas wins Senate seat.

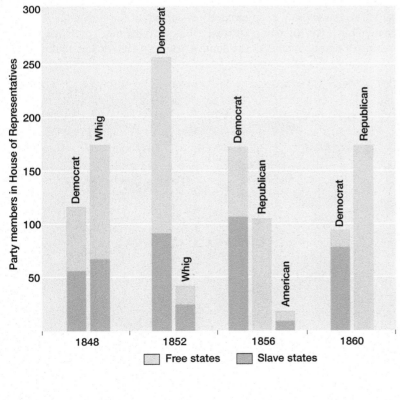

FIGURE 14.1 ◄ Changing Political Landscape, 1848–1860

The polarization of American politics between free states and slave states occurred in little more than a decade.

What upset the balance between slave and free states?

How did the party system change in the 1850s?

Why did northern fear of the "Slave Power" intensify in the 1850s?

Why did some southern states secede immediately after Lincoln's election?

Conclusion: Why did political compromise fail?

"Bleeding Kansas," 1850s

"Bleeding Kansas"
Term for the bloody struggle between proslavery and antislavery factions in Kansas following its organization in the fall of 1854.

PLACE EVENTS IN CONTEXT

What political and ideological developments influenced John Brown and his actions in Kansas?

Emigrant aid societies sprang up to promote settlement from free states or slave states. Missourians especially thought it important to secure Kansas for slavery. Thousands of rough frontiersmen, egged on by Missouri senator David Rice Atchison, invaded Kansas. "There are eleven hundred coming over from Platte County to vote," Atchison reported, "and if that ain't enough we can send five thousand—enough to kill every God-damned abolitionist in the Territory." Not surprisingly, proslavery candidates swept the territorial elections in November 1854. When Kansas's first territorial legislature met, it enacted a raft of proslavery laws, including one prohibiting antislavery men from holding office or serving on juries. President Pierce endorsed the work of the fraudulently elected legislature. Free-soil Kansans did not. They elected their own legislature, which promptly banned both slaves and free blacks from the territory. Organized into two rival governments and armed to the teeth, Kansans verged on civil war.

Fighting broke out on the morning of May 21, 1856, when several hundred proslavery men raided the town of Lawrence, the center of free-state settlement. Only one man died, but the "Sack of Lawrence," as free-soil forces called it, inflamed northern opinion. Elsewhere in Kansas, news of events in Lawrence provoked John Brown, a free-soil settler, to announce that "it was better that a score of bad men should die than that one man who came here to make Kansas a Free State should be driven out" and to lead the posse that massacred five allegedly proslavery settlers along Pottawatomie Creek.

Just as "Bleeding Kansas" gave the fledgling Republican Party fresh ammunition for its battle against the Slave Power, so too did an event that occurred in the national capital. In May 1856, Senator Charles Sumner of Massachusetts delivered a speech titled "The Crime against Kansas," which included a scalding personal attack on South Carolina senator Andrew P. Butler. Sumner described Butler as a "Don Quixote" who had taken as his mistress "the harlot, slavery."

Preston Brooks, a young South Carolina member of the House and a kinsman of Butler's, felt compelled to defend the honor of his aged relative. On May 22, Brooks entered the Senate, where he found Sumner working at his desk. He beat Sumner over the head with his cane until Sumner lay bleeding and unconscious on the floor. Brooks resigned his seat in the House, only to be promptly reelected. In the North, the southern hero became a villain. Like "Bleeding Kansas," "Bleeding Sumner" provided the Republican Party with a potent symbol of the South's "twisted and violent civilization."

▶ **Members of the Anti-Slavery Free-Soil Party, 1856** Rifles, pistols, and knives flooded "Bleeding Kansas," but cannons were not unknown. Violent confrontation between pro- and antislavery forces began years before the outbreak of the Civil War. In Kansas Territory, "Border Ruffians" fought "Free-Staters" to determine the status of slavery in the new territory. Peter Newark American Pictures/Bridgeman Images.

Why did the acquisition of land from Mexico contribute to sectional tensions?

The *Dred Scott* Decision

Political debate over slavery in the territories became heated in part because the Constitution lacked precision on the issue. In 1857, in the case of *Dred Scott v. Sandford*, the Supreme Court announced its understanding of the meaning of the Constitution regarding slavery in the territories. The Court's decision demonstrated that it had not escaped the sectional and partisan passions that were convulsing the land.

In 1833, an army doctor bought the slave Dred Scott in St. Louis, Missouri, and took him as his personal servant to Fort Armstrong, Illinois, and then to Fort Snelling in Minnesota Territory. Back in St. Louis in 1846, Scott, with the help of white friends, sued to prove that he and his family were legally entitled to their freedom. Scott argued that living in Illinois, a free state, and Minnesota, a free territory, had made his family free, and that they remained free even after returning to Missouri, a slave state.

In 1857, Chief Justice Roger B. Taney, who hated Republicans and detested racial equality, wrote the Court's *Dred Scott* decision. First, the Court ruled that Scott could not legally claim violation of his constitutional rights because he was not a citizen of the United States. When the Constitution was written, Taney said, blacks "were regarded as beings of an inferior order . . . so far inferior, that they had no rights which the white man was bound to respect." Second, the laws of Dred Scott's home state, Missouri, determined his status, and thus his travels in free areas did not make him free. Third, Congress's power to make "all needful rules and regulations" for the territories did not include the right to prohibit slavery. The Court explicitly declared the Missouri Compromise unconstitutional, even though the Kansas-Nebraska Act had already voided it.

The Taney Court's extreme proslavery decision outraged Republicans. By denying the federal government the right to exclude slavery in the territories, it cut the legs

Dred Scott decision
1857 Supreme Court decision that validated the South's most extreme argument for its rights in the territories. It denied the federal government's right to exclude slavery from the territories and declared that African Americans were not citizens.

ANALYZE EVIDENCE

What does "Bleeding Kansas" suggest about how the conflict between proslavery and free-soil forces had evolved in the short period between 1848, when the Mexican-American War ended, and 1856?

◀ **Dred Scott** This portrait of Dred Scott was painted in 1857, the year of the Supreme Court's decision. The Court's ruling particularly alarmed African Americans in the North. Although the Court rejected Scott's suit, he gained his freedom in May 1857 when a white man purchased and freed Scott and his family. Portrait: © Collection of the New-York Historical Society, USA/Bridgeman Images.

What upset the balance between slave and free states?	How did the party system change in the 1850s?	**Why did northern fear of the "Slave Power" intensify in the 1850s?**	Why did some southern states secede immediately after Lincoln's election?	Conclusion: Why did political compromise fail?

out from under the Republican Party. As the *New York Tribune* lamented, the decision cleared the way for "all our Territories . . . to be ripened into Slave States." Particularly frightening to African Americans in the North was the Court's declaration that free blacks were not citizens and had no rights.

The Republican rebuttal to the *Dred Scott* ruling relied heavily on the dissenting opinion of Justice Benjamin R. Curtis. Scott *was* a citizen of the United States, Curtis argued. At the time of the writing of the Constitution, free black men could vote in five states and participated in the ratification process. Scott *was* free. Because slavery was prohibited in Minnesota, the "involuntary servitude of a slave, coming into the Territory with his master, should cease to exist." The Missouri Compromise *was* constitutional. The Founders had meant exactly what they said: Congress had the power to make "*all* needful rules and regulations" for the territories, including barring slavery.

Unmoved by Curtis's dissent, the Court, in a seven-to-two decision, validated an extreme statement of the South's territorial rights. John C. Calhoun's claim that Congress had no authority to exclude slavery became the law of the land. White Southerners cheered. One gloated that the *Dred Scott* decision was the "funeral sermon of Black Republicanism . . . crushing and annihilating the antislavery platform." Ironically, the *Dred Scott* decision actually strengthened the young Republican Party. Indeed, that "outrageous decision," one Republican argued, was "the best thing that could have happened," for it provided powerful evidence of the Republicans' claim that a hostile Slave Power conspired against northern liberties.

CONSIDER CAUSE AND EFFECT

Why did the *Dred Scott* decision further inflame the tensions between proslavery and free-soil forces?

Prairie Republican: Abraham Lincoln

By reigniting the sectional flames, the Kansas-Nebraska Act in 1854 and the *Dred Scott* case in 1857 provided Republican politicians with fresh challenges and fresh opportunities. Abraham Lincoln, convinced that slavery was a "monstrous injustice," a "great moral wrong," and an "unqualified evil to the negro, the white man, and the State," condemned the Kansas-Nebraska Act of 1854 for giving slavery a new life and in 1856 joined the Republican Party. He accepted that the Constitution permitted slavery in those states where it existed, but he believed that Congress could contain its spread.

Lincoln envisioned the western territories as "places for poor people to go to, and better their conditions." But slavery's expansion threatened free men's opportunity. The *Dred Scott* decision, which denied Congress's right to ban slavery in the territories, persuaded him that slaveholders were engaged in a dangerous conspiracy to nationalize slavery. The next step, Lincoln warned, would be "another Supreme Court decision, declaring that the Constitution of the United States does not permit a State to exclude slavery from its limits." Unless the citizens of Illinois woke up, he warned, the Supreme Court would make "Illinois a slave State."

Republicans could even point to evidence that Southerners sought to spread slavery beyond the nation's borders. In the 1850s, thousands of Americans became "filibusters" (from the Spanish *filibustero*, meaning "freebooter" or "pirate"), adventurers who joined private armies that invaded foreign countries throughout the Western Hemisphere. Increasingly, filibusters were Southerners and proslavery. The most successful of all filibusters was William Walker of Tennessee, who in 1855 invaded Nicaragua, became president, legalized slavery, and called on Southerners to come raise cotton, sugar, and coffee in "a magnificent country." Filibusters confirmed Republicans' view of Southerners as dangerous cutthroats willing to do anything to expand slavery.

Why did the acquisition of land from Mexico contribute to sectional tensions?

▶ **Lincoln** Alexander Hesler took this photograph in Springfield, Illinois, less than two years after the Lincoln-Douglas debates. Lincoln's law partner, William T. Herndon, observed: "There is the peculiar curve of the lower lip, the lone mole on the right cheek, and a pose of the head so essentially Lincolnian; no other artist has ever caught it." Library of Congress, 3a09621.

In Lincoln's view, the nation could not "endure, permanently half slave and half free." Either opponents of slavery would arrest its spread and place it on the "course of ultimate extinction," or its advocates would see that it became legal in "*all* the States, *old* as well as *new—North* as well as *South*." Lincoln's convictions that slavery was wrong and that Congress must stop its spread formed the core of the Republican ideology. In 1858, Republicans in Illinois chose him to challenge the nation's premier Democrat, who was seeking reelection to the U.S. Senate.

The Lincoln-Douglas Debates

When Stephen Douglas learned that the Republican Abraham Lincoln would be his opponent for the Senate, he observed: "He is the strong man of the party—full of wit, facts, dates—and the best stump speaker, with his droll ways and dry jokes, in the West. He is as honest as he is shrewd, and if I beat him my victory will be hardly won."

Not only did Douglas have to contend with a formidable foe, but during the previous year, the nation had experienced a sharp economic downturn, the panic of 1857. Thousands of businesses had failed, and many were unemployed. As a Democrat, Douglas had to go before the voters as a member of the party whose policies stood accused of causing the panic of 1857.

Douglas's response to another crisis in 1857, however, helped shore up his standing in Illinois. Proslavery forces in Kansas met in the town of Lecompton, drafted a proslavery constitution, and applied for statehood. Everyone knew that free-soilers outnumbered proslavery settlers, but President Buchanan instructed Congress to admit Kansas as the sixteenth slave state. Senator Douglas broke with the Democratic administration and denounced the Lecompton constitution; Congress killed the Lecompton bill. (When Kansans reconsidered the Lecompton constitution in an honest election, they rejected it six to one. Kansas entered the Union in 1861 as a free state.) By denouncing the fraudulent proslavery constitution, Douglas declared his independence from the South and, he hoped, made himself acceptable at home.

> "'Slavery is wrong,' Lincoln repeated, because 'a man has the right to the fruits of his own labor.'"

A relative unknown and a decided underdog in the Illinois election, Lincoln challenged Douglas to debate him face-to-face. The two met in seven communities for what would become a legendary series of debates. To the thousands who stood straining to see and hear, they must have seemed an odd pair. Douglas was five feet four inches tall, broad, and stocky; Lincoln was six feet four, angular, and lean. Douglas was in perpetual motion, darting across the platform, shouting, and jabbing the air; Lincoln stood still and spoke deliberately. Douglas wore the latest fashion and dazzled audiences with his flashy vests. Lincoln wore good suits but managed to look rumpled anyway.

What upset the balance between slave and free states?	How did the party system change in the 1850s?	**Why did northern fear of the "Slave Power" intensify in the 1850s?**	Why did some southern states secede immediately after Lincoln's election?	Conclusion: Why did political compromise fail?

The two men debated the crucial issues of the age—slavery and freedom. Lincoln badgered Douglas with the question of whether he favored the spread of slavery. He tried to force Douglas into the damaging admission that the Supreme Court had repudiated Douglas's own territorial solution, popular sovereignty. At Freeport, Illinois, Douglas admitted that settlers could not now pass legislation barring slavery, but he argued that they could ban slavery just as effectively by not passing protective laws, such as those found in slave states. Southerners condemned Douglas's "Freeport Doctrine" and charged him with trying to steal the victory they had gained with the *Dred Scott* decision. Lincoln chastised his opponent for his "don't care" attitude about slavery, for "blowing out the moral lights around us."

Douglas worked the racial issue. He called Lincoln an abolitionist and an egalitarian enamored of "our colored brethren." Lincoln held what were moderate racial views for his time, but put on the defensive, he reaffirmed his faith in white rule: "I will say, then, that I am not, nor ever have been, in favor of bringing about in any way the social and political equality of the white and black race." Lincoln tried to steer the debate back to what he considered the true issue: the morality and future of slavery. "Slavery is wrong," Lincoln repeated, because "a man has the right to the fruits of his own labor."

As Douglas predicted, the election was hard-fought and closely contested. Until the adoption of the Seventeenth Amendment in 1911, citizens voted for state legislators, who in turn selected U.S. senators. Since Democrats won a slight majority in the Illinois legislature, the members returned Douglas to the Senate. But the Lincoln-Douglas debates thrust Lincoln, the prairie Republican, into the national spotlight.

UNDERSTAND POINTS OF VIEW

How did Lincoln's political and racial views reflect the North's free-labor ideology?

Lincoln-Douglas debates
Series of debates on the issue of slavery and freedom between Democrat Stephen Douglas and Republican Abraham Lincoln, held during the 1858 Illinois senatorial race. Douglas became senator, but the debates helped catapult Lincoln to national attention.

QUICK REVIEW

What evidence did Republicans have for a "Slave Power" conspiracy?

Why did some southern states secede immediately after Lincoln's election?

CHRONOLOGY

1859
– John Brown raids Harpers Ferry.

1860
– Abraham Lincoln elected president.
– South Carolina secedes from Union.

1861
– Six other Lower South states secede.
– Confederate States of America formed.

Republicans believed that they had irrefutable evidence of the South's aggressive promotion of slavery. White Southerners, of course, saw things differently. They were the ones who were under siege, they declared. They believed that Northerners were itching to use their numerical advantage to attack slavery, and not just in the territories. Republicans had made it clear that they were unwilling to accept the *Dred Scott* ruling as the last word on the issue of slavery expansion. And John Brown's attempt to incite a slave insurrection in Virginia in 1859 proved to Southerners that Northerners would do anything to end slavery.

Talk of leaving the Union had been heard for years, but until the final crisis, Southerners had used secession as a ploy to gain concessions within the Union, not to destroy it. Then the 1850s delivered powerful blows to Southerners' confidence that they could remain in the Union and protect slavery. When the Republican Party won the White House in 1860, many Southerners concluded that they would have to leave.

Why did the acquisition of land from Mexico contribute to sectional tensions?

The Aftermath of John Brown's Raid

For his failing attack on Harpers Ferry, Virginia, in 1859, John Brown stood trial for treason, murder, and incitement of slave insurrection. "To hang a fanatic is to make a martyr of him and fledge another brood of the same sort," cautioned one newspaper, but on December 2, 1859, Virginia executed Brown. In life, he was a ne'er-do-well, but as the poet Stephen Vincent Benét observed, "he knew how to die." Brown told his wife that he was "determined to make the utmost possible out of a defeat." He said to the court: "If it is deemed necessary that I should forfeit my life for the furtherance of the ends of justice, and mingle my blood further with the blood of . . . millions in this

▲ **John Brown Going to His Hanging, by Horace Pippin, 1942** The grandparents of Horace Pippin, a Pennsylvania artist, were slaves. His grandmother witnessed the hanging of John Brown, and this painting recalls the scene she so often described to him. Pippin used a muted palette to establish the bleak setting, but he also managed to convey its striking intensity. Historically accurate, the painting depicts Brown tied and sitting erect on his coffin, passing resolutely before the silent, staring white men. The black woman in the lower right corner presumably is Pippin's grandmother. Romare Bearden, another African American artist, recalled the central place of John Brown in black memory: "Lincoln and John Brown were as much a part of the actuality of the Afro-American experience, as were the domino games and the hoe cakes for Sunday morning breakfast. I vividly recall the yearly commemorations for John Brown." Courtesy of the Pennsylvania Academy of the Fine Arts, Philadelphia, www.pafa.org. John Lambert Fund.

READING THE IMAGE: What was the artist trying to convey about the tone of John Brown's execution? According to the painting, what were the feelings of those gathered to witness the event?

CONNECTIONS: How did Brown's trial and execution contribute to the growing split between North and South?

What upset the balance between slave and free states?	How did the party system change in the 1850s?	Why did northern fear of the "Slave Power" intensify in the 1850s?	**Why did some southern states secede immediately after Lincoln's election?**	Conclusion: Why did political compromise fail?

slave country whose rights are disregarded by wicked, cruel, and unjust enactments, I say, let it be done."

After Brown's execution, Americans across the land contemplated the meaning of his life and death. Some Northerners celebrated his "splendid martyrdom." Ralph Waldo Emerson likened Brown to Christ when he declared that Brown made "the gallows as glorious as the cross." Most Northerners did not advocate bloody rebellion, however. Like Lincoln, they concluded that Brown's noble antislavery ideals could not "excuse violence, bloodshed, and treason."

Still, when northern churches marked John Brown's hanging with tolling bells and prayer vigils, white Southerners contemplated what they had in common with people who "regard John Brown as a martyr and a Christian hero, rather than a murderer and robber." Georgia senator Robert Toombs announced solemnly that Southerners must "never permit this Federal government to pass into the traitorous hands of the black Republican party."

Republican Victory in 1860

When the Democrats converged on Charleston for their convention in April 1860, fire-eating Southerners denounced Stephen Douglas and demanded a platform that included federal protection of slavery in the territories, a goal of extreme proslavery Southerners for years. "Ours are the institutions which are at stake; ours is the property that is to be destroyed; ours is the honor at stake," shouted the Alabaman William Lowndes Yancy. When the delegates approved a platform with popular sovereignty, representatives from the entire Lower South and Arkansas stomped out of the convention. The remaining Democrats adjourned to meet a few weeks later in Baltimore, where they nominated Douglas for president.

When bolting southern Democrats reconvened, they approved a platform with a federal slave code and nominated Vice President John C. Breckinridge of Kentucky. Southern moderates, however, refused to support Breckinridge. They formed the Constitutional Union Party to provide voters with a Unionist choice. Instead of adopting a platform and confronting the slavery question, the Constitutional Union Party merely approved a vague resolution pledging "to recognize no political principle other than *the Constitution . . . the Union . . . and the Enforcement of the Laws.*" For president, they nominated former senator John Bell of Tennessee.

PLACE EVENTS IN CONTEXT
What factions emerged out of the shattered Democratic Party, and what were their policy goals?

The Republicans smelled victory, but they needed to carry nearly all the free states to win. To make their party more appealing, they expanded their platform beyond antislavery. They hoped that free homesteads, a protective tariff, a transcontinental railroad, and a guarantee of immigrant political rights would provide an agenda broad enough to unify the North. While reasserting their commitment to stop the spread of slavery, they also denounced John Brown's raid as "among the gravest of crimes" and confirmed the security of slavery in the South.

The foremost Republican, William H. Seward, had made enemies with his radical "higher law" doctrine, which claimed that there was a higher moral law than the Constitution, and with his "irrepressible conflict" speech, in which he declared that North and South were fated to collide. Lincoln, however, since bursting onto the national scene in 1858, had demonstrated his clear purpose, good judgment, and solid Republican credentials. That and his residence in Illinois, a crucial state, made him attractive to the party. On the third ballot, the delegates chose Lincoln. Defeated by Douglas in a state contest less than two years earlier, Lincoln now stood ready to take him on for the presidency.

Why did the acquisition of land from Mexico contribute to sectional tensions?

The election of 1860 was like none other in American politics. It took place in the midst of the nation's severest crisis. Four major candidates crowded the presidential field. Rather than a four-cornered contest, however, the election broke into two contests, each with two candidates. In the North, Lincoln faced Douglas; in the South, Breckinridge confronted Bell. So outrageous did Southerners consider the Republican Party that they did not even permit Lincoln's name to appear on the ballot in ten of the fifteen slave states.

On November 6, 1860, Lincoln swept all of the eighteen free states except New Jersey, which split its electoral votes between him and Douglas. Although Lincoln received only 39 percent of the popular vote, he won easily in the electoral college with 180 votes, 28 more than he needed for victory (**Map 14.5**). Lincoln did not win because his opposition was splintered. Even if the votes of his three opponents had been combined, Lincoln still would have won. He won because his votes were concentrated in the free states, which contained a majority of electoral votes. Ominously, however, Breckinridge, running on a southern-rights platform, won the entire Lower South, plus Delaware, Maryland, and North Carolina.

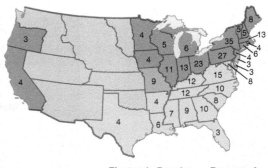

Candidate	Electoral Vote	Popular Vote	Percent of Popular Vote
Abraham Lincoln (Republican)	180	1,866,452	39.9
John C. Breckinridge (Southern Democrat)	72	847,953	18.1
Stephen A. Douglas (Northern Democrat)	12	1,375,157	29.4
John Bell (Constitutional Union)	39	590,631	12.6

MAP 14.5 ▲ The Election of 1860

Secession Winter

Anxious Southerners immediately began debating what to do. Although Breckinridge had carried the South, a vote for "southern rights" was not necessarily a vote for secession. Besides, slightly more than half of the Southerners who had voted had cast ballots for Douglas and Bell, two stout defenders of the Union. "The people of the South have too much sense to attempt the ruin of the government," Lincoln predicted.

Southern Unionists tried to calm the fears that Lincoln's election triggered. Former congressman Alexander Stephens of Georgia asked what Lincoln had done to justify something as extreme as secession. Had he not promised to respect slavery where it existed? In Stephens's judgment, secession might lead to war, which would possibly open the door to slave insurrection. "Revolutions are much easier started than controlled," he warned. "I consider slavery much more secure in the Union than out of it."

Secessionists emphasized the dangers of delay. "Mr. Lincoln and his party assert that this doctrine of equality applies to the negro," former Georgia governor Howell Cobb declared, "and necessarily there can exist no such thing as property in our equals." Lincoln's election without a single electoral vote from the South meant that Southerners were powerless to defend themselves within the Union, Cobb argued. Why wait, he asked, for abolitionists to attack? As for war, there would be none. The Union was a voluntary compact, and Lincoln would not coerce loyalty from Southerners. If Northerners did resist with force, secessionists argued, one southern woodsman could whip five of Lincoln's greasy mechanics.

For all their differences, southern whites agreed that they had to defend slavery. John Smith Preston of South Carolina spoke for the overwhelming majority when he declared, "The South cannot exist without slavery." They disagreed about whether the

CONSIDER CAUSE AND EFFECT

Why did the Republican Party choose to nominate Abraham Lincoln as its presidential candidate in 1860?

| What upset the balance between slave and free states? | How did the party system change in the 1850s? | Why did northern fear of the "Slave Power" intensify in the 1850s? | **Why did some southern states secede immediately after Lincoln's election?** | Conclusion: Why did political compromise fail? |

Southerners Debate Secession

The election of the Republican Abraham Lincoln to the presidency of the United States in November 1860 precipitated the greatest crisis in the nation's history. All eyes focused on the South. Lincoln declared that Southerners were too smart to break up the Union, but others were not so sure.

DOCUMENT 1

William L. Harris, Speech before the General Assembly of Georgia, 1860

Forces for and against immediate secession were almost evenly divided in Georgia, and Mississippi sent William L. Harris, a noted orator and native Georgian, to persuade Georgia to follow it out of the Union. Harris argued that secession was necessary to save slavery and also the South's racial order. He began with his analysis of what Lincoln's election meant.

. . . [The Republicans] have demanded, and now demand, equality between the white and negro races, under our Constitution; equality in representation, equality in the right of suffrage, equality in the honors and emoluments [rewards] of office, equality in the social circle, equality in the rights of matrimony. The cry has been, and now is, 'that slavery must cease, or American liberty must perish,' that 'the success of Black Republicanism is the triumph of anti-slavery.' . . .

To-day our government stands *totally revolutionized* in its main features, and our Constitution broken and overturned. The new administration, which has effected this revolution, only awaits the 4th of March for the inauguration of the new government, the new principles, and the new policy, upon the success of which they have proclaimed the freedom of the slave, but eternal degradation for you and for us. . . .

Our fathers made this a government for the white man, rejecting the negro, as an ignorant, inferior, barbarian race, incapable of self-government, and not, therefore, entitled to be associated with the white man upon terms of civil, political, or social equality. . . .

Mississippi is firmly convinced that there is but one alternative:

This *new union*, with Lincoln Black Republicans and free negroes, *without slavery*; or, slavery under our old constitutional bond of union, *without* Lincoln Black Republicans, or free negroes either, to molest us. . . .

Source: *Address of Hon. W. L. Harris, Commissioner from the State of Mississippi, Delivered before the General Assembly of the State of Georgia, on Monday, Dec. 17th, 1860* (Milledgeville, Ga., 1860).

DOCUMENT 2

Alexander H. Stephens, Speech in the Legislative Hall, Milledgeville, Georgia, 1860

Anti-secessionists in Georgia denied that Georgians had sufficient cause to leave the Union. Alexander H. Stephens believed that the secessionists were trying to create a false sense of urgency that would stampede Southerners out of the Union. He urged caution and careful consideration of the value of the Union.

The first question that presents itself is, Shall the people of the South secede from the Union in consequence of the election

Confederate States of America
Government formed by Lower South states on February 7, 1861, following their secession from the Union. Secessionists argued that the election of a Republican to the presidency imperiled slavery and that the South no longer had political protection within the Union.

mere presence of a Republican in the White House made it necessary to exercise what they considered a legitimate right to secede.

The debate about what to do was briefest in South Carolina, which seceded from the Union on December 20, 1860. By February 1861, the six other Lower South states followed in South Carolina's footsteps. In general, slaveholders spearheaded secession, while nonslaveholders in the Piedmont and mountain counties, where slaves were relatively few, displayed the greatest attachment to the Union. **(See "Analyzing Historical Evidence: Southerners Debate Secession" above.)**

In February, representatives from South Carolina, Georgia, Florida, Alabama, Mississippi, Louisiana, and Texas met in Montgomery, Alabama, where they created the **Confederate States of America**. Mississippi senator Jefferson Davis became

Why did the acquisition of land from Mexico contribute to sectional tensions?

of Mr. Lincoln to the Presidency of the United States? I tell you frankly, candidly, and earnestly, that I do not think they ought. In my judgment, the election of no man, constitutionally chosen to that high office, is sufficient cause for any State to separate from the Union. . . .

But it is said that Mr. Lincoln's policy and principles are against the Constitution, and that, if he carries them out, it will be destructive of our rights. Let us not anticipate a threatened evil. If he violates the Constitution, then will come our time to strike. . . . I do not anticipate that Mr. Lincoln will do anything to jeopard[ize] our safety or security, whatever may be his spirit to do it; for he is bound by the constitutional checks which are thrown around him, which at this time render him powerless to do any great mischief. . . .

I will never myself consent, as much as I admire this Union, for the glories of the past or the blessings of the present, as much as it has done for civilization, as much as the hopes of the world hang upon it; I would never submit to aggression upon my rights to maintain it longer; and if they cannot be maintained in the Union . . . I would be in favor of disrupting every tie which binds the States together.

Source: Richard M. Johnson and William H. Brown, *Life of Alexander H. Stephens* (Philadelphia: J. B. Lippincott, 1878), 564–68.

DOCUMENT 3

"Declaration of Causes which Induced the Secession of South Carolina" (1860)

State by state, the slave states made their decisions. South Carolina was first to leave. It issued a declaration justifying its decision.

A geographical line has been drawn across the Union, and all the States north of that line have united in the election of a man to the high office of President of the United States whose opinions and purposes are hostile to Slavery. . . .

On the 4th of March next this party will take possession of the Government. It has announced that the South shall be excluded from the common territory, that the Judicial tribunal shall be made sectional, and that a war must be waged against Slavery until it shall cease throughout the United States. . . .

We, therefore, the people of South Carolina, by our delegates in Convention assembled, appealing to the Supreme Judge of the world for the rectitude of our intentions, have solemnly declared that the Union heretofore existing between this State and the other States of North America is dissolved. . . .

Source: Frank H. Moore, ed., *The Rebellion Record*, vol. 1 (New York: G. P. Putnam, 1861), 3–4.

Questions for Analysis

CONSIDER THE CONTEXT: Why, in the opinion of William Harris, was an attack on slavery in the South also an attack on white supremacy?

SUMMARIZE THE ARGUMENT: Why, according to Alexander Stephens, was immediate secession both ill-advised and wrong?

RECOGNIZE VIEWPOINTS: According to South Carolina's "Declaration of Causes," why had "the line" (the Mason-Dixon line) become so menacing to the South?

---

president, and Alexander Stephens of Georgia, who had spoken so eloquently about the dangers of revolution, became vice president. In March 1861, Stephens declared that the Confederacy's "cornerstone" was "the great truth that the negro is not equal to the white man; that slavery, subordination to the superior race, is his natural and moral condition."

Lincoln's election had split the Union. Now secession split the South. Seven slave states seceded during the winter, but the eight slave states of the Upper South rejected secession, at least for the moment. The Upper South had a smaller stake in slavery. Barely half as many white families in the Upper South held slaves (21 percent) as in the Lower South (37 percent). Slaves represented twice as large a percentage of the population in the Lower South (48 percent) as in

| What upset the balance between slave and free states? | How did the party system change in the 1850s? | Why did northern fear of the "Slave Power" intensify in the 1850s? | **Why did some southern states secede immediately after Lincoln's election?** | Conclusion: Why did political compromise fail? |

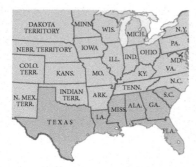

**Secession of the Lower South,
December 1860–February 1861**

**CONSIDER CAUSE
AND EFFECT**

What factors influenced the
South Carolinian fire-eaters'
insistence that secession
was the only logical course
for the South?

the Upper South (23 percent). Consequently, whites in the Upper South had fewer fears that Republican ascendancy meant economic catastrophe, social chaos, and racial war. Lincoln would need to do more than just be elected to provoke them into secession.

The nation had to wait until March 4, 1861, when Lincoln took office, to see what he would do. (Presidents-elect waited four months to take office until 1933, when the Twentieth Amendment to the Constitution shifted the inauguration to January 20.) He chose to stay in Springfield after his election and to say nothing. "Lame-duck" president James Buchanan sat in Washington and did nothing. Congress's efforts at cobbling together a peace-saving compromise came to nothing.

Lincoln began his inaugural address with reassurances to the South. He had "no lawful right" to interfere with slavery where it existed, he declared again, adding for emphasis that he had "no inclination to do so." Conciliatory about slavery in the South, Lincoln proved inflexible about the Union. The Union, he declared, was "perpetual." Secession was "anarchy" and "legally void." The Constitution required him to execute the law "in all the States."

The decision for war or peace rested in the South's hands, Lincoln said. "You can have no conflict, without being yourselves the aggressors. *You* have no oath registered in Heaven to destroy the government, while I shall have the most solemn one to 'preserve, protect, and defend' it."

QUICK REVIEW

Why were the states of the Lower and Upper South divided
on the question of secession during the winter of 1860–61?

Conclusion: Why did political compromise fail?

As their economies, societies, and cultures diverged in the nineteenth century, Northerners and Southerners expressed different concepts of the American promise and the place of slavery within it. Their differences crystallized into political form in 1846 when David Wilmot proposed banning slavery in any territory won in the Mexican-American War. "As if by magic," a Boston newspaper observed, "it brought to a head the great question that is about to divide the American people." Discovery of gold and other precious metals in the West added urgency to the controversy over slavery in the territories. Congress attempted to address the issue with the Compromise of 1850, but the Fugitive Slave Act and the publication of *Uncle Tom's Cabin* hardened northern sentiments against slavery and confirmed southern suspicions of northern ill will. The bloody violence that erupted in Kansas in 1856 and the incendiary *Dred Scott* decision in 1857 further eroded hope for a solution to this momentous question.

During the extended crisis of the Union that stretched from 1846 to 1861, the traditional Whig and Democratic parties struggled to hold together as new parties,

Why did the acquisition
of land from Mexico
contribute to sectional
tensions?

most notably the Republican Party, emerged. Politicians fixed their attention on the expansion of slavery, but from the beginning Americans recognized that the controversy had less to do with slavery in the territories than with the future of slavery in the nation.

For more than seventy years, statesmen had found compromises that accepted slavery and preserved the Union. But as each section grew increasingly committed to its labor system, Americans discovered that accommodation had limits. In 1859, John Brown's militant antislavery pushed white Southerners to the edge. In 1860, Lincoln's election convinced whites in the Lower South that slavery and the society they had built on it were at risk in the Union, and they seceded. But it remained to be seen whether disunion would mean war.

| What upset the balance between slave and free states? | How did the party system change in the 1850s? | Why did northern fear of the "Slave Power" intensify in the 1850s? | Why did some southern states secede immediately after Lincoln's election? | **Conclusion: Why did political compromise fail?** |

STEP 1

EXPLAIN WHY IT MATTERS

Put your reading into practice. Identify each term below, and then explain why it matters in U.S. history.

TERM	WHO OR WHAT & WHEN	WHY IT MATTERS
Wilmot Proviso (p. 392)		
free labor (p. 392)		
popular sovereignty (p. 393)		
Compromise of 1850 (p. 395)		
Fugitive Slave Act (p. 396)		
Uncle Tom's Cabin (p. 397)		
Kansas-Nebraska Act (p. 399)		
Republican Party (p. 401)		
"Bleeding Kansas" (p. 406)		
Dred Scott decision (p. 407)		
Lincoln-Douglas debates (p. 410)		
Confederate States of America (p. 414)		

STEP 2

MOVE BEYOND THE BASICS

To demonstrate a more advanced understanding, use the table below to sketch the political landscape of the 1850s. How did slavery help transform the American political landscape?

Party	Supporters	Position on Slavery	Views on Expansion	Perspectives on Immigration
Democratic Party				
Whig Party				
Republican Party				
American (Know-Nothing) Party				

STEP 3

PUT IT ALL TOGETHER

Now, explain the big picture. Remember to use specific examples from the chapter in your answers.

EXPANSION AND SECTIONALISM

- Why was the Wilmot Proviso so controversial? What did the response to the proviso reveal about the diverging visions of America in the North and the South?

- Why was the expansion of slavery not only a moral issue for abolitionists but also an economic concern to both Northerners and Southerners?

POLITICAL INSTABILITY

- Why did the Compromise of 1850 ultimately fail?

- What were the consequences of the events of the 1840s and 1850s for America's political parties? How did the party system change under the pressure of the sectional divide?

THE ROAD TO SECESSION

- If most Northerners and Southerners wanted to avoid war, why did war begin?

- Why did so many Southerners see the election of Abraham Lincoln as a threat to their way of life? Why did more than half of the southern electorate vote for pro-Union candidates?

LOOKING BACKWARD, LOOKING AHEAD

- Why, in the early nineteenth century, was compromise on the issue of slavery possible? Why did so many reject compromise in the 1840s and 1850s?

- What consequences might Southerners have imagined would follow from secession? What might have led them to underestimate Lincoln's determination to fight for the Union?

STEP 4

CONNECT THESE EVENTS

How did the territory taken from Mexico in 1848 disrupt the American political system?

STEP 5

CONNECT TO THE PRESENT

Does the Mason-Dixon line still divide the nation today? If so, in what ways?

15

THE CRUCIBLE OF WAR

1861–1865

How did the Civil War change the nation, North and South? Chapter 15 traces the course of the Civil War, exploring the connections between events on the battlefield and the political, social, and economic developments on the home fronts. It explains how the war became a fight for black freedom and examines why the North ultimately won the war.

This chapter will explore the following questions:

- Why did both the Union and the Confederacy consider control of the border states crucial?
- Why did each side expect to win?
- How did each side fare in the early years of the war?
- How did the war for union become a fight for black freedom?
- What problems did the Confederacy face at home?
- How did the war affect the economy and politics of the North?
- How did the Union finally win the war?
- Conclusion: In what ways was the Civil War a "Second American Revolution"?

AN AMERICAN STORY

Just before dawn on May 13, 1862, Robert Smalls, a twenty-three-year-old enslaved man, maneuvered a Confederate sidewheel steamer named the *Planter* away from a Charleston wharf. He and the other enslaved crew members had decided, Smalls remembered later, that they would "be free or die." They had waited for the moment when the ship's three white officers left to spend the night ashore. Then Smalls, who was an experienced pilot, took the helm and impersonated the captain by wearing his wide-brimmed straw hat. Smalls then steered the ship to a rendezvous point where he picked up his wife and children and the families of the other crew members. Finally, they sailed the *Planter* across Charleston harbor and out into the Atlantic where they intended to deliver the Confederate ship to the U.S. Navy, which was blockading the port.

Navigating the ten miles from the wharf to the Atlantic meant sailing under the noses of several heavily armed Confederate fortifications. To present the *Planter* as a Confederate vessel, the crew raised two rebel flags. When the ship approached Fort Sumter, whose guns could easily blast the steamer out of the water, Smalls seized the whistle cord and offered "two long blows and a short one," the Confederate signal for safe passage that Smalls had learned on previous trips.

Once beyond the Confederate guns, the crew rushed to take down the rebel flags and hoisted a white sheet to signal surrender. The danger was that the U.S. Navy would fire on the Confederate ship before it recognized that the *Planter* was friendly. Fortunately, the captain of the USS *Onward* ordered the *Planter* to come alongside and took the crew and passengers aboard. Despite the odds, slaves had successfully hijacked a Confederate ship from one of the most heavily fortified places in America.

Smalls had done more than liberate a handful of slaves. His actions required courage, intelligence, and skill and helped convince many doubting white Northerners that African Americans could and would fight for their freedom. Such was his fame that Smalls soon sat at a conference table next to the great African American leader, Frederick Douglass, as they tried to convince President Lincoln to allow black men to join the fight. In 1863, Smalls returned to South Carolina to pilot U.S. Navy ships during the successful siege of Charleston, participating in seventeen battles.

Smalls's wartime story was extraordinary, but he was only one of many African Americans who fought in the Civil War. Like Smalls, they saw the war as a fight to abolish slavery. For the first eighteen months of the war, however, the Lincoln government officially fought only to uphold the Constitution and preserve the nation. Only with the Emancipation Proclamation in 1863 did the northern war effort take on a dual purpose: to save the Union and to free the slaves.

As the world's first modern war, the Civil War transformed America. It mobilized the entire populations of North and South, harnessed the productive capacities of both regions, and produced battles with 200,000 soldiers and casualties in the tens of thousands. The slaughter lasted four years and cost the nation approximately 750,000 lives. The war helped mold the modern American nation-state, and the federal government emerged with new power and responsibility over national life.

All Americans endured the crucible of war, but the war affected no group more than the nearly 4 million African Americans who saw its beginning as slaves and emerged as free people.

▼ **Robert Smalls and the *Planter*** Born a slave in Beaufort, South Carolina, in 1839, Robert Smalls was sent to Charleston when he was twelve. He worked at a variety of city jobs until 1861 when he became a deckhand on the *Planter*. He developed into an expert navigator, one of the best pilots in Charleston Bay, a skill he dramatically demonstrated on the night of May 13, 1862. Library of Congress, 3c17998.

ROBERT SMALLS, CAPTAIN OF THE GUN-BOAT "PLANTER"   THE GUN-BOAT "PLANTER" RUN OUT OF CHARLESTON, S. C., BY ROBERT SMALLS, MAY, 1862.

Why did both the Union and the Confederacy consider control of the border states crucial?

CHRONOLOGY

1861
- Fort Sumter attacked.
- Four Upper South states join Confederacy.

Abraham Lincoln faced the worst crisis in the history of the nation: disunion. He revealed his strategy to save the Union in his inaugural address on March 4, 1861. First, he declared the Union "perpetual," denied the right of secession, and sought to stop its spread by avoiding any act that would push the skittish Upper South (North Carolina, Virginia, Maryland, Delaware, Kentucky, Tennessee, Missouri, and Arkansas) out of the Union. Second, he sought to reassure the seceding Lower South (South Carolina, Georgia, Florida, Alabama, Mississippi, Louisiana, and Texas) that his government would not abolish slavery. Lincoln believed that his assurance would help Unionists there assert themselves and overturn the secession decision.

His counterpart, Jefferson Davis, fully intended to establish the Confederate States of America as an independent slaveholding republic. To succeed, Davis had to sustain the secession fever that had carried the Lower South out of the Union. Even if the Lower South held firm, however, the Confederacy would remain weak without additional states. Davis watched for opportunities to add new stars to the Confederate flag.

Neither man sought war; both wanted to achieve their objectives peacefully. As Lincoln later observed, "Both parties deprecated war, but one of them would *make* war rather than let the nation survive, and the other would *accept* war rather than let it perish. And the war came."

Attack on Fort Sumter

Fort Sumter
Union fort on an island at the entrance to Charleston harbor in South Carolina. After Confederate leaders learned President Lincoln intended to resupply Fort Sumter, Confederate forces attacked the fort on April 12, 1861, initiating the Civil War.

Major Robert Anderson and some eighty U.S. soldiers occupied **Fort Sumter** at the entrance to Charleston harbor. The fort with its American flag became a hated symbol of the nation that Southerners had abandoned, and they wanted federal troops out. Sumter was also a symbol to Northerners, a beacon affirming federal authority in the seceded states.

Lincoln decided to hold the fort. In early April 1861, Lincoln authorized a peaceful expedition to deliver badly needed supplies, but not military reinforcements, to the fort. The president understood that in seeking to relieve the fort he risked war, but his plan honored his inaugural promises to defend federal property and to avoid using military force unless first attacked. Masterfully, Lincoln had shifted the fateful decision of war or peace to Jefferson Davis.

On April 9, Davis and his cabinet met to consider the situation in Charleston harbor. Davis argued for military action, but his secretary of state, Robert Toombs of Georgia, countered: "Mr. President, at this time it is suicide, murder, and will lose us every friend at the North. You will wantonly strike a hornet's nest which extends from mountain to ocean, and legions now quiet will swarm out and sting us to death." But Davis ordered Confederate troops to take the fort before the relief expedition arrived. Thirty-three hours of bombardment on April 12 and 13 reduced the fort to rubble. On April 14, Major Anderson offered his surrender and lowered the U.S. flag. The Confederates had Fort Sumter, but they also had war.

On April 15, when Lincoln called for 75,000 militiamen to serve for ninety days to put down the rebellion, several times that number rushed to defend the flag.

ANALYZE EVIDENCE

What does the clash over Fort Sumter suggest about Jefferson Davis's and Abraham Lincoln's respective priorities and goals in the spring of 1861?

Why did both the Union and the Confederacy consider control of the border states crucial?	Why did each side expect to win?	How did each side fare in the early years of the war?

Democrats responded as fervently as Republicans. Stephen A. Douglas, the recently defeated Democratic candidate for president, pledged his support and noted, "There can be no neutrals in this war, *only patriots—or traitors.*"

Stephen A. Douglas noted, "There can be no neutrals in this war, *only patriots—or traitors.*"

The Upper South Chooses Sides

With the outbreak of war, the Upper South faced a horrendous choice: either to fight against the Lower South or to fight against the Union. Many who only months earlier had rejected secession now embraced the Confederacy. To vote against southern independence was one thing, to fight fellow Southerners quite another. Thousands felt betrayed, believing that Lincoln had promised to achieve a peaceful reunion by waiting patiently for Unionists to retake power in the seceding states. It was a "politician's war," one man declared, but he conceded that "this is no time now to discuss the causes, but it is the duty of all who regard Southern institutions of value to side with the South, make common cause with the Confederate States and sink or swim with them."

Virginia, Arkansas, Tennessee, and North Carolina joined the Confederacy (**Map 15.1**). But in the border states of Delaware, Maryland, Kentucky, and Missouri, Unionism triumphed. Only in Delaware, where slaves accounted for less than 2 percent of the population, was the victory easy. In Maryland, Unionism needed a helping hand. Lincoln suspended the writ of habeas corpus, essentially setting aside constitutional guarantees that protect citizens from arbitrary arrest and detention, and he ordered U.S. troops into Baltimore. Maryland's legislature rejected secession.

The struggle turned violent in the West. In Missouri, Unionists won a narrow victory, but southern-sympathizing guerrilla bands roamed the state for the duration of the war, terrorizing civilians and soldiers alike. In Kentucky, Unionists also narrowly defeated secession, but the prosouthern minority claimed otherwise. Throughout the

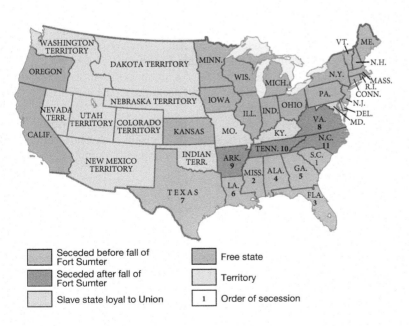

MAP 15.1 ◀ Secession, 1860–1861

After Lincoln's election, the fifteen slave states debated what to do. Seven states quickly left the Union, four left after the firing on Fort Sumter, and four remained loyal to the Union.

Legend:
- Seceded before fall of Fort Sumter
- Seceded after fall of Fort Sumter
- Slave state loyal to Union
- Free state
- Territory
- 1 Order of secession

| How did the war for union become a fight for black freedom? | What problems did the Confederacy face at home? | How did the war affect the economy and politics of the North? | How did the Union finally win the war? | Conclusion: In what ways was the Civil War a "Second American Revolution"? |

border states, secession divided families. Seven of Kentuckian Henry Clay's grandsons fought: four for the Confederacy and three for the Union.

Lincoln understood that the border states—particularly Kentucky—contained indispensable resources, population, and wealth; in addition, they controlled major rivers and railroads. "I think to lose Kentucky is nearly the same as to lose the whole game," Lincoln said. "Kentucky gone, we can not hold Missouri, nor, as I think, Maryland. These all against us, . . . we would as well consent to separation at once."

In the end, only eleven of the fifteen slave states joined the Confederacy. The four seceding Upper South states contained significant numbers of people who felt little affection for secession. Dissatisfaction was so rife in the western counties of Virginia that in 1863, citizens there voted to create the separate state of West Virginia, loyal to the Union. Still, the acquisition of four new states greatly strengthened the Confederacy's drive for national independence.

CONSIDER CAUSE AND EFFECT

What factors explain southern states' decisions whether to secede from the Union?

QUICK REVIEW

Why did the attack on Fort Sumter force the Upper South to choose sides?

Why did each side expect to win?

Only slaveholders had a direct economic stake in preserving slavery, but most whites in the Confederacy defended the institution, the way of life built on it, and the Confederate nation. The degraded status of blacks elevated the status of the poorest whites. One Southerner declared, "It is enough that one simply belongs to the superior and ruling race, to secure consideration and respect." Moreover, Yankee "aggression" was no longer a mere threat; it was real and at the South's door.

For Northerners, the South's failure to accept the democratic election of a president and its firing on the nation's flag challenged the rule of law, the authority of the Constitution, and the ability of the people to govern themselves. As an Indiana soldier told his wife, a "good government is the best thing on earth. Property is nothing without it, because it is not protected; a family is nothing without it, because they cannot be educated." Only a Union victory, Lincoln declared, would secure America's promise "to elevate the condition of man."

Northerners and Southerners rallied behind their separate flags, fully convinced that they were in the right and that God was on their side. Yankees took heart from their superior power, but the rebels believed they had advantages that nullified every northern strength.

How They Expected to Win

The balance sheet of northern and southern resources reveals enormous advantages for the Union (**Figure 15.1**). The twenty-three states remaining in the Union had a population of 22.3 million; the eleven Confederate states had a population of only 9.1 million, of whom 3.67 million (40 percent) were slaves. The North's economic advantages were even more overwhelming. Yet Southerners expected to win for some good reasons—and they came very close to doing so.

| Why did both the Union and the Confederacy consider control of the border states crucial? | **Why did each side expect to win?** | How did each side fare in the early years of the war? |

Total population	71%	29%	2.4 to 1
Free males	81%	19%	4.3 to 1
Wealth produced	75%	25%	3 to 1
Industrial workers	92%	8%	11.5 to 1
Factory production	91%	9%	10.1 to 1
Textile production	93%	7%	13.3 to 1
Firearms production	97%	3%—	32.3 to 1
Railroad mileage	71%	29%	2.4 to 1
Iron production	94%	6%	15.7 to 1
Coal production	97%	3%—	32.3 to 1
Livestock	60%	40%	1.5 to 1
Farm acreage	75%	25%	3 to 1
Wheat	81%	19%	4.3 to 1
Corn	67%	33%	2 to 1
Cotton	—4%	96%	1 to 24
Merchant ship tonnage	90%	10%	9 to 1
Naval ship tonnage	96%	4%—	24 to 1

Union   Confederacy

FIGURE 15.1 ◀ Resources of the Union and the Confederacy

The Union's enormous statistical advantages failed to convince Confederates that their cause was doomed.

Southerners knew they bucked the military odds, but hadn't the liberty-loving colonists in 1776 also done so? "Britain could not conquer three million," a Louisianan proclaimed, and "the world cannot conquer the South." How could anyone doubt the outcome of a contest between lean, hard, country-born rebel warriors defending family, property, and liberty, and soft, flabby, citified Yankee mechanics waging an unconstitutional war?

The South's confidence also rested on its belief that northern prosperity depended on the South's cotton. Without cotton, New England textile mills would stand idle. Without planters purchasing northern manufactured goods, northern factories would drown in their own unsold surpluses. And without the revenue earned by the overseas sales of cotton, the financial structure of the entire Yankee nation would collapse. In the South's ability to "withhold the benefits of our trade," one Virginian said, "we hold a power over the North more powerful than a powerful army in the field."

Cotton would also make Europe a powerful ally of the Confederacy, Southerners reasoned. Of the 900 million pounds of cotton Britain imported annually, more than 700 million pounds came from the American South. If the supply was interrupted, economic necessity would make Britain and perhaps France Confederate allies. And because the British navy ruled the seas, the North would find Britain a formidable foe.

The Confederacy recognized that a Union victory required the North to defeat and subjugate the South, but a Confederate victory required only that the South stay at home, blunt invasions, avoid battles that risked annihilating its army, and outlast the North's will to fight. When an opportunity presented itself, the South would strike the invaders. Like the American colonists, the South could win independence by not losing the war.

The Lincoln administration countered with an aggressive strategy designed to take advantage of its superior resources. Lincoln declared a naval blockade of the

How did the war for union become a fight for black freedom?	What problems did the Confederacy face at home?	How did the war affect the economy and politics of the North?	How did the Union finally win the war?	Conclusion: In what ways was the Civil War a "Second American Revolution"?

Confederacy to deny it the ability to sell cotton abroad, giving the South far fewer dollars to pay for war goods. Lincoln also ordered the Union army into Virginia, at the same time planning a march through the Mississippi valley that would cut the Confederacy in two.

Most Americans thought of war in terms of their most recent experience, the Mexican-American War in the 1840s. In Mexico, fighting had taken relatively small numbers of lives and had inflicted only light damage on the countryside. They could not imagine the four ghastly years of bloodletting that lay ahead.

Lincoln and Davis Mobilize

Mobilization required effective political leadership, and at first glance the South appeared to have the advantage. Jefferson Davis was a West Point graduate and an authentic hero of the Mexican-American War. He also brought to the Confederate presidency a distinguished political career, including experience in the U.S. Senate. Dignified and ramrod straight, with "a jaw sawed in steel," Davis appeared to be everything a nation could want in a wartime leader.

By contrast, Abraham Lincoln could show one lackluster term in the House of Representatives and almost no administrative experience. His sole brush with the military was as a captain in the militia in the Black Hawk War, a brief struggle in Illinois in 1832, in which whites expelled the last Indians from the state. The lanky, disheveled Illinois lawyer-politician looked anything but military or presidential.

Davis, however, proved to be less than he appeared. Although he worked hard, he had no gift for military strategy, yet intervened often in military affairs. He was an even less able political leader. Quarrelsome and proud, he had an acid tongue that made enemies the Confederacy could ill afford. In his defense, the Confederacy's intimidating problems might have defeated an even more talented leader.

With Lincoln, the North got far more than met the eye. He proved himself a master politician and a superb leader. When forming his cabinet, Lincoln chose the ablest men, even if they were often his chief rivals and critics. He appointed Salmon P. Chase secretary of the treasury, knowing that Chase had presidential ambitions. As secretary of state, he chose his chief opponent for the Republican nomination in 1860, William H. Seward. Despite his civilian background, Lincoln displayed an innate understanding of military strategy. No one was more crucial in mapping the Union war plan.

Lincoln and Davis began gathering their military forces. Confederates had to build almost everything from scratch, and Northerners had to channel their superior numbers and industrial resources to war. On the eve of the war, the federal army numbered only 16,000 men. The U.S. Navy was in better shape. Forty-two ships were in service, and a large merchant marine would in time provide more ships and sailors for the Union. Possessing a much weaker navy, the South pinned its hopes on its armies.

The Confederacy made impressive efforts to build factories to supply its armies with tents, blankets, shoes, and uniforms, but even when factories produced what soldiers needed, southern railroads often could not deliver the goods. And each year, more railroads were captured, destroyed, or left in disrepair. Food production proved less of a problem, but food sometimes rotted before it reached the soldiers. The one bright spot was the Confederacy's Ordnance Bureau, headed by Josiah Gorgas. In April 1864, Gorgas proudly observed: "Where three years ago we were not making a gun, a pistol nor a sabre, no shot nor shell . . . we now make all these in quantities to meet the demands of our large armies."

| Why did both the Union and the Confederacy consider control of the border states crucial? | **Why did each side expect to win?** | How did each side fare in the early years of the war? |

◀ Federal Recruiting Poster With the American flag flying proudly, this poster from the 36th Regiment, New York Volunteers, reaches out to potential recruits. It promises a nine-month enlistment (relatively short) and the "usual bounty" (an enlistment bonus). And it warns, "Don't wait to be drafted!" Being drafted was shameful; volunteering was manly and patriotic. Private Collection/Peter Newark Military Pictures/Bridgeman Images.

Recruiting and supplying huge armies required enormous new revenues. The Union and the Confederacy sold war bonds, which essentially were loans from patriotic citizens. In addition, both sides turned to taxes. Eventually, both began printing paper money. Inflation soared, but the Confederacy suffered more because it financed a greater part of its wartime costs through the printing press. Prices in the Union rose by about 80 percent during the war, while inflation in the Confederacy topped 9,000 percent.

Within months of the bombardment of Fort Sumter, both sides found men to fight and ways to supply them. But the underlying strength of the northern economy gave the Union the decided advantage. With their military and industrial muscles beginning to ripple, Northerners became itchy for action that would smash the rebellion. Horace Greeley's *New York Tribune* began to chant: "Forward to Richmond! Forward to Richmond!"

COMPARE AND CONTRAST
What were the greatest strengths and most significant weaknesses of each side at the start of the Civil War?

QUICK REVIEW

Why did the South believe it could win the war despite numerical disadvantages?

How did the war for union become a fight for black freedom?	What problems did the Confederacy face at home?	How did the war affect the economy and politics of the North?	How did the Union finally win the war?	Conclusion: In what ways was the Civil War a "Second American Revolution"?

How did each side fare in the early years of the war?

CHRONOLOGY

1861
- First battle of Bull Run (Manassas) fought.

1862
- Grant captures Fort Henry and Fort Donelson.
- Battle of Glorieta Pass fought.
- Battle of Pea Ridge fought.
- Battle of Shiloh fought.
- Virginia peninsula campaign waged.
- Battle of Antietam fought.

battle of Bull Run (Manassas)
First major battle of the Civil War, fought at a railroad junction in northern Virginia on July 21, 1861. The Union suffered a sobering defeat, while the Confederates felt affirmed in their superiority and the inevitability of Confederate nationhood.

Peninsula Campaign, 1862

During the first year and a half of the war, armies fought major campaigns in both the East and West. While the eastern campaign was more dramatic, Lincoln had trouble finding a capable general, and the fighting ended in a stalemate. Battles in the West proved more decisive. Union general Ulysses S. Grant won important victories in Kentucky and Tennessee. As Yankee and rebel armies pounded each other on land, the navies fought on the seas and on the rivers of the South. In Europe, Confederate and U.S. diplomats competed for advantage in the corridors of power. All the while, casualty lists on both sides reached appalling lengths.

Stalemate in the Eastern Theater

In the summer of 1861, Lincoln ordered the 35,000 Union troops assembling outside Washington to attack the 20,000 Confederates defending Manassas, a railroad junction in Virginia about thirty miles from Washington, D.C. On July 21, the army forded Bull Run, a branch of the Potomac River, and engaged the southern forces (**Map 15.2**). But fast-moving southern reinforcements blunted the Union attack and then counterattacked. What began as an orderly Union retreat turned into a panicky stampede.

By Civil War standards, the casualties (wounded and dead) at the **battle of Bull Run** (or **Manassas**, as Southerners called the battle) were light, about 2,000 Confederates and 1,600 Federals. The significance of the battle lay in the lessons Northerners and Southerners drew from it. For Southerners, it confirmed the superiority of rebel fighting men and the inevitability of Confederate nationhood. Manassas was "*one of the decisive battles of the world,*" a Georgian proclaimed. It "*has* secured our independence." On the other hand, defeat sobered Northerners. It was a major setback, admitted the *New York Tribune*, but "let us go to work, then, with a will." Within four days of the disaster, the president authorized the enlistment of 1 million men for three years.

Lincoln also found a new general, the young George B. McClellan, whom he appointed commander of the newly named Army of the Potomac. Having graduated from West Point second in his class, the thirty-four-year-old McClellan believed that he was a great soldier and that Lincoln was a dunce, the "original Gorilla." A superb administrator and organizer, McClellan energetically whipped his dispirited soldiers into shape, but for all his energy, McClellan lacked decisiveness. Lincoln wanted a general who would advance, take risks, and fight, but McClellan went into winter quarters. "If General McClellan does not want to use the army I would like to *borrow* it," Lincoln declared in frustration.

Finally, in May 1862, McClellan launched his long-awaited offensive. He transported his highly polished army, now 130,000 strong, to the mouth of the James River and began slowly moving up the Yorktown peninsula toward Richmond. When he was within six miles of the Confederate capital, General Joseph Johnston hit him like a hammer. In the assault, Johnston was wounded and was replaced by Robert E. Lee, who would become the South's most celebrated general.

The contrast between Lee and McClellan could hardly have been greater. McClellan brimmed with conceit; Lee was courteous and reserved. On the battlefield, McClellan grew timid, and Lee became aggressive, even reckless. And Lee had at his side in the peninsula campaign military men of real talent: Thomas J. Jackson, nicknamed "Stonewall" for holding the line at Manassas, and

| Why did both the Union and the Confederacy consider control of the border states crucial? | Why did each side expect to win? | **How did each side fare in the early years of the war?** |

◀ **Dead Confederate Soldier** This young soldier lies with his rifle in a trench at Fort Mahone, near Petersburg, Virginia, on April 2, 1865, just days before the end of the war. Photography like this brought the horrors of war into the lives of civilians far from the battlefields. Library of Congress, 1s02706.

James E. B. ("Jeb") Stuart, a dashing young cavalry commander who rode circles around Yankee troops.

Lee's assault initiated the Seven Days Battle (June 25–July 1) and began McClellan's march back down the peninsula. By the time McClellan reached safety, 30,000 men from both sides had died or been wounded. Although Southerners suffered twice the casualties of Northerners, Lee had saved Richmond. Lincoln fired McClellan and replaced him with General John Pope.

In August, north of Richmond, at the second battle of Bull Run, Lee's smaller army battered Pope's forces and sent them scurrying back to Washington. Lincoln ordered Pope to Minnesota to pacify the Indians and restored McClellan to command. Lincoln had not changed his mind about McClellan's capacity as a warrior, but he had concluded, "There is no man in the Army who can lick these troops of ours into shape half as well as he. . . . If he can't fight himself, he excels in making others ready to fight."

Believing that he had the enemy on the run, Lee pushed his army across the Potomac and invaded Maryland. A victory on northern soil would dislodge Maryland from the Union, Lee reasoned, and might even cause Lincoln to sue for peace. On September 17, 1862, McClellan's forces engaged Lee's army at Antietam Creek (see Map 15.2). With "solid shot . . . cracking skulls like eggshells," according to one observer, the armies went after each other. At Miller's Cornfield, the firing was so intense that "every stalk of corn in the . . . field was cut as closely as could have been done with a knife." By nightfall, 6,000 men lay dead or dying on the battlefield, and 17,000 more had been wounded. The **battle of Antietam** would be the bloodiest day of the war and sent the battered Army of Northern Virginia limping back home. McClellan claimed to have saved the North, but Lincoln again removed him from command and appointed General Ambrose Burnside.

Though bloodied, Lee found an opportunity in December to punish the enemy at Fredericksburg, Virginia, where Burnside's 122,000 Union troops faced 78,500 Confederates dug in behind a stone wall on the heights above the Rappahannock River. Half a mile of open ground separated the armies. "A chicken could not live on that field when we open on it," a Confederate artillery officer predicted. Yet Burnside ordered a frontal assault. The Federals counted nearly 13,000 casualties, the Confederates fewer than 5,000. The battle of Fredericksburg was one of the Union's

battle of Antietam
Battle fought in Maryland on September 17, 1862, between the Union forces of George McClellan and Confederate troops of Robert E. Lee. The battle, a Union victory that left 6,000 dead and 17,000 wounded, was the bloodiest day of the war.

How did the war for union become a fight for black freedom?	What problems did the Confederacy face at home?	How did the war affect the economy and politics of the North?	How did the Union finally win the war?	Conclusion: In what ways was the Civil War a "Second American Revolution"?

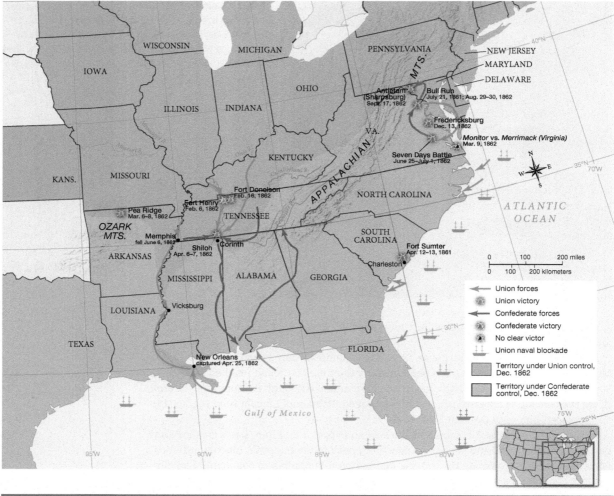

MAP 15.2 ▲ The Civil War, 1861–1862 While most eyes were focused on the eastern theater, especially the ninety-mile stretch of land between Washington, D.C., and the Confederate capital of Richmond, Virginia, Union troops were winning strategic victories in the West.

READING THE MAP: In which states did the Confederacy and the Union each win the most battles during this period? Which side used or followed water routes most for troop movements and attacks?

CONNECTIONS: Which major cities in the South and West fell to Union troops in 1862? Which strategic area did those Confederate losses place in Union hands? How did this outcome affect the later movement of troops and supplies?

worst defeats. As 1862 ended, the North seemed no nearer to ending the rebellion than it had been when the war began. Rather than checkmate, military struggle in the East had reached a stalemate.

Union Victories in the Western Theater

The decisive early encounters of the war were taking place between the Appalachian Mountains and the Ozarks (see Map 15.2). Confederates wanted Missouri and Kentucky, states they claimed but did not control. Federals wanted to split Arkansas,

| Why did both the Union and the Confederacy consider control of the border states crucial? | Why did each side expect to win? | How did each side fare in the early years of the war? |

Louisiana, and Texas from the Confederacy by taking control of the Mississippi River and to occupy Tennessee, one of the Confederacy's main producers of food, mules, and iron—all vital resources.

Before Union forces could march on Tennessee, they needed to secure Missouri. Union troops swept across Missouri to the border of Arkansas, where in March 1862 they encountered a 16,000-man Confederate army, which included three regiments of Indians from the so-called Five Civilized Tribes—the Choctaw, Chickasaw, Creek, Seminole, and Cherokee. The Union victory at the battle of Pea Ridge left Missouri free of Confederate troops, but guerrilla bands led by the notorious William Clarke Quantrill and "Bloody Bill" Anderson burned, tortured, scalped, and murdered Union civilians and soldiers until the final year of the war.

Even farther west, Confederate armies sought to extend their slaveholding empire all the way to the Pacific. Both sides recognized the immense value of the gold and silver mines of California, Nevada, and Colorado. And both sides bolstered their armies in the Southwest with Mexican Americans. A quick strike by Texas troops took Santa Fe, New Mexico, in the winter of 1861–62. Then in March 1862, a band of Colorado miners ambushed and crushed southern forces at Glorieta Pass, outside Santa Fe, effectively ending dreams of a Confederate empire beyond Texas.

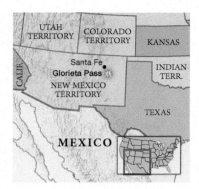

Battle of Glorieta Pass, 1862

The principal western battles took place in Tennessee, where General Ulysses S. Grant emerged as the key northern commander. Grant, a West Point graduate who served in Mexico, was a thirty-nine-year-old dry-goods clerk in Galena, Illinois, when the war began. Gentle at home, he became pugnacious on the battlefield. "The art of war is simple," he said. "Find out where your enemy is, get at him as soon as you can and strike him as hard as you can, and keep moving on." Grant's philosophy of war as attrition would take a huge toll in human life, but it played to the North's superiority in manpower. Later, to critics who wanted Lincoln to sack Grant because of his drinking, the president would say, "*I can't spare this man. He fights.*"

In February 1862, operating in tandem with U.S. Navy gunboats, Grant captured Fort Henry on the Tennessee River and Fort Donelson on the Cumberland (see Map 15.2). Defeat forced the Confederates to withdraw from all of Kentucky and most of Tennessee, but Grant followed.

On April 6, General Albert Sidney Johnston's army surprised Grant at Shiloh Church in Tennessee. Union troops were badly mauled the first day, but Grant remained cool and brought up reinforcements throughout the night. The next morning, the Union army counterattacked, driving the Confederates before it. The **battle of Shiloh** was terribly costly to both sides. The 20,000 casualties included General Johnston. After Shiloh, Grant "gave up all idea of saving the Union except by complete conquest."

Although no one knew it at the time, Shiloh ruined the Confederacy's bid to control the western theater. The Yankees quickly captured the strategic town of Corinth, Mississippi; the river city of Memphis; and the South's largest city, New Orleans. By the end of 1862, the far West and most—but not all—of the Mississippi valley lay in Union hands. At the same time, the outcome of the struggle in another theater of war was also becoming clearer.

battle of Shiloh
Battle at Shiloh Church, Tennessee, on April 6–7, 1862, between Albert Sidney Johnston's Confederate forces and Ulysses S. Grant's Union army. The Union army ultimately prevailed, though at great cost to both sides. Shiloh ruined the Confederacy's bid to control the war in the West.

The Atlantic Theater

When the war began, the U.S. Navy's blockade fleet consisted of about three dozen ships to patrol more than 3,500 miles of southern coastline, and rebel merchant ships were able to slip in and out of southern ports nearly at will. Taking on cargoes in the Caribbean, sleek Confederate blockade runners brought in vital supplies—guns and medicine. But with the U.S. Navy commissioning a new blockader almost weekly, the

COMPARE AND CONTRAST
What were the military strategies of Union and Confederate leaders during the first two years of the Civil War? Which was more successful, and why?

| How did the war for union become a fight for black freedom? | What problems did the Confederacy face at home? | How did the war affect the economy and politics of the North? | How did the Union finally win the war? | Conclusion: In what ways was the Civil War a "Second American Revolution"? |

▲ **Battle of Fredericksburg, 1862** This painting by Private John Richards of the New York Volunteers captures the behind-the-lines Union activity at the battle of Fredericksburg. Long rows of fresh troops await orders to march up the hill to join the fighting underway in the distance. Barely visible, the cavalry charges off into one of the Union's greatest failures. These foot soldiers will follow the cavalry soon. Private Collection/ Peter Newark Military Pictures/Bridgeman Images.

READING THE IMAGE: What does the artist portray in the lower left of the painting? What are the lines of wagons hauling?

CONNECTIONS: At Fredericksburg, General Ambrose Burnside joined the list of failed Union generals. What other Union defeats can be attributed, at least in part, to failed Union leadership?

naval fleet eventually numbered 150 ships on duty, and the Union navy dramatically improved its score.

Unable to build a conventional navy equal to the expanding U.S. fleet, the Confederates experimented with a radical new maritime design: the ironclad warship. At Norfolk, Virginia, Southerners layered the wooden hull of the *Merrimack* with two-inch-thick armor plate. Rechristened *Virginia*, the ship steamed out in March 1862 and sank two wooden federal ships (see Map 15.2). When the *Virginia* returned to finish off the federal blockaders the next morning, it was challenged by the *Monitor*, a federal ironclad of even more radical design, topped with a revolving turret holding two eleven-inch guns. On March 9, the two ships hurled shells at each other for two hours, but the battle ended in a draw.

| Why did both the Union and the Confederacy consider control of the border states crucial? | Why did each side expect to win? | **How did each side fare in the early years of the war?** |

The Confederacy never found a way to break the Union blockade despite exploring many naval innovations, including a new underwater vessel—the submarine. By 1865, the blockaders were intercepting about half of the southern ships attempting to break through. The Union navy, a southern naval officer observed, "shut the Confederacy out from the world, deprived it of supplies, weakened its military and naval strength."

International Diplomacy

What the Confederates could not achieve on the seas, they sought to achieve through international diplomacy. They based their hope for European intervention on King Cotton. In theory, cotton-starved European nations would have no choice but to break the Union blockade and recognize the Confederacy. Southern hopes were not unreasonable, for at the height of the "cotton famine" in 1862, when 2 million British workers were unemployed, Britain tilted toward recognition. Along with several other European nations, Britain granted the Confederacy "belligerent" status, which enabled it to buy goods and build ships in European ports. But no country challenged the Union blockade or recognized the Confederacy as a nation, a bold act that probably would have meant war.

King Cotton diplomacy failed for several reasons. When the war began, the warehouses of British textile manufacturers bulged with surplus cotton. In 1862, when a cotton shortage did occur, European manufacturers found new sources in India, Egypt, and elsewhere (**Figure 15.2**). In addition, the development of a brisk trade

Union blockade
The United States' use of its navy to patrol the southern coastline to restrict Confederate trade. The blockade became increasingly effective and succeeded in depriving the Confederacy of vital supplies and revenue.

King Cotton diplomacy
Confederate diplomatic strategy built on the hope that European nations starving for cotton would break the Union blockade and recognize the Confederacy. This strategy failed as Europeans held stores of surplus cotton and developed new sources outside the South.

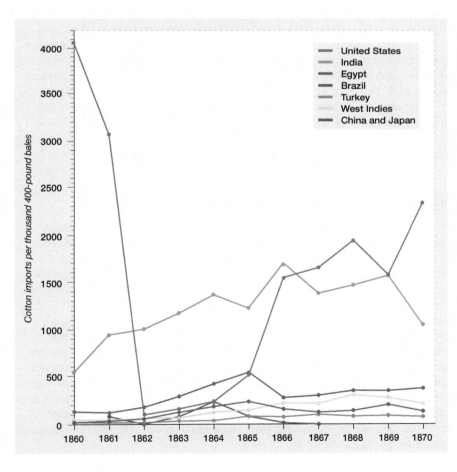

FIGURE 15.2 ◄ **Global Comparison: European Cotton Imports, 1860–1870**

In 1860, the South enjoyed a near monopoly in supplying cotton to Europe's textile mills, but the Civil War almost entirely halted its exports. Figures for Europe's importation of cotton from 1861 to 1865 reveal one of the reasons the Confederacy's King Cotton diplomacy failed: Europeans found other sources of cotton. Which countries were most important in filling the void? When the war ended in 1865, cotton production resumed in the South, and exports to Europe again soared. Did the South regain its near monopoly? How would you characterize the United States' competitive position five years after the war?

| How did the war for union become a fight for black freedom? | What problems did the Confederacy face at home? | How did the war affect the economy and politics of the North? | How did the Union finally win the war? | Conclusion: In what ways was the Civil War a "Second American Revolution"? |

ANALYZE EVIDENCE

Why did the Confederacy's bid for international support fail?

between the Union and Britain—British war materiel for American grain and flour—helped offset the decline in textiles and encouraged Britain to remain neutral.

Europe's temptation to intervene disappeared for good in 1862. Union military successes in the West made Britain and France think twice about linking their fates to the struggling Confederacy. In September 1862, Lincoln announced a new policy that made an alliance with the Confederacy an alliance with slavery—a commitment the French and British, who had outlawed slavery in their empires and looked forward to its eradication worldwide, were not willing to make.

QUICK REVIEW

After a year and a half of fighting, who had the advantage in the war?

How did the war for union become a fight for black freedom?

CHRONOLOGY

1861
– First Confiscation Act passes.

1862
– Second Confiscation Act passes.
– Militia Act passes.

1863
– Emancipation Proclamation announced.

For a year and a half, Lincoln insisted that the North fought strictly to save the Union and not to abolish slavery. Nevertheless, the war for union became a war for African American freedom. Each month the conflict dragged on, it became clearer that the Confederate war machine depended heavily on slavery. Rebel armies used slaves to build fortifications and haul supplies. On the southern home front, slaves labored in ironworks and shipyards, and they grew the food that fed both soldiers and civilians. As Frederick Douglass put it, slavery was the "stomach of this rebellion." Slavery undergirded the Confederacy as certainly as it had the Old South. In the field among Union military commanders, in the halls of Congress, and in the White House, the truth gradually came into focus: To defeat the Confederacy, the North would have to destroy slavery. "I am a slow walker," Lincoln said, "but I never walk back."

From Slaves to Contraband

Lincoln detested human bondage, but as president he felt compelled to act prudently in the interests of the Union. He doubted his right under the Constitution to abolish slavery, even in states in rebellion. An astute politician, Lincoln worked within the tight limits of public opinion. The issue of black freedom was particularly explosive in the loyal border states, where slaveholders threatened to jump into the arms of the Confederacy at even the hint of emancipation.

Black freedom also raised alarms in the free states. The Democratic Party gave notice that emancipation would make the war strictly a Republican affair. Many white Northerners were not about to risk their lives to satisfy what they considered abolitionist "fanaticism." "We Won't Fight to Free the Nigger," one racist banner read. They feared that emancipation would propel "two or three million semi-savages" northward, where they would crowd into white neighborhoods, compete for white jobs, and mix with white "sons and daughters." Thus, emancipation threatened to dislodge the loyal slave states from the Union, alienate the Democratic Party, deplete the armies, and perhaps even spark race warfare in the North.

| Why did both the Union and the Confederacy consider control of the border states crucial? | Why did each side expect to win? | How did each side fare in the early years of the war? |

Yet proponents of emancipation pressed Lincoln as relentlessly as did the anti-emancipation forces. Abolitionists argued that by seceding, Southerners had forfeited their right to the protection of the Constitution and that Lincoln could—as the price of their treason—legally confiscate their slaves. When Lincoln refused, abolitionists scalded him. Frederick Douglass labeled him "the miserable tool of traitors and rebels."

The Republican-dominated Congress sometimes moved more vigorously against slavery than President Lincoln. In August 1861, Congress approved the Confiscation Act, which allowed the seizure of any slave employed directly by the Confederate military. It also fulfilled the free-soil dream of prohibiting slavery in the territories and abolished slavery in Washington, D.C. Democrats and border-state representatives voted against even these mild measures.

Slaves, not politicians, became the most insistent force for emancipation. By running away to Union lines, they forced slavery on the North's wartime agenda. Runaways made Northerners answer a crucial question: Were the

> "One African American responded, 'This is our country as much as it is yours, and we will not leave it.'"

runaways now free, or were they still slaves who, according to the fugitive slave law, had to be returned to their masters? At first, Yankee military officers sent the fugitives back. But Union armies needed laborers, and at Fort Monroe, Virginia, General Benjamin F. Butler called runaways **contraband of war**, meaning "confiscated property," and put them to work. Congress made Butler's practice national policy in March 1862 when it forbade returning fugitive slaves to their masters. Slaves were still not legally free, but there was a tilt toward emancipation. Lincoln's policy of noninterference with slavery gradually crumbled. To calm Northerners' racial fears, Lincoln offered colonization, the deportation of African Americans from the United States to Haiti, Panama, or elsewhere. In the summer of 1862, he told a delegation of black visitors that racial prejudice among whites made it impossible for blacks to achieve equality in the United States. One African American responded, "This is our country as much as it is yours, and we will not leave it." Congress voted a small amount of money to underwrite colonization, but practical limitations and stiff black opposition sank the scheme.

contraband of war
General Benjamin F. Butler's term for runaway slaves, whom he considered confiscated property of war, not fugitives, and put to work in the Union army. This policy proved to be a step on the road to emancipation.

While Lincoln was developing his own antislavery initiatives, he snuffed out actions that he believed would jeopardize northern unity. He was particularly alert to Union commanders who tried to dictate slavery policy from the field. In August 1861, when John C. Frémont, former Republican presidential nominee and now commander of federal troops in Missouri, freed the slaves belonging to Missouri rebels, Lincoln forced the general to revoke his edict. Events moved so rapidly, however, that Lincoln found it impossible to control federal policy on slavery.

From Contraband to Free People

On August 22, 1862, Lincoln replied to an angry abolitionist who demanded that he attack slavery. "My paramount objective in this struggle *is* to save the Union," Lincoln said, "and is *not* either to save or destroy slavery. If I could save the Union without freeing *any* slave I would do it, and if I could save it by freeing *all* the slaves I would do it; and if I could save it by freeing some and leaving others alone I would also do that." At first glance, Lincoln seemed to restate his old position that union was the North's sole objective. Instead, Lincoln announced that slavery was no longer untouchable and that he would emancipate every slave if doing so would preserve the Union.

By the summer of 1862, events were tumbling rapidly toward emancipation. On July 17, Congress adopted the second Confiscation Act. The first had confiscated slaves employed by the Confederate military; the second declared all slaves of rebel

| How did the war for union become a fight for black freedom? | What problems did the Confederacy face at home? | How did the war affect the economy and politics of the North? | How did the Union finally win the war? | Conclusion: In what ways was the Civil War a "Second American Revolution"? |

masters "forever free of their servitude." In theory, this breathtaking measure freed most Confederate slaves, for slaveholders formed the backbone of the rebellion. Congress had traveled far since the war began.

Lincoln had, too. By July 1862, the president had come to believe that emancipation was "a military necessity, absolutely essential to the preservation of the Union." The lengthening casualty lists had finally brought him around. In September, he announced his preliminary Emancipation Proclamation that promised to free *all* the slaves in the seceding states on January 1, 1863. The limitations of the proclamation—it exempted the loyal border states and the Union-occupied areas of the Confederacy—caused some to ridicule the act. The *Times* (London) observed cynically, "Where he has no power Mr. Lincoln will set the negroes free, where he retains power he will consider them as slaves." But Lincoln had no power to free slaves in loyal states, and invading Union armies would liberate slaves in the Confederacy as they advanced.

By presenting emancipation as a "military necessity," Lincoln hoped to disarm his conservative critics. Emancipation would deprive the Confederacy of valuable slave laborers, shorten the war, and thus save lives. Democrats, however, fumed that the "shrieking and howling abolitionist faction" had captured the White House and made it "a nigger war." When Democrats gained thirty-four congressional seats in the November 1862 elections, House Democrats quickly proposed a resolution branding emancipation "a high crime against the Constitution." The Republicans, who maintained narrow majorities in both houses of Congress, barely beat it back.

As promised, on New Year's Day 1863, Lincoln issued the final Emancipation Proclamation. In addition to freeing the slaves in the rebel states, the Emancipation Proclamation also committed the federal government to the fullest use of African Americans to defeat the Confederate enemy.

Emancipation Proclamation
President Lincoln's proclamation issued on January 1, 1863, declaring all slaves in Confederate-controlled territory free. The proclamation made the Civil War a war for abolition, as well as a war for union.

Major Battles of the Civil War, 1861–1862	
April 12–13, 1861	Attack on Fort Sumter
July 21, 1861	First battle of Bull Run (Manassas)
February 6, 1862	Battle of Fort Henry
February 16, 1862	Battle of Fort Donelson
March 6–8, 1862	Battle of Pea Ridge
March 9, 1862	Battle of the *Merrimack* (the *Virginia*) and the *Monitor*
March 26, 1862	Battle of Glorieta Pass
April 6–7, 1862	Battle of Shiloh
May–July 1862	McClellan's peninsula campaign
June 6, 1862	Fall of Memphis
June 25–July 1, 1862	Seven Days Battle
August 29–30, 1862	Second battle of Bull Run (Manassas)
September 17, 1862	Battle of Antietam
December 13, 1862	Battle of Fredericksburg

Why did both the Union and the Confederacy consider control of the border states crucial?	Why did each side expect to win?	How did each side fare in the early years of the war?

The War of Black Liberation

Even before Lincoln proclaimed emancipation a Union war aim, African Americans in the North had volunteered to fight. But the War Department, doubtful of blacks' abilities and fearful of white reaction to serving side by side with them, refused to make black men soldiers. Instead, the army employed black men as manual laborers; black women sometimes found employment as laundresses and cooks. The navy, however, accepted blacks from the outset, including runaway slaves.

As white casualties increased, Northerners gradually and reluctantly turned to African Americans. With the Militia Act of July 1862, Congress authorized enrolling blacks in "any military or naval service for which they may be found competent." After the Emancipation Proclamation, whites—like it or not—were fighting and dying for black freedom, and few insisted that blacks remain out of harm's way. Indeed, whites insisted that blacks share the danger, especially after March 1863, when Congress resorted to the draft to fill the Union army.

The military was far from color-blind. The Union army established segregated black regiments, paid black soldiers $10 per month rather than the $13 it paid whites, refused blacks the opportunity to become commissioned officers, punished blacks as if they were slaves, and assigned blacks to labor battalions rather than to combat units. Still, when the war ended, 179,000 African American men had served in the Union army. An astounding 71 percent of black men aged eighteen to forty-five in the free states wore Union blue, a participation rate substantially higher than that of white men.

In time, whites allowed blacks to put down their shovels and to shoulder rifles. Robert Smalls's hijacking of the *Planter* contradicted whites' prejudices. Likewise, the battles of Port Hudson and Milliken's Bend on the Mississippi River and Fort Wagner

CONSIDER CAUSE AND EFFECT

What was the importance of African Americans' active participation in winning their own freedom?

▲ **Black Dockworkers, Virginia** Hundreds of thousands of able-bodied free blacks and runaways cleared forests, built roads, erected bridges, constructed fortifications, and transported supplies for the U.S. Army. Their labor became indispensable to the war effort, and as one Northerner remembered, "The truth was we never could get enough of them." These men unloaded Union ships at an unnamed Virginia dock. National Archives photo no. 111-B-400.

How did the war for union become a fight for black freedom?	What problems did the Confederacy face at home?	How did the war affect the economy and politics of the North?	How did the Union finally win the war?	Conclusion: In what ways was the Civil War a "Second American Revolution"?

The Right to Fight: Black Soldiers in the Civil War

"A war undertaken and brazenly carried on for the perpetual enslavement of colored men, calls logically and loudly for colored men to help suppress it," black leader Frederick Douglass declared at the beginning of the Civil War. But it was only in 1863 that the lengthening casualty lists finally convinced the Lincoln administration to begin aggressively recruiting black soldiers.

In February 1863, James Henry Gooding, a twenty-six-year-old seaman from New Bedford, enlisted in the 54th Massachusetts Colored Regiment. Like most black soldiers, Gooding viewed military service as an opportunity to strike blows against slavery. The destruction of slavery, he believed, "depends on the free black men of the North" because "those who are in bonds must have some one to open the door; when the slave sees the white soldier approach, he dares not trust him and why? Because he has heard that *some* have treated him worse than their owners in rebellion. But if the slave sees a black soldier, he knows he has got a friend."

▲ The Lincoln administration was slow to accept black soldiers into the Union army, but eventually the valor of black troops eroded white skepticism. Here the 64th Colored Infantry stands in formation in front of their rough winter cabins, with their stacked rifles in the foreground. Library of Congress, LC-DIG-ppmsca-34152.

Fighting for the Union also offered a chance to attack white racism. In military service lay "the germs of the elevation of a downtrodden and despised race," Gooding believed, the chance for African Americans "to make themselves a people." Fighting, Gooding said, offered blacks the opportunity to destroy the "foul aspersion that they were not men."

According to the white commander of the 59th U.S. Colored Infantry, when an ex-slave put on a uniform of army blue, the change was dramatic: "Yesterday a filthy, repulsive 'nigger,' to-day a neatly-attired man; yesterday a slave, to-day a freeman; yesterday a civilian, to-day a soldier." Others noticed the same transformation: "Put a United States uniform on his back and the *chattel* is a man." Black veterans agreed. "This was the biggest thing that ever happened in my life," one ex-soldier remembered. "I felt like a man with a uniform and a gun in my hand." Another said, "I felt freedom in my bones."

---

in Charleston harbor demonstrated black courage under fire. More than 38,000 black soldiers died in the Civil War, a mortality rate that was higher than that of white troops. Blacks played a crucial role in the triumph of the Union and the destruction of slavery in the South. **(See "Spotlight: The Right to Fight: Black Soldiers in the Civil War" above.)**

When black men became soldiers, they and their families gained new confidence and self-esteem. Military service taught them new skills and introduced them to political struggle as they battled for their rights within the army. Wartime experiences stood them in good stead when the war of liberation was over and the battle for equality

Why did both the Union and the Confederacy consider control of the border states crucial?	Why did each side expect to win?	How did each side fare in the early years of the war?

Black courage under fire ended skepticism about the capabilities of African American troops. As one white officer observed after a battle, "They seemed like men who were fighting to vindicate their manhood and they did it well." Another remarked, "they have fought their way into the respect of all the army." After the 54th served courageously in South Carolina, Gooding reported: "It is not for us to blow our horn; but when a regiment of white men gave us three cheers as we were passing them, it shows that we did our duty as men should."

Yet discrimination within the Union army continued. When the government refused to pay blacks the same as whites, the 54th refused to accept unequal pay. Gooding wrote to President Lincoln himself to explain his regiment's decision: "Now the main question is, Are we Soldiers, or are we Labourers? . . . Now your Excellency, we have done a Soldier's Duty. Why Can't we have a Soldier's pay?" The 54th's principled stance helped reverse the government's position, and in June 1864 Congress equalized the pay of black and white soldiers.

As Union troops advanced deeper into the Confederacy, former slaves greeted black soldiers as heroes. In March 1865, the white officer of a black regiment in North Carolina reported that black soldiers "stepped like lords & conquerors. The frantic demonstrations of the negro population will never die out of my memory. Their cheers & heartfelt 'God bress ye's' & cries of 'De chains is broke; De chains is broke' mingled sublimely with the lusty shout of our brave soldiery." Hardened and disciplined by their military service, black soldiers drew tremendous strength from their participation in the Union effort. Despite their second-class status, they found army life a great counterweight to the degradation and dependency of slavery.

Eager to shoulder the rights, privileges, and responsibilities of freedom, black veterans often took the lead in the hard struggle for equality after the war. Blacks in the Union army that occupied the South after 1865 assumed a special obligation to protect former slaves. "The fact is," one black chaplain said, "when colored soldiers are about they [whites] are afraid to kick colored women and abuse colored people on the Streets, as they usually do." Black veterans believed that their military service entitled African Americans not only to freedom but also to civil and political rights. Sergeant Henry Maxwell announced: "We want two more boxes besides the cartridge box—the ballot and the jury box." Black men had demonstrated what they could do when permitted to become soldiers; they now demanded the chance to perform as citizens.

James Henry Gooding did not have a chance to participate in the postwar struggle for equal rights. Wounded and captured at the battle of Olustee in Florida, he was sent to the infamous Confederate prison Andersonville, where he died on July 19, 1864.

Questions for Analysis

RECOGNIZE VIEWPOINTS: Why did the Union resist enrolling black troops?

ANALYZE THE EVIDENCE: What specific benefits or opportunities did black men encounter as a result of military service?

CONSIDER THE CONTEXT: Why was the right to fight so important to black men? In what ways do you think military service by black men would have been important to the entire black community?

began. But first there was a rebellion to put down. Victory depended as much on what happened behind the lines as on the battlefields.

QUICK REVIEW

Why did the Union change policy in 1863 to allow black men to serve in the army?

| How did the war for union become a fight for black freedom? | What problems did the Confederacy face at home? | How did the war affect the economy and politics of the North? | How did the Union finally win the war? | Conclusion: In what ways was the Civil War a "Second American Revolution"? |

What problems did the Confederacy face at home?

CHRONOLOGY

1862
– Confederate Congress authorizes draft.

1863
– Bread riots break out in South.

By seceding, Southerners brought on themselves a firestorm of unimaginable fury. Monstrous losses on the battlefield nearly bled the Confederacy to death. Southerners on the home front also suffered, even at the hands of their own government. Efforts by the Davis administration in Richmond to centralize power in order to fight the war caused some men and women to charge Richmond with tyranny. War also meant severe economic hardship. Shortages and inflation hurt everyone, some more than others. By 1863, unequal suffering meant that planters and yeomen who had stood together began to drift apart. Most disturbing of all, slaves became open participants in the destruction of slavery and the Confederacy.

Revolution from Above

As a Confederate general observed, Southerners were engaged in a total war "in which the whole population and the whole production . . . are to be put on a war footing, where every institution is to be made auxiliary to war." Jefferson Davis faced the task of building an army and a navy from almost nothing, supplying them from factories that were scarce and puny, and paying for it all from a treasury that did not exist. Finding eager soldiers proved easiest. Hundreds of officers defected from the U.S. Army, and hundreds of thousands of eager young rebels volunteered to follow them.

▶ **John Wallace Comer, C.S.A., with His Servant, Burrell** Many slaveholders took personal servants with them to war. These slaves cooked, washed, and cleaned for their owners. Owners sometimes dressed their servants in uniforms, as Comer did, which led some observers to conclude incorrectly that slaves were members of the Confederate military. Alabama Department of Archives and History, Montgomery, Alabama.

| Why did both the Union and the Confederacy consider control of the border states crucial? | Why did each side expect to win? | How did each side fare in the early years of the war? |

The Confederacy's economy and finances proved tougher problems. Because of the Union blockade, the government had no choice but to build an industrial sector itself. Government-owned clothing and shoe factories, mines, arms manufacturers, and powder works sprang up. The government also harnessed private companies, such as the huge Tredegar Iron Works in Richmond, to the war effort. Paying for the war became the most difficult task. A flood of paper money caused debilitating inflation. By Christmas 1864, a Confederate soldier's monthly pay no longer bought a pair of socks. The Confederacy manufactured much more than most people imagined possible, but it never produced all that the rebels needed.

Richmond's war-making effort brought unprecedented government intrusion into the private lives of Confederate citizens. In April 1862, the Confederate Congress passed the first conscription (draft) law in American history. All able-bodied white males between the ages of eighteen and thirty-five (later seventeen and fifty) were liable to serve in the rebel army. The government adopted a policy of impressment, which allowed officials to confiscate food, horses, and wagons from private citizens and to pay what they wanted. After March 1863, the Confederacy legally impressed slaves, employing them as military laborers.

Richmond's centralizing efforts ran head-on into the South's traditional values of states' rights and unfettered individualism. Southerners lashed out at what Georgia governor Joseph E. Brown denounced as the "dangerous usurpation by Congress of the reserved right of the States." Richmond and the states struggled for control of money, supplies, and soldiers, with damaging consequences for the war effort.

Hardship Below

Hardships on the home front fell most heavily on the poor. The draft stripped yeoman farms of men, leaving the women and children to grow what they ate. Government agents took 10 percent of harvests as a "tax-in-kind" on agriculture. Like inflation, shortages afflicted the entire population, but the rich lost luxuries while the poor lost necessities. In the spring of 1863, bread riots broke out in a dozen cities and villages across the South. In Richmond, a mob of nearly a thousand hungry women broke into shops and took what they needed.

"Men cannot be expected to fight for the Government that permits their wives & children to starve," one woman observed. Although a few wealthy individuals shared their bounty and the Confederate and state governments made efforts at social welfare, every attempt fell short. In late 1864, one desperate farmwife wrote her husband, "I have always been proud of you, and since your connection with the Confederate army, I have been prouder of you than ever before. I would not have you do anything wrong for the world, but before God, Edward, unless you come home, we must die." When the war ended, one-third of the soldiers had already gone home. A Mississippi deserter explained, "We are poor men and are willing to defend our country but our families [come] first." **(See "Analyzing Historical Evidence: Home and Country" on page 442.)**

Small white farmers perceived a profound inequality of sacrifice. They called it "a rich man's war and a poor man's fight." The draft law permitted a man who had money to hire a substitute to take his place. The "twenty-Negro law" exempted one white man on every plantation with twenty or more slaves. The government intended this law to provide protection for white women and to see that slaves tended the crops, but yeomen perceived it as rich men evading military service. In fact, most slaveholders went off to war, but the extreme suffering of common folk and the relative immunity of planters increased class friction.

| How did the war for union become a fight for black freedom? | **What problems did the Confederacy face at home?** | How did the war affect the economy and politics of the North? | How did the Union finally win the war? | Conclusion: In what ways was the Civil War a "Second American Revolution"? |

Home and Country

Christian Marion Epperly and his wife, Mary Epperly, lived in the Blue Ridge Mountains of Virginia. Although neither was a passionate secessionist, Marion entered the Confederate army as a private early in 1862. He hated army life and longed for his wife and children. Mary was equally heartsick without Marion. Despite their limited schooling, the couple's letters reveal how plain folks wrestled with the tangled issues of loyalty and obligation.

DOCUMENT 1

Letter from Chickahominy Creek, Virginia, May 16, 1862

During the peninsula campaign in Virginia, as Union general George B. McClellan was approaching the Confederate capital of Richmond, Marion wrote to Mary from near the action.

I think the people will be bound to suffer for something to eat[;] the grain is all destroid and nearly all the fenses is burnt up from yorktown to Richmond: it looks distressing just to travel along the road: the wheat up waist hi some of it and horses and cattle has eat the most of it to the ground and I think the yankees will make a finish of the ballans [balance] that is left but the[y] cant doo much more damage than our army did[;] our own men killed all the cattle and hogs & sheep that the farmers had[,] even took ther chickens[;] every thing is totally destroid in this part of the State. . . .

I hope and pray this awful war will soon come to a close some way or another[,] any way to get pease in the world wonst more[;] it seems to me I had drather be at home and live on bred and water than to have this war hanging over us but I pray god pease will soon be made[.] I dont think the war can last long.

DOCUMENT 2

Letter from Camp near Bells Bridge, Tennessee, August 15, 1863

By the summer of 1863, Marion's regiment had moved to Tennessee, where he notices increasing war-weariness, desertions, and disillusionment with the Confederacy.

You don't know how glad I would be if I was just thar with you this morning to see the sun rise over the hills in Virginia again[,] for everry thing seames so sad and desolate here this morning; it seames like the absens of dear friends and the present condition of things has brought deep refletion and sadnes upon everry heart, and [men] are growing weary and getting out of heart and leaving the Army everry day. I cant tell wheather it will be for the better or wheather it will make things wors: but I hope it is a way god has provided to bring this war and time of sorrow to an end and to give us pease in our land again: Thoug I believe the south first started on a just course but our own wickedness and disobedians has brought us to what we are and I firmly believe wee will be bound to give up to subjugation[.] I don't think the south will stand much longer, and I am sorrow to say it for wee will be a ruined people while time ma [may] last, but wee ought to submit to any thing to have this awwful war ended.

DOCUMENT 3

Letter from Floyd County, Virginia, August 16, 1863

Mary longs for peace and argues that desertion will end the war.

Oh how much beter satisfied would I be if you was just hear with me this beatiful Sabath morning. I feel as if my

---

COMPARE AND CONTRAST
How did white Southerners' experiences of the Civil War vary by class and status?

The Richmond government hoped that the crucible of war would mold a region into a nation. Officials actively promoted Confederate nationalism to "excite in our citizens an ardent and enduring attachment to our Government and its institutions." Clergymen assured their congregations that God had blessed slavery and the new nation. Jefferson Davis claimed that the Confederacy was part of a divine plan and asked citizens to observe national days of fasting and prayer. But these efforts failed to win over thousands of die-hard Unionists and an increasing number of alienated yeomen. As animosity between yeomen and planters increased, the war also threatened to rip the southern social fabric along its racial seam.

Why did both the Union and the Confederacy consider control of the border states crucial?	Why did each side expect to win?	How did each side fare in the early years of the war?

troubles on earth would all be over if you was just at home to stay wonst more[,] but god sent it upon us and we will have to bear with it the best we can but I do pray that he may soon end this destressing time some way[.] I would be willing for it to end most any way just so it would end[.] Dear Marion I think if the head men dont soon end this war that the soldiers will for they are runing way from down east by hundreds[;] they was five hundard went through hear last weak and well armed and they say they wont go back any more and I dont blame them for it[.] I wish they would all runaway and these head men would be oblige to fight it out but as long as they can stay at home and speculate off of the poor soulders they dont care how long the war lasts[.] Serious Smith wrote a leter the 9 of this month and he wrote that they had to pay 15 dolars for a bushel of taters . . . how can the poor soulders make out and only get a leven [eleven] dolars a month[?]

DOCUMENT 4

Letter from Outskirts of Dalton, Georgia, March 25, 1864

As his regiment is backing toward Atlanta, trying to fend off Sherman, Marion considers what has gone wrong with the Confederacy.

I dont think it will last much longer if the souldiers doo what they say they will doo[;] they are all verry tired of this war and the way it is carried on[.] I think wee all have stud it about as long as we can unless our leading men dos a heap better than they ever have yet: if they wer God fearing men I would think wee would prosper but so long as they [seek] the Bottom of a Whiskey Barl and frolick around bad places just so long we will hafto fight and suffer. . . . we was all Born in a free land and I think wee ought to stil be free

and not be bound down wors than slaves[;] we wonst had a union and was living happy and had all man can wish for[;] now we are cut off from that union and what are wee nothing but a ruend people as long as we shal live . . . dissatisfaction and wickedness all over the south[;] may God show us our errors and put us in the rite way and Bring us Back to our old union again.

Despite his doubts about the Confederacy and continued affection for the Union, Marion left the army without authorization only once, and after a few weeks at home in 1863, he returned to his regiment. Like many disillusioned soldiers, he fought in the rebel army to the very end.

Source: Christian M. Epperly Correspondence, Gilder Lehrman Collection, Pierpont Morgan Library, New York.

Questions for Analysis

ANALYZE THE EVIDENCE: How does Marion contrast his previous life in the Union with life in the Confederacy? What specific differences does he note?

RECOGNIZE VIEWPOINTS: How does the Epperlys' perspective on the Confederacy reflect their social position as plain folk in Virginia society?

CONSIDER THE CONTEXT: Marion makes clear why he had such affection for his home; he is much less clear about why he fought for the Confederacy. What might some of his reasons have been?

The Disintegration of Slavery

The legal destruction of slavery was the product of presidential proclamation, congressional legislation, and eventually constitutional amendment, but the practical destruction of slavery was the product of war, what Lincoln called war's "friction and abrasion." Slaves took advantage of the upheaval to reach for freedom. Some half a million of the South's 4 million slaves ran away to Union military lines. More than 100,000 runaways took up arms as federal soldiers and sailors. Other men and women stayed in the slave quarter, where they also staked their claim to freedom.

How did the war for union become a fight for black freedom?	What problems did the Confederacy face at home?	How did the war affect the economy and politics of the North?	How did the Union finally win the war?	Conclusion: In what ways was the Civil War a "Second American Revolution"?

TRACE CHANGE
OVER TIME

How did the day-to-day
experiences of enslaved
African Americans change
over the course of the
Civil War?

War disrupted slavery in a dozen ways. Almost immediately, it called the master away, leaving the mistress to assume responsibility for the plantation. But mistresses could not maintain traditional standards of slave discipline in wartime, and the balance of power shifted. Slaves got to the fields late, worked indifferently, and quit early. Some slaveholders responded violently; most saw no alternative but to strike bargains—offering gifts or part of the crop—to keep slaves at home and at work. An Alabaman complained that she "begged . . . what little is done." When the war began, a North Carolina woman praised her slaves as "diligent and respectful." When it ended, she said, "As to the idea of a *faithful servant, it is all a fiction.*" Whites' greatest fear—retaliatory violence—rarely occurred, but slaves gradually undermined white mastery and expanded control over their own lives.

QUICK REVIEW

How did wartime hardship in the South contribute to class friction?

How did the war affect the economy and politics of the North?

CHRONOLOGY

1863

– National Banking Act
  passes.
– Congress authorizes draft.
– New York City draft riots
  erupt.

Although little fighting took place on northern soil, almost every family had a son, husband, father, or brother in uniform. As in the South, men marched off to fight, but preserving the country was also women's work. For civilians as well as soldiers, for women as well as men, war was transforming.

The need to build and fuel the Union war machine strengthened the federal government and boosted the economy. The Union sent nearly two million men into the military and still increased production in almost every area. But because the rewards and burdens of patriotism were distributed unevenly, the North experienced sharp, even violent, divisions. Workers confronted employers, whites confronted blacks, and Democrats confronted Republicans. Still, Northerners on the home front remained fervently attached to the Union.

The Government and the Economy

When the war began, the United States had no national banking system, no national currency, and no federal income tax. But the secession of eleven slave states cut the Democrats' strength in Congress in half and destroyed their capacity to resist Republican economic programs. The Legal Tender Act of February 1862 created a national currency, paper money that Northerners called "greenbacks." With the passage of the National Banking Act in February 1863, Congress established a system of national banks that by the 1870s had largely replaced the antebellum system of decentralized state banks. Congress also enacted a series of sweeping tax laws.

The Republicans' wartime legislation also aimed at integrating the West into the Union. In May 1862, Congress approved the Homestead Act, which offered 160 acres of public land to settlers who would live and labor on it. The Homestead Act bolstered western loyalty and in time resulted in more than a million new farms. The Pacific Railroad Act in July 1862 provided massive federal assistance for building a transcontinental railroad that ran from Omaha to San Francisco when completed in 1869. Congress further bound East and West by subsidizing the Pony Express mail service and a transcontinental telegraph.

Why did both the Union and the Confederacy consider control of the border states crucial?	Why did each side expect to win?	How did each side fare in the early years of the war?

Congress also created the Department of Agriculture and passed the Land-Grant College Act (also known as the Morrill Act after its sponsor, Representative Justin Morrill of Vermont), which set aside public land to support universities that emphasized "agriculture and mechanical arts." As the Lincoln administration strengthened the North's ability to win the war, it also permanently changed the nation.

Women and Work at Home and at War

More than a million farm men were called to the military, and farm women added men's chores to their own. "I met more women driving teams on the road and saw more at work in the fields than men," a visitor to Iowa reported in the fall of 1862. Rising production testified to their success in plowing, planting, and harvesting. Rapid mechanization assisted farm women in their new roles. Cyrus McCormick sold 165,000 of his reapers during the war years. The combination of high prices for farm products and increased production ensured that war and prosperity joined hands in the rural North.

In cities, women stepped into jobs vacated by men, particularly in manufacturing. In addition, women entered essentially new occupations such as government secretaries and clerks. The number of women working for wages rose 40 percent during the war. As more and more women entered the workforce, employers cut wages. In 1864, New York seamstresses working fourteen-hour days earned only $1.54 a week, not enough "to sustain life," they said. Urban workers resorted increasingly to strikes to wrench decent salaries from their employers, but their protests rarely succeeded.

▲ **Women Doing Laundry for Federal Soldiers, ca. 1861** Some northern women were forced by their desperate financial circumstances to wash soldiers' dirty clothes to make a living. Army camps were difficult places for "respectable" women to work. One Union soldier discouraged his wife even from visiting, noting, "It is not a fit place for any woman, for there is all kinds of talk, songs and everything not good for them 2 hear." Corbis via Getty Images.

TRACE CHANGE OVER TIME

How did the new legislation adopted by the U.S. Congress during the Civil War change the role of the federal government?

| How did the war for union become a fight for black freedom? | What problems did the Confederacy face at home? | **How did the war affect the economy and politics of the North?** | How did the Union finally win the war? | Conclusion: In what ways was the Civil War a "Second American Revolution"? |

Most middle-class white women stayed home and contributed to the war effort in traditional ways. They sewed, wrapped bandages, and sold homemade goods at local fairs to raise money to aid the soldiers. Other women expressed their patriotism in an untraditional way. Defying prejudices about female delicacy, thousands of women on both sides volunteered to nurse the wounded. Many northern female volunteers worked through the U.S. Sanitary Commission, a huge civilian organization that bought and distributed clothing, food, and medicine, recruited doctors and nurses, and buried the dead.

Some volunteers went on to become paid military nurses. Dorothea Dix, well known for her efforts to reform insane asylums, was named superintendent of female nurses in April 1861. By 1863, some 3,000 nurses served under her. Most nurses worked in hospitals behind the battle lines, but some, like Clara Barton, who later founded the American Red Cross, worked in battlefield units.

Politics and Dissent

At first, the bustle of economic and military mobilization seemed to silence politics, but bipartisan unity did not last. Within a year, Democrats were labeling the Republican administration a "reign of terror" and denouncing as unconstitutional Republican policies expanding federal power, subsidizing private business, and emancipating the slaves. In turn, Republicans were calling Democrats the party of "Dixie, Davis, and the Devil."

When the Republican-dominated Congress enacted the draft law in March 1863, Democrats had another grievance. The law required that all men between the ages of twenty and forty-five enroll in a lottery that would decide who went to war. It also allowed a draftee to hire a substitute or simply to pay a $300 fee and get out of his military obligation. As in the South, common folk could be heard chanting, "A rich man's war and a poor man's fight."

ANALYZE EVIDENCE

What do events like the New York City draft riots and other public acts of opposition to the war reveal about divisions in northern society?

New York City draft riots
Four days of rioting in New York City in July 1863, triggered by efforts to enforce the military draft. Democratic Irish workingmen, suffering economic hardship, infuriated by the draft, and opposed to fighting for black freedom, killed at least 105 people, most of them black.

Linking the draft and emancipation, Democrats argued that Republicans employed an unconstitutional means (the draft) to achieve an unconstitutional end (emancipation). In the summer of 1863, antidraft, antiblack mobs went on rampages in northern cities. In July in New York City, Democratic Irish workingmen—crowded into filthy tenements, gouged by inflation, enraged by the draft, and dead set against fighting to free blacks—erupted in four days of rioting. The New York City draft riots killed at least 105 people, most of them black.

Lincoln called Democratic opposition to the war "the fire in the rear" and believed that it was even more threatening to national survival than were Confederate armies. The antiwar wing of the Democratic Party, the Peace Democrats—whom some called "Copperheads," after the poisonous snake—found their chief spokesman in Ohio congressman Clement Vallandigham, who demanded: "Stop fighting. Make an armistice. . . . Withdraw your army from the seceding States."

In September 1862, in an effort to stifle opposition to the war, Lincoln placed under military arrest any person who discouraged enlistments, resisted the draft, or engaged in "disloyal" practices. Before the war ended, his administration imprisoned nearly 14,000 individuals, most in the border states. The administration's heavy-handed tactics suppressed free speech, but the campaign fell short of a reign of terror, for the majority of the prisoners were not northern Democratic opponents but Confederates, blockade runners, and citizens of foreign countries, and most of those arrested gained quick release. Still, the administration's net captured Vallandigham, who was arrested, convicted of treason, and banished.

QUICK REVIEW

Why was the U.S. Congress able to pass such a bold legislative agenda during the war?

| Why did both the Union and the Confederacy consider control of the border states crucial? | Why did each side expect to win? | How did each side fare in the early years of the war? |

How did the Union finally win the war?

I n the early months of 1863, the Union's prospects looked bleak, and the Confederate cause stood at high tide. Then, in July 1863, the tide began to turn. The military man most responsible for this shift was Ulysses S. Grant. Elevated to supreme command in 1864, Grant knit together a powerful war machine that integrated a sophisticated command structure, modern technology, and complex logistics and supply systems. Grant's arithmetic was simple: Killing more of the enemy than he killed of you equaled "the complete over-throw of the rebellion."

The North ground out the victory battle by bloody battle. Still, Southerners were not deterred. The fighting escalated in the last two years of the war. As national elections approached in the fall of 1864, Lincoln expected a war-weary North to reject him. Instead, northern voters declared their willingness to continue the war in the defense of the ideals of union and freedom. Lincoln lived to see victory, but only days after Lee surrendered, the president died from an assassin's bullet.

Vicksburg and Gettysburg

Vicksburg, Mississippi, situated on the eastern bank of the Mississippi River, stood between Union forces and complete control of the river. In May 1863, Union forces under Grant laid siege to the city. As the siege of Vicksburg dragged on, civilians ate mules and rats to survive. After six weeks, on July 4, 1863, nearly 30,000 rebels marched out of Vicksburg, stacked their arms, and surrendered unconditionally. A Yankee captain wrote home to his wife: "The backbone of the Rebellion is this day broken. The Confederacy is divided. . . . Vicksburg is ours. The Mississippi River is opened, and Gen. Grant is to be our next President."

On the same Fourth of July, word arrived that Union forces had crushed General Lee at Gettysburg, Pennsylvania (**Map 15.3**). Emboldened by his victory at Chancellorsville in May, Lee and his 75,000-man army had invaded Pennsylvania. On June 28, Union forces under General George G. Meade intercepted the Confederates at the small town of Gettysburg, where Union soldiers occupied the high ground. In three days of furious fighting, the Confederates failed to dislodge the Federals. The battle of Gettysburg cost Lee more than one-third of his army—28,000 casualties. "It's all my fault," he lamented. On the night of July 4, 1863, he marched his battered army back to Virginia.

The twin disasters at Vicksburg and Gettysburg proved to be the turning point of the war. The Confederacy could not replace the nearly 60,000 soldiers who were captured, wounded, or killed. It is hindsight, however, that permits us to see the pair of battles as decisive. At the time, the Confederacy still controlled the heartland of the South, and Lee still had a vicious sting. War-weariness threatened to erode the North's will to win before Union armies could destroy the Confederacy's ability to go on.

Grant Takes Command

In the fall of 1863, General U. S. Grant, who was now commander of Union forces between the Mississippi River and the Appalachians, won a decisive victory at Chattanooga, Tennessee. The victory opened the door to Georgia. In March 1864, Lincoln asked Grant to come east to become the general in chief of all Union armies.

In Washington, General Grant implemented his grand strategy for a war of attrition. He ordered a series of simultaneous assaults from Virginia to Louisiana. Two

CHRONOLOGY

1863
- Vicksburg falls to Union forces.
- Lee defeated at battle of Gettysburg.

1864
- Grant appointed Union general in chief.
- Wilderness campaign launches.
- Atlanta falls to Union forces.
- Lincoln reelected.

1865
- Richmond falls to Union forces.
- Lee surrenders at Appomattox Court House.
- Lincoln assassinated; Andrew Johnson becomes president.

siege of Vicksburg
Six-week siege by General Grant intended to starve out Vicksburg. On July 4, 1863, the 30,000 Confederate troops holding the city surrendered. The victory gave the Union control of the Mississippi River and, together with Gettysburg, marked a major turning point of the war.

battle of Gettysburg
Battle fought at Gettysburg, Pennsylvania (July 1–3, 1863), between Union forces under General Meade and Confederate forces under General Lee. The Union emerged victorious and Lee lost more than one-third of his men. Together with Vicksburg, Gettysburg marked a major turning point of the war.

| How did the war for union become a fight for black freedom? | What problems did the Confederacy face at home? | How did the war affect the economy and politics of the North? | **How did the Union finally win the war?** | Conclusion: In what ways was the Civil War a "Second American Revolution"? |

Vicksburg Campaign, 1863

Legend:
→ Union advance
→ Confederate advance
◂--- Confederate retreat
✳ Union victory

actions proved particularly significant. In one, General William Tecumseh Sherman, whom Grant appointed his successor to command the western armies, plunged southeast toward Atlanta. In the other, Grant, who took control of the Army of the Potomac, went head-to-head with Lee in Virginia in May and June of 1864.

The fighting between Grant and Lee was particularly savage. At the battle of the Wilderness, where thick forest often made it impossible to see more than ten paces, the armies pounded away at each other until approximately 18,000 Yankees and 11,000 rebels had fallen. At Spotsylvania Court House, frenzied men fought hand to hand for eighteen hours in the rain. One veteran remembered men "piled upon each other in some places four layers deep, exhibiting every ghastly phase of mutilation." Spotsylvania cost Grant another 18,000 casualties and Lee 10,000. Grant kept moving and attacked Lee again at Cold Harbor, where he suffered 13,000 additional casualties to Lee's 5,000.

Twice as many Union soldiers as rebel soldiers died in four weeks of fighting in Virginia, but because Lee had only half as many troops as Grant, his losses were equivalent to Grant's. Grant knew that the South could not replace the losses. The campaign carried Grant to the outskirts of Petersburg, just south of Richmond, where he abandoned the costly tactic of the frontal assault and began a siege that immobilized both armies and dragged on for nine months.

Simultaneously, Sherman invaded Georgia. Skillful maneuvering, constant skirmishing, and one pitched battle, at Kennesaw Mountain, brought Sherman to Atlanta, which fell on September 2. Intending to "make Georgia howl," Sherman marched out of Atlanta on November 15 with 62,000 battle-hardened veterans, heading for Savannah, 285 miles away on the Atlantic coast. One veteran remembered, "[We]

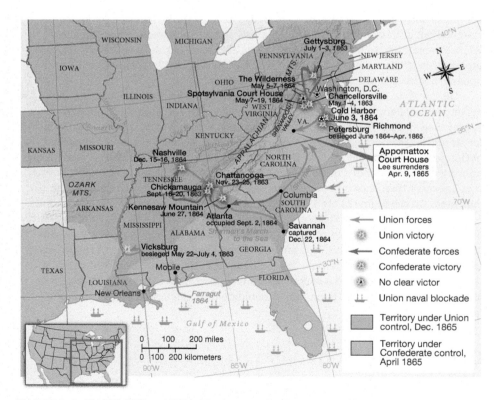

MAP 15.3 ▲ The Civil War, 1863–1865

Ulysses S. Grant's victory at Vicksburg divided the Confederacy at the Mississippi River. William Tecumseh Sherman's march from Chattanooga to Savannah divided it again. In northern Virginia, Robert E. Lee fought fiercely, but Grant's larger, better-supplied armies prevailed.

Why did both the Union and the Confederacy consider control of the border states crucial?	Why did each side expect to win?	How did each side fare in the early years of the war?

destroyed all we could not eat, stole their niggers, burned their cotton & gins, spilled their sorghum, burned & twisted their R. Roads and raised Hell generally." **Sherman's March to the Sea** aimed at destroying the will of white Southerners to continue the war. A few weeks earlier, General Philip H. Sheridan had carried out his own scorched-earth campaign in the Shenandoah Valley of Virginia. When Sherman's troops entered an undefended Savannah in mid-December, the general telegraphed Lincoln that he had "a Christmas gift" for him. A month earlier, Union voters had bestowed on the president an even greater gift.

The Election of 1864

In the summer of 1864, with Sherman temporarily checked outside Atlanta and Grant bogged down in the siege of Petersburg, the Democratic Party smelled victory in the fall elections. Lincoln himself concluded, "It seems exceedingly probable that this administration will not be re-elected."

The Democrats were badly divided, however. Peace Democrats insisted on a truce, while "war" Democrats supported the conflict but opposed Republican means of fighting it. The party tried to paper over the chasm by nominating a war candidate, General George McClellan, but adopting a peace platform that demanded that "immediate efforts be made for a cessation of hostilities." Republicans denounced the peace plank as a cut-and-run plan that "virtually proposed to surrender the country to the rebels in arms against us."

The capture of Atlanta in September turned the political tide in favor of the Republicans. Lincoln received 55 percent of the popular vote, but his electoral margin was a whopping 212 to McClellan's 21 (**Map 15.4**). Lincoln's resounding victory gave him a mandate to continue the war until slavery and the Confederacy were dead.

The Confederacy Collapses

As 1865 dawned, military disaster littered the Confederate landscape. With the destruction of John B. Hood's army at Nashville in December 1864, the interior of the Confederacy lay in Yankee hands (see Map 15.3). Sherman's troops, resting momentarily in Savannah, eyed South Carolina hungrily. Farther north, Grant had Lee's army pinned down in Petersburg, a few miles from Richmond.

Some Confederates turned their backs on the rebellion. News from the battlefields made it difficult not to conclude that the Yankees had beaten them. When soldiers' wives begged their husbands to return home to keep their families from starving, the stream of deserters grew dramatically. Still, white Southerners had demonstrated a remarkable endurance for their cause. Half of the Confederate soldiers were casualties of war, and the sacrifices of ragged, hungry women and children were obvious to all.

The end came with a rush. On February 1, 1865, Sherman's troops stormed out of Savannah into South Carolina, the "cradle of the Confederacy." In Virginia, Lee abandoned Petersburg on April 2, and Richmond fell on April 3. Grant pursued Lee until he surrendered on April 9, 1865, at Appomattox Court House, Virginia. Grant offered generous peace terms. He allowed Lee's men to return home and to keep their horses to help "put in a crop to carry themselves and their families through the next winter." With Lee gone, the remaining Confederate armies lost hope and gave up within two weeks. After four years, the war was over.

No one was more relieved than Lincoln, but his celebration was restrained. He told his cabinet that his postwar burdens would weigh almost as heavily as those of wartime. Seeking a distraction, Lincoln attended Ford's Theatre on the evening of Good Friday, April 14, 1865. John Wilkes Booth, an actor with southern sympathies, slipped

Sherman's March to the Sea
Military campaign from September through December 1864 in which Union forces under General Sherman marched from Atlanta, Georgia, to the coast at Savannah. Carving a path of destruction as it progressed, Sherman's army aimed at destroying white Southerners' will to continue the war.

Battle of Gettysburg, July 1–3, 1863

PLACE EVENTS IN CONTEXT

How important was the military leadership of Sherman and Grant in securing the North's victory?

How did the war for union become a fight for black freedom?	What problems did the Confederacy face at home?	How did the war affect the economy and politics of the North?	**How did the Union finally win the war?**	Conclusion: In what ways was the Civil War a "Second American Revolution"?

▲ **The Dead Line, by Robert Sneden, Andersonville Prison, 1864** Union soldier Robert Sneden arrived at Andersonville in February 1864. Soon the sixteen-and-a-half acres were crammed with 33,000 Union prisoners. Sneden sketched this scene of a man being shot by a guard while trying to take part of a fence (the "dead line" that prisoners could not cross) for firewood. More than 13,000 prisoners perished at Andersonville. Virginia Historical Society, Richmond, Virginia, USA/Bridgeman Images.

READING THE IMAGE: What does the painting suggest were among the hazards to the health of the prisoners at Andersonville?

CONNECTIONS: How might the state of the Confederate economy have affected conditions at Andersonville?

into the president's box and shot Lincoln, who died the next morning. Vice President Andrew Johnson became president. The man who had led the nation through the war would not lead it during the postwar search for a just peace.

The War's Bloody Toll

The war cost Lincoln and approximately 750,000 soldiers and sailors their lives, more than in all the nation's other wars combined. Several factors explain why so many died.

The sheer size of the armies—some battles involved more than 200,000 soldiers—ensured huge casualties. What most Americans expected to be a short war extended

▶ **Surgical Kit** Misery did not end when the cannons ceased firing. Northern and southern surgeons performed approximately 60,000 amputations with simple instruments such as those included in this surgical kit. © Chicago History Museum, USA/Bridgeman Images.

Why did both the Union and the Confederacy consider control of the border states crucial?	Why did each side expect to win?	How did each side fare in the early years of the war?

for four full years. In addition, armies fought according to antiquated Napoleonic strategy. Soldiers advanced with their comrades in compact formation, but by the 1860s weapons with rifled barrels were replacing smoothbore muskets and cannons, and the new weapons' greater range and accuracy made sitting ducks of charging infantry.

When the war began, Union and Confederate medical departments could not cope with large-scale battles. They had no ambulance corps to remove the wounded. They had no field hospitals. Wounded soldiers often lay on the battlefields for hours, sometimes days. Gradually, both sides organized effective ambulance corps, built hospitals, and hired trained surgeons and nurses.

Soldiers did not always count speedy transportation to a hospital a blessing, however. As one Union soldier said, "I had rather risk a battle than the Hospitals." Field doctors gained a reputation as butchers, but a wounded man's real enemy was medical ignorance. Unaware of basic germ theory, surgeons spread infections almost every time they operated. They wore the same dirty smocks for days and washed their scalpels and saws in buckets of filthy water.

The growing ranks of nurses increased men's odds and alleviated their suffering. Still, nearly one of every five wounded rebel soldiers died, and one of every six wounded Yankees. A century later, in Vietnam, only one wounded American soldier in four hundred died.

Soldiers who avoided battlefield wounds and hospital infections still faced sickness. Dysentery, typhoid fever, pneumonia, and malaria cut down many. Disease killed nearly twice as many soldiers as did battle. Many who died of disease were prisoners of war. Some 30,000 Northerners died in Confederate prisons, and some 26,000 Southerners died in Union prisons.

The soldiers' cultural attitudes and values also played a role in the war's huge death toll. The nineteenth-century code of masculinity propelled bravery on the battlefields, and patriotism, for either the Union or the Confederacy, moved soldiers to risk everything. Soldiers' religious beliefs helped them deal with dying. The triumph of evangelical Protestantism meant that many soldiers believed in a heaven that promised bodily resurrection and family reunion. The assurance of everlasting life surrounded by family made it easier to face death.

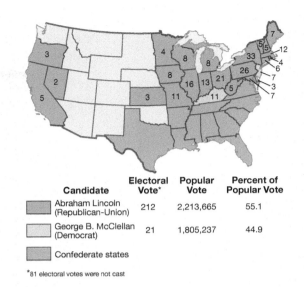

Candidate	Electoral Vote*	Popular Vote	Percent of Popular Vote
Abraham Lincoln (Republican-Union)	212	2,213,665	55.1
George B. McClellan (Democrat)	21	1,805,237	44.9
Confederate states			

*81 electoral votes were not cast

MAP 15.4 ▲ The Election of 1864

◄ **Lee Surrendering to Grant at Appomattox (ca. 1870)** Artist Alonzo Chappel captures the quiet dignity of the moment when Ulysses S. Grant and Robert E. Lee met in the simple parlor of Wilmer McLean's home in Appomattox Court House, Virginia. After four years of fighting, Lee surrendered his army, and Grant offered terms even more generous than Lee had hoped for. Smithsonian American Art Museum, Washington, D.C./Art Resource, NY.

How did the war for union become a fight for black freedom?

What problems did the Confederacy face at home?

How did the war affect the economy and politics of the North?

How did the Union finally win the war?

Conclusion: In what ways was the Civil War a "Second American Revolution"?

Major Battles of the Civil War, 1863–1865	
May 1–4, 1863	Battle of Chancellorsville
July 1–3, 1863	Battle of Gettysburg
July 4, 1863	Fall of Vicksburg
September 16–20, 1863	Battle of Chickamauga
November 23–25, 1863	Battle of Chattanooga
May 5–7, 1864	Battle of the Wilderness
May 7–19, 1864	Battle of Spotsylvania Court House
June 3, 1864	Battle of Cold Harbor
June 27, 1864	Battle of Kennesaw Mountain
September 2, 1864	Fall of Atlanta
November–December 1864	Sheridan sacks Shenandoah Valley; Sherman's March to the Sea
December 15–16, 1864	Battle of Nashville
December 22, 1864	Fall of Savannah
April 2–3, 1865	Fall of Petersburg and Richmond
April 9, 1865	Lee surrenders at Appomattox Court House

QUICK REVIEW

Why were the siege of Vicksburg and the battle of Gettysburg crucial to the outcome of the war?

Conclusion: In what ways was the Civil War a "Second American Revolution"?

A transformed nation emerged from the crucible of war. Antebellum America was decentralized politically and loosely integrated economically. To bend the resources of the country to a Union victory, Congress enacted legislation that reshaped the nation's political and economic character. It created a transcontinental railroad and miles of telegraph lines to bind the West to the rest of the nation. The massive changes brought about by the war—the creation of a truly national government, a national economy, and a national spirit—led one historian to call the American Civil War the "Second American Revolution."

Why did both the Union and the Confederacy consider control of the border states crucial?	Why did each side expect to win?	How did each side fare in the early years of the war?

The Civil War also had a profound effect on individual lives. Millions of men put on blue or gray uniforms and fought and suffered for what they passionately believed was right. The war disrupted families, leaving some women with additional responsibilities and providing others wartime work in factories, offices, and hospitals. It offered blacks new and more effective ways to resist slavery and agitate for equality.

The war devastated the South. Three-fourths of southern white men of military age served in the Confederate army, and half of them became casualties. The war destroyed two-fifths of the South's livestock, wrecked half of the farm machinery, and blackened dozens of cities and towns. The struggle also cost the North a heavy price in lives, but rather than devastating the land, the war set the countryside and cities humming with business activity. The radical shift in power from South to North signaled a new direction in American development: the long decline of agriculture and the rise of industrial capitalism.

Most revolutionary of all, the war ended slavery. Ironically, the South's war to preserve slavery destroyed it. Nearly 200,000 black men dedicated their military service to its eradication. Because slavery was both a labor and a racial system, the institution was entangled in almost every aspect of southern life. Slavery's uprooting inevitably meant fundamental change. But the full meaning of abolition remained unclear in 1865, and the status of ex-slaves would be the principal task of reconstruction.

| How did the war for union become a fight for black freedom? | What problems did the Confederacy face at home? | How did the war affect the economy and politics of the North? | How did the Union finally win the war? | Conclusion: In what ways was the Civil War a "Second American Revolution"? |

CHAPTER 15 STUDY GUIDE

STEP 1

EXPLAIN WHY IT MATTERS

Put your reading into practice. Identify each term below, and then explain why it matters in U.S. history.

TERM	WHO OR WHAT & WHEN	WHY IT MATTERS
Fort Sumter (p. 422)		
battle of Bull Run (Manassas) (p. 428)		
battle of Antietam (p. 429)		
battle of Shiloh (p. 431)		
Union blockade (p. 433)		
King Cotton diplomacy (p. 433)		
contraband of war (p. 435)		
Emancipation Proclamation (p. 436)		
New York City draft riots (p. 446)		
siege of Vicksburg (p. 447)		
battle of Gettysburg (p. 447)		
Sherman's March to the Sea (p. 449)		

STEP 2

MOVE BEYOND THE BASICS

To demonstrate a more advanced understanding, assess the strengths and weaknesses of the North and South at the outset of the Civil War.

Category	South	North
Population		
Industry		
Financial Resources		
Leadership		
War Strategy		

PUT IT ALL TOGETHER

Now, explain the big picture. Remember to use specific examples from the chapter in your answers.

THE EARLY YEARS OF THE WAR

• Why did the North, with all its advantages, fail to achieve rapid victory over the South?

• Why did the South fail to attract international support for its cause?

THE HOME FRONT

• Why did Lincoln decide to issue the Emancipation Proclamation? How did Northerners respond to this decision?

• Why did conditions in the South deteriorate as the war went on? How did problems on the home front undermine the South's war effort?

UNION VICTORY

• What was Grant's strategy? How did it turn the tide of the war?

• Is it possible to identify a "turning point" that predicted a Union victory? Explain your reasoning.

LOOKING BACKWARD, LOOKING AHEAD

• Argue for or against the following statement: "The root cause of the Civil War was the failure of the architects of the Constitution to resolve the issue of slavery once and for all."

CONNECT THESE EVENTS

How did emancipation affect the outcome of the war?

CONNECT TO THE PRESENT

What changes brought about by the Civil War continue to shape the nation today?

16

RECONSTRUCTION

1863–1877

What were the achievements and failures of Reconstruction? Chapter 16 explores the era of Reconstruction, in which the nation struggled to define the defeated South's status and the meaning of freedom for ex-slaves. Following the Civil War, the nation entered one of its most confused and violent periods as victorious Northerners, defeated white Southerners, and newly freed African Americans battled to shape the postwar South.

This chapter will explore the following questions:

- Why did Congress object to Lincoln's wartime plan for reconstruction?
- How did the North respond to the passage of black codes in the southern states?
- How radical was congressional reconstruction?
- What brought the elements of the South's Republican coalition together?
- Why did Reconstruction collapse?
- Conclusion: Was Reconstruction "a revolution but half accomplished"?

AN AMERICAN STORY

In 1856, John Rapier, a free black barber in Florence, Alabama, urged his four freeborn sons to flee the increasingly repressive and dangerous South. Nineteen-year-old James T. Rapier chose Canada, where he went to live with his uncle in a largely black community and studied in a log schoolhouse. In a letter to his father, he vowed, "I will endeavor to do my part in solving the problems [of African Americans] in my native land."

The Union victory in the Civil War gave James Rapier the opportunity to redeem his pledge. In 1865, after more than eight years of exile, Rapier returned to Alabama, where he presided over the first political gathering of former slaves in the state. He soon discovered, however, that Alabama's whites found it agonizingly difficult to accept defeat and black freedom. They responded to the revolutionary changes under the banner "White Man—Right or Wrong—Still the White Man!"

During the elections of 1868, when Rapier and other Alabama blacks vigorously supported the Republican ticket, the recently organized Ku Klux Klan went on a bloody rampage. A mob of 150 outraged whites raced through Rapier's neighborhood seeking four black politicians they claimed were trying to "Africanize Alabama." They caught and hanged three, but the "nigger carpetbagger from Canada" escaped. After briefly considering fleeing the state, Rapier decided to stay and fight for his rights. In 1872, Rapier won election to the House of Representatives, where he joined six other black congressmen in Washington, D.C. Defeated for reelection in 1874 in a campaign marked by ballot-box stuffing, Rapier turned to cotton farming. But unrelenting racial violence convinced him that blacks could never achieve equality and prosperity in the South. He purchased land in Kansas and urged Alabama's blacks to escape with him. In 1883, however, before he could leave Alabama, the forty-five-year-old Rapier died of tuberculosis.

In 1865, Union general Carl Schurz had foreseen many of the troubles Rapier encountered in the postwar South. The Civil War, Schurz observed, was "a revolution but half accomplished." He meant that while northern victory had freed the slaves, it had not changed former slaveholders' minds about blacks' unfitness for freedom. Left to themselves, whites would "introduce some new system of forced labor, not perhaps exactly slavery in its old form but something similar to it," Schurz predicted.

To defend their freedom, blacks would need federal protection, land of their own, and voting rights. Until whites "cut loose from the past, it will be a dangerous experiment to put Southern society upon its own legs."

As Schurz understood, the end of the war did not mean peace. Indeed, the nation entered one of its most turbulent and violent eras—Reconstruction. Answers to the era's central questions—about the defeated South's status within the Union and the meaning of freedom for ex-slaves—came from many directions and often clashed. In Washington, D.C., the federal government played an active role, passing the Fourteenth and Fifteenth Amendments to the Constitution that strengthened the claim of African Americans to equal rights. But state legislatures and county seats across the South also featured blacks and whites vigorously disagreeing about the future of the South. The struggle over the future also took place on the South's farms and plantations, where former slaves sought to become free workers while former slaveholders clung to old, oppressive habits. Whites often backed their opinions with racial violence. In the end, the efforts of African Americans and their allies to secure full citizenship and racial equality failed. In the contest to determine the consequences of Confederate defeat and emancipation, white Southerners prevailed.

▼ **James T. Rapier** In 1874, when Representative James T. Rapier spoke before Congress on behalf of a civil rights bill, he described the humiliation of being denied service at inns all along his route from Montgomery to Washington. Elsewhere in the world, he said, class and religion were invoked to defend discrimination. But in America, "our distinction is color." Alabama Department of Archives and History, Montgomery, Alabama.

Why did Congress object to Lincoln's wartime plan for reconstruction?

Reconstruction did not wait for the end of war. As the odds of a northern victory increased, thinking about reunification quickened. But who had authority to devise a plan for reconstructing the Union? President Abraham Lincoln firmly believed that reconstruction was a matter of executive responsibility. Congress just as firmly asserted its jurisdiction. Fueling the argument were significant differences about the terms of reconstruction.

In their eagerness to formulate a plan for political reunification, neither Lincoln nor Congress gave much attention to the South's land and labor problems. Yet the war rapidly eroded slavery, and Yankee military commanders in the Union-occupied areas of the Confederacy had no choice but to oversee the emergence of a new labor system.

"To Bind Up the Nation's Wounds"

As early as 1863, Lincoln began contemplating how "to bind up the nation's wounds" and achieve "a lasting peace." While deep compassion for the enemy guided his thinking about peace, his plan for reconstruction aimed primarily at shortening the war and ending slavery.

Lincoln's Proclamation of Amnesty and Reconstruction in December 1863 set out his terms. He offered a full pardon, restoring property (except slaves) and political rights, to most rebels willing to renounce secession and to accept emancipation. When 10 percent of a state's voting population had taken an oath of allegiance, the state could organize a new government and be readmitted into the Union. Lincoln's plan did not require ex-rebels to extend civil rights to ex-slaves, nor did it anticipate a program of long-term federal assistance to freedmen. Clearly, the president looked forward to the rapid, forgiving restoration of the broken Union.

Lincoln's easy terms enraged abolitionists such as Wendell Phillips of Boston, who charged that the president "makes the negro's freedom a mere sham." He "is willing that the negro should be free but seeks nothing else for him." Comparing Lincoln to the Union's most passive general, Phillips declared, "What McClellan was on the battlefield—'Do as little hurt as possible!'—Lincoln is in civil affairs—'Make as little change as possible!'" Phillips and other northern Radicals called instead for a thorough overhaul of southern society. Their ideas proved to be too drastic for most Republicans during the war years, but Congress agreed that Lincoln's plan was inadequate.

In July 1864, Congress put forward a plan of its own. Congressman Henry Winter Davis of Maryland and Senator Benjamin Wade of Ohio jointly sponsored a bill that demanded that at least half of the voters in a conquered rebel state take the oath of allegiance before reconstruction could begin. The Wade-Davis bill also banned almost all ex-Confederates from participating in the drafting of new state constitutions. Finally, the bill guaranteed the equality of freedmen before the law. Congress's reconstruction would be neither as quick nor as forgiving as Lincoln's. When Lincoln refused to sign the bill and let it die, Wade and Davis charged the president with tyranny.

Undeterred, Lincoln continued to nurture the formation of loyal state governments under his own plan. Four states—Arkansas, Louisiana, Tennessee, and Virginia—fulfilled the president's requirements, but Congress refused to seat representatives from the "Lincoln states." Lincoln admitted that a government based on only 10 percent was not ideal, but he argued, "We shall sooner have the fowl by hatching the egg than by smashing it." Massachusetts senator Charles Sumner responded,

COMPARE AND CONTRAST
How did Lincoln's vision for reconstruction differ from that put forth in the Wade-Davis bill? What factors account for the differences?

Why did Congress object to Lincoln's wartime plan for reconstruction?

CHAPTER 16
458 RECONSTRUCTION

▲ **Wartime Reconstruction** This cartoon from the presidential campaign of 1864 shows the "Rail Splitter" Abraham Lincoln leveraging the broken nation back together while his running mate, Andrew Johnson, who once was a tailor by trade, stitches the Confederate states securely back into the Union. Optimism that the task of reconstructing the nation after the war would be both quick and easy shines through the cartoon. The Granger Collection, New York.

"The eggs of crocodiles can produce only crocodiles." In his last public address in April 1865, Lincoln defended his plan but expressed his endorsement of voting rights for southern blacks, at least "the very intelligent, and . . . those who serve our cause as soldiers." The announcement demonstrated that Lincoln's thinking about reconstruction was still evolving. Four days later, he was dead.

Land and Labor

Of all the problems raised by the North's victory in the war, none proved more critical than the South's transition from slavery to free labor. As federal armies occupied the Confederacy, hundreds of thousands of slaves became free workers. In addition, Union armies controlled vast territories in the South where legal title to land had become unclear. The Confiscation Acts passed during the war punished "traitors" by taking away their property. The question of what to do with federally occupied land and how to organize labor on it engaged ex-slaves, ex-slaveholders, Union military commanders, and federal government officials long before the war ended.

In the Mississippi valley, occupying federal troops announced a new labor code. It required landholders to give up whipping, sign contracts with ex-slaves, pay wages, and provide food, housing, and medical care. The code also required black laborers to enter

| How did the North respond to the passage of black codes in the southern states? | How radical was congressional reconstruction? | What brought the elements of the South's Republican coalition together? | Why did Reconstruction collapse? | Conclusion: Was Reconstruction "a revolution but half accomplished"? |

▶ **The Lord Is My Shepherd, 1863** Maine-born Eastman Johnson (1824–1906) did this painting only months after the Emancipation Proclamation. Its title comes from Psalm 23, which begins, "The Lord is my shepherd; I shall not want." The painting captures a humble black man quietly reading his Bible and reminds us of one of the reasons freedmen struggled so hard for literacy. Smithsonian American Art Museum, Washington, D.C./Art Resource, NY.

READING THE IMAGE: What is the artist saying about ex-slaves' capacity to live as free people?

CONNECTIONS: Why did southern whites in the Reconstruction era consider literacy for former slaves less a religious impulse than a dangerous political act?

into contracts, work diligently, and remain subordinate and obedient. The Union military clearly had no intention of promoting a social or economic revolution. Instead, they sought to restore traditional plantation agriculture with wage labor. The effort resulted in a hybrid system that one contemporary called "compulsory free labor," which satisfied no one.

Planters complained because the new system fell short of slavery. Blacks could not be "transformed by proclamation," a Louisiana sugar planter declared. Without the right to whip, he argued, the new labor system did not have a chance. Either Union soldiers must "*compel* the negroes to work," or the planters themselves must "be authorized and sustained in using force."

African Americans found the new regime too similar to slavery to be called free labor. Its chief deficiency, they believed, was the failure to provide them with land of their own. Freedmen believed they had a moral right to land because they and their ancestors had worked it without pay for centuries. "What's the use of being free if you don't own land enough to be buried in?" one man asked. Several wartime developments led freedmen to believe that the federal government planned to defend black freedom with landownership.

In January 1865, General William Tecumseh Sherman set aside part of the coast south of Charleston for black settlement. By June, some 40,000 freedmen sat on 400,000 acres of "Sherman land." In addition, in March 1865, Congress passed a bill establishing the Bureau of Refugees, Freedmen, and Abandoned Lands. The **Freedmen's Bureau**, as it was called, distributed food and clothing to destitute Southerners and eased the transition of blacks from slaves to free persons. Congress also authorized the agency to divide abandoned and confiscated land into 40-acre plots, to rent them to freedmen, and eventually to sell them "with such title as the United States can convey." By June 1865, the Bureau had situated nearly 10,000 black families on one-half million acres.

Despite the flurry of activity, wartime reconstruction failed to produce agreement about whether the president or Congress had the authority to devise policy or what proper policy should be.

Freedmen's Bureau
Government organization created in March 1865 to distribute food and clothing to destitute Southerners and to ease the transition of slaves to free persons.

Why did Congress object to Lincoln's wartime plan for reconstruction?

The African American Quest for Autonomy

Ex-slaves never had any doubt about what they wanted from freedom. They had only to contemplate what they had been denied as slaves. **(See "Analyzing Historical Evidence: The Meaning of Freedom" on page 462.)** Slaves had to remain on their plantations; freedom allowed blacks to see what was on the other side of the hill. Slaves had to be at work in the fields by dawn; freedom permitted blacks to sleep through a sunrise. Freedmen also tested the etiquette of racial subordination. "Lizzie's maid passed me today when I was coming from church *without speaking to me*," huffed one plantation mistress.

To whites, emancipation looked like pure anarchy. Blacks, they said, had reverted to their natural condition: lazy, irresponsible, and wild. Actually, former slaves were experimenting with freedom, but they could not long afford to roam the countryside, neglect work, and casually provoke whites. Soon, most were back at work in whites' kitchens and fields.

But they continued to dream of land and independence. "The way we can best take care of ourselves is to have land," one former slave declared in 1865, "and turn it and till it by our own labor." A South Carolina freedman agreed, declaring that ex-slaves wanted land, "not a Master or owner[,] Neither a driver with his Whip."

Slavery had deliberately kept blacks illiterate, and freedmen emerged from bondage eager to learn to read and write. "I wishes the Childern all in School,"

▲ **Harry Stephens and Family, 1866** The seven members of the Stephens family sit proudly for a photograph just after the Civil War ended. Many black families were not as fortunate as these Virginians. Separated by slavery or war, former slaves desperately sought news of missing family members through newspaper advertisements. The Metropolitan Museum of Art, Gilman Collection, Purchase, The Horace W. Goldsmith Foundation Gift, through Joyce and Robert Menschel, 2005.

How did the North respond to the passage of black codes in the southern states?	How radical was congressional reconstruction?	What brought the elements of the South's Republican coalition together?	Why did Reconstruction collapse?	Conclusion: Was Reconstruction "a revolution but half accomplished"?

The Meaning of Freedom

Although the Emancipation Proclamation itself did not free any slaves, it transformed the character of the war. Black people resolutely focused on the possibilities of freedom even before the war ended.

DOCUMENT 1

Letter from John Q. A. Dennis to Edwin M. Stanton, July 26, 1864

John Q. A. Dennis, formerly a slave in Maryland, wrote to ask Secretary of War Edwin M. Stanton for help in reuniting his family.

Boston. Dear Sir I am Glad that I have the Honour to Write you a few line I have been in troble for about four yars my Dear wife was taken from me Nov 19th 1859 and left me with three Children and I being a Slave At the time Could Not do Anny thing for the poor little Children for my master it was took me Carry me some forty mile from them So I Could Not do for them and the man that they live with half feed them and half Cloth them & beat them like dogs & when I was admitted to go to see them it use to brake my heart & Now I say again I am Glad to have the honour to write to you to see if you Can Do Anny thing for me or for my poor little Children I was keap in Slavy untell last Novr 1863. then the Good lord sent the Cornel borne [federal colonel William Birney?] Down their in Marland in worsester Co So as I have been recently freed I have but letle to live on but I am Striveing Dear Sir but what I went too know of you Sir is it possible for me to go & take my Children from those men that keep them in Savery if it is possible will you pleas give me a permit from your hand then I think they would let them go. . . . I want get the little Children out of Slavery. . . .

Source: *Freedom: A Documentary History of Emancipation, 1861–1867,* ser. 1, vol. 1, *The Destruction of Slavery,* edited by Ira Berlin, Joseph P. Reidy, and Leslie S. Rowland 386. Copyright © 1985.

DOCUMENT 2

Report from the Reverend A. B. Randall, February 28, 1865

A. B. Randall, the white chaplain of a black regiment stationed in Little Rock, Arkansas, affirmed the importance of legal marriage to freed slaves and emphasized their conviction that emancipation was only the first step toward full freedom.

Weddings, just now, are very popular, and abundant among the Colored People. They have just learned, of the Special Order No. 15. of Gen Thomas [Adjutant General Lorenzo Thomas] by which, they may not only be lawfully married, but have their Marriage Certificates, Recorded; in a book furnished by the Government. . . . I have married, during the month, at this Post; Twenty five couples; mostly, those, who have families; & have been living together for years. . . . The Colord People here, generally consider, this war not only; their exodus, from bondage; but the road, to Responsibility; Competency; and an honorable Citizenship—God grant that their hopes and expectations may be fully realized.

Source: *Freedom: A Documentary History of Emancipation, 1861–1867,* ser. 2, vol. 1, *The Black Military Experience,* edited by Ira Berlin, Joseph P. Reidy, and Leslie S. Rowland, 712. Copyright © 1982.

UNDERSTAND POINTS OF VIEW

What were African Americans' primary concerns during the transition from slavery to freedom, and how did they envision their lives as free people?

one black military veteran asserted. "It is beter for them then [than] to be their Surveing a mistes [mistress]." Freedmen looked on schools as "first proof of their *independence.*"

The restoration of broken families was another persistent black aspiration. Thousands of freedmen took to the roads in 1865 to look for kin who had been sold or to free those who were being held illegally as slaves. A black soldier from Missouri wrote his daughters that he was coming for them. "I will have you if it cost me my life," he declared. "Your Miss Kitty said that I tried to steal you," he told them. "But I'll let her know that god never intended for a man to steal his own flesh and blood." And he swore that "if she meets me with ten thousand soldiers, she [will] meet her enemy."

Why did Congress object to Lincoln's wartime plan for reconstruction?

DOCUMENT 3

Petition "to the Union Convention of Tennessee Assembled in the Capitol at Nashville," January 9, 1865

In January 1865, black Tennesseans petitioned a convention of white Unionists debating the reorganization of state government.

We the undersigned petitioners, American citizens of African descent, natives and residents of Tennessee, and devoted friends of the great National cause, do most respectfully ask a patient hearing of your honorable body in regard to matters deeply affecting the future condition of our unfortunate and long suffering race. . . .

In the contest between the nation and slavery, our unfortunate people have sided, by instinct, with the former. . . . We will work, pray, live, and, if need be, die for the Union, as cheerfully as ever a white patriot died for his country. The color of our skin does not lessen in the least degree, our love either for God or for the land of our birth. . . .

We know the burdens of citizenship, and are ready to bear them. We know the duties of the good citizen, and are ready to perform them cheerfully, and would ask to be put in a position in which we can discharge them more effectually. . . .

This is a democracy—a government of the people. It should aim to make every man, without regard to the color of his skin, the amount of his wealth, or the character of his religious faith, feel personally interested in its welfare. Every man who lives under the Government should feel that it is his property, his treasure, the bulwark and defence of himself and his family. . . .

This is not a Democratic Government if a numerous, law-abiding, industrious, and useful class of citizens, born and bred on the soil, are to be treated as aliens and enemies, as an inferior degraded class, who must have no voice in the Government which they support, protect and defend, with all their heart, soul, mind, and body, both in peace and war. . . .

The possibility that the negro suffrage proposition may shock popular prejudice at first sight, is not a conclusive argument against its wisdom and policy. No proposition ever met with more furious or general opposition than the one to enlist colored soldiers in the United States army. The opponents of the measure exclaimed on all hands that the negro was a coward; that he would not fight; that one white man, with a whip in his hand could put to flight a regiment of them. . . . Yet the colored man has fought so well. . . .

The Government has asked the colored man to fight for its preservation and gladly has he done it. It can afford to trust him with a vote as safely as it trusted him with a bayonet.

Source: *Freedom: A Documentary History of Emancipation, 1861–1867*, ser. 2, vol. 1, *The Black Military Experience*, edited by Ira Berlin, Joseph P. Reidy, and Leslie S. Rowland, 811–16. Copyright © 1982.

Questions for Analysis

ANALYZE THE EVIDENCE: What does John Q. A. Dennis's interpretation of his responsibility as a father say about slavery's ability to destroy slave families?

CONSIDER THE CONTEXT: Why was legal marriage so important to ex-slaves?

RECOGNIZE VIEWPOINTS: According to petitioners to the Union Convention of Tennessee, why was the experience of black soldiers relevant to black voting rights?

Independent worship was another dream. African Americans greeted freedom with a mass exodus from white churches, where they had been required to worship when slaves. Some joined the newly established southern branches of all-black northern churches, such as the African Methodist Episcopal Church. Others formed black versions of the major southern denominations, Baptists and Methodists.

QUICK REVIEW

To what extent did Lincoln's wartime plan for reconstruction reflect the concerns of newly freed slaves?

| How did the North respond to the passage of black codes in the southern states? | How radical was congressional reconstruction? | What brought the elements of the South's Republican coalition together? | Why did Reconstruction collapse? | Conclusion: Was Reconstruction "a revolution but half accomplished"? |

How did the North respond to the passage of black codes in the southern states?

CHRONOLOGY

1865
- Lincoln assassinated; Andrew Johnson becomes president.
- First black codes enacted.
- Thirteenth Amendment becomes part of Constitution.

1866
- Civil Rights Act passes.

Abraham Lincoln died on April 15, 1865, just hours after John Wilkes Booth shot him at a Washington, D.C., theater. Vice President Andrew Johnson of Tennessee became president. Congress had adjourned in March and would not reconvene until December. Throughout the summer and fall, Johnson drew up and executed a plan of reconstruction without congressional advice.

Congress returned to the capital in December to find that, as far as the new president and former Confederates were concerned, reconstruction was over. Most Republicans, however, thought Johnson's plan made far too few demands of ex-rebels and made a mockery of the sacrifice of Union soldiers. They claimed that Johnson's leniency had encouraged the rebirth of the Old South, that he had achieved political reunification at the cost of black freedom. Republicans in Congress then proceeded to dismantle Johnson's program and substitute a program of their own.

Johnson's Program of Reconciliation

Born in 1808 in Raleigh, North Carolina, Andrew Johnson was the son of illiterate parents. Self-educated and ambitious, Johnson moved to Tennessee, where he worked as a tailor, accumulated a fortune in land and five slaves, and built a career in politics championing the South's common white people and assailing its planter class. The only senator from a Confederate state to remain loyal to the Union, Johnson held planters responsible for secession. Less than two weeks before he became president, he announced what he would do to planters if he ever had the chance: "I would arrest them—I would try them—I would convict them and I would hang them."

"As one freedman observed, 'Things was hurt by Mr. Lincoln getting killed.'"

A Democrat all his life, Johnson occupied the White House only because the Republican Party in 1864 had needed a vice presidential candidate who would appeal to Union-supporting Democrats. Johnson vigorously defended states' rights (but not secession) and opposed Republican efforts to expand the power of the federal government. A steadfast supporter of slavery, Johnson had owned slaves until 1862, when Tennessee rebels, angry at his Unionism, confiscated them. When he grudgingly accepted emancipation, it was more because he hated planters than sympathized with slaves. "Damn the negroes," he said. "I am fighting those traitorous aristocrats, their masters." The new president harbored unshakable racist convictions. Africans, Johnson said, were "inferior to the white man in point of intellect—better calculated in physical structure to undergo drudgery and hardship."

Like Lincoln, Johnson stressed the rapid restoration of civil government in the South. Like Lincoln, he promised to pardon most, but not all, ex-rebels. Johnson recognized the state governments created by Lincoln but set out his own requirements for restoring the other rebel states to the Union. All that the citizens of a state had to do was to renounce the right of secession, repudiate the debts of the Confederacy, and ratify the Thirteenth Amendment abolishing slavery, which became part of the Constitution in December 1865.

Johnson also returned all confiscated and abandoned land to pardoned ex-Confederates, even if it was in the hands of freedmen. Reformers were shocked. Instead of punishing planters as he had promised, Johnson canceled the promising beginnings

Why did Congress object to Lincoln's wartime plan for reconstruction?

made by General Sherman and the Freedmen's Bureau to settle blacks on land of their own. As one freedman observed, "Things was hurt by Mr. Lincoln getting killed."

White Southern Resistance and Black Codes

In the summer of 1865, white Southerners drew up the new state constitutions Johnson's plan of reconstruction required. But they refused to accept even the president's mild requirements. Refusing to renounce secession, the South Carolina and Georgia conventions merely "repudiated" their secession ordinances, preserving in principle their right to secede. South Carolina and Mississippi refused to disown their Confederate war debts. Mississippi rejected the Thirteenth Amendment, and Alabama rejected it in part. Despite this defiance, Johnson did nothing. White Southerners began to think that by standing up for themselves they could shape the terms of reconstruction.

New state governments across the South adopted a series of laws known as **black codes**, which denied black rights. The codes sought to keep ex-slaves subordinate to whites by subjecting them to every sort of discrimination. Several states made it illegal for blacks to own a gun. Mississippi made insulting gestures and language

black codes
Laws passed by state governments in the South in 1865 and 1866 that sought to keep ex-slaves subordinate to whites. At the core of the black codes lay the desire to force freedmen back to the plantations.

▲ **The Black Codes** Titled *Selling a Freeman to Pay His Fine at Monticello, Florida,* this 1867 drawing from a northern magazine equates black codes with the reinstitution of slavery. The laws stopped short of reenslavement but sharply restricted blacks' freedom. In southern states, certain acts, such as breaking a labor contract, were made criminal offenses, the penalty for which could be involuntary plantation labor for a year. The Granger Collection, New York.

How did the North respond to the passage of black codes in the southern states?	How radical was congressional reconstruction?	What brought the elements of the South's Republican coalition together?	Why did Reconstruction collapse?	Conclusion: Was Reconstruction "a revolution but half accomplished"?

by blacks a criminal offense. The codes barred blacks from jury duty. Not a single southern state granted any black the right to vote.

At the core of the black codes, however, lay the matter of labor. Legislators sought to hustle freedmen back to the plantations. South Carolina attempted to limit blacks to either farmwork or domestic service by requiring them to pay annual taxes of $10 to $100 to work in any other occupation. Mississippi declared that blacks who did not possess written evidence of employment could be declared vagrants and be subject to involuntary plantation labor. Under so-called apprenticeship laws, courts bound thousands of black children—orphans and others whose parents were deemed unable to support them—to work for planter "guardians."

Johnson refused to intervene. A staunch defender of states' rights, he believed that citizens of every state should be free to write their own constitutions and laws. He was as eager as other white Southerners to restore white supremacy. "White men alone must manage the South," he declared.

UNDERSTAND POINTS OF VIEW

What did Andrew Johnson hope to accomplish with his plan of presidential reconstruction?

Johnson also recognized that his do-nothing response offered him political advantage. A conservative Tennessee Democrat at the head of a northern Republican Party, he had begun to look southward for political allies. Despite tough talk about punishing traitors, he personally pardoned fourteen thousand wealthy or high-ranking ex-Confederates. By pardoning powerful whites, by accepting state governments even when they failed to satisfy his minimal demands, and by acquiescing in the black codes, he won useful southern friends.

In the fall elections of 1865, white Southerners dramatically expressed their mood. To represent them in Congress, they chose former Confederates. Of the eighty senators and representatives they sent to Washington, fifteen had served in the Confederate army, ten of them as generals. Another sixteen had served in civil and judicial posts in the Confederacy. Nine others had served in the Confederate Congress. One— Alexander Stephens—had been vice president of the Confederacy. As one Georgian remarked, "It looked as though Richmond had moved to Washington."

Expansion of Federal Authority and Black Rights

White Southerners had blundered monumentally. They had assumed that what Andrew Johnson was willing to accept, northern Republicans would accept as well. But southern resistance compelled even moderates to conclude that ex-rebels were a "generation of vipers," still disloyal and dangerous. The black codes became a symbol of southern intentions to "restore all of slavery but its name." "We tell the white men of Mississippi," the *Chicago Tribune* roared, "that the men of the North will convert the State of Mississippi into a frog pond before they will allow such laws to disgrace one foot of the soil in which the bones of our soldiers sleep and over which the flag of freedom waves."

The moderate majority of the Republican Party wanted only assurance that slavery and treason were dead. They did not champion black equality, the confiscation of plantations, or black voting, as did the Radical minority within the party. But southern resistance had succeeded in forging unity (at least temporarily) among Republican factions. In December 1865, Republicans refused to seat the Southerners elected in the fall elections. Rather than accept Johnson's claim that the "work of restoration" was done, Congress challenged Johnson's reconstruction.

PLACE EVENTS IN CONTEXT

What circumstances led even moderate Republicans to support the Civil Rights Act of 1866?

Republican senator Lyman Trumbull declared that the president's policy meant that an ex-slave would "be tyrannized over, abused, and virtually reenslaved without some legislation by the nation for his protection." Early in 1866, the moderates produced two bills that strengthened the federal shield. The Freedmen's Bureau bill prolonged the life of the agency established by the previous Congress. Arguing that

Why did Congress object to Lincoln's wartime plan for reconstruction?

the Constitution never contemplated a "system for the support of indigent persons," President Andrew Johnson vetoed the bill. Congress failed by a narrow margin to override the president's veto.

The moderates designed their second measure, the Civil Rights Act of 1866, to nullify the black codes by affirming African Americans' rights to "full and equal benefit of all laws and proceedings for the security of person and property as is enjoyed by white citizens." The act boldly required the end of racial discrimination in state laws and represented an extraordinary expansion of black rights and federal authority. The president argued that the civil rights bill amounted to "unconstitutional invasion of states' rights" and vetoed it. In essence, he denied that the federal government had the authority to protect the civil rights of African Americans.

In April 1866, an outraged Republican Party again pushed the civil rights bill through Congress and overrode the presidential veto. In July, it passed another Freedmen's Bureau bill and overrode Johnson's veto. For the first time in American history, Congress had over-turned presidential vetoes of major legislation. As a worried South Carolinian observed, Johnson's vetoes would probably touch off "a fight this fall such as has never been seen."

Civil Rights Act of 1866
Legislation passed by Congress in 1866 that nullified the black codes and affirmed that black Americans should have equal benefit of the law. President Andrew Johnson vetoed this expansion of black rights and federal authority, but Congress later overrode his veto.

QUICK REVIEW

When the southern states passed the black codes, how did the U.S. Congress respond?

How radical was congressional reconstruction?

By the summer of 1866, President Andrew Johnson and Congress had dropped their gloves and stood toe-to-toe in a bare-knuckle contest unprecedented in American history. Johnson made it clear that he would not budge on either executive authority or policy. Moderate Republicans responded by amending the Constitution. But Johnson's and white Southerners' stubbornness pushed Republican moderates ever closer to the Radicals and to acceptance of additional federal inter-vention in the South. To end presidential interference, Congress voted to impeach the president for the first time in the nation's history. Soon after, Congress debated whether to make voting rights color-blind, while women championed making voting sex-blind as well.

The Fourteenth Amendment and Escalating Violence

In June 1866, Congress passed the Fourteenth Amendment to the Constitution, and two years later the states ratified it. The most important provisions of this complex amendment made all native-born or naturalized persons American citizens and prohib-ited states from abridging the "privileges and immunities" of citizens, depriving them of "life, liberty, or property without due process of law," and denying them "equal protection of the laws." By making blacks national citizens, the amendment provided a national guarantee of equality before the law. In essence, it protected blacks against violation by southern state governments.

CHRONOLOGY

1866
- Congress approves Fourteenth Amendment.
- American Equal Rights Association founded.

1867
- Military Reconstruction Act passes.
- Tenure of Office Act passes.

1868
- Impeachment trial of President Johnson held.

1869
- Congress approves Fifteenth Amendment.

| How did the North respond to the passage of black codes in the southern states? | **How radical was congressional reconstruction?** | What brought the elements of the South's Republican coalition together? | Why did Reconstruction collapse? | Conclusion: Was Reconstruction "a revolution but half accomplished"? |

467

The **Fourteenth Amendment** also dealt with voting rights. It gave Congress the right to reduce the congressional representation of states that withheld suffrage from some of its adult male population. In other words, white Southerners could either allow black men to vote or see their representation in Washington slashed. Whatever happened, Republicans stood to benefit. If southern whites granted voting rights to freedmen, Republicans would gain valuable black votes. If whites refused, the number of southern Democrats in Congress would plunge.

The Fourteenth Amendment's suffrage provisions ignored the small band of women who had emerged from the war demanding "the ballot for the two disenfranchised classes, negroes and women." Founding the American Equal Rights Association in 1866, Susan B. Anthony and Elizabeth Cady Stanton lobbied for "a government by the people, and the whole people; for the people and the whole people." They felt betrayed when their old antislavery allies refused to work for woman suffrage. "It was the Negro's hour," Frederick Douglass explained. Senator Charles Sumner suggested that woman suffrage could be "the great question of the future."

Tennessee approved the Fourteenth Amendment in July, and Congress promptly welcomed the state's representatives and senators back. Had President Johnson counseled other southern states to ratify the amendment, they might have listened. Instead, Johnson advised Southerners to reject the Fourteenth Amendment and to rely on him to trounce the Republicans in the fall congressional elections.

PLACE EVENTS IN CONTEXT

What political constituencies in the United States showed strong support for the Fourteenth Amendment, and which provisions, in particular, appealed to those groups?

Johnson had decided to make the Fourteenth Amendment the overriding issue of the 1866 elections and to gather its white opponents into a new conservative party, the National Union Party. The president's strategy suffered a setback when whites in several southern cities went on rampages against blacks. Mobs killed thirty-four blacks in New Orleans and forty-six blacks in Memphis. The slaughter shocked Northerners and renewed skepticism about Johnson's claim that southern whites could be trusted. "Who doubts that the Freedmen's Bureau ought to be abolished forthwith," a New Yorker observed sarcastically, "and the blacks remitted to the paternal care of their old masters, who 'understand the nigger, you know, a great deal better than the Yankees can.'"

The 1866 elections resulted in an overwhelming Republican victory. Johnson had bet that Northerners would not support federal protection of black rights and that a racist backlash would punish the Republican Party. But the war was still fresh in northern minds, and as one Republican explained, southern whites "with all their intelligence were traitors, the blacks with all their ignorance were loyal."

Radical Reconstruction and Military Rule

When Johnson continued to urge Southerners to reject the Fourteenth Amendment, every southern state except Tennessee voted it down. "The last one of the sinful ten," thundered Representative James A. Garfield

◀ **Elizabeth Cady Stanton and Susan B. Anthony, 1870** Stanton, left, and Anthony were lifelong friends and veteran reformers who advocated, among other things, improved working conditions for labor, married women's property rights, liberalization of divorce laws, and women's admission to colleges and trade schools. Their broad agenda led some conservatives to oppose women's political equality because they equated the suffragist cause with radicalism in general. Bettmann / Getty Images.

Why did Congress object to Lincoln's wartime plan for reconstruction?

of Ohio, "has flung back into our teeth the magnanimous offer of a generous nation." After the South rejected the moderates' program, the Radicals seized the initiative.

Each act of defiance by southern whites had boosted the standing of the Radicals within the Republican Party. Except for freedmen themselves, no one did more to make freedom the "mighty moral question of the age." Radicals such as Massachusetts senator Charles Sumner and Pennsylvania representative Thaddeus Stevens united in demanding civil and political equality. Southern states were "like clay in the hands of the potter," Stevens declared in January 1867, and he called on Congress to begin reconstruction all over again.

In March 1867, Congress overturned the Johnson state governments and initiated military rule of the South. The **Military Reconstruction Act** (and three subsequent acts) divided the ten unreconstructed Confederate states into five military districts. Congress placed a Union general in charge of each district and instructed him to "suppress insurrection, disorder, and violence" and to begin political reform. After the military had completed voter registration, which would include black men, voters in each state would elect delegates to conventions that would draw up new state constitutions. Each constitution would guarantee black suffrage. When the voters of each state had approved the constitution and the state legislature had ratified the Fourteenth Amendment, Congress could seat the state's senators and representatives, and political reunification would be completed.

Radicals proclaimed the provision for black suffrage "a prodigious triumph," for it extended far beyond the limited voting provisions of the Fourteenth Amendment. When combined with the disfranchisement of thousands of ex-rebels, it promised to cripple any neo-Confederate resurgence and guarantee Republican state governments in the South.

Despite its bold suffrage provision, the Military Reconstruction Act of 1867 disappointed those who also advocated the confiscation of southern plantations and their redistribution to ex-slaves. Thaddeus Stevens agreed with the freedman who said, "Give us our own land and we take care of ourselves, but without land, the old masters can hire us or starve us, as they please." But most Republicans believed they had provided blacks with all they needed: equal legal rights and the ballot. Besides, confiscation was too radical, even for some Radicals. Taking private property, declared the *New York Times*, "strikes at the root of all property rights in both sections. It concerns Massachusetts quite as much as Mississippi." If blacks were to get land, they would have to gain it themselves.

Declaring that he would rather sever his right arm than sign such a formula for "anarchy and chaos," Andrew Johnson vetoed the Military Reconstruction Act, but Congress overrode his veto. With the passage of the Reconstruction Acts of 1867, congressional reconstruction was virtually completed. Congress left whites owning most of the South's land but, in a departure that justified the term *radical reconstruction*, had given black men the ballot.

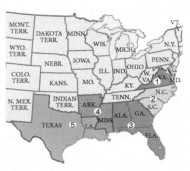

Reconstruction Military Districts, 1867

Military Reconstruction Act
Congressional act of March 1867 that initiated military rule of the South. Congressional reconstruction divided the ten unreconstructed Confederate states into five military districts, each under the direction of a Union general. It also established the procedure by which unreconstructed states could reenter the Union.

TRACE CHANGE OVER TIME
How and why did Reconstruction evolve and change between 1865 and 1867?

Impeaching a President

Despite his defeats, Andrew Johnson had no intention of yielding control of reconstruction. In a dozen ways, he sabotaged Congress's will and encouraged southern whites to resist. He issued a flood of pardons, waged war against the Freedmen's Bureau, and replaced Union generals eager to enforce Congress's Reconstruction Acts with conservative officers eager to block them. Johnson claimed that he was merely defending the "violated Constitution." At bottom, however, the president acted to protect southern whites from what he considered the horrors of "Negro domination."

| How did the North respond to the passage of black codes in the southern states? | **How radical was congressional reconstruction?** | What brought the elements of the South's Republican coalition together? | Why did Reconstruction collapse? | Conclusion: Was Reconstruction "a revolution but half accomplished"? |

▶ **Reconstruction Cartoon** This 1865 cartoon pokes fun at two Richmond ladies as they pass by a Union officer on their way to receive free government rations. One says sourly to the other, "Don't you think that Yankee must feel like shrinking into his boots before such high-toned Southern ladies as we?" The New York Public Library/Art Resource, NY.

READING THE IMAGE: Just a step behind is a smiling black woman. What does her expression say about her impression of the scene taking place in front of her?

CONNECTIONS: What do these white women suggest about the white South's attitude toward defeat and reconstruction?

Radicals argued that Johnson's abuse of his power and his failure to fulfill constitutional obligations to enforce the law were impeachable offenses. According to the Constitution, the House of Representatives can impeach and the Senate can try any federal official for "treason, bribery, or other high crimes and misdemeanors." But moderates interpreted the Constitution to mean violation of criminal statutes. As long as Johnson refrained from breaking the law, impeachment (the process of bringing formal charges of wrongdoing against the president or another federal official) remained stalled.

In August 1867, Johnson suspended Secretary of War Edwin M. Stanton from office. As required by the Tenure of Office Act, which demanded the approval of the Senate for the removal of any government official who had been appointed with Senate approval, the president requested the Senate to consent to Stanton's dismissal. When the Senate declined, Johnson removed Stanton anyway. "Is the President crazy, or only drunk?" asked a dumbfounded Republican moderate. "I'm afraid his doings will make us all favor impeachment."

News of Johnson's open defiance of the law convinced every Republican in the House to vote for a resolution impeaching the president. Supreme Court chief justice Salmon Chase presided over the Senate trial, which lasted from March until May 1868. When the vote came, thirty-five senators voted guilty and nineteen not guilty. Impeachment fell one vote short of the two-thirds needed to convict.

After his trial, Johnson called a truce, and for the remaining ten months of his term, congressional reconstruction proceeded unhindered by presidential interference. Without interference from Johnson, Congress revisited the suffrage issue.

Fifteenth Amendment
Constitutional amendment passed in February 1869 prohibiting states from depriving any citizen of the right to vote because of "race, color, or previous condition of servitude." It extended black suffrage nationwide.

The Fifteenth Amendment and Women's Demands

In February 1869, Republicans passed the Fifteenth Amendment to the Constitution, which prohibited states from depriving any citizen of the right to vote because of "race, color, or previous condition of servitude." The Reconstruction Acts of 1867 already

Why did Congress object to Lincoln's wartime plan for reconstruction?

required black suffrage in the South; the Fifteenth Amendment extended black voting nationwide.

Some Republicans, however, found the final wording of the Fifteenth Amendment "lame and halting." Rather than guaranteeing the right to vote, the amendment merely prohibited exclusion on grounds of race. The distinction would prove to be significant. In time, white Southerners would devise tests of literacy and property and other apparently nonracial measures that would effectively disfranchise blacks yet not violate the Fifteenth Amendment. But an amendment that guaranteed the right to vote courted defeat outside the South. Rising antiforeign sentiment—against the Chinese in California and European immigrants in the Northeast—caused states to resist giving up control of suffrage requirements. In March 1870, after three-fourths of the states had ratified it, the Fifteenth Amendment became part of the Constitution.

Woman suffrage advocates, however, condemned the Fifteenth Amendment's failure to extend voting rights to women. Elizabeth Cady Stanton and Susan B. Anthony rejected the Republicans' "negro first" strategy and pointed out that women remained "the only class of citizens wholly unrepresented in the government." Activist women concluded that woman "must not put her trust in man." The Fifteenth Amendment severed the early feminist movement from its abolitionist roots. Over the next several decades, feminists established an independent suffrage crusade that drew millions of women into political life.

After the Fifteen Amendment, Republicans concluded that black suffrage was the "last great point that remained to be settled of the issues of the war" and promptly scratched the "Negro question" from the agenda of national politics. Even that steadfast crusader for equality Wendell Phillips reasoned that the black man now held "sufficient shield in his own hands. . . . Whatever he suffers will be largely now, and in future, his own fault." Northerners had no idea of the violent struggles that lay ahead in the South.

CONSIDER CAUSE AND EFFECT

Why did many woman's rights activists, most of whom had cut their political teeth in the abolitionist movement, strike out on their own in the late 1860s?

QUICK REVIEW

Why did Congress impeach President Andrew Johnson?

What brought the elements of the South's Republican coalition together?

Northerners believed they had discharged their responsibilities with the Reconstruction Acts and the amendments to the Constitution, but Southerners knew that the battle had just begun. Black suffrage had destroyed traditional southern politics and established the foundation for the rise of the Republican Party. Gathering outsiders and outcasts, southern Republicans won elections, wrote new state constitutions, and formed new state governments.

Challenging the established class for political control was dangerous business. Equally dangerous were the confrontations that took place on southern farms and

| How did the North respond to the passage of black codes in the southern states? | How radical was congressional reconstruction? | **What brought the elements of the South's Republican coalition together?** | Why did Reconstruction collapse? | Conclusion: Was Reconstruction "a revolution but half accomplished"? |

471

1866
- Ku Klux Klan founded.

1867
- Southern African Americans gain voting rights under Military Reconstruction Act.
- Southern states hold elections for state convention delegates.

1875
- One-half of South Carolina's and Mississippi's children, the majority black, attend school.
- Sharecropping is dominant labor system for rural southern blacks.

carpetbaggers
Southerners' pejorative term for northern migrants who sought opportunity in the South after the Civil War. Northern migrants formed an important part of the southern Republican Party.

scalawag
A derogatory term that Southerners applied to southern white Republicans, who were seen as traitors to the South. Most were yeoman farmers.

Ku Klux Klan
A social club of Confederate veterans that quickly developed into a paramilitary organization supporting Democrats. With too few Union troops in the South to control the region, the Klan went on a rampage of violence to defeat Republicans and restore white supremacy.

UNDERSTAND POINTS OF VIEW

What did Southerners who supported the Republican Party have in common, and how did they differ?

plantations, where blacks sought to give fuller meaning to their newly won legal and political equality. Ex-masters had their own ideas about the labor system that should replace slavery, and freedom remained contested territory. Southerners fought pitched battles with one another to determine the contours of their new world.

Freedmen, Yankees, and Yeomen

African Americans made up the majority of southern Republicans. After gaining voting rights in 1867, nearly all eligible black men registered to vote as Republicans, grateful to the party that had freed them and granted them the franchise. "It is the hardest thing in the world to keep a negro away from the polls," observed a critical Alabama white man. Southern blacks did not all have identical political priorities, but they united in their desire for education and equal treatment before the law.

Northern whites who made the South their home after the war were a second element of the South's Republican Party. Most white Southerners called them **carpetbaggers**, opportunists who stuffed all their belongings in a single carpet-sided suitcase and headed south to "fatten on our misfortunes." But most Northerners who moved south were young men who looked upon the South as they did the West—as a promising place to make a living. Northerners in the southern Republican Party supported programs that encouraged vigorous economic development along the lines of the northern free-labor model.

Southern whites made up the third element of the South's Republican Party. Approximately one out of four white Southerners voted Republican. The other three condemned the one who did as a traitor to his region and his race and called him a **scalawag**, a term for runty horses and low-down, good-for-nothing rascals. Yeoman farmers accounted for the majority of southern white Republicans. Some were Unionists who emerged from the war with bitter memories of Confederate persecution. Others were small farmers who wanted to end state governments' favoritism toward plantation owners. Yeomen supported initiatives for public schools and for expanding economic opportunity in the South.

The South's Republican Party, then, was made up of freedmen, Yankees, and yeomen—an improbable coalition. The mix of races, regions, and classes inevitably meant friction as each group maneuvered to define the party. Still, Reconstruction represented an extraordinary moment in American politics: Blacks and whites joined together in the Republican Party to pursue political change. Formally, of course, only men participated in politics—casting ballots and holding offices—but white and black women also played a part in the political struggle by joining in parades and rallies, attending stump speeches, and even campaigning.

Most whites in the South condemned southern Republicans as illegitimate and felt justified in doing whatever they could to stamp them out. Violence against blacks—the "white terror"—took brutal institutional form in 1866 with the formation in Tennessee of the **Ku Klux Klan**, a group of Confederate veterans that quickly developed into a paramilitary organization supporting Democrats. The Klan went on a rampage of whipping, hanging, shooting, burning, and throat-cutting to defeat Republicans and restore white supremacy. **(See "Spotlight: What Did the Ku Klux Klan Really Want?" on page 474.)**

Rapid demobilization of the Union army after the war left only a handful of troops to patrol the entire South. Without effective military protection, southern Republicans had to take care of themselves.

Republican Rule

In the fall of 1867, southern states held elections for delegates to state constitutional conventions, as required by the Reconstruction Acts. About 40 percent of the white electorate stayed home because they had been disfranchised or because they had

Why did Congress object to Lincoln's wartime plan for reconstruction?

decided to boycott politics. Republicans won three-fourths of the seats. About 15 percent of the Republican delegates to the conventions were Northerners who had moved south, 25 percent were African Americans, and 60 percent were white Southerners. As a British visitor observed, the delegate elections reflected "the mighty revolution that had taken place in America."

The conventions brought together serious, purposeful men who hammered out the legal framework for a new society. The reconstruction constitutions introduced two broad categories of changes in the South: those that reduced aristocratic privilege and increased democratic equality and those that expanded the state's responsibility for the general welfare. In the first category, the constitutions adopted universal male suffrage, abolished property qualifications for holding office, and made more offices elective and fewer appointed. In the second category, they enacted prison reform; made the state responsible for caring for orphans, the insane, and the deaf and mute; and exempted debtors' homes from seizure.

To Democrats, these progressive constitutions looked like wild revolution. They were blind to the fact that no constitution confiscated and redistributed land, as virtually every former slave wished, or disfranchised ex-rebels wholesale, as most southern Unionists advocated. Yet Democrats were convinced that the new constitutions initiated "Negro domination." In fact, although 80 percent of Republican voters were black men, only 6 percent of Southerners in Congress during Reconstruction were black (**Figure 16.1**). The sixteen black men in Congress included exceptional men, such as Representative James T. Rapier of Alabama. No state legislature experienced "Negro rule," despite black majorities in the populations of some states.

Southern voters ratified the new state constitutions and swept Republicans into power. When the former Confederate states ratified the Fourteenth Amendment, Congress readmitted them. Southern Republicans then turned to a staggering array of problems at home. Wartime destruction littered the landscape. Making matters worse, racial harassment and reactionary violence dogged Southerners who sought reform. Democrats mocked Republican officeholders as ignorant field hands who had only "agricultural degrees" and "brick yard diplomas," but Republicans began a serious effort to rebuild and reform the region.

Activity focused on three areas—education, civil rights, and economic development. Every state inaugurated a system of public education. Before the Civil War, whites had deliberately kept slaves illiterate, and planter-dominated governments rarely spent tax money to educate the children of yeomen. By 1875, half of Mississippi's and South Carolina's eligible children were attending school. Although schools were underfunded, literacy rates rose sharply. Public schools were racially segregated, but education remained for many blacks a deeply satisfying benefit of freedom and Republican rule.

State legislatures also attacked racial discrimination and defended civil rights. Republicans resisted efforts to segregate blacks from whites, especially in public transportation. Mississippi levied fines and jail terms for owners of railroads and steamboats that pushed blacks into "smoking cars" or to lower decks. But passing color-blind laws was one thing; enforcing them was another. A Mississippian complained: "Education amounts to nothing, good behavior counts for nothing, even money cannot buy for a colored man or woman decent treatment and the comforts that white people claim and can obtain." Despite the laws, segregation—later called Jim Crow—developed at white insistence. Determined to underscore the social inferiority of blacks, whites saw to it that separation by race became a feature of southern life long before the end of the Reconstruction era.

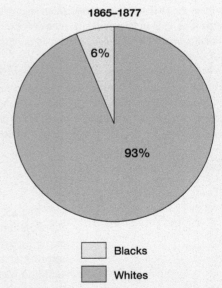

1865–1877

6%

93%

Blacks

Whites

FIGURE 16.1 ▲ Southern Congressional Delegations, 1865–1877

The statistics contradict the myth of black domination of congressional representation during Reconstruction.

How did the North respond to the passage of black codes in the southern states?	How radical was congressional reconstruction?	**What brought the elements of the South's Republican coalition together?**	Why did Reconstruction collapse?	Conclusion: Was Reconstruction "a revolution but half accomplished"?

What Did the Ku Klux Klan Really Want?

In 1866 in Pulaski, Tennessee, six Confederate veterans founded the Ku Klux Klan for fun and fellowship. By 1868, when congressional reconstruction went into effect, the Klan had spread across the South, and members had turned to more serious matters.

According to former Confederate general and Georgia Democratic politician John B. Gordon, the Klan owed its popularity to the "instinct of self-preservation . . . the sense of insecurity and danger, particularly in those neighborhoods where the Negro population largely predominated." Everywhere whites looked, he said, they saw "great crime." According to Gordon, Republican politicians marched ignorant freedmen to the polls, where they voted as they were told. Ex-slaves drove overseers from plantations and claimed the land for themselves. Black rapists made white women cower behind barred doors. It was necessary, Gordon declared, "in order to protect our families from outrage and preserve our own lives, to have something that we could regard as a brotherhood—a combination of the best men of the country, to act purely in self-defense."

Behind the Klan's claim of self-defense, however, lay another agenda, revealed in their actions, not their words. Klansmen embarked on a campaign to reverse history. Garbed in robes and hoods, they engaged in guerrilla warfare against free labor, civil equality, and political democracy. They aimed to terrorize their enemies—ex-slaves and white Republicans—into submission. Changes in four particular areas of southern life proved flash points for Klan violence: racial etiquette, education, labor, and politics.

The Klan punished blacks and whites who broke the Old South's racial code. It considered "impudence" a punishable offense. Asked to define "impudence" before a congressional investigating committee, one white man responded: "Well, it is considered impudence for a negro not to be polite to a

▲ During Reconstruction, Klansmen wore robes of various designs and colors. Uniform white robes came later. These counterrevolutionary terrorists fought to beat back free labor, democracy, and republicanism and to force the South back into its antebellum channels. Dallas Historical Society, Texas, USA/Bridgeman Images.

Republican governments also launched ambitious programs of economic development. They envisioned a South of diversified agriculture, roaring factories, and booming towns. State legislatures chartered scores of banks and industrial companies, appropriated funds to fix ruined levees and drain swamps, and went on a railroad-building binge. These efforts fell far short of solving the South's economic troubles, however. Republican spending to stimulate economic growth meant rising taxes and enormous debt that siphoned funds from schools and other programs.

The southern Republicans' record was mixed. To their credit, the biracial party adopted an ambitious agenda to change the South. But money was scarce, the Democrats continued their vicious harassment, and differences threatened the Republican Party from within. Corruption infected Republican governments. Nonetheless, the

Why did Congress object to Lincoln's wartime plan for reconstruction?

white man—not to pull off his hat and bow and scrape to a white man, as was done formerly." Klansmen whipped blacks for speaking disrespectfully, refusing to yield the sidewalk, and dressing well. Black women who "dress up and fix up like ladies" risked a midnight visit from the Klan. The Klan sought to restore racial subordination in every aspect of private and public life.

Klansmen also took aim at black education. They found the sight of blacks in classrooms hard to stomach. Schools were easy targets, and they burned scores of them. They whipped teachers, male and female. Klansmen drove northern-born teacher Alonzo B. Corliss from North Carolina for "teaching niggers and making them like white men." Planters wanted ex-slaves back in the fields, not at desks. In 1869, an Alabama newspaper announced that the burning of a black school should be "a warning for them to stick hereafter to 'de shovel and de hoe,' and let their dirty-backed primers go."

Planters also turned to the Klan as part of their effort to preserve plantation agriculture. An Alabama white admitted that in his area the Klan was "intended principally for the negroes who failed to work." Hooded bands "punished Negroes whose landlords had complained of them." Sharecroppers who disputed their share at "settling up time" risked a visit from the night riders. It was dangerous for freedmen to consider changing employers. "If we got out looking for some other place to go," an ex-slave from Texas remembered, "them KKK they would tend to Mister negro good and plenty."

Above all, the Klan terrorized Republicans. Klansmen became the military arm of the Democratic Party. They drove blacks from the polls on election day and assaulted Republican officeholders. Klansmen gave Andrew Flowers, a black politician in Chattanooga, a brutal beating and told him that they "did not intend any nigger to hold office in the United States." Jack Dupree, president of the Republican Club in Monroe County, Mississippi, a man known to "speak his mind," had his throat cut and was disemboweled while his wife was forced to watch.

Political violence reached astounding levels. Arkansas experienced nearly three hundred political killings during the fall elections in 1868. Louisiana was even bloodier, suffering more than one thousand killings in the same year. In Georgia, the Klan murdered three scalawag members of the legislature and drove ten others from their homes. As one Georgia Republican commented after a Klan attack: "We don't call them [D]emocrats, we call them southern murderers."

It proved hard to arrest Klansmen and harder still to convict them. "If a white man kills a colored man in any of the counties of this State," observed a Florida sheriff, "you cannot convict him." Federal intervention—in the Ku Klux Klan Acts of 1870 and 1871—signaled an end to much of the Klan's power but not to counterrevolutionary violence in the South. Other groups continued the terror in the cause of white supremacy.

Questions for Analysis

SUMMARIZE THE ARGUMENT: According to the author, what were the primary goals of the Ku Klux Klan?

ANALYZE THE EVIDENCE: Why did Klansmen believe that their actions were justified? What specific "crimes" did they aim to address? Why do you think they hid their identities?

CONSIDER THE CONTEXT: How did the Ku Klux Klan serve the counterrevolutionary goals of the South's Democratic Party?

Republican Party made headway in its efforts to purge the South of aristocratic privilege and racist oppression. Republican governments had less success in overthrowing the long-established white oppression of black farm laborers in the rural South.

White Landlords, Black Sharecroppers

Ex-slaves who wished to escape slave labor and ex-masters who wanted to reinstitute old oppressions clashed repeatedly. Except for having to pay subsistence wages, planters had not been required to offer many concessions to emancipation. They continued to believe that African Americans would not work without coercion. A Tennessee man

| How did the North respond to the passage of black codes in the southern states? | How radical was congressional reconstruction? | **What brought the elements of the South's Republican coalition together?** | Why did Reconstruction collapse? | Conclusion: Was Reconstruction "a revolution but half accomplished"? |

475

▲ **Students at a Freedmen's School in Virginia, ca. 1870s** "The people are hungry and thirsty after knowledge," a former slave observed immediately after the Civil War. African American leader Booker T. Washington remembered "a whole race trying to go to school." Students at this Virginia school stand in front of their log-cabin classroom, reading books. For people long forbidden to learn to read and write, literacy symbolized freedom. Photo12/UIG/Getty Images.

declared two years after the war ended that blacks were "a trifling set of lazy devils who will never make a living without Masters."

Some planters were so discouraged about the prospect of farming with free black labor that they fled the South. Their determination "to get away from the free Negro" carried them around the world, but especially to Brazil, which seemed to offer the best chance of resurrecting antebellum southern society because slavery was still legal there. Firsthand experience in Brazil shocked most southern migrants, however. They found "decay" everywhere, race relations that challenged their notions of white supremacy, and most important, abolition on the horizon. By 1870, most migrating planters were back home, where they joined those who had stayed in their efforts to restore as much of slavery as they could get away with.

Ex-slaves resisted every effort to turn back the clock. They argued that if any class could be described as "lazy," it was the planters, who, as one former slave noted, "lived in idleness all their lives on stolen labor." Freedmen believed that land of their own would anchor their economic independence and end planters' interference in their personal lives. They could then, for example, make their own decisions about whether women and children would labor in the fields. Indeed, within months after the war, perhaps one-third of black women abandoned field labor to work on chores in their own cabins just as poor white women did. Black women also negotiated about work ex-mistresses wanted done

ANALYZE EVIDENCE

What do the policies southern reconstruction legislators pursued suggest about what kind of society they hoped to create in the new South?

Why did Congress object to Lincoln's wartime plan for reconstruction?

in the big house. Hundreds of thousands of black children enrolled in school. But without their own land, ex-slaves had little choice but to work on plantations.

Although forced to return to the planters' fields, they resisted efforts to restore slavelike conditions. Instead of working for wages, a South Carolinian observed, "the negroes all seem disposed to rent land," which increased their independence from whites. Out of this tug-of-war between white landlords and black laborers emerged a new system of southern agriculture.

Sharecropping was a compromise that offered something to both ex-masters and ex-slaves, but satisfied neither. Under the new system, planters divided their cotton plantations into small farms that freedmen rented, paying with a share of each year's crop, usually half. Sharecropping gave blacks more freedom than the system of wages and labor gangs and released them from day-to-day supervision by whites. Black families abandoned the old slave quarters and built separate cabins for themselves on the land they rented (**Map 16.1**). Still, most black families remained dependent on white landlords, who had the power to evict them at the end of each growing season.

sharecropping
Labor system that emerged in the South during Reconstruction. Under this system, planters divided their plantations into small farms that freedmen rented, paying with a share of each year's crop. Sharecropping gave blacks some freedom, but they remained dependent on white landlords and country merchants.

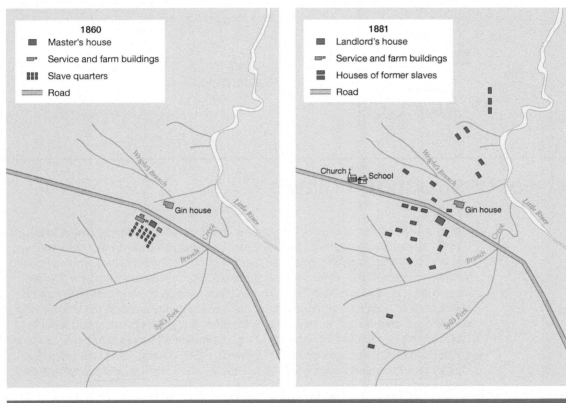

1860
- ■ Master's house
- ◧ Service and farm buildings
- ▥ Slave quarters
- ▨ Road

1881
- ■ Landlord's house
- ◧ Service and farm buildings
- ▤ Houses of former slaves
- ▨ Road

MAP ACTIVITY

MAP 16.1 ▲ A Southern Plantation in 1860 and 1881 These maps of the Barrow cotton plantation in Georgia illustrate some of the ways in which ex-slaves expressed their freedom. Freedmen and freedwomen deserted the clustered living quarters behind the master's house, scattered over the plantation, built family cabins, and farmed rented land. The former Barrow slaves also worked together to build a school and a church.

READING THE MAP: Compare the number and size of the slave quarters in 1860 with the homes of the former slaves in 1881. How do they differ? Which buildings were prominently located along the road in 1860, and which could be found along the road in 1881?

CONNECTIONS: How might the former master feel about the new configuration of buildings on the plantation in 1881? In what ways did the new system of sharecropping replicate the old system of plantation agriculture? In what ways was it different?

| How did the North respond to the passage of black codes in the southern states? | How radical was congressional reconstruction? | **What brought the elements of the South's Republican coalition together?** | Why did Reconstruction collapse? | Conclusion: Was Reconstruction "a revolution but half accomplished"? |

For planters, sharecropping offered a way to resume agricultural production, but it did not allow them to restore the old slave plantation.

Sharecropping introduced the country merchant into the agricultural equation. Landlords supplied sharecroppers with land, mules, seeds, and tools, but sharecroppers also needed credit to obtain essential food and clothing before they harvested their crops. Under an arrangement called a crop lien, a merchant would advance goods in exchange for a *lien*, or legal claim, on the sharecropper's future crop. Some merchants charged exorbitant rates of interest, as much as 60 percent, on the goods they sold. At the end of the growing season, after the landlord had taken half of the farmer's crop for rent, the merchant took most of the rest. Sometimes, the farmer did not earn enough to repay the debt to the merchant, so he would have to borrow more from the merchant and begin the cycle again.

An experiment at first, sharecropping soon dominated the cotton South. Lien merchants forced tenants to plant cotton, which was easy to sell, instead of food crops. The result was excessive production of cotton and falling cotton prices, developments that cost thousands of small white farmers their land and pushed them into the great army of poor sharecroppers. The new sharecropping system of agriculture took shape just as the political power of Republicans in the South began to buckle under Democratic pressure.

COMPARE AND CONTRAST
How did the new system of sharecropping compare to the old system of plantation slavery, considering its impact on African Americans, planters, and the southern economy?

QUICK REVIEW

How did Reconstruction shape politics and economic change in the South?

Why did Reconstruction collapse?

By 1870, after a decade of war and reconstruction, Northerners wanted to put "the southern problem" behind them. Businessmen came to dominate the Republican Party, replacing the band of reformers and idealists who had been prominent in the 1860s. Civil War hero Ulysses S. Grant succeeded Andrew Johnson as president in 1869 and quickly became an issue himself, proving that brilliance on the battlefield does not necessarily translate into accomplishment in the White House. As northern commitment to defend black freedom eroded, southern commitment to white supremacy intensified. Without northern protection, southern Republicans were no match for the Democrats' economic coercion, political fraud, and bloody violence. One by one, Republican state governments fell in the South. The election of 1876 both confirmed and completed the collapse of reconstruction.

Grant's Troubled Presidency

In 1868, the Republican Party's presidential nomination went to Ulysses S. Grant, the North's favorite general. His Democratic opponent, Horatio Seymour of New York, ran on a platform that blasted reconstruction as "a flagrant usurpation of power . . . unconstitutional, revolutionary, and void." The Republicans answered by "waving the bloody shirt"—that is, they reminded voters that the Democrats were "the party of rebellion." Despite a reign of terror in the South, costing hundreds of Republicans their lives, Grant gained a narrow 309,000-vote margin in the popular vote and a substantial victory (214 votes to 80) in the electoral college (**Map 16.2**).

Why did Congress object to Lincoln's wartime plan for reconstruction?

The talents Grant had demonstrated on the battlefield—decisiveness, clarity, and resolution—were less obvious in the White House. While Grant sought both justice for blacks and sectional reconciliation, he surrounded himself with fumbling kinfolk and old friends from his army days and made a string of dubious appointments that led to a series of damaging scandals. Charges of corruption tainted his vice president, Schuyler Colfax, and brought down two of his cabinet officers. Though never personally implicated in any scandal, Grant was naive and blind to the rot that filled his administration. Republican congressman James A. Garfield declared: "His imperturbability is amazing. I am in doubt whether to call it greatness or stupidity."

In 1872, anti-Grant Republicans bolted and launched the Liberal Party. To clean up the corruption, Liberals proposed ending the spoils system, by which victorious parties rewarded loyal workers with public office, and replacing it with a nonpartisan civil service commission that would oversee competitive examinations for appointment to office. Liberals also demanded that the federal government remove its troops from the South and restore "home rule" (southern white control). Democrats liked the Liberals' southern policy and endorsed the Liberal presidential candidate, Horace Greeley, the longtime editor of the *New York Tribune*. The nation, however, still felt enormous affection for the man who had saved the Union and reelected Grant with 56 percent of the popular vote.

Northern Resolve Withers

Although Grant genuinely wanted to protect blacks' civil and political rights, he understood that most Northerners had grown weary of reconstruction. Citizens wanted to shift their attention to other issues, especially after the nation slipped into a devastating economic depression in 1873. More than eighteen thousand businesses collapsed, leaving more than a million workers on the streets. Northern businessmen wanted to invest in the South but believed that repeated federal intrusion was itself a major cause of instability in the region. Republican leaders began to question the wisdom of their party's alliance with the South's lower classes—its small farmers and sharecroppers. One member of Grant's administration proposed allying with the "thinking and influential native southerners . . . the intelligent, well-to-do, and controlling class."

Congress, too, wanted to leave reconstruction behind, but southern Republicans made that difficult. When the South's Republicans begged for federal protection from increasing Klan violence, Congress enacted three laws in 1870 and 1871 that were intended to break the back of white terrorism. The severest of the three, the Ku Klux Klan Act (1871), made interference with voting rights a felony. Federal marshals arrested thousands of Klansmen and came close to destroying the Klan, but they did not end terrorism against blacks. Congress also passed the Civil Rights Act of 1875, which boldly outlawed racial discrimination in transportation, public accommodations, and juries. Federal authorities never enforced the law aggressively, however, and segregation remained the rule throughout the South.

By the early 1870s, the Republican Party had lost its leading champions of African American rights to death or defeat at the polls. Other Republicans concluded that the quest for black equality was mistaken or hopelessly naive. In May 1872, Congress restored the right of officeholding to all but three hundred ex-rebels. Many Republicans had come to believe that traditional white leaders offered the best hope for honesty, order, and prosperity in the South.

CHRONOLOGY

1868
– Ulysses S. Grant elected president.

1871
– Ku Klux Klan Act passes.

1872
– Liberal Party formed.
– President Grant reelected.

1873
– Economic depression sets in.
– *Slaughterhouse* cases decided.
– Colfax massacre kills more than eighty blacks.

1874
– Democrats win majority in House of Representatives.

1877
– Republican Rutherford B. Hayes inaugurated president and Reconstruction ends.

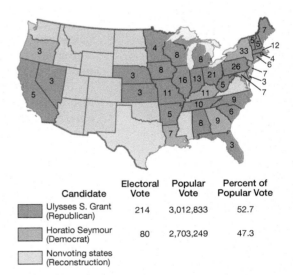

Candidate	Electoral Vote	Popular Vote	Percent of Popular Vote
Ulysses S. Grant (Republican)	214	3,012,833	52.7
Horatio Seymour (Democrat)	80	2,703,249	47.3
Nonvoting states (Reconstruction)			

MAP 16.2 ▲ The Election of 1868

How did the North respond to the passage of black codes in the southern states?	How radical was congressional reconstruction?	What brought the elements of the South's Republican coalition together?	**Why did Reconstruction collapse?**	Conclusion: Was Reconstruction "a revolution but half accomplished"?

Underlying the North's abandonment of reconstruction was unyielding racial prejudice. Northerners had learned to accept black freedom during the war, but deep-seated prejudice prevented many from accepting black equality. Even the actions they took on behalf of blacks often served partisan political advantage. Northerners generally supported Indiana senator Thomas A. Hendricks's harsh declaration that "this is a white man's Government, made by the white man for the white man."

The U.S. Supreme Court also did its part to undermine reconstruction. The Court issued a series of decisions that significantly weakened the federal government's ability to protect black Southerners. In the *Slaughterhouse* cases (1873), the Court distinguished between national and state citizenship and ruled that the Fourteenth Amendment protected only those rights that stemmed from the federal government, such as voting in federal elections and interstate travel. Since the Court decided that most rights derived from the states, it sharply curtailed the federal government's authority to defend black citizens. Even more devastating, the *United States v. Cruikshank* ruling (1876) said that the reconstruction amendments gave Congress the power to legislate against discrimination only by states, not by individuals. The "suppression of ordinary crime," such as assault, remained a state responsibility. The Supreme Court did not declare reconstruction unconstitutional but eroded its legal foundation.

The mood of the North found political expression in the election of 1874, when for the first time in eighteen years the Democrats gained control of the House of Representatives. As one Republican observed, the people had grown tired of the "negro question, with all its complications, and the reconstruction of Southern States, with all its interminable embroilments." Rather than defend reconstruction from its southern enemies, Northerners steadily backed away from the challenge. By the early 1870s, southern Republicans faced the forces of southern racism largely on their own.

"The people had grown tired of the 'negro question, with all its complications, and the reconstruction of Southern States, with all its interminable embroilments.'"

PLACE EVENTS IN CONTEXT
Why did the Fourteenth and Fifteenth Amendments fail to protect the freedpeople in the South?

White Supremacy Triumphs

To most white Southerners, Reconstruction meant intolerable insults: Black militiamen patrolled town streets, black laborers negotiated contracts with former masters, black maids stood up to former mistresses, black voters cast ballots, and black legislators such as James T. Rapier helped enact laws. Whites fought back by extolling the "great Confederate cause," or Lost Cause. They celebrated their soldiers, "the noblest band of men who ever fought," and made an idol of Robert E. Lee, the embodiment of the southern gentleman.

But the most important way white Southerners responded to reconstruction was their assault on Republican governments in the South. These biracial governments attracted more hatred than did any other political regimes in American history. The northern retreat from reconstruction permitted southern Democrats to set things right. Taking the name **Redeemers**, Democrats in the South promised to replace "bayonet rule" (a few federal troops continued to be stationed in the South) with "home rule." They promised that honest, thrifty Democrats would supplant corrupt tax-and-spend Republicans. Above all, Redeemers swore to save southern civilization from a descent into "African barbarism." As one man put it, "We must render this either a white man's government, or convert the land into a Negro man's cemetery."

Southern Democrats adopted a multipronged strategy to overthrow Republican governments. First, they sought to polarize the parties around race. They went about gathering all the South's white voters into the Democratic Party, leaving the Republicans to depend on blacks, who made up a minority of the population in almost every

Redeemers
Name taken by southern Democrats who harnessed white rage in order to overthrow Republican rule and black political power and thus, they believed, save southern civilization.

Why did Congress object to Lincoln's wartime plan for reconstruction?

southern state. To dislodge whites from the Republican Party, Democrats fanned the flames of racism. A South Carolina Democrat crowed that his party appealed to the "proud Caucasian race, whose sovereignty on earth God has proclaimed."

Democrats also exploited the severe economic plight of small white farmers by blaming it on Republicans. Government spending soared during Reconstruction, and small farmers saw their tax burden skyrocket. "This is tax time," a South Carolinian reported. "They are so high & so little money to pay with" that farmers were "selling every egg and chicken they can get." In 1871, Mississippi reported that one-seventh of the state's land—3.3 million acres—had been forfeited for nonpayment of taxes. The small farmers' economic distress had a racial dimension. Because few freedmen succeeded in acquiring land, they rarely paid taxes. In Georgia in 1874, blacks made up 45 percent of the population but paid only 2 percent of the taxes. From the perspective of a small white farmer, Republican rule meant that he was not only paying more taxes but paying them to aid blacks.

If racial pride and financial hardship proved insufficient to drive yeomen from the Republican Party, Democrats turned to terrorism. "Night riders" targeted white Republicans as well as blacks for murder and assassination. Whether white or black, a "dead Radical is very harmless," South Carolina Democratic leader Martin Gary told his followers.

Still, the primary victims of white violence were black Republicans. Violence escalated to an unprecedented ferocity on Easter Sunday in 1873 in tiny Colfax, Louisiana. When Democrats turned to fraud to win a local election, black Republicans refused to accept the result and occupied the courthouse. After three weeks, 165 white men attacked and set the courthouse on fire. When the blacks tried to surrender, the attackers murdered them. At least 81 black men were slaughtered that day. Although the federal government indicted the white killers, the Supreme Court ruled that it did not have the right to prosecute. And since local whites would not prosecute neighbors who killed blacks, the defendants in the Colfax massacre went free.

Even before adopting the all-out white supremacist tactics of the 1870s, Democrats had taken control of the governments of Virginia, Tennessee, and North Carolina. The new campaign brought fresh gains. The Redeemers retook Georgia in 1871, Texas in 1873, and Arkansas and Alabama in 1874. As the state election approached in Mississippi in 1876, the Republican governor appealed to Washington for federal troops to control

CONSIDER CAUSE AND EFFECT
What factors led to the demise of Reconstruction, and which played the most important role?

◀ **"Of Course He Wants to Vote the Democratic Ticket"** This Republican cartoon from the October 21, 1876, issue of *Harper's Weekly* comments sarcastically on the possibility of honest elections in the South. The caption reads: "You're free as air, ain't you? Say you are or I'll blow yer black head off." The cartoon demonstrates not only some Northerners' concern that violence would deliver the election to the Democrats but also the perception that white Southerners were crude, drunken, ignorant brutes. The Granger Collection, New York.

| How did the North respond to the passage of black codes in the southern states? | How radical was congressional reconstruction? | What brought the elements of the South's Republican coalition together? | **Why did Reconstruction collapse?** | Conclusion: Was Reconstruction "a revolution but half accomplished"? |

MAP 16.3 ▶ The Reconstruction of the South

Myth has it that Republican rule of the former Confederacy was not only harsh but long. In most states, however, conservative southern whites stormed back into power in months or just a few years. By the election of 1876, Republican governments could be found in only three states, and they soon fell.

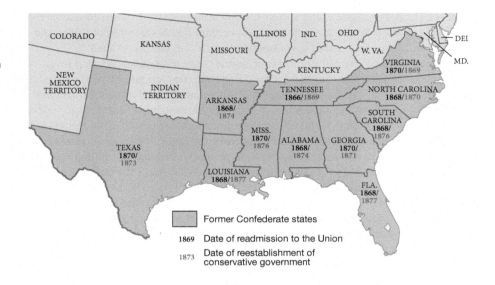

	Former Confederate states
1869	Date of readmission to the Union
1873	Date of reestablishment of conservative government

the violence, only to hear from the attorney general that the "whole public are tired of these annual autumnal outbreaks in the South." Abandoned, Mississippi Republicans succumbed to the Democratic onslaught in the fall elections. By 1876, only three Republican state governments survived in the South (**Map 16.3**).

An Election and a Compromise

The year 1876 witnessed one of the most chaotic elections in American history. The election took place in November, but not until March 2 of the following year did the nation know who would be inaugurated president on March 4. Sixteen years after Lincoln's election, Americans feared that a presidential election would again precipitate civil war.

The Democrats nominated New York's governor, Samuel J. Tilden, who targeted the corruption of the Grant administration and the "despotism" of Republican reconstruction. The Republicans put forward Rutherford B. Hayes, governor of Ohio. Privately, Hayes considered "bayonet rule" a mistake but concluded that waving the bloody shirt remained the Republicans' best political strategy.

On election day, Tilden tallied 4,288,590 votes to Hayes's 4,036,298. But in the all-important electoral college, Tilden fell one vote short of the majority required for victory. The electoral votes of three states—South Carolina, Louisiana, and Florida, the only remaining Republican governments in the South—remained in doubt because both Republicans and Democrats in those states claimed victory. To win, Tilden needed only one of the nineteen contested votes. Hayes had to have all of them.

Congress had to decide who had actually won the elections in the three southern states and thus who would be president. The Constitution provided no guidance. Democrats controlled the House, and Republicans controlled the Senate. Congress created a special electoral commission to arbitrate the disputed returns. All of the commissioners voted their party affiliation, giving every state to the Republican Hayes and putting him over the top in electoral votes (**Map 16.4**).

Some outraged Democrats vowed to resist Hayes's victory. Rumors flew of an impending coup and renewed civil war.

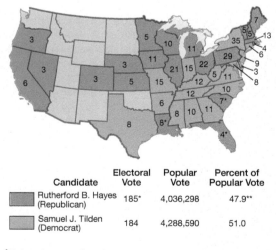

Candidate	Electoral Vote	Popular Vote	Percent of Popular Vote
Rutherford B. Hayes (Republican)	185*	4,036,298	47.9**
Samuel J. Tilden (Democrat)	184	4,288,590	51.0

*19 electoral votes were disputed.

**Percentages do not total 100 because some popular votes went to other parties.

MAP 16.4 ▲ The Election of 1876

Why did Congress object to Lincoln's wartime plan for reconstruction?

482 CHAPTER 16 RECONSTRUCTION

But the impasse was broken when negotiations behind the scenes resulted in an informal understanding known as the Compromise of 1877. In exchange for a Democratic promise not to block Hayes's inauguration and to deal fairly with the freedmen, Hayes vowed to refrain from using the army to uphold the remaining Republican regimes in the South and to provide the South with substantial federal subsidies for railroads.

Stubborn Tilden supporters bemoaned the "stolen election" and damned "His Fraudulency," Rutherford B. Hayes. Old-guard Radicals such as William Lloyd Garrison denounced Hayes's bargain as a "policy of compromise, of credulity, of weakness, of subserviency, of surrender." But the nation as a whole celebrated, for the country had weathered a grave crisis. The last three Republican state governments in the South fell quickly once Hayes withdrew the U.S. Army. Reconstruction came to an end.

Compromise of 1877
Informal agreement in which Democrats agreed not to block Rutherford Hayes's inauguration and to deal fairly with freedmen; in return, Hayes vowed not to use the army to uphold the remaining Republican regimes in the South and to provide the South with substantial federal subsidies for railroads. The compromise brought the Reconstruction era to an end.

QUICK REVIEW

How did the Supreme Court undermine Reconstruction?

Conclusion: Was Reconstruction "a revolution but half accomplished"?

In 1865, when General Carl Schurz visited the South, he discovered, he said, "a revolution but half accomplished." White Southerners resisted the passage from slavery to free labor, from white racial despotism to equal justice, and from white political monopoly to biracial democracy. The old elite wanted to get "things back as near to slavery as possible," Schurz reported, while African Americans such as James T. Rapier and some whites were eager to exploit the revolutionary implications of defeat and emancipation.

Although the northern-dominated Republican Congress refused to provide for blacks' economic welfare, it employed constitutional amendments to require ex-Confederates to accept legal equality and share political power with black men. Congress was not willing to extend such power to women, however. Conservative southern whites fought ferociously to recover their power and privilege. When Democrats regained control of politics, whites used both state power and private violence to wipe out many of the gains of Reconstruction, leading one observer to conclude that the North had won the war but the South had won the peace.

The Redeemer counterrevolution, however, did not mean a return to slavery. Northern victory in the Civil War ensured that ex-slaves no longer faced the auction block and could send their children to school, worship in their own churches, and work independently on their own rented farms. Sharecropping, with all its hardships, provided more autonomy and economic welfare than bondage had. It was limited freedom, to be sure, but it was not slavery.

The Civil War and emancipation set in motion the most profound upheaval in the nation's history. War destroyed the largest slave society in the New World. The world of masters and slaves gave way to that of landlords and sharecroppers. Washington increased its role in national affairs, and the victorious North set the nation's compass toward the expansion of industrial capitalism and the final conquest of the West.

Despite massive changes, however, the Civil War remained only a "half accomplished" revolution. By not fulfilling the promises, the nation seemed to hold out to black Americans at war's end, Reconstruction represents a tragedy of enormous proportions. The failure to protect blacks and guarantee their rights had enduring consequences. It was the failure of the first reconstruction that made the modern civil rights movement necessary.

| How did the North respond to the passage of black codes in the southern states? | How radical was congressional reconstruction? | What brought the elements of the South's Republican coalition together? | Why did Reconstruction collapse? | **Conclusion: Was Reconstruction "a revolution but half accomplished"?** |

STEP 1

EXPLAIN WHY IT MATTERS

Put your reading into practice. Identify each term below, and then explain why it matters in U.S. history.

TERM	WHO OR WHAT & WHEN	WHY IT MATTERS
Freedmen's Bureau (p. 460)		
black codes (p. 465)		
Civil Rights Act of 1866 (p. 467)		
Fourteenth Amendment (p. 468)		
Military Reconstruction Act (p. 469)		
Fifteenth Amendment (p. 470)		
carpetbaggers (p. 472)		
scalawag (p. 472)		
Ku Klux Klan (p. 472)		
sharecropping (p. 477)		
Redeemers (p. 480)		
Compromise of 1877 (p. 483)		

STEP 2

MOVE BEYOND THE BASICS

To demonstrate a more advanced understanding, indicate below how each phase of Reconstruction addressed the key issues involved.

Phase of Reconstruction	Requirements for Readmission	Role/Rights of Freedmen	Achievements	Failures
Wartime Reconstruction (Lincoln)				
Presidential Reconstruction (Johnson)				
Congressional Reconstruction				

STEP 3

PUT IT ALL TOGETHER

Now, explain the big picture. Remember to use specific examples from the chapter in your answers.

PRESIDENTIAL AND CONGRESSIONAL RECONSTRUCTION

• What role did the black codes play in shaping the course of Reconstruction?

• What steps did Congress take between 1865 and 1869 to assist ex-slaves in their lives as freedmen? Were these actions effective?

SOUTHERN RECONSTRUCTION IN ACTION

• How did white Southerners respond during Reconstruction? Consider both Democrats and Republicans in your response.

• How did southern African Americans attempt to shape their own lives during Reconstruction?

THE END OF RECONSTRUCTION

• How and why did the decline of northern support for Reconstruction help southern Democrats "redeem" the South?

• Why did white supremacy become the foundation of southern politics in the 1870s?

LOOKING BACKWARD, LOOKING AHEAD

• How did long-held racial views among whites, in both the South and the North, shape Reconstruction?

• What were the lasting accomplishments of Reconstruction? What were its most important failures?

STEP 4

CONNECT THESE EVENTS

How did the response of a majority of white Southerners to President Johnson's plan of reconstruction in 1865 preview the response of southern whites for the remainder of reconstruction?

STEP 5

CONNECT TO THE PRESENT

If Reconstruction was "a revolution but half accomplished," has the nation completed the revolution today?

DIRECTORY

DOCUMENTS

THE DECLARATION OF INDEPENDENCE

In Congress, July 4, 1776,

THE UNANIMOUS DECLARATION OF THE THIRTEEN UNITED STATES OF AMERICA

When in the course of human events, it becomes necessary for one people to dissolve the political bands which have connected them with another, and to assume, among the powers of the earth, the separate and equal station to which the laws of nature and of nature's God entitle them, a decent respect to the opinions of mankind requires that they should declare the causes which impel them to the separation.

We hold these truths to be self-evident, that all men are created equal; that they are endowed by their Creator with certain unalienable rights; that among these, are life, liberty, and the pursuit of happiness. That, to secure these rights, governments are instituted among men, deriving their just powers from the consent of the governed; that, whenever any form of government becomes destructive of these ends, it is the right of the people to alter or to abolish it, and to institute a new government, laying its foundation on such principles, and organizing its powers in such form, as to them shall seem most likely to effect their safety and happiness. Prudence, indeed, will dictate that governments long established, should not be changed for light and transient causes; and, accordingly, all experience hath shown, that mankind are more disposed to suffer, while evils are sufferable, than to right themselves by abolishing the forms to which they are accustomed. But, when a long train of abuses and usurpations, pursuing invariably the same object, evinces a design to reduce them under absolute despotism, it is their right, it is their duty, to throw off such government and to provide new guards for their future security. Such has been the patient sufferance of these colonies, and such is now the necessity which constrains them to alter their former systems of government. The history of the present King of Great Britain is a history of repeated injuries and usurpations, all having, in direct object, the establishment of an absolute tyranny over these States. To prove this, let facts be submitted to a candid world: He has refused his assent to laws the most wholesome and necessary for the public good.

He has forbidden his governors to pass laws of immediate and pressing importance, unless suspended in their operation till his assent should be obtained; and, when so suspended, he has utterly neglected to attend to them.

He has refused to pass other laws for the accommodation of large districts of people, unless those people would relinquish the right of representation in the legislature; a right inestimable to them, and formidable to tyrants only.

He has called together legislative bodies at places unusual, uncomfortable, and distant from the depository of their public records, for the sole purpose of fatiguing them into compliance with his measures.

He has dissolved representative houses repeatedly for opposing, with manly firmness, his invasions on the rights of the people.

He has refused, for a long time after such dissolutions, to cause others to be elected; whereby the legislative powers, incapable of annihilation, have returned to the people at large for their exercise; the state remaining in the mean-time exposed to all the danger of invasion from without, and convulsions within.

He has endeavored to prevent the population of these States; for that purpose, obstructing the laws for naturalization of foreigners, refusing to pass others to encourage their migration hither, and raising the conditions of new appropriations of lands.

He has obstructed the administration of justice, by refusing his assent to laws for establishing judiciary powers.

He has made judges dependent on his will alone, for the tenure of their offices, and the amount and payment of their salaries.

He has erected a multitude of new offices, and sent hither swarms of officers to harass our people, and eat out their substance.

He has kept among us, in times of peace, standing armies, without the consent of our legislature.

He has affected to render the military independent of, and superior to, the civil power.

He has combined, with others, to subject us to a jurisdiction foreign to our Constitution, and unacknowledged by our laws; giving his assent to their acts of pretended legislation:

For quartering large bodies of armed troops among us:

For protecting them by a mock trial, from punishment, for any murders which they should commit on the inhabitants of these States:

For cutting off our trade with all parts of the world:

For imposing taxes on us without our consent:

For depriving us, in many cases, of the benefit of trial by jury:

For transporting us beyond seas to be tried for pretended offences:

For abolishing the free system of English laws in a neighboring province, establishing therein an arbitrary government, and enlarging its boundaries, so as to render it at once an example and fit instrument for introducing the same absolute rule into these colonies:

For taking away our charters, abolishing our most valuable laws, and altering, fundamentally, the powers of our governments:

For suspending our own legislatures, and declaring themselves invested with power to legislate for us in all cases whatsoever.

He has abdicated government here, by declaring us out of his protection, and waging war against us.

He has plundered our seas, ravaged our coasts, burnt our towns, and destroyed the lives of our people.

He is, at this time, transporting large armies of foreign mercenaries to complete the works of death, desolation, and tyranny, already begun, with circumstances of cruelty and perfidy scarcely paralleled in the most barbarous ages, and totally unworthy the head of a civilized nation.

He has constrained our fellow citizens, taken captive on the high seas, to bear arms against their country, to become the executioners of their friends, and brethren, or to fall themselves by their hands.

He has excited domestic insurrections amongst us, and has endeavored to bring on the inhabitants of our frontiers, the merciless Indian savages, whose known rule of warfare is an undistinguished destruction of all ages, sexes, and conditions.

In every stage of these oppressions, we have petitioned for redress; in the most humble terms; our repeated petitions have been answered only by repeated injury. A prince, whose character is thus marked by every act which may define a tyrant, is unfit to be the ruler of a free people.

Nor have we been wanting in attention to our British brethren. We have warned them, from time to time, of attempts made by their legislature to extend an unwarrantable jurisdiction over us. We have reminded them of the circumstances of our emigration and settlement here. We have appealed to their native justice and magnanimity, and we have conjured them, by the ties of our common kindred, to disavow these usurpations, which would inevitably interrupt our connections and correspondence. They, too, have been deaf to the voice of justice and consanguinity. We must, therefore, acquiesce in the necessity which denounces our separation, and hold them as we hold the rest of mankind, enemies in war, in peace, friends.

We, therefore, the representatives of the United States of America, in general Congress assembled, appealing to the Supreme Judge of the world for the rectitude of our intentions, do, in the name, and by authority of the good people of these colonies, solemnly publish and declare, that these united colonies are, and of right ought to be, free and independent states: that they are absolved from all allegiance to the British Crown, and that all political connection between them and the state of Great Britain is, and ought to be, totally dissolved; and that, as free and independent states, they have full power to levy war, conclude peace, contract alliances, establish commerce, and to do all other acts and things which independent states may of right do. And, for the support of this declaration, with a firm reliance on the protection of Divine Providence, we mutually pledge to each other our lives, our fortunes, and our sacred honor.

The foregoing Declaration was, by order of Congress, engrossed, and signed by the following members:

JOHN HANCOCK

New Hampshire
Josiah Bartlett
William Whipple
Matthew Thornton

Massachusetts Bay
Samuel Adams
John Adams
Robert Treat Paine
Elbridge Gerry

Rhode Island
Stephen Hopkins
William Ellery

Connecticut
Roger Sherman
Samuel Huntington
William Williams
Oliver Wolcott

New York
William Floyd
Phillip Livingston
Francis Lewis
Lewis Morris

New Jersey
Richard Stockton
John Witherspoon
Francis Hopkinson
John Hart
Abraham Clark

Pennsylvania
Robert Morris
Benjamin Rush
Benjamin Franklin
John Morton
George Clymer
James Smith

George Taylor
James Wilson
George Ross

Delaware
Caesar Rodney
George Read
Thomas M'Kean

Maryland
Samuel Chase
William Paca
Thomas Stone
Charles Carroll,
of Carrollton

North Carolina
William Hooper
Joseph Hewes
John Penn

South Carolina
Edward Rutledge
Thomas Heyward, Jr.
Thomas Lynch, Jr.
Arthur Middleton

Virginia
George Wythe
Richard Henry Lee
Thomas Jefferson
Benjamin Harrison
Thomas Nelson, Jr.
Francis Lightfoot Lee
Carter Braxton

Georgia
Button Gwinnett
Lyman Hall
George Walton

Resolved, That copies of the Declaration be sent to the several assemblies, conventions, and committees, or councils of safety, and to the several commanding officers of the continental troops; that it be proclaimed in each of the United States, at the head of the army.

THE CONSTITUTION OF THE UNITED STATES*

Agreed to by Philadelphia Convention, September 17, 1787. Implemented March 4, 1789.

Preamble

We the people of the United States, in order to form a more perfect union, establish justice, insure domestic tranquility, provide for the common defense, promote the general welfare, and secure the blessings of liberty to ourselves and our posterity, do ordain and establish this Constitution for the United States of America.

Article I

Section 1 All legislative powers herein granted shall be vested in a Congress of the United States, which shall consist of a Senate and a House of Representatives.

Section 2 The House of Representatives shall be composed of members chosen every second year by the people of the several States, and the electors in each State shall have the qualifications requisite for electors of the most numerous branch of the State Legislature.

No person shall be a Representative who shall not have attained to the age of twenty-five years, and been seven years a citizen of the United States, and who shall not, when elected, be an inhabitant of that State in which he shall be chosen.

Representatives and direct taxes shall be apportioned among the several States which may be included within this Union, according to their respective numbers, *which shall be determined by adding to the whole number of free persons, including those bound to service for a term of years and excluding Indians not taxed, three-fifths of all other persons.* The actual enumeration shall be made within three years after the first meeting of the Congress of the United States, and within every subsequent term of ten years, in such manner as they shall by law direct. The number of Representatives shall not exceed one for every thirty thousand, but each State shall have at least one Representative; *and until such enumeration shall be made, the State of New Hampshire shall be entitled to choose three, Massachusetts eight, Rhode Island and Providence Plantations one, Connecticut five, New York six, New Jersey four, Pennsylvania eight, Delaware one, Maryland six, Virginia ten, North Carolina five, South Carolina five, and Georgia three.*

When vacancies happen in the representation from any State, the Executive authority thereof shall issue writs of election to fill such vacancies.

The House of Representatives shall choose their Speaker and other officers; and shall have the sole power of impeachment.

Section 3 The Senate of the United States shall be composed of two Senators from each State, *chosen by the legislature thereof,* for six years; and each Senator shall have one vote.

Immediately after they shall be assembled in consequence of the first election, they shall be divided as equally as may be into three classes. The seats of the Senators of the first class shall be vacated at the expiration of the second year, of the second class at the expiration of the fourth year, and of the third class at the expiration of the sixth year, so that one-third may be chosen every second year; *and if vacancies happen by resignation or otherwise, during the recess of the legislature of any State, the Executive thereof may make temporary appointments until the next meeting of the legislature, which shall then fill such vacancies.*

No person shall be a Senator who shall not have attained to the age of thirty years, and been nine years a citizen of the United States, and who shall not, when elected, be an inhabitant of that State for which he shall be chosen.

The Vice-President of the United States shall be President of the Senate, but shall have no vote, unless they be equally divided.

The Senate shall choose their other officers, and also a President pro tempore, in the absence of the Vice-President, or when he shall exercise the office of President of the United States.

The Senate shall have the sole power to try all impeachments. When sitting for that purpose, they shall be on oath or affirmation. When the President of the United States is tried, the Chief Justice shall preside: and no person shall be convicted without the concurrence of two-thirds of the members present.

Judgment in cases of impeachment shall not extend further than to removal from the office, and disqualification to hold and enjoy any office of honor, trust or profit under the United States: but the party convicted shall nevertheless be liable and subject to indictment, trial, judgment and punishment, according to law.

Section 4 The times, places and manner of holding elections for Senators and Representatives shall be prescribed in each

---

Passages no longer in effect are in italic type.

State by the legislature thereof; but the Congress may at any time by law make or alter such regulations, except as to the places of choosing Senators.

The Congress shall assemble at least once in every year, and such meeting *shall be on the first Monday in December, unless they shall by law appoint a different day.*

Section 5 Each house shall be the judge of the elections, returns and qualifications of its own members, and a majority of each shall constitute a quorum to do business; but a smaller number may adjourn from day to day, and may be authorized to compel the attendance of absent members, in such manner, and under such penalties, as each house may provide.

Each house may determine the rules of its proceedings, punish its members for disorderly behavior, and with the concurrence of two-thirds, expel a member.

Each house shall keep a journal of its proceedings, and from time to time publish the same, excepting such parts as may in their judgment require secrecy; and the yeas and nays of the members of either house on any question shall, at the desire of one-fifth of those present, be entered on the journal.

Neither house, during the session of Congress, shall, without the consent of the other, adjourn for more than three days, nor to any other place than that in which the two houses shall be sitting.

Section 6 The Senators and Representatives shall receive a compensation for their services, to be ascertained by law and paid out of the treasury of the United States. They shall in all cases except treason, felony and breach of the peace, be privileged from arrest during their attendance at the session of their respective houses, and in going to and returning from the same; and for any speech or debate in either house, they shall not be questioned in any other place.

No Senator or Representative shall, during the time for which he was elected, be appointed to any civil office under the authority of the United States, which shall have been created, or the emoluments whereof shall have been increased, during such time; and no person holding any office under the United States shall be a member of either house during his continuance in office.

Section 7 All bills for raising revenue shall originate in the House of Representatives; but the Senate may propose or concur with amendments as on other bills.

Every bill which shall have passed the House of Representatives and the Senate, shall, before it become a law, be presented to the President of the United States; if he approve he shall sign it, but if not he shall return it with objections to that house in which it shall have originated, who shall enter the objections at large on their journal, and proceed to reconsider it. If after such reconsideration two-thirds of that house shall agree to pass the bill, it shall be sent, together with the objections, to the other house, by which it shall likewise be reconsidered, and, if approved by two-thirds of that house, it shall become a law. But in all such cases the votes of both houses shall be determined by yeas and nays, and the names of the persons voting

for and against the bill shall be entered on the journal of each house respectively. If any bill shall not be returned by the President within ten days (Sundays excepted) after it shall have been presented to him, the same shall be a law, in like manner as if he had signed it, unless the Congress by their adjournment prevent its return, in which case it shall not be a law.

Every order, resolution, or vote to which the concurrence of the Senate and House of Representatives may be necessary (except on a question of adjournment) shall be presented to the President of the United States; and before the same shall take effect, shall be approved by him, or being disapproved by him, shall be repassed by two-thirds of the Senate and House of Representatives, according to the rules and limitations prescribed in the case of a bill.

Section 8 The Congress shall have power

To lay and collect taxes, duties, imposts, and excises, to pay the debts and provide for the common defense and general welfare of the United States; but all duties, imposts and excises shall be uniform throughout the United States;

To borrow money on the credit of the United States;

To regulate commerce with foreign nations, and among the several States, and with the Indian tribes;

To establish an uniform rule of naturalization, and uniform laws on the subject of bankruptcies throughout the United States;

To coin money, regulate the value thereof, and of foreign coin, and fix the standard of weights and measures;

To provide for the punishment of counterfeiting the securities and current coin of the United States;

To establish post offices and post roads;

To promote the progress of science and useful arts by securing for limited times to authors and inventors the exclusive right to their respective writings and discoveries;

To constitute tribunals inferior to the Supreme Court;

To define and punish piracies and felonies committed on the high seas and offences against the law of nations;

To declare war, grant letters of marque and reprisal, and make rules concerning captures on land and water;

To raise and support armies, but no appropriation of money to that use shall be for a longer term than two years;

To provide and maintain a navy;

To make rules for the government and regulation of the land and naval forces;

To provide for calling forth the militia to execute the laws of the Union, suppress insurrections and repel invasions;

To provide for organizing, arming, and disciplining the militia, and for governing such part of them as may be employed in the service of the United States, reserving to the States respectively the appointment of the officers, and the authority of training the militia according to the discipline prescribed by Congress;

To exercise exclusive legislation in all cases whatsoever, over such district (not exceeding ten miles square) as may, by cession of particular States, and the acceptance of Congress, become the seat of the government of the United States, and to exercise like authority over all places purchased by the consent of the legislature of the State, in which the same shall be, for erection of forts, magazines, arsenals, dock-yards, and other needful buildings;—and

To make all laws which shall be necessary and proper for carrying into execution the foregoing powers, and all other powers vested by this Constitution in the government of the United States, or in any department or officer thereof.

Section 9 *The migration or importation of such persons as any of the States now existing shall think proper to admit shall not be prohibited by the Congress prior to the year one thousand eight hundred and eight; but a tax or duty may be imposed on such importation, not exceeding ten dollars for each person.*

The privilege of the writ of habeas corpus shall not be suspended, unless when in cases of rebellion or invasion the public safety may require it.

No bill of attainder or ex post facto law shall be passed.

No capitation, or other direct, tax shall be laid, unless in proportion to the census or enumeration herein before directed to be taken.

No tax or duty shall be laid on articles exported from any State.

No preference shall be given by any regulation of commerce or revenue to the ports of one State over those of another; nor shall vessels bound to, or from, one State be obliged to enter, clear, or pay duties in another.

No money shall be drawn from the treasury, but in consequence of appropriations made by law; and a regular statement and account of the receipts and expenditures of all public money shall be published from time to time.

No title of nobility shall be granted by the United States: and no person holding any office of profit or trust under them, shall, without the consent of the Congress, accept of any present, emolument, office, or title, of any kind whatever, from any king, prince, or foreign state.

Section 10 No State shall enter into any treaty, alliance, or confederation; grant letters of marque and reprisal; coin money; emit bills of credit; make anything but gold and silver coin a tender in payment of debts; pass any bill of attainder, ex post facto law, or law impairing the obligation of contracts, or grant any title of nobility.

No State shall, without the consent of Congress, lay any imposts or duties on imports or exports, except what may be absolutely necessary for executing its inspection laws: and the net produce of all duties and imposts, laid by any State on imports or exports, shall be for the use of the treasury of the United States; and all such laws shall be subject to the revision and control of the Congress.

No State shall, without the consent of Congress, lay any duty of tonnage, keep troops, or ships of war in time of peace, enter into any agreement or compact with another State, or with a foreign power, or engage in war, unless actually invaded, or in such imminent danger as will not admit of delay.

Article II

Section 1 The executive power shall be vested in a President of the United States of America. He shall hold his office during the term of four years, and, together with the Vice-President, chosen for the same term, be elected as follows:

Each State shall appoint, in such manner as the legislature thereof may direct, a number of electors, equal to the whole number of Senators and Representatives to which the State may be entitled in the Congress; but no Senator or Representative, or person holding an office of trust or profit under the United States, shall be appointed an elector.

The electors shall meet in their respective States, and vote by ballot for two persons, of whom one at least shall not be an inhabitant of the same State with themselves. And they shall make a list of all the persons voted for, and of the number of votes for each; which list they shall sign and certify, and transmit sealed to the seat of government of the United States, directed to the President of the Senate. The President of the Senate shall, in the presence of the Senate and House of Representatives, open all the certificates, and the votes shall then be counted. The person having the greatest number of votes shall be the President, if such number be a majority of the whole number of electors appointed; and if there be more than one who have such majority, and have an equal number of votes, then the House of Representatives shall immediately choose by ballot one of them for President; and if no person have a majority, then from the five highest on the list said house shall in like manner choose the President. But in choosing the President the votes shall be taken by States, the representation from each State having one vote; a quorum for this purpose shall consist of a member or members from two-thirds of the States, and a majority of all the States shall be necessary to a choice. In every case, after the choice of the President, the person having the greatest number of votes of the electors shall be the Vice-President. But if there should remain two or more who have equal votes, the Senate shall choose from them by ballot the Vice-President.

The Congress may determine the time of choosing the electors, and the day on which they shall give their votes; which day shall be the same throughout the United States.

No person except a natural-born citizen, *or a citizen of the United States at the time of the adoption of this Constitution,* shall be eligible to the office of President; neither shall any person be eligible to that office who shall not have attained to the age of thirty-five years, and been fourteen years a resident within the United States.

In cases of the removal of the President from office or of his death, resignation, or inability to discharge the powers and duties of the said office, the same shall devolve on the Vice-President, and the Congress may by law provide for the case of removal, death, resignation, or inability, both of the President and Vice-President, declaring what officer shall then act as President, and such officer shall act accordingly, until the disability be removed, or a President shall be elected.

The President shall, at stated times, receive for his services a compensation, which shall neither be increased nor diminished during the period for which he shall have been elected, and he shall not receive within that period any other emolument from the United States, or any of them.

Before he enter on the execution of his office, he shall take the following oath or affirmation:—"I do solemnly swear (or affirm) that I will faithfully execute the office of the President of the United States, and will to the best of my ability preserve, protect and defend the Constitution of the United States."

Section 2 The President shall be commander in chief of the army and navy of the United States, and of the militia of the several States, when called into the actual service of the United States; he may require the opinion, in writing, of the principal officer in each of the executive departments, upon any subject relating to the duties of their respective offices, and he shall have power to grant reprieves and pardons for offences against the United States, except in cases of impeachment.

He shall have power, by and with the advice and consent of the Senate, to make treaties, provided two-thirds of the Senators present concur; and he shall nominate, and by and with the advice and consent of the Senate, shall appoint ambassadors, other public ministers and consuls, judges of the Supreme Court, and all other officers of the United States, whose appointments are not herein otherwise provided for, and which shall be established by law: but Congress may by law vest the appointment of such inferior officers, as they think proper, in the President alone, in the courts of law, or in the heads of departments.

The President shall have power to fill up all vacancies that may happen during the recess of the Senate, by granting commissions which shall expire at the end of their next session.

Section 3 He shall from time to time give to the Congress information of the state of the Union, and recommend to their consideration such measures as he shall judge necessary and expedient; he may, on extraordinary occasions, convene both houses, or either of them, and in case of disagreement between them, with respect to the time of adjournment, he may adjourn them to such time as he shall think proper; he shall receive ambassadors and other public ministers; he shall take care that the laws be faithfully executed, and shall commission all the officers of the United States.

Section 4 The President, Vice-President and all civil officers of the United States shall be removed from office on impeachment for, and on conviction of, treason, bribery, or other high crimes and misdemeanors.

Article III

Section 1 The judicial power of the United States shall be vested in one Supreme Court, and in such inferior courts as the Congress may from time to time ordain and establish. The judges, both of the Supreme and inferior courts, shall

hold their offices during good behavior, and shall, at stated times, receive for their services a compensation which shall not be diminished during their continuance in office.

Section 2 The judicial power shall extend to all cases, in law and equity, arising under this Constitution, the laws of the United States, and treaties made, or which shall be made, under their authority;—to all cases affecting ambassadors, other public ministers and consuls;—to all cases of admiralty and maritime jurisdiction;—to controversies to which the United States shall be a party;—to controversies between two or more States;—*between a State and citizens of another State*;—between citizens of different States;— between citizens of the same State claiming lands under grants of different States, and between a State, or the citizens thereof, and foreign states, citizens or subjects.

In all cases affecting ambassadors, other public ministers and consuls, and those in which a State shall be party, the Supreme Court shall have original jurisdiction. In all the other cases before mentioned, the Supreme Court shall have appellate jurisdiction, both as to law and fact, with such exceptions, and under such regulations, as the Congress shall make.

The trial of all crimes, except in cases of impeachment, shall be by jury; and such trial shall be held in the State where said crimes shall have been committed; but when not committed within any State, the trial shall be at such place or places as the Congress may by Law have directed.

Section 3 Treason against the United States shall consist only in levying war against them, or in adhering to their enemies, giving them aid and comfort. No person shall be convicted of treason unless on the testimony of two witnesses to the same overt act, or on confession in open court.

The Congress shall have power to declare the punishment of treason, but no attainder of treason shall work corruption of blood, or forfeiture except during the life of the person attainted.

Article IV

Section 1 Full faith and credit shall be given in each State to the public acts, records, and judicial proceedings of every other State. And the Congress may by general laws prescribe the manner in which such acts, records, and proceedings shall be proved, and the effect thereof.

Section 2 The citizens of each State shall be entitled to all privileges and immunities of citizens in the several States.

A person charged in any State with treason, felony, or other crime, who shall flee from justice, and be found in another State, shall on demand of the executive authority of the State from which he fled, be delivered up, to be removed to the State having jurisdiction of the crime.

No Person held to service or labor in one State, under the laws thereof, escaping into another, shall, in consequence of any law or regulation therein, be discharged from such service or labor, but shall be delivered up on claim of the party to whom such service or labor may be due.

Section 3 New States may be admitted by the Congress into this Union; but no new State shall be formed or erected within the jurisdiction of any other State; nor any State be formed by the junction of two or more States, or parts of States, without the consent of the legislatures of the States concerned as well as of the Congress.

The Congress shall have power to dispose of and make all needful rules and regulations respecting the territory or other property belonging to the United States; and nothing in this Constitution shall be so construed as to prejudice any claims of the United States, or of any particular State.

Section 4 The United States shall guarantee to every State in this Union a republican form of government, and shall protect each of them against invasion; and on application of the legislature, or of the executive (when the legislature cannot be convened), against domestic violence.

Article V

The Congress, whenever two-thirds of both houses shall deem it necessary, shall propose amendments to this Constitution, or, on the application of the legislatures of two-thirds of the several States, shall call a convention for proposing amendments, which, in either case, shall be valid to all intents and purposes, as part of this Constitution, when ratified by the legislatures of three-fourths of the several States, or by conventions in three-fourths thereof, as the one or the other mode of ratification may be proposed by the Congress; provided *that no amendments which may be made prior to the year one thousand eight hundred and eight shall in any manner affect the first and fourth clauses in the ninth section* of the first article; and that no State, without its consent, shall be deprived of its equal suffrage in the Senate.

Article VI

All debts contracted and engagements entered into, before the adoption of this Constitution, shall be as valid against the United States under this Constitution, as under the Confederation.

This Constitution, and the laws of the United States which shall be made in pursuance thereof; and all treaties made, or which shall be made, under the authority of the United States, shall be the supreme law of the land; and the judges in every State shall be bound thereby, anything in the Constitution or laws of any State to the contrary notwithstanding.

The Senators and Representatives before mentioned, and the members of the several State legislatures, and all executive and judicial officers, both of the United States and of the several States, shall be bound by oath or affirmation to support this Constitution; but no religious test shall ever be required as a qualification to any office or public trust under the United States.

Article VII

The ratification of the conventions of nine States shall be sufficient for the establishment of this Constitution between the States so ratifying the same.

Done in convention by the unanimous consent of the States present, the seventeenth day of September in the year of our Lord one thousand seven hundred and eighty-seven and of the Independence of the United States of America the twelfth. In witness whereof we have hereunto subscribed our names.

GEORGE WASHINGTON
President and Deputy from Virginia

New Hampshire
John Langdon
Nicholas Gilman

Massachusetts
Nathaniel Gorham
Rufus King

Connecticut
William Samuel Johnson
Roger Sherman

New York
Alexander Hamilton

New Jersey
William Livingston
David Brearley

William Paterson
Jonathan Dayton

Pennsylvania
Benjamin Franklin
Thomas Mifflin
Robert Morris
George Clymer
Thomas FitzSimons
Jared Ingersoll
James Wilson
Gouverneur Morris

Delaware
George Read
Gunning Bedford, Jr.
John Dickinson

Richard Bassett
Jacob Broom

Maryland
James McHenry
Daniel of St. Thomas Jenifer
Daniel Carroll

Virginia
John Blair
James Madison, Jr.

North Carolina
William Blount
Richard Dobbs Spaight
Hugh Williamson

South Carolina
John Rutledge
Charles Cotesworth Pinckney
Charles Pinckney
Pierce Butler

Georgia
William Few
Abraham Baldwin

AMENDMENTS TO THE CONSTITUTION WITH ANNOTATIONS
(including the six unratified amendments)

▶ *IN THEIR EFFORT TO GAIN Antifederalists' support for the Constitution, Federalists frequently pointed to the inclusion of Article 5, which provides an orderly method of amending the Constitution. In contrast, the Articles of Confederation, which were universally recognized as seriously flawed, offered no means of amendment. For their part, Antifederalists argued that the amendment process was so "intricate" that one might as easily roll "sixes an hundred times in succession" as change the Constitution.*

The system for amendment laid out in the Constitution requires that two-thirds of both houses of Congress agree to a proposed amendment, which must then be ratified by three-quarters of the legislatures of the states. Alternatively, an amendment may be proposed by a convention called by the legislatures of two-thirds of the states. Since 1789, members of Congress have proposed thousands of amendments. Besides the seventeen amendments added since 1789, only the six "unratified" ones included here were approved by two-thirds of both houses and sent to the states for ratification.

Among the many amendments that never made it out of Congress have been proposals to declare dueling, divorce, and interracial marriage unconstitutional as well as proposals to establish a national university, to acknowledge the sovereignty of Jesus Christ, and to prohibit any person from possessing wealth in excess of $10 million.*

Among the issues facing Americans today that might lead to constitutional amendment are efforts to balance the federal budget, to limit the number of terms elected officials may serve, to limit access to or prohibit abortion, to establish English as the official language of the United States, and to prohibit flag burning. None of these proposed amendments has yet garnered enough support in Congress to be sent to the states for ratification.

Although the first ten amendments to the Constitution are commonly known as the Bill of Rights, only Amendments 1–8 actually provide guarantees of individual rights. Amendments 9 and 10 deal with the structure of power within the constitutional system. The Bill of Rights was promised to appease Antifederalists who refused to ratify the Constitution without guarantees of individual liberties and limitations to federal power. After studying more than two hundred amendments recommended by the ratifying conventions of the states, Federalist James Madison presented a list of seventeen to Congress, which used Madison's list as the foundation for the twelve amendments that were sent to the states for ratification. Ten of the twelve were adopted in 1791. The first on the list of twelve, known as the Reapportionment Amendment, was never adopted (see page A-11). The second proposed amendment was adopted in 1992 as Amendment 27 (see page A-19).

---

*Richard B. Bernstein, *Amending America* (New York: Times Books, 1993), *177–81.*

Amendment I

Congress shall make no law respecting an establishment of religion, or prohibiting the free exercise thereof; or abridging the freedom of speech, or of the press; or the right of the people peaceably to assemble, and to petition the government for a redress of grievances.

◆◆◆

▶ *The First Amendment is a potent symbol for many Americans. Most are well aware of their rights to free speech, freedom of the press, and freedom of religion and their rights to assemble and to petition, even if they cannot cite the exact words of this amendment.*

The First Amendment guarantee of freedom of religion has two clauses: the "free exercise clause," which allows individuals to practice or not practice any religion, and the "establishment clause," which prevents the federal government from discriminating against or favoring any particular religion. This clause was designed to create what Thomas Jefferson referred to as "a wall of separation between church and state." In the 1960s, the Supreme Court ruled that the First Amendment prohibits prayer (see Engel v. Vitale, *online) and Bible reading in public schools.*

Although the rights to free speech and freedom of the press are established in the First Amendment, it was not until the twentieth century that the Supreme Court began to explore the full meaning of these guarantees. In 1919, the Court ruled in Schenck v. United States *(online) that the government could suppress free expression only where it could cite a "clear and present danger." In a decision that continues to raise controversies, the Court ruled in 1990, in* Texas v. Johnson, *that flag burning is a form of symbolic speech protected by the First Amendment.*

Amendment II

A well-regulated militia being necessary to the security of a free State, the right of the people to keep and bear arms shall not be infringed.

◆◆◆

▶ *Fear of a standing army under the control of a hostile government made the Second Amendment an important part of the Bill of Rights. Advocates of gun ownership claim that the amendment prevents the government from regulating firearms. Proponents of gun control argue that the amendment is designed only to protect the right of the states to maintain militia units.*

In 1939, the Supreme Court ruled in United States v. Miller *that the Second Amendment did not protect the right of an individual to own a sawed-off shotgun, which it argued was not ordinary militia equipment.*

Since then, the Supreme Court has refused to hear Second Amendment cases, while lower courts have upheld firearms regulations. Several justices currently on the bench seem to favor a narrow interpretation of the Second Amendment, which would allow gun control legislation. The controversy over the impact of the Second Amendment on gun owners and gun control legislation will certainly continue.

Amendment III

No soldier shall, in time of peace, be quartered in any house without the consent of the owner, nor in time of war, but in a manner to be prescribed by law.

◆ ◆ ◆

▶ *The Third Amendment was extremely important to the framers of the Constitution, but today it is nearly forgotten. American colonists were especially outraged that they were forced to quarter British troops in the years before and during the American Revolution. The philosophy of the Third Amendment has been viewed by some justices and scholars as the foundation of the modern constitutional right to privacy. One example of this can be found in Justice William O. Douglas's opinion in* Griswold v. Connecticut *(online).*

Amendment IV

The right of the people to be secure in their persons, houses, papers, and effects, against unreasonable searches and seizures, shall not be violated, and no warrants shall issue but upon probable cause, supported by oath or affirmation, and particularly describing the place to be searched, and the persons or things to be seized.

◆ ◆ ◆

▶ *In the years before the Revolution, the houses, barns, stores, and warehouses of American colonists were ransacked by British authorities under "writs of assistance," or general warrants. The British, thus empowered, searched for seditious material or smuggled goods that could then be used as evidence against colonists who were charged with a crime only after the items were found. The first part of the Fourth Amendment protects citizens from "unreasonable" searches and seizures.*

The Supreme Court has interpreted this protection as well as the words search *and* seizure *in different ways at different times. At one time, the Court did not recognize electronic eavesdropping as a form of search and seizure, though it does today. At times, an "unreasonable" search has been almost any search carried out without a warrant, but in the two decades before 1969, the Court sometimes sanctioned warrantless searches that it considered reasonable based on "the total atmosphere of the case."*

The second part of the Fourth Amendment defines the procedure for issuing a search warrant and states the requirement of "probable cause," which is generally viewed as evidence indicating that a suspect has committed an offense.

The Fourth Amendment has been controversial because the Court has sometimes excluded evidence that has been seized in violation of constitutional standards. The justification is that excluding such evidence deters violations of the amendment, but doing so may allow a guilty person to escape punishment.

Amendment V

No person shall be held to answer for a capital, or otherwise infamous crime, unless on a presentment or indictment of a grand jury, except in cases arising in the land or naval forces, or in the militia, when in actual service in time of war or public danger; nor shall any person be subject for the same offence to be twice put in jeopardy of life or limb; nor shall be compelled in any criminal case to be a witness against himself, nor be deprived of life, liberty, or property, without due process of law; nor shall private property be taken for public use without just compensation.

◆ ◆ ◆

▶ *The Fifth Amendment protects people against government authority in the prosecution of criminal offenses. It prohibits the state, first, from charging a person with a serious crime without a grand jury hearing to decide whether there is sufficient evidence to support the charge and, second, from charging a person with the same crime twice. The best-known aspect of the Fifth Amendment is that it prevents a person from being "compelled . . . to be a witness against himself." The last clause, the "takings clause," limits the power of the government to seize property.*

Although invoking the Fifth Amendment is popularly viewed as a confession of guilt, a person may be innocent yet still fear prosecution. For example, during the Red-baiting era of the late 1940s and 1950s, many people who had participated in legal activities that were associated with the Communist Party claimed the Fifth Amendment privilege rather than testify before the House Un-American Activities Committee because the mood of the times cast those activities in a negative light. Since "taking the Fifth" was viewed as an admission of guilt, those people often lost their jobs or became unemployable. (See chapter 26.) Nonetheless, the right to protect oneself against self-incrimination plays an important role in guarding against the collective power of the state.

Amendment VI

In all criminal prosecutions, the accused shall enjoy the right to a speedy and public trial, by an impartial jury of the State and district wherein the crime shall have been committed, which district shall have been previously ascertained by law, and to be informed of the nature and cause of the accusation; to be confronted with the witnesses against him; to have compulsory process for obtaining witnesses in his favor, and to have the assistance of counsel for his defence.

◆ ◆ ◆

▶ *The original Constitution put few limits on the government's power to investigate, prosecute, and punish crime. This process was of great concern to the early Americans, however, and of the twenty-eight rights specified in the first eight amendments, fifteen have to do with it. Seven rights are specified in the Sixth Amendment. These include the right to a speedy trial, a public trial, a jury trial, a notice of accusation, confrontation by opposing witnesses, testimony by favorable witnesses, and the assistance of counsel.*

Although this amendment originally guaranteed these rights only in cases involving the federal government, the adoption of the Fourteenth Amendment began a process of applying the protections of the Bill of Rights to the states through court cases such as Gideon v. Wainwright *(online).*

Amendment VII

In suits at common law, where the value in controversy shall exceed twenty dollars, the right of trial by jury shall be preserved, and no fact tried by a jury shall be otherwise reexamined in any court of the United States, than according to the rules of the common law.

◆ ◆ ◆

▶ *This amendment guarantees people the same right to a trial by jury as was guaranteed by English common law in 1791. Under common law, in civil trials (those involving money damages) the role of the judge was to settle questions of law and that of the jury was to settle questions of fact. The amendment does not specify the size of the jury or its role in a trial, however. The Supreme Court has generally held that those issues be determined by English common law of 1791, which stated that a jury consists of twelve people, that a trial must be conducted before a judge who instructs the jury on the law and advises it on facts, and that a verdict must be unanimous.*

Amendment VIII

Excessive bail shall not be required, nor excessive fines imposed, nor cruel and unusual punishments inflicted.

◆ ◆ ◆

▶ *The language used to guarantee the three rights in this amendment was inspired by the English Bill of Rights of 1689. The Supreme Court has not had a lot to say about "excessive fines." In recent years it has agreed that, despite the provision against "excessive bail," persons who are believed to be dangerous to others can be held without bail even before they have been convicted.*

Although opponents of the death penalty have not succeeded in using the Eighth Amendment to achieve the end of capital punishment, the clause regarding "cruel and unusual punishments" has been used to prohibit capital punishment in certain cases (see Furman v. Georgia, *online) and to require improved conditions in prisons.*

Amendment IX

The enumeration in the Constitution, of certain rights, shall not be construed to deny or disparage others retained by the people.

◆ ◆ ◆

▶ *Some Federalists feared that inclusion of the Bill of Rights in the Constitution would allow later generations of interpreters to claim that the people had surrendered any rights not specifically enumerated there. To guard against this, Madison added language that became the Ninth Amendment. Interest in this heretofore largely ignored amendment revived in 1965 when it was used in a concurring opinion in* Griswold v. Connecticut *(online). While Justice William O. Douglas called on the Third Amendment to support the right to privacy in deciding that case, Justice Arthur Goldberg, in the concurring opinion, argued that the right to privacy regarding contraception was an unenumerated right that was protected by the Ninth Amendment.*

In 1980, the Court ruled that the right of the press to attend a public trial was protected by the Ninth Amendment. While some scholars argue that modern judges cannot identify the unenumerated rights that the framers were trying to protect, others argue that the Ninth Amendment should be read as providing a constitutional "presumption of liberty" that allows people to act in any way that does not violate the rights of others.

Amendment X

The powers not delegated to the United States by the Constitution, nor prohibited by it to the States, are reserved to the States respectively, or to the people.

◆ ◆ ◆

▶ *The Antifederalists were especially eager to see a "reserved powers clause" explicitly guaranteeing the states control over their internal affairs. Not surprisingly, the Tenth Amendment has been a frequent battleground in the struggle over states' rights and federal supremacy. Prior to the Civil War, the Democratic Republican Party and Jacksonian Democrats invoked the Tenth Amendment to prohibit the federal government from making decisions about whether people in individual states could own slaves. The Tenth Amendment was virtually suspended during Reconstruction following the Civil War. In 1883, however, the Supreme Court declared the Civil Rights Act of 1875 unconstitutional on the grounds that it violated the Tenth Amendment. Business interests also called on the amendment to block efforts at federal regulation.*

The Court was inconsistent over the next several decades as it attempted to resolve the tension between the restrictions of the Tenth Amendment and the powers the Constitution granted to Congress to regulate interstate commerce and levy taxes. The Court upheld the Pure Food and Drug Act (1906), the Meat Inspection Acts (1906 and 1907), and the White Slave Traffic Act (1910), all of which affected the states, but struck down an act prohibiting interstate shipment of goods produced through child labor. Between 1934 and 1935, a number of New Deal programs created by Franklin D. Roosevelt were declared unconstitutional on the grounds that they violated the Tenth Amendment. (See chapter 24.) As Roosevelt appointees changed the composition of the Court, the Tenth Amendment was declared to have no substantive meaning. Generally, the amendment is held to protect the rights of states to regulate internal matters such as local government, education, commerce, labor, and business, as well as matters involving families such as marriage, divorce, and inheritance within the state.

Unratified Amendment

Reapportionment Amendment (proposed by Congress September 25, 1789, along with the Bill of Rights)
After the first enumeration required by the first article of the Constitution, there shall be one Representative for every thirty thousand, until the number shall amount to one hundred, after which the proportion shall be so regulated by Congress, that there shall be not less than one hundred Representatives, nor less than one Representative for every forty thousand persons, until the number of Representatives shall amount to two hundred; after which the proportion shall be so regulated by Congress, that there shall not be less than two hundred Representatives, nor more than one Representative for every fifty thousand persons.

◆ ◆ ◆

▶ *If the Reapportionment Amendment had passed and remained in effect, the House of Representatives today would have more than 5,000 members rather than 435.*

Amendment XI

[Adopted 1798]
The judicial power of the United States shall not be construed to extend to any suit in law or equity, commenced or prosecuted against one of the United States by citizens of another State, or by citizens or subjects of any foreign state.

◆ ◆ ◆

▶ *In 1793, the Supreme Court ruled in favor of Alexander Chisholm, executor of the estate of a deceased South Carolina merchant. Chisholm was suing the state of Georgia because the merchant had never been paid for provisions he had supplied during the Revolution. Many regarded this Court decision as an error that violated the intent of the Constitution.*

Antifederalists had long feared a federal court system with the power to overrule a state court.

When the Constitution was being drafted, Federalists had assured worried Antifederalists that section 2 of Article 3, which allows federal courts to hear cases "between a State and citizens of another State," did not mean that the federal courts were authorized to hear suits against a state by citizens of another state or a foreign country. Antifederalists and many other Americans feared a powerful federal court system because they worried that it would become like the British courts of this period, which were accountable only to the monarch. Furthermore, Chisholm v. Georgia *prompted a series of suits against state governments by creditors and suppliers who had made loans during the war.*

In addition, state legislators and Congress feared that the shaky economies of the new states, as well as the country as a whole, would be destroyed, especially if loyalists who had fled to other countries sought reimbursement for land and property that had been seized. The day after the Supreme Court announced its decision, a resolution proposing the Eleventh Amendment, which overturned the decision in Chisholm v. Georgia, *was introduced in the U.S. Senate.*

Amendment XII

[Adopted 1804]
The electors shall meet in their respective States, and vote by ballot for President and Vice-President, one of whom, at least, shall not be an inhabitant of the same State with themselves; they shall name in their ballots the person voted for as President, and in distinct ballots the person voted for as Vice-President, and they shall make distinct lists of all persons voted for as President, and of all persons voted for as Vice-President, and of the number of votes for each, which lists they shall sign and certify, and transmit sealed to the seat of government of the United States, directed to the President of the Senate;—the President of the Senate shall, in the presence of the Senate and House of Representatives, open all the certificates and the votes shall then be counted;—the person having the greatest number of votes for President shall be the President, if such number be a majority of the whole number of electors appointed; and if no person have such majority, then from the persons having the highest numbers not exceeding three on the list of those voted for as President, the House of Representatives shall choose immediately, by ballot, the President. But in choosing the President, the votes shall be taken by States, the representation from each State having one vote; a quorum for this purpose shall consist of a member or members from two-thirds of the States, and a majority of all the States shall be necessary to a choice. And if the House of Representatives shall not choose a President whenever the right of choice shall devolve upon them, before the fourth day of March next following, then the Vice-President shall act as President, as in the case of the death or other constitutional disability of the President.

The person having the greatest number of votes as Vice-President shall be the Vice-President, if such number be a majority of the whole number of electors appointed; and if no person have a majority, then from the two highest numbers on the list the Senate shall choose the Vice-President; a quorum for the purpose shall consist of two-thirds of the whole number of Senators, and a majority of the whole number shall be necessary to a choice. But no person constitutionally ineligible to the office of President shall be eligible to that of Vice-President of the United States.

◆ ◆ ◆

▶ The framers of the Constitution disliked political parties and assumed that none would ever form. Under the original system, electors chosen by the states would each vote for two candidates. The candidate who won the most votes would become president, while the person who won the second-highest number of votes would become vice president. Rivalries between Federalists and Antifederalists led to the formation of political parties, however, even before George Washington had left office. Though Washington was elected unanimously in 1789 and 1792, the elections of 1796 and 1800 were procedural disasters because of party maneuvering (see chapters 9 and 10). In 1796, Federalist John Adams was chosen as president, and his great rival, the Antifederalist Thomas Jefferson (whose party was called the Republican Party), became his vice president. In 1800, all the electors cast their two votes as one of two party blocs. Jefferson and his fellow Republican nominee, Aaron Burr, were tied with 73 votes each. The contest went to the House of Representatives, which finally elected Jefferson after 36 ballots. The Twelfth Amendment prevents these problems by requiring electors to vote separately for the president and vice president.

Unratified Amendment

Titles of Nobility Amendment (proposed by Congress May 1, 1810)

If any citizen of the United States shall accept, claim, receive or retain any title of nobility or honor or shall, without the consent of Congress, accept and retain any present, pension, office or emolument of any kind whatever, from any emperor, king, prince or foreign power, such person shall cease to be a citizen of the United States, and shall be incapable of holding any office of trust or profit under them or either of them.

♦♦♦

▶ This amendment would have extended Article 1, section 9, clause 8 of the Constitution, which prevents the awarding of titles by the United States and the acceptance of such awards from foreign powers without congressional consent. Historians speculate that general nervousness about the power of the emperor Napoleon, who was at that time extending France's empire throughout Europe, may have prompted the proposal. Though it fell one vote short of ratification, Congress and the American people thought the proposal had been ratified, and it was included in many nineteenth-century editions of the Constitution.

The Civil War and Reconstruction Amendments (Thirteenth, Fourteenth, and Fifteenth Amendments)

▶ In the four months between the election of Abraham Lincoln and his inauguration, more than 200 proposed constitutional amendments were presented to Congress as part of a desperate attempt to hold the rapidly dissolving Union together. Most of these were efforts to appease the southern states by protecting the right to own slaves or by disfranchising African Americans through constitutional amendment. None were able to win the votes required from Congress to send them to the states. The relatively innocuous Corwin Amendment seemed to be the only hope for preserving the Union by amending the Constitution.

The northern victors in the Civil War tried to restructure the Constitution just as the war had restructured the nation. Yet they were often divided in their goals. Some wanted to end slavery; others hoped for social and economic equality regardless of race; others hoped that extending the power of the ballot box to former slaves would help create a new political order. The debates over the Thirteenth, Fourteenth, and Fifteenth Amendments were bitter. Few of those who fought for these changes were satisfied with the amendments themselves; fewer still were satisfied with their interpretation. Although the amendments put an end to the legal status of slavery, it took nearly a hundred years after the amendments' passage before most of the descendants of former slaves could begin to experience the economic, social, and political equality the amendments had been intended to provide.

Unratified Amendment

Corwin Amendment (proposed by Congress March 2, 1861)

No amendment shall be made to the Constitution which will authorize or give to Congress the power to abolish or interfere, within any State, with the domestic institutions thereof, including that of persons held to labor or service by the laws of said State.

♦♦♦

▶ Following the election of Abraham Lincoln, Congress scrambled to try to prevent the secession of the slaveholding states. House member Thomas Corwin of Ohio proposed the "unamendable" amendment in the hope that by protecting slavery where it existed, Congress would keep the southern states in the Union. Lincoln indicated his support for the proposed amendment in his first inaugural address. Only Ohio and Maryland ratified the Corwin Amendment before it was forgotten.

Amendment XIII

[Adopted 1865]

Section 1 Neither slavery nor involuntary servitude, except as a punishment for crime whereof the party shall have been duly convicted, shall exist within the United States, or any place subject to their jurisdiction.

Section 2 Congress shall have power to enforce this article by appropriate legislation.

♦♦♦

▶ Although President Lincoln had abolished slavery in the Confederacy with the Emancipation Proclamation of 1863, abolitionists wanted to rid the entire country of slavery. The Thirteenth Amendment did this in a clear and straightforward manner. In February 1865, when the proposal was approved by the House, the gallery of the House was newly opened to black Americans who had a chance at last to see their government at work. Passage of the proposal was greeted by wild cheers from the gallery as well as tears on the House floor, where congressional representatives openly embraced one another.

The problem of ratification remained, however. The Union position was that the Confederate states were part of the country of thirty-six states. Therefore, twenty-seven states were needed to ratify the amendment. When Kentucky and Delaware rejected it, backers realized that without approval from at least four former Confederate states, the amendment would fail. Lincoln's successor, President Andrew Johnson, made ratification of the Thirteenth Amendment a condition for southern states to rejoin the Union. Under those terms, all the former Confederate states except Mississippi accepted the Thirteenth Amendment, and by the end of 1865 the amendment had become part of the Constitution and slavery had been prohibited in the United States.

Amendment XIV

[Adopted 1868]

Section 1 All persons born or naturalized in the United States, and subject to the jurisdiction thereof, are citizens of the United States and of the State wherein they reside. No State shall make or enforce any law which shall abridge the privileges or immunities of citizens of the United States; nor shall any State deprive any person of life, liberty, or property, without due process of law; nor deny to any person within its jurisdiction the equal protection of the laws.

Section 2 Representatives shall be appointed among the several States according to their respective numbers, counting the whole number of persons in each State, excluding Indians not taxed. But when the right to vote at any election for the choice of Electors for President and Vice-President of the United States, Representatives in Congress, the executive and judicial officers of a State, or the members of the legislature thereof, is denied to any of the male inhabitants of such State, being twenty-one years of age and citizens of the United States, or in any way abridged, except for participation in rebellion, or other crime, the basis of representation therein shall be reduced in the proportion which the number of such male citizens shall bear to the whole number of male citizens twenty-one years of age in such State.

Section 3 No person shall be a Senator or Representative in Congress, or Elector of President and Vice-President, or hold any office, civil or military, under the United States, or under any State, who, having previously taken an oath, as a member of Congress, or as an officer of the United States, or as a member of any State legislature, or as an executive or judicial officer of any State, to support the Constitution of the United States, shall have engaged in insurrection or rebellion against the same, or given aid or comfort to the enemies thereof. Congress may, by a vote of two-thirds of each house, remove such disability.

Section 4 The validity of the public debt of the United States, authorized by law, including debts incurred for payment of pensions and bounties for services in suppressing insurrection or rebellion, shall not be questioned. But neither the United States nor any State shall assume or pay any debt or obligation incurred in aid of insurrection or rebellion against the United States, or any claim for the loss or emancipation of any slave; but all such debts, obligations, and claims shall be held illegal and void.

Section 5 The Congress shall have power to enforce, by appropriate legislation, the provisions of this article.

◆ ◆ ◆

► *Without Lincoln's leadership in the reconstruction of the nation following the Civil War, it soon became clear that the Thirteenth Amendment needed additional constitutional support. Less than a year after Lincoln's assassination, Andrew Johnson was ready to bring the former Confederate states back into the Union with few changes in their governments or politics. Anxious Republicans drafted the Fourteenth Amendment to prevent that from happening. The most important provisions of this complex amendment made all native-born or naturalized persons American citizens and prohibited states from abridging the "privileges or immunities" of citizens; depriving them of "life, liberty, or property, without due process of law"; and denying them "equal protection of the laws." In essence, it made all ex-slaves citizens and protected the rights of all citizens against violation by their own state governments.*

As occurred in the case of the Thirteenth Amendment, former Confederate states were forced to ratify the amendment as a condition of representation in the House and the Senate. The intentions of the Fourteenth Amendment, and how those intentions should be enforced, have been the most debated point of constitutional history. The terms due process and equal protection have been especially troublesome. Was the amendment designed to outlaw racial segregation? Or was the goal simply to prevent the leaders of the rebellious South from gaining political power?

The framers of the Fourteenth Amendment hoped Article 2 would produce black voters who would increase the power of the Republican Party. The federal government, however, never used its power to punish states for denying blacks their right to vote. Although the Fourteenth Amendment had an immediate impact in giving black Americans citizenship, it did nothing to protect blacks from the vengeance of whites once Reconstruction ended. In the late nineteenth and early twentieth centuries, section 1 of the Fourteenth Amendment was often used to protect business interests and strike down laws protecting workers on the grounds that the rights of "persons," that is, corporations, were protected by "due process." More recently, the Fourteenth Amendment has been used to justify school desegregation and affirmative action programs, as well as to dismantle such programs.

Amendment XV

[Adopted 1870]

Section 1 The right of citizens of the United States to vote shall not be denied or abridged by the United States or by any State on account of race, color, or previous condition of servitude.

Section 2 The Congress shall have power to enforce this article by appropriate legislation.

♦ ♦ ♦

▶ The Fifteenth Amendment was the last major piece of Reconstruction legislation. While earlier Reconstruction acts had already required black suffrage in the South, the Fifteenth Amendment extended black voting rights to the entire nation. Some Republicans felt morally obligated to do away with the double standard between North and South since many northern states had stubbornly refused to enfranchise blacks. Others believed that the freedman's ballot required the extra protection of a constitutional amendment to shield it from white counterattack. But partisan advantage also played an important role in the amendment's passage, since Republicans hoped that by giving the ballot to northern blacks, they could lessen their political vulnerability.

Many women's rights advocates had fought for the amendment. They had felt betrayed by the inclusion of the word "male" in section 2 of the Fourteenth Amendment and were further angered when the proposed Fifteenth Amendment failed to prohibit denial of the right to vote on the grounds of sex as well as "race, color, or previous condition of servitude." In this amendment, for the first time, the federal government claimed the power to regulate the franchise, or vote. It was also the first time the Constitution placed limits on the power of the states to regulate access to the franchise. Although ratified in 1870, the amendment was not enforced until the twentieth century.

The Progressive Amendments (Sixteenth–Nineteenth Amendments)

▶ No amendments were added to the Constitution between the Civil War and the Progressive Era. America was changing, however, in fundamental ways. The rapid industrialization of the United States after the Civil War led to many social and economic problems. Hundreds of amendments were proposed, but none received enough support in Congress to be sent to the states. Some scholars believe that regional differences and rivalries were so strong during this period that it was almost impossible to gain a consensus on a constitutional amendment. During the Progressive Era, however, the Constitution was amended four times in seven years.

Amendment XVI

[Adopted 1913]

The Congress shall have power to lay and collect taxes on incomes, from whatever source derived, without apportionment among the several States, and without regard to any census or enumeration.

♦ ♦ ♦

▶ Until passage of the Sixteenth Amendment, most of the money used to run the federal government came from customs duties and taxes on specific items, such as liquor. During the Civil War, the federal government taxed incomes as an emergency measure. Pressure to enact an income tax came from those who were concerned about the growing gap between rich and poor in the United States. The Populist Party began campaigning for a graduated income tax in 1892, and support continued to grow. By 1909, thirty-three proposed income tax amendments had been presented in Congress, but lobbying by corporate and other special interests had defeated them all. In June 1909, the growing pressure for an income tax, which had been endorsed by Presidents Roosevelt and Taft, finally pushed an amendment through the Senate. The required thirty-six states had ratified the amendment by February 1913.

Amendment XVII

[Adopted 1913]

Section 1 The Senate of the United States shall be composed of two Senators from each State, elected by the people thereof, for six years; and each Senator shall have one vote. The electors in each State shall have the qualifications requisite for electors of [voters for] the most numerous branch of the State legislatures.

Section 2 When vacancies happen in the representation of any State in the Senate, the executive authority of such State shall issue writs of election to fill such vacancies: Provided, that the Legislature of any State may empower the executive thereof to make temporary appointments until the people fill the vacancies by election as the Legislature may direct.

Section 3 This amendment shall not be so construed as to affect the election or term of any Senator chosen before it becomes valid as part of the Constitution.

♦ ♦ ♦

▶ The framers of the Constitution saw the members of the House as the representatives of the people and the members of the Senate as the representatives of the states. Originally senators were to be chosen by the state legislators. According to reform advocates, however, the growth of private industry and transportation conglomerates during the Gilded Age had created a network of corruption in which wealth and power were exchanged for influence and votes in the Senate. For example, Senator Nelson Aldrich, who represented Rhode Island in the late nineteenth and early twentieth centuries, was known as "the senator from Standard Oil" because of his open support of special business interests.

Efforts to amend the Constitution to allow direct election of senators had begun in 1826, but since any proposal had to be approved by the Senate, reform seemed impossible. Progressives tried to gain influence in the Senate by instituting party caucuses and primary elections, which gave citizens the chance to express their choice of a senator who could then be officially elected by the state legislature. By 1910, fourteen of the country's thirty senators received popular votes through a state primary before the state legislature made its selection. Despairing of getting a proposal through the Senate, supporters of a direct election amendment had begun in 1893 to seek a convention of representatives from two-thirds of the states to propose an amendment that could then be ratified. By 1905, thirty-one of forty-five states had endorsed such an amendment. Finally, in 1911, despite extraordinary opposition, a proposed amendment passed the Senate; by 1913, it had been ratified.

Amendment XVIII

[Adopted 1919; repealed 1933 by Amendment XXI]

Section 1 After one year from the ratification of this article the manufacture, sale, or transportation of intoxicating liquors within, the importation thereof into, or the exportation thereof from the United States and all territory subject to the jurisdiction thereof, for beverage purposes, is hereby prohibited.

Section 2 The Congress and the several States shall have concurrent power to enforce this article by appropriate legislation.

Section 3 This article shall be inoperative unless it shall have been ratified as an amendment to the Constitution by the legislatures of the several States, as provided by the Constitution, within seven years from the date of the submission thereof to the States by the Congress.

♦ ♦ ♦

▶ *The Prohibition Party, formed in 1869, began calling for a constitutional amendment to outlaw alcoholic beverages in 1872. A prohibition amendment was first proposed in the Senate in 1876 and was revived eighteen times before 1913. Between 1913 and 1919, another thirty-nine attempts were made to prohibit liquor in the United States through a constitutional amendment. Prohibition became a key element of the progressive agenda as reformers linked alcohol and drunkenness to numerous social problems, including the corruption of immigrant voters. While opponents of such an amendment argued that it was undemocratic, supporters claimed that their efforts had widespread public support. The admission of twelve "dry" western states to the Union in the early twentieth century and the spirit of sacrifice during World War I laid the groundwork for passage and ratification of the Eighteenth Amendment in 1919. Opponents added a time limit to the amendment in the hope that they*

could thus block ratification, but this effort failed. (See also Amendment XXI.)

Amendment XIX

[Adopted 1920]

Section 1 The right of citizens of the United States to vote shall not be denied or abridged by the United States or by any State on account of sex.

Section 2 Congress shall have the power to enforce this article by appropriate legislation.

♦ ♦ ♦

▶ *Advocates of women's rights tried and failed to link woman suffrage to the Fourteenth and Fifteenth Amendments. Nonetheless, the effort for woman suffrage continued. Between 1878 and 1912, at least one and sometimes as many as four proposed amendments were introduced in Congress each year to grant women the right to vote. While over time women won very limited voting rights in some states, at both the state and federal levels opposition to an amendment for woman suffrage remained very strong. President Woodrow Wilson and other officials felt that the federal government should not interfere with the power of the states in this matter. Others worried that granting suffrage to women would encourage ethnic minorities to exercise their own right to vote. And many were concerned that giving women the vote would result in their abandoning traditional gender roles. In 1919, following a protracted and often bitter campaign of protest in which women went on hunger strikes and chained themselves to fences, an amendment was introduced with the backing of President Wilson. It narrowly passed the Senate (after efforts to limit the suffrage to white women failed) and was adopted in 1920 after Tennessee became the thirty-sixth state to ratify it.*

Unratified Amendment

Child Labor Amendment (proposed by Congress June 2, 1924)

Section 1 The Congress shall have power to limit, regulate, and prohibit the labor of persons under eighteen years of age.

Section 2 The power of the several States is unimpaired by this article except that the operation of State laws shall be suspended to the extent necessary to give effect to legislation enacted by Congress.

♦ ♦ ♦

▶ *Throughout the late nineteenth and early twentieth centuries, alarm over the condition of child workers grew. Opponents of child labor argued that children worked in dangerous and unhealthy conditions, that they took jobs from adult workers, that they depressed wages in certain industries, and that states that allowed child labor had an economic advantage over those that* did not. Defenders of child labor claimed that children provided needed income in many families, that working at a young age developed character, and that the effort to prohibit the practice constituted an invasion of family privacy.

In 1916, Congress passed a law that made it illegal to sell goods made by children through interstate commerce. The Supreme Court, however, ruled that the law violated the limits on the power of Congress to regulate interstate commerce. Congress then tried to penalize industries that used child labor by taxing such goods. This measure was also thrown out by the Court. In response, reformers set out to amend the Constitution. The proposed amendment was ratified by twenty-eight states, but by 1925, thirteen states had rejected it. Passage of the Fair Labor Standards Act in 1938, which was upheld by the Supreme Court in 1941, made the amendment irrelevant.

Amendment XX

[Adopted 1933]

Section 1 The terms of the President and Vice-President shall end at noon on the 20th day of January, and the terms of Senators and Representatives at noon on the 3rd day of January, of the years in which such terms would have ended if this article had not been ratified; and the terms of their successors shall then begin.

Section 2 The Congress shall assemble at least once in every year, and such meeting shall begin at noon on the 3rd day of January, unless they shall by law appoint a different day.

Section 3 If, at the time fixed for the beginning of the term of the President, the President-elect shall have died, the Vice-President-elect shall become President. If a President shall not have been chosen before the time fixed for the beginning of his term, or if the President-elect shall have failed to qualify, then the Vice-President-elect shall act as President until a President shall have qualified; and the Congress may by law provide for the case wherein neither a President-elect nor a Vice-President-elect shall have qualified, declaring who shall then act as President, or the manner in which one who is to act shall be selected, and such person shall act accordingly until a President or Vice-President shall have qualified.

Section 4 The Congress may by law provide for the case of the death of any of the persons from whom the House of Representatives may choose a President whenever the right of choice shall have devolved upon them, and for the case of the death of any of the persons from whom the Senate may choose a Vice-President whenever the right of choice shall have devolved upon them.

Section 5 Sections 1 and 2 shall take effect on the 15th day of October following the ratification of this article.

Section 6 This article shall be inoperative unless it shall have been ratified as an amendment to the Constitution by the Legislatures of three-fourths of the several States within seven years from the date of its submission.

♦ ♦ ♦

▶ *Until 1933, presidents took office on March 4. Since elections are held in early November and electoral votes are counted in mid-December, this meant that more than three months passed between the time a new president was elected and when he took office. Moving the inauguration to January shortened the transition period and allowed Congress to begin its term closer to the time of the president's inauguration. Although this seems like a minor change, an amendment was required because the Constitution specifies terms of office. This amendment also deals with questions of succession in the event that a president-elect or vice president-elect dies before assuming office. Section 3 also clarifies a method for resolving a deadlock in the electoral college.*

Amendment XXI

[Adopted 1933]

Section 1 The eighteenth article of amendment to the Constitution of the United States is hereby repealed.

Section 2 The transportation or importation into any State, Territory, or Possession of the United States for delivery or use therein of intoxicating liquors, in violation of the laws thereof, is hereby prohibited.

Section 3 This article shall be inoperative unless it shall have been ratified as an amendment to the Constitution by conventions in the several States, as provided in the Constitution, within seven years from the date of the submission thereof to the States by the Congress.

♦ ♦ ♦

▶ *Widespread violation of the Volstead Act, the law enacted to enforce prohibition, made the United States a nation of lawbreakers. Prohibition caused more problems than it solved by encouraging crime, bribery, and corruption. Further, a coalition of liquor and beer manufacturers, personal liberty advocates, and constitutional scholars joined forces to challenge the amendment. By 1929, thirty proposed repeal amendments had been introduced in Congress, and the Democratic Party made repeal part of its platform in the 1932 presidential campaign. The Twenty-First Amendment was proposed in February 1933 and ratified less than a year later. The failure of the effort to enforce prohibition through a constitutional amendment has often been cited by opponents of subsequent efforts to shape public virtue and private morality.*

Amendment XXII

[Adopted 1951]

Section 1 No person shall be elected to the office of the President more than twice, and no person who has held the office of President, or acted as President, for more than two years of a term to which some other person was elected President shall be elected to the office of President more than once. But this article shall not apply to any person holding the office of President when this Article was proposed by the Congress, and shall not prevent any person who may be holding the office of President, or acting as President, during the term within which this Article becomes operative from holding the office of President or acting as President during the remainder of such term.

Section 2 This article shall be inoperative unless it shall have been ratified as an amendment to the Constitution by the legislatures of three-fourths of the several States within seven years from the date of its submission to the States by the Congress.

◆ ◆ ◆

▶ *George Washington's refusal to seek a third term of office set a precedent that stood until 1912, when former president Theodore Roosevelt sought, without success, another term as an independent candidate. Democrat Franklin Roosevelt was the only president to seek and win a fourth term, though he did so amid great controversy. Roosevelt died in April 1945, a few months after the beginning of his fourth term. In 1946, Republicans won control of the House and the Senate, and early in 1947 a proposal for an amendment to limit future presidents to two four-year terms was offered to the states for ratification. Democratic critics of the Twenty-Second Amendment charged that it was a partisan posthumous jab at Roosevelt.*

Since the Twenty-Second Amendment was adopted, however, the only presidents who might have been able to seek a third term, had it not existed, were Republicans Dwight Eisenhower, Ronald Reagan, and George W. Bush, and Democrat Bill Clinton. Since 1826, Congress has entertained 160 proposed amendments to limit the president to one six-year term. Such amendments have been backed by fifteen presidents, including Gerald Ford and Jimmy Carter.

Amendment XXIII

[Adopted 1961]

Section 1 The District constituting the seat of Government of the United States shall appoint in such manner as the Congress may direct: A number of electors of President and Vice-President equal to the whole number of Senators and Representatives in Congress to which the District would be entitled if it were a State, but in no event more than the least populous State; they shall be in addition to those appointed by the States, but they shall be considered for the purposes of the election of President and Vice-President, to be electors appointed by a State; and they shall meet in the District and perform such duties as provided by the twelfth article of amendment.

Section 2 The Congress shall have the power to enforce this article by appropriate legislation.

◆ ◆ ◆

▶ *When Washington, D.C., was established as a federal district, no one expected that a significant number of people would make it their permanent and primary residence. A proposal to allow citizens of the district to vote in presidential elections was approved by Congress in June 1960 and was ratified on March 29, 1961.*

Amendment XXIV

[Adopted 1964]

Section 1 The right of citizens of the United States to vote in any primary or other election for President or Vice-President, for electors for President or Vice-President, or for Senator or Representative in Congress, shall not be denied or abridged by the United States or any State by reason of failure to pay any poll tax or other tax.

Section 2 The Congress shall have the power to enforce this article by appropriate legislation.

◆ ◆ ◆

▶ *In the colonial and Revolutionary eras, financial independence was seen as necessary to political independence, and the poll tax was used as a requirement for voting. By the twentieth century, however, the poll tax was used mostly to bar poor people, especially southern blacks, from voting. While conservatives complained that the amendment interfered with states' rights, liberals thought that the amendment did not go far enough because it barred the poll tax only in national elections and not in state or local elections. The amendment was ratified in 1964, however, and two years later, the Supreme Court ruled that poll taxes in state and local elections also violated the equal protection clause of the Fourteenth Amendment.*

Amendment XXV

[Adopted 1967]

Section 1 In case of the removal of the President from office or of his death or resignation, the Vice-President shall become President.

Section 2 Whenever there is a vacancy in the office of the Vice-President, the President shall nominate a Vice-President who shall take office upon confirmation by a majority vote of both Houses of Congress.

Section 3 Whenever the President transmits to the President pro tempore of the Senate and the Speaker of the House of Representatives his written declaration that he is unable to discharge the powers and duties of his office, and until he transmits to them a written declaration to the contrary, such powers and duties shall be discharged by the Vice-President as Acting President.

Section 4 Whenever the Vice-President and a majority of either the principal officers of the executive departments or of such other body as Congress may by law provide, transmit to the President pro tempore of the Senate and the Speaker of the House of Representatives their written declaration that the President is unable to discharge the powers and duties of his office, the Vice-President shall immediately assume the powers and duties of the office as Acting President.

Thereafter, when the President transmits to the President pro tempore of the Senate and the Speaker of the House of Representatives his written declaration that no inability exists, he shall resume the powers and duties of his office unless the Vice-President and a majority of either the principal officers of the executive department[s] or of such other body as Congress may by law provide, transmit within four days to the President pro tempore of the Senate and the Speaker of the House of Representatives their written declaration that the President is unable to discharge the powers and duties of his office. Thereupon Congress shall decide the issue, assembling within forty-eight hours for that purpose if not in session. If the Congress, within twenty-one days after receipt of the latter written declaration, or, if Congress is not in session, within twenty-one days after Congress is required to assemble, determines by two-thirds vote of both Houses that the President is unable to discharge the powers and duties of his office, the Vice-President shall continue to discharge the same as Acting President; otherwise, the President shall resume the powers and duties of his office.

◆ ◆ ◆

▶ *The framers of the Constitution established the office of vice president because someone was needed to preside over the Senate. The first president to die in office was William Henry Harrison, in 1841. Vice President John Tyler had himself sworn in as president, setting a precedent that was followed when seven later presidents died in office. The assassination of President James A. Garfield in 1881 posed a new problem, however. After he was shot, the president was incapacitated for two months before he died; he was unable to lead the country, while his vice president, Chester A. Arthur, was unable to assume leadership. Efforts to resolve questions of succession in the event of a presidential disability thus began with the death of Garfield.*

In 1963, the assassination of President John F. Kennedy galvanized Congress to action. Vice President Lyndon Johnson was a chain-smoker with a history of heart trouble. According to the 1947 Presidential Succession Act, the two men who stood in line to succeed him were the seventy-two-year-old Speaker of the House and the eighty-six-year-old president of the Senate. There were serious concerns that any of these men might become incapacitated while serving as chief executive. The first time the Twenty-Fifth Amendment was used, however, was not in the case of presidential death or illness, but during the Watergate crisis. When Vice President Spiro T. Agnew was forced to resign following allegations of bribery and tax violations, President Richard M. Nixon appointed House minority leader Gerald R. Ford vice president. Ford became president following Nixon's resignation eight

months later and named Nelson A. Rockefeller as his vice president. Thus, for more than two years, the two highest offices in the country were held by people who had not been elected to them.

Amendment XXVI

[Adopted 1971]

Section 1 The right of citizens of the United States, who are eighteen years of age or older, to vote shall not be denied or abridged by the United States or by any State on account of age.

Section 2 The Congress shall have power to enforce this article by appropriate legislation.

◆ ◆ ◆

▶ *Efforts to lower the voting age from twenty-one to eighteen began during World War II. Recognizing that those who were old enough to fight a war should have some say in the government policies that involved them in the war, Presidents Eisenhower, Johnson, and Nixon endorsed the idea. In 1970, the combined pressure of the antiwar movement and the demographic pressure of the baby boom generation led to a Voting Rights Act lowering the voting age in federal, state, and local elections.*

In Oregon v. Mitchell (1970), the state of Oregon challenged the right of Congress to determine the age at which people could vote in state or local elections. The Supreme Court agreed with Oregon. Since the Voting Rights Act was ruled unconstitutional, the Constitution had to be amended to allow passage of a law that would lower the voting age. The amendment was ratified in a little more than three months, making it the most rapidly ratified amendment in U.S. history.

Unratified Amendment

Equal Rights Amendment (proposed by Congress March 22, 1972; seven-year deadline for ratification extended to June 30, 1982)

Section 1 Equality of rights under the law shall not be denied or abridged by the United States or by any State on account of sex.

Section 2 The Congress shall have the power to enforce, by appropriate legislation, the provisions of this article.

Section 3 This amendment shall take effect two years after the date of ratification.

◆ ◆ ◆

▶ *In 1923, soon after women had won the right to vote, Alice Paul, a leading activist in the woman suffrage movement, proposed an amendment requiring equal treatment of men and women. Opponents of the proposal argued that such an amendment would invalidate laws that protected women and would make women subject to the military draft. After the 1964 Civil*

Rights Act was adopted, protective workplace legislation was removed anyway.

The renewal of the women's movement, as a byproduct of the civil rights and antiwar movements, led to a revival of the Equal Rights Amendment (ERA) in Congress. Disagreements over language held up congressional passage of the proposed amendment, but on March 22, 1972, the Senate approved the ERA by a vote of 84 to 8, and it was sent to the states. Six states ratified the amendment within two days, and by the middle of 1973 the amendment seemed well on its way to adoption, with thirty of the needed thirty-eight states having ratified it. In the mid-1970s, however, a powerful "Stop ERA" campaign developed. The campaign portrayed the ERA as a threat to "family values" and traditional relationships between men and women. Although thirty-five states ultimately ratified the ERA, five of those state legislatures voted to rescind ratification, and the amendment was never adopted.

Unratified Amendment

D.C. Statehood Amendment (proposed by Congress August 22, 1978)

Section 1 For purposes of representation in the Congress, election of the President and Vice-President, and article V of this Constitution, the District constituting the seat of government of the United States shall be treated as though it were a State.

Section 2 The exercise of the rights and powers conferred under this article shall be by the people of the District constituting the seat of government, and as shall be provided by Congress.

Section 3 The twenty-third article of amendment to the Constitution of the United States is hereby repealed.

Section 4 This article shall be inoperative, unless it shall have been ratified as an amendment to the Constitution by the legislatures of three-fourths of the several states within seven years from the date of its submission.

◆ ◆ ◆

▶ *The 1961 ratification of the Twenty-Third Amendment, giving residents of the District of Columbia the right to vote for a president and vice president, inspired an effort to give residents of the district full voting rights. In 1966, President Lyndon Johnson appointed a mayor and city council; in 1971, D.C. residents were allowed*

to name a nonvoting delegate to the House; and in 1981, residents were allowed to elect the mayor and city council. Congress retained the right to overrule laws that might affect commuters, the height of federal buildings, and selection of judges and prosecutors. The district's nonvoting delegate to Congress, Walter Fauntroy, lobbied fiercely for a congressional amendment granting statehood to the district. In 1978, a proposed amendment was approved and sent to the states. A number of states quickly ratified the amendment, but, like the ERA, the D.C. Statehood Amendment ran into trouble.

Opponents argued that section 2 created a separate category of "nominal" statehood. They argued that the federal district should be eliminated and that the territory should be reabsorbed into the state of Maryland. Although these theoretical arguments were strong, some scholars believe that racist attitudes toward the predominantly black population of the city were also a factor leading to the defeat of the amendment.

Amendment XXVII

[Adopted 1992]

No law, varying the compensation for the services of the Senators and Representatives, shall take effect, until an election of Representatives shall have intervened.

◆ ◆ ◆

▶ *While the Twenty-Sixth Amendment was the most rapidly ratified amendment in U.S. history, the Twenty-Seventh Amendment had the longest journey to ratification. First proposed by James Madison in 1789 as part of the package that included the Bill of Rights, this amendment had been ratified by only six states by 1791. In 1873, however, it was ratified by Ohio to protest a massive retroactive salary increase by the federal government. Unlike later proposed amendments, this one came with no time limit on ratification.*

In the early 1980s, Gregory D. Watson, a University of Texas economics major, discovered the "lost" amendment and began a single-handed campaign to get state legislators to introduce it for ratification. In 1983, it was accepted by Maine. In 1984, it passed the Colorado legislature. Ratifications trickled in slowly until May 1992, when Michigan and New Jersey became the thirty-eighth and thirty-ninth states, respectively, to ratify. This amendment prevents members of Congress from raising their own salaries without giving voters a chance to vote them out of office before they can benefit from the raises.

GOVERNMENT AND DEMOGRAPHICS

Presidential Elections						
Year	Candidates	Parties	Popular Vote	Percentage of Popular Vote	Electoral Vote	Percentage of Voter Participation
1789	**GEORGE WASHINGTON (Va.)***				69	
	John Adams				34	
	Others				35	
1792	**GEORGE WASHINGTON (Va.)**				132	
	John Adams				77	
	George Clinton				50	
	Others				5	
1796	**JOHN ADAMS (Mass.)**	Federalist			71	
	Thomas Jefferson	Democratic-Republican			68	
	Thomas Pinckney	Federalist			59	
	Aaron Burr	Dem.-Rep.			30	
	Others				48	
1800	**THOMAS JEFFERSON (Va.)**	Dem.-Rep.			73	
	Aaron Burr	Dem.-Rep.			73	
	John Adams	Federalist			65	
	C. C. Pinckney	Federalist			64	
	John Jay	Federalist			1	
1804	**THOMAS JEFFERSON (Va.)**	Dem.-Rep.			162	
	C. C. Pinckney	Federalist			14	
1808	**JAMES MADISON (Va.)**	Dem.-Rep.			122	
	C. C. Pinckney	Federalist			47	
	George Clinton	Dem.-Rep.			6	
1812	**JAMES MADISON (Va.)**	Dem.-Rep.			128	
	DeWitt Clinton	Federalist			89	
1816	**JAMES MONROE (Va.)**	Dem.-Rep.			183	
	Rufus King	Federalist			34	
1820	**JAMES MONROE (Va.)**	Dem.-Rep.			231	
	John Quincy Adams	Dem.-Rep.			1	
1824	**JOHN Q. ADAMS (Mass.)**	Dem.-Rep.	108,740	30.5	84	26.9
	Andrew Jackson	Dem.-Rep.	153,544	43.1	99	
	William H. Crawford	Dem.-Rep.	46,618	13.1	41	
	Henry Clay	Dem.-Rep.	47,136	13.2	37	
1828	**ANDREW JACKSON (Tenn.)**	Dem.-Rep.	647,286	56.0	178	57.6
	John Quincy Adams	National Republican	508,064	44.0	83	

*State of residence when elected president.

Year	Candidates	Parties	Popular Vote	Percentage of Popular Vote	Electoral Vote	Percentage of Voter Participation
1832	**ANDREW JACKSON (Tenn.)**	Dem.-Rep.	687,502	55.0	219	55.4
	Henry Clay	National Republican	530,189	42.4	49	
	John Floyd	Independent			11	
	William Wirt	Anti-Mason	33,108	2.6	7	
1836	**MARTIN VAN BUREN (N.Y.)**	Democratic	765,483	50.9	170	57.8
	W. H. Harrison	Whig			73	
	Hugh L. White	Whig	739,795	49.1	26	
	Daniel Webster	Whig			14	
	W. P. Mangum	Independent			11	
1840	**WILLIAM H. HARRISON (Ohio)**	Whig	1,274,624	53.1	234	78.0
	Martin Van Buren	Democratic	1,127,781	46.9	60	
	J. G. Birney	Liberty	7,069		—	
1844	**JAMES K. POLK (Tenn.)**	Democratic	1,338,464	49.6	170	78.9
	Henry Clay	Whig	1,300,097	48.1	105	
	J. G. Birney	Liberty	62,300	2.3	—	
1848	**ZACHARY TAYLOR (La.)**	Whig	1,360,099	47.4	163	72.7
	Lewis Cass	Democratic	1,220,544	42.5	127	
	Martin Van Buren	Free-Soil	291,263	10.1	—	
1852	**FRANKLIN PIERCE (N.H.)**	Democratic	1,601,274	50.9	254	69.6
	Winfield Scott	Whig	1,386,580	44.1	42	
	John P. Hale	Free-Soil	155,825	5.0	—	
1856	**JAMES BUCHANAN (Pa.)**	Democratic	1,836,169	45.3	174	78.9
	John C. Frémont	Republican	1,341,264	33.1	114	
	Millard Fillmore	American	874,534	21.6	8	
1860	**ABRAHAM LINCOLN (Ill.)**	Republican	1,866,452	39.9	180	81.2
	Stephen A. Douglas	Democratic	1,375,157	29.4	12	
	John C. Breckinridge	Democratic	847,953	18.1	72	
	John Bell	Union	590,631	12.6	39	
1864	**ABRAHAM LINCOLN (Ill.)**	Republican	2,213,665	55.1	212	73.8
	George B. McClellan	Democratic	1,805,237	44.9	21	
1868	**ULYSSES S. GRANT (Ill.)**	Republican	3,012,833	52.7	214	78.1
	Horatio Seymour	Democratic	2,703,249	47.3	80	
1872	**ULYSSES S. GRANT (Ill.)**	Republican	3,597,132	55.6	286	71.3
	Horace Greeley	Democratic; Liberal Republican	2,834,125	43.9	66	
1876	**RUTHERFORD B. HAYES (Ohio)**	Republican	4,036,298	47.9	185	81.8
	Samuel J. Tilden	Democratic	4,288,590	51.0	184	
1880	**JAMES A. GARFIELD (Ohio)**	Republican	4,454,416	48.5	214	79.4
	Winfield S. Hancock	Democratic	4,444,952	48.1	155	
1884	**GROVER CLEVELAND (N.Y.)**	Democratic	4,874,986	48.5	219	77.5
	James G. Blaine	Republican	4,851,981	48.3	182	
1888	**BENJAMIN HARRISON (Ind.)**	Republican	5,439,853	47.9	233	79.3
	Grover Cleveland	Democratic	5,540,309	48.6	168	

Year	Candidates	Parties	Popular Vote	Percentage of Popular Vote	Electoral Vote	Percentage of Voter Participation
1892	**GROVER CLEVELAND (N.Y.)**	Democratic	5,555,426	46.1	277	74.7
	Benjamin Harrison	Republican	5,182,690	43.0	145	
	James B. Weaver	People's	1,029,846	8.5	22	
1896	**WILLIAM McKINLEY (Ohio)**	Republican	7,104,779	51.1	271	79.3
	William J. Bryan	Democratic-People's	6,502,925	47.7	176	
1900	**WILLIAM McKINLEY (Ohio)**	Republican	7,207,923	51.7	292	73.2
	William J. Bryan	Dem.-Populist	6,358,133	45.5	155	
1904	**THEODORE ROOSEVELT (N.Y.)**	Republican	7,623,486	57.9	336	65.2
	Alton B. Parker	Democratic	5,077,911	37.6	140	
	Eugene V. Debs	Socialist	402,283	3.0	—	
1908	**WILLIAM H. TAFT (Ohio)**	Republican	7,678,908	51.6	321	65.4
	William J. Bryan	Democratic	6,409,104	43.1	162	
	Eugene V. Debs	Socialist	420,793	2.8	—	
1912	**WOODROW WILSON (N.J.)**	Democratic	6,293,454	41.9	435	58.8
	Theodore Roosevelt	Progressive	4,119,538	27.4	88	
	William H. Taft	Republican	3,484,980	23.2	8	
	Eugene V. Debs	Socialist	900,672	6.1	—	
1916	**WOODROW WILSON (N.J.)**	Democratic	9,129,606	49.4	277	61.6
	Charles E. Hughes	Republican	8,538,221	46.2	254	
	A. L. Benson	Socialist	585,113	3.2	—	
1920	**WARREN G. HARDING (Ohio)**	Republican	16,143,407	60.5	404	49.2
	James M. Cox	Democratic	9,130,328	34.2	127	
	Eugene V. Debs	Socialist	919,799	3.4	—	
1924	**CALVIN COOLIDGE (Mass.)**	Republican	15,725,016	54.0	382	48.9
	John W. Davis	Democratic	8,386,503	28.8	136	
	Robert M. La Follette	Progressive	4,822,856	16.6	13	
1928	**HERBERT HOOVER (Calif.)**	Republican	21,391,381	57.4	444	56.9
	Alfred E. Smith	Democratic	15,016,443	40.3	87	
	Norman Thomas	Socialist	881,951	2.3	—	
1932	**FRANKLIN D. ROOSEVELT (N.Y.)**	Democratic	22,821,857	57.4	472	56.9
	Herbert Hoover	Republican	15,761,841	39.7	59	
	Norman Thomas	Socialist	881,951	2.2	—	
	William Z. Foster	Communist	102,991	0.3	—	
1936	**FRANKLIN D. ROOSEVELT (N.Y.)**	Democratic	27,751,597	60.8	523	61.0
	Alfred M. Landon	Republican	16,679,583	36.5	8	
	William Lemke	Union	882,479	1.9	—	
1940	**FRANKLIN D. ROOSEVELT (N.Y.)**	Democratic	27,244,160	54.8	449	62.5
	Wendell Willkie	Republican	22,305,198	44.8	82	
1944	**FRANKLIN D. ROOSEVELT (N.Y.)**	Democratic	25,602,504	53.5	432	55.9
	Thomas E. Dewey	Republican	22,006,285	46.0	99	
1948	**HARRY S. TRUMAN (Mo.)**	Democratic	24,105,695	49.5	303	53.0
	Thomas E. Dewey	Republican	21,969,170	45.1	189	
	J. Strom Thurmond	States' Rights	1,169,021	2.4	39	
	Henry A. Wallace	Progressive	1,156,103	2.4	—	
1952	**DWIGHT D. EISENHOWER (N.Y.)**	Republican	33,936,252	55.1	442	63.3
	Adlai Stevenson	Democratic	27,314,992	44.4	89	

Year	Candidates	Parties	Popular Vote	Percentage of Popular Vote	Electoral Vote	Percentage of Voter Participation
1956	**DWIGHT D. EISENHOWER (N.Y.)**	Republican	35,575,420	57.6	457	60.6
	Adlai Stevenson	Democratic	26,033,066	42.1	73	
	Other	—	—		1	
1960	**JOHN F. KENNEDY (Mass.)**	Democratic	34,227,096	49.9	303	62.8
	Richard M. Nixon	Republican	34,108,546	49.6	219	
	Other	—	—		15	
1964	**LYNDON B. JOHNSON (Texas)**	Democratic	43,126,506	61.1	486	61.7
	Barry M. Goldwater	Republican	27,176,799	38.5	52	
1968	**RICHARD M. NIXON (N.Y.)**	Republican	31,770,237	43.4	301	60.9
	Hubert H. Humphrey	Democratic	31,270,533	42.7	191	
	George Wallace	American Indep.	9,906,141	13.5	46	
1972	**RICHARD M. NIXON (N.Y.)**	Republican	47,169,911	60.7	520	55.2
	George S. McGovern	Democratic	29,170,383	37.5	17	
	Other	—	—		1	
1976	**JIMMY CARTER (Ga.)**	Democratic	40,830,763	50.1	297	53.5
	Gerald R. Ford	Republican	39,147,793	48.0	240	
	Other	—	1,575,459	2.1	—	
1980	**RONALD REAGAN (Calif.)**	Republican	43,901,812	51.0	489	54.0
	Jimmy Carter	Democratic	35,483,820	41.0	49	
	John B. Anderson	Independent	5,719,722	7.0	—	
	Ed Clark	Libertarian	921,188	1.1	—	
1984	**RONALD REAGAN (Calif.)**	Republican	54,455,075	59.0	525	53.1
	Walter Mondale	Democratic	37,577,185	41.0	13	
1988	**GEORGE H. W. BUSH (Texas)**	Republican	47,946,422	54.0	426	50.2
	Michael S. Dukakis	Democratic	41,016,429	46.0	112	
1992	**WILLIAM J. CLINTON (Ark.)**	Democratic	44,909,889	43.0	370	55.9
	George H. W. Bush	Republican	39,104,545	37.5	168	
	H. Ross Perot	Independent	19,742,257	18.9	—	
1996	**WILLIAM J. CLINTON (Ark.)**	Democratic	47,401,185	49.2	379	49.0
	Robert Dole	Republican	39,197,469	40.7	159	
	H. Ross Perot	Independent	8,085,294	8.4	—	
2000	**GEORGE W. BUSH (Texas)**	Republican	50,456,062	47.8	271	51.2
	Al Gore	Democratic	50,996,862	48.4	267	
	Ralph Nader	Green Party	2,858,843	2.7	—	
	Patrick J. Buchanan	Reform Party	438,760	0.4	—	
2004	**GEORGE W. BUSH (Texas)**	Republican	61,872,711	50.7	286	60.3
	John F. Kerry	Democratic	58,894,584	48.3	252	
	Other	—	1,582,185	1.3	—	
2008	**BARACK OBAMA (Ill.)**	Democratic	69,456,897	52.9	365	56.8
	John McCain	Republican	59,934,314	45.7	173	
2012	**BARACK OBAMA (Ill.)**	Democratic	65,899,660	51.1	332	57.5
	Willard Mitt Romney	Republican	60,932,152	47.2	206	
2016	**DONALD J. TRUMP (N.Y.)**	Republican	62,984,825	46.1	304*	61.4%
	Hillary Clinton	Democratic	65,853,516	48.2	227	
	Gary Johnson	Libertarian	4,489,221	3.3	—	
	Jill Stein	Green Party	1,457,216	1.1	—	

*There were 7 electors who did not vote for either Trump or Clinton.

Supreme Court Justices

Name	Service	Appointed by	Name	Service	Appointed by
John Jay*	1789–1795	Washington	Henry B. Brown	1890–1906	B. Harrison
James Wilson	1789–1798	Washington	George Shiras	1892–1903	B. Harrison
John Blair	1789–1796	Washington	Howell E. Jackson	1893–1895	B. Harrison
John Rutledge	1790–1791	Washington	Edward D. White	1894–1910	Cleveland
William Cushing	1790–1810	Washington	Rufus W. Peckham	1896–1909	Cleveland
James Iredell	1790–1799	Washington	Joseph McKenna	1898–1925	McKinley
Thomas Johnson	1791–1793	Washington	Oliver W. Holmes	1902–1932	T. Roosevelt
William Paterson	1793–1806	Washington	William R. Day	1903–1922	T. Roosevelt
John Rutledge†	1795	Washington	William H. Moody	1906–1910	T. Roosevelt
Samuel Chase	1796–1811	Washington	Horace H. Lurton	1910–1914	Taft
Oliver Ellsworth	1796–1799	Washington	Charles E. Hughes	1910–1916	Taft
Bushrod Washington	1798–1829	J. Adams	Willis Van Devanter	1910–1937	Taft
Alfred Moore	1799–1804	J. Adams	**Edward D. White**	1910–1921	Taft
John Marshall	1801–1835	J. Adams	Joseph R. Lamar	1911–1916	Taft
William Johnson	1804–1834	Jefferson	Mahlon Pitney	1912–1922	Taft
Henry B. Livingston	1806–1823	Jefferson	James C. McReynolds	1914–1941	Wilson
Thomas Todd	1807–1826	Jefferson	Louis D. Brandeis	1916–1939	Wilson
Gabriel Duval	1811–1836	Madison	John H. Clarke	1916–1922	Wilson
Joseph Story	1811–1845	Madison	**William H. Taft**	1921–1930	Harding
Smith Thompson	1823–1843	Monroe	George Sutherland	1922–1938	Harding
Robert Trimble	1826–1828	J. Q. Adams	Pierce Butler	1923–1939	Harding
John McLean	1829–1861	Jackson	Edward T. Sanford	1923–1930	Harding
Henry Baldwin	1830–1844	Jackson	Harlan F. Stone	1925–1941	Coolidge
James M. Wayne	1835–1867	Jackson	**Charles E. Hughes**	1930–1941	Hoover
Roger B. Taney	1836–1864	Jackson	Owen J. Roberts	1930–1945	Hoover
Philip P. Barbour	1836–1841	Jackson	Benjamin N. Cardozo	1932–1938	Hoover
John Catron	1837–1865	Van Buren	Hugo L. Black	1937–1971	F. Roosevelt
John McKinley	1837–1852	Van Buren	Stanley F. Reed	1938–1957	F. Roosevelt
Peter V. Daniel	1841–1860	Van Buren	Felix Frankfurter	1939–1962	F. Roosevelt
Samuel Nelson	1845–1872	Tyler	William O. Douglas	1939–1975	F. Roosevelt
Levi Woodbury	1845–1851	Polk	Frank Murphy	1940–1949	F. Roosevelt
Robert C. Grier	1846–1870	Polk	Harlan F. Stone	1941–1946	F. Roosevelt
Benjamin R. Curtis	1851–1857	Fillmore	James F. Byrnes	1941–1942	F. Roosevelt
John A. Campbell	1853–1861	Pierce	Robert H. Jackson	1941–1954	F. Roosevelt
Nathan Clifford	1858–1881	Buchanan	Wiley B. Rutledge	1943–1949	F. Roosevelt
Noah H. Swayne	1862–1881	Lincoln	Harold H. Burton	1945–1958	Truman
Samuel F. Miller	1862–1890	Lincoln	**Frederick M. Vinson**	1946–1953	Truman
David Davis	1862–1877	Lincoln	Tom C. Clark	1949–1967	Truman
Stephen J. Field	1863–1897	Lincoln	Sherman Minton	1949–1956	Truman
Salmon P. Chase	1864–1873	Lincoln	**Earl Warren**	1953–1969	Eisenhower
William Strong	1870–1880	Grant	John Marshall Harlan	1955–1971	Eisenhower
Joseph P. Bradley	1870–1892	Grant	William J. Brennan Jr.	1956–1990	Eisenhower
Ward Hunt	1873–1882	Grant	Charles E. Whittaker	1957–1962	Eisenhower
Morrison R. Waite	1874–1888	Grant	Potter Stewart	1958–1981	Eisenhower
John M. Harlan	1877–1911	Hayes	Byron R. White	1962–1993	Kennedy
William B. Woods	1880–1887	Hayes	Arthur J. Goldberg	1962–1965	Kennedy
Stanley Matthews	1881–1889	Garfield	Abe Fortas	1965–1969	L. Johnson
Horace Gray	1882–1902	Arthur	Thurgood Marshall	1967–1991	L. Johnson
Samuel Blatchford	1882–1893	Arthur	**Warren E. Burger**	1969–1986	Nixon
Lucius Q. C. Lamar	1888–1893	Cleveland	Harry A. Blackmun	1970–1994	Nixon
Melville W. Fuller	1888–1910	Cleveland	Lewis F. Powell Jr.	1972–1988	Nixon
David J. Brewer	1889–1910	B. Harrison	William H. Rehnquist	1972–1986	Nixon

*Chief Justices appear in bold type.

†Acting Chief Justice; Senate refused to confirm appointment.

Name	Service	Appointed by	Name	Service	Appointed by
John Paul Stevens	1975–2010	Ford	Stephen Breyer	1994–	Clinton
Sandra Day O'Connor	1981–2006	Reagan	**John G. Roberts Jr.**	2005–	G. W. Bush
William H. Rehnquist	1986–2005	Reagan	Samuel Anthony Alito Jr.	2006–	G. W. Bush
Antonin Scalia	1986–2016	Reagan			
Anthony M. Kennedy	1988–2018	Reagan	Sonia Sotomayor	2009–	Obama
David H. Souter	1990–2009	G. H. W. Bush	Elena Kagan	2010–	Obama
Clarence Thomas	1991–	G. H. W. Bush	Neil Gorsuch	2018–	Trump
Ruth Bader Ginsburg	1993–	Clinton	Brett Kavanaugh	2018–	Trump

Admission of States to the Union

State	Date of Admission	State	Date of Admission
Delaware	December 7, 1787	Michigan	January 16, 1837
Pennsylvania	December 12, 1787	Florida	March 3, 1845
New Jersey	December 18, 1787	Texas	December 29, 1845
Georgia	January 2, 1788	Iowa	December 28, 1846
Connecticut	January 9, 1788	Wisconsin	May 29, 1848
Massachusetts	February 6, 1788	California	September 9, 1850
Maryland	April 28, 1788	Minnesota	May 11, 1858
South Carolina	May 23, 1788	Oregon	February 14, 1859
New Hampshire	June 21, 1788	Kansas	January 29, 1861
Virginia	June 25, 1788	West Virginia	June 19, 1863
New York	July 26, 1788	Nevada	October 31, 1864
North Carolina	November 21, 1789	Nebraska	March 1, 1867
Rhode Island	May 29, 1790	Colorado	August 1, 1876
Vermont	March 4, 1791	North Dakota	November 2, 1889
Kentucky	June 1, 1792	South Dakota	November 2, 1889
Tennessee	June 1, 1796	Montana	November 8, 1889
Ohio	March 1, 1803	Washington	November 11, 1889
Louisiana	April 30, 1812	Idaho	July 3, 1890
Indiana	December 11, 1816	Wyoming	July 10, 1890
Mississippi	December 10, 1817	Utah	January 4, 1896
Illinois	December 3, 1818	Oklahoma	November 16, 1907
Alabama	December 14, 1819	New Mexico	January 6, 1912
Maine	March 15, 1820	Arizona	February 14, 1912
Missouri	August 10, 1821	Alaska	January 3, 1959
Arkansas	June 15, 1836	Hawai'i	August 21, 1959

Population

FROM AN ESTIMATED 4,600 white inhabitants in 1630, the country's population grew to a total of more than 308 million in 2010. It is important to note that the U.S. census, first conducted in 1790, and the source of these figures, counted blacks, both free and slave, but did not include American Indians until 1860. The years 1790 to 1900 saw the most rapid population growth, with an average increase of 25 to 35 percent per decade. In addition to "natural" growth—birthrate exceeding death rate—immigration was also a factor in that rise, especially between 1840 and 1860, 1880 and 1890, and 1900 and 1910. The twentieth century witnessed slower growth, partly a result of 1920s immigration restrictions and a decline in the birthrate, especially during the depression era and the 1960s and 1970s. The U.S. population is expected to pass 340 million by the year 2020.

Population Growth, 1630–2010

Year	Population	Percent Increase	Year	Population	Percent Increase
1630	4,600	—	1830	12,866,020	33.5
1640	26,600	473.3	1840	17,069,453	32.7
1650	50,400	89.1	1850	23,191,876	35.9
1660	75,100	49.0	1860	31,443,321	35.6
1670	111,900	49.1	1870	39,818,449	26.6
1680	151,500	35.4	1880	50,155,783	26.0
1690	210,400	38.9	1890	62,947,714	25.5
1700	250,900	19.3	1900	75,994,575	20.7
1710	331,700	32.2	1910	91,972,266	21.0
1720	466,200	40.5	1920	105,710,620	14.9
1730	629,400	35.0	1930	122,775,046	16.1
1740	905,600	43.9	1940	131,669,275	7.2
1750	1,170,800	30.0	1950	150,697,361	14.5
1760	1,593,600	36.1	1960	179,323,175	19.0
1770	2,148,100	34.8	1970	203,302,031	13.4
1780	2,780,400	29.4	1980	226,542,199	11.4
1790	3,929,214	41.3	1990	248,718,302	9.8
1800	5,308,483	35.1	2000	281,422,509	13.1
1810	7,239,881	36.4	2010	308,745,538	9.7
1820	9,638,453	33.1			

Sources: *Historical Statistics of the U.S.* (1960); *Historical Statistics of the U.S., Colonial Times to 1970* (1975); *Statistical Abstract of the U.S., 1996* (1996); *Statistical Abstract of the U.S., 2003* (2003); and United States Census (2010).

Major Trends in Immigration, 1820–2010

THE QUANTITY AND CHARACTER of immigration to the United States has varied greatly over time. During the first major influx, between 1840 and 1860, newcomers hailed primarily from northern and western Europe. From 1880 to 1915, when rates soared even more dramatically, the profile changed, with 80 percent of the "new immigration" coming from central, eastern, and southern Europe. Following World War I, strict quotas reduced the flow considerably. Note also the significant falloff during the years of the Great Depression and World War II. The sources of immigration during the last half century have changed significantly, a result of changes to immigration laws as well as geopolitical developments, with the majority of arrivals coming from Latin America, the Caribbean, and Asia. The latest surge during the 1980s and 1990s brought more immigrants to the United States than in any period since the early twentieth century. Immigrants were 13.2 percent of the U.S. population by 2014. Latinos constituted the largest group, although the largest number of new arrivals after 2010 came from Asia.

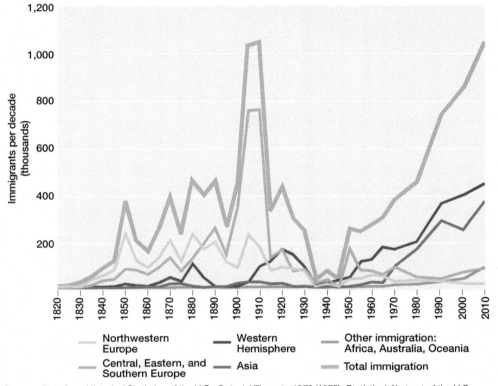

SOURCES: Data from *Historical Statistics of the U.S., Colonial Times to 1970* (1975); *Statistical Abstract of the U.S., 1999* (1999); and *Statistical Abstract of the U.S., 2011* (2011).

SELECTED BIBLIOGRAPHY

Chapter 1

GENERAL WORKS

Thomas D. Dillehay, *The Settlement of the Americas: A New Prehistory* (2000).

Thomas D. Dillehay, ed., *Where the Land Meets the Sea: Fourteen Millennia of Human History at Haca Prieta, Peru* (2017).

Brian Fagan, *The First North Americans: An Archaeological Journey* (2012).

Tim Flannery, *The Eternal Frontier: An Ecological History of North America and Its Peoples* (2001).

Charles C. Mann, *1491: New Revelations of the Americas before Columbus* (2006).

Francis McManamon et al., eds., *Archaeology in America* (2008).

Steven Mithen, *After the Ice: A Global Human History, 20,000–5000 BC* (2003).

David Reich, *Who We Are and How We Got Here: Ancient DNA and the New Science of the Human Past* (2018).

Daniel K. Richter, *Before the Revolution: America's Ancient Pasts* (2011).

Adam Rutherford, *A Brief History of Everyone Who Ever Lived: The Human Story Retold through Our Genes* (2017).

Christina Snyder, *Slavery in Indian Country: The Changing Face of Captivity in Early America* (2010).

Nicholas Wade, *Before the Dawn: Recovering the Lost History of Our Ancestors* (2006).

NATIVE AMERICAN CULTURES IN TERRITORY OF PRESENT-DAY UNITED STATES

Kenneth M. Ames and Herbert D. G. Maschner, *Peoples of the Northwest Coast: Their Archaeology and Prehistory* (2000).

Sally A. Kitt Chappell, *Cahokia: Mirror of the Cosmos* (2002).

Andrew Clark and Douglas Bamforth, *Archaeological Perspectives on Warfare on the Great Plains* (2018).

Linda S. Cordell, *Archaeology of the Southwest* (2009).

E. James Dixon, *Bones, Boats, and Bison: Archeology and the First Colonization of Western North America* (2000).

Thomas E. Emerson et al., eds., *Late Woodland Societies: Tradition and Transformation across the Midcontinent* (2008).

Brian Fagan, *Chaco Canyon: Archaeologists Explore the Lives of an Ancient Society* (2005).

Sarah A. Kerr, *Beyond Chaco: Great Kiva Communities on the Mogollon Rim Frontier* (2001).

Marcel Kornfeld and George C. Frison, *Prehistoric Hunter-Gatherers of the High Plains* (2009).

Steven A. LeBlanc, *Prehistoric Warfare in the American Southwest* (2007).

Jerald T. Milanich, *Florida Indians and the Invasion from Europe* (2018).

Timothy R. Pauketat, *Cahokia: Ancient America's Greatest City on the Mississippi* (2009).

Marvin T. Smith, *Coosa: The Rise and Fall of a Southeastern Mississippian Chiefdom* (2000).

THE MEXICA

David Carrasco, *Aztecs: A Very Short Introduction* (2011).

Michael D. Coe and Rex Koontz, *Mexico: From the Olmecs to the Aztecs* (6th ed., 2013).

Susan Toby Evans, *Ancient Mexico and Central America: Archaeology and Culture History* (2nd ed., 2008).

Eduardo Matos Moctezuma and Felipe Solis Olguin, *Aztecs* (2002).

Michael E. Smith, *The Aztecs* (2011).

Chapter 2

GENERAL WORKS

Jorge Canizares-Esguerra and Erik R. Seeman, eds., *The Atlantic in Global History: 1500–2000* (2018).

J. H. Elliott, *Empires of the Atlantic World: Britain and Spain in America, 1491–1830* (2006).

Mark G. Hanna, *Pirate Nests and the Rise of the British Empire, 1570–1740* (2015).

John L. Kessell, *Spain in the Southwest: A Narrative History of Colonial New Mexico, Arizona, Texas, and California* (2002).

Diarmaid MacCulloch, *Christianity: The First Three Thousand Years* (2009).

David Parrott, *The Business of War: Military Enterprise and Military Revolution in Early Modern Europe* (2013).

John K. Thornton, *A Cultural History of the Atlantic World, 1250–1820* (2012).

David J. Weber, *The Spanish Frontier in North America* (2009).

EXPLORERS AND EMPIRES

Roger Crowley, *Conquerors: How Portugal Forged the First Global Empire* (2015).

James Horn, *A Kingdom Strange: The Brief and Tragic History of the Lost Colony of Roanoke* (2010).

Henry Arthur Francis Kamen, *Empire: How Spain Became a World Power, 1492–1763* (2004).

Karen Ordahl Kupperman, *Roanoke: The Abandoned Colony* (2nd ed., 2007).

Francesc Relaño, *The Shaping of Africa: Cosmographic Discourse and Cartographic Science in Late Medieval and Early Modern Europe* (2002).

Hugh Thomas, *Rivers of Gold: The Rise of the Spanish Empire from Columbus to Magellan* (2004).

EUROPEANS ENCOUNTER THE NEW WORLD

Stephen R. Berry, *Path in the Mighty Waters: Shipboard Life and Atlantic Crossings to the New World* (2015).

Nicolás Wey Gomez, *The Tropics of Empire: Why Columbus Sailed South to the Indies* (2008).

Charles C. Mann, *1493: Uncovering the New World Columbus Created* (2012).

Michael Leroy Oberg, *The Head in Edward Nugent's Hand: Roanoke's Forgotten Indians* (2008).

Gene Waddell, *The Taino in 1492* (2015).

CONQUEST AND NEW SPAIN

Ida Altman, *The War for Mexico's West: Indians and Spaniards in New Galicia, 1524–1550* (2010).

Herman L. Bennett, *Colonial Blackness: A History of Afro-Mexico* (2010).

Richard Flint and Shirley Cushing Flint, *The Coronado Expedition* (2003).

John L. Kessell, *Pueblos, Spaniards, and the Kingdom of New Mexico* (2010).

Miguel Leon-Portilla and Lysander Kemp, *The Broken Spears: The Aztec Account of the Conquest of Mexico* (2006).

Andrés Reséndez, *The Other Slavery: The Uncovered Story of Indian Enslavement in America* (2016).

Matthew Restall, *Seven Myths of the Spanish Conquest* (2004).

Matthew Restall and Kris Lane, *Latin America in Colonial Times* (2011).

Stuart B. Schwartz, *All Can Be Saved: Religious Tolerance and Salvation in the Iberian Atlantic World* (2009).

John TePaske, *A New World of Gold and Silver* (2010).

Hugh Thomas, *World without End: Spain, Philip II, and the First Global Empire* (2015).

Charles A. Truxillo, *By the Sword and the Cross: The Historical Evolution of the Catholic World Monarchy in Spain and the New World, 1492–1825* (2001).

David Wheat, *Atlantic Africa and the Spanish Caribbean, 1570–1640* (2016).

Stephanie Gail Wood, *Transcending Conquest: Nahua Views of Spanish Colonial Mexico* (2003).

Chapter 3

CHESAPEAKE SOCIETY

Bernard Bailyn, *The Barbarous Years: The Peopling of British North America: The Conflict of Civilizations, 1600–1675* (2012).

Alison Games, *The Web of Empire: English Cosmopolitans in the Age of Expansion, 1560–1660* (2009).

Alexander B. Haskell, *For God, King, and People: Forging Commonwealth Bonds in Renaissance Virginia* (2017).

April Hatfield, *Atlantic Virginia: Intercolonial Relations in the Seventeenth Century* (2003).

James Horn, *A Land as God Made It: Jamestown and the Birth of America* (2006).

Karen Ordahl Kupperman, *The Jamestown Project* (2010).

Peter C. Mancall, *The Atlantic World and Virginia, 1550–1624* (2007).

Debra Meyers, *Common Whores, Vertuous Women, and Loveing Wives: Free Will Christian Women in Colonial Maryland* (2003).

Marcy Norton, *Sacred Gifts, Profane Pleasures: A History of Tobacco and Chocolate in the Atlantic World* (2010).

Geoffrey Parker, *Global Crisis: War, Climate Change and Catastrophe in the Seventeenth Century* (2013).

L. H. Roper, *Advancing Empire: English Interests and Overseas Expansion, 1613–1688* (2017).

Steve Sarson, *British America, 1500–1800: Creating Colonies, Imagining an Empire* (2005).

Terri L. Snyder, *Brabbling Women: Disorderly Speech and the Law in Early Virginia* (2003).

Christopher L. Tomlins, *Freedom Bound: Law, Labor, and Civic Identity in Colonizing English America, 1580–1865* (2010).

Lorena S. Walsh, *Motives of Honor, Pleasure, and Profit: Plantation Management in the Colonial Chesapeake, 1607–1763* (2010).

INDIANS

Alan Gallay, *The Indian Slave Trade: The Rise of the English Empire in the American South, 1670–1717* (2002).

Joseph M. Hall Jr., *Zamumo's Gifts: Indian-European Exchange in the Colonial Southeast* (2012).

Karen Ordahl Kupperman, *Indians and English: Facing Off in Early America* (2000).

Andrew Lipman, *The Saltwater Frontier: Indians and the Contest for the American Coast* (2015).

Helen C. Rountree, *Pocahontas, Powhatan, Opechancanough: Three Indian Lives Changed by Jamestown* (2005).

Kristalyn Marie Shefveland, *Anglo-Native Virginia: Trade, Conversion, and Indian Slavery in the Old Dominion, 1646–1722* (2016).

David Silverman, *Thundersticks: Firearms and the Violent Transformation of Native America* (2016).

Christina Snyder, *Slavery in Indian Country: The Changing Face of Captivity in Early America* (2010).

Jayme A. Sokolow, *The Great Encounter: Native Peoples and European Settlers in the Americas, 1492–1800* (2003).

Jessica Yirush Stern, *The Lives in Objects: Native Americans, British Colonists, and Cultures of Labor and Exchange in the Southeast* (2017).

Margaret Holmes Williamson, *Powhatan Lords of Life and Death: Command and Consent in Seventeenth-Century Virginia* (2003).

SLAVERY AND INDENTURED SERVITUDE

Susan Dwyer Amussen, *Caribbean Exchanges: Slavery and the Transformation of English Society, 1640–1700* (2007).

James F. Brooks, *Captives and Cousins: Slavery, Kinship, and Community in the Southwest Borderlands* (2002).

Tim Hashaw, *The Birth of Black America: The First African Americans and the Pursuit of Freedom at Jamestown* (2007).

Linda M. Heywood and John K. Thornton, *Central Africans, Atlantic Creoles, and the Foundation of the Americas* (2007).

Russell R. Menard, *Migrants, Servants, and Slaves: Unfree Labor in Colonial British America* (2001).

Jennifer L. Morgan, *Laboring Women: Reproduction and Gender in New World Slavery* (2004).

Simon P. Newman, *A New World of Labor: The Development of Plantation Slavery in the British Atlantic* (2013).

Gregory E. O'Malley, *Final Passages: The Intercolonial Slave Trade of British America, 1619–1807* (2014).

John Ruston Pagan, *Anne Orthwood's Bastard: Sex and Law in Early Virginia* (2003).

CAROLINA SOCIETY AND THE WEST INDIES

Cara Anzilotti, *In the Affairs of the World: Women, Patriarchy, and Power in Colonial South Carolina* (2002).

S. Max Edelson, *Plantation Enterprise in Colonial South Carolina* (2006).

Adrian Finucane, *The Temptations of Trade: Britain, Spain, and the Struggle for Empire* (2016).

Kirsten Fischer, *Suspect Relations: Sex, Race, and Resistance in Colonial North Carolina* (2002).

Michael Jarvis, *In the Eye of All Trade: Bermuda, Bermudians, and the Maritime Atlantic World, 1680–1783* (2010).

Russell K. Menard, *Sweet Negotiations: Sugar, Slavery, and Plantation Agriculture in Early Barbados* (2006).

Matthew Mulcahy, *Hubs of Empire: The Southeastern Low Country and British Caribbean* (2014).

Chapter 4

GENERAL WORKS

Virginia DeJohn Anderson, *Creatures of Empire: How Domestic Animals Transformed Early America* (2004).

Bernard Bailyn, *The Barbarous Years: The Peopling of British North America: The Conflict of Civilizations, 1600–1675* (2012).

Eric Jay Dolin, *Fur, Fortune, and Empire: The Epic History of the Fur Trade in America* (2010).

Robert S. DuPlessis, *The Material Atlantic: Clothing, Commerce, and Colonization in the Atlantic World, 1650–1800* (2016).

Max Edelson, *The New Map of Empire: How Britain Imagined America before Independence* (2017).

Peter C. Mancall, *Nature and Culture in the Early Modern Atlantic* (2017).

Peter Moogk, *La Nouvelle France: The Making of French Canada—A Cultural History* (2000).

Christopher L. Pastore, *Between Land and Sea: The Atlantic Coast and the Transformation of New England* (2014).

Carla Gardina Pestana, *The English Atlantic in the Age of Revolution, 1640–1661* (2004).

James Pritchard, *In Search of Empire: The French in the Americas, 1670–1730* (2007).

Sam White, *A Cold Welcome: The Little Ice Age and Europe's Encounter with North America* (2017).

Anya Zilberstein, *A Temperate Empire: Making Climate Change in Early America* (2016).

NATIVE AMERICANS

Russell Bourne, *Gods of War, Gods of Peace: How the Meeting of Native and Colonial Religions Shaped Early America* (2002).

Roger M. Carpenter, *The Renewed, the Destroyed, and the Remade: The Three Thought Worlds of the Huron and the Iroquois, 1609–1675* (2004).

Daniel R. Mandell, *King Philip's War: Colonial Expansion, Native Resistance, and the End of Indian Sovereignty* (2010).

Michael McDonnell, *Masters of Empire: Great Lakes Indians and the Making of America* (2015).

Donna Merwick, *The Shame and the Sorrow: Dutch-Amerindian Encounters in New Netherland* (2006).

Ann Marie Plane, *Colonial Intimacies: Indian Marriages in Early New England* (2000).

NEW ENGLAND

Louise A. Breen, *Transgressing the Bounds: Subversive Enterprises among the Puritan Elite in Massachusetts, 1630–1692* (2001).

Nick Bunker, *Making Haste from Babylon: The Mayflower Pilgrims and Their World* (2010).

Lisa M. Gordis, *Opening Scriptures: Bible Reading and Interpretive Authority in Puritan New England* (2003).

Katherine Grandjean, *American Passage: The Communications Frontier in Early New England* (2015).

David D. Hall, *A Reforming People: Transformation of Public Life in New England* (2013).

Susan Juster, *Sacred Violence in Early America* (2016).

Eve LaPlante, *American Jezebel: The Uncommon Life of Anne Hutchinson, the Woman Who Defied the Puritans* (2005).

Mary Beth Norton, *In the Devil's Snare: The Salem Witchcraft Crisis of 1692* (2002).

Nathaniel Philbrick, *Mayflower: A Story of Courage, Community, and War* (2006).

Nancy Shoemaker, *Native American Whalemen and the World: Indigenous Encounters and the Contingency of Race* (2017).

Wendy Warren, *New England Bound: Slavery and Colonization in Early America* (2016).

Michael P. Winship, *Making Heretics: Militant Protestantism and Free Grace in Massachusetts, 1636–1641* (2002).

MIDDLE COLONIES

Evan Haefeli, *New Netherland and the Dutch Origins of American Religious Liberty* (2012).

Ned C. Landsman, *Crossroads of Empire: The Middle Colonies in British North America* (2010).

Peter C. Mancall, *Fatal Journey: The Final Expedition of Henry Hudson* (2009).

Russell Shorto, *The Island at the Center of the World: The Epic Story of Dutch Manhattan and the Forgotten Colony That Shaped America* (2004).

Chapter 5

GENERAL WORKS

Jennifer L. Anderson, *Mahogany: The Costs of Luxury in Early America* (2012).

Ira Berlin, *Generations of Captivity: A History of African-American Slaves* (2003).

Holly Brewer, *By Birth or Consent: Children, Law, and the Anglo-American Revolution in Authority* (2005).

Martin Brückner, *The Social Life of Maps in America, 1750–1860* (2017).

Richard Lyman Bushman, *The American Farmer in the Eighteenth Century: A Social and Cultural History* (2018).

Eric Jay Dolin, *Fur, Fortune, and Empire: The Epic History of the Fur Trade in America* (2010).

Robert S. DuPlessis, *The Material Atlantic: Clothing, Commerce, and Colonization in the Atlantic World, 1650–1800* (2016).

Kathleen DuVal, *The Native Ground: Indians and Colonists in the Heart of the Continent* (2006).

Adrian Finucane, *The Temptations of Trade: Britain, Spain, and the Struggle for Empire* (2016).

Patrick Griffin, *The People with No Name: Ireland's Ulster Scots, America's Scots Irish, and the Creation of a British Atlantic World, 1689–1764* (2001).

David Hancock, *Oceans of Wine: Madeira and the Emergence of American Trade and Taste* (2009).

Brendan McConville, *The King's Three Faces: The Rise and Fall of Royal America, 1688–1776* (2007).

Robert Woods Sayre, *Modernity and Its Other: The Encounter with North American Indians in the Eighteenth Century* (2017).

Peter Silver, *Our Savage Neighbors: How Indian War Transformed Early America* (2008).

Christina Snyder, *Slavery in Indian Country: The Changing Face of Captivity in Early America* (2012).

Caroline Winterer, *American Enlightenments: Pursuing Happiness in the Age of Reason* (2016).

Michael Witgen, *An Infinity of Nations: How the Native New World Shaped Early North America* (2013).

NEW ENGLAND

Phyllis Whitman Hunter, *Purchasing Identity in the Atlantic World: Massachusetts Merchants, 1670–1780* (2001).

Lisa Norling, *Captain Ahab Had a Wife: New England Women and the Whale Fishery, 1720–1870* (2000).

Timothy L. Shannon, *Indian Captive, Indian King: Peter Williamson in America and Britain* (2017).

Jennifer Van Horn, *The Power of Objects in Eighteenth-Century British America* (2017).

Daniel Vickers, *Young Men and the Sea: Yankee Seafarers in the Age of Sail* (2005).

Douglas L. Winiarski, *Darkness Falls on the Land of Light: Experiencing Religious Awakenings in Eighteenth-Century New England* (2016).

MIDDLE COLONIES

Zara Anishanslin, *Portrait of a Woman in Silk: Hidden Histories of the British Atlantic World* (2016).

Katherine Carté Engel, *Religion and Profit: Moravians in Early America* (2009).

Leslie M. Harris, *In the Shadow of Slavery: African Americans in New York City, 1626–1863* (2003).

Jill Lepore, *New York Burning: Liberty, Slavery, and Conspiracy in Eighteenth-Century Manhattan* (2005).

Jane T. Merritt, *At the Crossroads: Indians and Empires on a Mid-Atlantic Frontier, 1700–1763* (2003).

Donna Merwick, *The Shame and the Sorrow: Dutch-Amerindian Encounters in New Netherland* (2006).

Simon P. Newman, *Embodied History: The Lives of the Poor in Early Philadelphia* (2003).

SOUTHERN COLONIES

Alejandra Dubcovsky, *Informed Power: Communication in the Early American South* (2016).

Steven W. Hackel, *Children of Coyote, Missionaries of Saint Francis: Indian-Spanish Relations in Colonial California, 1769–1850* (2005).

Robert H. Jackson, *Missions and the Frontiers of Spanish America* (2005).

Sean M. Kelley, *The Voyage of the Slave Ship* Hare: *A Journey into Captivity from Sierra Leone to South Carolina* (2016).

Catherine Kerrison, *Claiming the Pen: Women and Intellectual Life in the Early American South* (2006).

Brett Rushforth, *Bonds of Alliance: Indigenous and Atlantic Slaveries in New France* (2012).

Randy J. Sparks, *The Two Princes of Calabar: An Eighteenth-Century Atlantic Odyssey* (2004).

——, *Africans in the Old South: Mapping Exceptional Lives across the Atlantic World* (2016).

Bradford J. Wood, *This Remote Part of the World: Regional Formation in Lower Cape Fear, North Carolina, 1725–1775* (2004).

Chapter 6

GENERAL WORKS

Edward Countryman, *The American Revolution* (2003).

Merrill Jensen, *The Founding of a Nation: A History of the American Revolution, 1763–1776* (2004).

Robert Middlekauff, *The Glorious Cause: The American Revolution, 1763–1789* (2005).

Gordon Wood, *The Radicalism of the American Revolution* (1993).

Alfred F. Young, *Liberty Tree: Ordinary People and the American Revolution* (2006).

NATIVE AMERICANS AND THE SEVEN YEARS' WAR

Fred Anderson, *Crucible of War: The Seven Years' War and the Fate of Empire in British North America, 1754–1766* (2001).

Colin G. Calloway, *The Scratch of a Pen: 1763 and the Transformation of America* (2007).

Gregory Evans Dowd, *War under Heaven: Pontiac, the Indian Nations, and the British Empire* (2004).

Eric Hinderaker, *The Two Hendricks: Unraveling a Mohawk Mystery* (2010).

James H. Merrell, *Into the American Woods: Negotiators on the Pennsylvania Frontier* (2000).

David Preston, *Braddock's Defeat: The Battle of the Monongahela and the Road to Revolution* (2015).

Timothy J. Shannon, *Indians and Colonists at the Crossroads of Empire: The Albany Congress of 1754* (2002).

Peter Silver, *Our Savage Neighbors: How Indian War Transformed Early America* (2009).

Richard White, *The Middle Ground: Indians, Empires, and Republics in the Great Lakes Region, 1650–1815* (1991).

THE REVOLUTIONARY CRISIS OF THE 1760S AND 1770S

Richard Archer, *As If an Enemy's Country: The British Occupation of Boston and the Origins of Revolution* (2010).

Bernard Bailyn, *The Ordeal of Thomas Hutchinson* (1976).

Carol Berkin, *Revolutionary Mothers: Women in the Struggle for America's Independence* (2006).

T. H. Breen, *American Insurgents, American Patriots: The Revolution of the People* (2010).

Benjamin L. Carp, *Defiance of the Patriots: The Boston Tea Party and the Making of America* (2010).

John E. Ferling, *The First of Men: A Life of George Washington* (1988).

David Hackett Fischer, *Paul Revere's Ride* (1995).

Robert A. Gross, *The Minutemen and Their World* (2001).

Joan Gundersen, *To Be Useful to the World: Women in Revolutionary America, 1740–1790* (1996).

Eric Hinderaker, *Boston's Massacre* (2017).

Woody Holton, *Forced Founders: Indians, Debtors, Slaves, and the Making of the American Revolution in Virginia* (1999).

Pauline Maier, *From Resistance to Revolution: Colonial Radicals and the Development of American Opposition to Britain, 1765–1776* (1992).

Mary Beth Norton, *Liberty's Daughters: The Revolutionary Experience of American Women, 1750–1800* (1996).

Andrew Jackson O'Shaughnessy, *The Men Who Lost America: British Leadership, the American Revolution, and the Fate of the Empire* (2013).

Gautham Rao, *National Duties: Customs Houses and the Making of the American State* (2016).

Alfred F. Young, *The Shoemaker and the Tea Party: Memory and the American Revolution* (2000).

SLAVERY

Ira Berlin, *Many Thousands Gone: The First Two Centuries of Slavery in North America* (2000).

Douglas R. Egerton, *Death or Liberty: African Americans and Revolutionary America* (2009).

Sylvia Frey, *Water from the Rock: Black Resistance in a Revolutionary Age* (1991).

Philip Morgan, *Slave Counterpoint* (1998).

Chapter 7

GENERAL WORKS

Carol Berkin, *Revolutionary Mothers: Women in the Struggle for America's Independence* (2005).

Elijah Gould, *Among the Powers of the Earth: The American Revolution and the Making of a New World Empire* (2012).

Jonathan Israel, *The Expanding Blaze: How the American Revolution Ignited the World, 1775–1848* (2017).

Gary B. Nash, *The Unknown American Revolution: The Unruly Birth of Democracy and the Struggle to Create America* (2005).

Robert G. Parkinson, *The Common Cause: Creating Race and Nation in the American Revolution* (2016).

Jack Rakove, *Revolutionaries: A New History of the Invention of America* (2010).

Charles Royster, *A Revolutionary People at War: The Continental Army and American Character, 1775–1783* (1996).

Alan Taylor, *American Revolutions: A Continental History, 1750–1804* (2016).

Gordon S. Wood, *The Radicalism of the American Revolution* (1992).

Alfred F. Young, Gary B. Nash, and Ray Raphael, *Revolutionary Founders: Rebels, Radicals, and Reformers in the Making of the Nation* (2011).

THE WARTIME CONFEDERATION AND ITS LEADERS

Colin G. Calloway, *The Indian World of George Washington* (2018).

Ron Chernow, *Washington: A Life* (2010).

Joseph J. Ellis, *His Excellency: George Washington* (2004).

Edith Gelles, *Portia: The World of Abigail Adams* (1992).

Woody Holton, *Abigail Adams* (2010).

Jackson Turner Main, *The Sovereign States, 1775–1783* (1973).

Sheila L. Skemp, *The Making of a Patriot: Benjamin Franklin at the Cockpit* (2012).

CAMPAIGNS, BATTLES, AND SOLDIERS

Wayne K. Bodle, *The Valley Forge Winter: Civilians and Soldiers in War* (2004).

W. Jeffrey Bolster, *Black Jacks: African American Seamen in the Age of Sail* (1998).

Colin G. Calloway, *The American Revolution in Indian Country: Crisis and Diversity in Native American Communities* (1995).

Kathleen DuVal, *Independence Lost: Lives on the Edge of the American Revolution* (2015).

Elizabeth A. Fenn, *Pox Americana: The Great Smallpox Epidemic of 1775–1782* (2002).

David Hackett Fischer, *Washington's Crossing* (2004).

Robert Gross, *The Minutemen and Their World* (2001).

Holger Hoock, *Scars of Independence: America's Violent Birth* (2017).

Myra Jasanoff, *Liberty's Exiles: American Loyalists in the Revolutionary World* (2012).

Jane Kamensky, *A Revolution in Color: The World of John Singleton Copley* (2016).

David McCullough, *1776* (2005).

Nathan Perl-Rosenthal, *Citizen Sailors: Becoming American in the Age of Revolution* (2015).

Cassandra Pybus, *Epic Journeys of Freedom: Runaway Slaves of the American Revolution and Their Global Quest for Liberty* (2006).

Claudio Saunt, *West of the Revolution: An Uncommon History of 1776* (2014).

Alfred F. Young, *Masquerade: The Life and Times of Deborah Sampson, Continental Soldier* (2004).

Chapter 8

GENERAL WORKS

Lance Banning, *The Sacred Fire of Liberty: James Madison and the Founding of the Federal Republic* (1995).

Max Edling, *A Revolution in Favor of Government: Origins of the U.S. Constitution and the Making of the American State* (2008).

Gary B. Nash, *The Unknown American Revolution: The Unruly Birth of Democracy and the Struggle to Create America* (2006).

Peter S. Onuf, *Statehood and Union: A History of the Northwest Ordinance* (1987).

Jack Rakove, *Revolutionaries: A New History of the Invention of America* (2010).

Robert E. Shalhope, *The Roots of Democracy: American Thought and Culture, 1760–1800* (2004).

Gordon Wood, *The Creation of the American Republic, 1776–1787* (1969).

NATIVE AMERICAN AND U.S. EXPANSION

Gregory Evans Dowd, *War under Heaven: Pontiac, the Indian Nations and the British Empire* (2002).

Patrick Griffith, *American Leviathan: Empire, Nation, and Revolutionary Frontier* (2007).

Laurence Hauptman, *Conspiracy of Interests: Iroquois Dispossession and the Rise of New York State* (1999).

Eric Hinderaker, *Elusive Empires: Constructing Colonialism in the Ohio Valley* (1997).

Leonard J. Sadosky, *Revolutionary Negotiations: Indians, Empires, and Diplomats in the Founding of America* (2009).

Alan Taylor, *The Divided Ground: Indians, Settlers, and the Northern Borderland of the American Revolution* (2006).

Karim M. Tiro, *The People of the Standing Stone: The Oneida Nation from the Revolution through the Era of Removal* (2011).

Richard White, *The Middle Ground: Indians, Empires, and Republics in the Great Lakes Region* (1991).

CITIZENSHIP

Lawrence B. A. Hatter, *Citizens of Convenience: The Imperial Origins of American Nationhood on the U.S.-Canadian Border* (2017).

Kate Haulman, *The Politics of Fashion in Eighteenth-Century America* (2014).

Catherine O'Donnell Kaplan, *Men of Letters in the Early Republic: Cultivating Forums of Citizenship* (2012).

Linda K. Kerber, *Women of the Republic: Intellect and Ideology in Revolutionary America* (1980).

Leonard L. Richards, *Shays's Rebellion: The American Revolution's Final Battle* (2002).

Marylynn Salmon, *Women and the Law of Property in Early America* (1986).

David Waldstreicher, *Slavery's Constitution: From Revolution to Ratification* (2009).

Rosemarie Zagarri, *Revolutionary Backlash: Women and Politics in the Early American Republic* (2007).

THE CONSTITUTION AND RATIFICATION

Richard Beeman, *Plain, Honest Men: The Making of the American Constitution* (2010).

Carol Berkin, *A Brilliant Solution: Inventing the American Constitution* (2003).

Mary Sarah Bilder, *Madison's Hand: Revising the Constitutional Convention* (2015).

Saul Cornell, *The Other Founders: Anti-Federalism and the Dissenting Tradition in America, 1788–1828* (1999).

Jonathan Gienapp, *The Second Creation: Fixing the American Constitution in the Founding Era* (2018).

Woody Holton, *Unruly Americans and the Origins of the Constitution* (2007).

Michael J. Klarman, *The Framers' Coup: The Making of the United States Constitution* (2016).

Pauline Maier, *Ratification: The People Debate the Constitution, 1787–1788* (2011).

Jackson Turner Main, *The Antifederalists: Critics of the Constitution, 1781–1788* (2006).

Melvin Yazawa, *Contested Conventions: The Struggle to Establish the Constitution and Save the Union, 1787–1789* (2016).

Chapter 9

POLITICS

Terry Bouton, *Taming Democracy: "The People," the Founders, and the Troubled Ending of the American Revolution* (2007).

Ron Chernow, *Alexander Hamilton* (2004).

Seth Cotlar, *Tom Paine's America: The Rise and Fall of Transatlantic Radicalism in the Early Republic* (2011).

Laurent Dubois, *Avengers of the New World: The Story of the Haitian Revolution* (2004).

James Alexander Dun, *Dangerous Neighbors: Making the Haitian Revolution in Early America* (2016).

Stanley Elkins and Eric McKitrick, *The Age of Federalism: The Early American Republic, 1788–1800* (1993).

Todd Estes, *The Jay Treaty Debate, Public Opinion, and the Evolution of Early American Political Culture* (2006).

Don E. Fehrenbacher, *The Slaveholding Republic: An Account of the United States Government's Relations to Slavery* (2001).

John E. Ferling, *Adams vs. Jefferson: The Tumultuous Election of 1800* (2005).

Ronald Angelo Johnson, *Diplomacy in Black and White: John Adams, Toussaint Louverture, and Their Atlantic World Alliance* (2014).

Tim Matthewson, *A Proslavery Foreign Policy: Haitian-American Relations during the Early Republic* (2003).

David McCullough, *John Adams* (2001).

Jeffrey L. Pasley, *The First Presidential Contest: 1796 and the Founding of American Democracy* (2013).

Jeffrey L. Pasley, Andrew W. Robertson, and David Waldstreicher, *Beyond the Founders: New Approaches to the Political History of the Early American Republic* (2004).

Gordon Wood, *Empire of Liberty: A History of the Early Republic, 1789–1815* (2009).

SOCIETY, ECONOMY, AND CULTURE

Susan Branson, *These Fiery Frenchified Dames: Women and Political Culture in Early National Philadelphia* (2001).

Andrew Cayton, *Love in the Time of Revolution: Transatlantic Literary Radicalism and Historical Change, 1793–1818* (2013).

Rachel Hope Cleves, *The Reign of Terror in America: Visions of Violence from Anti-Jacobinism to Antislavery* (2009).

Nancy F. Cott, *The Bonds of Womanhood: "Woman's Sphere" in New England, 1780–1835* (2nd ed., 1997).

Erica Armstrong Dunbar, *Never Caught: The Washingtons' Relentless Pursuit of Their Runaway Slave, Ona Judge* (2017).

Robin Einhorn, *American Taxation, American Slavery* (2006).

Joanne B. Freeman, *Affairs of Honor: National Politics in the New Republic* (2001).

Cassandra A. Good, *Founding Friendships: Friendships between Men and Women in the Early American Republic* (2015).

Mary Kelley, *Learning to Stand and Speak: Women, Education, and Public Life in America's Republic* (2006).

Clare A. Lyons, *Sex among the Rabble: An Intimate History of Gender and Power in the Age of Revolution, Philadelphia, 1730–1830* (2006).

Gautham Rao, *National Duties: Custom Houses and the Making of the American State* (2016).

Ashli White, *Encountering Revolution: Haiti and the Making of the Early Republic* (2012).

INDIANS AND THE FRONTIER

Fred Anderson and Andrew R. L. Cayton, *The Dominion of War: Empire and Liberty in North America, 1500–2000* (2005).

Stuart Banner, *How the Indians Lost Their Land: Law and Power on the Frontier* (2005).

Tyler Boulware, *Deconstructing the Cherokee Nation: Town, Region, and Nation among Eighteenth-Century Cherokees* (2015).

Catherine Cangany, *Frontier Seaport: Detroit's Transformation into an Atlantic Entrepôt* (2014).

Allan Greer, *Property and Dispossession: Natives, Empires and Land in Early Modern North America* (2018).

James E. Lewis, *The American Union and the Problem of Neighborhood: The United States and the Collapse of the Spanish Empire, 1783–1829* (1998).

Kristofer Ray, *Middle Tennessee, 1775–1825: Progress and Popular Democracy on the Southwestern Frontier* (2007).

Malcolm J. Rohrbough, *Trans-Appalachian Frontier: People, Societies, and Institutions, 1775–1850* (3rd ed., 2008).

Bethel Saler, *The Settlers' Empire: Colonialism and State Formation in America's Old Northwest* (2015).

Chapter 10

POLITICS

John L. Brooke, *Columbia Rising: Civil Life on the Upper Hudson from the Revolution to the Age of Jackson* (2012).

Andrew Burstein and Nancy Isenberg, *Madison and Jefferson* (2010).

Saul Cornell, *The Other Founders: Anti-Federalism and the Dissenting Tradition in America, 1788–1828* (1999).

Caitlin Fitz, *Our Sister Republics: The United States in an Age of American Revolution* (2016).

Joanne B. Freeman, *Affairs of Honor: National Politics in the New Republic* (2001).

Nancy Isenberg, *Fallen Founder: The Life of Aaron Burr* (2008).

Alexander Keyssar, *The Right to Vote: The Contested History of Democracy in the United States* (2000).

Frank Lambert, *The Barbary Wars: American Independence in the Atlantic World* (2005).

Edward J. Larson, *A Magnificent Catastrophe: The Tumultuous Election of 1800, America's First Presidential Campaign* (2007).

James E. Lewis Jr., *The Burr Conspiracy: Uncovering the Story of an Early American Crisis* (2017).

Jeffrey L. Pasley, Andrew W. Robertson, and David Waldstreicher, *Beyond the Founders: New Approaches to the Political History of the Early American Republic* (2003).

Jay Sexton, *The Monroe Doctrine: Empire and Nation in Nineteenth-Century America* (2011).

Sean Wilentz, *The Rise of American Democracy: Jefferson to Lincoln* (2005).

INDIANS, THE WAR OF 1812, AND THE WEST

James F. Brooks, *Captives and Cousins: Slavery, Kinship, and Community in the Southwest Borderlands* (2002).

Kathleen DuVal, *The Native Ground: Indians and Colonists in the Heart of the Continent* (2007).

Eberhard L. Faber, *Building the Land of Dreams: New Orleans and the Transformation of Early America* (2016).

Elizabeth A. Fenn, *Encounters at the Heart of the World: A History of the Mandan People* (2014).

Anne Farrar Hyde, *Empires, Nations, and Families: A History of the North American West, 1800–1860* (2011).

Pekka Hämäläinen, *The Comanche Empire* (2008).

Alan Taylor, *The Civil War of 1812: American Citizens, British Subjects, Irish Rebels, and Indian Allies* (2010).

SLAVERY

Robert Pierce Forbes, *The Missouri Compromise and Its Aftermath: Slavery and the Meaning of America* (2007).

Annette Gordon-Reed, *The Hemingses of Monticello: An American Family* (2009).

John Craig Hammond, *Slavery, Freedom, and Expansion in the Early American West* (2007).

Alan Taylor, *The Internal Enemy: Slavery and War in Virginia, 1772–1832* (2013).

John R. Van Atta, *Wolf by the Ears: The Missouri Crisis* (2015).

WOMEN, MARRIAGE, AND RELIGION

Catherine Allgor, *Dolley Madison: The Problem of National Unity* (2013).

Nancy Cott, *Public Vows: A History of Marriage and the Nation* (2001).

Mary Kelley, *Learning to Stand and Speak: Women, Education, and Public Life in America's Republic* (2006).

Susan E. Klepp, *Revolutionary Conceptions: Women, Fertility, and Family Limitation in America, 1760–1820* (2009).

Mary Beth Sievens, *Stray Wives: Marital Conflict in Early National New England* (2005).

Rosemarie Zagarri, *Revolutionary Backlash: Women and Politics in the Early American Republic* (2007).

Chapter 11
ECONOMY

Edward J. Balleisen, *Navigating Failure: Bankruptcy and Commercial Society in Antebellum America* (2001).

Sven Beckert, *Empire of Cotton: A Global History* (2014).

John Lauritz Larson, *The Market Revolution in America: Liberty, Ambition, and the Eclipse of the Common Good* (2009).

Jessica M. Lepler, *The Many Panics of 1837: People, Politics, and the Creation of a Transatlantic Financial Crisis* (2013).

Stephen Mihm, *A Nation of Counterfeiters: Capitalists, Con Men, and the Making of the United States* (2009).

Brian Phillips Murphy, *Building the Empire State: Political Economy in the Early Republic* (2015).

Seth Rockman, *Scraping By: Wage Labor, Slavery, and Survival in Early Baltimore* (2008).

Caitlin Rosenthal, *Accounting for Slavery: Masters and Management* (2018).

Joshua D. Rothman, *Flush Times and Fever Dreams: A Story of Capitalism and Slavery in the Age of Jackson* (2012).

Calvin Schermerhorn, *The Business of Slavery and the Rise of American Capitalism, 1815–1860* (2015).

POLITICS

Stuart Banner, *How the Indians Lost Their Land: Law and Power on the Frontier* (2005).

Andrew Burstein, *The Passions of Andrew Jackson* (2003).

Cynthia Cumfer, *Separate Peoples, One Land: The Minds of Cherokees, Blacks, and Whites on the Tennessee Frontier* (2007).

Daniel Walker Howe, *What Hath God Wrought: The Transformation of America, 1815–1845* (2009).

Walter Johnson, *River of Dark Dreams: Slavery and Empire in the Cotton Kingdom* (2013).

Sean Michael O'Brien, *In Bitterness and in Tears: Andrew Jackson's Destruction of the Creeks and Seminoles* (2003).

J. M. Opal, *Avenging the People: Andrew Jackson, the Rule of Law, and the American Nation* (2017).

Sean Wilentz, *The Rise of American Democracy, Jefferson to Lincoln* (2005).

Michael Zakim, *Ready-Made Democracy: A History of Men's Dress in the American Republic, 1760–1860* (2003).

CULTURE, RELIGION, AND REFORM

Patricia Cline Cohen, Timothy J. Gilfoyle, and Helen Lefkowitz Horowitz, *The Flash Press: Sporting Male Weeklies in 1840s New York* (2008).

Bruce Dorsey, *Reforming Men and Women: Gender in the Antebellum City* (2002).

Stephen David Kantrowitz, *More Than Freedom: Fighting for Black Citizenship in a White Republic, 1829–1889* (2012).

Bruce Laurie, *Beyond Garrison: Antislavery and Social Reform* (2005).

Gerda Lerner, *The Grimké Sisters from South Carolina: Pioneers for Women's Rights and Abolition* (2009).

Caleb McDaniel, *The Problem of Democracy in the Age of Slavery: Garrisonian Abolitionists and Transatlantic Reform* (2013).

Richard S. Newman, *The Transformation of American Abolitionism: Fighting Slavery in the Early Republic* (2002).

Mark Perry, *Lift Up Thy Voice: The Sarah and Angelina Grimké Family's Journey from Slaveholders to Civil Rights Leaders* (2002).

Alisse Portnoy, *Their Right to Speak: Women's Activism in the Indian and Slave Debates* (2005).

Patrick Rael, *Black Identity and Black Protest in the Antebellum North* (2002).

Stacey M. Robertson, *Hearts Beating for Liberty: Women Abolitionists in the Old Northwest* (2010).

Scott A. Sandage, *Born Losers: A History of Failure in America* (2005).

Manisha Sinha, *The Slave's Cause: A History of Abolition* (2016).

Kathryn Kish Sklar and James Brewer Stewart, *Women's Rights and Transatlantic Slavery in the Era of Emancipation* (2007).

Richard B. Stott, *Jolly Fellows: Male Milieus in Nineteenth-Century America* (2009).

Daniel S. Wright, *"The First of Causes to Our Sex": The Female Moral Reform Movement in the Antebellum Northeast, 1834–1848* (2006).

Ronald J. Zboray and Mary Saracino Zboray, *Literary Dollars and Social Sense: A People's History of the Mass Market Book* (2005).

Chapter 12

THE ECONOMY AND FREE LABOR

Sean Patrick Adams, *Old Dominion, Industrial Commonwealth: Coal, Politics, and Economy in Antebellum America* (2009).

Stanley L. Engerman and Robert E. Gallman, eds., *The Cambridge Economic History of the United States: The Long Nineteenth Century* (2000).

J. Matthew Gallman, *Receiving Erin's Children: Philadelphia, Liverpool, and the Irish Famine Migration, 1854–1855* (2000).

Jonathan Hughes and Louis P. Cain, *American Economic History* (2011).

Robert A. Margo, *Wages and Labor Markets in the United States, 1820–1860* (2000).

David R. Meyer, *The Roots of American Industrialization* (2003).

Scott A. Sandage, *Born Losers: A History of Failure in America* (2005).

Robert J. Steinfeld, *Coercion, Contract, and Free Labor in the Nineteenth Century* (2010).

Kenneth J. Winkle, *The Young Eagle: The Rise of Abraham Lincoln* (2001).

WESTWARD EXPANSION AND THE MEXICAN-AMERICAN WAR

Gary Anderson, *The Conquest of Texas: Ethnic Cleansing in the Promised Land, 1820–1875* (2005).

Peter J. Blodgett, *Land of Golden Dreams: California in the Gold Rush Decade, 1848–1858* (1999).

H. W. Brand, *Lone Star Nation* (2004).

Richard L. Bushman, *Joseph Smith: Rough Stone Rolling* (2005).

Catherine M. Cameron, Paul Kelton, and Alan C. Swedlund, eds., *Beyond Germs: Native Depopulation in North America* (2015).

David C. Clary, *Eagles and Empire: The United States, Mexico, and the Struggle for a Continent* (2009).

Peter Cozzens, *The Earth Is Weeping: The Epic Story of the Indian Wars for the American West* (2016).

Geoff Cunfer and Bill Waiser, eds., *Bison and People on the North American Great Plains: A Deep Environmental History* (2016).

David Dary, *The Oregon Trail: An American Saga* (2004).

Brian DeLay, *War of a Thousand Deserts: Indian Raids and the U.S.-Mexican War* (2008).

Paul W. Foos, *A Short, Offhand, Killing Affair: Soldiers and Social Conflict during the Mexican-American War* (2002).

Sarah Barringer Gordon, *The Mormon Question: Polygamy and Constitutional Conflict in Nineteenth-Century America* (2002).

Amy S. Greenberg, *Manifest Manhood and the Antebellum American Empire* (2005).

——, *A Wicked War: Polk, Clay, Lincoln and the 1846 U.S. Invasion of Mexico* (2013).

Timothy J. Henderson, *A Glorious Defeat: Mexico and Its War with the United States* (2007).

Albert Hurtado, *John Sutter: A Life on the North American Frontier* (2006).

Benjamin Heber Johnson, *Revolution in Texas: How a Forgotten Rebellion and Its Bloody Suppression Turned Mexicans into Americans* (2003).

Susan Lee Johnson, *Roaring Camp: The Social World of the California Gold Rush* (2000).

Kent G. Lightfoot, *Indians, Missionaries, and Merchants: The Legacy of Colonial Encounters on the California Frontier* (2005).

Benjamin Madley, *An American Genocide: The United States and the California Indian Catastrophe, 1846–1873* (2016).

Robert W. Merry, *A Country of Vast Designs: James K. Polk, the Mexican War, and the Conquest of the American Continent* (2009).

Andres Resendez, *Changing National Identities at the Frontier: Texas and New Mexico, 1800–1850* (2005).

Malcolm Rohrbough, *Days of Gold: The California Gold Rush and the American Nation* (1997).

James A. Sandos, *Converting California: Indians and Franciscans in the Missions* (2004).

Virginia Scharff and Carolyn Brucken, *Home Lands: How Women Made the West* (2010).

Joel H. Sibley, *Storm over Texas: The Annexation Controversy and the Road to Civil War* (2005).

Stacey L. Smith, *Freedom's Frontier: California and the Struggle over Unfree Labor, Emancipation, and Reconstruction* (2013).

Michael L. Tate, *Indians and Emigrants: Encounters on the Overland Trail* (2006).

John G. Turner, *Brigham Young: Pioneer Prophet* (2012).

Richard White, *"It's Your Misfortune and None of My Own": A New History of the American West* (1993).

Richard Bruce Winders, *Mr. Polk's Army: The American Military Experience in the Mexican War* (1997).

Steven E. Woodworth, *Manifest Destinies: America's Westward Expansion and the Road to Civil War* (2010).

ANTEBELLUM CULTURE AND REFORM

Bruce Dorsey, *Reforming Men and Women: Gender in the Antebellum City* (2002).

Lori D. Ginzberg, *Elizabeth Cady Stanton: An American Life* (2009).

Bruce Laurie, *Beyond Garrison: Antislavery and Social Reform* (2005).

Sally McMillen, *Seneca Falls and the Origins of the Women's Rights Movement* (2008).

Patrick Rael, *Black Identity and Black Protest in the Antebellum North* (2002).

Susan M. Ryan, *The Grammar of Good Intentions: Race and the Antebellum Culture of Benevolence* (2003).

Beth A. Salerno, *Sister Societies: Women's Antislavery Organizations in Antebellum America* (2005).

Manisha Sinha, *The Slave's Cause: A History of Abolition* (2016).

Susan Zaeske, *Signatures of Citizenship: Petitioning, Antislavery, and Women's Political Identity* (2003).

Chapter 13

SLAVEHOLDERS AND THE ECONOMY

Edward E. Baptist, *The Half Has Never Been Told: Slavery and the Making of American Capitalism* (2014).

Sven Beckert, *Empire of Cotton: A Global History* (2014).

David L. Carlton and Peter A. Coclanis, *The South, the Nation, and the World: Perspectives on Southern Economic Development* (2003).

Steven Deyle, *Carry Me Back: The Domestic Slave Trade in American Life* (2005).

Richard Follett, *The Sugar Masters: Planters and Slaves in Louisiana's Cane World, 1820–1860* (2005).

Walter Johnson, *River of Dark Dreams: Slavery and Empire in the Cotton South* (2013).

Aaron W. Marrs, *Railroads in the Old South: Pursuing Progress in a Slave Society* (2009).

James David Miller, *South by Southwest: Planter Emigration and Identity in the Slave South* (2002).

Calvin Schermerhorn, *The Business of Slavery and the Rise of American Capitalism, 1815–1860* (2015).

Gavin Wright, *Slavery and American Economic Development* (2006).

SLAVES, SLAVERY, AND RACE RELATIONS

David F. Allmendinger Jr., *Nat Turner and the Rising in Southhampton County* (2014).

Ira Berlin, *Generations of Captivity: A History of African-American Slaves* (2003).

Patrick H. Breen, *The Land Shall Be Deluged in Blood: A New History of the Nat Turner Revolt* (2016).

Diane Mutti Burke, *On Slavery's Border: Missouri's Small-Slaveholding Households, 1815–1865* (2011).

Stephanie M. H. Camp, *Closer to Freedom: Enslaved Women and Everyday Resistance in the Plantation South* (2004).

Erskine Clarke, *Dwelling Place: A Plantation Epic* (2005).

Laurent DuBois, *The Banjo: America's African Instrument* (2016).

Sharla Fett, *Working Cures: Healing, Health, and Power on Southern Slave Plantations* (2002).

Jeff Forret, *Slave against Slave: Plantation Violence in the Old South* (2015).

Eugene D. Genovese, *Roll, Jordan, Roll: The World the Slave Made* (1974).

Kenneth S. Greenberg, ed., *Nat Turner: A Slave Rebellion in History and Memory* (2003).

Gwendolyn Midlo Hall, *Slavery and African Ethnicities in the Americas: Restoring the Links* (2005).

Anthony E. Kaye, *Joining Places: Slave Neighborhoods in the Old South* (2007).

Sydney Nathans, *To Free a Family: The Journey of Mary Walker* (2012).

Dylan C. Penningroth, *The Claims of Kinfolk: African American Property and Community in the Nineteenth-Century South* (2003).

Brenda E. Stevenson, *Life in Black and White: Family and Community in the Slave South* (1996).

SOCIETY AND CULTURE

Ira Berlin, *Slaves without Masters: The Free Negro in the Antebellum South* (1974).

Charles C. Bolton and Scott P. Culclasure, eds., *The Confessions of Edward Isham: A Poor White Life of the Old South* (1998).

Alfred L. Brophy, *University, Court, and Slave: Pro-Slavery Thought in Southern Colleges and Courts and the Coming of Civil War* (2016).

Christine Jacobson Carter, *Southern Single Blessedness: Unmarried Women in the Urban South, 1800–1865* (2006).

Laura F. Edwards, *The People and Their Peace: Legal Culture and the Transformation of Inequality in the Post-Revolutionary South* (2009).

Robert Elder, *The Sacred Mirror: Evangelicalism, Honor, and Identity in the Deep South, 1790–1860* (2016).

Craig T. Friend and Lorri Glover, eds., *Southern Manhood: Perspectives on Masculinity in the Old South* (2004).

Tim Alan Garrison and Greg O'Brien, eds., *The Native South: New Histories and Enduring Legacies* (2017).

Steven Hahn, *The Roots of Southern Populism: Yeoman Farmers and the Transformation of the Georgia Upcountry, 1850–1890* (1983).

Christine Leigh Heyrman, *Southern Cross: The Beginnings of the Bible Belt* (1997).

Anya Jabour, *Scarlett's Sisters: Young Women in the Old South* (2007).

Michael P. Johnson and James L. Roark, *Black Masters: A Free Family of Color in the Old South* (1984).

Stephanie McCurry, *Masters of Small Worlds: Yeoman Households, Gender Relations, and the Political Culture of the Antebellum South* (1995).

Glenn McNair, *Criminal Injustice: Slaves and Free Blacks in Georgia's Criminal Justice System* (2009).

Keri Leigh Merritt, *Masterless Men: Poor Whites and Slavery in the Antebellum South* (2017).

Seth Rockman, *Scraping By: Wage Labor, Slavery, and Survival in Early Baltimore* (2009).

Adam Rothman, *Slave Country: American Expansion and the Deep South* (2005).

Joshua D. Rothman, *Notorious in the Neighborhood: Sex and Families across the Color Line in Virginia, 1787–1861* (2002).

Loren Schweninger, *Families in Crisis in the Old South: Divorce, Slavery, and the Law* (2012).

Michael D. Thompson, *Working on the Dock of the Bay: Labor and Enterprise in an Antebellum Southern Port* (2015).

Jonathan Daniel Wells, *Origins of the Southern Middle Class, 1800–1861* (2004).

Julie Winch, *Between Slavery and Freedom: Free People of Color in America from Settlement to the Civil War* (2014).

Eva Sheppard Wolf, *Almost Free: A Story about Family and Race in Antebellum Virginia* (2012).

Bertram Wyatt-Brown, *Southern Honor: Ethics and Behavior in the Old South* (1982).

Jeffrey Robert Young, *Domesticating Slavery: The Master Class in Georgia and South Carolina, 1670–1837* (1999).

POLITICS AND POLITICAL CULTURE

Anthony Gene Carey, *Parties, Slavery, and the Union in Antebellum Georgia* (1997).

William J. Cooper Jr., *Liberty and Slavery: Southern Politics to 1860* (1983).

Lacy K. Ford Jr., *Deliver Us from Evil: The Slavery Question in the Old South* (2009).

Michael Perman, *Pursuit of Unity: A Political History of the American South* (2009).

Elizabeth R. Varon, *We Mean to Be Counted: White Women and Politics in Antebellum Virginia* (1998).

Peter Wallenstein, *From Slave South to New South: Public Policy in Nineteenth-Century Georgia* (1987).

Chapter 14

GENERAL WORKS

Don E. Fehrenbacher, *The Slaveholding Republic: An Account of the United States Government's Relations to Slavery* (2001).

Michael Holt, *The Fate of Their Country: Politicians, Slavery Extension, and the Coming of the Civil War* (2004).

Bruce C. Levine, *Half Slave and Half Free: The Roots of the Civil War* (1992).

James M. McPherson, *Ordeal by Fire: The Civil War and Reconstruction* (1982).

Mark E. Neely, *Boundaries of American Political Culture in the Civil War Era* (2005).

David M. Potter, *The Impending Crisis: America before the Civil War, 1848–1861* (2011).

Eric H. Walther, *The Shattering of the Union: America in the 1850s* (2004).

Sean Wilentz, *The Rise of American Democracy: Jefferson to Lincoln* (2005).

NORTHERN SECTIONALISM

Bonnie Anderson, *The Rabbi's Daughter: Ernestine Rose, Internationalist Feminist Pioneer* (2017).

Tom Chaffin, *Pathfinder: John Charles Frémont and the Course of American Empire* (2002).

Rodney O. Davis and Douglas L. Wilson, eds., *The Lincoln-Douglas Debates* (2008).

Eric Foner, *Free Soil, Free Labor, Free Men: The Ideology of the Republican Party before the Civil War* (1970).

——, *Gateway to Freedom: The Hidden History of the Underground Railroad* (2015).

William E. Gienapp, *The Origins of the Republican Party, 1852–1856* (1987).

R. Blakeslee Gilpin, *John Brown Still Lives! America's Long Reckoning with Violence, Equality, and Change* (2011).

Susan-Mary Grant, *North over South: Northern Nationalism and American Identity in the Antebellum Era* (2000).

David Grimsted, *American Mobbing, 1828–1865: Toward Civil War* (1998).

Joan D. Hedrick, *Harriet Beecher Stowe: A Life* (1994).

Pamela Herr, *Jessie Benton Frémont: A Biography* (1987).

Steven Lubet, *The "Colored Hero" of Harper's Ferry: John Anthony Copeland and the War against Slavery* (2015).

Kristen Tegtmeier Oertel, *Harriet Tubman: Slavery, the Civil War, and Civil Rights in the Nineteenth Century* (2016).

David S. Reynolds, *John Brown, Abolitionist: The Man Who Killed Slavery, Sparked the Civil War, and Seeded Civil Rights* (2005).

Leonard L. Richards, *The California Gold Rush and the Coming of the Civil War* (2007).

Brian Schoen, *The Fragile Fabric of Union: Cotton, Federal Politics, and the Global Origins of the Civil War* (2009).

James Brewer Stewart, *Wendell Phillips, Liberty's Hero* (1986).

Wendy Hamand Venet, *Neither Ballots nor Bullets: Women Abolitionists and the Civil War* (1991).

Kenneth J. Winkle, *The Young Eagle: The Rise of Abraham Lincoln* (2001).

SOUTHERN SECTIONALISM

Robert E. Bonner, *Mastering America: Southern Slaveholders and the Crisis of American Nationhood* (2009).

William J. Cooper Jr., *The South and the Politics of Slavery, 1828–1856* (1978).

John Patrick Daly, *When Slavery Was Called Freedom: Evangelicalism, Proslavery, and the Causes of the Civil War* (2002).

Lacy K. Ford Jr., *Origins of Southern Radicalism: The South Carolina Upcountry, 1800–1860* (1988).

William W. Freehling, *The Road to Disunion*, 2 vols. (1990–2007).

Matthew Pratt Guterl, *American Mediterranean: Southern Slaveholders in the Age of Emancipation* (2008).

David S. Heidler and Jeanne T. Heidler, *Henry Clay: The Essential American* (2010).

Matthew Karp, *This Vast Southern Empire: Slaveholders at the Helm of American Foreign Policy* (2016).

William A. Link, *Roots of Secession: Slavery and Politics in Antebellum Virginia* (2002).

Robert E. May, *Manifest Destiny's Underworld: Filibustering in Antebellum America* (2002).

Christopher J. Olsen, *Political Culture and Secession in Mississippi: Masculinity, Honor, and the Antiparty Tradition, 1830–1860* (2002).

George Rable, *Damn Yankees! Demonization and Defiance in the Confederate South* (2015).

Edward Rugemer, *The Problem of Emancipation: The Caribbean Roots of the American Civil War* (2008).

Mitchell Snay, *Gospel of Disunion: Religion and Separatism in the Antebellum South* (1993).

SECESSION

Shearer Davis Bowman, *At the Precipice: Americans North and South during the Secession Crisis* (2010).

Daniel Crofts, *Reluctant Confederates: Upper South Unionists in the Secession Crisis* (1989).

Charles B. Dew, *Apostles of Disunion: Southern Secession Commissioners and the Causes of the Civil War* (2001).

Michael P. Johnson, *Toward a Patriarchal Republic: The Secession of Georgia* (1977).

Russell McClintock, *Lincoln and the Decision for War: The Northern Response to Secession* (2008).

Carl Lawrence Paulus, *The Slaveholding Crisis: Fear of Insurrection and the Coming of the Civil War* (2017).

David M. Potter, *Lincoln and His Party in the Secession Crisis* (1942).

Lorman A. Ratner and Dwight L. Teeter Jr., *Fanatics and Fire-Eaters: Newspapers and the Coming of the Civil War* (2003).

Chapter 15
GENERAL WORKS

Orville Vernon Burton, *The Age of Lincoln* (2007).

Allen C. Guelzo, *A New History of the Civil War and Reconstruction* (2012).

Steven Hahn, *A Nation without Borders: The U.S. and Its World in an Age of Civil War, 1830–1910* (2016).

James M. McPherson, *The Battle Cry of Freedom: The Civil War Era* (1988).

Scott Nelson and Carol Sheriff, *A People at War: Civilians and Soldiers in America's Civil War* (2007).

Adam I. P. Smith, *The American Civil War* (2007).

MILITARY HISTORY

Thomas F. Army Jr., *Engineering Victory: How Technology Won the Civil War* (2016).

Ron Chernow, *Grant* (2017).

Mark Grimsley, *The Hard Hand of War: Union Military Policy toward Southern Civilians, 1861–1865* (1995).

Joseph T. Glatthaar, *General Lee's Army: From Victory to Collapse* (2008).

Earl J. Hess, *Civil War Infantry Tactics: Training, Combat, and Small-Unit Effectiveness* (2015).

Chandra Manning, *What This Cruel War Was Over: Soldiers, Slavery, and the Civil War* (2007).

James M. McPherson, *Tried by War: Abraham Lincoln as Commander-in-Chief* (2008).

Williamson Murray and Wayne Wei-siang Hsieh, *A Savage War: A Military History of the Civil War* (2016).

Mark E. Neely Jr., *The Civil War and the Limits of Destruction* (2007).

Christopher Phillips, *The Civil War in the Border South* (2013).

Brooks D. Simpson, *Ulysses S. Grant: Triumph over Adversity, 1822–1865* (2000).

Donald Stoker, *The Grand Design: Strategy and the U.S. Civil War* (2010).

Daniel E. Sutherland, *A Savage Conflict: The Decisive Role of Guerrillas in the American Civil War* (2009).

William G. Thomas, *The Iron Way: Railroads, the Civil War, and the Making of Modern America* (2011).

Russell F. Weigley, *A Great Civil War: A Military and Political History, 1861–1865* (2000).

John Fabian Witt, *Lincoln's Code: The Laws of War* (2012).

THE NORTH AND SOUTH AT WAR

Iver Bernstein, *The New York City Draft Riots: Their Significance for American Society and Politics in the Age of the Civil War* (1990).

William A. Blair, *Virginia's Private War: Feeding Body and Soul in the Confederacy, 1861–1865* (1998).

——, *With Malice toward Some: Treason and Loyalty in the Civil War Era* (2014).

Michael Bonner, *Confederate Political Economy: Creating and Managing a Southern Corporatist Nation* (2016).

William J. Cooper, *Jefferson Davis, American* (2000).

Daniel W. Crofts, *Lincoln and the Politics of Slavery* (2017).

D. H. Dilbeck, *A More Civil War: How the Union Waged a Just War* (2016).

Drew Gilpin Faust, *This Republic of Suffering: Death and the American Civil War* (2008).

William W. Freehling, *The South vs. the South: How Anti-Confederate Southerners Shaped the Course of the Civil War* (2001).

Gary W. Gallagher, *The Confederate War* (1997).

Judith Ann Giesberg, *Civil War Sisterhood: The U.S. Sanitary Commission and Women's Politics in Transition* (2000).

William C. Harris, *Lincoln and the Border States: Preserving the Union* (2012).

——, *Lincoln and Congress* (2017).

Libra R. Hilde, *Worth a Dozen Men: Women and Nursing in the Civil War South* (2012).

R. Douglas Hurt, *Agriculture and the Confederacy: Policy, Productivity, and Power in the Civil War South* (2015).

Jacqueline Jones, *Saving Savannah: The City and the Civil War* (2008).

Bruce Levine, *The Fall of the House of Dixie: The Civil War and the Social Revolution That Transformed the South* (2013).

Stephanie McCurry, *Confederate Reckoning: Power and Politics in the Civil War* (2010).

Mark E. Neely Jr., *The Fate of Liberty: Abraham Lincoln and Civil Liberties* (1991).

Megan Kate Nelson, *Ruin Nation: Destruction and the American Civil War* (2012).

George C. Rable, *God's Almost Chosen People: A Religious History of the American Civil War* (2010).

Heather Cox Richardson, *The Greatest Nation of the Earth: Republican Economic Policies during the Civil War* (1997).

Anne Sarah Rubin, *A Shattered Nation: The Rise and Fall of the Confederacy, 1861–1868* (2005).

Mark S. Schantz, *Awaiting the Heavenly Country: The Civil War and America's Culture of Death* (2008).

Nina Silber, *Daughters of the Union: Northern Women Fight the Civil War* (2006).

Walter Stahr, *Seward: Lincoln's Indispensable Man* (2012).

Yael A. Sternhell, *Routes of War: The World of Movement in the Confederate South* (2012).

Margaret M. Storey, *Loyalty and Loss: Alabama's Unionists in the Civil War and Reconstruction* (2004).

Amy Murrell Taylor, *The Divided Family in Civil War America* (2005).

Jennifer L. Weber, *Copperheads: The Rise and Fall of Lincoln's Opponents in the North* (2008).

THE STRUGGLE FOR FREEDOM

Edward Ayers, *The Thin Light of Freedom: The Civil War and Emancipation in the Heart of America* (2017).

Ira Berlin, *The Long Emancipation: The Demise of Slavery in the U.S.* (2015).

Ira Berlin et al., eds., *Freedom: A Documentary History of Emancipation, 1861–1867,* 5 vols. (1982–2008).

Eric Foner, *The Fiery Trial: Abraham Lincoln and American Slavery* (2010).

Joseph T. Glatthaar, *Forged in Battle: The Civil War Alliance of Black Soldiers and White Officers* (1990).

Allen C. Guelzo, *Lincoln's Emancipation Proclamation: The End of Slavery in America* (2004).

Steven Hahn, *The Political Worlds of Slavery and Freedom* (2009).

Bruce Levine, *Confederate Emancipation: Southern Plans to Free and Arm Slaves during the Civil War* (2006).

Cate Lineberry, *Be Free or Die: The Amazing Story of Robert Smalls' Escape from Slavery to Union Hero* (2017).

Chandra Manning, *Troubled Refuge: Struggling for Freedom in the Civil War* (2016).

William S. McFeely, *Frederick Douglass* (1991).

James Oakes, *The Radical and the Republican: Frederick Douglass, Abraham Lincoln, and the Triumph of Antislavery Politics* (2007).

Chapter 16

GENERAL WORKS

Thomas J. Brown, ed., *Reconstructions: New Perspectives on the Postbellum United States* (2006).

Gregory P. Downs and Kate Masur, eds., *The World the Civil War Made* (2015).

Michael W. Fitzgerald, *Splendid Failure: Postwar Reconstruction in the American South* (2007).

Eric Foner, *Reconstruction: America's Unfinished Revolution* (1988).

Martha Hodes, *Mourning Lincoln* (2015).

Sharon D. Kennedy-Nolle, *Writing Reconstruction: Race, Gender, and Citizenship in the Postwar South* (2015).

James M. McPherson, *Ordeal by Fire: The Civil War and Reconstruction* (3rd ed., 2000).

John David Smith, ed., *Interpreting American History: Reconstruction* (2016).

Mark Wahlgren Summers, *The Ordeal of Reunion: A New History of Reconstruction* (2014).

THE MEANING OF FREEDOM

Ira Berlin et al., eds., *Freedom: A Documentary History of Emancipation, 1861–1867*, 5 vols. (1982–2008).

Ronald E. Butchart, *Schooling the Freed People: Teaching, Learning, and the Struggle for Black Freedom, 1861–1876* (2010).

Jim Downs, *Sick for Freedom: African-American Illness and Suffering during the Civil War and Reconstruction* (2012).

Laura F. Edwards, *A Legal History of the Civil War and Reconstruction: A Nation of Rights* (2015).

Thavolia Glymph, *Out of the House of Bondage: The Transformation of the Plantation Household* (2008).

Steven Hahn, *A Nation under Our Feet: Black Political Struggles in the Rural South, from Slavery to the Great Migration* (2003).

Leon F. Litwack, *Been in the Storm So Long: The Aftermath of Slavery* (1979).

Sydney Nathans, *A Mind to Stay: White Plantations, Black Homeland* (2017).

Susan Eva O'Donovan, *Becoming Free in the Cotton South* (2007).

Howard N. Rabinowitz, *Race Relations in the Urban South, 1865–1890* (1978).

Roger L. Ransom and Richard Sutch, *One Kind of Freedom: The Economic Consequences of Emancipation* (1977).

Martin Ruef, *Between Slavery and Capitalism: The Legacy of Emancipation in the American South* (2014).

Leslie Schwalm, *A Hard Fight for We: Women's Transition from Slavery to Freedom in South Carolina* (1997).

Loren Schweninger, *James T. Rapier and Reconstruction* (1978).

Rebecca J. Scott, *Degrees of Freedom: Louisiana and Cuba after Slavery* (2005).

THE POLITICS OF RECONSTRUCTION

Stephen V. Ash, *A Massacre in Memphis: The Race Riot That Shook the Nation* (2013).

Justin Behrend, *Reconstructing Democracy: Grassroots Black Politics in the Deep South after the Civil War* (2015).

Richard F. Bensel, *Yankee Leviathan: The Origins of Central State Authority in America, 1859–1877* (1990).

Luis-Alejandro Dinnella-Borrego, *The Risen Phoenix: Black Politics in the Post–Civil War South* (2016).

Philip Dray, *Capitol Men: The Epic Story of Reconstruction through the Lives of the First Black Congressmen* (2008).

Gregory P. Downs, *After Appomattox: Military Occupation and the Ends of War* (2015).

Ellen Carol DuBois, *Feminism and Suffrage: The Emergence of an Independent Women's Movement in America, 1848–1869* (1978).

Laura Edwards, *Gendered Strife and Confusion: The Political Culture of Reconstruction* (1997).

Michael W. Fitzgerald, *Reconstruction in Alabama: From Civil War to Redemption in the Cotton South* (2017).

James K. Hogue, *Uncivil War: Five New Orleans Street Battles and the Rise and Fall of Radical Reconstruction* (2006).

Richard L. Hume and Jerry B. Gough, *Blacks, Carpetbaggers, and Scalawags: The Constitutional Conventions of Radical Reconstruction* (2008).

Elaine Frantz Parsons, *Ku-Klux: The Birth of the Klan during Reconstruction* (2016).

Heather Cox Richardson, *The Death of Reconstruction: Race, Labor, and Politics in the Post–Civil War North, 1865–1901* (2001).

Leslie A. Schwalm, *Emancipation's Diaspora: Race and Reconstruction in the Upper Midwest* (2009).

Brooks D. Simpson, *The Reconstruction Presidents* (1998).

Mark Wahlgren Summers, *A Dangerous Stir: Fear, Paranoia, and the Making of Reconstruction* (2009).

Michael Vorenberg, *Final Freedom: The Civil War, the Abolition of Slavery, and the Thirteenth Amendment* (2001).

C. Vann Woodward, *Reunion and Reaction: The Compromise of 1877 and the End of Reconstruction* (1951).

THE STRUGGLE IN THE SOUTH

James Alex Baggett, *The Scalawags: Southern Dissenters in the Civil War and Reconstruction* (2003).

Nancy D. Bercaw, *Gendered Freedoms: Race, Rights, and the Politics of Household in the Delta, 1861–1875* (2003).

Stephen Budiansky, *The Bloody Shirt: Terror after the Civil War* (2008).

Jane Turner Censer, *The Reconstruction of White Southern Womanhood, 1865–1895* (2003).

Paul A. Cimbala, *Under the Guardianship of the Nation: The Freedmen's Bureau and the Reconstruction of Georgia, 1865–1870* (1997).

Jane E. Dailey, *Before Jim Crow: The Politics of Race in Post-emancipation Virginia* (2000).

Carole Faulkner, *Women's Radical Reconstruction: The Freedmen's Aid Movement* (2004).

Sarah E. Gardner, *Blood and Irony: Southern White Women's Narratives of the Civil War, 1861–1937* (2004).

Moon-Ho Jung, *Coolies and Cane: Race, Labor, and Sugar in the Age of Emancipation* (2006).

Stephen Kantrowitz, *Ben Tillman and the Reconstruction of White Supremacy* (2000).

Charles Lane, *The Day Freedom Died: The Colfax Massacre, the Supreme Court, and the Betrayal of Reconstruction* (2008).

Amy Feely Morsman, *The Big House after Slavery: Virginian Plantation Families and Their Postbellum Domestic Experiences* (2010).

George C. Rable, *But There Was No Peace: The Role of Violence in the Politics of Reconstruction* (1984).

Hannah Rosen, *Terror in the Heart of Freedom: Citizenship, Sexual Violence, and the Meaning of Race in the Postemancipation South* (2009).

Hyman Rubin III, *South Carolina Scalawags* (2006).

Christopher M. Span, *From Cotton Field to Schoolhouse: African American Education in Mississippi, 1862–1875* (2009).

Peter Wallenstein, *From Slave South to New South: Public Policy in Nineteenth-Century Georgia* (1987).

GLOSSARY

Acoma pueblo revolt Revolt against the Spanish by Indians living at the Acoma pueblo in 1599.

Algonquian Indians People who inhabited the coastal plain of present-day Virginia, near the Chesapeake Bay, when English colonists first settled the region.

Alien and Sedition Acts 1798 laws passed to suppress political dissent. The Sedition Act criminalized conspiracy and criticism of government leaders. The two Alien Acts extended the waiting period for citizenship and empowered the president to deport or imprison without trial any foreigner deemed a danger.

American Colonization Society Organization that sent freed slaves and other black Americans to Liberia in West Africa.

American system The practice of manufacturing and then assembling interchangeable parts.

American Temperance Society Organization founded in 1826 by Lyman Beecher that linked drinking with poverty, idleness, ill health, and violence. The temperance movement had considerable success, contributing to a sharp drop in American alcohol consumption.

Antifederalists Opponents of the ratification of the Constitution. Antifederalists feared that a powerful and distant central government would be out of touch with the needs of citizens. They also complained that the Constitution failed to guarantee individual liberties in a bill of rights.

antinomians Individuals who believed that Christians could be saved by faith alone and did not need to act in accordance with God's law as set forth in the Bible.

Archaic Indians Hunting and gathering peoples who descended from Paleo-Indians and dominated the Americas from 10,000 BP to between 4000 and 3000 BP.

Articles of Confederation The written document defining the structure of the government during and after the Revolution. Under the Articles, the Union was a confederation of equal states, with no president and with limited powers, existing mainly to foster a common defense.

Bacon's Rebellion A rebellion in 1676 led by frontier settler Nathaniel Bacon, who sought to attack both Indians and wealthy planters favored by the Virginia government.

Barbados Island in the English West Indies that produced sugar during the seventeenth century and provided a major source of wealth for England.

battle of Antietam Battle fought in Maryland on September 17, 1862, between the Union forces of George McClellan and Confederate troops of Robert E. Lee. The battle, a Union victory that left 6,000 dead and 17,000 wounded, was the bloodiest day of the war.

battle of Bull Run (Manassas) First major battle of the Civil War, fought at a railroad junction in northern Virginia on July 21, 1861. The Union suffered a sobering defeat, while the Confederates felt affirmed in their superiority and the inevitability of Confederate nationhood.

battle of Bunker Hill Early battle of the war, on June 17, 1775, involving a massive British attack on New England militia units on a hill facing Boston. The militiamen finally yielded the hill, but not before inflicting heavy casualties on the British.

battle of Gettysburg Battle fought at Gettysburg, Pennsylvania (July 1–3, 1863), between Union forces under General Meade and Confederate forces under General Lee. The Union emerged victorious and Lee lost more than one-third of his men. Together with Vicksburg, Gettysburg marked a major turning point of the war.

battle of Long Island First major engagement of the new Continental army, which fought 45,000 British troops newly arrived on western Long Island (today Brooklyn). The Continentals retreated with high casualties and many taken prisoner.

battle of New Orleans The final battle in the War of 1812, fought and won by General Andrew Jackson and his militiamen against the much larger British army in New Orleans. The celebrated battle made no difference since the peace had already been negotiated.

battle of Oriskany A punishing defeat for Americans in New York in August 1777. Mohawk and Seneca Indians ambushed German American militiamen and allied Oneida warriors, and four hundred on the revolutionary side were killed. It marked the beginning of bitter frontier warfare with sharp racial overtones.

battle of Saratoga A two-stage battle in New York ending with the decisive defeat and surrender of British general John Burgoyne on October 17, 1777. This victory convinced France to ally with the American side in the war, turning the American Revolution into a global war.

battle of Shiloh Battle at Shiloh Church, Tennessee, on April 6–7, 1862, between Albert Sidney Johnston's Confederate forces and Ulysses S. Grant's Union army. The Union army ultimately prevailed, though at great cost to both sides. Shiloh ruined the Confederacy's bid to control the war in the West.

battle of Tippecanoe An attack on Shawnee Indians at Prophetstown on the Tippecanoe River in 1811 by American forces headed by William Henry Harrison, Indiana's territorial governor. Tenskwatawa, the Prophet, fled with his followers. Tecumseh, his brother, deepened his resolve to make war on the United States.

battle of Yorktown October 1781 battle that sealed American victory. French and American troops and the French navy trapped the British army at Yorktown, Virginia.

Beringia The land bridge between Siberia and Alaska that allowed people to migrate into the Western Hemisphere.

Bill of Rights The first ten amendments to the Constitution, officially ratified by 1791. The First through Eighth Amendments dealt with individual liberties, and the Ninth and Tenth concerned the boundary between federal and state authority.

black codes Laws passed by state governments in the South in 1865 and 1866 that sought to keep ex-slaves subordinate to whites. At the core of the black codes lay the desire to force freedmen back to the plantations.

Black Death A disease in the mid-fourteenth century that killed about a third of the European population.

"Bleeding Kansas" Term for the bloody struggle between proslavery and antislavery factions in Kansas following its organization in the fall of 1854.

Boston Massacre March 1770 incident in Boston in which British soldiers fired on an American crowd, killing five. The Boston Massacre became a rallying point for colonists who increasingly saw the British government as tyrannical and illegitimate.

burial mounds Earthen mounds constructed by ancient American peoples, especially throughout the gigantic drainage of the Ohio and Mississippi rivers, after about 2500 BP.

Cahokia The largest ceremonial site in ancient North America, located near the Mississippi River across from present-day St. Louis, where thousands of inhabitants built hundreds of earthen mounds between about AD 800 and AD 1500.

California gold rush Mining rush initiated by James Marshall's discovery of gold in the foothills of the Sierra Nevada in 1848.

Calvinism Doctrines of John Calvin emphasizing predestination, namely the idea that God had determined which souls would receive eternal salvation.

carpetbaggers Southerners' pejorative term for northern migrants who sought opportunity in the South after the Civil War. Northern migrants formed an important part of the southern Republican Party.

chiefdom Hierarchical social organization headed by a chief. Archaeologists believe Woodland chiefdoms commanded the labor required to construct burial mounds.

chivalry The South's romantic ideal of male-female relationships. Chivalry's underlying assumptions about the weakness of white women and the protective authority of men resembled the paternalistic defense of slavery.

Civil Rights Act of 1866 Legislation passed by Congress in 1866 that nullified the black codes and affirmed that black Americans should have equal benefit of the law. President Andrew Johnson vetoed this expansion of black rights and federal authority, but Congress later overrode his veto.

Clovis point Distinctively shaped spearhead used by Paleo-Indians and named for the place in New Mexico where it was first excavated.

Coercive Acts Four British acts of 1774 meant to punish Massachusetts for the destruction of three shiploads of tea. Known in America as the Intolerable Acts, they led to open rebellion in the northern colonies.

Columbian exchange The transatlantic exchange of goods, people, and ideas that began when Columbus arrived in the Caribbean, ending the age-old separation of the hemispheres by the Atlantic Ocean.

Comanchería Indian empire based on trade in horses, hides, guns, and captives that stretched from the Canadian plains to Mexico in the eighteenth century. By 1865, fewer than five thousand Comanches lived in the empire, which ranged from west Texas north to Oklahoma.

committees of correspondence A communications network established among towns in Massachusetts and among colonial capital towns in 1772–1773. Providing for the rapid dissemination of important political news, these committees politicized ordinary townspeople, sparking a revolutionary language of rights.

Common Sense A pamphlet written by Thomas Paine in 1776 that laid out the case for independence. In it, Paine rejected monarchy, urging its replacement with republican government based on the consent of the people. The wildly popular pamphlet influenced public opinion throughout the colonies.

Compromise of 1850 Laws passed in 1850 meant to resolve disputes about the place of slavery in the nation. Key elements included the admission of California as a free state and the Fugitive Slave Act.

Compromise of 1877 Informal agreement in which Democrats agreed not to block Rutherford Hayes's inauguration and to deal fairly with freedmen; in return, Hayes vowed not to use the army to uphold the remaining Republican regimes in the South and to provide the South with substantial federal subsidies for railroads. The compromise brought the Reconstruction era to an end.

Confederate States of America Government formed by Lower South states on February 7, 1861, following their secession from the Union. Secessionists argued that the election of a Republican to the presidency imperiled slavery and that the South no longer had political protection within the Union.

conquistadors Spanish explorers and soldiers who conquered Native Americans in the New World.

Continental army The army created in June 1775 by the Second Continental Congress to fight the British. Virginian George Washington, commander in chief, had the task of turning local militias and untrained volunteers into a disciplined force.

contraband of war General Benjamin F. Butler's term for runaway slaves, whom he considered confiscated property of war, not fugitives, and put to work in the Union army. This policy proved to be a step on the road to emancipation.

cotton kingdom Term that reflected the dominance of cotton in the southern economy. Cotton was particularly important in the tier of states from South Carolina west to Texas. Cotton cultivation was the key factor in the growth of slavery.

Creek War Part of the War of 1812 involving the Creek nation in the Mississippi Territory and Tennessee militiamen. General Andrew Jackson's forces defeated the Creeks at the Battle of Horseshoe Bend in 1814, forcing them to sign away much of their land.

creoles Children born to Spanish parents in the New World who, with the *peninsulares*, made up the tiny portion of the population at the top of the colonial social hierarchy.

Declaration of Independence A document containing philosophical principles and a list of grievances that declared and justified the colonies' independence from Britain. The Second Continental Congress adopted the Declaration on July 4, 1776, abandoning the moderates' policy of reconciliation and turning the rebellion into a revolution.

Declaratory Act 1766 law issued by Parliament to assert its unassailable right to legislate for its British colonies "in all cases whatsoever." The act put Americans on notice that Britain retained the power to govern the colonies despite repealing the Stamp Act.

Democrats Political party that evolved out of the Democratic Republicans after 1834. Strongest in the South and West, the Democrats embraced Andrew Jackson's vision of limited government, expanded political participation for white men, and the promotion of an ethic of individualism.

***Dred Scott* decision** 1857 Supreme Court decision that validated the South's most extreme argument for its rights in the territories. It denied the federal government's right to exclude slavery from the territories and declared that African Americans were not citizens.

Emancipation Proclamation President Lincoln's proclamation issued on January 1, 1863, declaring all slaves in Confederate-controlled territory free. The proclamation made the Civil War a war for abolition, as well as a war for union.

Embargo Act of 1807 Act of Congress that prohibited U.S. ships from traveling to foreign ports and effectively banned overseas trade in an attempt to deter Britain from halting U.S. ships at sea. The embargo caused grave hardships for Americans engaged in overseas commerce.

encomienda A system that allowed the Spanish *encomendero,* or "owner" of a town, to collect tribute from the town in return for providing law and order and encouraging "his" Indians to convert to Christianity.

English Reformation Abolished the Catholic Church in England and declared King Henry VIII head of the new Church of England.

Enlightenment An eighteenth-century philosophical movement that emphasized the use of reason to reevaluate previously accepted doctrines and traditions.

Erie Canal Canal finished in 1825, covering 350 miles between Albany and Buffalo and linking the port of New York City with the entire Great Lakes region. The canal turned New York City into the country's premier commercial city.

Federalists Originally the term for the supporters of the ratification of the U.S. Constitution in 1787–1788. In the 1790s, it became the name for one of the two dominant political groups that emerged during that decade. Federalists supported Britain in foreign policy and commercial interests at home. Prominent Federalists included George Washington, Alexander Hamilton, and John Adams.

feme covert Legal doctrine grounded in British common law that held that a wife's civic life was subsumed by her husband's. Married women lacked independence to own property, make contracts, or keep wages earned. The doctrine shaped women's status in the early Republic.

First Continental Congress September 1774 gathering of colonial delegates in Philadelphia to discuss the crisis precipitated by the Coercive Acts. The congress produced a declaration of rights and an agreement to impose a limited boycott of trade with Britain.

Fort Sumter Union fort on an island at the entrance to Charleston harbor in South Carolina. After Confederate leaders learned President Lincoln intended to resupply Fort Sumter, Confederate forces attacked the fort on April 12, 1861, initiating the Civil War.

free black An African American who was not enslaved. State legislatures stemmed the growth of the free black population and shrank the liberty of free blacks.

free labor Term referring to work conducted free from constraint and according to a voluntary contract between employer and laborer. The ideal of free labor lay at the heart of the North's argument that slavery should not be extended into the western territories.

Freedmen's Bureau Government organization created in March 1865 to distribute food and clothing to destitute Southerners and to ease the transition of slaves to free persons.

Fugitive Slave Act A law included in the Compromise of 1850 to strengthen provisions for capturing runaway slaves in the North.

Gabriel's rebellion Planned rebellion organized by an enslaved blacksmith named Gabriel and inspired by the Haitian Revolution. When the alleged conspiracy was revealed, the accused slaves defended themselves by comparing their violent resistance to slavery with the American Revolution.

gradual emancipation Laws passed in five northern states that provided a multistage process for freeing slaves. Gradual emancipation laws were seen as a middle path, balancing enslaved peoples' rights to liberty with slave owners' rights to "property": two fundamental rights enshrined by the Revolution.

Great Awakening Wave of revivals that began in Massachusetts and spread through the colonies in the 1730s and 1740s.

Haitian Revolution Uprising in the French colony of Saint Domingue that began in 1791 and led to the creation of the Republic of Haiti in 1804. Unlike the French and American Revolutions, the Haitian Revolution committed itself to the liberty of slaves and equality for people of African descent. It fueled fears of slave insurrections in the United States.

Halfway Covenant A compromise that allowed the unconverted children of visible saints to become "halfway" members of the church and baptize their own children, even though they were not full church members.

Hartford Convention A secret meeting of New England Federalist politicians held in late 1814 to discuss constitutional changes to reduce the South's political power and thus help block policies that injured northern commercial interests.

headright Fifty acres of free land granted by the Virginia Company to planters for each indentured servant they purchased.

Homestead lockout 1892 lockout of workers at the Homestead, Pennsylvania, steel mill after Andrew Carnegie refused to renew the union contract and workers prepared to strike. Union supporters attacked the Pinkerton National Detective Agency guards hired to protect the mill, but the National Guard soon broke the strike.

House of Burgesses Virginia's assembly of representatives elected by inhabitants that was established by the Virginia Company and continued after the settlement became a royal colony.

hunter-gatherer A way of life that involved hunting game and gathering food from naturally occurring sources.

Incan empire A region under the control of the Incas and their emperor, Atahualpa, that stretched along the western coast of South America.

indentured servants Poor immigrants who signed contracts known as indentures, in which they agreed to four to seven years of labor in North America in exchange for transportation from England, as well as food and shelter during their period of servitude.

Indian Removal Act of 1830 Act that directed the forced relocation of eastern tribes to territory west of the Mississippi. Jackson insisted that his goal was to save the Indians. Indians resisted the controversial act, but in the end most were forced to comply.

Jamestown The first permanent English settlement in North America, established in 1607 by colonists sponsored by the Virginia Company.

Jay Treaty 1795 treaty between the United States and Britain negotiated by John Jay. It secured limited trading rights in the West Indies but failed to accomplish most other U.S. objectives. Bitterly denounced by its opponents, it sharply divided Americans and hastened the formation of political parties.

Kansas-Nebraska Act 1854 law that divided Indian Territory into Kansas and Nebraska, repealed the Missouri Compromise, and left the new territories to decide the issue of slavery on the basis of popular sovereignty.

King Cotton diplomacy Confederate diplomatic strategy built on the hope that European nations starving for cotton would break the Union blockade and recognize the Confederacy. This strategy failed as Europeans held stores of surplus cotton and developed new sources outside the South.

King Philip's War War begun by Metacomet (King Philip) in 1675, in which the colonists finally prevailed after much bloodshed.

Ladies Association A women's organization in Philadelphia that collected donations in 1780 for Continental troops. A leader authored a declaration, "The Sentiments of an American Woman," to justify women's unexpected entry into political life.

Lewis and Clark expedition 1804–1806 expedition led by Meriwether Lewis and William Clark that explored the trans-Mississippi West for the U.S. government. The expedition's mission was scientific, political, and geographic.

Lincoln-Douglas debates Series of debates on the issue of slavery and freedom between Democrat Stephen Douglas and Republican Abraham Lincoln, held during the 1858 Illinois senatorial race. Douglas became senator, but the debates helped catapult Lincoln to national attention.

Lone Star Republic Independent republic, also known as the Republic of Texas, that was established by a rebellion of Texans against Mexican rule.

Louisiana Purchase 1803 purchase of French territory west of the Mississippi River that stretched from the Gulf of Mexico to Canada. The Louisiana Purchase nearly doubled the size of the United States and opened the way for future American expansion west.

Lowell mills Water-powered textile mills constructed along the Merrimack River in Lowell, Massachusetts, that pioneered the extensive use of female laborers. By 1836, the eight mills there employed more than five thousand young women, who lived in boardinghouses under close supervision.

loyalists Colonists who remained loyal to Britain during the Revolutionary War, probably numbering around one-fifth of the population in 1776. Colonists supported Britain for many reasons, and loyalists could be found in every region of the country.

manifest destiny Term coined in 1845 by journalist John L. O'Sullivan to justify American expansion.

Marbury v. Madison 1803 Supreme Court case that established the concept of judicial review in finding that parts of the Judiciary Act of 1789 were in conflict with the Constitution. The Supreme Court assumed legal authority to overrule acts of other branches of the government.

Mason-Dixon line A surveyor's mark that had established the boundary between Maryland and Pennsylvania in colonial times. By the 1830s, the boundary divided the free North and the slave South.

mechanical reaper Machine that allowed farmers to harvest up to twelve acres of wheat a day.

Mexica The Mexica commanded an empire that stretched from coast to coast across central Mexico and encompassed as many as six million people.

Middle Passage The Atlantic crossing by slave ships traveling from West Africa to the Americas.

Military Reconstruction Act Congressional act of March 1867 that initiated military rule of the South. Congressional reconstruction divided the ten unreconstructed Confederate states into five military districts, each under the direction of a Union general. It also established the procedure by which unreconstructed states could reenter the Union.

miscegenation Interracial sex. Proslavery spokesmen argued that abolition would lead to miscegenation. In reality, slavery led to considerable sexual abuse of black women by their white masters.

Missouri Compromise 1820 congressional compromise engineered by Henry Clay that paired Missouri's entrance into the Union as a slave state with Maine's entrance as a free state. The compromise also established Missouri's southern border as the permanent line dividing slave states from free states.

Monroe Doctrine President James Monroe's 1823 declaration that the Western Hemisphere was closed to further colonization or interference by European powers. In exchange, Monroe pledged that the United States would not become involved in European struggles. The United States strengthened the doctrine during the late nineteenth century.

Mormons Members of the Church of Jesus Christ of Latter-Day Saints founded by Joseph Smith in 1830.

National American Woman Suffrage Association (NAWSA) Organization formed in 1890 that united the National Woman Suffrage Association and the American Woman Suffrage Association. The NAWSA pursued state-level campaigns to gain the vote for women. With successes in Idaho, Colorado, and Utah, woman suffrage had become more accepted by the 1890s.

natural increase Growth of population through reproduction, as opposed to immigration.

Navigation Acts English laws passed in the 1650s and 1660s requiring that English colonial goods be shipped through English ports on English ships in order to benefit English merchants, shippers, and seamen.

New Jersey Plan Alternative plan drafted by delegates from small states, retaining the confederation's single-house congress with one vote per state. Like the Virginia Plan, it proposed enhanced congressional powers, including the right to tax, regulate trade, and use force on unruly state governments.

new Negroes Term given to newly arrived African slaves in the colonies.

New Netherland Dutch colony on Manhattan Island.

New Spain Spanish colony in the New World that governed for the benefit of Spain.

New York City draft riots Four days of rioting in New York City in July 1863, triggered by efforts to enforce the military draft. Democratic Irish workingmen, suffering economic hardship, infuriated by the draft, and opposed to fighting for black freedom, killed at least 105 people, most of them black.

New York Female Moral Reform Society An organization of religious women inspired by the Second Great Awakening to eradicate sexual sin and male licentiousness. Formed in 1833, it spread to hundreds of auxiliaries across the country.

Newburgh Conspiracy A threatened coup planned by Continental army officers and leaders in the Continental Congress in 1782–1783. General Washington defused the threat by appealing to the officers' commitment to republicanism and their sense of honor. As a result, his fame grew to new heights.

Northwest Confederacy Coalition of Native American nations defending their territory situated between the Ohio River and the Great Lakes from U.S. expansion. With the assistance of British officers in forts along the Great Lakes, it fought to preserve a zone of Native American sovereignty.

Northwest Ordinance Land act of 1787 that established a three-stage process by which settled territories would become states. It also banned slavery in the Northwest Territory. The ordinance guaranteed that new states joining the United States would not become colonial dependencies.

nullification Theory asserting that states could nullify acts of Congress that exceeded its constitutional powers. South Carolina advanced the theory of nullification in 1828 in response to an unfavorable federal tariff. A show of force by Andrew Jackson, combined with tariff revisions, ended the crisis.

Oneida community Utopian community organized by John Humphrey Noyes in New York in 1848.

Open Door policy Policy successfully insisted upon by Secretary of State John Hay in 1899–1900 recommending that the major powers of the United States, Britain, Japan, Germany, France, and Russia all have access to trade with China and that Chinese sovereignty be maintained.

Oregon Trail Route from Independence, Missouri, to Oregon traveled by American settlers starting in the late 1830s.

Paleo-Indians Archaeologists' term for the first migrants into North America and their descendants who spread across the Americas between about 15,000 BP and 13,500 BP.

panic of 1837 Major economic crisis that led to several years of hard times in the United States from 1837 to 1841. Sudden bankruptcies, contraction of credit, and runs on banks led to hardships nationwide. The causes were multiple and global and not well understood.

partible inheritance System of inheritance in which land was divided equally among sons.

paternalism The theory of slavery that emphasized reciprocal duties and obligations between masters and their slaves. Whites employed the concept of paternalism to deny that the slave system was brutal and exploitative.

Pennsylvania Dutch Name given by other colonists to German immigrants to the middle colonies.

People's Party (Populist Party) Political party formed in St. Louis in 1892 by the Farmers' Alliance to advance the goals of the Populist movement. Populists sought economic democracy, promoting land, electoral, banking, and monetary reform. Republican victory in the presidential election of 1896 effectively destroyed the People's Party.

plantation Large farm worked by twenty or more slaves. Although small farms were far more numerous, plantations produced more than 75 percent of the South's export crops.

plantation belt Flatlands that spread from South Carolina to east Texas and were dominated by large plantations.

planter A substantial landowner who tilled his estate with twenty or more slaves. Although small in number, planters dominated the economic, social, and political world of the South.

Pontiac's War The continued war of Native American peoples in the northwest after France capitulated at the end of the Seven Years' War. The war heightened Britain's determination to create a boundary between colonists and Indians, embodied in the Royal Proclamation of 1763.

popular sovereignty The idea that government is subject to the will of the people. Applied to the territories, popular sovereignty meant that the residents of a territory should determine, through their legislature, whether to allow slavery.

predestination Doctrine stating that God determined whether individuals were destined for salvation or damnation before their birth.

presidios Spanish forts built to block Russian advance into California.

Protestant Reformation A religious rupture that began in 1517 with Martin Luther's critiques of the Roman Catholic Church, and precipitated the enduring division between Protestants and Catholics.

Pueblo Bonito The largest residential and ceremonial site, containing more than six hundred rooms and thirty-five kivas, in the major Anasazi cultural center of Chaco Canyon in present-day New Mexico.

Pueblo Revolt The revolt of Pueblo Indians in 1680 against the Spanish in New Mexico, under the leadership of Popé.

pueblos Multiunit dwellings, storage spaces, and ceremonial centers—often termed *kivas*—built by ancient Americans in the Southwest for centuries around AD 1000.

Pullman boycott Nationwide railroad workers' boycott of trains carrying Pullman cars in 1894 after Pullman workers, suffering radically reduced wages, joined the American Railway Union (ARU) and union leaders were fired in response. The boycott ended after the U.S. Army fired on strikers and ARU leader Eugene Debs was jailed.

Puritan Revolution English civil war which began in 1642 and ended with the execution of Charles I in 1649, resulting in Puritan rule in England until 1660.

Puritans Dissenters from the Church of England who wanted a genuine Protestant Reformation rather than the partial Reformation sought by Henry VIII.

Quakers Members of the Society of Friends who believed that God spoke directly to each individual through an "inner light."

Reconquest The centuries-long drive by the Christian kingdoms of Spain and Portugal to expel Muslims from the Iberian Peninsula.

Redeemers Name taken by southern Democrats who harnessed white rage in order to overthrow Republican rule and black political power and thus, they believed, save southern civilization.

redemptioners A kind of indentured servant.

Report on Manufactures Hamilton's 1791 proposal to encourage the production of American-made goods by subsidizing manufacturers and imposing tariffs on imports. Its vision of a future manufacturing society broke sharply from the nation's agrarian economy. Congress rejected the measure.

Report on Public Credit Hamilton's 1790 report recommending that the national debt be funded at full value, but not repaid immediately. Hamilton's goal was to make the new country creditworthy, not debt-free, and tie the interests of wealthy bondholders to the new government. Critics complained that it would benefit speculators.

republicanism A political philosophy founded on the principle of government by the consent of the people. It embraced representative institutions (as opposed to monarchy) and required a citizenry willing to put the public good ahead of its private interests.

Republican motherhood Ideology emphasizing the importance of female education to equip women to raise educated and enlightened male citizens. Even as it opened pathways for women's education, the ideology reinforced existing hierarchies of gender.

Republican Party Antislavery party formed in 1854 following passage of the Kansas-Nebraska Act. The Republicans attempted to unite all those who opposed the extension of slavery into any territory of the United States.

Republicans Sometimes called Democratic-Republicans, they emerged as a political party in the 1790s in opposition to the Federalists. Republicans supported the revolutionaries in France and agrarian interests at home. Prominent Republicans included Thomas Jefferson and James Madison.

royal colony A colony ruled by a king or queen and governed by officials appointed to serve the monarchy and represent its interests.

Royal Proclamation of 1763 A law that reserved lands to the west of the Appalachian Mountains as Native American territory. By forbidding colonial settlement and land purchases, the Proclamation helped to settle Pontiac's War, but it inflamed tensions between British settlers and the imperial government.

scalawag A derogatory term that Southerners applied to southern white Republicans, who were seen as traitors to the South. Most were yeoman farmers.

Scots-Irish Protestant immigrants from northern Ireland, Scotland, and northern England.

second Bank of the United States National bank chartered in 1816. Intended to help regulate the economy, the bank became a major issue in Andrew Jackson's 1832 reelection campaign.

Second Continental Congress Legislative body that governed the American colonies from May 1775 through the end of the war. It established an army, created its own money, and declared independence. It also conducted the nation's foreign policy, entering into a critical alliance with France.

Second Great Awakening Unprecedented religious revival in the 1820s and 1830s that promised access to salvation. It was a major impetus for reform movements of the era, inspiring efforts to combat drinking, sexual sin, and slavery.

Seneca Falls Declaration of Sentiments Declaration issued in 1848 at the first national woman's rights convention in the United States, which was held in Seneca Falls, New York.

separate spheres Ideology that posited a sharp separation between the masculine, public sphere of the workplace and the feminine, domestic sphere of the home. Both consequence and facilitator of the rapid economic changes of the early nineteenth century, it transformed gender and family relations.

Separatists Puritans who sought to withdraw or separate from the Church of England.

Seven Years' War War (1756–1763) between Britain and France that shattered the French empire in North America. Known in America as the French and Indian War (fighting in America began and ended earlier than it did elsewhere in the world), it ended with the spectacular victory of Great Britain but planted the seeds of future imperial troubles.

sharecropping Labor system that emerged in the South during Reconstruction. Under this system, planters divided their plantations into small farms that freedmen rented, paying with a share of each year's crop. Sharecropping gave blacks some freedom, but they remained dependent on white landlords and country merchants.

Shays's Rebellion Uprising (1786–1787) led by farmers centered in western Massachusetts. Dissidents protested tax policies of the eastern elites who controlled the state's government. Shays's Rebellion caused leaders throughout the country to worry about the confederation's ability to handle civil disorder.

Sherman's March to the Sea Military campaign from September through December 1864 in which Union forces under General Sherman marched from Atlanta, Georgia, to the coast at Savannah. Carving a path of destruction as it progressed, Sherman's army aimed at destroying white Southerners' will to continue the war.

siege of Vicksburg Six-week siege by General Grant intended to starve out Vicksburg. On July 4, 1863, the 30,000 Confederate troops holding the city surrendered. The victory gave the Union control of the Mississippi River and, together with Gettysburg, marked a major turning point of the war.

slave codes Laws enacted in southern states to strengthen the institution of slavery that required the total submission of slaves.

slavery Lifelong bondage and coerced labor imposed on captured Africans and usually inherited by their New World descendants.

Stamp Act 1765 British law imposing a tax on all paper used for official documents, for the purpose of raising revenue. Widespread resistance to the Stamp Act led to its repeal in 1766.

Stono Rebellion Slave uprising in Stono, South Carolina, in 1739.

Sugar (Revenue) Act 1764 British law that decreased the duty on French molasses, making it more attractive for shippers to obey the law, and at the same time raised penalties for smuggling. The Sugar Act regulated trade but was also intended to raise revenue.

Tainos Indians who inhabited San Salvador and were the first people Columbus encountered in the New World.

task system A system of labor that assigned slaves a daily task and allowed them to do as they wished if their task was completed.

Tea Act of 1773 British act that lowered the existing tax on tea to entice boycotting Americans to buy it. Resistance to the Tea Act led to the passage of the Coercive Acts and imposition of military rule in Massachusetts.

three-fifths clause A clause in the Constitution stipulating that all free persons plus "three-fifths of all other Persons" would constitute the numerical base for apportioning both representation and taxation. The clause tacitly acknowledged the existence of slavery in the United States and gave extra representation to slaveholding states.

Townshend duties British law that established new duties on tea, glass, lead, paper, and painters' colors imported into the colonies. The Townshend duties led to boycotts and heightened tensions between Britain and the American colonies.

Trail of Tears Forced westward journey of Cherokees from their lands in Georgia to present-day Oklahoma in 1838. Despite a Supreme Court decision in their favor, federal troops forced the Cherokees on a grueling 1,200-mile march. Nearly one-quarter died en route.

Treaty of Amity and Commerce Treaty between the United States and France signed on February 6, 1778. Along with the treaty of alliance, it provided French military and financial aid for the rebellious colonies, and mutual trade agreements to promote a permanent alliance. The U.S. promised not to make a separate peace with Britain.

Treaty of Fort Stanwix A 1784 treaty between the United States and the Iroquois Confederacy that resulted in large land cessions in western New York and northwestern Pennsylvania. Tribes not present at Fort Stanwix disavowed the treaty.

Treaty of Greenville 1795 treaty between the United States and nations of the Northwest Confederacy. The United States gave Native Americans treaty goods valued at $25,000. In exchange, the Indians ceded most of Ohio. The treaty brought only temporary peace to the region.

Treaty of Guadalupe Hidalgo February 1848 treaty that ended the Mexican-American War.

Treaty (Peace) of Paris, 1783 September 3, 1783, treaty between the U.S. and Britain that ended the Revolutionary War. The treaty acknowledged America's independence, set its boundaries, and promised the quick withdrawal of British troops from American soil. It failed to recognize Indians as players in the conflict.

Treaty of Tordesillas The 1494 treaty drew an imaginary line west of the Canary Islands; land discovered west of the line belonged to Spain, and land to the east belonged to Portugal.

tribute The goods, ranging from food and luxury items to candidates for human sacrifice, that the Mexica collected from people they conquered.

Uncle Tom's Cabin Enormously popular antislavery novel written by Harriet Beecher Stowe and published in 1852. It helped to solidify northern sentiment against slavery and to confirm white Southerners' sense that no sympathy remained for them in the free states.

underground railroad Network consisting mainly of black homes, churches, and neighborhoods that helped slaves escape to the North.

Union blockade The United States' use of its navy to patrol the southern coastline to restrict Confederate trade. The blockade became increasingly effective and succeeded in depriving the Confederacy of vital supplies and revenue.

United States Constitution The document written in 1787 and subsequently ratified by the original thirteen states that laid out the governing structure of the United States in separate legislative, executive, and judicial branches.

upcountry The hills and mountains of the southern interior whose higher elevation, colder climate, rugged terrain, and poor transportation made the region less hospitable than the flatlands to slavery and plantations.

Virginia and Kentucky Resolutions 1798 resolutions condemning the Alien and Sedition Acts submitted to the federal government by the Virginia and Kentucky state legislatures. The resolutions advanced the idea that state legislatures could judge the constitutionality of federal laws and nullify them.

Virginia Company A joint-stock company organized by London investors in 1606 that received a land grant from King James I in order to establish English colonies in North America.

Virginia Plan Plan drafted by James Madison proposing a powerful three-branch government, with representation in both houses of the congress tied to population. This plan eclipsed the voice of small states in national government.

virtual representation The theory that all British subjects were represented in Parliament, whether they had elected representatives in that body or not. American colonists rejected the theory of virtual representation, arguing that only direct representatives had the right to tax the colonists.

visible saints Puritans who had passed the tests of conversion and church membership and therefore appeared to be among God's elect.

War Hawks Young men newly elected to the Congress of 1811 who were eager for war against Britain in order to end impressments, fight Indians, and expand into neighboring

British territory. Leaders included Henry Clay of Kentucky and John C. Calhoun of South Carolina.

Whigs Political party that evolved out of the National Republicans after 1834. With a northeastern power base, the Whigs supported federal action to promote commercial development and generally looked favorably on the reform movements associated with the Second Great Awakening.

Whiskey Rebellion July 1794 uprising by farmers in western Pennsylvania in response to enforcement of an unpopular tax on whiskey. Fearing it might spark a revolution against the new government in the west, President Washington responded with overwhelming force to quash the rebellion and avoid bloodshed.

Wilmot Proviso Proposal put forward by Representative David Wilmot of Pennsylvania in August 1846 to ban slavery in territory acquired from the Mexican-American War.

XYZ affair A 1797 incident in which French officials demanded bribes from the United States as the price for peace negotiations. American diplomats refused. News of the incident caused widespread outrage in the United States and led to an undeclared war with France, known as the Quasi-War.

yeomen Farmers who owned and worked on their own small plots of land. Yeomen living within the plantation belt were more dependent on planters than were yeomen in the upcountry, where small farmers dominated.

INDEX

A note about the index: Names of individuals appear in boldface. Letters in parentheses following pages refer to: *(i)* illustrations, including photographs and artifacts *(f)* figures; including charts and graphs; *(m)* maps; *(b)* boxed features (such as "Analyzing Historical Evidence"); *(t)* tables.

Arobe, Francisco de, 49*(i)*
Arrows, and bows, Archaic Indians and, 9
Articles of Confederation, 205*(i)*, 206–209
Artifact(s)
  in archaeology versus history, 3
  Cahokia mother and child statue, 3*(i)*
  from Chaco Canyon, New Mexico, 16–17*(b)*
  Clovis point as, 7*(i)*
  Folsom point as, 7*(i)*
  Inca goddess, 36*(i)*
  Ozette carving as, 11*(i)*
  from Seven Years' War, 143*(i)*
  weaving kit as, 21*(i)*
Ashley, John, 212*(b)*
Asia. *See also specific countries*
  European trade with, 30, 31*(m)*
  human migration to, 5–6
  Portuguese exploration of, 32
Assemblies, colonial, 135–136
Atahualpa, 39
Atchison, David Rice, 406
Athapascan Indians, 21
Atlanta, Georgia, Yankee capture of, 448*(m)*, 449, 452*(t)*
Atlantic Ocean
  Civil War and, 429*(m)*, 433
  sea bridge across, 36
  slave trade across, in 18th century, 120–123, 121*(m)*, 121*(t)*
Attorney general, creation of, 239
Attucks, Crispus, 159–160, 160*(i)*
Augusta, Georgia, British capture of, 193
Austin, Stephen F., 341
Ayllón, Lucas Vázquez de, 35*(m)*, 40

Bache, Benjamin, 258*(b)*
Bacon, Nathaniel, 68–72
Bacon's Laws, 69
Bacon's Rebellion, 67, 68–72
Balboa, Vasco Núñez, 35*(m)*, 36
Ball courts, 18*(i)*
Baltimore, Lord, 66–67
Baltimore and Ohio Railroad, building of, 300
Banknotes, as currency, 302–303, 311, 312
Bank of the United States
  creation of first, 245*(i)*, 245–246
  creation of second, 304
  end of second, 311–312
Bankruptcy, panic of 1819 and, 304
Banks and banking
  in 1790s, 241

Bank of the United States and. *See* Bank of the United States
  economic growth of, in 1790s, 241
  increase of, in early 19th century, 302–304
  national, creation of, 444
Baptists and Baptist Church
  black churches of, 463
  in colonial America in 18th century, 130
  plain folk in South as, 381
  Second Great Awakening and, 316
  slaves as, 377
  women in church governance and, 284
Barbados
  African slaves brought to Carolina colonies from, 72
  immigrants from, in Carolina colonies, 74
  sugar from, 74
Barbary Wars, 270–271
Barton, Clara, 446
Baskets, Indian, 8
Batalla del Sacramento (Michaud), 345*(i)*
Battles. *See specific locations of battles*
Bay Psalm book, 83*(i)*
Bearden, Romare, 412*(i)*
Bear Flag Revolt, 342, 344*(m)*
Beecher, Lyman, 316
Bell, John, 400*(m)*, 411, 413, 413*(m)*
Benét, Stephen Vincent, 411
Benezet, Anthony, 125*(b)*
Benton, Thomas Hart, 337
Beringia, 5–6, 6*(m)*
Berkeley, William, 67, 68–72, 69*(i)*
Bernard, Francis
  Sons of Liberty and, 159
  Stamp Act and, 152, 153
  Townshend duties and, 157
Bethlehem, Pennsylvania, in 18th century, 119*(i)*
Bett, Mum (Elizabeth Freeman), 212, 212*(i)*, 212–213*(b)*
Bibb, Henry, 354
Bible
  King James Version of, 85
  Protestant Reformation and, 49–50
  slavery and, 377
"The Bible Argument: or, Slavery in the Light of Divine Revelation" (Stringfellow), 365*(b)*
Big house, plantation life and, 369–370, 370*(f)*
Bill of Rights
  Antifederalists on, 231

  First Congress and, 239
  in state constitutions, 210
Birney, James G., 343
Births, to slave mothers, 123
Bison. *See* Buffalo
Black codes, 465*(i)*, 465–467
Black Death, 30
Blackfeet Indians, 20
Black Hawk (Saux and Fox Indian leader), 308
Black Hawk War, 308
Black market, during Revolutionary War, 187
Blacks
  as African Americans. *See* African Americans
  as emancipated slaves. *See* Freedmen
  as nonslaves during slavery. *See* Free blacks
  as slaves born in Africa. *See* African slaves; Slaves and slavery
  as slaves born in America. *See* African American slaves; Slaves and slavery
  voting rights of. *See* African American suffrage
Black skin color, 70–71*(b)*
Black soldiers, 187*(i)*
Blade, on moral reform, 319*(b)*
"Bleeding Kansas," 406, 406*(i)*, 406*(m)*
"Bleeding Sumner," 406
Blue Jacket (Shawnee chief), 250, 251
Board of Trade, colonial government and, 136
Boarman, Richard, 64–65*(b)*
Boleyn, Anne, 84
Bonds, *Report on Public Credit* and, 242
The Book of Mormon, 340
Boonesborough, Kentucky, Cherokee attack on, 191
Booth, John Wilkes, 451, 464
Boré, Étienne de, 367
Boston, Massachusetts
  British military occupation of, 159–160
  Dominion of New England and, 105–106
  Puritans and, 87
  Shays's Rebellion and, 224
  slave rebellions in, 169
  Stamp Act and, 152–153
  tea dumped in harbor at, 162
  Townshend duties and, 156–157, 159–160
  War of 1812 and, 280–281*(b)*
  wealthy merchants in, 116

California gold rush
  beginning and consequences of, 348–350
  Chinese immigrants and, 349(i)
  firsthand experiences of, 350–351(b)
  Indian deaths from, 349
California Indians
  in 1490s, 19(f), 21
  California gold rush and, 349
  culture of, 9(m), 9–11
California Territory
  Mexican-American War and, 344(m), 346
  ranchos in, 342
  Spanish missions in, 133, 133(m), 134–135(b), 136(i)
  Treaty of Guadalupe Hidalgo and, 347, 348(m)
California Trail, 338(m), 342
Californios, discrimination against, 349
Calvin, John, 88
Calvinists and Calvinism, 88
Camden, South Carolina, battle of, 194, 194(m)
Camp followers, of British army, 189
Camp followers, of Continental army, 179
Canada
  black loyalists in, 214(i)
  invasion of, War of 1812 and, 278, 279(m)
  Paleo-Indians and, 6
Canal boats, 298(i), 299, 299(m)
Cape of Good Hope, Dias and, 32
Cape Verde, Portuguese exploration of, 32
Caravels, 32
Caribbean area
  Columbus and, 34
  sugar from, 74
Carleton, Guy, 197
Carmel Mission, 136(i)
Carney, Kate, 372
Carolina colonies. *See also* North Carolina colony; South Carolina colony
  African slaves and, 72
  early settlement of, 74–76, 75(m)
Carpetbaggers, 472
Cartier, Jacques, 35(m), 50
Cass, Lewis, 393–394, 394(m), 400(m)
Catholic missionaries. *See also* Catholics and Catholicism
  in California Territory, 133, 134–135(b)

in New Spain, 45
Catholics and Catholicism
  Church of England and, 84–85
  in colonial America in 18th century, 130
  encomienda and, 45
  in Florida and New Mexico in 17th century, 72–73
  as immigrants, from 1845 to 1855, 401
  as immigrants from Ireland, 336
  in Maryland, 66–67
  as missionaries. *See* Catholic missionaries; Christian missionaries
  Protestant Reformation and, 49–50
  Quebec Act and, 163
Catlin, George, 275(i), 278(i), 339, 340(i)
Cayuga Indians, 19, 184
Census of 1810, 277
Certificates of debt
  Report on Public Credit and, 242, 244
  Revolutionary War and, 187
Ceuta, Portuguese conquest of, 31
Chaco Canyon, New Mexico, Pueblo Bonito in, 13, 16(i), 16–17(b)
Chancellorsville, Virginia, battle of, 447, 448(m), 451(t)
Chappel, Alonzo, 452(i)
Chapultepec Castle, battle at, 347
Charles I, king of England
  Lord Baltimore and, 66
  Puritanism and, 85
  Puritan Revolution and, 93
Charles I, king of Spain, 49
Charles II, king of England
  Barbados and, 74
  King Philip's War and, 104–106
  New Netherlands and, 99
  Penn and, 101
Charleston, South Carolina
  British evacuation of, 200
  establishment of, 74, 75(m)
  pro–French Revolution sentiments in, 253
  slave demonstrations in, 156
  Stamp Act and, 154
  Townshend duties and, 158
Charleston Mercury, on slavery, 360
Charles Towne, 74, 75(m). *See also* Charleston, South Carolina
Charles V, emperor, 49–50
Charter of Privileges, in Pennsylvania colony, 102
Chase, Salmon P.
  Andrew Johnson and, 470

on Henry Clay's plan, 394
  in Lincoln's cabinet, 426
  on slavery, 394
Chattanooga, Tennessee, battle of, 447, 448(m), 451(t)
Cherokee Indians
  Confederate army and, 431
  Continental army and, 91–92
  Indian Removal Act of 1830 and, 308–310, 309(m), 310(i)
  Northwest Confederacy and, 220
  Yamasee War and, 132
Cherry Valley, New York, Indian attack on, 190–191
Chesapeake (ship), 276, 277(m)
Chesapeake Bay, defense of, 196
Chesapeake colonies, 55–79
  in 17th century, 61(m)
  at end of 17th century, 103(m)
  exports from, in 18th century, 129(f)
  Jamestown and, 56–59
  preferred slaves in, 123
  Puritans in, 87
  ratio of blacks to whites in, in 18th century, 120
  slave labor system in, 72–78
  social hierarchy and inequality in, 67–72
  tobacco growing and, 60–67
Chesnut, Mary Boykin, 373, 386
Cheyenne Indians
  in 1490s, 20
  westward migration of settlers and, 339
Chicago, Illinois, transcontinental railroad and, 398
Chicago Tribune, on slavery in Mississippi, 466
Chickamauga, Alabama, battle of, 448(m), 451(t)
Chickasaw Indians
  in 1490s, 19
  in Confederate army, 431
  Indian Removal Act of 1830 and, 308–309, 309(m), 310
Chiefdom, 12, 13–18
Child, Lydia Maria, 353, 404(i)
Child labor, in Great Britain, 368(b)
China
  European trade with, 31(m)
  immigrants from. *See* Chinese immigrants
  per capita production of, in 1850s, 334(b)
  Portuguese trade with, 32, 33(i)
Chinese immigrants, California gold rush and, 349, 349(i)
Chippewa Indians, 19, 220

Conestoga Indians, 149
Confederacy. *See also* Confederate army
  challenges of, 440–441
  collapse of, 449–451
  creation of, 415–416, 416*(m)*
  states of Upper South and, 423*(m)*, 423–424
Confederacy's Ordnance Bureau, 426
Confederate army. *See also* Civil War; Confederacy
  attack on Fort Sumter by, 422–423
  battles of 1861-1862, 428–430, 429*(m)*, 431*(t)*. *See also specific battles*
  battles of 1863-1865, 447*(t)*, 447–453, 448*(m)*, 451*(t)*. *See also specific battles*
  black soldiers fighting against, 436–439, 438–439*(b)*
  effect of war on southern states and, 440–444
  military strategy of, 424–425
  reasons it expected to win, 424–427
  recruiting and supplying of, 426–427
  resources of, 424–425, 425*(f)*
Confederate States of America, 414–415, 416*(m)*. *See also* Confederacy
Confederation (of states), 205–233
  Articles of Confederation for, 206–209
  problems of, 215–225
  ratification of Constitution in, 228–232
  sovereign states in, 209–215
  United States Constitution for, 225–228
Confiscation Act of 1861, 435
Confiscation Act of 1862, 436
Confiscation Acts, 459
Confiscation of property, from loyalists, 186
Congregationalism, in colonial America in 18th century, 130
Congress. *See also* House of Representatives; Senate
  actions of, during Civil War, 444–445
  creation of, by Constitution, 226
  during Reconstruction, blacks versus whites in, 473, 473*(f)*
  reconstruction plan of, 458

slavery in Southwest and, 392–393
Connecticut. *See also* Connecticut colony
  New Jersey Plan and, 226
  ratification of Constitution by, 229, 229*(m)*
  state laws on slavery in, 211
  tax requisition of 1785 and, 221
Connecticut colony
  New Haven, Townshend duties and, 157
  sale of land by, 114
  Stamp Act and, 154
Conquest, by Spain, official justification of, 46–47*(b)*
Conquistadors
  encomienda and, 45
  Spanish, 39–42
Conscription. *See* Military draft
Constitutional Union Party, 411, 413*(m)*
Constitution of United States
  amendments to, from First Congress, 239
  checks and balances in, 227–228
  Fifteenth Amendment and, 470–471
  Fourteenth Amendment and, 468–469, 473, 480
  Madison and, 205
  proposals for, 225–228
  ratification of, 228–232, 229*(m)*
  Thirteenth Amendment and, 464, 465
  writing of, 225–226
Continental army. *See also* Revolutionary War
  blacks, recruitment of, 187
  Bunker Hill, battle of, 175
  Camden, battle of, 194, 194*(m)*
  capture of Montreal by, 180, 181*(m)*
  characteristics of, 178–179
  Cowpens, battle of, 194*(m)*
  creation of, 174
  Fort Stanwix, battle of, 189
  King's Mountain, battle of, 194*(m)*, 195
  Long Island, battle of, 180
  military pay in arrears for, 215–216
  Oriskany, battle of, 189
  Saratoga, battle of, 189, 190*(m)*
  Yorktown, battle of, 196, 196*(m)*
Continental Association, 166
Continental Congress
  Articles of Confederation and, 206–207

First, 166
James Madison and, 205
Second, 174–178
tax requisition of 1785 and, 221–224
Treaty of Fort Stanwix and, 216–217
Continental currency
  depreciation of, 187
  issuance of, 174
Continental drift, 5, 5*(m)*
Contraband of war, fugitive slaves as, 435
Conversion, Puritanism and, 88, 95–96. *See also* Catholic missionaries; Christian missionaries
Coode, John, 106
Copley, John Singleton, 240*(i)*
Copperheads (Peace Democrats), 446
Corinth, Mississippi, Yankee capture of, 429*(m)*, 433
Corliss, Alonzo B., 475*(b)*
Corn
  in ancient America, 14–15*(b)*
  artifacts used with, 16–17*(b)*
  Jamestown and, 57–59
  from New World to Europe, 37
  southwestern Indians and, 12
Cornplanter (Seneca negotiator), Treaty of Fort Stanwix and, 217, 217*(i)*
Cornstalk (Shawnee chief), 191
Cornwallis, Charles, 194*(m)*, 195–196
Coronado, Francisco Vasquez de, 35*(m)*, 42, 42*(i)*
Corporations, growth in, 304
"Corrupt bargain," 291
Cortés, Hernán
  explorations of, 35*(m)*, 38–39, 39*(i)*, 39*(m)*, 44
  success of, 40–41*(b)*
Cortés Montezuma, Isabel Tolsa, 43
Cotton
  importance of, during Civil War, 425
  increased growth of, 241
  international cloth industry and, 368–369*(b)*
  international diplomacy during Civil War and, 433–434, 434*(f)*
  plantations for, 366*(m)*, 366–367, 367*(i)*
  sharecroppers and, 478
  westward migration and, 360–361

Nahuatl, Cortés and, 38
Nannies, slaves as, in South, 372(i)
Napoleon, 271, 272, 276
Naranjo, Joseph, 137(i)
Narragansett Indians, 104
Narrative of the Life of Frederick Douglass, as Told by Himself (Douglass), 398
Narváez, Pánfilo de, 35(m), 40
Nashville, Tennessee, battle of, 448(m), 449, 451(t)
Natchez Indians, 19–20
National Banking Act, 444
National banks, creation of first, 245
National currency, creation of, 444
National domain, 207
National government. *See* Government
Nationalism, spirit of, after War of 1812, 282
National Negro Convention, in 1830, 317
National Republicans, 305
National Union Party, 468
Native Americans. *See also* Indian and colonist relationship; *specific tribes and persons*
in 1490s, 18–22, 19(f), 20(m)
as allies of Cortés, 41(b)
California gold rush and, 349
California missions and, 133
Columbian exchange and, 36
conflict among, 22
cultural similarities, 21–22
discrimination against, in Chesapeake colonies, 70–71(b)
diseases brought from Europe to, 36, 37(i), 41(b)
early use of term of, 70(b)
effect of diseases on. *See* Diseases
forced labor from, in New Spain, 45
Jackson administration and, 307–310
Jamestown and, 57(i), 58–59
land speculation in Northwest Territory and, 220
languages of, 38
Lewis and Clark expedition and, 274
as loyalists, 183–185
named "Indians" by Columbus, 34
Northwest Ordinance and, 220–221
Pennsylvania colony and, 102
Pennsylvania proclamation against, 190(i)
repartimiento and, 45

in Revolutionary War, 183–185
Seven Years' War and, 142–150, 144(m)
social status of, in New Spain, 47–48
tension with British after Treaty of Paris and, 149
trade with colonists in 18th century and, 131–132
Treaty of Paris and, 147, 197, 200
variety of, 9
violence between Chesapeake colonists and, 68–69
after War of 1812, 177
war with, during Revolutionary War, 190–192, 191(m)
war with, in 1790s, 246–251
Nativism, Know-Nothing Party and, 401
Natural increase
of population in colonial America, 112
of population in New England colonies, 113–114
of slave population, from 1830 to 1860, 361
of slave population, in early 18th century, 123
of slave population, paternalism and, 370
Nature, colonists' view of, 90–91(b)
Nauvoo, Illinois, Mormons in, 340
Navajo Indians, 21
Navigation Acts, 68, 104, 133, 151
Navigational aids, maritime, invention of, 31
Navy (U.S.)
black soldiers in Civil War and, 436–439
Civil War and, 425–426, 429(m), 433
fugitive slaves as sailors in, 421, 421(i)
Nebraska, as territory, creation of, 398, 399(m)
Negro, early use of term of, 71(b)
Neolin (Delaware prophet), 149
Netherlands
immigration from, from 1492 to 1700, 76(f)
Revolutionary War and, 192
Net worth, personal, voting rights and, 210
Neutrality Proclamation, 253
Neville, John, 247

New Amsterdam. *See also* New York City
Puritans in, 87
as trading center, 97
Newburgh Conspiracy, 216
Newburyport, Massachusetts, party antagonism in, 257
New England Anti-Slavery Society, 317
New England colonies
in 18th century, 112–116
attempt to isolate by British army, 188–190
Coercive Acts and, 162–164
at end of 17th century, 103(m)
England's direct government of, 105–106
evolution of society in, 88–97
exports from, in 18th century, 129(f)
map of, in 17th century, 87(m)
population of, in 17th century, 94(f)
Puritans and Puritanism in, 84–88
Newfoundland
Cabot and, 35(m), 36
Gilbert and, 35(m), 51
Norse exploration of, 30
New France
colonial America and, 131, 132–133
English colonies and, 114
Ohio Country and, 142–143
relation with Indians in 18th century in, 142
zones of, 132(m)
New Hampshire
as colony, Boston Port Act and, 165(b)
New Jersey Plan and, 226
ratification of Constitution by, 229(m), 231
state laws on slavery in, 211
tax requisition of 1785 and, 221
New Haven, Connecticut, Townshend duties and, 157
New Jersey. *See also* New Jersey colony
Articles of Confederation and, 207
early statehood of, voting rights in, 211
New Jersey Plan and, 226–227
ratification of Constitution by, 229, 229(m)
state laws on slavery in, 213–214
tax requisition of 1785 and, 221

Preston, John Smith, 413
Preston, Thomas, 159, 160, 162
Prices, during Revolutionary War, 187
Printing press, invention of, 30–31
Prisoners of war
    in Civil War, 450(i)
    in Civil War, disease and, 452
Proclamation of 1763, 150
Proclamation of Amnesty and Reconstruction, 458
Property confiscation, from loyalists, 186
Property owners, voting rights of, 210
Prophetstown, Indiana, attack on, 278
Prostitution, moral reform of, in early 19th century, 316
Protestant Association, 106
Protestant Reformation
    Puritanism and, 84
    Spanish response to, 49–50
Protestants and Protestantism
    in Chesapeake colonies, 66
    Civil War casualties and, 453
    in colonial America in 18th century, 128–131
    German immigrants and, 334
    immigration of, from 1845-1855, 401
    immigration of, in 18th century, 117
    in Maryland, in 17th century, 66
    Puritanism and, 84–85, 88–90
    Second Great Awakening and, 315
    women in church governance and, 284–285
Public debt, First Congress and, 241–244
Public schools. See also Education
    in 1830s, 314–315
    female education and. See Female education
    free labor and, 332–333
    plain folk in South and, 381
    in South during Reconstruction, 473, 476(i)
Public securities, Revolutionary War and, 187
Public virtue, 240
Pueblo Bonito, 13, 16(i), 16–17(b)
Pueblo Revolt, 73
Pueblos, 12, 13
Puritan Revolution, 93
Puritans and Puritanism
    in 18th century, 130

beliefs and practices of, 88–89
economic changes and religious controversies for, 93–97
government by and for, 90–92
meeting house, 92(i)
origins of, 84–85
settlement of New England colonies and, 84–88
splintering of, 92–93
Pynchon, William, 91

Quakers
    beliefs and practices of, 101, 101(i)
    financial success of, 119–120
    in New England colonies, 96
    Penn and, 101
    in Pennsylvania colony, 101–102
    views on slavery of, 125(b)
    women in church governance and, 284
Quantrill, William Clarke, 431
Quartering Act of 1765, 162–163
Quasi-War with France, 257, 261
Quebec, American attempted capture of, 180, 181(m)
Quebec, Battle of, 147(i)
Quebec Act, 162, 163, 197
Quincy, Josiah, 160

Racial and ethnic discrimination
    against African Americans, after Civil War, 473
    against African Americans, in Southwest, 392
    against African slaves, 77, 118
    against black soldiers in Civil War, 421, 437, 439(b)
    against Californios, 349
    Fourteenth Amendment and, 468
    against free blacks in 1840s and 1850s, 354–355
    against Indians, in Chesapeake colonies, 70–71(b)
    against Mexican Americans, 349
    against Spanish immigrants, 349
Radicals within Republican Party, Reconstruction and, 469–470
Railroads
    in 1840s and 1850s, 330–332
    in 1860, 331(m)
    in early 19th century, 300
    transcontinental, Pierce administration and, 398–399
Raleigh, Walter, 35(m), 51
Rammasay, Cato, 214(i)
Rancheros, 342, 349
Ranchos, 342

Randall, A. B., 462(b)
Randolph, Edmund, 239, 371
Rapier, James T., 457, 457(i), 473
Rapier, John, 457
Reading and writing, freedmen and, 461–462
Rebels of Civil War. See Confederate army
Reconquest, 31
Reconstruction, 457–483
    during Civil War, 458–463
    collapse of, 478–483, 482(m)
    by Congress, 467–471
    political cartoons and, 467(i)
    by presidents, 464–467
    struggle in South during, 471–478
Reconstruction Acts of 1867, 470
Redcoats. See British army
Redeemers, 480–481
Redemptioners, 117
Red Hawk (Shawnee chief), 191
Red River, expedition of, 274
Reed, Esther DeBerdt, 182
Religion. See also specific religions or denominations
    Civil War casualties and, 453
    in colonial America in 18th century, 127, 128–131
    freedmen and, 463
    Mexica Indian warfare and, 41(b)
    of Native Americans, 149
    plain folk in South and, 381–382, 382(i)
    revivals and, in 18th century, 130–131
    Second Great Awakening and, 315–316
    slaves and, 377
    toleration of, in New Netherland, 98–100
    toleration of, in Pennsylvania colony, 101–102
    women in church governance and, 284–285
Repartimiento, 45
Report on Manufactures (Hamilton), 245–246
Report on Public Credit (Hamilton), 241–244
Report on the Causes and Reasons for War, 278
Representation, Constitution and, 226
Republican government, Jefferson's vision of, 267–270

Slave rebellions
    fear of, 383
    free blacks, 383
    Gabriel's rebellion, 266
    infrequency of, 378–379
    Nat Turner and, 359
    pre-Revolutionary period, 167–169
    Stono Rebellion, 124–125
Slaves and slavery
    abolitionist movement and. *See*
        Abolitionist movement
    African born. *See* African slaves
    alliance with, if allied with
        Confederate army, 434
    American born. *See* African
        American slaves
    annexation of Texas and, 343
    in Brazil, 476
    Caribbean, 38
    in Constitution, 227
    cotton kingdom and, 360–361,
        361*(m)*
    in Declaration of Independence,
        177
    Declaration of Independence and,
        177
    differences between South and
        North and, 360–368
    disintegration of, 443–444
    early state constitutions and,
        211–215, 214*(m)*
    emancipated. *See* Freedmen
    few critics of, in 18th century,
        124–125*(b)*
    freed. *See* Freedmen
    freedom from, for fighting with
        British, 168
    Haitian Revolution and, 254
    Lincoln-Douglas debates and,
        409–410
    marriage and, 284, 376–377
    masters and mistresses and,
        369–374
    in Missouri, statehood and, 288
    Northwest Ordinance and,
        222–223*(b)*
    in Northwest Territory, 221
    plain folk and, 379–382
    politics of, from 1820 to 1860,
        384–386
    preservation of Union and, 434–439
    punishment of, 371, 371*(i)*
    rebellions of, in Virginia, 359, 359*(i)*
    Republican Party and, 402–403
    runaway. *See* Fugitive slaves
    slave quarters and daily life for,
        374–379

southern defense of, 362–365,
    364–365*(b)*
underground railroad and, 355
in West Indies, 74
Slave states, balance of free states
    and, 288
Slave trade
    from Africa, 111, 111*(i)*
    across Atlantic, 121*(m)*, 121*(t)*,
        121–122
    few critics of, in 18th century,
        124–125*(b)*
Smallpox
    brought from Europe to New
        World, 36, 37*(i)*, 41*(b)*
    in New Spain, 48–49
    Revolutionary War and, 175, 180,
        196
    slaves in British army and, 169
Smalls, Robert, 421*(i)*, 437
Smith, Gerrit, 354*(i)*
Smith, John
    Jamestown and, 57
    Powhatan and, 57
Smith, Joseph Jr., 340, 506
Smoking. *See* Tobacco and tobacco
    industry
Smuggling, Sugar Act and, 151
Sneden, Robert, 450*(i)*
Social inequality, in Chesapeake
    colonies, 67–72. *See also*
    Discrimination; Racial and
    ethnic discrimination
Social status, in New Spain,
    47–48
Society of Friends. *See* Quakers
Sons of Liberty, 156
    Boston Massacre and, 159–160
    Stamp Act and, 152
    Tea Act of 1773 and, 162
    Townshend duties and, 158, 159
South. *See also specific states*
    Civil War and, 440–444. *See also*
        Civil War; Confederacy;
        Confederate army
    colonies of, in 17th century. *See*
        Southern colonies in 17th
        century
    colonies of, in 18th century. *See*
        Southern colonies in 18th
        century
    effect of Civil War on, 453
    Missouri Compromise and, 288
    slavery in Southwest and,
        394–395
    struggle in, during Reconstruction,
        471–478

talk of secession by, 413–416,
    414–415*(b)*
South, from 1820 to 1860, 359–387
    differences between North and,
        360–368
    free blacks in, 382–384
    masters and mistresses and,
        369–374
    party system in, 399–404
    plain folk in, 379–382
    politics of slavery and, 384–386
    slaves and slave quarters in,
        374–379
South America. *See also specific
    countries*
    Vespucci and, 35*(m)*, 36
South Carolina. *See also* Carolina
    colonies; South Carolina
    colony
    black codes and, 465–466
    Confederate States of America
        and, 414, 416*(m)*
    "Declaration of Causes which
        Induced the Secession of
        South Carolina," 415*(b)*
    federal tariffs and, 310–311
    population of blacks and whites
        in, in 1860, 362*(f)*
    ratification of Constitution by, 229,
        229*(m)*
    secession of, 414
    state laws on slavery in, 214
    whiskey tax and, 247
South Carolina colony
    British capture of, 193, 194*(m)*
    Camden, battle of, 194, 194*(m)*
    Charleston. *See* Charleston, South
        Carolina
    Cowpens, battle of, 194*(m)*
    early settlement of, 74–76, 75*(m)*
    guerrilla warfare in, 195
    Iroquois Indians in, 19
    patterns of settlement, 118*(m)*
    population of, in 18th century, 120
    preferred slaves in, 123
    slave demonstrations in, 156
    slavery and, 121
    Stamp Act and, 156
    Stono Rebellion in, 124–125
    voting in 18th century in, 127
Southeast Indians, in 1490s,
    population of, 19*(f)*
Southern colonies in 17th century,
    55–79
    Jamestown and, 56–59
    population of, 94*(f)*
    slave labor system in, 72–78

Fifteenth Amendment and, 471
during Reconstruction, 468
after Revolutionary War, 210–211
unmarried women and, 210(i), 211
Women
    abolitionist work of, 319–320, 327
    in Chesapeake colonies, 63
    church governance and, 284–285
    domestic role of, in early 19th
        century, 313
    in military. See Women in military
    on Oregon Trail and in Oregon
        Country, 339
    patriotism during Revolutionary
        War and, 182
    petitions against Indian Removal
        Act and, 309
    Puritanism and, 92–93
    Quakers and, 96
    republican ideals and, 239–240
    Republican Party and, 403
    rights of. See Women's rights
    separate spheres, 313–315, 314(i)
    in South, expected qualities of,
        372–374
    on upcountry farms, 380
    voting rights of. See Woman
        suffrage
    in workforce. See Women in
        workforce
Women in military
    in Civil War camps, as laborers,
        445(i)
    in Continental and British armies,
        179
    Sampson, 173, 173(i)

Women in workforce
    black women after Civil War,
        476–477
    in early 19th century, 313
    as farmers and employees during
        Civil War, 445–446
    in textile and shoe industries, 301
Women's rights
    in 1790s, 242–243(b)
    abolitionist movement and, 320
    activists for, in 1840s and 1850s,
        353, 353(i)
    Adams, Abigail, on, 176
    equality with men and, 297
    in France and Britain in 1790s,
        242–243(b)
    legal status of women in 1820s
        and, 283–286
    property ownership by married
        women and, 210–211,
        402–403(b)
    right to own property and,
        402–403(b)
    as spouses of loyalists, property
        ownership and, 186
    to vote. See Woman suffrage
Woodhenges, 17–18
Woodland Indians. See Eastern
    Woodland Indians
Wood products, colonial American
    exports of, 129(f)
Woods, Daniel B., 351(b)
Woodworking, Pacific Northwest
    Indians and, 11
Woolman, John, 125(b)
Worcester v. Georgia, 309

Work. See Employment; Free
    labor; Labor; Unemployment;
    specific industries and jobs
Workforce, women in. See Women in
    workforce
The World Turn'd Upside Down, 89(i)
Worship. See Religion
Wounded, in Civil War, high death
    rates for, 449(i), 451–453
Writing, ancient America and, 4

XYZ affair, 256–257

Yamasee Indians, 132
Yamasee War, 132
Yancy, William Lowndes, 411
Yankees
    during Civil War. See Union army
    living in South during
        Reconstruction, 472
Yeomen
    in Chesapeake colony, in 17th
        century, 67
    hardships of war on families of, 441
    as plain folk, 379–380
    in plantation belt, 379, 379(m)
    pressured to be Democrats, 481
    as Republicans, 472
    in upcountry, 380, 380(m)
York (slave), 274
Yorktown, Virginia, battle of, 196,
    196(m)
Young, Brigham, 340
Young, Lewis, 375

Zemis, 34
Zuñi Indians, 42, 42(i)

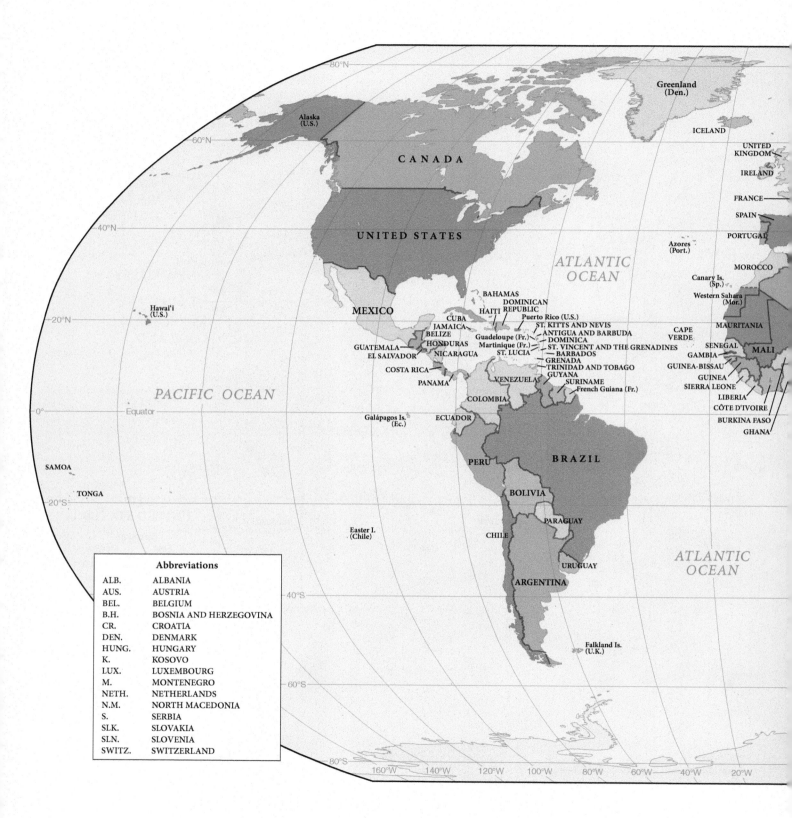

80°N

Greenland
(Den.)

Alaska
(U.S.)

60°N

ICELAND

UNITED
KINGDOM

IRELAND

CANADA

FRANCE

SPAIN

40°N

PORTUGAL

UNITED STATES

ATLANTIC
OCEAN

Azores
(Port.)

MOROCCO

Canary Is.
(Sp.)

Western Sahara
(Mor.)

Hawai'i
(U.S.)

20°N

BAHAMAS

DOMINICAN
REPUBLIC

MEXICO

HAITI

CUBA

Puerto Rico (U.S.)

ST. KITTS AND NEVIS

MAURITANIA

JAMAICA

BELIZE

Guadeloupe (Fr.)

ANTIGUA AND BARBUDA

DOMINICA

CAPE
VERDE

HONDURAS

Martinique (Fr.)

ST. VINCENT AND THE GRENADINES

SENEGAL

GUATEMALA

ST. LUCIA

BARBADOS

GAMBIA

MALI

EL SALVADOR

NICARAGUA

GRENADA

GUINEA-BISSAU

TRINIDAD AND TOBAGO

COSTA RICA

GUYANA

GUINEA

SIERRA LEONE

VENEZUELA

SURINAME

PANAMA

French Guiana (Fr.)

LIBERIA

COLOMBIA

CÔTE D'IVOIRE

0° Equator

PACIFIC OCEAN

Galápagos Is.
(Ec.)

ECUADOR

BURKINA FASO

GHANA

PERU

BRAZIL

SAMOA

BOLIVIA

20°S

TONGA

Easter I.
(Chile)

PARAGUAY

CHILE

ATLANTIC
OCEAN

URUGUAY

40°S

ARGENTINA

Falkland Is.
(U.K.)

60°S

80°S

160°W **140°W** **120°W** **100°W** **80°W** **60°W** **40°W** **20°W**

Abbreviations	
ALB.	ALBANIA
AUS.	AUSTRIA
BEL.	BELGIUM
B.H.	BOSNIA AND HERZEGOVINA
CR.	CROATIA
DEN.	DENMARK
HUNG.	HUNGARY
K.	KOSOVO
LUX.	LUXEMBOURG
M.	MONTENEGRO
NETH.	NETHERLANDS
N.M.	NORTH MACEDONIA
S.	SERBIA
SLK.	SLOVAKIA
SLN.	SLOVENIA
SWITZ.	SWITZERLAND

ARCTIC OCEAN

RUSSIAN FEDERATION

NORWAY
SWEDEN
FINLAND
ESTONIA
LATVIA
LITHUANIA
DEN.
NETH.
GERMANY
BEL.
LUX.
POLAND BELARUS
CZECHIA
AUS. SLK.
HUNG. UKRAINE
SWITZ. SLN. MOLDOVA
ITALY CR. ROMANIA
B.H. S. BULGARIA
M. K. N.M.
ALB. GREECE
TUNISIA MALTA
CYPRUS
ISRAEL
Gaza Strip
West Bank
JORDAN
GEORGIA
ARMENIA
TURKEY AZERBAIJAN
SYRIA
LEBANON
IRAQ

KAZAKHSTAN

MONGOLIA

UZBEKISTAN KYRGYZSTAN
TURKMENISTAN TAJIKISTAN

N. KOREA
S. KOREA
JAPAN

CHINA

PACIFIC OCEAN

ALGERIA
LIBYA
EGYPT

IRAN
AFGHANISTAN
PAKISTAN

KUWAIT
SAUDI ARABIA
QATAR
UNITED ARAB
EMIRATES
BAHRAIN
OMAN

NEPAL
BHUTAN
BANGLADESH
INDIA
MYANMAR
(BURMA)

TAIWAN

LAOS
VIETNAM
THAILAND
CAMBODIA

Mariana Is.
(U.S.)

Guam
(U.S.)

MARSHALL
IS.

NIGER
CHAD
SUDAN
ERITREA
YEMEN
DJIBOUTI

NIGERIA
BENIN
TOGO
CAMEROON
CENTRAL
AFRICAN REP.
SOUTH
SUDAN
ETHIOPIA
SOMALIA

MALDIVES

SRI
LANKA

PHILIPPINES

BRUNEI

MALAYSIA

PALAU

FEDERATED STATES
OF MICRONESIA

EQ.
GUINEA
GABON
CONGO
SÃO
TOMÉ
& PRÍNCIPE
DEM. REP. OF
THE CONGO
RWANDA
BURUNDI
UGANDA
KENYA
TANZANIA
COMOROS
SEYCHELLES

SINGAPORE

INDONESIA

EAST
TIMOR

PAPUA
NEW
GUINEA

NAURU

SOLOMON
IS.

KIRIBATI

TUVALU

ANGOLA
ZAMBIA
MALAWI
ZIMBABWE
MADAGASCAR

INDIAN OCEAN

VANUATU

FIJI

NAMIBIA
BOTSWANA
MOZAMBIQUE
ESWATINI
LESOTHO
SOUTH
AFRICA

MAURITIUS

AUSTRALIA

New Caledonia
(Fr.)

NEW
ZEALAND

Tasmania
(Aust.)

0   1,500   3,000 miles
0   1,500   3,000 kilometers

ANTARCTICA

20°E   40°E   60°E   80°E   100°E   120°E   140°E   160°E

ABOUT THE AUTHORS

James L. Roark (Ph.D., Stanford University) is Samuel Candler Dobbs Professor Emeritus of American History at Emory University. He received his university's Emory Williams Distinguished Teaching Award, and in 2001–2002 he was Pitt Professor of American Institutions at Cambridge University. He has written *Masters without Slaves: Southern Planters in the Civil War and Reconstruction* and coauthored *Black Masters: A Free Family of Color in the Old South* with Michael P. Johnson. He has also co-edited *No Chariot Let Down: Charleston's Free People of Color on the Eve of the Civil War* with Michael P. Johnson.

Michael P. Johnson (Ph.D., Stanford University) is Professor of History at Johns Hopkins University. His publications include *Toward a Patriarchal Republic: The Secession of Georgia*; *Abraham Lincoln, Slavery, and the Civil War: Selected Speeches and Writings*; and *Reading the American Past: Selected Historical Documents*, the documents reader for *The American Promise*. He has also coedited *No Chariot Let Down: Charleston's Free People of Color on the Eve of the Civil War* with James L. Roark.

François Furstenberg (Ph.D., Johns Hopkins University) is Professor of History at Johns Hopkins University. From 2003–2014 he taught at the Université de Montréal. His publications include *In the Name of the Father: Washington's Legacy, Slavery, and the Making of a Nation*; and *When the United States Spoke French: Five Refugees who Shaped a Nation*.

Patricia Cline Cohen (Ph.D., University of California, Berkeley) is Professor Emeritus of History at the University of California, Santa Barbara, where she received the Distinguished Teaching Award in 2005–2006. She has written *A Calculating People: The Spread of Numeracy in Early America* and *The Murder of Helen Jewett: The Life and Death of a Prostitute in Nineteenth-Century New York*, and she has coauthored *The Flash Press: Sporting Male Weeklies in 1840s New York*.

Sarah Stage (Ph.D., Yale University) has taught U.S. history at Williams College and the University of California, Riverside, and she was a visiting professor at Beijing University and Szechuan University. Currently she is Professor of Women's Studies at Arizona State University. Her books include *Female Complaints: Lydia Pinkham and the Business of Women's Medicine* and *Rethinking Home Economics: Women and the History of a Profession*.

Susan M. Hartmann (Ph.D., University of Missouri) is Arts and Humanities Distinguished Professor Emeritus of History at Ohio State University. In 1995 she won the university's Exemplary Faculty Award in the College of Humanities. Her publications include *Truman and the 80th Congress*; *The Home Front and Beyond: American Women in the 1940s*; *From Margin to Mainstream: American Women and Politics since 1960*; and *The Other Feminists: Activists in the Liberal Establishment*.

Sarah E. Igo (Ph.D., Princeton University) is the Andrew Jackson Professor of American History and Director of American Studies at Vanderbilt University. Previously, she was an associate professor at the University of Pennsylvania, where she won the Richard S. Dunn Award for Distinguished Teaching in 2003. She is the author of *The Averaged American: Surveys, Citizens and the Making of a Mass Public* and *The Known Citizen: A History of Privacy in Modern America*.